Love between Enemies

T0372736

Love between Enemies explores the forbidden relationships that formed between foreign prisoners of war and German women during the Second World War. From the desire to have fun to deep love commitments, this study examines the range of motivations that lay behind these relationships, tapping into new documents and drawing on thousands of court cases to offer a transnational analysis of personal relations between enemies. Highlighting gender roles, the contradictory reactions of the communities surrounding the couples, and the diplomatic tensions resulting from the severe punishments, this is a history of everyday life that throws light on this subversive aspect of intimacy in wartime Nazi Germany. Comparing the "transgressing" couples to other groups persecuted for their cultural or private choices, Raffael Scheck demonstrates how the relationships were silenced or justified in the postwar memory of prisoners, while the German women, who had been publicly shamed, continued to live with the stigma, and even illegitimate children, for the years that followed.

RAFFAEL SCHECK is Audrey Wade Hittinger Katz and Sheldon Toby Katz Distinguished Teaching Professor of History at Colby College. He is the author of six books including *Hitler's African Victims: The German Army Massacres of Black French Soldiers in 1940* (2006) and *French Colonial Soldiers in German Captivity during World War II* (2014). He is currently working on a new book project on the meaning of the German victory in the West in 1940.

Love between Enemies

Western Prisoners of War and German Women in World War II

Raffael Scheck

Colby College

CAMBRIDGE
UNIVERSITY PRESS

Shaftesbury Road, Cambridge CB2 8EA, United Kingdom

One Liberty Plaza, 20th Floor, New York, NY 10006, USA

477 Williamstown Road, Port Melbourne, VIC 3207, Australia

314–321, 3rd Floor, Plot 3, Splendor Forum, Jasola District Centre, New Delhi – 110025, India

103 Penang Road, #05–06/07, Visioncrest Commercial, Singapore 238467

Cambridge University Press is part of Cambridge University Press & Assessment, a department of the University of Cambridge.

We share the University's mission to contribute to society through the pursuit of education, learning and research at the highest international levels of excellence.

www.cambridge.org
Information on this title: www.cambridge.org/9781108795289

DOI: 10.1017/9781108894821

First published 2021
First paperback edition 2024

A catalogue record for this publication is available from the British Library

Library of Congress Cataloging-in-Publication data
Names: Scheck, Raffael, 1960– author.
Title: Love between enemies : Western Prisoners of War and German women in
    World War II / Raffael Scheck, Colby College, Maine.
Other titles: Western Prisoners of War and German women in World War II
Description: Cambridge, United Kingdom ; New York, NY : Cambridge
    University Press, 2021. | Includes bibliographical references and index.
Identifiers: LCCN 2020021925 (print) | LCCN 2020021926 (ebook) |
    ISBN 9781108841757 (hardback) | ISBN 9781108795289 (paperback) |
    ISBN 9781108894821 (ebook)
Subjects: LCSH: World War, 1939-1945–Prisoners and prisons, German. |
    Prisoners of war–History–20th century. | Prisoners of
    war–Germany–Sexual behavior–History–20th century. | Man-woman
    relationships–Germany–History–20th century. | Women and war–Germany–
    History–20th century. | World War, 1939-1945–Social aspects. |
    National socialism and justice. | World War, 1939-1945–Concentration
    camps–Germany.
Classification: LCC D805.G3 S364 2020 (print) | LCC D805.G3 (ebook) |
    DDC 940.54/7243–dc23
LC record available at https://lccn.loc.gov/2020021925
LC ebook record available at https://lccn.loc.gov/2020021926

ISBN   978-1-108-84175-7   Hardback
ISBN   978-1-108-79528-9   Paperback

To the fifteen Soviet prisoners of war who saved the life of my grandfather, August Wache, in April or May 1945

Contents

Acknowledgments

My greatest debt is to the archivists from the twenty archives I used. In particular, I want to thank Bartłomiej Warzecha, a retired archivist and historian from Katowice, Michael Scholz from Darmstadt, and Rainer Hering from Schleswig who went out of their way to help me get access to a range of precious documents I would otherwise not have been able to see because of time and budget constraints. Moreover, I had the pleasure of sharing my work with several friends and colleagues who provided advice and help, especially Julia Torrie, Fabien Théofilakis, Doris Bergen, Eric Jennings, Olivier Wieviorka, Jeffrey Herf, Caroline Nilsen, Timothy Schroer, Kara Ritzheimer, Mark Roseman, Nicholas Stargardt, Richard Wetzell, Maria Prieler-Woldan, Matthias Reiss, Brian Feltman, Lisa Todd, Elisabeth Schöggl-Ernst, Gwendoline Cicottini, Annette Timm, and Geoffrey Megargee. Thomas Kohut allowed me to consult his new manuscript on historical empathy, which helped me approach the sensitive aspects of my topic. Rüdiger Overmans gracefully answered some special queries. Jim and Sue Balan read an earlier version of the manuscript and provided encouragement. Gabe Stowe from Colby's interlibrary loan department fielded a stream of orders from me. My endowed chair at Colby College, a generous gift of Audrey Wade Hittinger Katz and Sheldon Toby Katz, provided most valuable research support, as did a summer grant from the American Philosophical Association and from the Andersonville National Historical Site foundation. My family, especially Lori and Sophia Scheck, graciously accompanied me on summer research trips, and my older children, Anselm and Adelia Scheck, have followed my research with a warm interest. Annie Ahn, one of my students, helped during the preparation of the index. It has been a pleasure and privilege working with Liz Friend-Smith, the senior commissioning editor, and Atifa Jiwa, the senior editorial assistant, from Cambridge University Press.

While writing this book, I could not avoid thinking of my maternal grandfather, August Wache, who guarded prisoners of war (POWs) during World War II. He was born on August 31, 1906, as the eighth child of a landless laborer in a tiny village in East Prussia, very close to the German–Russian border and in one of the poorest regions of pre-1914 Germany (today in the southeastern corner of the Russian Kaliningrad exclave, not far from the Polish and Lithuanian border). August Wache experienced the Russian invasion in August 1914. When Russian soldiers arrived and asked him for a match, he feared they would burn down the village, as had happened in other places. But the Russians just made a fire in the central square to prepare cocoa taken from the village store (a scene also described, albeit in a different village, in Aleksandr Solzhenitsyn's great novel *August 1914*[1]). When August Wache saw the Russians retreat after the battle of Tannenberg a few days later, with many wounded, he felt sorry for them. He vividly remembered their sad faces, and he witnessed some Russians being hit by the shots of the pursuing German troops.

After the war, in which he lost a brother, August Wache became a gardener. He wanted to get a master's degree in gardening, but there was no money for that. Finding no steady work in East Prussia, he moved to Berlin, but he remained unemployed or underemployed for many years there, too. During the Great Depression, he lived with one of his sisters, sleeping in a cubbyhole and looking every day for an opportunity to earn a few marks with random work. In 1934, he finally received employment by the still secretive German air force and was tasked with planting green foliage on top of air force bunkers for camouflage. His job allowed him to get married, to have a child (my mother), and to rent a small apartment in a working-class neighborhood of Berlin-Haselhorst.

When the war broke out, he continued working as a gardener for the air force. He did not have to fight because he was blind in one eye (a result of a kick in the face by a horse during his childhood). In early 1943, however, he was drafted into a guard unit and assigned to a work detachment of fifteen Soviet POWs on a nobleman's estate northwest of Berlin. He realized that the prisoners were starving, and he secretly supplied them with peas from the barn of the estate. When one of the prisoners became sick, he took him to Berlin on the suburban commuter train, so that my grandmother could prepare her chicken soup for him – a risky act that would have led to severe punishment for all three. He sent my mother to the corner store to buy milk for the prisoner, and my mother was so honored by this task that she proudly told the lady running the store that she needed milk for a Soviet prisoner her father had brought home. My mother was sorely disappointed when the lady

[1] Alexander Solzhenitsyn, *August 1914* (New York: Farrar, Straus and Giroux, 1972), 306.

admonished her never to say this in public, but nobody denounced my grandfather, and the prisoner recovered. On the last New Year's Eve of the war, an allied plane dropped a bomb in the courtyard of the estate, but the bomb did not explode. Together with volunteers among his POWs, August Wache loaded the bomb onto a hay cart and transported it to a nearby swamp. He received a medal for this action (which he threw away later during his flight). When the Red Army approached Berlin, the prisoners warned him that he would be killed by their troops if they captured him. The prisoners gave him their secret possessions – charms and food – and urged him to run away. He fled westward and became a British POW south of Hamburg, but he soon escaped and walked back to Berlin across the Soviet occupation zone because he wanted to know whether his wife and daughter were still alive. He found them in their apartment, which was undamaged except for the windows, which had been blown out by the bombs hitting houses nearby. They shared the apartment with two other families, refugees from eastern Germany.

What happened to the fifteen Soviet POWs is unknown. They may very well have ended up in the Gulag as alleged traitors. August Wache, like a number of guards who appear in this book, felt a humane duty to care for the POWs under his command, an attitude severely condemned by the Nazi authorities. In turn, the POWs saved his life.

Abbreviations

AN	*Archives nationales*, French state archives, Pierrefitte-sur-Seine
BA-MA	*Bundesarchiv-Militärarchiv*, German military archives, Freiburg im Breisgau
BAR	*Bundesarchiv* Bern, Swiss Federal Archives, Bern
BLHA	*Brandenburgisches Landeshauptarchiv*, Brandenburg main state archives, Potsdam
BStA	*Bayerisches Staatsarchiv*, Bavarian state archives
CEGESOMA	*Centre d'études et de documentation guerres et sociétés contemporaines/Studie- en Dokumentatiecentrum oorlog en hedendaagse Maatschappij*, Center for Historical Research and Documentation on War and Contemporary Society, Brussels
DSLP	*Délégation du Service de liaison avec les prisonniers de guerre*, Belgian commission for prisoners of war
HHStA	*Hessisches Hauptstaatsarchiv* Wiesbaden, Hessian main state archives
HStAD	*Hessisches Staatsarchiv* Darmstadt, Hessian state archive Darmstadt
ICRC	International Committee of the Red Cross
IMI	*Italienischer Militärinternierter*, Italian Military Internee
KStVO	*Kriegsstrafverfahrensordnung*
LASH	*Landesarchiv Schleswig-Holstein*, state archives of Schleswig Holstein, Schleswig
NACP	National Archives College Park (Maryland)
NLA	*Niedersächsisches Landesarchiv*, state archives of Lower Saxony (Oldenburg and Hannover)
OKW	*Oberkommando der Wehrmacht*, German High Command
OTAD	*Office des Travaux de l'armée démobilisée*, Office for the (Belgian) demobilized army

PAAA	*Politisches Archiv des Auswärtigen Amtes*, German Foreign Office archives, Berlin
POW	prisoner of war
RSHA	*Reichssicherheitshauptamt* (Reich Main Security Office), a central office of the SS
SA	*Sturmabteilung* (storm troopers)
SD	*Sicherheitsdienst* (security service of the SS)
SDGP	*Service Diplomatique des Prisonniers de Guerre* (Diplomatic Service for Prisonners of War)
SHD	*Service Historique de la Défense – Division des Archives des Victimes des Conflits Contemporains*, archives for French victims of war, Caen
StLA	*Steiermärkisches Landesarchiv* Graz, county archive of Styria
STO	*Service du travail obligatoire*, mandatory labor service for France
WStLA	*Wiener Stadt- und Landesarchiv*, Vienna city and country archives

Current Place Names

Note: for an interactive map with all major German POW camps, see Moosburg online (www.moosburg.org/info/stalag/laglist.html)

Mechtal – Miechowice (Poland)
Memel – Klaipeda (Lithuania)
Neisse – Nysa (Poland)
Neustettin – Szczecinek (Poland)
Odrau (Sudetenland) – Odry (Czech Republic)
Pless – Pszczyna (Poland)
Posen – Poznań (Poland)
Reichenau (Sudetenland) – Rychnov u Jablonce nad Nisou
Reichenberg (Sudetenland) – Liberec (Czech Republic)
Sagan – Żagań (Poland)
Schubin – Szubin (Poland)
Stettin – Szczecin (Poland)
Stolp – Słupsk (Poland)
Stuhm – Sztum (Poland)
Teplitz-Schönau (Sudetenland) – Teplice (Czech Republic)
Teschen – Český Těšín (Czech Republic)
Thorn – Toruń (Poland)
Trebnitz – Trzebnica (Poland)
Troppau (Sudetenland) – Opava (Czech Republic)
Znaim (Sudetenland) – Znojmo (Czech Republic)

Major sites of military tribunals and courts mentioned in the text

Introduction

The Problem

Despite a strict prohibition and harsh punishments, thousands of western prisoners of war (POWs) and German women started forbidden relations with each other during World War II. An estimated 15,000–20,000 French, Belgian, and British POWs and an equal number of women had to stand trial, and there were undoubtedly many more relations that remained undiscovered or never came to trial. Given their large number and their increasingly lax guarding, French POWs were the predominant "offenders," with more than 80 percent of all court martial cases.[1] The Belgians, detained under similar conditions to the French, engaged in forbidden relations in an even higher proportion, and the British POWs, once they became more integrated into German work life and were less strictly guarded (in 1943), followed in their footsteps. Many German women, facing a shortage of local men in their age bracket, defied Nazi propaganda that stigmatized the foreign POW as an implacable enemy. They also disregarded the omnipresent warning notices and the public posters and newspaper articles providing detailed accounts of the "shameful," "unpatriotic" activities and harsh punishments of women who had become involved with a POW. These texts included the full names of the women.

What motivated these international love relations, these "collaborations of the heart," in the midst of war?[2] The Belgian officer and historian of captivity E. Gillet reduced it to a simple formula: "Human

---

[1] Prisoners of war had to stand trial in front of a court martial (*Feldgericht*) of the German reserve army, staffed by a military judge and two assistants. The same courts also sentenced German soldiers on home leave. Following the example of some works on POWs, I use the term court martial, but military tribunal would also be a fine translation. Throughout the book, I also use the terms relation and relationship interchangeably, often adding an adjective to the former for clarification.

[2] Raffael Scheck, "Collaboration of the Heart: The Forbidden Love Affairs of French Prisoners of War and German Women in Nazi Germany," *The Journal of Modern History* 90, no. 2 (2018).

nature preserved its rights."[3] The former Belgian prisoner representative in East Prussia, Georges Smets, agreed and, in a television program in 1975, appealed to his audience not to judge these relationships too harshly. Smets' open discussion of the relationships provoked outrage among former comrades. One of them wrote him an angry letter denying that love relations existed except in the case of a few evil collaborators. Smets answered:

Noble love could very well exist between a Belgian POW and a German woman. Love knows neither boundaries nor races. That is what I tried to explain in the TV program, not more and not less. It would be a serious error to suggest to the wider public that we were all saints. Of course, the opposite is true, and this also applies to quite a few wives of our POWs.[4]

But Smets, a keen observer of the POW psyche and of German wartime society, also stressed other factors than "human nature," such as the German population's growing acceptance of Belgian and French POWs (who predominated in his region), its increasing war-weariness, and the indispensability of the foreign POWs, who, according to Smets, were largely in charge of his province by 1944. Smets refused to condemn his fellow prisoners for having loved a German woman; the "Don Juans," as he called them, were all-too-human, uprooted, and far away from home. Reflecting on this topic in the mid-1970s, Smets saw the love between enemies as an encouraging sign for humanity. Yet, his revelation in the television program caused a scandal. POWs were supposed to have been heroic or stoic victims, fostering a spirit of defiance and always looking for a way to escape and to fool the German guards. At least, that was the tenor in memoirs, fiction, and historical publications.

French postwar works often portrayed the amorous relations as a "conquest," making up for the defeat of 1940 and the symbolic emasculation of the captured soldiers. Authors took special delight in the thought of having "cuckolded" German soldiers and officers, and they portrayed German women as all-too-eager accomplices.[5] An early and influential example is the autobiographic novel *Les grandes Vacances 1939–1945* (The Great Holidays, 1939–1945) by French NCO Francis

---

[3] Musée Royal de l'Armée et d'Histoire Militaire, Evere, Fonds Gillet, boîte 1, #4, "Histoire des prisonniers de guerre 40–45."

[4] Georges Smets to Mr. Georges Paulus, January 11, 1976, in Musée Royal de l'Armée et d'Histoire Militaire, Brussels, Fonds Hautecler, Farde 34.

[5] Patrice Arnaud, "Die deutsch-französischen Liebesbeziehungen der französischen Zwangsarbeiter und beurlaubten Kriegsgefangenen im 'Dritten Reich': vom Mythos des verführerischen Franzosen zur Umkehrung der Geschlechterrolle," in *Nationalsozialismus und Geschlecht: Zur Politisierung und Ästhetisierung von Körper, "Rasse" und Sexualität im "Dritten Reich" und nach 1945*, ed. Elke Frietsch and Christina Herkommer (Bielefeld: transcript Verlag, 2009), 184–8.

Ambrière, which won the Prix Goncourt of French literature in 1946.
Drawing from a rich collection of stories he heard from comrades,
Ambrière gleefully tells of French POWs wearing the uniform of a husband serving in the Wehrmacht or SS while carrying on an erotic relationship with the wife, perhaps surprising the husband with a new baby "in
whose procreation the husband had no part." Ambrière described German
women as crude and lecherous beings with "the large, heavy breasts that
are the default in this race" and who see French POW camps as studs for
their primitive desire: "it has to be said that the compliant and dumb
sentimentality of the German women, together with their sometimes
bestial sensuality, provided the Frenchmen with prey that they did not
need to coerce and that most often sought to surrender themselves."[6]
Ambrière reverses Nazi racial arrogance by integrating the encounters
of French POWs with German women into a narrative of the more
refined French who surpass the Germans in everything except brutality.
The French POWs, who demonstrate their superior technical expertise in
all jobs and make themselves increasingly indispensable, feel equally
revolted by the animalistic vulgarity of German women (he once calls
them "sows") as by their cuisine, which cooks all meat in water.

Ambrière may have appealed to a still hateful French public, including
many of his former comrades. Portraying German women as animals was
his answer to the Nazi propaganda of 1940, which had depicted the
French as a "degenerate" and "negroized" race.[7] It is notable that he
consistently depicts German women as the active force in the forbidden
relationships. He tells of his own experience bathing in the Rhine River
with a few comrades in a sector the guard had allowed them to use.
Suddenly, three young German women appeared. Despite the admonishments of the guard, the scantily dressed women smiled at the prisoners and repeatedly swam into "their" sector. After drying off, the three
women walked right through the beach area reserved for the prisoners,
provoking another confrontation with the guard.[8] From comrades,
Ambrière heard many similar stories, for example of a stout waitress
who forced a homosexual French POW into her room and into her
bed, and of some farm women who selected one prisoner after the other
for their farm primarily to exploit them sexually. Experiencing the vivid

[6] "... il faut bien dire que la sentimentalité complaisante et niaise des Allemandes, autant
que leur sensualité parfois bestiale, rendait au Français des proies qu'ils n'avaient nul mal
à forcer et qui le plus souvent conspiraient d'elles-mêmes à se rendre." Francis Ambrière,
Les grandes Vacances 1939–1945 (Paris: Les Éditions de la Nouvelle France, 1946), 200.
[7] Raffael Scheck, "La victoire allemande de 1940 comme justification de l'idéologie raciale
nazie," in *La Guerre de 40: Se battre, subir, se souvenir*, ed. Stefan Martens and Steffen
Prauser (Villeneuve d'Asq: Presses universitaires du Septentrion, 2014).
[8] Ambrière, *Les grandes Vacances*, 201.

desire of German women for French men must have been balm for the morale of the prisoners, similar to the frequent requests of German employers for French POWs as workers, but this perspective erases the often very active role of the prisoners.

At least Ambrière acknowledges the forbidden relations. He even considers them to have been extremely widespread and believes that only a small fraction went to trial. He claims that the trials were meant to be less a deterrent for the POWs and the women than a way to reassure German soldier-husbands that the state was watching over the fidelity of their wives or girlfriends while they were serving at the front. Although he points out many collaborators and opportunists among the prisoners, Ambrière weaves the forbidden relationships into an overarching narrative that stresses French resistance and patriotism in captivity, undermining the perception he cynically references in his book title, namely that the time spent in Germany was "the great holidays."

Although Ambrière insinuates that German employers and guards used the lure of sexual experiences to make POWs work more happily for the German war effort, he recognizes that there were numerous romantic and sincere relationships and that some couples wanted to marry. Despite his demeaning and racist descriptions of German women, he also asks some intriguing questions about their motivation. Did the behavior of German women arise from "an internal revolt against the absurdity and ignominious nature of the Hitler régime? Was this for the women a way to protest in the name of human nature, and to repair with the gift of themselves all the evil of which their race had become guilty?"[9] Ambrière did not provide a definitive answer, but he suggested that at least in some cases this factor might have played a role.

The motivations for the forbidden relationships are hard to trace, and they can be contradictory and ambivalent. Examples of women who felt compassion for the POWs are indeed easy to find, although it is just as easy to identify prisoners feeling compassion for a woman. The relationships ran the gamut from cursory physical encounters to deeply committed love with marriage plans. Every couple negotiated their relationship in their own way, and often in a dynamic process. A seemingly deep love

---

[9] "Cela répondait-il à quelque révolte intérieure contre l'absurdité et l'ignominie du régime hitlérien? Était-ce pour elles comme une façon de protester au nom de la nature humaine, et de réparer par le don d'elles-mêmes tout ce dont leur race se rendait coupable?" Ambrière, *Les grandes Vacances*, 206–7. Antje Zühl raises a similar question with respect to all foreign laborers on German farms: Antje Zühl, "Zum Verhältnis der deutschen Landbevölkerung gegenüber Zwangsarbeitern und Kriegsgefangenen," in *Faschismus und Rassismus: Kontroversen um Ideologie und Opfer*, ed. Werner Röhr et al. (Berlin: Akademie-Verlag, 1992), 352.

could turn into mudslinging once the partners faced a court hearing and were pressed to explain contradictory statements. An apparently superficial sexual contact could reveal a more sincere and caring dimension when it came to trial. The POWs have simultaneously been accused of collaboration for loving enemy women and praised as resisters for seducing them. The women may have engaged in an act of revolt or defiance, but they may occasionally have exploited their position as free civilians in relations with the prisoners. The distinction is sometimes murky, as suggested by Ambrière's experience with the three bathers.

The POWs who became involved with a German woman were sentenced for "disobedience," which suggested an act of insubordination or revolt. Most of the women meanwhile had to stand trial in special courts, which specialized in the ruthless and quick prosecution of political dissent and treasonous acts. Yet, most couples probably did not think very much about the political implications of their actions. A number of POWs punished by the courts martial, especially in 1941 and 1942, had a track record of being avidly pro-German, and some women tried by the special courts were NSDAP (Nazi Party) members and played an active role in the *NS-Frauenschaft*, the party's organization for women. And yet, their personal acts were political not only because they constituted a serious crime under Nazi law but above all because they challenged Nazi policies designed to preserve "racial purity" and a national solidarity defined by exclusion and resentment of all outsiders.[10]

The task of this book is to explore and explain the forbidden relationships as well as their legal and diplomatic context. It focuses on amorous liaisons between western POWs and women, although there were also forbidden relations between German women and Polish or Soviet POWs and civilian laborers. But these relationships were even more stigmatized by Nazi propaganda than those with western POWs and led to draconic punishment: while the Polish and Soviet POWs were often executed, many of the women involved with them were sent to a concentration camp, in both cases usually without a trial.[11] The book also does not consider the forbidden relations between POWs and German or non-German men that came to trial, with the exception of a short section on homosexual relations. German men could also be sentenced for forbidden contact with a prisoner on other grounds, for example by helping him escape, transporting his letters, or giving him food or cigarettes. The

---

[10] For a good overview, see Annette F. Timm, *The Politics of Fertility in Twentieth-Century Berlin* (Cambridge and New York: Cambridge University Press, 2010), 118–38.

[11] See the section "Other Prisoners" in Chapter 1, "The Prisoners of War and the German Women."

POW would hardly be punished for this kind of contact except for homosexual acts, which were severely penalized in Nazi Germany. Nazi legislation and propaganda targeted the relations between POWs and German women because the Nazi regime considered them to be a particular danger to the German home front. As a consequence, the thousands of German women and POWs who disregarded the prohibition at great risk brought to light tensions and contradictory reactions in German wartime society. As Georges Smets explained to his outraged comrade after revealing the love relations in the television program: "I am often asked to write my memoirs, but for this chapter alone I could easily write a volume of 300 pages."[12]

The Literature

The forbidden relations lie at a crossroads of historiographies that are rarely explored comprehensively and in correspondence with each other. A body of literature focuses on the special courts and on the efforts of the Nazi system to prevent and punish German women's relations with foreigners, usually POWs as well as forced laborers. Second, there is a rich literature on German military justice, although rarely with a focus on courts martial against POWs. Third, there are many works on POWs, most with a focus on policy, diplomacy, and the treatment of POWs by Nazi Germany, but only a few that address relations of POWs to civilians.[13]

Aside from some generic publications on the Nazi special courts, which usually judged the women involved with prisoners, most of the works on these institutions are fine local studies, but a forbidden relationship with a POW was only one among many offenses that came before them.[14] The primary interest in these works is typically to explore the role of the justice system in political repression and the latitude of the

[12] Georges Smets to Mr. Georges Paulus, January 11, 1976, in Musée Royal de l'Armée et d'Histoire Militaire, Brussels, Fonds Hautecler, Farde 34.
[13] Notable exceptions are the works by Yves Durand (noted below), Antje Zühl (noted above), and Jean Marie d'Hoop: Jean-Marie d'Hoop, "Prisonniers de guerre français témoins de la défaite allemande (1945)," *Guerres mondiales et conflits contemporains* 38, no. 150 (1988); d'Hoop, "Les prisonniers français et la communauté rurale allemande (1940–1945)," *Guerres mondiales et conflits contemporains*, no. 147 (1987). See also Edith Petschnigg, *Von der Front aufs Feld. Britische Kriegsgefangene in der Steiermark 1941–1945* (Graz: Verein zur Förderung der Forschung von Folgen nach Konflikten und Kriegen, 2003), and Petschnigg, "'The Spirit of Comradeship'. Britische Kriegsgefangene in der Steiermark 1941 bis 1945," in *Kriegsgefangene des Zweiten Weltkrieges: Gefangennahme, Lagerleben, Rückkehr*, ed. Günter Bischof et al. (Munich: Oldenbourg, 2005).
[14] Gerd Weckbecker, *Zwischen Freispruch und Todesstrafe: Die Rechtsprechung der nationalsozialistischen Sondergerichte Frankfurt/Main und Bromberg* (Baden-Baden: Nomos, 1998).

judges.[15] A few articles deal specifically with trials against women involved with prisoners. Bernd Boll, for example, analyzes several cases from the court of Offenburg (Baden). He focuses on the trials against women but also looks at a few courts martial against the POWs, as far as they are accessible in local archives.[16] There are similar articles by Eckard Colmorgen and Klaus-Detlev Godau-Schüttke and by Iris Siemssen

---

[15] Freia Anders, *Strafjustiz im Sudetengau 1938–1945* (Munich: Oldenbourg, 2008); Klaus Bästlein, "Zur 'Rechts'-Praxis des Schleswig-Holsteinischen Sondergerichts 1937–1945," in *Strafverfolgung und Strafverzicht: Festschrift zum 125-jährigen Bestehen der Staatsanwaltschaft Schleswig-Holstein*, ed. Heribert Ostendorf (Köln: Heymann, 1992); Helmut Beer, *Widerstand gegen den Nationalsozialismus in Nürnberg 1933–1945* (Nürnberg: Stadtarchiv Nürnberg, 1976); Justizbehörde Hamburg, ed., *"Von Gewohnheitsverbrechern, Volksschädlingen und Asozialen ...": Hamburger Justizurteile im Nationalsozialismus* (Hamburg: Ergebnisse Verlag, 1995); Peter Lutz Kalmbach, "Das System der NS-Sondergerichtsbarkeiten," *Kritische Justiz* 50, no. 2 (2017); Karl-Heinz Keldungs, *Das Duisburger Sondergericht 1942–1945* (Baden-Baden: Nomos, 1998); Angelika Kleinz, *Individuum und Gemeinschaft in der juristischen Germanistik: die Geschworenengerichte und das "Gesunde Volksempfinden"* (Heidelberg: Winter, 2001); Gertraud Lehmann, "Von der 'Ehre der deutschen Frau': Nürnbergerinnen vor dem Sondergericht 1933–1945," in *Am Anfang war Sigena: Ein Nürnberger Frauengeschichtsbuch*, ed. Nadja Bennewitz and Gaby Franger (Nürnberg: Anthologie ars vivendi, 1999); Michael Löffelsender, *Strafjustiz an der Heimatfront: Die strafrechtliche Verfolgung von Frauen und Jugendlichen im Oberlandesgerichtsbezirk Köln 1939–1945* (Tübingen: Mohr Siebeck, 2012); Hans-Ulrich Ludewig and Dieter Kuessner, *'Es sei also jeder gewarnt': Das Sondergericht Braunschweig 1933–1945* (Braunschweig: Selbstverlag des Braunschweigischen Geschichtsvereins, 2000); Nina Lutz, "Das Sondergericht Nürnberg 1933–1945: Eingespielte Justizmaschinerie der gelenkten Rechtspflege," in *Justizpalast Nürnberg. Ein Ort der Weltgeschichte wird 100 Jahre: Festschrift zum 100. Jahrestag der feierlichen Eröffnung des Justizpalastes in Nürnberg durch König Ludwig III. am 11. September 1916*, ed. Ewald Behrschmidt (Neustadt an der Aisch: VDS Verlagsdruckerei Schmidt, 2016); Andreas Müller, "Das Sondergericht Graz von 1939 bis 1945" (Magisterarbeit Universität Graz, 2005); Jürgen Sandweg, "Schwabacher vor dem Sondergericht: Der Alltag der Denunziation und die 'Justiz des gesunden Volksempfindens'," in *Vergessen und verdrängt? Schwabach 1918–1945*, ed. Sabine Weigand-Karg, Sandra Hoffmann, and Jürgen Sandweg (Schwabach: Stadtmuseum Schwabach, 1997); Bernd Schimmler, *Recht ohne Gerechtigkeit: Zur Tätigkeit der Berliner Sondergerichte im Nationalsozialismus* (Berlin: Wissenschaftlicher Autoren-Verlag, 1984); Hans Wrobel, Henning Maul-Backer, and Ilka Renken, eds., *Strafjustiz im totalen Krieg: Aus den Akten des Sondergerichts Bremen 1940 bis 1945*, 3 vols., vol. 2 (Bremen: Bremen Verlags- und Buchhandelsgesellschaft, 1994); Hans Wüllenweber, *Sondergerichte im Dritten Reich: Vergessene Verbrechen der Justiz* (Frankfurt (M): Luchterhand, 1990); Wolf-Dieter Mechler, *Kriegsalltag an der "Heimatfront": Das Sondergericht Hannover im Einsatz gegen "Rundfunkverbrecher," "Schwarzschlachter," "Volksschädlinge" und andere "Straftäter" 1939 bis 1945* (Hannover: Hahn'sche Buchhandlung, 1997); Gedenkstätte Roter Ochse, ed., *"... das gesunde Volksempfinden gröblichst verletzt": "verbotener Umgang mit Kriegsgefangenen" im Sondergerichtsbezirk Halle* (Halle: Heinrich-Böll-Stiftung Sachsen-Anhalt, Stiftung Gedenkstätten Sachsen-Anhalt, 2009).

[16] Bernd Boll, "'... das gesunde Volksempfinden auf das Gröbste verletzt'. Die Offenburger Strafjustiz und der 'verbotene Umgang mit Kriegsgefangenen' während des Zweiten Weltkrieges," *Die Ortenau: Zeitschrift des Historischen Vereins für Mittelbaden* 71 (1991).

on trials at the special courts in Kiel and Altona and by Andreas Heusler on Munich.[17] These studies provide important facts and observations on the courts, but they remain limited to a specific area and usually say little about the POWs.

The literature on the expectations and restrictions for German women in relations with foreigners is also rich and helpful but has remained largely isolated from studies on POWs. The book on German soldiers' wives in both world wars by Birthe Kundrus, for example, provides much detail on the social expectations placed on these women, and her article on forbidden love in Nazi Germany highlights the relations between German women and foreign prisoners and laborers, but both works are not concerned with the prisoners' perspective and their diplomatic representation.[18] Silke Schneider's in-depth study of forbidden contacts between German women and foreign prisoners and laborers is very good on Nazi ideas regarding "sexual treason" or "racial treason," but it focuses only on the trials against women and pursues a broader aim insofar as the book also includes relations with foreign civilian laborers.[19] A fascinating case study by Maria Prieler-Wolan follows the fate of an Austrian mountain farm woman, a widow, sentenced for forbidden relations with three French POWs working on her farm or nearby, but it does not contain much information about the prisoners. Moreover, it is difficult to generalize from this one case.[20]

Cornelie Usborne's article "Female Desire and Male Honor: German Women's Illicit Love Affairs with Prisoners of War during the Second World War" draws from trials against women in front of the special court

---

[17] Eckard Colmorgen and Klaus-Detlev Godau-Schüttke, "'Verbotener Umgang mit Kriegsgefangenen'. Frauen vor dem Schleswig-Holsteinischen Sondergericht (1940–1945)," *Demokratische Geschichte: Jahrbuch zur Arbeiterbewegung und Demokratie in Schleswig-Holstein* 9 (1995); Iris Siemssen, "Das Sondergericht und die Nähe: Die Rechtsprechung bei 'verbotenem Umgang mit Kriegsgefangenen' am Beispiel von Fällen aus dem Kreis Plön," in *"Standgericht der inneren Front": Das Sondergericht Altona/Kiel 1932–1945*, ed. Robert Bohn and Uwe Danker (Hamburg: Ergebnisse-Verlag, 1998); Andreas Heusler, "'Strafbestand' Liebe: Verbotene Kontake zwischen Münchnerinnen und ausländischen Kriegsgefangenen," in *Zwischen den Fronten. Münchner Frauen in Krieg und Frieden 1900–1950*, ed. Sybille Krafft (Munich: Buchendorfer Verlag, 1995).

[18] Birthe Kundrus, *Kriegerfrauen: Familienpolitik und Geschlechterverhältnisse im Ersten und Zweiten Weltkrieg* (Hamburg: Christians, 1995), and Kundrus, "Forbidden Company: Romantic Relationships between Germans and Foreigners, 1939 to 1945," *Journal of the History of Sexuality* 11, no. 1/2 (2002).

[19] Silke Schneider, *Verbotener Umgang: Ausländer und Deutsche im Nationalsozialismus. Diskurse um Sexualität, Moral, Wissen und Strafe* (Baden-Baden: Nomos, 2010).

[20] Maria Prieler-Woldan, *Das Selbstverständliche tun: Die Salzburger Bäuerin Maria Etzer und ihr verbotener Einsatz für Fremde im Nationalsozialismus* (Innsbruck, Vienna, Bozen: StudienVerlag, 2018).

in Munich. Usborne, who is particularly interested in the history of emotions, highlights the active role of many women in these forbidden relationships, suggesting that a shift in female sexual behavior and expectations occurred in wartime Germany. With reference to findings of Dagmar Herzog, she stresses the destructive effects of the war on traditional constraints and communal controls and the Janus-faced Nazi approach to sexuality, with conservative and prudish messages mixing with more progressive narratives of sexual fulfillment in a popular culture that raised corresponding expectations.[21] Usborne provides good observations of the behavior and the motivations of German women but does not use the files of the prisoners involved with them, which are often an enlightening corrective to the trial records of the women. Drawing from literature that does not properly distinguish between western POWs and civilian laborers (the prohibition applied only to the former), she concludes that the punishment of POWs, if they were punished at all, was generally lenient.[22] Moreover, she takes a critical approach toward the active role of the women, suggesting that these women sometimes were complicit in Nazi racism and even took advantage of it by engaging in erotic relations with men in unfreedom whose punishment could be savage, especially in the case of Poles and Soviet POWs.[23] But the punishment for the women was harsh, too, and the power relation between German women and western POWs, who had some rights and privileges, was highly dynamic and not one-sided. Some POWs, for example by hiding in a woman's apartment after an escape, also brought particularly severe punishments upon the women.[24]

Older works on German military justice are dominated by the controversy regarding the degree of Nazification of military justice and its role in ensuring discipline and obedience within the German armed forces (*Wehrmacht*) to the last days of the Third Reich. The important study by Manfred Messerschmidt, which argues that the military justice system

[21] Cornelie Usborne, "Female Sexual Desire and Male Honor: German Women's Illicit Love Affairs with Prisoners of War during the Second World War," *Journal of the History of Sexuality* 26, no. 3 (2017): 476–7 and 482–4; see also Dagmar Herzog, "Introduction: War and Sexuality in Europe's Twentieth Century," in *Brutality and Desire: War and Sexuality in Europe's Twentieth Century*, ed. Dagmar Herzog (New York: Palgrave Macmillan, 2009), 5. For an exaggerated insistence on Nazi prudishness and condemnation of sexual pleasure, see Stefan Maiwald and Gerd Mischler, *Sexualität unter dem Hakenkreuz: Manipulation und Vernichtung der Intimsphäre im NS-Staat* (Hamburg and Vienna: Europa Verlag, 1999), for example 59–60, 103.
[22] Usborne, "Female Sexual Desire and Male Honor," 460–1, especially note 19.
[23] Ibid., 486–7.
[24] See Chapter 3 on "The Relations," especially the section "Gender Dynamics."

was strongly Nazified, mentions courts martial against POWs only in passing.[25] More recently, Peter Lutz Kalmbach, who has also published on civilian courts, has taken a broader perspective by interpreting military justice in the context of Nazi preparations for total war, which required utmost discipline both on the war and home front. Kalmbach addresses the courts martial against POWs involved with German women and reveals that Hitler personally took interest in the matter and pushed for a faster sentencing of the POWs in 1943, which was, however, difficult to achieve because of the delays required by the 1929 Geneva Convention on POWs and the often intricate correlation between the courts martial and the special courts trying the women.[26] David Raub Snyder's study *Sex Crimes under the Wehrmacht* deals mostly with trials against German soldiers and argues that military utility and pragmatism, more than ideology, were the guiding criteria of Nazi military justice, which reacted with surprising leniency in many cases of German soldiers having sex with racially stigmatized groups. Snyder suggests that the military tribunals were more lenient and less ideological than civilian courts in this matter, but this impression does not agree with my findings on courts martial against POWs. These cases, however, are outside the scope of Snyder's book, which focuses on sex crimes (not consensual relations) by German soldiers.[27] Birgit Beck's study of the Wehrmacht and sexual violence includes a section on forbidden relations between German women and foreign men as a comparative angle to the trials against German soldiers accused of sex crimes. Like Kundrus and Schneider, Beck stresses the double morality of German courts, which harshly punished undesirable relations when German women were involved but was more lenient with Wehrmacht soldiers abroad. She demonstrates how the notion of "sexual honor" was also defined much more restrictively with respect to German women than to non-German women attacked by German soldiers – with important distinctions between western and eastern Europeans. Beck highlights the fact that the judges adjudicating sex crimes of German soldiers treated the soldiers' "sexual

[25] Manfred Messerschmidt, *Die Wehrmachtjustiz 1933–1945* (Paderborn: Schöningh, 2005), 312 and 319.

[26] Peter Lutz Kalmbach, *Wehrmachtjustiz* (Berlin: Metropol-Verlag, 2012), 150–3. See also Kalmbach, "'Schutz der geistigen Wehrkraft': NS-Strafrechtsreformen für den 'totalen Krieg'," *Juristenzeitung* 17 (2015); Kalmbach, "The German Courts-Martial and Their Cooperation with the Police Organizations during the World War II," *Journal on European History of Law* 8, no. 1 (2017); Kalmbach, "Das System der NS-Sondergerichtsbarkeiten."

[27] David Raub Snyder, *Sex Crimes under the Wehrmacht* (Lincoln and London: University of Nebraska Press, 2007), 190–200.

need" as a mitigating factor.[28] The book on military justice on the "home front" by Kerstin Theis deals precisely with the military tribunals that tried POWs, among many other groups. Theis focuses on the military tribunals in Bonn and Marburg and argues, as Ambrière suggested, that the courts martial for forbidden relations mostly took place to serve as deterrent examples. These two tribunals, however, did not sentence a large number of POWs. Still, Theis provides interesting background data on the judges and procedures of the courts martial on the territory of the Reich – as opposed to the courts martial near the frontlines and in occupied countries.[29]

There is a rich literature on POWs in Nazi Germany. Rüdiger Overmans, in a chapter for the multi-volume work *Germany and the Second World War*, analyzes German policy regarding POWs of different nations and argues that, with respect to western prisoners, German officials were still to some extent motivated by national conservative, not Nazi, ideas inherited from World War I. These ideas clashed occasionally with Hitler's desire for a harsher treatment that would have violated the Geneva Convention on POWs of 1929 that Germany had ratified in 1934. Overmans also consistently stresses the economic utility of the POWs as workers.[30] Bob Moore provides a helpful overview on the treatment of POWs in the western European theater of war, arguing that the terms of the Geneva Convention were generally upheld, with notable exceptions mostly in the context of the capture of enemy soldiers and at the end of the war, when the German government ceased to exist altogether.[31]

Many studies focus on the POWs from a specific nation. For a long time, the history of British (including Commonwealth) and American POWs in Germany was dominated by a focus on heroic escapes and acts of defiance against petty, dumb, and brutal German guards ("goon baiting"). This focus provided attractive material for films and television

---

[28] Birgit Beck, *Wehrmacht und sexuelle Gewalt: Sexualverbrechen vor deutschen Militärgerichten 1939–1945* (Paderborn: Schöningh, 2004), 281–92. Snyder, however, argues that the Wehrmacht administered draconic punishment to German soldiers who raped Soviet women – not out of empathy for the women but because of concerns for discipline and worries about enticing more partisan opposition: Snyder, *Sex Crimes under the Wehrmacht*, 138–44.

[29] Kerstin Theis, *Wehrmachtjustiz an der "Heimatfront": Die Militärgerichte des Ersatzheeres im Zweiten Weltkrieg* (Berlin and Boston: De Gruyter/Oldenbourg, 2016), 383–9.

[30] Rüdiger Overmans, "Die Kriegsgefangenenpolitik des Deutschen Reiches 1939 bis 1945," in *Das Deutsche Reich und der Zweite Weltkrieg*, ed. Jörg Echternkamp (Munich: Deutsche Verlags-Anstalt, 2005), 735–6.

[31] Bob Moore, "The Treatment of Prisoners of War in the Western European Theatre of War, 1939–1945," in *Prisoners in War*, ed. Sibylle Scheipers (Oxford and New York: Oxford University Press, 2010).

series, but it supported a one-sided and elitist image of captivity. It is the merit of Simon Paul MacKenzie's book *The Colditz Myth* and other thorough studies, such as the books by Arieh Kochavi, Vasilis Vourkou-tiotis, Neville Wylie, and Clare Makepeace on British or American POWs, and Jonathan Vance and Peter Monteath on Canadian and Australian POWs respectively, to have replaced this image with a more rigorous analysis of the captivity experience and a deeper understanding of the diplomatic aspects pertaining to POWs.[32] Still, romantic adventures seemed irrelevant in this sober and harsh context. Makepeace's book, which analyzes POW memoirs and diaries, does not address them. Midge Gillies' book *The Barbed-Wire University: The Real Lives of Allied Prisoners of War in the Second World War*, briefly mentions some affairs of British POWs, but German women appear mostly as intruders into an all-male camp world: "Prisoners could go for months without glimpsing a woman so that when a female entered the camp – perhaps the wife or daughter of a German guard who had been invited to a concert or display of craft work – they were gawked at like an alien."[33] MacKenzie suggests that many POWs in retrospect argued that hunger made the sex drive go away and tells the story of a beautiful German woman passing in front of the barbed wire enclosing a British POW camp on her way home from the bakery; all the prisoners stared – at the bread. If British POWs did undertake erotic relations, MacKenzie argues, it was mostly with Polish or other non-German women.[34] David Rolf, in a study that despite its broad title (*Prisoners of the Reich: Germany's Captives 1939–1945*) deals above all with British POWs, mentions some sexual adventures of

---

[32] Arieh J. Kochavi, *Confronting Captivity: Britain and the United States and Their POWs in Nazi Germany* (Chapel Hill and London: University of North Carolina Press, 2005); Simon Paul MacKenzie, *The Colditz Myth: British and Commonwealth Prisoners of War in Nazi Germany* (Oxford and New York: Oxford University Press, 2004); Clare Makepeace, *Captives of War: British Prisoners of War in Europe in the Second World War* (Cambridge: Cambridge University Press, 2017); Vasilis Vourkoutiotis, *Prisoners of War and the German High Command: The British and American Experience* (New York: Palgrave, 2003); Vourkoutiotis, "What the Angels Saw: Red Cross and Protective Power Visits to Anglo-American POWs, 1939–1945," *Journal of Contemporary History* 40, no. 4 (2005); Neville Wylie, *Barbed Wire Diplomacy: Britain, Germany, and the Politics of Prisoners of War, 1939–1945* (Oxford and New York: Oxford University Press, 2010); Jonathan Vance, *Objects of Concern: Canadian Prisoners of War through the Twentieth Century* ([no place]: UBC Press, 1994); Peter Monteath, *P.O.W.: Australian Prisoners of War in Hitler's Reich* (Sydney: Macmillan, 2011).

[33] Midge Gillies, *The Barbed-Wire University: The Real Lives of Allied Prisoners of War in the Second World War* (London: Aurum Press, 2011), 48–9. The title is misleading because the book only deals with (mostly elite) British POWs and not Soviet, American, or other Allied POWs.

[34] MacKenzie, *Colditz Myth*, 213–15; for the story of the woman with the bread, see also Petschnigg, *Von der Front aufs Feld*, 232.

prisoners, mostly secret visits to brothels, often with the complicity of guards. But Rolf says little about relations with German women outside the venal context.[35] An article by Karen Horn on South African POWs in a camp on the outskirts of Dresden stresses the amicable relations between the POWs and the commander, the guards, and for a while also local civilians. But bombing attacks, especially the devastating raids on Dresden in February 1945, triggered hostility from civilians. Horn mentions that the commander tacitly tolerated an illicit love relation of a POW with a German woman but does not explain whether this case was an exception and if there ever were trials against any of the South Africans from this camp.[36]

Yet, the archival files show that British POWs did not lose their sexual appetite and that they did end up in front of military tribunals in increasing numbers. It is true that many British POWs sought contact with women who might have appeared to be Polish or Czech, as MacKenzie suggests, but we have to consider that most British POWs were held on the eastern periphery of the Reich where national identity was often ambiguous; many women whose background was partly Polish, Czech, or Yugoslav did in fact have German citizenship, and contact with them was therefore punishable. Moreover, two military district commanders in the German–Polish border areas (military districts XX and XXI), frustrated by these ambiguities, decreed that *all* POW relations to women, regardless of citizenship, were forbidden.[37]

The key works on French POWs in Nazi Germany are more dated and also say little about the amorous relations, with the exception of the two books by Yves Durand from the 1980s, which provide interesting material on the everyday lives of the French POWs and mention the forbidden relations in the context of POW relations with civilians. Durand did not yet have access to the judicial files for the POWs, however, and he downplays the erotic dimension of the forbidden relations. His discretion is not surprising if one considers that his work was commissioned by the association of former POWs and appeared at a time when most former

[35] David Rolf, *Prisoners of the Reich: Germany's Captives 1939–1945* (London: Cooper, 1988), 73, 104–6.
[36] Karen Horn, "'History from the Inside': South African Prisoner-of-War Experience in Work Camp 1169, Dresden, 1943–1945," *War & Society* 33, no. 4 (2014): 276, 280–1.
[37] Hans K. Frey, *Die disziplinarische und gerichtliche Bestrafung von Kriegsgefangenen. Die Anwendung des Kriegsgefangenenabkommens von 1929 auf die angelsächsischen und deutschen Kriegsgefangenen während des Zweiten Weltkrieges* (Vienna: Springer, 1948), 61. Frey mentions only district XX. For the corresponding order applying to district XXI, see Feldurteil, Posen, April 6, 1944, in BAR Bern, Bestand Vertretung Berlin, 72b.

POWs were still alive.[38] A more recent study of the memoirs of French
POWs and civilian laborers by Patrice Arnaud argues that the Frenchmen in Germany retrospectively described the love relations as a reversal
of the military defeat through erotic "conquests." Arnaud suggests that,
in reality, a reversal of gender roles often took place, given that the
woman was a member of the dominant society and the Frenchman a
captive soldier or worker. The reversal of gender roles expressed itself in
the active part of the woman in the relationships and also in her occasional function as provider of extra food. Many French memoirs, as
Arnaud points out, also stress the reputation of French men among
German women as excellent lovers.[39]

Belgian POWs in World War II have received very little scholarly
attention. There were efforts in the 1970s and 1980s to produce a
comprehensive history of the Belgian POWs similar to what Yves Dur-
and was doing at the time for French POWs. Georges Hautecler and
E. Gillet, both retired officers and former POWs, gathered archival
documents and testimonies, but nothing substantial materialized, except
for a well-researched but short series of articles by Gillet in the Belgian
military history journal in 1987–90, an anecdotal book by Hautecler on
spectacular prisoner escapes, and an article on the religious life of the
prisoners, also by Hautecler.[40]

A few scholarly works have looked at both, the realms of the German
women and the POWs. Almost all of these studies reference the pathbreaking work by Ulrich Herbert about foreign laborers (both POWs and

[38] Yves Durand, *La Captivité: histoire des prisonniers de guerre français, 1939–1945* (Paris: Fédération nationale des combattants et prisonniers de guerre et combattants d'Algérie, de Tunisie et du Maroc, 1982), 414–20; Durand, *Les Prisonniers de guerre dans les Stalags, les Oflags et les Kommandos, 1939–1945* (Paris: Hachette, 1987), 250–4. See also Fabien Théofilakis, "Le Prisonnier de guerre dans l'historiographie française et allemande: Étudier la Seconde Guerre mondiale à front renversé," *Guerres mondiales et conflits contemporains*, no. 274 (2019): 19–20. The older work by Pierre Gascar does mention love relations but is not precise and contains no references: Pierre Gascar, *Histoire de la captivité des Français en Allemagne (1939–1945)* (Paris: Gallimard, 1967), 110–16; Gascar also mentions many relations of French POWs with Ukrainian and Polish forced laborers: 149.
[39] Arnaud, "Die deutsch-französischen Liebesbeziehungen," 186–9. See also Patrice Arnaud, *Les STO. Histoire des Français requis en Allemagne nazie 1942–1945* (Paris: CNRS Editions, 2010), 241–50 and 441.
[40] E. Gillet, "Histoire des sous-officiers et soldats belges prisonniers de guerre, 1940–1945," *Belgisch tijdschrift voor militaire geschiedenis/Revue belge d'histoire militaire* XXVII (1987–8): 227–54, 299–320; 355–79; XXVIII (1989–90): 45–78, 123–66, 217–54, 299–335, 351–82; Georges Hautecler, *Évasions réussies* (Liège: Éditions Solédi, 1966); Hautecler, "La Vie religieuse des prisonniers de guerre Belges (1940–1945). Faits et documents," *Cahiers d'Histoire de la Seconde Guerre mondiale* 3 (1974). See also the brief article by X. Buckinx, "Belgen in duitse Krijgsgevangenschap 1940–1945," *Spiegel Historiael*, no. 11 (1984).

civilians) in Nazi Germany, which presented some information on forbidden relations and efforts of the Nazi regime to negotiate the tension
between its desire for racial homogeneity and its dependence on the
large-scale presence of foreign laborers.[41] Very useful and insightful is
Fabrice Virgili's book *Naître ennemi*, dealing with Franco-German children born in World War II. Virgili, who had already published a book on
the head-shaving of French women accused of "horizontal collaboration"
with Germans, examines sexual relations between French and German
nationals and the fate of their offspring in both countries during and
immediately after the war. As in the book on shorn women, he addresses
public concerns about sexual boundaries and gender roles in wartime
and postwar societies, showing that Franco-German children grew up in
an atmosphere of suspicion, stigmatized as children of treason and
shame. Virgili's book is well documented but favors the French perspective and French materials (as he admits). It reveals more about the
children of German men in France than about the children of French
men in Germany, and it does not consider trials against German women
and the numerous local studies available in German.[42]

The French journalist Jean-Paul Picaper, an expert on German politics, wrote a book about the love relations between French men and
German women in Nazi Germany for a popular audience. Picaper found
some surviving lovers and their children, interviewed them, and even
helped some of the children to track down their missing parent or family.
Many families had no idea that they have relatives in the other country.
The reunions prompted by Picaper's discoveries could foster warm
friendships and bonds, but they could also cause mean-spirited rejection
motivated by the fear of rival heirs. Picaper's book focuses on POWs and
civilian laborers, and it does not always make the necessary distinctions
between them. For example, Picaper repeatedly claims that contacts
between French civilian workers and German women were forbidden.
Picaper also mistakenly claims that German women involved with
French men, and sometimes their French partners, would be sent to a
concentration camp if convicted. This was only true for some women
involved with Polish or Soviet POWs or eastern laborers. Still, Picaper's

[41] Ulrich Herbert, *Hitler's Foreign Workers: Enforced Foreign Labor in Germany under the Third Reich*, trans. William Templer (Cambridge and New York: Cambridge University Press, 1997), especially 124–6. The book was orginially published in German in 1986.
[42] Fabrice Virgili, *Naître ennemi: Les enfants des couples franco-allemands nés pendant la Seconde Guerre mondiale* (Paris: Editions Payot, 2009). See also Virgili, *La France "virile": Des femmes tondues à la Libération* (Paris: Éditions Payot & Rivage, 2004), translated into English as *Shorn Women: Gender and Punishment in Liberation France*, trans. John Flower (Oxford and New York: Berg, 2002).

book comes closest to analyzing the lived reality of Franco-German love relations, and it highlights what was often sincere love in very difficult circumstances.[43]

An inspiring work that connects sexuality to international relations, albeit not with a focus on POWs, is Mary Louise Roberts' book *What Soldiers Do: Sex and the American GI in World War II France*.[44] Roberts touches on similar themes to my book, from sex and race to power in an international framework. She argues that the image of France, especially Paris, as a promiscuous place of sexual adventure featured as a great attraction to American soldiers in 1944–5 and helped motivate them to fight. At least, this worked for white soldiers; black soldiers found themselves easily accused of rape and punished draconically in flimsy courts martial that, I would add in light of the evidence in my book, compared rather badly with the average German court martial, which generally followed rules of evidence and featured engaged defense attorneys. Roberts shows how blaming black soldiers for rapes and the unsavory aspects of the American army presence provided something like a lighting rod appreciated by American army leaders as well as by many French people, who were more racist than African Americans believed them to be on the basis of memories from World War I. Roberts argues that the frequent encounters with desperate French women prostituting themselves instilled, or confirmed, in the American soldiers an image of a decadent and weak France that needed strong American leadership, and she argues that this type of relationship had international consequences insofar as it allowed American leaders to dismiss France as a serious international player. Of course, the relationship between a soldier of a liberating, victorious, and very well-supplied army to a woman from a liberated, humiliated, poor, and relatively powerless country features very different gender dynamics than the relationship between a POW and a woman of the detaining state. Roberts' efforts to tie sexual relations to international politics are inspiring and aspirational, but her book deals mostly with the American push to dismantle the French regulated prostitution system and not with the higher diplomatic level. I would argue that the notion of a weak France (and not only in American eyes) owes much more to France's quick and surprising defeat of May–June 1940 than to the sexual relations of GIs and French women in 1944–5. Also, Roberts focuses almost exclusively on narrowly sexual

[43] Jean-Paul Picaper, *Le Crime d'aimer: Les enfants du STO* (Paris: Éditions des syrtes, 2005). For references to concentration camps, see pp. 31, 139, 159, 295, 306.

[44] Mary Louise Roberts, *What Soldiers Do: Sex and the American GI in World War II France* (Chicago: The University of Chicago Press, 2013).

encounters, while the relations between western POWs and German women encompassed a much broader spectrum and included only very few cases of rape.

The Prison Camp Paradigm and Alternative Reality

One problem that has made it difficult to integrate the different avenues of scholarship is what I propose to call the "prison camp paradigm" of POW history, namely the widespread notion that POWs, unlike civilian laborers, were groups insulated behind barbed wire and separated from German civilian society. Memoirs and psychological research on former POWs have stressed the effects of long-term confinement, popularly called "barbed-wire disease," arising from years of isolation in an all-male group of comrades. Research on gender roles, homoerotic relations, and female impersonators in POW theaters has provided insights into the creative ways in which POWs coped with this situation, always assuming a rather isolated sphere in which POWs spent their days. The prison camp paradigm was useful to former POWs in their efforts to portray themselves as victims of Nazism qualifying for indemnification because the POW camp appeared to belong to the same spectrum as the concentration camp. It also helped to cover up the degree of freedom many POWs had and the choices they made, especially in terms of love relations. But the prison camp paradigm is misleading and rests on an often implicit focus on the privileged and articulate elites, mostly officers.[45] The Geneva Convention stipulated that officers did not have to work, and except for a minority who volunteered to work, officers were indeed secluded in camp complexes or castles on forbidding hilltops, such as the famous Colditz castle in Saxony that inspired films and television series.[46] Much of the literature on the POW experience, especially on the British and Americans, focuses on these officers, their escape plans, their ingenious book projects, their theater productions, and their attempts to fill their idle time through bird-watching, sports, reading, or university-level courses.[47] Some of the more educated

---

[45] For this reason, much of the interesting literature on camps is not useful for my project. See, for example, Bettina Greiner and Alan Kramer, eds., *Die Welt der Lager: Zur "Erfolgsgeschichte" einer Institution* (Hamburg: Hamburger Edition, 2013); Joël Kotek and Pierre Rigoulot, *Le Siècle des camps: Détention, concentration, extermination. Cent ans de mal radical* ([Paris]: Lattès, 2000).

[46] MacKenzie, *Colditz Myth*, 93–4. See also Simon P. MacKenzie, "British Prisoners of War in Nazi Germany," *Archives* 28 (2003): 184–5.

[47] For some examples among many: David A. Foy, *For You the War Is Over: American Prisoners of War in Nazi Germany* (New York: Stein and Day, 1984); Makepeace, *Captives of War*, 69–73.

rank-and-file prisoners experienced captivity in similar ways to officers because they were charged with administrative duties in the camps, for example as translators, secretaries, or scribes.

Granted, there were many great artists, scientists, writers, and historians among the POWs, and they deserve attention because the enforced idleness of a POW camp could be a remarkably creative and productive period despite hardships. In *The Barbed-Wire University*, Gillies presents an impressive list of artistic and scientific achievements of British (officer) POWs.[48] A cursory look at eminent French POWs reads like a who's-who of intellectual and political life of the postwar period. The historian Fernand Braudel, for example, developed his pathbreaking ideas about history as a social science in lectures to his fellow prisoners in an officer camp in Lübeck. For the philosopher Louis Althusser, who worked as a translator and assistant prisoner representative (man of confidence) in various camps in Schleswig-Holstein, captivity also was an intellectual gestation period. He studied, among other subjects, German literature and used his POW diary to formulate new ideas – between reports about passionate soccer matches against Belgian, Serbian, and Polish officers.[49] The philosopher Emmanuel Levinas spent most of the war in the officer barracks of the POW camp Fallingbostel near Hannover and drafted his work *Existence and Existents* (1947) in captivity.[50] The philosopher Jean-Paul Sartre spent a few months in the POW camp of Trier and formed a diverse and lively intellectual circle there.[51] The poet, philosopher, and later statesman Léopold Sédar Senghor, the first president of Senegal (1960–80), also experienced captivity – in his case in the midst of French colonial prisoners in German-occupied France – as a transforming period for his ideas about being black, African, and French, although he, like others, tended to mystify his captivity experience in postwar accounts.[52]

By privileging the experience of illustrious or elite POWs, the prison camp paradigm has tended to suppress the interactions of POWs and

---

[48] Gillies, *Barbed-Wire University*, 84–96, 271–304.

[49] Peter Schöttler, "Der französische Historiker Fernand Braudel als Kriegsgefangener in Lübeck," *Zeitschrift für Lübeckische Geschichte* 95 (2015); Louis Althusser, *Journal de Captivité. Stalag XA/1940–1945. Carnets, correspondances, textes* (n. p.: Stock/ IMEC, 1992).

[50] Bettina Bergo, "Emmanuel Levinas," *The Stanford Encyclopedia of Philosophy* (Fall 2017 Edition), Edward N. Zalta (ed.), plato.stanford.edu/archives/fall2017/entries/levinas/ (last visited on 13 May 2019). Yves Durand also recognizes the creative aspect of captivity: Durand, *Captivité*, 289–307; Durand, *Prisonniers de Guerre*, 183–93.

[51] Marius Perrin, *Avec Sartre au Stalag 12D* (Paris: Delarge, 1980), 29–42.

[52] Raffael Scheck, "Léopold Sédar Senghor prisonnier de guerre allemand. Une nouvelle approche fondée sur un texte inédit," *French Politics, Culture & Society* 31, no. 2 (2014).

civilians. The able-bodied prisoners without rank all had to work, and this brought them into contact with German civilians. During their long work days (ten to twelve hours, Monday to Saturday), these POWs interacted with the German labor force, including an increasing number of German women and foreigners (interactions between POWs and non-German civilian workers, both women and men, still await a focused exploration). Spontaneous conversations in broken German arose during routine tasks or over breaks. Prisoners might also meet civilians on their way to and from work. On farms, the separation between POWs and civilians was impossible to maintain from the start, as the POW might work alone with a woman in the fields or vineyards and sleep on the farm. A shortage of guards made close supervision of working prisoners nearly impossible, although foremen and farmers were usually contracted as auxiliary guards. Even prisoners who were locked up in sleeping quarters at night could find ways to sneak out and return before daybreak.

Working prisoners, the vast majority, obviously had no problems related to idleness in an isolated all-male sphere, and their living conditions did not favor the outbreak of "barbed-wire disease." Instead, they shared many of the problems and concerns of German working people. Even Ambrière acknowledged this, speaking about solidarity between French POWs, many of them farmers, and German farmers, all united in an age-old hatred of tax collectors and urban meddlers – "those people who always take and never give."[53] Not surprisingly, most of the women involved with POWs belonged to the working population – employees, industrial workers, and especially farmwomen and maids – although a number of housewives without regular employment, some of them from the social elites, also had to stand trial for a forbidden relationship.

Given the integration of POWs into German work life, captivity slowly turned into an alternative reality. Connections to home and the old life were tenuous, and an end of the new life for a long time seemed distant and insecure, although many prisoners at least initially hoped that liberation would come soon.[54] Many married prisoners had doubts about the fidelity of their wives, and some knew for sure that their wife or girlfriend was involved with somebody else – for French or Belgian POWs quite possibly a German soldier stationed in their home country.[55] The daily

---

[53] Ambrière, *Les grandes Vacances*, 193.

[54] Ibid 197. On the expectation of a quick liberation in the case of British POWs, see Makepeace, *Captives of War*, 42–52.

[55] Sarah Fishman has explored the paternalistic attention to POW wives by the Vichy government, which appears to mirror Kundrus' findings about warrior wives in Nazi Germany: Sarah Fishman, *We Will Wait: Wives of French Prisoners of War, 1940–1945* (New Haven and London: Yale University Press, 1991); Fishman, "Grand Delusions:

experience of common work with German civilians led them to identify to some degree with their concerns. Most prisoners picked up some German over long years of captivity, and many spoke it quite well. Historian Jean-Marie d'Hoop has shown that empathy developed between French prisoners and the German civilians particularly in the context of the catastrophic German defeat. The research of Durand, based on written and oral testimonies of former French POWs, confirms this impression, as does the study of Württemberg in the Second World War by Jill Stephenson.[56] Although most prisoners probably missed home and wanted to return, they adapted to a new life in Germany. The two realities co-existed next to each other and without much connection. Many married prisoners, who would probably not have contemplated infidelity or even divorce under normal circumstances, felt driven into passionate amorous entanglements in their present and immediate reality. Many couples wanted to marry after the war, but this was rarely possible because military regulations insisted on prompt repatriation of the POW alone, and the strong public hostility to Germans in France, Belgium, and Britain ruled out acceptance of a German bride for some time.

It was harder for British POWs than for Frenchmen and Belgians to settle into an alternative reality during captivity, and it would seem that their POW lives always remained more provisional. The British army forbade "fraternization" with the enemy, and British POWs faced tighter regimentation and guarding. The German "enemy remains enemy" propaganda found more resonance given that Britain remained in the war and given that new British POWs kept arriving from various fronts. Under these conditions, one would expect to see a higher proportion of superficial erotic encounters of the British POWs, as compared to French and Belgian POWs. Yet, a significant number of British POWs did grow very close to their German girlfriends, and many German–British couples developed marriage plans. Whether this happened more rarely than in relations involving French and Belgian POWs is hard to ascertain. The recollections of British POWs seem to reflect on predominantly hostile "German" civilians (although one needs to consider that many British prisoners stayed on the eastern periphery of the Reich and dealt

---

The Unintended Consequences of Vichy France's Prisoner of War Propaganda," *Journal of Contemporary History* 26, no. 2 (1991). See also Gerlinda Swillen, *De Wieg van WO II. Oorlogskinderen op de as Brussel-Berlijn* (Brussels: ASP, 2016).

[56] d'Hoop, "Prisonniers de guerre français témoins de la défaite allemande," 77; Durand, *Captivité*, 401–21; Durand, *Prisonniers de Guerre*, 241–55; Jill Stephenson, *Hitler's Home Front : Württemberg under the Nazis* (London and New York: Hambledon Continuum, 2006), 279 and 84. See also, albeit with a focus on all foreign laborers: Zühl, "Zum Verhältnis der deutschen Landbevölkerung," 351–2.

with many people who were German only in a broader sense), but there is much evidence that British POWs were well received in some rural areas, for example in Austria. Historian Edith Petschnigg has discovered only relatively few court cases involving Austrian women and British POWs, but she argues that there were many relations that did not come to trial. While the SS Security Service ascribed the low number of trials to the restraint of British prisoners rooted in national pride, her findings suggest that, as elsewhere, popular acceptance of the POWs led to a cover of silence. She even found a case of an Australian POW who remained in Austria after the war and married his village sweetheart and of a New Zealander who married his Austrian lover and took her home with him after the war.[57] Some British POWs promised their farming families that they would protect them once Allied troops arrived.[58]

The Sources

The source material for this project is immense. I therefore had to select certain places and source groups. I started with the fifty-five volumes in the German Foreign Office Archives in Berlin dealing with trials against French POWs.[59] These files contain more than one thousand court martial judgments as well as much contextual material such as diplomatic exchanges between Germany and France and internal German communications about specific policies and judgments, mostly between the Foreign Office and the High Command. For unclear reasons, this collection stops in February 1942, with the exception of a few court martial sentences from a few months later, mostly in cases where the German High Command considered an earlier sentence too lenient and asked for a retrial. Around 75 percent of the cases in this collection concern trials for consensual relations with women. Poaching, resistance to a guard, theft, and political offenses (insults to the German army or leadership), as well as a few cases of rape, child abuse, and homosexual relations make up the remaining 25 percent. The first trials in this collection date from the summer of 1940, but forbidden relations appeared only in late 1940. The same archives also contain much smaller collections for Belgian (five volumes) and British POWs (four volumes). The Belgian files are similar to the French, but the British files contain

---

[57] Petschnigg, *Von der Front aufs Feld*, 224–37, especially 225–6, 236; Petschnigg, "The Spirit of Comradeship," 430, 432–4.

[58] See, for example, the testimony of the guard Fraebel, February 10, 1945, in Steiermärkisches Landesarchiv (StLA) Graz, Sondergericht, KLs 250/45 K.3, case against Maria H.

[59] Politisches Archiv des Auswärtigen Amtes (PAAA) Berlin, R 40860–40914.

mostly courts martial regarding resistance to a guard, theft, and political offenses, and not a single court martial relating to a forbidden relation. The Belgian and British collections, like the French, end in early 1942 and are incomplete even for the period they cover.[60]

The Archives nationales in Pierrefitte-sur-Seine, outside Paris, hold a vast collection pertaining to French POWs and the French agencies that dealt with POW matters, primarily the so-called Scapini Mission, which on December 10, 1940, assumed the role of protecting power for the French POWs, a role normally played by a neutral country according to the Geneva Convention. These materials contain more than 17,000 trial records, correspondence between the Scapini Mission and German defense attorneys as well as French legal advisors in the POW camps, diplomatic documents, internal memos, inspection reports, and eyewitness accounts. Access to some of these materials, especially the court martial records, was for a long time restricted for legal reasons. I obtained permission in 2015 to consult specific files selected by name. The legal restrictions expired not much later, but the material condition of the documents, printed on low-quality paper that tends to disintegrate whenever one turns a page, led to restricted access again. It is therefore impossible to examine these records systematically. But I did explore select files from these holdings, and I extensively analyzed the diplomatic documents and the correspondence of the Scapini Mission, which were in better physical shape and mostly accessible without special permission. A curious mix of files concerning French POWs and German women also exists in the *Bureau des Archives des victimes des conflits contemporains* in Caen, a branch of the French military archives. This collection contains the richest materials on POW trials and also seemingly random files of women from the northwest and south of Germany who became involved with French POWs. This archive also holds a registry of French soldiers, including their POW identity cards, which often provide information on the fate of the prisoner after the court martial.[61]

For the Belgian POWs, I consulted five archives in greater Brussels. Although American military trucks dropped off boxes with German court martial files in front of the War Ministry in Brussels in July 1945, this collection was divided up and can no longer be traced in the archives.[62]

---

[60] PAAA, R 40851–40855 (Belgians) and R 40856–40859 (British).

[61] Gaël Eismann and Corinna von List, "Les Fonds des tribunaux allemands (1940–1945) conservés au BAVCC à Caen," *Francia* 39 (2012).

[62] See Georges Hautecler, "Sources de l'histoire de la captivité de guerre belge 1940–1945" (1969), in Centre d'études et de documentation guerres et sociétés contemporaines/Studie- en Dokumentatiecentrum Oorlog en hedendaagse Maatschappij (CEGESOMA), Brussels, AB 270.

Clearly, some files were used, and preserved, in connection with restitution claims by ex-POWs who served time in German prisons or penitentiaries.[63] Many papers, however, were destroyed by a fire at the Belgian military archives in Evere outside of Brussels.[64] The most extensive collection relevant to Belgian POWs lies in the Center for Historical Research and Documentation on War and Society (CEGESOMA) in Brussels. A precious find are the notes of Georges Smets, the man of confidence of the Belgians in Stalag I-A in East Prussia, conserved partly at the CEGESOMA and partly at the Brussels branch of the Royal Museum of the Armed Forces and Military History. Smets' descriptions from the war and his postwar reflections are a humane voice from a POW representative who was centrally concerned with helping POWs accused of forbidden relations.

For the British POWs, the records of the Swiss legation in Berlin, which acted as protecting power for the British after the entry of the United States into the war, contain the richest material. These records are preserved in the Swiss Federal Archives in Bern. They show a proliferation of love-related trials in 1943, getting most intense by early 1945. The Swiss Federal Archives also contain diplomatic exchanges between the governments in London and Berlin pertaining to POW matters as well as inspection reports of military prisons and civil penitentiaries by the Swiss delegates and the International Committee of the Red Cross (ICRC). The Swiss archives also have material on American POWs, but given the late arrival, stricter guarding, and the more controlled deployment of most American POWs, trials for forbidden relations involving Americans were rare.

In addition, I consulted some smaller collections from the American National Archives in College Park (Maryland) pertaining to French, Belgian, and British POWs when the United States was still their protecting power, and to American POWs in Germany. The German military archives in Freiburg im Breisgau contain some normative material (on the treatment of POWs) and some legal files, which used to belong to a collection of records located in Aachen-Kornelimünster. These collections are very incomplete. A new POW document collection in the British National Archives in Kew is gradually being opened, and I have

---

[63] These documents are part of the collection of the "Service Archives des victimes de la guerre" in Brussels-Anderlecht, Square de l'Aviation 31.
[64] Among the materials destroyed by the fire in Evere are: Musée Royal de l'Armée et d'Histoire Militaire, Evere, Dossier I, #7 Liste de condamnations; #8 Demandes de diminution de peine, #9 Pièces judicières diverses, and Dossier IX #1 Jurisprudence.

consulted it for some specific prisoners, mostly to trace their path after conviction by a German court martial.

The trial materials for the women are much richer than most POW files. They contain denunciation letters, love letters between the POW and the woman, and detailed interrogation reports and reference letters from mayors or police officials. They therefore allow for a closer analysis of the social context of the love affair and its discovery. The women's court files also contain post-trial materials, such as clemency pleas and requests for rehabilitation or indemnification after the war. Some of the women's files include the court martial sentence for the prisoner and interrogation reports of the prisoner and some of his comrades.

Despite significant wartime losses – the Reich Ministry of Justice ordered the destruction of legal documents in 1945 – many state archives in Germany hold extensive collections of trial records from the special courts and from some district courts.[65] The richness of these collections forced me to select certain archives. I initially was worried chiefly about getting materials from industrial areas as well as agricultural areas, but I found that every collection I used contains a mix of both because the special courts, which normally tried the women in the more severe cases, covered a fairly large area including cities as well as villages, offering a mix of work situations. I therefore had to worry most about geographic variety. I started out with the collections in Schleswig, Nürnberg, and Vienna, a mix of predominantly Lutheran (Schleswig) and Catholic (Vienna) regions (Nürnberg covered a mixed religious area). Given the limits on my time and archival restrictions, I was not able to explore all of these collections completely. In Vienna, for example, the access numbers for the relevant folders have to be searched in the reading room with the help of a three-volume registry written by hand in the late 1940s and including all trials of the special court. Yet, I gathered a diverse sample in terms of date and severity of sentence in these archives. In a second phase of research, I analyzed dossiers in Potsdam (covering the region of Brandenburg-Berlin, including areas east of the Oder River now part of Poland), Oldenburg, Hannover, Bremen, Graz (Austria), Darmstadt, and Wiesbaden. The collections in Oldenburg and Potsdam also contain some materials on efforts to put special court judges on trial after the war and on prisons and penitentiaries, but these files are not very rich.

---

[65] On the destruction order, see Martin F. Polaschek, *Im Namen der Republik Oesterreich! Die Volksgerichte in der Steiermark 1945 bis 1955* (Graz: LAD Zentralkanzlei, 1998), 105.

It is difficult to access materials from the eastern periphery of the former Reich, specifically from the areas now part of Poland and from former East Prussia. This is deplorable because it was in this area that many British POWs were tried, and I would have liked to see more files of the women involved with them. Of particular interest was the status of the women because many civilians in the eastern regions had mixed ancestry. Although most of the women tried by the special courts had German citizenship, some could have passed themselves off as Poles or Czechs to the prisoners given their mixed ancestry or their non-German last names. The archives in Wroclaw (formerly Breslau) claim that they lost their extensive collection of special court documents during a flood in 1997. Information from Gdansk (formerly Danzig) was too vague to justify a research trip, but I had the great luck of finding an extremely helpful retired archivist in Katowice (formerly Kattowitz) in eastern Upper Silesia who photographed relevant materials for me. Altogether, while there are a great many more files than I examined, this book includes a sample covering areas with different religious, social, and economic structures.

It is of course risky to rely so much on trial records given that people threatened with severe punishment will likely represent their case in a way that might lead to milder punishment and given the potential of abusive interrogators, especially for the women. But the trial records contain such broad and varied materials that it is possible to qualify the statements defendants made to the police interrogators or in front of the courts.[66] They include what the Germans call "ego documents" – such as love letters and other documents written not at all in view of a pending trial (although sometimes self-censored because of fear of discovery) – and they contain much material from legal advisors, attorneys, POW representatives, and diplomats who looked at the forbidden relations and the trials from a different perspective. Wherever possible, I have paired the court martial file of the POW with the court file of the woman to gain the most balanced and well-rounded picture.

Confidentiality rules differ slightly in Germany, Austria, France, Britain, Belgium, Poland, Switzerland, and the United States. But generally, I am not authorized to use full names for people on trial who are born less than one hundred years ago or passed away less than thirty years ago. The files usually disclose the birth date, but given that it is almost always

---

[66] Cornelie Usborne addresses this concern well, while stressing that even some of the statements recorded by police interrogators can be authentic: Usborne, "Female Sexual Desire and Male Honor," 462–3.

difficult to determine the date of a person's death, I have changed the last names of the prisoners and the German women who came before the courts. I have tried to select names that reflect the flavor of the original (for example, a Basque French name or the name of Polish–German woman). I apologize if I have selected implausible or, worse, nonsensical last names.

1 The Prisoners of War and the German Women

The French

Approximately 1.55 million French POWs came to Germany following the defeat of the western powers in May and June 1940. Close to one million of them were still in Germany in 1945.[1] The situation of French POWs in Nazi Germany was peculiar. As a part of the armistice agreement signed on June 22, 1940, France had to release all of its German prisoners while Germany kept its French POWs until a peace treaty was signed. The French government therefore had no direct reciprocity – the option to retaliate against POWs if the enemy mistreats its captives.[2] Moreover, the French government in Vichy adopted a policy of collaboration with Nazi Germany. The fact that Germany decided to retain its French POWs was crucial for this decision, and I have argued elsewhere that collaboration became a substitute reciprocity: major violations of the Geneva Convention would have threatened collaboration and involved a significant cost for Germany.[3] The importance of the POW question for Marshall Philippe Pétain and his government is evident in the fact that Pétain already in August 1940 selected Georges Scapini, a right-wing World War I veteran, as his special ambassador for POW questions. Scapini, blinded in battle in 1915, had been involved in Franco-German veterans' reunions and presided over a mutual friendship group directed by Otto Abetz, Foreign Minister Joachim von Ribbentrop's expert on

---

[1] For a brief survey of French POWs in Nazi Germany, see Overmans, "Kriegsgefangenenpolitik," 758–72. Most French POWs who returned home during the war benefited from the *relève*, an agreement that placed three civilian laborers at the disposal of German industry in exchange for one POW.

[2] For basic considerations on the role of reciprocity in POW matters (the "mutual hostage factor"), see Simon Paul MacKenzie, "The Treatment of Prisoners of War in World War II," *The Journal of Modern History* 66, no. 3 (1994): 495–7, 516.

[3] Raffael Scheck, "The Prisoner of War Question and the Beginnings of Collaboration: The Franco-German Agreement of 16 November 1940," *Journal of Contemporary History* 45, no. 2 (2010).

France. Abetz became *de facto* German ambassador in Paris. Scapini had met Hitler on two occasions before the war. According to Abetz, Hitler was deeply moved by his encounter with Scapini, perhaps on account of the temporary blindness that Hitler himself had experienced as a result of poison gas in 1918. Scapini, who spoke German quite well, became the key figure in French negotiations on POWs.[4]

The Geneva Convention arranged for a protecting power, normally a neutral country, to monitor the situation of the POWs and observance of the Convention (article 86). The first protecting power of the French (and also the Belgian and British) POWs was the United States. The American embassy in Berlin, under the direction of a chargé d'affaires – the United States had withdrawn its ambassador in protest against the anti-Jewish pogrom of November 9, 1938 – thus took over the inspection of the POW camps and the communication of grievances to the French government. The key official in this effort was the diplomat Jefferson Patterson. Patterson and the American consuls in the major German cities visited POW camps and worked hard to overcome the many shortcomings of the first months.[5]

As relations between Germany and the United States were deteriorating in the fall of 1940 because of the pro-British attitude of the American government, Hitler in early November 1940 demanded that the Vichy government itself take over the role of protecting power. This was a highly unusual arrangement, but the Vichy authorities knew that opposing it would be risky and hoped to use to their own advantage the more direct contact to the prisoners that the role of protecting power promised. Hitler indicated his willingness to reward Vichy's compliance with several concessions, among them the release of fathers and oldest brothers from poor families with four children. Scapini and Pétain expected that France could alleviate the situation of the prisoners through the more direct channels of communication open to representatives of a protecting power, and they also hoped to influence the prisoners politically and to win them over to the policies of Pétain. In the context of the personal meeting of Pétain and Hitler in Montoire at the end of October 1940, the Vichy authorities expected that collaboration would result in a series of liberations and improvements for the prisoners.[6]

With the Franco-German agreement of November 16, 1940, France assumed the role of protecting power for its own soldiers in German

---

[4] Ibid., 367–8.
[5] Raffael Scheck, *French Colonial Soldiers in German Captivity during World War II* (Cambridge and New York: Cambridge University Press, 2014), 45–53.
[6] Scheck, "The Prisoner of War Question," 374–5.

captivity. Scapini, who already had headquarters in Paris, set up an office
in Berlin and hired a group of camp inspectors who visited camps and
labor detachments in Germany. Members of the Scapini Mission regularly met with German officials in Paris and Berlin to present grievances
and to negotiate further liberations and improvements. Scapini
developed a cordial relationship with the German official in charge of
POWs, General Hermann Reinecke of the High Command, as well as
with Reinecke's representative in Paris and the principal accompanying
officer during camp inspections. Major new rewards from Germany did
not materialize, however, although Hitler agreed to some limited liberations in exchange for French concessions (World War I veterans, for
example). When French general Henri Giraud escaped from German
captivity in April 1942, Hitler flew into a fit of rage and suspended all
agreements benefiting French POWs and even some rights of the prisoners and the protecting power guarantied by the Geneva Convention
(such as camp inspections and the repatriation of sick prisoners). Scapini, deeply worried about the threat to the POWs, implored Giraud to
return into captivity and offered himself as a hostage to Hitler until
Giraud returned, but Hitler rejected the offer. Scapini noticed, however,
that Reinecke and other German officials ignored or watered down many
of Hitler's directives, and after a few months the usual contacts and
inspections resumed. In March 1943, Reinecke told Scapini in confidence that he had quietly cancelled the last of Hitler's vindictive
ordinances.[7]

The substitution of France for the United States as protecting power
eased the handling of complaints and shortcomings and offered Vichy
better and timelier access to information about the POWs, but it
deprived French prisoners of the protection of a neutral power. Scapini
eloquently defended the agreement during his postwar trials and in his
memoirs.[8] Scapini was probably right in arguing that the direct contacts
between the French and German POW officials offered some advantages
and that there would have been no real alternative to Vichy taking over as
its own protecting power, especially after the American entry into the war
in December 1941. The French and Belgian POWs shared the disadvantage that their country was defeated and occupied by Germany. While
the Belgian POWs retained the services of the American embassy in
Berlin until December 1941, it is dubious that they fared better than
the French. After Pearl Harbor, Germany refused to accept a new

[7] "Entretien Scapini-Reinecke," March 18, 1943, in Archives nationales, Pierrefitte-sur-
Seine (AN), F9, 2176.
[8] Georges Scapini, *Mission sans gloire* (Paris: Editions Morgan, 1960), 31–2.

protecting power for the Belgians, and this might have happened to the French POWs had Vichy refused to take on this role.

The severe penalties for contacts between POWs and civilians irked French officials, given that the two governments were collaborating. In his talks with Reinecke and other German officials, Scapini repeatedly questioned the prohibition and sought to mitigate its effects, for example by suggesting milder sentences and by working to improve conditions for the sentenced POWs. State collaboration was clearly undermining Nazi propaganda, which sought to stigmatize all POWs as enemies who could never be trusted. As Gaullist and British forces repeatedly attacked Vichy-controlled colonial territories, the Vichy government appeared as a friendly neutral, if not an ally. The fact that some French volunteers joined a Waffen-SS Division in 1942 and fought on the eastern front further bolstered the perception that the French were no longer enemies.[9] The integration of 95 percent of the French prisoners into the German economy, largely completed by the end of 1940, led to widespread acceptance and often appreciation of the French prisoners by the German population. On countless farms, the French prisoner filled the role of the absent farmer or of male helpers drafted into the German army. In many factories, French POWs became an indispensable labor force. Small businesses such as bakeries, beverage distributors, and public services, for example the construction departments of little towns, could not survive without them either.[10]

Trials for forbidden relations involving French prisoners began in earnest during the spring of 1941. Given that the French POW authorities numbered the court martial cases, one can detect the numerical trends despite the fact that the records are incomplete. Whereas a little more than 1,000 court martial cases had been recorded before the end of March 1941, including trials for crimes committed during the fighting in the west, 500 new cases accumulated in the half-year between April 1 and October 1, and more than 500 new cases came to trial in the last quarter of 1941 alone, with forbidden relations being the overwhelming majority after April 1, 1941. The pace continued to increase, reaching number 11,000 by the end of 1943, which meant that at least 9,000 new cases had come to trial in the two calendar years 1942 and 1943. Record-keeping became more precarious by the end of 1943 because the offices of the French delegation in Berlin were destroyed by bombs, necessitating a move to the village Letschin an der Oder, seventy-five kilometers east of

---

[9] Philippe Carrard, *The French Who Fought for Hitler: Memories from the Outcasts* (New York: Cambridge University Press, 2010).
[10] Durand, *Prisonniers de guerre*, 79–94, 241–6.

Berlin. Everything indicates that the intensity of courts martial remained very high throughout 1944 and early 1945, although hearings in the last months of the war often had to be postponed due to bombings and chaotic traffic conditions. An internal memorandum of the Scapini Mission stated in March 1944 that on average 450–500 new trials against French POWs occurred every month, which indicates an average of 5,000–6,000 trials per year, mostly for love relations. The number was so large that the budget of the Scapini Mission had to be increased significantly because it had to pay the attorney fees.[11] Although not all of the trials concerned forbidden relations, one has to consider that some love-related trials involved more than one prisoner. Given that the proportion of love-related trials against French POWs was between 75 and 80 percent, one can estimate that approximately 15,000 French POWs had to stand trial for forbidden relations in 1942–4. There was still a very large number of cases under prosecution in 1945 that did not lead to a verdict. The total number of French POWs facing prosecution for a forbidden relationship therefore was likely between 17,000 and 19,000.

For French POWs, as for all others, the discovered cases leading to prosecution form only the tip of the iceberg. One has to assume the existence of an unknown number of love relationships that never came to trial, especially in remote villages where communal solidarity and the farmers' fear of losing vitally important laborers may have created a camouflage net.[12] As a French POW priest noted with disgust in August 1943: "I know that in a certain village where 35 Frenchmen are working there are only three who are not sleeping with their farmwoman or a maid."[13] Ambrière also claimed that a large number of undiscovered or unprosecuted relations existed. He had met quite a few prisoners whose amorous affairs remained undiscovered or unpunished.[14]

Although soldiers of non-European descent were generally held in German POW camps in occupied France, the French captives in Germany mirrored much of the ethnic and national diversity of the French army. They included men with Polish, Italian, Spanish, or German ancestry, and some Jews. Some of these soldiers had French citizenship, others did not. The German military tribunals, as the Geneva

---

[11] "Note pour l'Ambassadeur," March 16, 1944, in AN, F9, 2185 (Affaires judiciaires).
[12] Kundrus, "Forbidden Company," 209; Jill Stephenson, *Hitler's Home Front: Württemberg under the Nazis* (London and New York: Hambledon Continuum, 2006), 285; Gisela Schwarze, *Es war wie eine Hexenjagd: Die vergessene Verfolgung ganz normaler Frauen im Zweiten Weltkrieg* (Münster: Ardey, 2009), 45 and 165.
[13] Virgili, *Naître ennemi*, 56–8, 250. For more testimonies about widespread tolerated relationships, even in industrial work detachments, see Durand, *Captivité*, 418.
[14] Ambrière, *Les grandes Vacances*, 197.

Convention required, treated the prisoners according to their uniform and made no significant differences in punishing them. In one case a French Catholic and a Hungarian Jew serving in the French army had an affair with an innkeeper's wife in southern Germany, one after the other. The military judge, although clearly biased against the Jew, gave both prisoners exactly the same punishment.[15]

For the majority of French POWs, captivity had little to do with large camps surrounded by barbed wire and watchtowers with mean and trigger-happy guards, although all prisoners experienced this setting in the first months. After distribution to work detachments, guarding of most rank-and-file French prisoners relaxed, and they dealt mostly with German civilians. Being a POW meant for many of them primarily a legal and administrative status. Work detachments in industry and public works would be housed in a school, a restaurant or hotel that made little business during the war, or a hall on the factory grounds. The prisoners, in groups of ten to fifty, would sleep in these buildings, guarded by one or two German soldiers who mostly had to make sure that all POWs checked in for the night. Many of these guards, usually older or disabled men, were friendly and supportive. The sleeping quarters of the French POWs were not secured well. Prisoners often found a window that could be opened, or they produced a picklock that could open the door while the guard was sleeping. In some cases, women were even able to sneak into the sleeping quarters of the POWs.[16] On Sundays, many French POWs could go out freely without a guard. Regulations for the guarding of French and Belgian prisoners became more relaxed in 1941 and even more in 1943, when the manpower shortage of the German army increased due to the high losses on the eastern front.[17]

On many farms, one or two French prisoners would move in and work like a German farm laborer. This was true especially in the western and southern parts of the Third Reich, where small family farms predominated. Legally, the farmer was the supervisor and substitute "guard" of the

[15] Feldurteil, Memmingen, January 9, 1942, in Politisches Archiv des Auswärtigen Amtes, Berlin (PAAA), R 40908.
[16] For an example, see the case of Marie K., Wiener Stadt- und Landesarchiv (WStLA), Sondergericht, vol. 6995. Marie K. visited the POW in his sleeping quarters and spent the night with him. A similar case is Helene A., in Landesarchiv Schleswig-Holstein, Schleswig (LASH), Abt. 358, Staatsanwaltschaft beim Sondergericht Altona/Kiel, vol. 2760.
[17] "Auflockerung der Bewachung kf. gef. Franzosen." Memo of the German High Command (OKW), October 3, 1941, in Niedersächsisches Landesarchiv (NLA) Oldenburg, Best. 135 B, and *Handbuch für Arbeitskommandoführer Wehrkreis XIII*, in AN, F9, 3644.

prisoner, but many farmers were drafted into the Wehrmacht, and the French prisoner often worked alone with the farmer's wife or daughter and a few employees, including a milkmaid and girls aged sixteen to eighteen performing their mandatory service year (*Pflichtjahr*).[18] Once the bombings of German towns increased, many farms would also house an evacuee from a big city, normally a woman, and often a mother with children. There were also some male employees on the farm, usually older farm laborers or *Schweizer* (experts in the handling of cattle). In many places, French POWs also worked alongside laborers from eastern Europe, particularly Poles and Ukrainians, mostly deported forced laborers (both male and female). Except in the two military districts XX and XXI (Danzig and Posen), POWs would not be punished for relations with these laborers because the prohibition only outlawed contact with German civilians, but the foreign laborers would still be punished because contact with POWs was forbidden to every civilian. A POW on a small farm would often meet comrades working in the same village on Sundays or in the evenings, but his social circle normally consisted mostly of Germans, predominantly women. On many small farms, the French (or Belgian) prisoner, often a man with experience in agricultural work, replaced the farmer who had been drafted into the Wehrmacht and perhaps gone missing or been killed in action. Guarding often consisted of a soldier on a bicycle stopping by from time to time to ensure the prisoner was still there and to inquire whether the prisoner or his employer had any complaints.[19]

Many French prisoners and their German lovers wanted to marry after the war, but Free French military regulations, popular sentiment in liberated France, and often also rejection of the German bride by the prisoner's family made it extremely difficult to realize these plans. Often the former prisoner, once at home, showed no interest any more in his German fiancée. Still, a few couples did marry and stayed together either in Germany or France.[20]

The Belgians

After the German army invaded Belgium on May 10, 1940, it captured approximately 225,000 Belgian prisoners. In July 1940, Hitler ordered the release of all Flemish (Dutch-speaking) prisoners except professional

[18] See OKW-Erlass, March 24, 1943, in NLA Oldenburg, Best. 135 B. This document reiterated earlier guidelines.
[19] Ambrière, *Les grandes Vacances*, 197.
[20] Virgili, *Naître ennemi*, 248–61; Picaper, *Le Crime d'aimer*, 34, 104–5.

soldiers as part of a policy to attract the Flemish population of Belgium to Germany. This order was carried out inconsistently, however. German officials overlooked some Flemings and freed some French-speakers (Walloons). Some Flemish POWs did not bother to apply for dismissal because, like all other western prisoners, they at first expected a swift end of the war and prompt release. Quite a few Belgians had mixed ancestry, moreover. Especially for soldiers from Brussels and its surroundings, bilingualism was common, and identification as a Fleming or Walloon made little sense.[21] Still, the majority of the 85,000 Belgian prisoners who remained in captivity after the dismissals stopped in February 1941 were French-speaking Walloons. Approximately 90 percent of the Belgian POWs were assigned to work detachments and individual farms and businesses in the same way as the French, with whom they often shared accommodation. Most of the Belgians, close to 70,000, were still in German captivity in early 1945 although Belgian POWs had also benefited from dismissals similar to those agreed between Vichy and Berlin (for example fathers of four children and World War I veterans).[22]

The protecting power for the Belgian POWs was the United States – until December 1941. The Belgian prewar government had gone into exile in London, but King Leopold III remained in the country. He set up an organization taking care of matters relating to the demobilized army under the leadership of General Maurice Keyaerts, the *Office des Travaux de l'armée démobilisée* (OTAD), which organized aid shipments to the prisoners of war. While the Belgian government in London wanted the Swiss to take over as protecting power when the United States entered the war, the German foreign ministry, which did not recognize the Belgian government-in-exile, refused to accept a new protecting power for the Belgian POWs. For several months, the Belgian POWs relied on the inspections and supplies from the International Committee of the Red Cross (ICRC) in Geneva, but in June 1942 the Germans agreed to recognize a commission set up by the OTAD as a partner in matters relating to the Belgian POWs, the *Délégation du Service de liaison avec les prisonniers de guerre* (DSLP).[23] The DSLP was headed by the retired officer Count de t'Serclaes et Wammerson, a descendant of general Johann Tilly (1559–1632), Austria's famous military leader in the first phase of the Thirty Years War. The Belgian government-in-exile

[21] Gillet, "Histoire des sous-officiers et soldats belges," XXVIII, 48–51; Overmans, "Kriegsgefangenenpolitik," 776.
[22] Gillet, "Histoire des sous-officiers et soldats belges," XXVIII, 53; Buckinx, "Belgen in duitse Krijgsgevangenschap," 506.
[23] Gillet, "Histoire des sous-officiers et soldats belges," XXVIII, 136–8.

and King Leopold always denied that the DSLP constituted a protecting power in the sense of the Geneva Convention and in analogy to the Scapini Mission, and the DSLP, unlike the Scapini Mission, did not see itself in a diplomatic role. Yet Count t'Serclaes and his officials performed some of same functions as the Scapini Mission, inspecting camps and following up with German officials about problems and complaints from the prisoners, and the German High Command dealt with them on similar terms as with the Scapini Mission.[24] In judicial matters, the DSLP supplied defense attorneys to the prisoners and monitored their prison terms. The DSLP set up offices in the Adlon hotel in Berlin, deliberately avoiding the Belgian embassy building, which would have been available, in order to underscore the point that it did not act as a diplomatic agency.[25] In November 1943, the DSLP had to move to Bellin, a village across the Oder from Letschin, where the Scapini Mission had been relocated after the bombing of the city center of Berlin, which had also destroyed the Adlon hotel.

As an organization headed by the king and set up without the approval of the government-in-exile, the DSLP encountered some hostility from POWs, but it did help the prisoners effectively until it met with increasing German suspicion because of its pro-Allied sympathies in 1944. After the liberation of Belgium by Allied troops in September 1944, the DSLP fell into disarray because many of its officials remained in Belgium. The German defense attorneys could no longer be paid; some of them sent their unpaid bills to the Belgian government after the end of the war, but to no avail.[26] The ICRC protected the interests of the Belgian POWs as far as this was possible in the chaotic circumstances of the last months of Nazi Germany. After the liberation of Belgium, the Belgian government began holding German prisoners on its territory and therefore could ensure some reciprocity.[27]

---

[24] Ibid., 135. "Note relative à la question posée et à l'avis émis par certains prisonniers, 'Quelle est notre puissance protectrice?'", CEGESOMA, AA 265; Overmans, "Kriegsgefangenenpolitik," 775–9.

[25] "Rapport du Lt. med. Van Doornick," in Musée Royal de l'Armée et d'Histoire Militaire, Evere, Dossier captivité, box 1, #12.

[26] See, for example, Dr. Hoge [attorney from Greifswald] to Belgian representative in Berlin, October 10, 1946, in Archives du Ministère des Affaires étrangères, Brussels, Film 409.

[27] Gillet, "Histoire des sous-officiers et soldats belges," XXVIII, 48–51. For more detail on the role of the DSLP, see CEGESOMA, AA 265, dossier IV (Aide et assistence aux prisonniers de guerre); Musée Royal de l'Armée et d'Histoire Militaire, Evere, Fonds Gillet, box 1, #7: La commission t'Serclaes; and "Rapport du Lt med Van Doornick," in Musée Royal de l'Armée et d'Histoire Militaire, Evere, Dossier captivité, box 1, #12. Van Doornick was the chief medical official of the DSLP.

Over time, Belgian prisoners appear to have been accepted in very similar ways as French POWs, especially in rural communities.[28] Georges Smets, reflecting on his experience as man of confidence of a big POW camp in East Prussia, explained in retrospect that the initially hostile and arrogant local population became friendlier and increasingly supportive after the tide of the war seemed to have turned. As the Belgian veteran and military historian Georges Hautecler wrote in a newspaper article in 1975 with allusion to the forbidden amorous liaisons: "The relations with the German population were good, sometimes too good."[29] Although the Belgian government had left the country, the Belgian administration remained in place and collaborated. It was difficult for Germans to perceive the Belgians as real enemies, given that Germany had attacked Belgium in May 1940. Hitler suggested in his Reichstag speech of July 19, 1940, on the basis of captured French diplomatic documents that the Belgian government had plotted war against Germany, but it seems doubtful that these absurd claims were widely believed.[30] There were Belgians, including Walloons, in the Waffen-SS fighting alongside German forces in the Soviet Union, and it appears that the German population perceived the Belgians very much like the French – as friendly neutrals, if not allies. French and Belgian POWs were often mixed in the same camps and work detachments even though article 9 of the Geneva Convention required whenever possible separate housing for POWs of different nationalities.[31]

Court records from trials against German women often refer to Belgian prisoners. The share of trials because of forbidden relations was exactly the same for the Belgians as for the French, between 75 and 80 percent of all cases.[32] Georges Smets testified that 6 percent of his comrades in Stalag I-A had to stand trial for forbidden relations and that three-quarters of his time as man of confidence was devoted to helping prisoners accused of forbidden relations. If his figure can be

[28] Gillet, "Histoire des sous-officiers et soldats belges," XXVIII, 128–9.
[29] Georges Hautecler, "Il y a trente ans le V Day: Les prisonniers de guerre," *La Libre Belgique*, May 7–8, 1975. Copy in CEGESOMA, AA 265, dossier X (coupures de presse); see also Buckinx, "Belgen in duitse Krijgsgevangenschap," 509.
[30] Max Domarus, ed., *Hitler: Speeches and Proclamations, 1932–1945*, vol. 3 (Wauconda: Bolchazy-Carducci, 1990–2), 2049–50.
[31] Durand, *Captivité*, 422–3.
[32] Jean Thisquen, "Poursuite pénales contre le P.G. en Allemagne," in *S'Unir*, Stalag X-A. #13, Nov.-Dez. 1944, in CEGESOMA, AA 257. Buckinx writes that more than 80 percent of all trials against Belgian POWs in Germany concerned forbidden relations to a German woman, but he gives no source: Buckinx, "Belgen in duitse Krijgsgevangenschap," 510.

generalized, it would place Belgians proportionally even above the French.[33] An official postwar survey of judicial matters directed by General Keyaerts concluded that more than 1,000 trials against Belgian POWs had occurred, the vast majority involving amorous relations, but this figure did not include the documents lost during or soon after the war.[34] An ICRC representative informed the Belgian government-in-exile in March 1944 that German courts martial opened between fifty and a hundred new judicial cases against Belgian POWs every month, which would suggest an average of 900 cases per year at least during the "busiest" period of 1942–4 and a total of 3,000–4,000 cases. This would be closer to Smets's proportion (6 percent of an average of 77,500 Belgian POWs would be 4,650).[35] A study focused on Schleswig-Holstein confirms that, if one correlates the number of cases to the number of prisoners, the Belgians were proportionally the biggest "offenders": there were always approximately eight times as many French POWs as Belgians in the area, yet the trial ratio between Frenchmen and Belgians was five and a half to one.[36]

Belgian rank-and-file POWs, like the French, experienced captivity as an alternative reality and developed a growing empathy with the German population. Many POWs were afraid that their wives were disloyal, and the men of confidence handled many divorce requests.[37] In 1945, some Belgian prisoners wanted to stay in Germany or Austria and marry their partners, particularly on farms where the POW might have taken the place of a killed or missing farmer. The military police forced most of them to go home, but a few Belgians did manage to marry their German partners after the war.[38]

The British

More than 164,000 British (including Commonwealth) servicemen became POWs in Germany.[39] The first major group was the 44,000

[33] Georges Smets to Mr. Georges Paulus, January 11, 1976, in Musée Royal de l'Armée et d'Histoire Militaire, Brussels, Fonds Hautecler, Farde 34.
[34] "Affaires juridiques," in Archives du Général Keyaerts, Musée Royal de l'Armée et d'Histoire Militaire, Evere, Box 6 (Affaires juridiques).
[35] Jean Cellerier (CICR London) to Belgian Ministry of Foreign Affairs, London, March 15, 1944, in Archives du Ministère des Affaires étrangères, Brussels, Film 409.
[36] Colmorgen and Godau-Schüttke, "Verbotener Umgang mit Kriegsgefangenen," 147.
[37] Gillet, "Histoire des sous-officiers et soldats belges," XXVIII, 241–2. For examples, see the dossier "Affaires juridiques Stalag V-B Villingen," in CEGESOMA, AA 252.
[38] Lt-col. Lescrauwaet to Baron de Guben, September 21, 1945, in Archives du Ministère des Affaires étrangères, Brussels, Film 408: Dossier général 1942–8. Gillet, "Histoire des sous-officiers et soldats belges," XXVIII, 362. See also the notes in Musée Royal de l'Armée et d'Histoire Militaire, Evere, Fonds Gillet, box 1, #4 affaires juridiques, 301.
[39] MacKenzie, Colditz Myth, 41.

British servicemen captured during the campaign in the west, particularly in the area of Dunkirk in early June 1940. But unlike French and Belgian prisoners, who were almost all captured in May and June 1940, the British POWs kept arriving. In Greece, another nearly 10,000 British soldiers came into German captivity in April and May 1941, and in the fall of 1943, 52,000 (of 80,000) British POWs from the North African theater held in Italy were transferred to Germany after the Italian capitulation.[40] Approximately 10,000 downed British airmen also ended up in German captivity, mostly in the last two years of the war, and new prisoners came from the fronts in Italy after July 1943 and western Europe after June 6, 1944.

Most British POWs were sent to the eastern periphery of the Third Reich, a broad strip from Wolfsberg in southern Austria to Danzig on the Baltic Sea, including the former German–Czechoslovak borderlands and the prewar German–Polish border region. The largest camps with British POWs were in Upper Silesia (especially Stalag VIII-B headquartered in Lamsdorf and Teschen), West Prussia (Thorn and Marienburg), and Schubin near Posen (Stalag XXI-B), in areas that had partly belonged to Poland before the war. Another nexus of British POWs existed in Saxony around Torgau, and there were also large groups of British POWs in camps near Berlin (Stalag III-A Luckenwalde) and Munich (Stalag VII-A Moosburg).[41]

Many of the POWs in British uniform were not from the United Kingdom itself. Among the prisoners captured in mainland Greece and on Crete, for example, were many Australians, New Zealanders, and people from Palestine (Jews and Arabs), Cyprus, Malta, and British India. South Africans, Canadians, and Irish also formed part of the British forces. Germany generally followed the Geneva Convention by treating these prisoners as members of the British army without glaring discrimination. As with other POWs, the German army and German employers supplied rations that were too low, but generous packages from the British Red Cross and other aid agencies made the prisoners largely independent of the German rations as long as the deliveries arrived, although there were difficult phases owing to overcrowding. The last months of captivity were particularly harsh because of shortages caused by disruptions of the German transport system and because of poorly prepared evacuations of POWs from the eastern areas of the Reich.[42]

[40] Overmans, "Kriegsgefangenenpolitik," 786–8, 97–9.
[41] Kochavi, *Confronting Captivity*, 33–6, 54, 60; MacKenzie, *Colditz Myth*, 93–120.
[42] Vourkoutiotis, "What the Angels Saw," 691.

Given that German hostilities with Britain continued, the British prisoners were guarded more strictly and had less contact with German
civilians, especially in the earlier years. Unlike the French and Belgians,
moreover, the British authorities considered it shameful for POWs to get
involved with enemy women. Section 40 of the Army Act forbade any
interaction between prisoners of war and enemy civilians, and the British
army urged its officers to warn soldiers not to approach German women.
The British government was therefore not keen on protesting against the
orders, although they did complain about the harshness of German
military justice in general.[43]

Before 1943, there were almost no trials against British POWs for
forbidden relations not only because of stricter guarding and separation
from German civilians but also because, initially, some camp commanders mistakenly used mild disciplinary punishments rather than courts
martial against the offenders. The disciplinary punishments did not
require notification of the protecting power and therefore often left no
trace in the archives. According to the historian Vasilis Vourkoutiotis,
German camp commanders received an order in January 1943 no longer
to use disciplinary punishments in cases of forbidden relations, and from
then on the British POWs involved with a German woman also had to
stand trial in front of courts martial.[44] The files of the Swiss Legation in
Berlin contain 453 cases (349 POWs with court martials and 104 pending
cases at the end of the war) beginning in 1943 and intensifying throughout 1944 and early 1945. The Swiss official Hans K. Frey, who was
responsible for overseeing the trials against British POWs in the last year
of the war, noted that on average thirty new love-related cases kept
arriving on his desk every month, many of them involving more than
one prisoner.[45] Of the 349 British and Commonwealth POWs who stood
in front of a court martial because of forbidden relations, 317 prisoners
were sentenced to penitentiary, prison, or prolonged arrest, and thirty-
two were acquitted. In 1943 eighty-two POWs stood trial, with seven
acquittals. The majority of POWs had to face a court martial in 1944
(234, with twenty-three acquittals), and there were still thirty-three
POWs tried in 1945 (with two acquittals), almost all in January. In
addition, 104 British POWs were under prosecution for a forbidden
relationship in late 1944 and early 1945, but the records contain no

---

[43] National Archives, Kew, WO 32/15294: Trials and punishments of British POWs in
Germany 1941–45, and Schweizerisches Bundesarchiv (BAR) Bern, Bestand Vertretung
Berlin, 78a to 87b.
[44] Vourkoutiotis, *Prisoners of War and the German High Command*, 82–3.
[45] Frey, *Die disziplinarische und gerichtliche Bestrafung von Kriegsgefangenen*, 62.

sentence either because the trials could not take place in the chaotic circumstances (many British POWs were in the first areas of the Reich attacked by the Soviet army) or because the judgments never arrived.[46] The records of the Swiss Legation are incomplete even for the earlier period because of losses in war-ravaged Germany. For example, the prosecution of fifteen (!) Arab POWs from the British army who had amorous relations with twelve German women in a chair factory near Offenburg in early 1944 (discovered by Bernd Boll) left no trace in the Swiss records.[47] As with the other POWs, we of course have to assume an unknown number of relationships that were never discovered.

Other Prisoners

Prisoners from other armies also had to appear in front of courts martial for a forbidden relationship. Although the German army captured nearly 95,000 American POWs, a little more than Belgians after the release of the Flemish soldiers, the Americans lacked the time and the opportunity to get close to German women in greater numbers. Three-quarters of the American POWs came to Germany after the Allied landings in Normandy on June 6, 1944, and more than a third of the American POWs were downed airmen (predominantly officers) who were guarded more strictly and toward whom the population felt particularly hostile because of the bombing attacks. An American survey completed on November 1, 1945, traced 92,965 American POWs in Germany. Of these, 60,235 were ground troops, with approximately 10 percent officers. Only 9,274 American ground troops were in German captivity before D-Day.[48] Given that ground troops (except officers) were the group most likely to come into contact with German civilians, it is relevant to note that 85 percent of approximately 54,000 American rank-and-file ground troops were captured after D-Day and therefore had very little time to become involved with German civilians.

Initially, American POWs came to the same camps as British prisoners (this arrangement facilitated translation services), but the German army soon reserved space in some special camps for Americans east and northeast of Berlin and near Vienna. After the start of the Soviet offensive in January 1945, the German army evacuated most American POWs

---

[46] BAR Bern, Bestand Vertretung Berlin, volumes 71–88.

[47] Boll, "… das gesunde Volksempfinden auf das Gröbste verletzt," 658–9.

[48] "American Prisoners of War in Germany," prepared by the Military Intelligence Department on November 1, 1945, in NACP, Record Group 389: Records of the Provost Marshal General, ID 893506, container identifier: 2197. See also Kochavi, *Confronting Captivity*, 71; Foy, *For You the War Is Over*, 42–3, 64.

from these areas and concentrated them near Magdeburg and Munich. These evacuations brought American POWs into contact with German civilians, but they were hardly conducive to amorous adventures because they involved long forced marches in extreme cold, insufficient shelter, overcrowding in the arrival camps, and inadequate food supplies. If forbidden relations with German women occurred on these marches, the conditions would have made prosecution nearly impossible. Even the Americans who arrived before January 1945 would have found it hard to engage closely with German civilians. It took several months to distribute POWs to the smaller work detachments and for closer relations to develop and to be discovered and prosecuted (this had taken approximately six months for the French and Belgian POWs under less strict guarding in 1940).

The memory of American POWs seems to be dominated by experiences with harsh guards or superiors and with hunger, not surprisingly given that most Americans experienced only the phase of captivity in which supplies were insufficient.[49] Trials against American POWs took place mostly for attacks against guards and foreman, disobedience, theft, and insults against the German state and army, which included insults against Hitler (§134 of the German law code). Only a few love-related trials against American prisoners occurred, and most involved relatively small matters such as the exchange of cigarettes and a quick kiss or hug. In his memoirs, for example, ex-POW Jack Dower reveals that it was possible for an American work detachment to get to work in German agriculture under relatively lax guarding, but his group of twenty POWs was sent to a big state domain in the village Benzin near Stolp (eastern Pomerania), where they worked together with German girls, Ukrainian women, and French POWs. Although the work detachment had only one (friendly) guard, German supervisors watched the POWs during work, and at night it would have been difficult, but not impossible, to leave the sleeping quarters. Dower admits some admiring looks at a German waitress and a flirtation with a Ukrainian woman across a fence, but he was apparently not interested enough to leave the American sleeping quarters to see either of them at night.[50] Yet, there were a few cases of Americans involved with German women, and there were more cases coming, considering the notifications of the protecting power regarding POWs who were formally accused of a forbidden relationship but never came to trial because of the chaos in early 1945. But most of the cases that did lead to a court martial hearing were relatively superficial and

[49] Kochavi, *Confronting Captivity*, 90–1, 97–102.
[50] Jack Dower, *Deliverance at Diepholz: A World War II's Prisoner of War Story* (Mechanicsburg, PA: Stackpole Books, 2016), 61, 71, 102–3.

coincidental.[51] For the Americans, captivity never quite evolved into the alternative reality that it became for many French and Belgian POWs, who had been captured in 1940, when the outcome of the war was much less clear than in 1944–5, and who were increasingly left to their own devices surrounded by German civilians.

The German army also captured a large number of soldiers from the Royal Yugoslav Army in April 1941. Many of the prisoners were quickly released, but Serbs were kept in German captivity, and small contingents of them were deployed in various parts of the Reich. Serbia had a collaborating government, but Germany did not recognize the Geneva Convention in its dealings with this government (unlike in the case of western POWs). There were numerous trials against Serbian prisoners involved with German women. Although a study of this topic remains to be done, it appears that the courts martial treated Serbian POWs in similar ways to the western POWs. Convicted Serbian POWs generally had to go to the Wehrmacht prison in Germersheim (south of Mannheim), not to the prison of Graudenz, where most convicted western POWs were sent. The case files of the court martial of Reserve Infantry Division 410 in Schleswig-Holstein indicate sentences for Serbian POWs tried for forbidden relations that seem to be in line with sentences against western POWs.[52] From the case files of the women involved with Serbs it emerges that they received the same punishments as women involved with western prisoners.[53] Although Serbs, as a Slavic people, occupied a low rank on the Nazi hierarchy, this did not affect the trials against the women involved with them.

After the capitulation of Italy to the Allies in September 1943, many Italian soldiers who did not want to fight for the puppet government under Mussolini installed in Salò were interned in Germany under harsh conditions. These so-called Badoglio Italians (after the name of the marshal who signed the agreement with the Allies) were considered to be traitors and stigmatized in Nazi propaganda and popular feeling. Germany denied them the status of POWs as defined by the Geneva Convention and categorized them as Italian Military Internees (IMIs).

---

[51] For these cases, see BAR Bern, Bestand Vertretung Berlin, 82a, 87a, and 88a, and NACP, RG 59, 711.62114A, Boxes 2219 and 2220.
[52] Bundesarchiv-Militärarchiv, Freiburg im Breisgau (BA-MA), RW 60, vols. 1799–1811. Most of these files contain no details, however.
[53] For examples of women tried for a relationship with a Serb POW, see Brandenburgisches Landeshauptarchiv (BLHA) Potsdam, 12C, Sondergericht Berlin, 221; Sondergericht Frankfurt an der Oder, 926, and WStLA Wien, Sondergericht, vols. 3385, 4194, 7949. See also Helmut Irmen, *Das Sondergericht Aachen 1941–1945* (Berlin: De Gruyter, 2018), 79.

Nevertheless, the prohibition of contacts with civilians applied to them as if they were regular POWs. A few cases of IMIs involved with German women came to trial. These trials led to punishments that seem to have been similar to punishments against Serbian and western prisoners.[54] The convicted IMIs often came to military prisons, including Graudenz, where most western POWs sentenced to prison had to go, but conditions were worse for them than for other convicted POWs. Historian Michela Ponzani has explored the experience of IMIs with German women in the framework of a larger project on children of enemies during World War II. She shows that loving German women, and some humane guards, often helped underfed and mistreated Italians. Some of the couples wanted to marry after the war, but widespread resentment against Germans in Italy made it very difficult for them. The relationships were quickly forgotten because loving German women did not fit the notion of brutal Nazis prevalent in postwar Italy.[55]

Polish prisoners involved with German women were treated much more harshly. Nazi Germany transformed most Polish rank-and-file prisoners into civilian forced laborers in the course of 1940, arguing that the Geneva Convention was no longer binding for Poles because the Polish state no longer existed and because Sweden, the protecting power for the Polish POWs, had decided to end its role in November 1939.[56] Polish prisoners were placed under a harsh statute specifically formulated for Poles and Jews. Whether a Pole involved with a German woman was still a POW or a civilian worker did not matter. He was usually handed over to the Gestapo and hanged, often in front of comrades and other foreign laborers. The only chance to save his life was inclusion on the German people's list (*Deutsche Volksliste*), but this involved a complicated procedure in which the SS was the arbiter.[57]

[54] Gerhard Schreiber, *Die italienischen Militärinternierten im deutschen Machtbereich 1943–1945* (Munich: Oldenbourg, 1990), 99, 339–41, 444–74, and 499–500; Dokumentationszentrum NS-Zwangsarbeit der Stiftung Topographie des Terrors, ed., *Zwischen allen Stühlen: Die Geschichte der italienischen Militärinternierten 1943–1945/Tra più fuochi: La storia degli internati militari italiani 1943–1945* (Berlin: Spree Druck, 2016). For examples of trials against women involved with Italians, see sentence against Marie S., Sondergericht Darmstadt, September 1, 1944, in HStAD Fonds G 24, Nr. 955/2 Mitteilungen in Strafsachen, and HStAD, G 27 Darmstadt, vol. 1419.
[55] Michela Ponzani, *Figli del nemico: le relazioni d'amore in tempo di guerra, 1943–1948* (Rome: Laterzo, 2015), 95–110.
[56] Overmans, "Kriegsgefangenenpolitik," 749.
[57] Thomas Muggenthaler and Jörg Skriebeleit, *Verbrechen Liebe: Von polnischen Männern und deutschen Frauen. Hinrichtungen und Verfolgung in Niederbayern und der Oberpfalz während der NS-Zeit* (Viechtach: Ed. Lichtung, 2010); Dietmut Majer, *"Non-Germans" under the Third Reich: The Nazi Judicial and Administrative System in Germany and Occupied Eastern Europe, with Special Regard to Occupied Poland, 1939–1945* (Baltimore

The woman involved with a Pole could face deportation to a concentration camp, often prefaced by public humiliations and shaming rituals inspired by Nazi officials – until Hitler forbade them in response to negative public reaction. Yet, there were some trials against women involved with Polish and Soviet POWs that led to penitentiary or prison sentences. The court files do not reveal why some women were put on trial while others were directly sent to a concentration camp, and it appears that other researchers have also not found a compelling explanation for the inconsistency.[58] Scholars disagree on the question as to whether the courts sentenced women involved with Polish or Soviet POWs more harshly (if they did come to trial) than women involved with western POWs.[59] My sample indicates that the legal practice of the German courts in cases involving relations with Polish or Soviet POWs was indeed harsher. These trials show that the courts criticized and punished these relations most severely. The standard formulations in the sentences stated that Poland had planned to annihilate Germany and had committed atrocious bestialities against the German people during the campaign, an allusion to the attacks on ethnic Germans by Poles at the time of the outbreak of war. The fact that a woman had become involved with a Polish or Soviet prisoner seemed to indicate to the judges that she was a "criminal type," sometimes leading to the conclusion that they could soften the usual standards of proof. Yet, in rural Catholic regions, Polish POWs often encountered a friendly German population and were widely accepted into the social circle of the farmers employing them.[60]

---

and London: The Johns Hopkins University Press, 2003), 369. See also Rolf Hochhuth, *Eine Liebe in Deutschland* (Reinbek bei Hamburg: Rowohlt, 1978), translated into English as *A German Love Story*, tr. John Brownjohn (Boston: Little and Brown, 1980).

[58] Löffelsender, *Strafjustiz an der Heimatfront*, 306, note 58.

[59] Michael Löffelsender argues for an inconsistent but not always worse practice based on (as he admits very few) cases in Cologne and Bonn, whereas Hans-Ulrich Ludewig and Dietrich Kuessner do see a harsher practice in Braunschweig: Löffelsender, *Strafjustiz an der Heimatfront*, 306–8; Ludewig and Kuessner, *"Es sei also jeder gewarnt,"* 146, 148–9.

[60] In the case of Anna W., sentenced to three years of penal servitude in October 1941, her brother had invited the Polish POWs working on the family farm to his wedding, including the prisoner with whom Anna had a relationship: Bayerisches Staatsarchiv (BStA) Nürnberg, Akten der Anklagebehörde beim Sondergericht, 1273. For other examples, see BStA Nürnberg, Akten der Anklagebehörde beim Sondergericht, 1088 and 2777, and BLHA Potsdam, 12 C, Sondergericht Berlin, 232, 232/1, 232/2, 302, 302/1, 302/2, 320, 320/1, 320/2, and 6187, 6187/1, 6187/2. See also Ela Hornung, Ernst Langthaler, and Sabine Schweitzer, "Zwangsarbeit in der Landwirtschaft," in *Das Deutsche Reich und der Zweite Weltkrieg: Die deutsche Kriegsgesellschaft 1939 bis 1945* (Munich: Deutsche Verlags-Anstalt, 2005), 614–15.

Nazi policies toward Soviet POWs were extremely brutal and recognized no legal restraints.[61] More than half of the prisoners perished or were murdered in German captivity, mostly in the first months of the German campaign against the Soviet Union. Despite Hitler's initial refusal to allow Soviet POWs on German soil, labor shortages led to their large-scale deployment in Germany, albeit under strict surveillance and brutal conditions. Germans and non-Germans were severely punished for giving bread or cigarettes to the often-starving Soviet prisoners. In February 1942, for example, fifty-nine-year-old German worker Hermann Gabriel from Wilhelmshaven was sentenced to five months in prison for having given a Soviet prisoner some buttered bread and cigarette butts; the grateful prisoner gave Gabriel a watch in return.[62] Only a few love relations came to trial, but they were among the most tragic. Some women committed suicide when the affair was discovered.[63] The prisoners were often executed.

A comparison of the sentences against women involved with Soviet POWs and the punishments of women involved with western prisoners shows that the former suffered significantly harsher punishment. Two women who had a relationship with a Soviet POW in Nürnberg (one of them was pregnant from the POW) received five years of penal servitude in 1943, while the usual punishment of this special court for a relationship with a western POW at this time ranged from eighteen months to three years of penal servitude. The fate of the POW is only known in the second case: he was shot to death by a guard who ambushed him when he walked to the fence of his camp to meet the woman. He had been denounced by fellow prisoners.[64] In August 1944, a woman who had a

---

[61] A widespread misunderstanding is that the Geneva Convention obliged all signatories to observe its provisions also in conflicts with non-signatory states. Article 82 of the Geneva Convention only demands that the convention remain in force between signatory states in case the parties in the war involve a non-signatory state, but this does not mean that Nazi Germany had an obligation to observe the Geneva Convention for Soviet POWs. Still, they should have been treated according to The Hague Regulations of 1907, which had become customary law even though the Soviet Union had refused to observe any treaty the tsarist government had signed. Although The Hague Convention is less specific on POWs, it does contain many humanitarian principles of the Geneva Convention. See Rüdiger Overmans, "The Treatment of Prisoners of War in the Eastern European Theatre of Operations, 1941–56," in *Prisoners in War*, edited by Sibylle Scheipers (Oxford and New York: Oxford University Press, 2010), 127–8, and Neville Wylie, "The 1929 Prisoner of War Convention and the Building of the Inter-war Prisoner of War Regime," in *Prisoners in War*, edited by Sibylle Scheipers (Oxford and New York: Oxford University Press, 2010), 103.

[62] Tagesmeldung 6 of Wilhelmshaven office for the Reichssicherheitshauptamt (RSHA), February 1942, in NLA Oldenburg, Best. 136, Nr. 2886b.

[63] Tagesmeldung 1 of Wilhelmshaven office for the RSHA, June 1943, in NLA Oldenburg, Best. 136, Nr. 2886b.

[64] BStA Nürnberg, Akten der Anklagebehörde beim Sondergericht, 2419 and 2423.

love affair with the Soviet POW who worked on her parents' farm was sentenced to two years of penal servitude by the special court in Frankfurt an der Oder, which at this time punished relations with western POW with fifteen to eighteen months of penal servitude. The prisoner was sent to a Gestapo penal labor camp and was slated to be transferred to the Mauthausen concentration camp in Austria to receive "special treatment" (murder), but the state prosecutor urged postponement at the end of October 1944 because he might still be needed as a witness because of a mysterious barn fire that had killed a Swiss farmworker who was also in love with the woman. The police suspected that the woman and the prisoner might have started the fire to cover up the murder of the Swiss farmworker. What ultimately happened to the POW is not clear.[65]

The German Women

The notion that war is men's business, that men fight to protect women, and that women have little to do with war except as victims has long been discarded. Already in the 1960s, studies showed that women played very active roles in both world wars, although the prevailing notion was that the greater latitude for women during war was always meant to be exceptional, meaning that postwar social discourse sought to reaffirm prewar gender hierarchies and social roles, albeit not always successfully. The introduction to the edited book *Behind the Lines: Gender and the Two World Wars* (1987) states with admirable clarity that gender relations in the world wars tended to reproduce traditional hierarchies insofar as the greater role of women on the home front always remained subordinate to the frontline struggle, which highlighted masculine virtues. Although women's situation objectively changed during war, the relations of subordination and domination remained.[66] Women's role in sustaining and supporting military culture, even their participation in atrocities, has also received due attention. At the same time, with respect to Word War II, the notion of women as victims remains highly significant in light of the dangers and deprivations on the home front. Moreover, the ideological aspect of the war as a fight for democracy and against fascism or, conversely, for a fascist system and racial exclusivity, also affected women's thoughts and actions. German women became witnesses and

[65] BLHA Potsdam, 12 C, Sondergericht Frankfurt an der Oder, 849.
[66] Margaret Randolph Higonnet et al., eds., *Behind the Lines: Gender and the Two World Wars* (New Haven and London: Yale University Press, 1987), 4, 6.

even to a degree participants in Nazi discrimination and violence.[67] With
respect to women in Nazi Germany, the debate has long moved beyond
the question as to whether German women were victims or perpetrators,
showing that they often appeared in variations of both roles.[68]

The Nazi regime placed racial hierarchies above gender hierarchies,
although there is no doubt that it promoted pro-natalism among the
racially valued population groups and favored a traditional patriarchal
gender order.[69] The German women who during the war became
involved with POWs had all heard admonishments to be racially mindful
when selecting a marriage partner and to produce many children.
Women considered hereditarily ill were targeted for sterilization and
forced abortion.[70] But while the regime prized the role of "racially
acceptable" women as mothers and housewives, it also pressured them
into the working world with increasing force, as labor shortages began to
afflict an economy running in high gear after 1936 and even more
drastically during the war.[71] The labor shortage was most severe in
agriculture because low wages and profits had promoted migration to
the cities during the 1930s. Family farms had to manage with few or no
employees, and women shouldered a large burden of unpaid or poorly
paid labor on these farms. A Nazi scheme forced nearly a quarter of a
million unmarried women under twenty-five who wanted to work in
industry to first perform a year of service in agriculture or domestic
service (*Pflichtjahr*), but not all drafted women were useful laborers on
the farms. The regime resisted the idea of labor conscription for all
German women, and generous payments to soldiers' wives and widows
ensured that many of them did not need employment. When the regime
finally did decide to conscript German women under the age of forty-
five, it allowed for so many exceptions as to make the effect of the
measure marginal.[72]

---

[67] Nicole Ann Dombrowski, ed., *Women and War in the Twentieth Century: Enlisted with or without Consent* (New York and London: Garland Publishing, 1999), 3, 8–12. See also Elizabeth Harvey, *Women and the Nazi East: Agents and Witnesses of Germanization* (New Haven: Yale University Press, 2003); Wendy Lower, *Hitler's Furies: German Women in the Nazi Killing Fields* (Boston, MA: Houghton Mifflin Harcourt, 2013).

[68] Angelika Ebbinghaus, ed., *Opfer und Täterinnen: Frauenbiographien des Nationalsozialismus* (Frankfurt am Main: Fischer, 1996); Adelheid von Saldern, *Victims or Perpetrators? Controversies about the Role of Women in the Nazi State* (London and New York: Routledge, 1994).

[69] Matthew Stibbe, *Women in the Third Reich* (London: Arnold, 2003), 50–4.

[70] Gisela Bock, *Zwangssterilisation im Nationalsozialismus: Studien zur Rassenpolitik und Frauenpolitik* (Opladen: Westdeutscher Verlag, 1986); Gisela Bock and Pat Thane, eds., *Maternity and Gender Policies: Women and the Rise of the European Welfare States, 1880–1950s* (London and New York: Routledge, 1991).

[71] Stibbe, *Women in the Third Reich*, 84–96.   [72] Ibid., 91, 94–5.

The fact that Nazi Germany refused to exploit the full potential of German women's labor increased the dependence of enterprises and farms on foreign laborers over the course of the war. Already in 1939, a large number of Poles, including POWs, had been forced to work in Germany. The German victory in the West brought new POWs and increasingly also civilian workers to Germany, first voluntary workers and later recruited or forced laborers. The vast German conquests in the Balkans and the Soviet Union until 1943 led to mass deportations of men and women from these regions for labor in the Reich, so that by 1944 six million foreign civilians including two million women worked in Germany, most of them under harsh conditions.[73] To this labor force must be added more than two million POWs, the vast majority rank-and-file soldiers, and of course the hundreds of thousands of concentration camp inmates. The presence of foreign POWs is therefore indirectly connected to a policy that sought to spare middle- and upper-class German women, especially the married, from employment.

One salient feature of German women's experience of the war was the growing absence of German men in their age group. As Elizabeth Heineman states: "In many ways, the Second World War created a generation of German women standing alone."[74] The Wehrmacht drafted nearly eighteen million men over the course of the war, and already by the end of 1944 almost two million were confirmed dead and one million seven hundred thousand missing in action or taken prisoner. The drafting of men went through several waves, but it meant that more and more German women were largely on their own. In the countryside, the farmer's wife had to manage the family farm, supervise the workers, decide which cow to slaughter, and fulfill the ever more pressing demands of a state-imposed system of quotas, prices, and rationing. Military husbands had home leaves, but the time between leaves tended to grow longer as the war progressed, and it was not unusual for spouses not to see each other for a full year or more. Although millions of letters circulated between the homes and the front, husbands could not manage everything from distance, and this led to much conflict during home leaves.

---

[73] Ibid., 91, 96; Herbert, *Hitler's Foreign Workers*, 278–82; Mark Spoerer, "Die soziale Differenzierung der ausländischen Zivilarbeiter, Kriegsgefangenen und Häftlinge im Deutschen Reich," in *Das Deutsche Reich und der Zweite Weltkrieg*, edited by Jörg Echternkamp (Munich: Deutsche Verlags-Anstalt, 2005).

[74] Elizabeth D. Heineman, *What Difference Does a Husband Make? Women and Marital Status in Nazi and Postwar Germany* (Berkeley and Los Angeles: University of California Press, 1999), 44–5.

As labor shortages in agriculture persisted despite the large-scale deployment of POWs and foreign laborers, women working in German agriculture experienced the war as an extremely stressful period. The same might be said for urban women, even though some of the challenges of everyday life were different for them. Urban women suffered from growing rationing, rising prices, and shortages of food and heating fuel, although food was usually available in sufficient quantities until almost the end of the war owing to the massive exploitation of resources in the occupied countries. Employed urban women had to work long hours. In most cities, their homes and workplaces were increasingly threatened by bombs. Their apartments might be damaged or destroyed, and they might have to move in with neighbors, family, or friends. Daily survival required ever more improvisation and sacrifice. Some women with young children were evacuated to the countryside, but this could involve a culture shock. The urban woman might encounter suspicions from her rural neighbors, and in many cases mentalities and lifestyles clashed.[75] For all German women, but particularly for those living in the eastern areas, the looming German defeat became a nightmarish thought. Fear of Soviet revenge led to mass flights in the eastern areas in late 1944 and early 1945, and the encounter with Soviet troops often meant massive sexual violence, murder, or deportation to labor camps in the Soviet Union.[76]

Many Germans began to resent the war, which had not been popular when it started and which lasted so much longer than expected.[77] The distress of German women sometimes exploded in unexpected ways. In April 1943, a spontaneous demonstration of several hundred women occurred in Dortmund after the ill-treatment of a soldier by an officer, prompting the women to scream that they wanted their drafted husbands or sons back.[78] Several of the women on trial for forbidden relations in court blamed their "crime" on the enforced separation from their husbands. As a soldier's wife on trial for a forbidden relationship with a French POW in Nürnberg said in response to moralizing reproaches

[75] Julia S. Torrie, "For Their Own Good": Civilian Evacuations in Germany and France, 1939–1945 (New York and Oxford: Berghahn Books, 2010), 73–6.
[76] Heineman, What Difference Does a Husband Make?, 81–2; Ingo von Münch, "Frau komm!" Die Massenvergewaltigungen deutscher Frauen und Mädchen 1944/45 (Graz: Ares, 2009); Norman Naimark, The Russians in Germany: A History of the Soviet Zone of Occupation (Cambridge, MA: Harvard University Press, 1995); Miriam Gebhardt, Crimes Unspoken: The Rape of German Women at the End of the Second World War, trans. Nick Somers (Cambridge: Polity Press, 2016).
[77] Nicholas Stargardt, The German War: A Nation under Arms, 1939–1945: Citizens and Soldiers (New York: Basic Books, 2015), 30–4 and chapter 12.
[78] Stibbe, Women in the Third Reich, 151.

from the judge: "just let our husbands come back to us." She had not seen her husband in a year.[79]

The long enforced separation put marriages to a test. The outbreak of war had triggered a sudden increase in marriages, especially if the man had received a draft notice. The newly weds usually had little time to settle in before being separated. When a husband came home after an increasingly long tour of duty, the precious few days the couple could spend together often failed to live up to the high expectations. The husband, who might be traumatized or brutalized, was difficult to reach and seemed to have become a different person. He might be irritable and resent the fact that his wife seemed to be coping without him. She herself might be frustrated by his meddling with everything that she had more or less under control while living alone. Infidelity was of course not uncommon among married soldiers. Soldiers stationed in occupation units often had affairs with local women, particularly in France, and rest days on the frontline also offered opportunities to visit a brothel or engage with local women. Paris and other French cities were popular destinations of German soldiers, partly for these reasons.[80] Although the Wehrmacht prosecuted and punished rape, German soldiers could use pressure and incentives to obtain sexual favors in areas where the local population was desperate.[81] Meanwhile, German soldiers' wives (and widows) found themselves under increasing public scrutiny. A nonchalant or promiscuous lifestyle produced resentment and could easily trigger a denunciation, especially if the woman's partner was a foreign man. Beginning in 1943, the state could impose retrospective divorce for war widows considered to be leading immoral lives, depriving them of the pensions and benefits to which they were entitled. Although

---

[79] Case of Käthe P., BStA Nürnberg, Akten der Anklagebehörde beim Sondergericht, 1278. The response angered the judge, who sentenced her to fourteen months of penal servitude even though no sexual intercourse was proven. The prisoner, Fernand R., received only three months in prison because the military tribunal saw the woman, who was ten years older, as the seducer: *Feldurteil* Nürnberg, January 6, 1942, in PAAA, R 40905.

[80] Julia S. Torrie, *German Soldiers and the Occupation of France, 1940–1944* (Cambridge and New York: Cambridge University Press, 2018), 83–7.

[81] Snyder, *Sex Crimes under the Wehrmacht*, 138; Beck, *Wehrmacht und sexuelle Gewalt*, 290; Regina Mühlhäuser, *Eroberungen: Sexuelle Gewalttaten und intime Beziehungen deutscher Soldaten in der Sowjetunion, 1941–1945* (Hamburg: Hamburger Edition, 2010); Mühlhäuser, "Between 'Racial Awareness' and Fantasies of Potency: Nazi Sexual Politics in the Occupied Territories of the Soviet Union, 1942–1945," in Herzog, *Brutality and Desire*, 197–220; Maren Röger, *Kriegsbeziehungen: Intimität, Gewalt und Prostitution im besetzten Polen 1939 bis 1945* (Frankfurt am Main: Fischer, 2015), 108–14; Dagmar Herzog, *Sex after Fascism: Memory and Morality in Twentieth-Century Germany* (Princeton and Oxford: Princeton University Press, 2005), 60.

German soldiers had considerable sexual freedom, their wives were expected to remain faithful. The Nazi authorities believed that a correlation existed between marital loyalty (of the woman) and the morale and fighting spirit of the husband, and therefore put a high premium on the social control of soldiers' wives.[82]

Wars tend to provide rich opportunities for sexual encounters.[83] These encounters often contradicted desires to preserve or upgrade what Nazi ideologues considered to be racial purity because they involved partners from different countries and from populations and races taken to be inferior. The double morality of the Nazi regime in dealing with this challenge did not go unnoticed. Some women on trial for forbidden relations openly confronted their judges by pointing out for example that while they would be sentenced to years of penal servitude for having slept with a Frenchman, German men were not punished for sleeping with a French woman. The fact that relations with western civilian workers were not forbidden while relations with POWs were severely penalized also struck many Germans as a glaring contradiction, especially considering that many western POWs were increasingly living and working like foreign civilian laborers. Although much of the literature on forbidden relations claims that relations with civilian laborers were also illegal, this is true only for Polish and Soviet workers. Of course, the Nazi police could intimidate and threaten western foreign laborers and German women even if their relations were not expressly forbidden. A Nazi law on analogy (1935) gave judges flexibility in prosecuting actions that did not openly violate a law but which resembled an illegal act.[84] But even though the SS considered a comprehensive ban on sexual relations with all foreign laborers desirable, it was never enacted for pragmatic reasons, including concerns for the image of Nazi Germany abroad and the fear that such a ban would strengthen the aversion of western and northern Europeans to working in Germany.[85]

---

[82] Stibbe, *Women in the Third Reich*, 158; Kundrus, *Kriegerfrauen*, 369–73; Heineman, *What Difference Does a Husband Make?*, 44 and 54–6; Löffelsender, *Strafjustiz an der Heimatfront*, 54–5, 57–8.

[83] Matthias Reiss, *Controlling Sex in Captivity: POWs and Sexual Desire in the United States During the Second World War* (London: Bloomsbury, 2018), 2; Dagmar Herzog, "Introduction: War and Sexuality in Europe's Twentieth Century," in Herzog, ed., *Brutality and Desire*, 2 and 11; Herzog, *Sex after Fascism*, 62; Dagmar Herzog, *Sexuality in Europe: A Twentieth-Century History* (Cambridge and New York: Cambridge University Press, 2011), 47.

[84] *Reichsgesetzblatt* 1935, I, No. 70, 839–43, at: https://de.wikisource.org/wiki/Gesetz_zur_%C3%84nderung_des_Strafgesetzbuchs_(1935) (last visited December 19, 2019).

[85] Herbert, *Hitler's Foreign Workers*, 130; Löffelsender, *Strafjustiz an der Heimatfront*, 57.

German women during the Third Reich perceived contradictory messages about sexuality. As Dagmar Herzog has shown, the older notion of Nazism as simply anti-sex does no longer hold, nor does the idea of Nazism merely manipulating "racially" accepted people into sex without pleasure for the purpose of racial hygienic procreation. Although Nazi physicians and publicists often espoused conservative sexual values (for example premarital abstention and marital fidelity, at least for women) and bemoaned the allegedly demoralizing "Jewish" influence on sexual mores before 1933, other Nazi publications and especially youth organizations accepted sexual satisfaction for its own sake and encouraged sex before marriage and promiscuity, as long as it happened in strictly heterosexual and racially conscious ways. The brutalization of the fighting front and the increasing moral perversion of a popular and brutal regime further loosened sexual mores over the course of the war, while also creating a backlash from the churches, parents of teenagers, and frontline soldiers worried about the infidelity of their wives.[86] As Herzog concludes:

No regime before or since did so much to intervene violently in the bodies and intimate relationships of its citizens, and of citizens of all the conquered and occupied and collaborating nations – while at the same time promising rapturous enjoyment and the right to break taboos to its own followers.[87]

---

[86] Herzog, *Sex after Fascism*, 10–63, in particular 55–63.
[87] Herzog, *Sexuality in Europe*, 66.

Why the Prohibition?

All armies during the two world wars restricted contacts between POWs and civilians, arguing that such contacts facilitated black market activity, espionage, and sabotage. They could also give prisoners access to useful objects for an escape, such as civilian clothing, local currency, a compass, and maps. In case of closer and more intimate contacts, civilians might display solidarity with the prisoners, allowing them to hide in their homes. The perception of the disarmed enemy as a decent human, perhaps even a friend, questioned the "us" versus "them" dichotomy and undermined propaganda aiming to vilify the enemy in order to boost support for the war effort. Solidarity between POWs and civilians might especially hurt the morale of frontline soldiers, whose lives were in danger while their disarmed enemies were safe and able to "pry" among the soldiers' wives or potential brides. Given that every army used older or slightly disabled soldiers to guard POWs, who tended to be frontline soldiers in their physical prime, the contrast between fit and strong enemies and "weak" guardians could produce a feeling of inferiority within the home population.[1] Women engaging in amorous relations with POWs challenged national sensibilities at a time when women were expected to play a special role on the home front, upholding morality and order.

British officials in World War II therefore restricted what they called "fraternization" with Axis prisoners – even though it usually involved amorous relations between foreign men and local women – by forbidding civilians access to places where POWs were held and by punishing POWs who fostered relations to civilians. Canadian, Australian, and American regulations were similar, but transgressions by POWs were mostly

---

[1] Matthias Reiss, "Bronzed Bodies behind Barbed Wire: Masculinity and the Treatment of German Prisoners of War in the United States during World War II," *Journal of Military History* 69, no. 2 (2005); Reiss, *Controlling Sex in Captivity*, 18–38, 46–7.

treated as disciplinary matters, which meant that they did not involve a court martial hearing and led only to a mild punishment of up to one month of arrest.[2] The legal framework for civilians contained many loopholes, moreover. For example, the laws forbidding civilians access to POWs remained vague in Britain; civilians only risked fines for approaching a POW, and many women, in particular, were not deterred. Moreover, there was a fundamental difference between Italian and German prisoners, given that the Italians were often "billeted" with individual households, meaning that the prohibition for civilians to access places where POWs were held made no sense. Relations between British women and Italian prisoners became widespread, especially as the Italians, similar to the French and Belgian POWs in Germany, were not generally perceived as "real" enemies, but these relations did create some outrage at the local level and among frontline troops. German prisoners, by contrast, were for a long time much more closely guarded and more separated from civilians because they were considered to be more dangerous and fanatical. But when security concerns lessened in the last months of the war and in the postwar period, German POWs also became more dispersed and worked in close contact with British civilians. Despite the continuing stigmatization of the German prisoners, many amorous liaisons occurred and created outrage. Press reports on relations of British women with Axis prisoners often highlighted the active role of the woman, which was considered reprehensible and unpatriotic.[3]

In the United States, the situation was complicated by the presence of large populations of German and Italian descent who found themselves under close scrutiny because many Americans feared they might feel solidarity with the captives from "their" people. Although some German and Italian Americans tried to defuse suspicions by adopting a harsh and distant attitude to the POWs, relations between civilians and POWs were overall very friendly, so friendly in fact that officials felt the need to launch press campaigns designed to undermine the notion especially of the German prisoner as a healthy, fit, and attractive man. Reports about

---

[2] Frey, *Die disziplinarische und gerichtliche Bestrafung*, 64.

[3] Bob Moore, "Illicit Encounters: Female Civilian Fraternization with Axis Prisoners of War in Second World War Britain," *Journal of Contemporary History* 48, no. 4 (2013); Moore, "Enforced Diaspora: The Fate of Italian Prisoners of War during the Second World War," *War in History* 22, no. 2 (2015). On the labor deployment of Italians and Germans in Britain, see also Renate Held, *Kriegsgefangenschaft in Großbritannien: Deutsche Soldaten des Zweiten Weltkriegs in britischem Gewahrsam* (München: Oldenbourg, 2008), 53–9.

flirtatious encounters between POWs and American women –sometimes even women in army uniform – did create a public relations crisis and caused concern among frontline troops. Reining in these relationships proved to be challenging, however. American officials encountered the same problem as German officials: Stricter guarding of the POWs would have required much more personnel, and POW labor was economically most useful if the prisoners were deployed in a decentralized way, which multiplied opportunities for encountering civilians. Despite some public outrage, prosecution of these relationships in the United States remained lax and punishments lenient, as long as no other transgressions were present, for example helping a POW to escape.[4]

In Britain and the United States, the principal concerns associated with prisoner–civilian contacts involved amorous relations with local women and the resulting damage to image and morale, which was always rather diffuse. As in Germany, the more concrete worries about espionage, sabotage, or black-market activity proved unfounded. Contacts with women did sometimes facilitate escapes, as feared, but most escaped POWs were recaptured without much delay. The primary concern was about morale and morality in a public discourse that delegated to women the role of guardians of national respectability and moral standards. The women "fraternizing" with enemy prisoners were shunned and ostracized, especially the British women involved with German POWs, but economic priorities and administrative limitations worked against strict enforcement of the bans and harsh punishments.

In Germany during World War I, friendly contacts between civilians and POWs had caused similar concerns. In a society that was highly worried about the fidelity of the warrior's wife during her husband's absence at the front, all adulterous relations of the wife triggered outrage, but a relationship with a disarmed enemy soldier, member of the same army that was trying to kill the husband, carried a particular stigma. While the reigning double morality might tolerate the husband's sexual exploits with enemy women, the warrior wife stood under special scrutiny.[5] As historian Lisa Todd has shown, the often cordial contacts between POWs and civilians on farms triggered outcries about the erosion of the home front and the friend–foe dichotomy, and women engaging with prisoners of war were accused of "sexual treason" and punished, although much more leniently than in World War II and

---

[4] Reiss, *Controlling Sex in Captivity*, 23–5, 60–73, 79–87.
[5] For this problem in general, see Kundrus, *Kriegerfrauen*, 377–84; Kundrus, "Forbidden Company," 207.

without the racialized context of Nazi justifications.[6] The memory of these relationships assumed a particular importance in light of the perceived causes of the German defeat in 1918. The notion that an allegedly undefeated German army had been stabbed in the back by a disorderly home front was common currency among right-wing opponents of Weimar democracy and almost became state doctrine with the coming to power of the Nazi party.[7] Official pamphlets published on the eve of World War II argued that prisoners of war had exploited the goodwill and compassion of German civilians, especially women, to carry out sabotage and espionage, to spread defeatist rumors, and to undermine German morality. A brochure on POWs commissioned by the High Command in 1939 and distributed to regional and local magistrates claimed that the French government in World War I had systematically instructed POWs to act as spies and saboteurs. The friendly reception of POWs by German civilians had allegedly facilitated this task. But, according to Nazi officials, the amorous relations between POWs and German women had also pursued a broader but no less vicious aim, namely to destabilize the German family and to pollute the German race.[8] The High Command brochure stressed that POWs had not just pursued amorous relations to gain sexual satisfaction but that they had carried out a sinister and systematic "effort to consciously bastardize the German people, disturb its family life, and destroy German custom. – Moral sabotage!"[9] The amorous relations of World War I were therefore

[6] Lisa M. Todd, *Sexual Treason in Germany during the First World War*, Gender and Sexualities in History (Cham: Palgrave MacMillan, 2017), 107–16, 23–4; Todd, "'The Soldier's Wife Who Ran Away with the Russian': Sexual Infidelities in World War I Germany," *Central European History* 44 (2011), 264–5, 277–8; Uta Hinz, *Gefangen im Großen Krieg: Kriegsgefangenschaft in Deutschland 1914–1921* (Essen: Klartext Verlag, 2006), 173–4, 185–6, 191–201. On similar concerns in Britain in World War I, despite lack of firm evidence for sexual encounters between German POWs and British women: Brian K. Feltman, "'We Don't Want Any German Off-Spring after These Prisoners Left Here': German Military Prisoners and British Women in the First World War," *Gender & History* 30 (2018), 110–11, 124–5.

[7] On the implications of the stab-in-the back myth for military justice, see Theis, *Wehrmachtjustiz an der "Heimatfront,"* 388; Kalmbach, *Wehrmachtjustiz,* 49; Messerschmidt, *Die Wehrmachtjustiz 1933–1945,* 8–9. For an overview, see George S. Vascik and Mark R. Sadler, eds., *The Stab-in-the-Back Myth and the Fall of the Weimar Republic: A History in Documents and Visual Sources* (London: Bloomsbury, 2016).

[8] For a sample, see NLA Oldenburg, Best. 135 B, especially the brochure "Kriegsgefangene" edited by the OKW (High Command) in 1939 and sent to the government of Oldenburg on November 13, 1939, and "Feind bleibt Feind." See also Todd, "The Soldier's Wife Who Ran Away with the Russian," 277.

[9] "Kriegsgefangene," in NLA Oldenburg, Best. 135 B, p. 16. Original: "die bewußte Absicht der Verbastardierung des deutschen Volkes, Störung seines Familienlebens und Zerstörung deutscher Sitte. – Sittensabotage!" See also Walter Kallfelz, "Strafbarer Umgang mit Kriegsgefangenen," *Deutsches Recht* 10, no. 43 (1940): 1813.

seen in the same light as the alleged French effort to "bastardize" the German race by promoting the aggressive sexual behavior of non-European occupation troops in the Rhineland after 1918, as highlighted by the obnoxious "black horror" campaign.[10]

The lessons Nazi officials derived from World War I induced them to severely punish contacts between POWs and civilians and to launch a sustained propaganda effort warning German women of the dangers of "fraternization" with enemy prisoners. As public announcements never tired of repeating: "the enemy remains the enemy!" (*"Feind bleibt Feind!"*). Prisoners of war faced a court martial under a German military justice system that had itself sharpened considerably as a consequence of the widespread belief that German military justice had been too lenient at the end of World War I, allowing discipline in the German army to disintegrate.[11] Women faced prosecution through a legal system geared toward harsh prosecution of dissent and dissidence. In both cases the prosecution was strengthened at the expense of the defense, and both justice systems faced tight screening from the highest offices of the armed forces and the government. It was known that Hitler shared a low opinion of the law profession; he spectacularly threatened in a Reichstag speech on April 26, 1942, to fire judges who did not recognize "the imperatives of the hour." The servile Reichstag promptly passed a resolution declaring that Hitler stood above the law.[12]

As a consequence, punishments for POWs and civilians who entered into relationships with each other were much harsher in Nazi Germany than in the western countries and in Germany itself during World War I. Whereas German POWs "fraternizing" with American or British women would at worst receive arrest (special confinement) for up to thirty days, western POWs in Nazi Germany would face a court martial and be sentenced to years in military prisons, where the treatment of the

---

[10] Jean-Yves Le Naour, *La honte noire: L'Allemagne et les troupes coloniales françaises 1914–1945* (Paris: Hachette Littérature, 2003); Gisela Lebzelter, "Die 'Schwarze Schmach': Vorurteile – Propaganda – Mythos," *Geschichte und Gesellschaft* 11, no. 1 (1985). On earlier efforts to interpret female promiscuity as a sign of degeneration and also counterarguments that explained the relations with POWs as a consequence of war conditions, see Todd, *Sexual Treason in Germany*, 123–7.

[11] Messerschmidt, *Die Wehrmachtjustiz 1933–1945*, 19–22; Kalmbach, *Wehrmachtjustiz*, 49; Boll, "... das gesunde Volksempfinden," 650.

[12] Nikolaus Wachsmann, *Hitler's Prisons: Legal Terror in Nazi Germany* (New Haven and London: Yale University Press, 2004), 214; Thomas Blanke, *Die juristische Aufarbeitung des Unrechts-Staats* (Baden-Baden: Nomos, 1998), 457; Ralph Angermund, *Deutsche Richterschaft 1919–1945: Krisenerfahrung, Illusion, politische Rechtsprechung* (Frankfurt am Main: Fischer Taschenbuch Verlag, 1990), 248–9.

inmates (German and foreign) betrayed the brutal legacy of an older Prussian military discipline system. German women usually had to appear before a special court (*Sondergericht*), a branch of the justice system built up before the war to deal above all with political dissent.[13] In the case of sexual intercourse with a prisoner, a woman had to expect a sentence ranging from one and a half to five years in the harshest institution of German law enforcement, the *Zuchthaus*, commonly translated as "penitentiary" or "penal servitude." A *Zuchthaus* sentence, usually coupled with a loss of civil rights at least until the end of the sentence, involved forced labor under harsh conditions far from home. Visits from family or friends were much more restricted than in a common prison, and a *Zuchthaus* sentence carried a big social stigma.[14] For deterrence and as an act of shaming and humiliation, the sentences of the special courts with the names of the punished women were published in the newspapers and on posters with a denigrating commentary.

The Order for the Prisoners of War

The Geneva Convention of 1929 was the principal legal framework for western POWs in German hands. Although a pre-Nazi government had negotiated this international treaty, the Hitler government had ratified it in 1934. The Geneva Convention stipulated that POWs had to obey the laws, regulations, and orders in force in the army of the detaining state and that trials against them had to follow the same procedures as trials against soldiers of the state's own army (article 45).[15] The convicted POW should serve his sentence under the same conditions as convicted soldiers of the detaining state's army, as long as these procedures ensured humane treatment. Corporal punishment and cruelty were specifically

---

[13] Wüllenweber, *Sondergerichte im Dritten Reich*, 193–8; Lutz, "Das Sondergericht Nürnberg 1933–1945, 252–3; Angermund, *Deutsche Richterschaft 1919–1945*, 133–57. It appears that in some judicial districts, such as in Cologne, only forbidden relations that had likely involved sexual intercourse or help for an escape came before the special court, while lighter cases were judged by the district courts: Löffelsender, *Strafjustiz an der Heimatfront*, 115. My research shows, however, that the special courts elsewhere often dealt with lighter cases, too.

[14] Wachsmann, *Hitler's Prisons*, 2, 237–8, and 56. Wachsmann argues, however, that even the harshest penitentiaries during the war were less deadly than the concentration camps (256).

[15] All references to the Geneva Convention refer to the text in Jonathan Vance, ed., *Encyclopedia of Prisoners of War and Internment* (Santa Barbara: ABC-CLIO, 2000), 508–27. The text can also be consulted online on the site of the International Committee of the Red Cross: ihl-databases.icrc.org/applic/ihl/dih.nsf/INTRO/305? OpenDocument (last visited April 10, 2019).

banned even if they constituted accepted practice in the detaining state (article 46).

The Geneva Convention distinguishes between disciplinary punishments and judicial proceedings. The former, usually pronounced by a higher officer without elaborate procedure, dealt with lighter offenses, especially those that may endanger discipline among the prisoners. Disciplinary punishments could not exceed thirty days of confinement. Prisoners serving a disciplinary sentence preserved the right to read and write and to exercise. They were locked up inside the POW camp but otherwise faced similar conditions as the rest of the POWs. They could not be transferred to a prison or penitentiary (articles 54–59). Disciplinary punishments were a common penalty for escapes or for violations of camp regulations. For more serious offenses, the detaining power had to organize judicial proceedings; it had to inform the prisoner's protecting power of the charges and the date and place of the hearing. This notification had to arrive at least three weeks before the court martial met. The prisoner had the right to a defense attorney and an interpreter, and representatives of the protecting power could attend the hearing. The Geneva Convention gave POWs the same right to appeal against a sentence as a soldier of the armed forces of the detaining power, but this meant nothing in Nazi Germany because defendants sentenced by a court martial had no right to appeal and to refer the case to a higher judicial authority. Once confirmed by the higher military authorities, the judgment against the POW had to be communicated to the protecting power. Under no circumstances could the legal regime deprive prisoners of their right to formulate complaints against the conditions of captivity and to communicate them to the protecting power (article 67, with reference to article 42), and the protecting power had the right to inspect the facilities in which convicted POWs were held. With these provisions, the Geneva Convention aimed to ensure international oversight for the trials and the enforcement of sentences.

The fact that the Geneva Convention stipulated that all laws in force in the detaining army applied to POWs meant that POWs in Germany were exposed to the entire repressive Nazi legislation, which was designed to prepare a national community for total war. Paragraph 158 of the German military law code subjected prisoners to the same laws as German soldiers and referred to §3, which placed German soldiers under all laws valid in Germany.[16] POWs were surprised to learn that they

---

[16] Georg Dörken and Werner Scherer, *Das Militärstrafgesetzbuch und die Kriegssonderstrafrechtsverordnung*, 4th ed. (Berlin: Verlag Franz Vahlen, 1943), 7, 152, 57. For the use of the law in the preparation for total war, see Kalmbach, "Schutz der

could be sentenced to prison for a joke about Hitler because Nazi laws included the prohibition to denigrate in public the German army and state, the Nazi party, or its leaders (treachery law of December 20, 1934, §134 a and b of the German civil law code, and §5 of the Special War Decree). Even a prisoner who voiced critical opinions in a letter to his family could be dragged in front of a court martial on the grounds that the recipient of the letter might spread false rumors and that therefore the seemingly private remarks in the letter assumed a "public" character.[17] German law also placed harsh punishments on acts that were considered relatively harmless elsewhere. For example, courts martial treated poaching almost as an act of sabotage because it counted as an attack on the food supply of the German people. Many French prisoners who were used to a lax hunting and trapping regime in France were surprised when they received up to a year in prison for setting traps in the forest. German laws against homosexual acts and abortion predated the Nazi regime but were sharpened after 1933 and became much more severe than laws in other countries. A series of laws and decrees promulgated at the start of the war penalized many other actions, for example listening to enemy radio, and drastically increased punishments for smaller crimes such as theft if the perpetrator had exploited the war circumstances, for example the chaos after a bombing attack. All of these actions were prosecuted under an accelerated trial procedure that reduced the rights of the defendant and increased the punishments, greatly extending the use of the death penalty. Similarly, violation of non-fraternization orders was treated as a severe crime.[18]

The bulk of trials against POWs, between 75 and 80 percent for Frenchmen and Belgians, and a little less for the British, concerned forbidden relations with German women, almost always consensual. Another common crime was poaching, which was the second largest offense of the French and Belgians, but very rare for the British, who seem to have had better food supplies and less opportunity for trapping. Theft, rebellious behavior against a supervisor or military superior (contumacy), criticism, and neglect leading to accidents also figured among

---

geistigen Wehrkraft." Article 1 of the Decree on Special Justice in War (*Kriegssonderstrafrechtsverordnung*) confirmed that German civil law was applicable to all persons falling under the purview of the military law code, including POWs.

[17] On this topic, see Scheck, "Western Prisoners of War Tried for Insults of the Führer and Criticism of Nazi Germany," *Journal of Contemporary History* (forthcoming), and Scheck, "The Treatment of Western Prisoners of War in Nazi Germany: Rethinking Reciprocity and Asymmetry," *War in History* (forthcoming).

[18] For a good survey of this special legislation, see Ludewig and Kuessner, "*Es sei also jeder gewarnt,*" 115–69.

the causes for prosecution. But all other crimes together accounted for far fewer courts martial than the love relations, and the punishments were generally lighter than for forbidden relations. This meant that the prisoners sentenced for these crimes would often already have served a major part of the sentence in pre-trial custody and would spend the rest of the sentence in the main camp rather than in the military prison or penitentiary because it was not worth while to transfer them to a distant penal institution for a short time. The bitter irony is therefore that the vast majority of POWs who had to spend years in the harsh German military prisons and penitentiaries (95 percent for the French and Belgians) were sentenced for love relations with German women. The courts martial meted out harsher penalties only for severe cases of sabotage and sexual assault (especially against minors) and for murder. But these crimes were very rare.

The legal foundation outlawing relations with German women was an order by Field Marshal Wilhelm Keitel, chief of the German High Command, dated January 10, 1940: "Prisoners of war are most strictly forbidden to approach German women or girls without authorization or to enter into communication with them."[19] When this order appeared, the German army held almost exclusively Polish POWs, and the High Command had already decided together with the SS to transfer Polish POWs involved with German women to the Security Service of the SS, which meant incarceration into a concentration camp or immediate execution if sexual intercourse had occurred. After the defeat of the western powers in May and June 1940, one million five hundred and fifty thousand French and more than 200,000 British and Belgian POWs came to Germany, and the High Command hardened the penal regime by specifying on July 22 that violations of the order of January 1940 constituted military disobedience, a crime defined under §92 of the Military Law Code. In peacetime, disobedience could carry up to ten years in prison, but during war, it could lead to life in penitentiary or even to a death sentence.[20] Two weeks later, Reinhard Heydrich, the second-in-command of the SS, instructed police and SS officials that Hitler had ordered that the rules for Polish POWs be applied also to western POWs: "In particular, I point out that according to an order of the Führer, captured French, English, and Belgian soldiers are to be punished with death just like Polish prisoners of war if they have sexual intercourse with

[19] Thomas Werther, "Kriegsgefangene vor dem Marburger Militärgericht," in *Militärjustiz im Nationalsozialismus: Das Marburger Militärgericht*, ed. Michael Eberlein (Marburg: Geschichtswerkstatt Marburg, 1994), 255.
[20] Ibid., 254.

German women and girls."[21] The police and SS officials addressed by Heydrich's directive, however, were not in charge of judicial proceedings against POWs, which was the realm of the High Command and the military justice system. Moreover, the legal division of the German Foreign Ministry also had some say in this matter because it communicated with the protecting powers. These agencies ignored Hitler's order, probably because they feared acts of retribution against German POWs in Allied hands and because they anticipated that it would challenge the Geneva Convention and cause a bad international reaction. There seems to be no paper trail in the Foreign Ministry and High Command documents pertaining to Hitler's order to kill western POWs having had sex with a German woman. The protecting power for all western POWs at this time, the United States, was carefully monitoring legal matters, and a death sentence for an act that was considered a mere disciplinary offense in other states would have triggered massive protests. To my knowledge, not a single western POW ever received a death sentence because of a consensual relationship with a German woman.[22]

Paragraph 92 of the German military law code was drafted with a view to serious acts of disobedience in combat, for example refusal to follow an order to attack. This is clear insofar as it stipulated that disobedience could only be prosecuted in a court martial if it had led to a "significant disadvantage"; otherwise it would carry only disciplinary punishments (§92, section 8).[23] When Keitel placed the forbidden relations under §92 of the military law code, this meant that courts martial had to justify why a kiss, an embrace, a love letter, or a serious love affair with marriage plans caused a "significant disadvantage" meriting severe punishment. At first, courts martial had difficulties justifying the sentences. Verdicts varied but tended to be less harsh than later – usually around one year in prison for sexual intercourse in late 1940. The High Command considered this practice too lenient, however. Confronted with a rapid increase of French and Belgian POWs being prosecuted for forbidden relations in the spring of 1941, Keitel published a new decree on June 5, 1941, clarifying that: "This order has been passed to protect the purity of

[21] Durand, *Captivité*, 402.
[22] Vasilis Vourkoutiotis reports that the High Command circulated a note in November 1944 in the POW camps stating that a Serb POW had been sentenced to death for relations with a German woman, but the circumstances are not specified: Vourkoutiotis, *Prisoners of War and the German High Command*, 93. For the communications on legal matters between the American embassy and the Foreign Ministry, see the documents in PAAA, R 40850a. Herbert also concludes that Hitler's order was not applied to western POWs: Herbert, *Hitler's Foreign Workers*, 129.
[23] On the relevance of "significant disadvantage," see Frey, *Die disziplinarische und gerichtliche Bestrafung*, 62.

the German blood and to make it impossible to attack the ability of the German people to resist in this war, which has been forced upon it." He emphasized that German women received severe punishments, usually several years of penal servitude, and that therefore the POW also needed to be punished harshly. A sentence of three years in prison was the minimum for sexual intercourse, although courts martial could go slightly below three years if the woman had clearly seduced the prisoner. Keitel reminded military judges that the range of punishments for disobedience in wartime included the death penalty (§92, section 2).[24] There were no similar guidelines for lesser offenses, but courts martial quickly established that a single kiss or a love letter merited three to six months in prison, hugs with kisses and letters approximately one year in prison, and touching each other's sexual organs at least two years in prison, although some judges punished them as harshly as what they called "completed" or "normal" sexual intercourse.

Given the need to demonstrate "significant disadvantage," courts martial either applied Keitel's phrase about the "purity of the German blood" verbatim or composed their own variations on this theme, for example by claiming that prisoners had through their amorous relations created the potential of "unwanted admixtures to the German gene pool" or had "compromised racial purity." Sometimes, these justifications appeared absurd even according to Nazi racial thinking. On a work detachment in a forest near Memmingen (Bavaria), for example, a woman regularly invited four French POWs to have sex with her in the brush during the summer of 1941. This woman was on record as being "feeble-minded," which meant that she was almost certainly sterilized. The court martial in Memmingen sentenced the prisoners to two or two and a half years in prison (the discrepancy being caused by different frequencies of contact), but it still argued that the order was meant to "prevent the mixing of German blood with foreign blood."[25] The same court martial, like many others, explained in another case the reasoning for the prohibition: "The purpose of the order is evidently to keep the German blood pure and especially to prevent the birth of children from a foreign race in German marriages, thus bringing a foreign element into the German family. Therefore, very far-reaching considerations of racial and population policy led to this prohibition."[26]

---

[24] Werther, "Kriegsgefangene vor dem Marburger Militärgericht," 255–6.
[25] Feldurteil, Memmingen, September 12, 1941, in PAAA, R 40884.
[26] "Zweck des Befehls ist einmal die Reinhaltung des deutschen Blutes, und insbes. die Verhinderung, dass in deutschen Ehen fremdstämmige Kinder zur Welt gebracht werden und dadurch ein fremdes Element in die deutsche Familie kommt. Es sind also sehr weittragende Erwägungen der Rassen- und Bevölkerungspolitik, die zu dem

These blatantly racist justifications, which appeared in the judgments sent to the protecting powers, soon produced diplomatic irritations with Vichy France. Clearly, blaming French prisoners for spoiling the German race did not sit well with the policy of collaboration. The Scapini Mission inquired about the decree of June 5, 1941, which some courts martial had mentioned in the judgments despite Keitel's admonishments to keep it secret, and the Foreign Office openly confronted the legal experts at the High Command about the racial pollution argument, pointing out that it was a diplomatic liability and misguided policy.[27] In January 1942, the Foreign Office began to regularly protest against the racial justifications and repeatedly asked the High Command to instruct the courts martial to avoid them. As the Foreign Office's legal expert, Alfred Lautz, wrote: "The Reich does not seek to reach its demographic development goals [in the sense of racial "purification"] through military orders. The order of January 10, 1940, rests on different motivations. Moreover, it is at present not advantageous to refer to the demographic goals of the Reich government in judgments against French POWs."[28] In an awkward effort, a Foreign Office official armed with a red pencil crossed out the offensive phrases from the judgments communicated to the Vichy authorities.[29]

Without retracting from the racial pollution argument, Keitel conceded in a secret directive to military justice officials on February 19, 1942, that due to foreign policy considerations the judgments should no longer mention "racial political" arguments. He repeated the need for harsh punishments (at least three years for sexual intercourse) because women received severe sentences and because a prison term was less onerous for a POW, who already faced restrictions on his mobility, than for a free person. As a matter of principle, Keitel stated that POWs satisfying their sexual desire with German women were always causing a "significant disadvantage" in three ways: by undermining the morale of frontline troops, by harming the dignity of the German people, and by

Verbot geführt haben." Feldurteil against Joseph B., Memmingen, December 5, 1941, in PAAA, R 40900.

[27] See, for example, Lautz to OKW, November 28, 1941, in PAAA, R 40893, and Lautz to OKW, January 7, 1942, in PAAA, R 40900.

[28] "Die bevölkerungspolitischen Ziele des Reichs werden nicht durch militärische Befehle zu erreichen versucht und der Befehl vom 10.1.1940 beruht auf anderen Gesichtspunkten. Im übrigen ist es zur Zeit auch außenpolitisch nicht unbedenklich, im Urteil gegen französische Kriegsgefangene auf bevölkerungspolitische Absichten der Reichsregierung hinzuweisen." Lautz to OKW, January 26, 1942, in PAAA, R 40905. See also Lautz to OKW, January 7, 1942, in PAAA, R 40898, and Lautz to OKW, January 9, 1942, in PAAA, R 40900.

[29] For examples, see AN, F9, 2407.

dishonoring the German woman. He offered a new template for justifications, namely that the accused POW had "harmed the dignity of the German people and therefore caused a significant disadvantage."[30]

This directive placed a more general concern about morale and social cohesion into the foreground, as captured in the term "moral sabotage" used in the High Command guidelines of 1939 with reference to relations between POWs and German women in World War I. It took time until courts martial purged the offensive language about racial pollution from their judgments, but by 1943 most of them had adopted the new template ("harm to the dignity of the German people"), usually with an additional reference to the prisoner having violated the honor of the German woman (Keitel's third point). But this justification also triggered problems given that the judgments often spoke of the woman with so much contempt that it seemed hypocritical to punish the prisoner for having violated her honor. The German Foreign Office heavily criticized this justification, and some defense attorneys tried to take advantage of this contradiction. An exemplary case was the court martial against French POW Charles Moreau, sentenced to two and a half years in prison on January 22, 1942, for sexual intercourse with the farmhand Gertrude Paulsen. The judgment stated that the woman was a prostitute and therefore had no honor, but that the POW's transgression constituted an attack on the honor of the German woman in general.[31] Lautz immediately protested against this phrase: "It seems unacceptable to call the relation of a POW with a German prostitute a violation of the honor of the German woman in general. The Foreign Office therefore has concerns about communicating the judgment."[32] The High Command and the courts martial, however, continued to insist on the notion of "honor of the German woman" that the POW had allegedly violated even if the woman in question was not considered to be honorable.

Classifying the amorous relations of POWs with German women as military disobedience allowed the Nazi regime to treat them with the full force of wartime military law by placing a POW's consensual relationship with a German woman on the same level as a soldier's refusal to obey an

---

[30] Werther, "Kriegsgefangene vor dem Marburger Militärgericht," 256–9.
[31] Court martial against Charles M., Kassel, January 22, 1942, in PAAA, R 40908. For the dossier of the trial against the woman, see BStA Nürnberg, Akten der Anklagebehörde beim Sondergericht, 1296. Interestingly, the civilian trial, which sentenced her to two years of penitentiary for the forbidden relationship, does not define the woman as a prostitute, although it mentions her "uninhibited sexual life."
[32] "Es erscheint untragbar, den Verkehr eines Kriegsgefangenen mit einer Prostituierten als eine Verletzung der Ehre der deutschen Frau schlechthin zu bezeichnen. Das A.A. hat deshalb Bedenken, das Urteil weiterzugeben." Lautz to OKW, February 23, 1942, in PAAA, R 40908.

order to attack. But the linkage with military disobedience contained a loophole that reflected again on the intended operational context of the paragraph. Quite simply: for disobedience to occur, the order had to be received. While the violation of a law is generally punishable regardless of whether a person knows the law code or not, a soldier or prisoner cannot be punished for not following an order of which he was unaware. Many prisoners on trial denied that they had received or understood the order of January 10, 1940. The prosecution therefore needed to prove that the defendant knew the order. This was sometimes difficult to do, especially in the early years of captivity. Although camp commanders received instructions to post the order with translations and to periodically lecture the prisoners about it, quite a few prisoners argued that they had not seen the posters or had not understood the warnings. Many prisoners had been sent to small work detachments before the posters appeared in the main camps and before German commanders told the prisoners about it during a roll call. In 1940 and early 1941, many prisoners had to be acquitted because their attorneys were able to create enough doubt that the POW had received and understood the order. One typical example is the case of Marcel Best, who had a sexual relation with a married farm-woman in a village of the Eifel Mountains from July to September 1940. Although the commander of the nearest larger camp claimed that all prisoners had been informed about the order, a closer investigation found that Best had been transferred to a work detachment before the commander made the announcement and that his local commander had neglected to confirm that all prisoners had been informed. Although the court martial in Koblenz felt that it was very likely that Best had heard about the order through comrades, it could not prove that he had received it and therefore acquitted him. Meanwhile, the woman received a sentence of two years of penal servitude.[33] As trials for forbidden relations began to multiply, however, courts martial increasingly dismissed the prisoners' denials by arguing that the order must have been discussed among the prisoners. Although the explanatory text of the military law code gave judges some flexibility by stating that it was sufficient for a defendant to have consciously provoked damage through action or inaction even if he was not fully aware of an order, this was legally insecure ground.[34]

The issue proved vexing enough for the High Command to launch a massive information campaign in all POW camps and work detachments. Camp commanders and work detachment leaders received orders

---

[33] Feldurteil, Koblenz-Ehrenbreitstein, September 9, 1941, in PAAA, R 40884.
[34] Dörken and Scherer, *Das Militärstrafgesetzbuch*, 80 (point 6).

to frequently remind the prisoners of the order and to make sure that it was posted in every camp and labor detachment. The High Command even printed cards with the order that prisoners had to sign. Under the heading "Renewed Admonishment!," the order was printed in German, French, Polish, English, and later in Serbo-Croatian and Russian, and the prisoner had to sign the card in the presence of a witness. Two thick black lines framed the order on both sides.[35] In case an accused prisoner still claimed not to have received the order, the prosecution could present these signed statements. But there were still some cases as late as 1944 in which some POW attorneys convinced the court martial that the prisoner had either not received or been unable to understand the order. For example, the attorney of a POW from French Flanders argued that his client, who had gone to school for only two years, knew too little French to understand the order. The attorney further argued that the defendant's comrades could hardly have alerted him to the order because he socialized only with fellow Dutch-speakers. The POW was acquitted.[36] British POWs who were transferred from Italian captivity to Germany in 1943 also often claimed ignorance of the order and pointed out that they had been able to mingle with civilians quite freely in Italy and that nobody there had punished them for amorous relations with Italian women. This defense usually did not help. For example, in the court martial of British POW Fred Lord, who had come from Italy in October 1943, the judges in Neisse argued: "The fact that he moved from the slacking conditions in Italy to the tightly organized Reich suggests with incontrovertible necessity that he must have heard about the order – if not from the camp commander, then at least from comrades."[37] In the later years of the war, it became very difficult for POWs to uphold their ignorance of the order because prosecutors became adept at using every bit of evidence that the POW had tried to keep his relationship secret as proof of his awareness that he was doing something forbidden. Defense attorneys countered that secrecy could be motivated by other factors, for example the desire to avoid a scandal, but judges usually sided with the prosecution, arguing that courts martial for forbidden love relations had become so common that POWs simply could no longer claim ignorance of the order.[38]

---

[35] For an example, see CEGESOMA, AA 265 (Archives de la captivité), in dossier VI (documents allemands).

[36] Case of Fidèle M., "Affaires passées au Tribunal Militaire de Danzig," mai–juillet 1944, in AN, F9, 2745, Dossier Stalag XX-B.

[37] Feldurteil, Neisse, February 15, 1944, in BAR Bern, Bestand Vertretung Berlin, 86b.

[38] Stéphane Delattre, *Ma Guerre sans fusil. Décembre 1942–avril 1945. Une chronique judiciaire de la captivité* (La Rochelle: Rumeur des Âges, 1991), 149 and 51.

The severity of Nazi Germany's legal practice against amorous liaisons shocked foreign diplomats and POW defense attorneys. Vichy officials, confronted with a growing flood of love-related trials against French POWs, protested repeatedly.[39] In a note to the Foreign Office and the High Command, Scapini, who was a lawyer himself, argued that the order of January 10, 1940, violated article 45 of the Geneva Convention ("Prisoners of war shall be subject to the laws, regulations and orders in force in the armed forces of the Detaining Power") because it criminalized an act that had no equivalent for German soldiers. The German authorities rejected Scapini's objection by pointing to regulations forbidding contact of German soldiers with women in occupied Poland.[40] This was technically true but not a good refutation because punishments for German soldiers involved with Polish women tended to be much more lenient while German soldiers in western and northern Europe went unpunished if they had relations with local women.[41] Later, the German Foreign Office categorically rejected Scapini's insistence that article 45 demanded that there had to be an equivalent between a POW and a soldier of the detaining state's army in this matter.[42]

Several German defense attorneys argued that the prohibition itself was not the problem but that the punishments were much too severe. Attorney Franz Peterson from Salzburg, for example, challenged the linkage of the order of January 10, 1940, with §92 of the military law code, arguing that §92 was meant to ensure obedience to special orders by a military superior, not compliance with a generic prohibition. Like other lawyers, he pointed out that the punishments were exorbitantly high given that a prisoner in a consensual relationship with a German woman – unlike a comrade who had deliberately injured another person or stolen something – was not committing what one would normally consider a crime, especially at a time when many prisoners were integrated into rural households and amicably sharing the burdens of wartime work with German civilians. Peterson explained to the Scapini Mission, however, that he was powerless to challenge the harsh judgments because the military judges were under higher orders.[43]

Many other defense attorneys likewise informed the French and Swiss delegations (the latter protecting the interests of British POWs) and the Belgian POW administration that their latitude was small because

---

[39] Untitled memorandum, July 17, 1942, in AN, F9, 2731.
[40] Procès-verbal de la Réunion du 2 juin 1944, in AN, F9, 2358.
[41] Röger, *Kriegsbeziehungen*, 144–9.
[42] Speth (German Foreign Office) to French delegation in Letschin, July 31, 1944, in AN, F9, 2731. This was the late answer to a renewed French inquiry dated June 12, 1943.
[43] Dr. Franz Peterson to SDPG, July 7, 1942, in AN, F9, 2731.

military judges had to mete out certain minimum sentences and because the High Command reversed all judgments it considered too lenient.[44] When the DSLP also protested to their liaison in the German Foreign Office about the hard punishments of Belgian POWs in April 1943, the German official was sympathetic but pointed out that the matter belonged to the domain of the military justice system, which he could not influence.[45] British agencies were stunned because no comparable punishments existed for German POWs in British hands, but they had no interest in challenging the German judgments because British regulations forbade closer relationships between its captured servicemen and enemy civilians. The British did protest against the harshness of German military courts in general but did not single out the sentences against soldiers tried for forbidden relations, although officials concerned with POW matters privately expressed their amazement. British POW officials discussed submitting a protest against the harsh punishments of forbidden relations in 1943, but they rejected the idea because they believed the protest would be ineffective. Instead, British POW officials sought to encourage officers to warn their men about the harsh legal consequences of forbidden relations. This was doubly desirable because the British government was also unhappy about the amount of food from the aid parcels to British POWs that ended up in the hands of German civilians.[46]

Members of the German Foreign Office criticized the hard penal regime against POWs involved with German women, especially with respect to French prisoners. Reflecting on the massive increase in love-related trials, Lautz complained to Otto Abetz, the German ambassador in Paris, that the courts martial still cast the French prisoner as an implacable enemy whose relationships with German women undermined the will of the German people to resist and offered opportunities for espionage. This made little sense, Lautz argued, at a time when French civilian workers came to Germany and faced no dating restrictions even though one could argue that they might just as likely contribute to demoralization and espionage as prisoners of war. "I am asking for an

---

[44] Attorney Neugebauer to SDPG, December 19, 1941; Dr. Schwital to SDPG, August 28, 1941; Dr. Melchert to SDPG, July 17, 1943; Attorney Knipp to SDPG, April 29, 1942, all in AN, F9, 2731. Attorney Nehlert to Swiss Delegation, May 5, 1944, BAR Bern, Bestand Vertretung Berlin, 80a.

[45] Musée Royal de l'Armée et d'Histoire Militaire, Evere, Fonds Gillet, Boîte 1, #7 La commission t'Serclaes, 301.

[46] Wylie, *Barbed Wire Diplomacy*, 174–5; MacKenzie, *Colditz Myth*, 215. Memo by H. L. Phillimore, undated [1943], in National Archives Kew, WO 32/15294: Trials and punishments of British POWs in Germany 1941–45.

evaluation of the question as to whether this type of prosecution may have a negative impact on Franco-German relations. Is it really irrelevant for the future political development between the two countries that judgments like those mentioned above continue to be passed?"[47] The archives do not contain Abetz's response, but Lautz's concerns likely resonated with him: Abetz himself was married to a French woman, and he had once revealed to Scapini with a dry smile that he did not consider Franco-German romances a problem.[48] But the German Foreign Office had little influence on the military justice system.

Over the course of the war, the punishments for the prisoners hardened. A directive by Hitler dated January 6, 1942, stipulated that the High Command could reverse all court martial sentences, even after confirmation by the supreme judicial officer of the military district (*Gerichtsherr*).[49] Although this directive was primarily meant to ensure stricter discipline in the German army at a time of crisis on the eastern front, it also ensured a harsher judicial practice against POWs. Many mild sentences against POWs were reversed by Keitel himself or by the chief of the reserve army, General Friedrich Fromm, who served as deputy of the High Command and the second highest level of jurisdiction for military trials on the home front. In these cases, the courts martial simply received instructions to retry the POW because the sentence was too mild. Without any new evidence, POWs were retried and received a harsher verdict. Sometimes the prisoner had already served the first sentence when he received notification of the new hearing. The Scapini Mission complained that this practice violated the Geneva Convention (article 52) and the common legal principle of "*non bis in idem*," the rule that no person can be tried for the same offense twice, but the German authorities countered that the prisoner was not really being tried twice because the first sentence had been cancelled. Even some military judges felt uncomfortable about this interference from the top but told defense attorneys confidentially that they had no power to oppose it.[50]

---

[47] "Es wird um Nachprüfung gebeten, ob diese Art der Strafverfolgung geeignet ist, die deutsch-französischen Beziehungen negativ zu beeinflussen oder ob es für die weitere politische Entwicklung zwischen beiden Ländern bedeutungslos erscheint, wenn Urteile der vorstehend näherbezeichneten Art ergehen." Lautz to Abetz, January 5, 1942, in PAAA, R 40878.

[48] Scapini, *Mission sans gloire*, 213.

[49] Martin Moll, *"Führer-Erlasse" 1939–1945: Edition sämtlicher überlieferter, nicht im Reichsgesetzblatt abgedruckter, von Hitler während des Zweiten Weltkrieges schriftlich erteilter Direktiven aus den Bereichen Staat, Partei, Wirtschaft, Besatzungspolitik und Militärverwaltung* (Stuttgart: Franz Steiner Verlag, 1997), 218 (#130).

[50] Attorney Neugebauer to SDPG, December 18, 1941, in AN, F9, 2731.

The penal regime continued to harden as the tide of the war turned against Germany. In 1943, Keitel frequently reversed judgments that sentenced POWs who had been involved with a soldier's wife to military prison and asked for a penitentiary sentence instead. On January 7, 1944, Keitel, likely in consultation with Hitler, provided a new directive that formalized this practice. He explained that "in such cases, where prisoners of war knowingly break into the marriages of frontline soldiers, prison sentences are not sufficient. For reasons of deterrence, it is necessary to pronounce penitentiary sentences."[51] The Scapini Mission quickly learned of this practice and induced German officials to release the original text of the secret decree to them. The French delegates protested against the hardening legal practice, arguing that punishments should be determined in consideration of the individual case and not according to a rigid scheme.[52]

When protests led nowhere, the Scapini Mission attempted to at least mitigate the application of the *Zuchthaus* decree. On June 2, 1944, Scapini asked General Reinecke to limit penitentiary sentences to cases where four conditions were met: (1) the relationship had involved sexual intercourse; (2) the husband in question was a frontline soldier (rather than a soldier deployed in an occupation army, for example); (3) the POW had known the preceding fact; (4) the intrusion of the prisoner had destroyed the soldier's marriage.[53] Many French legal advisors mistook this proposal for a signed agreement, but German officials never accepted it. They particularly balked at the fourth condition. Many soldier marriages were strained owing to long separation, and POWs or their attorneys often pointed out that the prisoner's contact with the soldier's wife had not destroyed the marriage. For example, some soldiers' wives admitted that they had already had German lovers before meeting the prisoner or claimed that their husbands had been unfaithful (a charge that the courts often found confirmed). Sometimes one of the spouses had already filed for divorce when the wife became involved with the prisoner, proving that the prisoner had not ruined the marriage. In other cases, it became clear during the court martial that the husband had forgiven his wife and wanted to continue the marriage, so that the prisoner's "intrusion" had clearly not ruined the marriage. The courts martial largely ignored these factors, however, arguing that one could not

---

[51] Werther, "Kriegsgefangene vor dem Marburger Militärgericht," 259.
[52] See, for example, "Note ordonnant de punir de travaux forcés les rapports avec les femmes de soldats allemands" [early 1944], in AN, F9, 2731.
[53] See, for example, Chef de Délégation to man of confidence, Stalag X-A Schleswig, September 13, 1944, in AN, F9, 2744.

allow the prisoner to be the judge of the condition of a marriage into which he was "intruding."[54] In this matter, the courts martial were operating contrary to German civilian courts, which tended to punish the "intruding" man very leniently if the marriage was already ruined.[55]

The courts martial even hardened the regime against POWs by applying the decree of January 7, 1944, to a widening circle of husbands; while the original directive had only referred to frontline soldiers, courts martial applied it to all mobilized men and, later, even to armaments workers. In this matter, the courts martial conformed to general judicial practice against adultery involving German partners. As a missive of Justice Minister Otto Thierack dated May 1, 1943, stated:

The term warrior's wife is not limited to wives whose husbands are soldiers in general or frontline soldiers in particular. Every wife who is forced by wartime circumstances to be separated from her husband … is to be considered a warrior's wife. The marriage and honor of an armaments worker who works in areas threatened by bombs and whose wife lives and works in less threatened areas are not worthy of lesser protection than the marriage and honor of a frontline soldier.[56]

The only factor that sometimes helped POWs was that the prosecution had to demonstrate that the prisoner had known that the woman was married to a soldier. Some soldiers' wives did not tell the prisoner that they were married or that their husbands served in the Wehrmacht. Others deliberately misled the prisoner, perhaps expecting that ignorance in this matter would protect him in case of a court martial or in an effort to overcome the prisoner's fear of harsh punishment. The prisoner might in these cases avoid the penitentiary, but he still received a long prison sentence.

The High Command even began to retroactively apply the decree about sex with a warrior wife by ordering retrials for the many French and Belgian POWs who had been sentenced to prison terms for such a relationship before the *Zuchthaus* decree. POWs still serving their sentence therefore had to stand trial again without any new evidence, without an attorney of their choice and often without a translator, just to get a penitentiary sentence. The protecting power received no notice of the new hearing, was not informed about the sentence and the transfer of the

[54] See, for example, Dr. Staud (Oberkommando des Heeres) to attorney Fischer in Hamburg, December 1, 1944, in AN, F9, 2731.
[55] The husband could sue the (German) rival merely for "insult," which carried relatively mild punishments (if any): Heinz Boberach, *Richterbriefe: Dokumente zur Beeinträchtigung der deutschen Rechtsprechung 1942–1944* (Boppard: Boldt, 1975), 122.
[56] Ibid., 118.

POW, and had no way of communicating with him. This practice affected in particular the French and Belgian POWs incarcerated in the military prison of Graudenz (West Prussia) and its work detachments.[57] Every aspect of this practice violated the Geneva Convention, as the Scapini Mission was quick to point out, but the German authorities replied that they had the right to apply to POWs procedures that were allowed in the prosecution and punishment of German soldiers.[58] Obviously, the military courts were following instructions from Keitel and likely from Hitler himself. The judges honored a widely accepted and often repeated maxim in Nazi Germany, namely that the will of the Führer was the highest law.[59]

The legal ambiguities regarding amorous relations between POWs and German women reached a new level when the German plenipotentiary for labor, Fritz Sauckel, and the Vichy government signed a deal that offered French POWs the "transformation" into a civilian worker in January 1943.[60] The transformation, euphemistically called "mitigated status" ("*erleichterer Statut*") by the German authorities, in some ways assimilated the POW to a civilian laborer. He was no longer guarded, and he received the salary of a German worker – which was much higher than the pay of a POW. The transformed prisoner could rent a room and enjoy greater freedom of movement. He could wear civilian clothes instead of a uniform. The German authorities hoped that the deal would save them even more guard personnel and allow them to occupy French POWs with fewer restrictions, for example in the armaments industry (article 31 of the Geneva Convention forbids employment of POWs in directly war-related occupations, but the Vichy authorities had already made significant concessions in this matter).[61] In June 1944, 221,443 French POWs were *transformés*, approximately one in six prisoners. They often worked on the same site as before. The problem was, however, that the *transformés* legally remained prisoners of war. They were merely *beurlaubt* (on leave), and the orders given to POWs still applied to them.

[57] It seems that the court martial often assigned a local defense attorney, a Dr. Mielke, to the POWs. Mielke was not on the list of attorneys approved by the Scapini Mission and did a poor job. See the materials in AN, F9, 2746.
[58] Chef de Délégation to man of confidence Stalag XX-B, May 31, 1944, in AN, F9, 2745, dossier Stalag XX-B, and SDPG to Auswärtiges Amt, October 26, 1944, in AN, F9, 2745, dossier Stalag 344.
[59] Messerschmidt, *Die Wehrmachtjustiz 1933–1945*, 54; Anders, *Strafjustiz im Sudetengau 1938–1945*, 29.
[60] Durand, *Captivité*, 331–3; Durand, *Prisonniers de Guerre*, 207–9.
[61] Scheck, "The Prisoner of War Question," 378–9.

Point 5 of their identity card specifically reminded them: "All dealings with German women are forbidden."[62]

This legal arrangement was deeply flawed. On trial, many transformed POWs defended themselves by pointing out the mixed messages they had received – namely that the transformation would turn them into civilian laborers (to whom the order of January 10, 1940, did not apply) even though they would legally remain POWs. Moreover, the prohibition to have "dealings" with German women (in German *Verkehr* and in French *commerce*) could be interpreted in a variety of ways. Quite a few POWs and their attorneys pointed out that the term *commerce* could allude to illegal trading, such as black-market transactions. A French legal advisor of POWs argued in court that only a Frenchman familiar with sixteenth- or seventeenth-century French authors would intuitively associate the term *commerce* with sexual relationships.[63] Stéphane Delattre, a French POW lawyer, targeted the formulation "German women" on the identity card of the *transformés* and requested acquittal for transformed POWs who had been involved with unmarried women. He pointed out that the order of January 10, 1940, had spoken of "German women *and girls*" and argued that the term woman (*femme*) was frequently used specifically for married women. He drew attention to the fact that German legal documents used a different term – *Frauenperson* – when they meant women regardless of marital status.[64] Delattre regularly placed his *Petit Larousse* dictionary on the rear basket of his bicycle when he rode to courts martial and during the hearings triumphantly took it out and read how it defined woman (*femme*) as "companion of man, wife, the one who is or was married." With this argumentation, Delattre achieved some acquittals of transformed POWs involved with unmarried women. Other French legal advisors and German defense attorneys began to exploit the legal ambiguities of transformed POWs in similar ways.

The German higher authorities were not amused. They reversed many judgments that resulted in acquittals or mild sentences for transformed POWs, dismissing arguments about unclear terms as a "lawyer's trick." The directives insisted that transformed prisoners had to be treated the same way as the others.[65] Prosecutors began to argue that there was no reason why *commerce* should only refer to women if the word was meant in the sense of illegal trade, and that if such superficial interactions were forbidden, then why would the accused prisoner have assumed that more

[62] Delattre, *Ma Guerre sans fusil*, 144.
[63] Jacques Laffont to Chief of the French Delegation, May 17, 1944, in AN, F9, 3644.
[64] Delattre, *Ma Guerre sans fusil*, 144–9, 151, 154–5.   [65] Ibid., 150 and 154.

intimate relationships were permitted?[66] As in other cases, prosecutors also exploited every indication that the accused had sought to hide the relationship as proof that he knew he was violating an order. But many transformed prisoners displayed through their behavior that they had not understood that the prohibition still applied to them. They often did nothing to hide a relationship, and some of them were caught when they walked hand in hand with their girlfriend into a town office to apply for a marriage license.[67]

Scapini, who had repeatedly asked General Reinecke for a more lenient penal regime for forbidden relations, explained to him on January 19, 1944, that the very close cooperation of French prisoners and German civilians made a strict prosecution of forbidden relations counterintuitive and damaging, especially in the case of transformed prisoners. Scapini highlighted that some French POWs had been punished for merely giving chocolate to German women and children, and pointed out that they had often helped German women and children during bombings. "In these tragic circumstances, it may be permitted to assume that friendly relations may develop between the savior and the saved. This is indeed the case, yet these relations lead the prisoner to a court martial and, later, to the prison of Graudenz." Reinecke seemed visibly impressed and promised to consider the question with his superiors.[68] Interestingly, the Security Service (SD) reports about the public mood detected a very positive German opinion of the French transformed POWs specifically in the aftermath of bombings. Some transformed POWs had openly expressed their solidarity with the German civilian population and many had helped to fight the fires, often far away from their own residences and on a completely voluntary basis.[69] Yet, the German military tribunals remained harsh toward the transformés until the very last days of the Third Reich.

After some delay, the "transformation" also became possible for Belgian prisoners. The Belgian POW authorities, however, discouraged Belgians from accepting it, and rumors about the disappointing experiences of French transformed POWs soon traveled back to joint Franco-Belgian work detachments. Some men of confidence, such as Georges Smets in East Prussia, openly criticized the transformation as an unpatriotic act. Smets followed the French collaborator General Henri Didelet

---

[66] See, for example, the trial of André P., November 15, 1944, in AN, F9, 2799.

[67] Delattre, *Ma Guerre sans fusil*, 152–3.

[68] "Entretien du 19 janvier 1944" and "Objet: Condamnation de prisonniers de guerre pour rapports amicaux avec femmes allemandes," January 19, 1944, in AN, F9, 2176.

[69] Heinz Boberach, ed., *Meldungen aus dem Reich 1938–1945: Die geheimen Lageberichte des Sicherheitsdienstes der SS.* (Herrsching: Pawlak, 1984), vol. 15, 6104.

from camp to camp in his district and countered Didelet's exhortations to sign up for the transformation. Of the 5,000 Belgian POWs in his district, only one accepted it.[70] In some cases, however, Belgian prisoners did get "transformed" without their consent because they belonged to a work detachment in which a majority of the French POWs had opted for the transformation. They could apply for return to normal POW status, but this was a slow and complicated process. While French *transformés* figured very prominently in courts martial prosecuting forbidden relations during the last months of the war, the same cannot be said of the Belgian *transformés*.[71]

In another legal ambiguity the prisoners and their representatives achieved a victory of sorts. The order of January 10, 1940, spoke of *German* women and girls. This could refer to citizenship, but in Nazi parlance, German could also refer to ancestry in the sense of *deutschblütig*, of German blood. In wartime Germany, POWs encountered many people with German ancestry and ethnicity from all parts of Europe, the so-called *Volksdeutsche*. When the courts martial began trying a large number of prisoners in 1941, some military judges convicted POWs who had sexual relations with women considered to be German by blood, for example German-speaking Swiss, ethnic Germans from eastern Europe, and women from Alsace-Lorraine. Not surprisingly, this practice angered the Vichy authorities. The Scapini Mission insisted that "German" in a legal document could only mean people with German citizenship and that Alsace-Lorraine was not legally part of Germany, meaning that women from Alsace-Lorraine could not count as German citizens (although the French knew that Germany had already granted German citizenship illegally to many residents of Alsace and Lorraine). The legal experts of the Foreign Office backed the French point of view.[72] The High Command grudgingly agreed and reversed the judgments against POWs involved with women who did not have German citizenship and with women from Alsace and Lorraine. The prisoners were acquitted. Keitel's directive of February 19, 1942, clarified that the order covered only contacts with women who had German citizenship, not with *Volksdeutsche*, and added in parentheses: "It is noted that under

[70] Musée Royal de l'Armée et d'Histoire Militaire, Brussels, Fonds Hautecler, Farde 33: Le questionnaire aux hommes de confiance. Réponse de Georges Smets (Stalag I-A), Question 12 (no pagination).

[71] Gillet, "Histoire des sous-officiers et soldats belges," XXVIII, 125–6.

[72] Lautz to OKW, November 4, 1941, in PAAA, R 40886, and Lautz to OKW, February 13, 1942, in PAAA, R 40907. See also "Note pour la délégation de Berlin," undated [late 1943?], in AN, F9, 2731. This folder also contains other materials relevant for this question in the dossier "Rapports des PG avec les femmes allemandes."

constitutional law Alsace-Lorraine so far has not yet been incorporated into the Reich."[73]

Given that the prohibition for POWs emanated from an order, however, the prosecutor had to demonstrate that the prisoner knew or could have known that the woman was a German citizen. This was not always easy, especially in regions with ambiguous and fluid national identities. In the Sudetenland, for example, a territory annexed by Nazi Germany in 1938, many people had Czech family connections, and there was a large presence of Czechs from the Protectorate of Bohemia and Moravia who had no German citizenship even though many of them spoke German fluently. In the eastern parts of Austria, ambiguities existed with respect to women who had partly Hungarian, Slovak, or Yugoslav heritage. Their names may have been recognizably non-German, and sometimes these women were called "the Hungarian" or "the Slovak" at work, even though they had German citizenship and spoke German. The most complicated situation existed in the parts of Poland that Nazi Germany had annexed in 1939. While people who had long self-identified as members of the ethnic German minority swiftly received German citizenship, the situation was ambiguous for people with mixed ancestry. Under heavy pressure – especially the threat of deportation to the General Government of Poland – many locals applied for inclusion on the German people's list, the *Deutsche Volksliste*. Officials randomly placed these people into category III or category IV of the list. Members of category III received German citizenship (revocable for ten years) in 1942, whereas members of category IV did not.[74]

Prisoners accused of intimate relations with women from these areas almost routinely claimed that they had considered the woman to be non-German. Some women, upon interrogation during the prisoner's court

[73] Werther, "Kriegsgefangene vor dem Marburger Militärgericht," 258.
[74] Gerhard Wolf, "*Volk* Trumps Race: The *Deutsche Volksliste* in Annexed Poland," in *Beyond the Racial State: Rethinking Nazi Germany*, edited by Devon O. Pendas, Mark Roseman, and Richard F. Wetzell, 431–54 (Cambridge and New York: Cambridge University Press, 2017); Richard Weikart, "Hitler's Struggle for Existence against Slavs: Racial Theory and Vacillations in Nazi Policy toward Czechs and Poles," in *Eradicating Differences: The Treatment of Minorities in Nazi-Dominated Europe*, edited by Anton Weiss-Wendt, 61–83 (Newcastle upon Tyne: Cambridge Scholars Publishing, 2010); Röger, *Kriegsbeziehungen*, 19–20; Robert Lewis Koehl, "The 'Deutsche Volksliste' German Nationality List in Poland, 1939–1945," *Journal of Central European Affairs* 15, no. 4 (1956); James Bjork, *Neither German nor Pole: Catholicism and National Indifference in a Central European Borderland* (Ann Arbor: University of Michigan Press, 2008), 4. See also the very good entry "Deutsche Volksliste" on the site "Online-Lexikon zur Kultur und Geschichte der Deutschen im östlichen Europa" at the University of Oldenburg, ome-lexikon.uni-oldenburg.de/begriffe/deutsche-volksliste/ (last visited: October 19, 2018).

martial, indeed admitted that they had lied about their citizenship in order to overcome the prisoner's fear of punishment. This admission usually led to acquittal for the prisoner, although it counted as an aggravating factor during the woman's own trial.[75] But most cases were less clear-cut. Prosecutors learned to use a variety of evidence to show that the prisoner could have known that the woman was German or that he at the very least should have inquired about her citizenship.

The problems with the citizenship of women led the commander of military district XX (Danzig-West Prussia) to prohibit relations with all women regardless of citizenship on March 25, 1942.[76] The commander of district XXI (Posen) followed suit on March 9, 1943. His order read: "the prisoners of war are strictly and specifically forbidden to have any contact with civilians, in particular sexual intercourse with women. It leads to harsh punishments, potentially even a death sentence."[77] Courts martial in these districts, however, punished relations of POWs with Polish women or forced laborers from the Soviet Union less harshly than relations with German women. The "significant disadvantage" was deemed less serious if the relationship involved a non-German woman. According to a POW attorney from Danzig, the local court martial sentenced POWs who had sex with Polish women to one and a half years in prison, half the standard punishment for sex with a German woman. The lower punishment also applied if the court martial believed that the prisoner had mistaken a woman with German citizenship (category III of the German ethnic list) for a Pole (in other areas the POW would have been acquitted in such a case).[78]

A German official told the Scapini Mission in 1943 that the High Command planned to follow the example of the commanders of district

---

[75] One case is Louise H. from the village Selb in Bavaria, who pretended to be Belgian to her French lover. Her mother was indeed Belgian, but she herself had German citizenship. The POW was shocked when she finally told him that she was German. She admitted having hidden this fact because she was afraid of losing him. See "Rapport novembre 1943," by the man of confidence Lenoble, Stalag XIII-B, in AN, F9, 2745.

[76] Frey, *Die disziplinarische und gerichtliche Bestrafung*, 61.

[77] "Ausser den allgemeinen Vergehen gegen die militärische Zucht und Ordnung ist den Kriegsgefangenen im Besonderen jede Fühlungnahme mit der Zivilbevölkerung, vor allem jeder Geschlechtsverkehr mit Frauen, streng verboten und führt zu schweren Strafen, kann sogar mit dem Tode bestraft werden." As quoted in Feldurteil, Posen, April 6, 1944, in BAR Bern, Bestand Vertretung Berlin, 72b.

[78] Klawitter to Swiss legation, September 20, 1944, and Feldurteil, Danzig, August 22, 1944, both in BAR Bern, Bestand Vertretung Berlin, 79a. Klawitter referred to the court martial of Harry K., who received only 15 months in prison for having had sex once with a 22-year-old woman who belonged to category III of the German ethnic list but had always spoken Polish. The woman had been very active in facilitating the encounter, which explains the lenient court martial sentence. She herself received one and a half years of penal servitude, a standard punishment for German women at this time.

XX and XXI and extend the order of January 1940 to all POW relations with women everywhere in the Reich, but this never happened.[79] Generally, the directive that the order applied only to relationships with women who had German citizenship held throughout the war. The British POWs benefited from it when their love-related trials began to multiply in 1943, although a large number of British POWs were punished for relationships with non-German women in military districts XX and XXI. German courts martial increased the pressure with respect to women from Alsace and Lorraine, however. Even though the Scapini Mission pointed out that conferring German citizenship to most remaining residents of these regions violated international law, some courts martial did convict French POWs who had relationships with women from Alsace and Lorraine. A local camp commander took a page from the book of his colleagues in districts XX and XXI and outlawed all relations to women, regardless of citizenship. Some courts martial in Alsace-Lorraine sentenced French POWs who had relations with women from this area who were on the German ethnic list, but acquitted the POW if the woman had always spoken French with him and if the POW could not have known that she was a German citizen, as was the practice in the German–Polish border regions. The Scapini Mission carefully watched court martial cases involving contact with women from Alsace and Lorraine, noting that German courts martial were inconsistent.[80]

Inconsistencies also characterized the prosecution of French prisoners involved with non-German women who had married a German citizen. In Germany, marriage automatically conferred the husband's citizenship to the wife, but in France the wife could retain her original citizenship. French prisoners involved with women who had become German through marriage therefore claimed that they had mistaken the woman's citizenship. Prosecutors and judges soon became impatient with this loophole, however, and began arguing that the prisoner had been in Germany long enough to understand the citizenship provision of German marriage law. But French prisoners involved with a married woman who had originally been a French citizen often received acquittals or lenient punishments.[81]

---

[79] "Renseignements concernant la visite à faire au Kriegsgerichtsrat Dr. Peterson, Tribunal Militaire de Graudenz," May 14, 1943, in AN, F9, 2721.

[80] For a collection of relevant sentences and hand-written observations, see AN, F9, 2731.

[81] The most instructive case: Feldurteil against Paul S., Marburg, February 9, 1944, in AN, F9, 2756. See also Stéphane Delattre, "Rapport sur la Défense des Prisonniers devant le tribunal militaire allemand," September 29, 1943, in AN, F9, 2743; case of Marcel J., in summary of courts martial of February 23 and 25, 1944 and March 1, 1944, and case of

The Legislation for German Women

For German women, the legal framework was the "Complementary Decree for the Protection of the German Will to Resist" (*Verordnung zur Ergänzung der Strafvorschriften zum Schutz der deutschen Wehrkraft*) promulgated on November 25, 1939. This decree elaborated on an earlier law designed to ensure strict discipline on the home front and among the troops during war, the Special War Decree (*Kriegssonderstrafrechtsverordnung*) of 1938. This decree defined the crime of *Wehrkraftzersetzung*, approximately translatable as "undermining the will to resist" – or simply subversion – namely any act "designed to paralyze or undermine in public the will of the German or allied people to armed self-assertion" (§5). This paragraph later served as a justification for thousands of death sentences against civilians and soldiers engaged in subversive actions or expressions.[82] The November 1939 addendum to this decree stipulated that all relationships with prisoners of war that "crudely violate the healthy feeling of the Volk" would lead to prison sentences and, in severe cases, to penitentiary. The maximum penalty was fifteen years in penitentiary.[83] An additional decree of May 11, 1940, signed by Himmler, stated that all communication with a POW that went beyond what was strictly necessary for work was forbidden to everybody (*"jedermann"*).[84] These decrees also applied to German men and foreigners, but foreign women generally received more lenient sentences than German women.[85] Yet the vast majority of trials involved German women who had amorous relations with prisoners. Although the term "severe cases" in the decree of November 25, 1939, lacked a clear definition, the courts quickly agreed that every relationship that had involved sexual intercourse qualified as a "severe case" and deserved a sentence in the penitentiary, except if the woman was very young. Punishments for the women were standardized later than the court martial sentences against the POWs and become relatively consistent only by

Gaston B., May 17, 1944, dossier "Stalag XVII-A," in AN, F9, 2745; case of Lucien L., Feldurteil, Neustadt an der Weinstraße, October 21, 1944, in AN, F9, 3644.

[82] Messerschmidt, *Die Wehrmachtjustiz 1933–1945*, 58; Dörken and Scherer, *Das Militärstrafgesetzbuch*, 157; Kalmbach, *Wehrmachtjustiz*, 48–9; Snyder, *Sex Crimes under the Wehrmacht*, 37–8.

[83] "Verordnung zur Ergänzung der Strafvorschriften zum Schutz der Wehrkraft des deutschen Volkes. Vom 25. November 1939," *Reichsgesetzblatt*, 238, November 30, 1939, p. 2319, §4. Boberach, *Richterbriefe*, 87; Kallfelz, "Strafbarer Umgang mit Kriegsgefangenen," 1813.

[84] "Verordnung über den Umgang mit Kriegsgefangenen. Vom 11. Mai 1940," *Reichsgesetzblatt*, 86, Mai 17, 1940, 769.

[85] For a few examples, see Scheck, "Collaboration of the Heart," 358, note 28.

1943. Special courts tended to give much harsher sentences in 1941 than in the last two years of the war.[86]

The decree of November 25, 1939, referred to a crucial concept of Nazi jurisprudence, namely "the healthy feeling of the Volk." It implied that the community of the people (*Volksgemeinschaft*), purified and purged of foreign and inferior members, would display an intuitive sense of justice that would condemn relations with POWs and promote outrage and denunciations. Legal scholar Robert Bartsch argued in 1940 that the "healthy feeling of the Volk" is the source of law and that it emanates from the feeling of that part of the people "that thinks justly and is filled with the National Socialist legal ideology." Bartsch believed in a shared natural sentiment of people with common ancestry, united in physical as well as spritual kinship. Like other Nazi jurists, he pointed out that the *predominant* feeling of the Volk did not necessarily equate the *healthy* feeling of the Volk and that the ultimate reference point was the will of the Führer, who by definition always reflected the "healthy feeling of the Volk."[87] The reference to the "healthy feeling of the Volk," however, was controversial even in Nazi Germany. Legal theorist Ferdinand Kadecka, for example, considered it vague. Unfortunately, Kadecka sought to ground the "healthy feeling of the Volk" in another extremely arbitrary concept, namely the Nazi theory of "criminal types." According to Kadecka, people displaying the characteristics of these "criminal types" should be punished even if their acts did not strictly violate the letter of the law. This was the "healthy feeling of the Volk" in action.[88] For trials against women involved with POWs, this meant giving added weight to the dubious character judgments provided by the police or mayor, which were usually based on local gossip.

Initially, Nazi officials tried to help along the "healthy feeling of the Volk" by encouraging public shaming rituals against women caught in relations with foreign POWs and laborers, especially eastern Europeans. SA members would shave the heads of these women and parade them through the streets with humiliating placards. These rituals were not universally popular, however, as police spies reported. While some citizens condemned the forbidden relations and approved of the harsh

[86] Löffelsender, *Strafjustiz an der Heimatfront*, 297–8.
[87] Robert Bartsch, "Das 'gesunde Volksempfinden' im Strafrecht," Dr. Phil. Dissertation (Universität Hamburg, 1940), 8–11, 13–16, 29–30, 35; Karl Peters, "Das gesunde Volksempfinden: Ein Beitrag zur Rechtsquellenlehre des 19. und 20. Jahrhunderts," *Deutsches Strafrecht: Strafrecht, Strafrechtspolitik, Strafprozeß* 5 (Neue Folge), no. 10/11 (1938): 341. See also Anders, *Strafjustiz im Sudetengau 1938–1945*, 30–1.
[88] Ferdinand Kadecka, "Gesundes Volksempfinden und gesetzlicher Grundgedanke," *Zeitschrift für die gesamte Strafrechtswissenschaft* 62 (1942/1944): 2–4, 20-24.

punishments, the shaming rituals also promoted sympathy for the woman and the prisoner and triggered critical comments about double morality in light of the sexual freedoms of German soldiers abroad. As a consequence, Hitler ordered in October 1941 that the shaming rituals be stopped.[89] The head shavings and public humiliation parades were very rare for women involved with western POWs, but they did occasionally happen even after Hitler's prohibition, targeting women who had already been ostracized by the community for allegedly immoral behavior. The crowd sometimes beat the women during the processions.[90]

Even without the head shavings, Nazi propaganda consistently sought to stigmatize relations with POWs, especially involving women. Propaganda pamphlets and posters reminded Germans that enemy prisoners had to be treated as hostile elements and pariahs, and claimed that POWs in World War I had exploited contacts with civilians to cause fires, spread sexual diseases, sabotage agricultural and industrial production, and undermine the cohesion of German families and communities. Amorous relations with German women had allegedly served as a gateway for these nefarious designs.[91] Posters pointed out that POWs had only recently taken up arms against the German people – echoing the fiction that Germany was waging a defensive war – and warned civilians to maintain a clear distance from them. It was forbidden to take a walk with a prisoner and to allow prisoners to eat at the family dining table; any private conversation had to be avoided, and any gift to POWs was forbidden unless it was a reward for particularly hard work. A guide sheet for guards stressed that no POW should ever be alone or in the company of women and children.[92] Some warnings specifically addressed women:

---

[89] Kundrus, *Kriegerfrauen*, 382–3; Schneider, *Verbotener Umgang*, 212–14. An Austrian judicial report, after such a shaming action by SA members against a woman in Sierning near Steyr, warned that such events would undermine the reputation of the NSDAP: Wolfgang Form and Oliver Uthe, eds., *NS-Justiz in Österreich: Lage- und Reiseberichte 1938–1945* (Vienna: LIT Verlag, 2004), 195–6 (report from Linz, February 23, 1940); Stargardt, *German War*, 142–4.

[90] For examples, see the case of Louise B. from Bad Homburg (north of Frankfurt am Main, August 1941 – before Hitler's prohibition), in Hessisches Hauptstaatsarchiv (HHStA) Wiesbaden, Abt. 461, Nr. 8285; case of Anna B. in Mudersbach (near Siegen, September 1944), HHStA Wiesbaden, Abt. 461, Nr. 9875; Anna Maria B. in Bürstadt (north of Mannheim, sentenced on May 26, 1944), in Hessisches Staatsarchiv Darmstadt (HStAD), Fonds G 24, Nr. 955/2. The first two women were involved with French POWs, the latter with a Belgian. The two latter women were married to soldiers and had a bad local reputation. In the Mudersbach case, the local NSDAP leader and the village teacher played the active role. The teacher ordered all the schoolchildren to line up and watch the humiliation.

[91] "Kriegsgefangene," 7–9 and 16–17, NLA Oldenburg, Best. 135 B.

[92] "Merkblatt für die Behandlung von Kriegsgefangenen beim Arbeitseinsatz im Wehrkreis VI," Münster, June 1, 1940, in NLA Oldenburg, Best. 135 B.

"Especially the German woman needs to be aware that she cannot enter into any relationship with a prisoner whatsoever. Otherwise, she will lose her highest asset, her honor. German woman, avoid even the deceptive appearance!"[93] Another poster from May 1942 reinforced this message:

German women who enter into relations with prisoners of war are excluding themselves from the *Volksgemeinschaft* and will receive their deserved punishment. Even the false appearance of a rapprochement needs to be avoided. ... Whoever treats them [the POWs] better than German workers becomes a traitor against the *Volksgemeinschaft*.[94]

To magnify the effect of these warnings, court judgments against women involved with POWs appeared in the newspapers and on posters with the full name of the "perpetrator."

In reality, the "healthy feeling of the Volk" did not manifest itself in quite the way the Nazi regime expected. It is true that POWs often encountered anger and contempt from Germans whipped up by hate propaganda during the campaign of May–June 1940, which "yielded" practically all French and Belgian prisoners and a quarter of the British POWs. The SD initially noted expressions of outrage provoked by news of decent treatment of French and British POWs.[95] Upon arrival in Germany, western POWs often faced angry crowds who spat and threw stones at them.[96] But hostility dissipated quickly as more and more POWs, first the Belgians and French and later the British, became integrated into German production sites and households. An SD report from October 1942 expressed concern about amicable relations between German civilians and foreign prisoners who worked with them or for them, highlighting in particular the compassion of women. The report concluded that many prisoners had through their work and behavior earned the confidence of German "Volk comrades" who tended to forget

---

[93] "Besonders die deutsche Frau muss sich bewusst sein, daß sie in keinerlei Beziehungen zu Kriegsgefangenen treten darf. Sie verliert sonst ihr höchstes Gut, ihre Ehre. Deutsche Frau, vermeide daher auch jeden falschen Schein!" Pamphlet "Verhalten gegenüber Kriegsgefangenen," in NLA Oldenburg, Best. 135 B.

[94] "Deutsche Frauen, die in Beziehungen zu Kriegsgefangenen treten, schließen sich von selbst aus der Volksgemeinschaft aus und erhalten ihre gerechte Bestrafung. Selbst der Schein einer Annäherung muß vermieden werden. [...] Wer sie besser behandelt als deutsche Arbeitskräfte, wird zum Verräter an der Volksgemeinschaft." Pamphlet "Verhalten gegenüber Kriegsgefangenen," Berlin, May 1942, in NLA Oldenburg, Best. 135 B.

[95] Heinz Boberach, ed., *Meldungen aus dem Reich: Auswahl aus den geheimen Lageberichten des Sicherheitsdienstes der SS 1939–1944* (Neuwied and Berlin: Luchterhand, 1965), 75.

[96] MacKenzie, *Colditz Myth*, 75; Hans-Hermann Stopsack, *Stalag VI A Hemer. Kriegsgefangenenlager 1939–1945; eine Dokumentation* (Hemer: Volkshochschule Menden-Hemer-Balve, 1995), 41, 70.

the "necessary racial political distance." The SD had to admit that the majority of women who entered into intimate relationships with prisoners could not be classified as inferior or criminal types but came from "racial biologically and socially impeccable families."[97] From the middle of 1941, as trials for forbidden relations exploded, it is clear that many Germans tolerated the relationships or warned the couple instead of denouncing them. A very large number of Germans did not accept the official propaganda that the POW was an enemy who even in captivity tried to cause maximum damage. This notion made little sense with respect to French and Belgian (and to some extent Serb) prisoners, whose countries were defeated and occupied by Germany and whose state officials collaborated with Germany in a variety of ways. Even British prisoners, at least those deployed on farms, were generally treated with appreciation for their help and not ostracized.[98]

By the summer of 1942, Justice Minister Thierack was concerned enough to consult the ultimate reference point for the "healthy feeling of the Volk," the Führer. But Hitler's thoughts in this matter remained unclear. While he consistently pushed for harder sentences against POWs, he was less certain about the punishment of women because he had difficulty ascribing any agency to them and because he thought that punishing married women infringed on the patriarchal authority of the husbands, who should be free to settle things with their adulterous wives themselves. When in August 1942 the special court in Leitmeritz (Sudetenland) sentenced a farmer's wife to four and a half years of penitentiary for an amorous liaison with the French POW assigned to the farm while her husband was fighting in Russia, Hitler ordered the woman to be set free immediately. The reason was that the husband had submitted a clemency plea for her, arguing that the marriage had been happy and that his wife had been seduced by the prisoner. Thierack, stunned and frustrated by this hair-raising interference in a completed special court case, requested clarification, and Hitler discussed the issue with his secretary Martin Bormann in November 1942. He pointed out that it was important to the front soldier that the authorities keep a close watch on the home front, including German women. Yet, he knew that many soldiers forgave their wives and submitted clemency pleas on their behalf. He therefore decided that the woman should still be punished but

[97] Boberach, *Meldungen aus dem Reich: Auswahl*, 310.
[98] Elisabeth Schöggl-Ernst, "Das Ende der persönlichen Freiheit: Zwangsarbeit und Kriegsgefangenschaft," in *Geschichte der Steiermark: Bundesland und Reichsgau. Demokratie, "Ständestaat" und NS-Herrschaft in der Steiermark 1918–1945*, edited by Alfred Ableitinger (Wien, Köln, Weimar: Böhlau, 2015), 491.

that the prosecutor's offices could be generous if the soldier husband forgave his wife and submitted a clemency plea.[99] As a consequence, the sentences against women became milder after 1942, with the default being one to two years in penitentiary. Many married women with a forgiving (and politically not objectionable) husband received an early release. The view of the man as the seducer and the notion of the passive female was consistent with Nazi legislation on forbidden sexual encounters.[100]

Following Hitler's intervention, Thierack looked for a different justification of the prohibition for German women. In a letter to all German judges from March 1, 1943, he no longer mentioned the "healthy feeling of the Volk" but stressed that the protection of the *Volksgemeinschaft* was the leading principle. This meant watching over security as well as "the dignity and purity of the German blood." Thierack asked whether the racial and national characteristics of the POW could influence the sentences against women and if, in particular, contact with French POWs could be treated more leniently in light of their strong integration into German society. Instead of providing a clear answer, he insisted on hard punishments:

The question here cannot be whether the contact with prisoners of war of a specific nationality or race is to be judged more leniently, but rather whether there should be harsher punishments for the contact with members of peoples who are racially distant to the German people, are culturally inferior to it, or have shown a particular political irreconcilability.

He reminded the judges that all POWs had once fought against Germany and that they had likely spilled "German blood," echoing the official "enemy remains enemy" propaganda. Thierack's missive did not prohibit judges from letting the racial and national characteristics of the POW influence their sentences against women as long as they did not use them as mitigating factors. Thierack also confirmed that relations involving sexual intercourse were considered to be severe cases (meriting penitentiary) because allegedly a seduced woman could easily fall into sexual subservience to the prisoner, who could then use her for espionage and an escape.[101]

---

[99] Petition of Josef Wolf to Hitler, July 24, 1942; Chef der Reichskanzlei an Reichsminister der Justiz, August 20, 1942; Thierack to Lammers, September 3, 1942, all in Bundesarchiv Berlin-Lichterfelde, R 43-II/ 1560.

[100] Maiwald and Mischler, *Sexualität unter dem Hakenkreuz*, 209.

[101] Boberach, *Richterbriefe*, 91–2.

Trials Involving Prisoners of War and Other Men

The order of January 10, 1940, applied specifically to contacts "with German women and girls," and therefore POWs tried under §92 of the German military law code had all become involved with a German woman or a girl older than 16 (or 14 if the girl appeared mature for her age[102]). By contrast, the decrees forbidding civilians to contact POWs, although they targeted primarily women, also applied to men, and a large group of German and foreign men had to stand trial for forbidden contacts with POWs, for example for transferring letters for a POW, giving a prisoner food and cigarettes, or facilitating an escape.

Homosexual acts fell under §175 and 175a of the German law code, which the Nazi regime had sharpened and extended.[103] Whereas §175 covered homosexual acts in general and punished them with a prison term, §175a applied to homosexual acts involving violence or the threat of violence and to acts involving a partner less than twenty-one years old, allowing up to ten years of penal servitude.[104] Sexual acts between prisoners in Nazi Germany rarely led to persecution, however. This is consistent with the findings of Matthias Reiss about German POWs in the United States, who sometimes feared being beaten up or ostracized by comrades but were only very rarely punished by the American military authorities even though homosexual acts were also forbidden in the American army (and hence to its POWs).[105] Nazi courts severely punished sexual contact between a POW and a civilian man or boy, but the overall number of cases was small: the Swiss records show twenty-three British POWs facing prosecution on the basis of §175 and 175a in 1944–5, resulting in six acquittals (compared to 453 POWs prosecuted for amorous relations with women). The Belgian POW files in the German Foreign Ministry archives contain only one trial for homosexual contact until February 1942. Of the approximately 1,000 trials against

---

[102] Sexual contact with younger children was punished under §176 of the German law code, and there were a few courts martial against POWs for illicit contacts with children.

[103] See Raffael Scheck, "The Danger of 'Moral Sabotage:' Western Prisoners of War on Trial for Homosexual Relations in Nazi Germany," *Journal of the History of Sexuality* (forthcoming).

[104] Burkhard Jellonnek and Rüdiger Lautmann, eds., *Nationalsozialistischer Terror gegen Homosexuelle: Verdrängt und ungesühnt* (Paderborn: Schöningh, 2002); John Fout, "Homosexuelle in der NS-Zeit: Neue Forschungsansätze über Alltagsleben und Verfolgung," in *Nationalsozialistischer Terror gegen Homosexuelle: Verdrängt und ungesühnt*, ed. Burkhard Jellonnek and Rüdiger Lautmann (Paderborn: Schöningh, 2002), 167.

[105] Reiss, *Controlling Sex in Captivity*, 128. Reiss focuses on same-sex activities among POWs, not between POWs and civilians.

French POWs in the same collection and during the same period, only sixteen concern homosexual acts (including one acquittal), and seven of these cases occurred in German POW camps in France between North African POWs and French men or boys. Of these sixteen cases, five involved contact with a boy or man under age twenty-one and were punished according to §175a. There were more cases involving Belgian and French POWs later on, but they always were a tiny fraction of the trials against POWs involved with women.

Two French POWs did receive a death sentence for a homosexual relationship with a minor. Although their acts fell under §175a, which allowed a maximum of ten years of penal servitude, they were judged under a new law promulgated on September 4, 1941, that allowed the death penalty against persons deemed to be habitual criminals or dangerous sex offenders "if the protection of the people's community [*Volksgemeinschaft*] or the need for just atonement require it."[106] On October 30, 1941, the German court martial in Nancy sentenced the Algerian POW Abdellah Rahimi to death on the basis of German law, which also applied to POWs held on French territory. Rahimi had lured a French ten-year-old boy into a forest and raped him while threatening him with a knife. The German military commander in France confirmed the death sentence, but after a lengthy exchange of communications between the German Foreign Ministry and the military authorities, the High Command commuted it to twelve years of penal servitude on June 1, 1942. The problem in the eyes of German officials was that Rahimi was sentenced under a paragraph (175a) that was meant to protect the German people, not the French people, and that the court martial had applied the law of September 4, 1941, allowing the death sentence, even though the act had occurred earlier (although Nazi legal practice, contrary to a fundamental legal principle, did condone the retroactive application of laws). Moreover, the German Foreign Ministry feared negative repercussions for a future German colonial policy because the sentence had stressed that the act was particularly ignominious because it was committed on a European boy by a non-European man. Rahimi's French defense attorney argued that a death sentence would be understandable for a European "but not for an indigenous man [*indigène*], for whom

---

[106] Gottfried Lorenz, *Todesurteile und Hinrichtungen wegen homosexueller Handlungen während der NS-Zeit: Mann-männliche Internetprostitution und andere Texte zur Geschichte und zur Situation der Homosexuellen in Deutschland* (Berlin and Münster: Lit Verlag, 2018), 13; Günther Grau and Claudia Schoppmann, eds., *Homosexualität in der NS-Zeit: Dokumente einer Diskriminierung und Verfolgung* (Frankfurt am Main: Fischer Taschenbuch Verlag, 1993), 93–6.

homosexuality does not have the same unnatural character as for a European."[107]

The other case involved René Lefèbvre, who had engaged in sexual acts with four German farm boys in a village near Magdeburg during the summer of 1941 (also before the law of September 4, 1941). The relations were discovered only much later and led to a court martial against Lefèbvre on March 2, 1943. The fact that some of the boys were under fourteen when the contacts started was an aggravating factor, and Lefèbre was sentenced to death. The Geneva Convention required a three-month delay before any death sentence against a POW could be carried out, but neither the Scapini Mission nor any German authority intervened in Lefèbre's favor, although his attorney tried to challenge the sentence, to no avail. Lefèbvre was beheaded in Halle on September 7, 1943, and buried in a local cemetery.[108] In both cases, the punishment was so severe because it had involved sexual contact with minors (§175a). In the case of Lefèbvre, the contact appeared to be consensual, but it involved four German boys and went on for a long time. The court believed that the prisoner had spoiled these boys for life.

In the case of consensual homosexual contacts between prisoners and adult men over twenty-one years, the prisoner and the German man were punished in similar ways as a POW and a German woman. Belgian POW Joseph Colette, for example, worked on a landed estate in the region of Regensburg in 1941 when he began a sexual relationship with the thirty-five-year-old German farmworker August Bachmeier. The relationship was discovered after more than a year. The court martial in Amberg sentenced Colette to three years of penal servitude on June 30, 1943, a sentence that would have been typical at this time for a POW involved with a German soldier's wife. The special court in Nürnberg sentenced Bachmeier to five years of penal servitude on July 7, 1943. This sentence is harsh but not excessive in comparison to a typical sentence for a woman at this time, considering that Bachmeier had once given Colette a pistol and a suit, items that could have been useful in an escape attempt, and this counted as an aggravating factor. In analogy to many trials against women, the special court claimed that his behavior had most seriously offended the dignity of the German man.[109]

---

[107] Feldurteil, Nancy, October 30, 1941, and correspondence between Foreign Ministry and High Command, in PAAA, R 40904; list of death sentences against POWs, in AN, F9, 2358; case file number 123, in AN, F9, 2560.

[108] Feldurteil, Magdeburg, March 2, 1943, in AN, F9, 2382.

[109] Feldurteil, Amberg, June 30, 1943, in Service Archives des victimes de la guerre, Brussels, folder Joseph C.; BStA Nürnberg, Akten der Anklagebehörde beim Sondergericht, 2174. A German employee who engaged in homosexual acts with a

Assessment

Obsessed with racial purity considerations and a repeat of the stab-in-the-back of 1918, the Nazi regime punished love relations between POWs and German women much more seriously than was usual in other wartime societies, including Germany in World War I. Initially, the racial motivation prevailed. As many court martial judgments stated, the prohibition was meant to "prevent unwanted admixtures to the German blood." The preservation of racial purity became a diplomatic liability, however, and it made little sense even in Nazi terms because the courts could not prosecute POWs involved with ethnic German women who had no German citizenship. Moreover, the racial justification seemed absurd in light of the increasing number of civilian workers from France and Belgium who faced no restriction on amorous relations with German women, and it provoked criticism because of the double morality allowing German men (soldiers and civilians alike) relations with western and northern European women.

The racial pollution argument also failed in light of the diversity of the prisoners. On the one side, there were many prisoners from the French and British armies on German territory whose sexual contacts with German women the Nazi authorities definitely wanted to prevent, in particular Jews and Poles. On the other side, there were many POWs with a racial background the Nazis considered desirable. The French, British, and Belgian armies all included people whose families had emigrated from the German lands, putting courts martial into the absurd position of having to sentence men "of German blood" for soiling the German race. There were also quite a few overlooked Flemish prisoners on trial even though their racial background was considered desirable. The same could be said of many British prisoners who came from England or the dominions. Some of them even had German ancestors. Given that the Geneva Convention prohibited racial discrimination, the courts martial could not legally apply a Nazi racial filter to the relationships, punishing only those that by Nazi standards did "pollute" the German race. The racial motivation worked little better in the trials against women given the ambiguity of national, racial, and ethnic categories and the difficulties of Nazi officials to sharply define them.

In light of these problems, the courts martial focused on the other justifications for the prohibition, namely that love relations between POWs and women favored sabotage, espionage, and escapes, and that

Soviet POW and with many German men received a sentence of six years in penitentiary a week later in Dresden: Fout, "Homosexuelle in der NS-Zeit," 163–4.

they attacked the dignity of the German people and the honor of the German woman and prepared a new stab in the back. These justifications were as absurd as the racial pollution argument. Not a single case in my sample involved sabotage or espionage.[110] There were a few cases of POW sabotage that the courts martial or the *Reich* War Court punished severely, but none of them involved a love relationship with a German woman.[111] The fear of espionage was also groundless because prisoners were hardly in a position to acquire sensitive information and to communicate it safely to their country. There were a number of cases involving an attempted, sometimes a successful, escape. Without a doubt, some prisoners used a relationship with a German woman to get civilian clothes and other accessories useful for an escape. But many escape plans resulted from the impossibility of living a love relationship openly, and quite a few of them involved plans to flee together or perhaps to allow the prisoner to return to Germany as a civilian worker, so that he could be with his partner without having to hide.[112] In the files of 168 women who had to stand trial for a forbidden relation with a POW in Hannover, Wolf-Dieter Mechler found only four cases that involved a POW escape, and in three of them the escape was motivated by the desire to live together. One Franco-German couple from the region of Hannover managed to flee successfully and settle in a village near Lille, but the French POW was killed during an Allied bombing attack on May 13, 1944, and the woman then returned to Germany and gave herself up to the police. The special court sentenced her to three years of penal servitude in October 1944.[113] In any case, for the POW, escape was not a crime (although it was a crime for a civilian to help a POW escape). The Geneva Convention, following a long tradition that saw it as the patriotic duty of the POW to make every attempt to rejoin his army, stipulated that even repeated escape attempts could only be punished as disciplinary violations (article 50) leading to no more than thirty days of arrest.

Punishing the prisoner for having attacked the dignity of the German people and the honor of the German woman made little sense either. Many relationships were deep and sincere and involved marriage plans.

---

[110] Wolf-Dieter Mechler reaches the same conclusion after his careful analysis of 168 cases of women tried for a forbidden relation by the special court in Hannover: Mechler, *Kriegsalltag an der "Heimatfront,"* 234.

[111] See, for example, Michael Eberlein, Norbert Haase, and Wolfgang Oleschinski, *Torgau im Hinterland des Zweiten Weltkriegs: Militärjustiz, Wehrmachtgefängnisse, Reichskriegsgericht* (Leipzig: Kiepenheuer, 1999), 83.

[112] Virgili, *Naître ennemi*, 60–1; Picaper, *Le Crime d'aimer*, 152.

[113] Mechler, *Kriegsalltag an der "Heimatfront,"* 234–5, 45–6.

It was difficult for prosecutors to argue in these cases that the prisoner had attacked the dignity of the German people and the honor of the German woman. Protecting the honor of the German woman sounded particularly hollow in light of the frequently demeaning treatment of the accused women by the courts martial and the special courts, as some defense attorneys pointed out. Judges usually claimed that the prisoner had attacked the honor of the German woman *in general* and not the honor of the particular woman, but this abstraction made little sense, especially if one wanted to argue for the causation of a "significant disadvantage."

What remained consistent was the desire to discipline the POWs and to protect German morale and the cohesion of the *Volksgemeinschaft*. Here, too, the prohibition made little sense, however. Although punishments for the prisoners hardened, the number of forbidden relations rose every year for the French and Belgian POWs until it stabilized at a very high level in 1943; for British prisoners, the trials for forbidden relations became frequent in 1943 and the number of cases increased throughout 1944. The plan to compensate with severe punishments for an increasing shortage of guard personnel and a growing integration of POWs into German workplaces and households failed. It is true that Nazi agencies saw themselves as taking the place of absent military husbands in their efforts to monitor the fidelity of soldiers' wives.[114] But the harsh penal practice targeted not only the affairs of POWs with married women (in fact, unmarried, divorced, or widowed women predominated); moreover, it is important to stress that women married to soldiers had no interest in the state playing the role of the absent husband because they often took a very active role in initiating and developing the forbidden relationship.[115] It was also well known that the Wehrmacht operated brothels, and many soldier wives may have felt that they had the same right to promiscuity as their husbands.[116]

Ulrich Herbert argues that the German authorities, confronted with an epidemic of forbidden relations, selected only some cases for prosecution, hoping to use them as a deterrent.[117] Although the investigative zeal of the Gestapo and the judicial officials seems to contradict the impression that only some exemplary cases came to trial, it is possible that in situations where the prosecution of all affairs would have paralyzed a

[114] Stargardt, *German War*, 141.
[115] A survey of women on trial for a forbidden relationship in Nürnberg, Vienna, and Kiel/Neumünster shows that of the women whose marital status is clear (a total of 193) 57 percent (110) were unmarried and 43 percent (83) married.
[116] Mechler, *Kriegsalltag an der "Heimatfront,"* 232.
[117] Herbert, *Hitler's Foreign Workers*, 125.

farming community or a factory, the authorities chose to prosecute only some cases as a deterrent. Usually, large clusters of forbidden relations also pointed to a problem with poor guarding and supervision, and the trials may have served as much as a warning to the factory management or local peasant leader as to the couples. But while press agents selected certain women for particularly elaborate public shaming, in most cases the Gestapo tried to prosecute all relationships. The officers asked every arrested woman whether she knew of any other women in the village or factory who might be engaged with POWs, and it usually investigated all affairs if the clues appeared plausible. Even trivial offenses came to trial, for example the case of a woman in Königshütte (eastern Upper Silesia) who had accepted chocolate and raisins from a British POW during work in a local factory. The special court in Kattowitz sentenced her to two months in prison on March 1, 1944.[118]

With respect to the POWs, the Nazi justice system was caught in a mode of repression enforced by orders from the highest authorities and gradually sharpened from 1941 to 1944. Toward the end of the war, the Nazi regime became more repressive toward POWs because it feared an uprising of POWs and foreign laborers once Allied troops set foot on German soil. In September 1944, Hitler therefore transferred the POW administration to the SS under Gottlob Berger.[119] But this transfer did not significantly influence military tribunals dealing with love relations. The fear of an uprising made no sense in the light of the love relations of prisoners who were strongly integrated into German communities. In fact, the prisoners involved with German women were almost all disciplined, productive, and supportive of their employers, and there were many cases of French POWs who protected the German civilians with whom they had worked for several years when the Allied armies arrived.[120] These prisoners would not only have found it hard to rally for an uprising, they would not have been interested in such a plan.

---

[118] Sentence against Magdalena Sch., March 1, 1944, Archiwum Państwowe w Katowicach (Poland), Sondergericht, 2302.

[119] Robert Kübler, ed., *Chef KGW: Das Kriegsgefangenenwesen unter Gottlob Berger. Nachlass* (Lindhorst: Askania, 1984), 17–18, 25, 87.

[120] Stephenson, *Hitler's Home Front*, 289–90. See also d'Hoop, "Prisonniers de guerre français témoins de la défaite allemande," 96–7. D'Hoop refers to the account of Gustave Folcher, *Les carnets de guerre de Gustave Folcher paysan languedocien (1939–1945)* (Paris: François Maspero, 1981), 256–7.

3   The Relations

Meeting Each Other

The most common way for POWs and German women to meet was through work. This was most natural on farms, where the POW spent many hours working on fields and in barns in the company of women, be it the farmwife, a maid, or a teenage girl performing her mandatory service year (*Pflichtjahr*). Those Frenchmen and Belgians who were allowed to live on small family farms had contact with German civilians day and night. Although official pamphlets constantly reminded German employers that the POW was not a member of the house community and should not be allowed to eat at the same table as the farmer's family, this prohibition was honored mostly in the breach. The farm community largely integrated POWs, whether they slept in a separate location or on the farm itself.

In small businesses and public services, POWs worked daily in the company of German women. The individual prisoner helped out in a shop or performed deliveries, and the business owner's daughter or wife might supervise him or work with him. As on the farms, some of these prisoners would have to return to their sleeping quarters after work while others lived on the premises where they worked. As demonstrated, it was often easy for those who were in group sleeping quarters to sneak out at night, and on Sundays, many prisoners were unsupervised and could go out and mingle with civilians.

In factories, POWs and German women spent long workdays together.[1] Despite the presence of foremen and watchdog officials who spied on the prisoners and the women, and were under strict instructions to prevent relations, flirting and the exchange of secret love notes were very common. Many factories offered hiding places, for example a storage room or attic. Couples might also withdraw to the bathrooms or

---

[1] German and foreign employees in industry worked 56–60 hours weekly: Herbert, *Hitler's Foreign Workers*, 226.

washrooms. Group dating most often occurred in factory settings because the POWs and the women encountered each other in groups. Violating the prohibition together with peers relieved the fear of punishment on both sides.[2] Women might tell each other about their secret crushes and, if things had developed further, their sexual experience with the prisoner. The discovery of one relationship, however, often led to a chain reaction. Many factories with lax supervision experienced a string of arrests among the prisoners and female workers, providing a powerful incentive for the factory managers to step up vigilance in the future. Of course, couples were not always dependent on meetings during work given that prisoners found ways to meet their loved one at night or on Sundays. Judges recognized that working together provided the strongest temptation for the prisoner and the woman to enter into a forbidden relationship. This did not mean that they punished such relationships less severely, but it meant that they reacted with particular harshness against relations that sprang up outside the sphere of common work.

Many relationships outside of work came into being through a spontaneous exchange of smiles during a chance encounter. For example, a prisoner marching to his workplace in the morning might notice a woman standing at her window every day. There were German women who deliberately walked or biked near a POW residence and sometimes waved to a prisoner. Sooner or later, the woman or the prisoner might drop a little note in an inconspicuous place, making sure that the other saw it. Prisoners and women would reveal their names and arrange for a secret meeting. Very often little gifts accompanied the notes, be it some chocolate or cigarettes that the prisoner had obtained through his aid parcels, or a sandwich or baked dessert that the woman left for the prisoner. Most relations started with such small exchanges of gifts and notes. In cases involving British POWs, gifts of chocolate and soap from the aid parcels of the POW almost always played a part at the start of a forbidden relationship. Although chocolate existed on the German market, the British POWs received a particularly tasty brand. According to information from the British Red Cross, the chocolate distributed to POWs was "Meltis" chocolate (milk or plain chocolate), a brand that was bought up by the Swiss company Suchard in the 1970s. (The brand name still exists but belongs to a different company now.[3]) Cigarettes

---

[2] For a typical case, see Feldurteil, Berlin, December 6, 1941, in PAAA, R 40907. In this case, the POW convinced the woman to have sex with him because he told her of two other couples in the same place, the metal screw factory in Finsterwalde outside of Berlin. The three couples met repeatedly at night in the apartment of one of the women.
[3] I thank the British Red Cross for this information: Mehzebin Adam to author, e-mail, September 19, 2018.

and real coffee – as opposed to the despised *Ersatz* coffee available to German civilians – were also popular gifts coming from POW aid parcels. For the prisoners, baked goods and sandwiches (in German: *belegte Brote*) were a much-appreciated gift from German women particularly in light of their sometimes-meager food supply. Cigarettes figured prominently in gifts of both, prisoners and women. Although the quality of foreign cigarettes was often better than what was available on the German market, POWs might occasionally appreciate the extra cigarettes provided to them by German women. Smoking can mitigate the pangs of hunger, and cigarettes could be used as an alternative currency among POWs or on the black market.

Relations outside the scope of common work could also start on the basis of services German women provided to prisoners. When many POWs started living more like a civilian worker than a prisoner, they began employing German women to wash their laundry and to mend their clothes. This was particularly true for the transformed prisoners. In cities and larger farms, the POW would bring his laundry to the woman's apartment and pick it up a few days later, paying for the service. The exchange of laundry provided a great opportunity to slip a note or a little gift to each other and to start a conversation. Many women asked the POW to come in and stay for coffee and cake.[4] A woman might also ask for the services of a POW. Given that the prisoner was often the only able-bodied man in the neighborhood (except perhaps for an eastern European forced laborer with whom contact was riskier), a woman might ask a POW working on a neighboring farm to perform some work typically carried out by men, such as splitting her firewood or repairing a damaged door or window. In cities, women might get a prisoner working for a utility company after calling for repair work. Many workers charged with fixing damages to windows, walls, and roofs after bombings were POWs assigned to a construction or roofing battalion (*Bau- und Arbeitsbataillon* or *Dachdecker-Bataillon*).[5]

The proximity of living spaces also was a frequent catalyst for forbidden relations. Some POWs were housed in a restaurant or hotel and

---

[4] For examples, see the following cases in LASH Schleswig, Abt. 358: Martha M., 5998; Erna K., 6050; Anna M., 6174; Ella B., 6572. See also the case against Maurice F., "Audience du Tribunal de Neustettin du 19 septembre 1944," in AN, F9, 2742, dossier "Stalag II-B," and "Audience du 24 janvier 1944," case of André P. and Paul J., in AN, F9, 2743, dossier "Stalag IV-C," and case of Armand B., BA-MA, PERS 15/7318.

[5] A typical example is André L., who began a relationship after having been called to do repair work in a woman's apartment: case against Frieda J. and Kreszenz S., LASH Schleswig, Abt. 358, 5801. For similar cases, see Justizbehörde Hamburg, "Von Gewohnheitsverbrechern, Volksschädlingen und Asozialen," 365–6, and Wrobel, *Strafjustiz im totalen Krieg*, vol. 2, 263.

dined in the company of civilians, allowing for flirting and conversations with the innkeeper's wife or daughter, a waitress, or female guests. Many of the small work detachments were housed adjacent to German civilian quarters. Meetings between POWs and women might occur in the courtyard, the staircase, or from window to window.[6] The presence of children often facilitated these contacts. The prisoner might give chocolate to the children of a woman he had seen and start a playful conversation with them. The mother might thank the prisoner and join in the conversation. Later, a child might become the courier between the two, transporting love notes and gifts. Contacts of POWs with children aroused less suspicion, although it happened that children discovered and sometimes denounced a forbidden relationship, inadvertently or deliberately.

The vast majority of encounters, however, occurred in the workplace and therefore involved German working women, predominantly rural workers and industrial laborers. The prisoners deployed in these jobs represented a broader social mix. The German army made efforts to assign POWs to types of work for which they were most qualified, and many POWs working on farms had some farm experience themselves, but a number of POWs with a higher education also performed manual labor on farms or in factories. A law student from a privileged family in Paris, for example, might become involved with an unskilled agricultural or industrial laborer in Germany. But relations could also cross social lines in the other direction, for example in the case of a woman owning a large estate in the eastern regions of Germany falling in love with a POW from a lower social background.

Communication between Foreigners

Most prisoners, except for the linguistically most challenged, picked up some German during years of work in German farms or enterprises. American POW Jack Dower, for example, remembers that his German increased "by leaps and bounds" while he was working with Germans: "I was adding some thirty or forty new words to my vocabulary daily without conscious effort."[7] The prisoner might speak a heavily accented and imperfect German, but it would suffice for basic conversations. Women and some POWs could purchase a dictionary to facilitate

[6] For an example of a woman from Hamburg (who had relocated to Kattowitz in 1942 to join her husband), see the case of Helene P., in Archiwum Państwowe w Katowicach (Poland), Sondergericht, 1330.
[7] Dower, *Deliverance at Diepholz*, 69.

communication. Dictionaries were often among the first gifts a woman made to a prisoner. Many love letters were written in an awkward mix of German words and foreign syntax because the prisoner used a dictionary to produce a word-by-word translation of his letter into German. Homonyms provided traps. A French prisoner with a poor mastery of French spelling, for example, consistently mixed up the French verb form "*je peux*" (as in "I can") with the adverb "*peu*" (a little), writing for example to his girlfriend in German: "I a little come tonight" instead of "I can come tonight."[8] German women who aspired to write in the prisoner's language faced similar challenges. Many couples became creative in their use of language and communicated in an unashamed linguistic mix.

Hertha Schmittke and French POW René Gerson, a physical education teacher from Paris, were particularly courageous in aspiring to write each other in the other person's language. Both worked in the cafeteria of a machine factory in Babelsberg, outside Berlin, he in the kitchen and she as a waitress. Hertha Schmittke was married to an employee of the film company UFA, but her husband had been drafted. Her closeness to the prisoner caught the attention of her superiors, who moved her to a different department of the company. This transfer spurned some of the most creative correspondence between a prisoner and a German woman, and some of their letters would fit into an anthology of Dadaist poems composed of cut-out words drawn from a hat. Her letters, written with a dictionary, show German syntax with French words, but not always the appropriate word. When her husband came on home leave, she wrote about "*mon homme*" ("my man") – given that in German the word for man and husband are the same. His letters also relied on a dictionary, which meant that he sometimes used poetic and rare words, for example "*grämlich*" (aggrieved) for "sad," when he could not see her for a couple of days. When asking her for a photo of herself, he used the old-fashioned and stuffy word for "photo shop" (*Lichtbildnerei*), and he repeatedly addressed her with "Dear expensive" ("*Liebe teuer*") because of a translation error of the French *amour cher* (dear loved one). Both lovers stubbornly stuck to the infinitive form of their verbs. But both were trying hard to learn the other's language. Among Hertha Schmittke's court files are papers on which she had written down common German phrases with French translations. It was a routine search of the prisoner's

---

[8] Case of Helene Sch. and Camille R., BLHA Potsdam, 12 C, Sondergericht Berlin II, 6845.

possessions that led to the couple's arrest because the guard found Hertha Schmittke's letters.[9]

There were some German women who spoke French or English, and quite a few of them used the desire to perfect the language of a prisoner as an excuse for engaging with him. Some prisoners already knew German, and that often marked them for selection as translators, which also facilitated contacts with German civilians. A woman involved with a prisoner who spoke German fluently would often benefit from the judge's inclination to use this fact as a mitigating circumstance because the lack of a linguistic barrier made the prisoner seem less alien. British prisoners found it easy to learn a little bit of German through analogous words, and those Belgians who knew Dutch managed to learn German rather easily, particularly in northern Germany, where local dialects resembled Dutch. Knowing some German words, of course, did not always facilitate a closer entente, as those prisoners experienced who tried to initiate sexual contacts with the crude proposal *"fick, fick?"* or the only slightly less offensive *"Du mir Madame machen?"* ("You make madam to me?").[10]

Erotic Encounters

Sexuality behind barbed wire has received much attention in the literature on POWs. There is no doubt that many prisoners, a relatively young group, suffered from prolonged abstinence. Scholars have probed into phenomena such as situational homoerotic relationships, particularly in the context of female theater impersonators, and various other outlets including masturbation.[11] But the enforced isolation of an enclosed all-male camp community, typical for the prison camp paradigm, does not correspond to the reality of most rank-and-file prisoners in Nazi Germany. POWs working in daily contact with women, often even

---

[9] An example from one of his letters: "Liebe Teuer. Glauben nicht sprache soldat für Alkohol mit du. Freitag viel grämlich vermögen nicht nähern Du. Verfluchen haben ein lange hosen für mich Bitte. Geben du Lichtbildnerei und adresse. Viel KuB. René." BLHA Potsdam, 12 C, Sondergericht Berlin II, 6207.

[10] See also Arnaud, "Die deutsch-französischen Liebesbeziehungen," 185.

[11] Reiss, *Controlling Sex in Captivity*, 3–6 and 59–73. On World War I: Brian K. Feltman, *The Stigma of Surrender: German Prisoners, British Captors, and Manhood in the Great War and Beyond* (Chapel Hill: The University of North Carolina Press, 2015), 129–32; Alon Rachamimov, "The Disruptive Comforts of Drag: (Trans)Gender Performances among Prisoners of War in Russia, 1914–1920," *American Historical Review* 111 (2006): 362–82; Fabien Théofilakis, "La Sexualité du prisonnier de guerre: Allemands et Français en captivité (1914–1918, 1940–1948)," *Vingtième Siècle, revue d'histoire* 99 (2008): 204–5, 209–11.

sleeping under the same roof with them, needed no female impersonators to fantasize about heterosexual relations, and they probably never saw a POW theater. Almost all POWs knew that closer contacts with German women were forbidden and severely punished, but it was difficult to resist the temptation provided by daily contact with the other sex. This applies in particular to rural settings, where the POW and a farm maid often worked alone in the fields or the barn. Some mountain farmers in the Alps near Salzburg even sent their POWs with young farm maids up into the summer pastures and let them sleep in the same hayloft without any supervision for weeks or even months.[12] The presence of women in the workplace and often near the sleeping quarters of the POW represented a constant temptation that was missing in the all-male enclosed camp.

In order to avoid punishment for himself, the prisoner might seek a relationship with a foreign civilian laborer. For Belgians and Frenchmen, this could mean getting involved with a co-national given that many Belgian and French civilians worked in Germany, first as volunteers and later forced laborers. But these relationships involved risks for the foreign women because the prohibition to interact with POWs applied to them, too. Forced laborers from eastern Europe risked the most severe punishments, especially in case of a pregnancy. But it was possible for a prisoner to maintain a relationship with an eastern woman if these workers were not strictly guarded. A number of Belgian POWs in East Prussia, for example, began intimate relations with a Russian or Ukrainian woman working in their vicinity. Georges Smets even reports of a Ukrainian woman, Natacha, who followed "her" prisoner, Marcel, from Königsberg to Belgium toward the end of the war, asking a friendly German priest to marry them on the way. Neither the American army liberating them nor the Belgian state recognized the marriage, and both insisted on her repatriation to the Soviet Union. Yet, Natacha went into hiding until she could legally marry Marcel in a civil ceremony in Belgium a few years after the war.[13]

German women, however, often sought out POWs. Many had experienced a long period of abstinence because their husbands or boyfriends served in the Wehrmacht, and many men were killed or missing in

---

[12] See, for example, Feldurteil against Pierre G., Salzburg, December 4, 1941, and Feldurteil against Henri L. and Jacques G., Salzburg, December 4, 1941, both in PAAA, R 40914.

[13] The story of Marcel and Natacha is included in the oral history collection of Georges Hautecler: CEGESOMA, AA 244 (Archives *de la Commission d'Histoire de la Captivité de Guerre 1940–1945: verslagen, corr., vragenlijsten, 06/1940–15/04/1970*). Georges Smets also refers to the story: "Journée du 14 mars [1945]," Musée Royal de l'Armée et d'Histoire Militaire, Brussels, Fonds Hautecler, Farde 34.

action. Given the severe shortage of German male partners, the foreigners represented a big temptation. As Luise Hartmann explained in front of the special court in Lübeck on October 16, 1944, she had left Berlin in 1942 because of there were hardly any German men in her age group. She had then moved in with her sister in the village Panten (Holstein) and had fallen in love with a French POW. In her defense, she remarked that all the men in the village were either POWs or forced laborers from Poland and the Soviet Union.[14] According to French POW Marcel Rebillard, a German soldier's wife one day seduced him by giving him wine to drink and saying: "Look, your wife is in France, my husband in Russia, and we are having no fun."[15]

Some relationships were primarily motivated by desire for fun and erotic adventure – on both sides. One such case came before the court martial in Königsberg in 1942. It involved two German women and four Belgian prisoners. The women, Hildegard Henkel and Martha Witulski, were both married; Henkel's husband was serving in the Wehrmacht. The Belgians were housed in a camp with 150 POWs in Tilsit and worked for various local businesses. At the end of March 1942, the two women went to the camp and began talking to a Belgian prisoner who happened to stand outside. This prisoner, twenty-one-year-old José Michelet, was a dental assistant from Namur who was now working for a coal distributor in Tilsit. The women told him that they had heard rumors that a very handsome POW was working at a local hair salon and asked him whether he knew this man. Michelet understood that they meant his comrade Jean ("Jonny") Descoteaux, but as a joke, he said that he himself was that handsome prisoner. Michelet and the women agreed to meet at night in the city park, and he promised to bring a comrade. Michelet brought along Roger Deniau, a town clerk, and the two prisoners and the women exchanged kisses and hugs until midnight. They agreed to meet again a few days later. This time, Michelet brought with him the hair stylist "Jonny" Descoteaux, whose reputation had attracted the women in the first place. They found some hiding places in the grass of the park. Michelet had sex with Frau Witulski and Descoteaux with Frau Henkel. A few days later, Michelet again showed up with Deniau, who had sex with Henkel while Michelet and Witulski retired to their previous hiding place. During the fourth meeting, Michelet brought yet another prisoner, the tailor Albert Duval. Since it was rainy, Frau Henkel suggested that they go to her apartment to be more comfortable. The nightly meetings from then on always took place in her apartment. Henkel continued to have sex with

[14] Luise H., LASH Schleswig, Abt. 358, 6111.
[15] Feldurteil, Graudenz, April 1, 1944, in AN, F9, 3644.

Deniau, and Michelet with Witulski. When Deniau was sick, Henkel sent him cigarettes and some civilian clothes belonging to her husband.

It is unclear whether this suspicious gift or complaints from neighbors led to discovery, but the POWs and the women were arrested in July, and the special court in Königsberg sentenced Henkel to five years of penal servitude on account of her involvement with several prisoners and her willingness to offer her apartment for the nightly meetings. Witulski received three years of penal servitude. The court martial in Königsberg sentenced Michelet and Duval to four and a half years and Deniau and Descoteaux to two and a half years in prison. During interrogation, the prisoners denied everything and emphatically claimed that they could never have left the camp at night. But soon they had to admit at least common walks with the women. Michelet then defended himself by claiming that he had taken Frau Witulski for a Pole because of her Polish name, while Deniau claimed he had thought that Henkel was Czech. The court martial interrogated the women as witnesses, but they both denied ever to have pretended not to be German.[16]

A similar case occurred in Danzig-Langfuhr, where three British POWs (Thomas Beacham, John Morris Haldane, and Frank Wilson) were working in a brewery alongside the German workers Helene Milkowski, Hildegard Schwenker, and Anna Janosch in early 1944. After some flirting, they talked about meeting at night in Janosch's apartment if the prisoners could find a way to leave their sleeping quarters. The prisoners did manage to produce a picklock for the external gate of their building. This gate could only be opened from the outside of the building, but the prisoners realized that Haldane, who was very thin, could slip outside through the bars of a window and then open the gate for the two others. There was still a fence to cross and some distance to walk where the prisoners might be recognized because of their uniforms, but two of the women agreed to throw over the fence a suitcase with civilian clothes belonging to Janosch's husband. The prisoners changed into the civilian clothes and climbed across the fence. They managed to have three nightly reunions with the women in March 1944, every time involving sex, until they were caught for unknown reasons. The POWs claimed to have mistaken the women for Poles, but the court martial did not accept the excuse and sentenced Beacham and Haldane to three years in prison and Wilson to three years of penal servitude because he had been involved with the wife of a soldier (Janosch).[17]

[16] Feldurteil, Gericht der Kommandantur der Befestigungen Ostpreußen, Königsberg, September 14, 1942, in CEGESOMA, AA 244.
[17] Feldurteil, Danzig, October 10, 1944, in BAR Bern, Bestand Vertretung Berlin, 78a.

In the pulp factory Waldhof in Mannheim, French prisoner Emil
Steffens, a bank accountant and NCO, worked in the presence of other
POWs, civilian workers, and young German women in 1941. He was
married, but he had not heard from his wife in a long time and believed
that his marriage was in trouble. In June, he noticed twenty-year-old
Elisabeth Filzgruber, who had just had a child out of wedlock by a
German soldier. They began flirting. She brought him sandwiches, and
they exchanged letters, kisses, and hugs during work. They occasionally
went into hiding in a dark place of the factory, and he reached under her
clothes and touched her skin. In October 1941, they were caught. In
front of the court martial in Mannheim, Steffens admitted everything but
asked the judges to make sure that the erotic temptations provided by
common work would stop. He pointed out that in one room of the
factory, where it was always hot and steamy, the young German women
(including Filzgruber) had been working in their bathing suits. This,
Steffens explained, had aroused him beyond control – after sixteen
months in captivity. The court martial acknowledged the temptation
provided by the working conditions and sentenced Steffens to only eight
months in prison. The special court gave Filzgruber the same punishment, a light sentence because of her youth.[18]

A spectacular court case involved eleven British POWs from all
corners of Britain and the Commonwealth working as carpenters and
metalworkers in a factory in Bautsch in the Sudetenland in the fall of
1943. Their "camp" was a building surrounded by barbed wire, adjacent
to the factory. The daughter of a retired railroad employee, Elisabeth
Paschek, lived with her parents across from the factory and occasionally
worked there. She and her housemaid, Marie Mittermaier, became the
key figures in a group affair with the POWs involving several local
women, including Paschek's sister and a woman who worked in the
factory cafeteria. Paschek became fond of Irishman Jack O'Leary and
one day invited him and some comrades to her apartment, and Marie
Mittermaier, who liked POW David Jackman, offered her own apartment
as a meeting place. The prisoners and a growing group of women thus
repeatedly met at night to drink, smoke, and exchange hugs and kisses.
The prisoners brought gifts from their aid parcels. They had no difficulty
leaving their sleeping quarters, which was perhaps not surprising given
that Elisabeth Paschek had been enlisted as an auxiliary guard! But the
nightly reunions came to the attention of neighbors and triggered local
gossip after the women and prisoners had organized a big party on the

[18] Feldurteil, Mannheim, December 19, 1941, in PAAA, R 40902.

occasion of Jackman's birthday in September 1943, with noisy celebrations until 5 AM. The commander of the POW work detachment heard about the rumors and started an investigation. The POWs, as usual, denied everything, but the prosecution exploited some tensions among them: one of the prisoners was from Jamaica; according to the police, he was dark-skinned, had "the black hair of an Indian," and was not liked by the others. This prisoner apparently broke the ring of silence and admitted the forbidden encounters, although he himself seems not to have had sex with any of the women. The two women who had offered their apartments received extremely high punishments – more than eight years of penal servitude – while the two prisoners who had had sex with one of the women were sentenced to three and a half years in prison each, and the others to six to nine months in prison. Certainly, the opportunity provided by the proximity of private meeting places and the group dating facilitated this encounter. The prisoners and the women seem to have been interested above all in having parties.[19]

Some encounters were rather crude and direct. In the tiny hamlet Münchshöfen southeast of Regensburg, French POWs and local farmworkers teased each other sexually. Magdalene Schmidt one day told the French POW André Collier that he should let his comrade Georges Levy know that he could do "*fick, fick*" with her if he brought her some chocolate. Levy told the police that he had no interest given that the woman was allegedly much too old for him (she was forty-three, he forty-one) and that she reminded him of a cow. It soon became clear, however, that Levy did have a sexual encounter with her and that the three other French POWs on the farm, Collier, Marceau Gendron, and Alexandre Duchastel, also had had forbidden relations either with Schmidt or with the farmhands Franziska Riegerl and Katharina Hickl. Schmidt told Riegerl that she had made love also with Duchastel and that he was much better than "Schorsch" (Georges Levy). Riegerl replied that Gendron was not a bad lover either. Schmidt was married and had two children, while Riegerl was a war widow with four children, three of them born out of wedlock. The relations on the farm had started in late 1940 and went on for well over a year. The special court in Nürnberg sentenced Schmidt and Riegerl to two and a half years of penal servitude on October 16, 1942. The investigation was complicated because Schmidt and Riegerl had a big fallout during the interrogation phase

---

[19] Feldurteil, Neisse, April 18, 1944, in BAR Bern, Bestand Vertretung Berlin, 78a. The case is summarized in Frey, *Die disziplinarische und gerichtliche Bestrafung*, 62–3.

and accused each other of ever-greater transgressions. In pre-trial custody, however, they reconciled and withdrew some of the allegations.[20]

Another case of teasing with sexual overtones involved four Cypriot POWs from the British army working in the kitchen of the train repair yard in Komotau (Sudetenland) in early 1944, one of the many workplaces where forbidden relations were widespread. The Cypriots, captured in Greece during the spring of 1941, worked together with four German girls aged sixteen to eighteen. While peeling potatoes, they started teasing each other, leading to repeated kisses and hugs. The prisoners also wrote letters to the girls and gave them chocolate from their aid parcels. The prisoners received relatively mild prison sentences ranging from five to ten months because the court martial could not prove more far-reaching sexual contacts.[21]

A chance encounter triggered an affair between French POW René Labatet (thirty-three) and the thirty-year-old Franziska Wildermuth in Freising, outside of Munich. Labatet was a waiter from Bordeaux, married, with two children. He worked in a local bakery. Wildermuth was married to an NCO serving in the Wehrmacht and had four young children. She lived across from the bakery. It all started with the POW smiling at the woman on his way to work one morning in September 1941. She smiled back. The next morning, he deposited a note in front of her apartment building asking for a meeting early on the following day. When he came back, she had written him a reply asking him to come a day later. He did visit her, and they had sex five or six times in her apartment, usually before work, while her children were still sleeping. As in quite a few other cases, an unexpected home leave of the husband led to discovery. Labatet was sentenced to three years in prison (prisoners involved with a soldier's wife were not yet sent to a penitentiary). The court martial acknowledged that he had felt sexual need after having been separated from his wife for one and a half years but counted the fact that he had broken into the marriage of a soldier as an aggravating factor despite the far-reaching cooperation of the woman.[22]

In other chance encounters, it was the woman who took the initiative. In a suburb of Wittenberg, Indian POW Shaktee Singh was digging a ditch in June 1944 when he noticed that a woman was watching him from

---

[20] BStA Nürnberg, Akten der Anklagebehörde beim Sondergericht, 1455 and 1716.

[21] Feldurteil against Hadji K., Teplitz-Schönau, April 18, 1944, in BAR Bern, Bestand Vertretung Berlin, 72b; Feldurteil against Mehmed S., Teplitz-Schönau, April 18, 1944, in BAR Bern, Bestand Vertretung Berlin, 81a; Feldurteil against Thassos L. and Charalambos N., Teplitz-Schönau, May 15, 1944, BAR Bern, Bestand Vertretung Berlin, 79a.

[22] Feldurteil, München, December 19, 1941, in PAAA, R 40903.

a nearby house. She smiled when he looked at her. He saw her again on the following days. In an unguarded moment, he threw some chocolate and soap through a window of her apartment. Then, he visited her, and they kissed and hugged. A few days later, they had sex. It is unclear whether a guard noticed him or whether a neighbor denounced them, but the affair was discovered. The court martial in Leipzig sentenced Singh to three years in prison on December 22, 1944. He denied everything, but she confessed, and, as usual, her confession was used as evidence against him.[23]

As Cornelie Usborne points out, some women exploited the sexual plight of the POW.[24] In a work detachment near Pless in Upper Silesia, British POW George Linton, an army cook, worked in the POW kitchen. His supervisor was Emilie Kuberski, a former Polish citizen now belonging to category III of the German people's list. When Kuberski, who was married, explained the job to Linton, she suddenly turned to him and asked him in a flirtatious tone whether he had ever had experiences with women. Mindful of the severe punishments, he ignored her advance, but she kept teasing him day in day out, for example by promising him a kiss if he helped her wash the dishes. The kitchen was isolated and unsupervised, allowing Frau Kuberski to pursue her advances without outside interference. After having gotten him to kiss her occasionally, she tempted Linton to visit her in her apartment during a night when her husband had a night shift. Linton hesitated but finally gave in on December 21, 1943. He slipped through a hole beneath the fence during the change of guards and visited her. They had sex, and he crawled back into the camp in the early morning hours. They repeated the encounter several times, but on December 27 they had a fight when she made a contemptuous remark about her husband. Linton took offense and, two days later, he turned himself in. The court martial in Kattowitz sentenced him to one year in prison on April 12, 1944, an extremely mild punishment that considered the active role of the woman as well as Linton's initial resistance and his honest attitude, as reflected by his turning himself in.[25]

[23] "Mitteilung," Leipzig, October 5, 1944, and attorney Rudof Weinoldt to Swiss Legation, December 22, 1944, both in BAR Bern, Bestand Vertretung Berlin, 81a. Weinoldt mentioned that the trial had taken place on the day on which he was writing and that the woman had received a penitentiary sentence. He did not indicate the length of her sentence. The court martial judgment apparently never arrived at the Swiss Legation.

[24] Usborne, "Female Sexual Desire and Male Honor," 487.

[25] Feldurteil, Kattowitz, April 12, 1944, in BAR Bern, Bestand Vertretung Berlin, 79a.

In the little village Scharndorf, between Vienna and Bratislava, a local farmwoman invited five French POWs to a traditional ritual with sexual connotations, the *Federschleißen*, a cleaning and sorting of duck and goose feathers. The event was known in this region as an opportunity for young people to sit together for a long time over several days, to tease each other, to drink, and to touch and kiss. The woman who invited the prisoners, Ottilie (Tilli) Haberl, was known to be on particularly good terms with the French POWs. Apparently, all POWs in the village knew her by her first name and greeted her with the local greeting "*Servus*, Tilli." After hearing rumors about the five POWs having been close to women at the event, the guards forbade them to attend the *Federschleißen*, but it was too late. Several forbidden relations had already sprung up, and four women and the five prisoners had to go to trial. The invitation of POWs to a flirtatious ritual that typically allowed the village youth to "check each other out" shows the degree to which the prisoners were included in the rural community.[26]

In many erotic relations with French prisoners, the notion of French men as excellent lovers played an important role. There had been a long-standing public discourse in Germany and elsewhere about "decadent" France, where couples enjoyed sex for its own sake and not for the purpose of reproduction. Paris had an international reputation for its nightlife and for being a city of sexual adventure, inspiring condemnation and fascination in equal measure. In the imagination of many German women, French prisoners were superb lovers. As an accused woman confessed to a female friend in an admiring tone: "the Frenchmen know how to make love very differently from the Germans." Sometimes Belgians also benefited from the fame of their French comrades. As another woman said in front of the judges: "The Germans make love like bulls, but the French and Belgians know how to make love without making children."[27] Some women openly admitted in front of the courts that "their" prisoners deserved their reputation. Not surprisingly, many French and Belgian prisoners found it difficult to live up to these high expectations. Still, the large-scale presence of increasingly "available" French-speaking prisoners represented a strong temptation for German

---

[26] Sentence of special court Vienna, July 22, 1942, in WStLA, Sondergericht, 6315.

[27] See, for example, Feldurteil against Joseph-Louis N., Münster, November 6, 1941, in PAAA, R 40895. These statements occasionally alluded to oral sex: Hildegard V., LASH Schleswig, Abt. 358, 5966. On the reputation of French men as lovers, see Virgili, *Naître ennemi*, 38; Arnaud, "Die deutsch-französischen Liebesbeziehungen," 189.

women. Ironically, German men in uniform at the same time also enjoyed a powerful sex appeal in some occupied countries.[28]

A telling example for the reputation of French lovers is the case of three women coming before the special court of Frankfurt am Main in August 1941. In Schwanheim near Frankfurt, a work detachment of French prisoners was housed in an athletic gymnasium and worked at the nearby IG Farben chemical plant. Gertrud Leicht and her friend Maria Konradi, employees of this company, were fascinated by the French men. Leicht was married to a soldier who was serving in the German occupation army in France at the time and who was later killed in action in Russia, shortly after the conclusion of her trial. Konradi had been engaged to a Luftwaffe soldier, but the engagement had been dissolved. After work, the two women climbed on their bicycles and visited the gymnasium where the POWs slept. At this time (March–April 1941), French POWs were still more strictly guarded, but Leicht talked to the guards and tried to find out as much as possible about the prisoners. Noticing Leicht's persistent interest in the POWs, the guards alerted the factory managers, who investigated but could not find evidence that she had approached a POW. But the fact that she was married to a soldier likely exposed her to special scrutiny. On April 3, 1941, an anonymous denunciation letter arrived at the police and accused Leicht and another woman of having secret meetings with French POWs Louis Ricardet and Francis Kergoat. The letter triggered a police investigation, which revealed that the prisoners had produced a picklock for the door of the gymnasium and gone outside during many nights, joined after a while by a third POW, Georges Pellerin, who had started a relationship with Anna Schwenkmann, also an IG Farben employee. The prisoners met the women at night either in Leicht's apartment or in the forest. During their encounters, the women expressed interest in exploring alternative forms of sex for which French men were famous. They boasted to each other about having had mutual oral sex – the so-called sixty-nine position – and anal sex with the prisoners. To the police, however, they claimed that the alternative sexual experiences had been disappointing and partly so painful that it became difficult for them to ride a bicycle, so that they had ultimately reverted to "normal" intercourse. The prisoners, meanwhile, boasted about their sexual exploits to their peers, which was careless because one comrade, a sergeant from Paris, later gave the police

---

[28] See, for example, Lulu Anne Hansen, "'Youth Off the Rails': Teenage Girls and German Soldiers – A Case Study in Occupied Denmark, 1940–1945," in *Brutality and Desire: War and Sexuality in Europe's Twentieth Century*, ed. Dagmar Herzog (New York: Palgrave Macmillan, 2009), 152; Stargardt, *German War*, 127–30.

much information about the nightly gatherings. The special court in Frankfurt sentenced Leicht to four years and Konradi to three years of penal servitude. Schwenkmann received one year of penal servitude. The prisoners were punished unusually harshly for this time: Ricardet and Kergoat received four years in prison, and Perrin three.[29]

The divorced waitress Ellen Kaufreuter, a mother of four young children, bluntly told several people that she found sex with French men highly rewarding. Kaufreuter worked in a restaurant in Worms in which French POWs on work detachments ate their lunch. This is how she befriended Emile Mollet. He visited her in her room (she was a boarder in an apartment rented by a couple). Kaufreuter also had an affair with French POW André Plombier, with whom she took long walks along the Rhine. Her landlady once noticed Kaufmann walking barely dressed across the apartment, and Kaufmann told her that the "*bel ami*" (handsome friend), her pet name for Mollet, was inside and that she had just "tried him out." To a friend, Kaufreuter said that she had "tried out the Frenchman and that the Frenchmen are better than the Germans; for her, only a Frenchman would be suitable in the future."[30]

In a similar case in Reichenwalde, a village southeast of Frankfurt an der Oder, the married farmwoman Berta Bremer told various friends in 1942 that the French were excellent lovers. She mentioned oral sex and claimed to finally have learned what "real love" was. She allegedly encouraged her friends to also "supply themselves with a Frenchman" because "the Frenchmen know how to do it much better than the Germans."[31]

Two women who dated French POWs in Lauf, not far from Nürnberg, boasted to each other about their lovers' sexual organs. The custodian of the school where they worked as cleaning ladies overheard them and denounced them. The POWs involved, Jules Soredi and Roger Salda, were both from the European minority in Algeria. One of the women, Gunda Hermann, was a war widow and mother of seven children. The other one, Anna Berkner, had three children; her husband was stationed on the eastern front. She had already had affairs with an Italian and with several Germans, and apparently had gathered some experience with

---

[29] HHStA Wiesbaden, Abt. 461, Nr. 8265, and Feldurteil, Frankfurt am Main, August 22, 1941, in AN, F9, 2380. The fact that Leicht was married to a Wehrmacht soldier and that she had offered her apartment for the secret reunions counted as aggravating factors, as did the fact that the women had given the prisoners civilian clothes, which could have facilitated an escape.

[30] Sentence, Sondergericht Darmstadt, November 19, 1943, in HStAD Fonds G 24, Nr. 955/2.

[31] BLHA Potsdam, 12 C, Sondergericht Frankfurt an der Oder, 125.

police interrogations (she told Hermann that it was essential to lie to the police officer while looking him straight into the eye). The sexual encounters with the two prisoners seem to have been less exciting than the women claimed in retrospect, however, not least because they were always worried about discovery. Hermann was pregnant when she went to the penitentiary, likely from Soredi.[32]

Another revealing example for the German imagination about French sexual practices, in particular oral sex, is the case of Elisabeth Gruppner, the wife of a garden center owner in Pottendorf, a small town south of Vienna. In January 1941, Elisabeth's husband Franz was sent to serve in the occupation forces in France. Elisabeth became concerned about the temptations that might ensnare him there because she heard from women in the neighborhood that their husbands had all seemed "spoiled" by the French women after coming back from France. Elisabeth's suspicion seemed confirmed when she found pornographic photos in her husband's luggage during his next leave. She became curious about the sexual experiences he might have had and feared that she might not be able to live up to his expectations any more. One night after his return, she started teasing him and asked him to kiss her genitals, a request that apparently stunned and confused Franz, who mentioned to the interrogating officer that his wife had never shown much interest in intimacy before. When Franz returned home after his next tour of duty, Elisabeth admitted to him that she had become intimate with French prisoner Pierre Fouché, who worked in their garden center. In court, she argued that she had taken up intimate relations with Fouché because she had heard that French women knew "perverse" sexual practices and that she felt she needed to learn about them with Fouché's help so that she would be able to satisfy her husband in the future. Elisabeth Gruppner was disappointed with what she learned from Fouché, however. She also asked him to kiss her genitals, which he apparently did to please her, but then he always performed "normal" intercourse. The court did not accept her excuse that she had only started the forbidden relation in the interest of making her husband happy and sentenced her to two years of penal servitude. That she was leader of the local NSDAP women's league (her husband was the NSDAP district leader) made her case particularly embarrassing, and the judge argued that she should be held to higher

---

[32] BStA Nürnberg, Akten der Anklagebehörde beim Sondergericht, 2383, judgment of November 25, 1943. The special court in Nürnberg sentenced Hermann to four years of penal servitude, a hard sentence that also considered a theft of clothing from the school where she worked. Berkner received two and a half years in prison for her relationship with Salda and also for being involved in the theft of clothes.

standards. The fact that she had confessed the affair to her husband and that she had tried to commit suicide thereafter worked as mitigating factors, however.[33]

Many relationships that seemed to be primarily about sexual exploration or satisfaction revealed more complex motivations on closer reading, however. Even in the case of Elisabeth Gruppner, the trial documents show that she felt compassion for Fouché, a sad and lonely farmer far away from his own family. Fouché had been allowed to eat at the family table, and Elisabeth had occasionally bought beer for him. The case of British POW Charles Collins from Wales also reveals a mix of motivations. Collins was a respected prisoner and had been appointed foreman in the hydrogenation plant of Blechhammer in Upper Silesia. He usually had to go to the management office to pick up the shift assignments for the day. In the office he met two German girls aged sixteen (almost seventeen) and nineteen in April 1943. He flirted with them and gave them chocolate. After two months, he and Edeltraut Zöllner, the younger of the two girls, agreed to meet secretly in the vast factory warehouse, which offered many hiding places. They had sex three times, always very rapidly in order to minimize the chances of discovery.

What led to the discovery, however, was not the encounters but the chocolate: usually, the girls ate the chocolate Collins gave them right away, but one day they wanted to take it home, and the guard who routinely controlled the workers leaving the plant discovered it when he searched their bags. This triggered a series of interrogations by plant officials and a woman supervisor responsible for the girls employed there. Her question: "for what exactly did you get English chocolate?" provoked Zöllner to admit that Collins had kissed her. After some more separate interrogations of the two girls, the woman supervisor tricked Zöllner into admitting the sexual encounters by pretending that the other girl had revealed them. On the surface, it appeared as if Collins had distributed chocolate to "buy" sexual favors, but the investigation revealed a more subtle and affectionate side of the affair. Collins had asked a Polish employee to find out Zöllner's birthdate and, on her seventeenth birthday, surprised her with an extra ration of chocolate and a beautiful ring made out of a French one-franc piece. He at the same time took the cheap metal ring that Zöllner wore and kept it. The exchange of rings, initiated by the thirty-year-old single prisoner, suggests that his interest in Zöllner was motivated by more than erotic desire. But Collins's steadfast denial of the affair did not allow the court

---

[33] Case of Elisabeth G., sentence of special court Vienna, September 30, 1941, WStLA, Sondergericht, 5991.

martial to explore this possibility, and it sentenced him to three and a half years of prison.[34]

A mix of motives also characterized the romance of Emma Marquardt with French POW Raymond Bouchard in Luckenwalde, just south of Berlin. Emma Marquardt was taking care of her husband's trading business after he had volunteered to join a reserve unit of the Wehrmacht (he was a fifty-six-year-old World War I veteran and did not need to serve). On the ground floor of their house was a screw factory that occupied French prisoners. Marquardt and her husband, who was stationed in France but came back relatively frequently, befriended Bouchard, one of the prisoners working on the ground floor. Marquardt's husband even broke the law by transporting letters for Bouchard when he went back to France. Meanwhile, Bouchard and Frau Marquardt became rather close. She told him that she had gotten married in 1930 but that her husband had quickly lost all interest in sex and that she suffered much from this. Her husband was eighteen years older, and he had told her that she just had to accept that he no longer felt any sexual desire. She wrote Bouchard tender and passionate letters. She spoke of trembling with excitement when he came into her apartment and mentioned the bliss of giving herself over to him completely. She called her body "young and unused" and expressed longing for "love and sun." She hinted how happy she would be if she had a child from him. Bouchard wrote of divorcing his wife and marrying Frau Marquardt and moving to France with her. She liked the thought of marrying him but was afraid that she might not be accepted by his family and that her French was too bad ("I can only so poorly *parler français*").

The relationship soon became part of the rumor mill in town. Bouchard was arrested in July 1941, but Frau Marquardt was allowed to remain at home until her trial on January 14, 1942, because her attorney argued that she was essential to her husband's business. Although her letters contained open allusions to erotic encounters, both Marquardt and Bouchard denied having had sex. The court martial ordered a psychiatric examination of Frau Marquardt by a university professor, who concluded that she was hysterical and tended to describe her wishful fantasies as reality. He therefore did not think that the letters proved that the couple had had sex (although both admitted having kissed each other). He also found out that she had a rather adventurous sexual live before her marriage and was indeed suffering from her husband's indifference. The special court in Berlin sentenced her to fifteen months in

---

[34] Feldurteil, Neisse, January 19, 1944, in BAR Bern, Bestand Vertretung Berlin, 78a.

prison. Bouchard received one year in prison, taking into account that Herr Marquardt had inadvertently facilitated the forbidden relation by inviting Bouchard into their apartment and that Frau Marquardt had been the driving force.[35]

Longing for Comfort and Emotional Warmth

As many of the more directly erotic encounters suggest, many women and prisoners felt a longing for comfort and emotional warmth. They were both facing an exceptional situation during the war. The normal life rhythms and contexts were disrupted for the women, while the men were living in an alternative reality, sharply separated from their peacetime lives. Women and prisoners may have looked to the future with anxiety. Would it be possible to slip back into the prewar routine? How much had changed? For many, of course, the prewar past was already irretrievably lost. Their spouse may have been dead, their home destroyed, the business ruined. For the prisoners, the reality of being in a foreign country without knowing when they would be released was depressing. Many had children and suffered from the reality that their children were growing up without their father, perhaps soon remembering nothing but the photo of him in the dining room. Some prisoners had a child they had never met because it was born after their last home leave. For women, the wartime pressures and frustrations also triggered a desire for comfort and emotional warmth. The increasing bombings, the threat of a German defeat and a vindictive foreign occupation and, potentially, ethnic cleansing provoked deep anxiety among German women toward the end of the war. Although the prisoners might look at an Allied victory with relief and yearn for their liberation, in the short run, they also had to brace the dangers of bombings and upheavals. For POWs in the east of Germany, the evacuations in early 1945 provoked much hardship and concern.[36] In addition, the prospect of being liberated by the Soviet army could cause special worries. Would they be distinguished from the Germans? Would they be punished as collaborators for having worked in the German war economy – a fear particularly widespread among French and Belgian prisoners? How would they get home, and how long would it take?[37]

---

[35] Feldurteil, Berlin, January 30, 1942, in PAAA, R 40910; BLHA Potsdam, 12 C, Sondergericht Berlin, 182.

[36] John Nichol and Tony Rennell, *The Last Escape: The Untold Story of Allied Prisoners of War in Europe 1944–1945* (New York: Viking, 2002).

[37] d'Hoop, "Prisonniers de guerre français témoins de la défaite allemande," 94–5.

The need for emotional warmth is evident already early in the captivity period. The French railroad employee Louis Arivault, for example, belonged to a work detachment housed in a restaurant in Oberwesel on the Rhine, south of Koblenz, in early 1941. He was married and had two children. In the restaurant he met twenty-year-old Luise Dammann. One day in March, he spontaneously kissed her hand when they met in the hallway. A few days later, she noticed that he had tear-stained eyes. She asked him about the cause of his grief, and he answered that he terribly missed his family and was worried about one of his children, who had a disease. Dammann tried to comfort him by stroking his hair. He placed his head on her shoulder, hugged her, and gave her a kiss. They met again, kissed and hugged. They never had sexual intercourse because they could not hide long enough, but they came fairly close. It appears that the affair was discovered when he tried to board a Rhine steamer with her in June 1941 in order to escape. Arivault was tried on September 9, 1941, and sentenced to one year in prison, a relatively mild punishment. The judges recognized his emotional distress and the genuine sympathy between the two, and they rewarded his open confession.[38]

A similar case involved Gustave Verstraeten (born in 1910), a textile worker from Dunkirk who was married and had five young children. In February 1941, Verstraeten had been assigned to a farm near Marchegg, east of Vienna. The farmwoman, sixty-one-year-old Barbara Waller, felt pity for the prisoner, who missed his family. One day, she proposed that he could sleep in bed with her. He accepted, and they had sexual intercourse five or six times. The court martial in Linz sentenced him to only eight months in prison on September 9, 1941. The fact that he could have been released as a father of five children (according to the agreement of November 16, 1940, that Scapini had negotiated with Hitler) served as a mitigating circumstance, as did his concern for his family and the fact that the age of the woman "had ruled out any danger for the German blood."[39]

In a battery factory in Hagen, French POW Fleuris Derocher, a barber from Lille, befriended the secretary Irmgard Schenker, who was engaged to a German soldier. Derocher gave her perfume, chocolate, and a photo of himself. Although his German was very poor, he wrote her a brief letter telling her that he had lost his parents at age seventeen and that he missed his home. She felt pity and sought to provide comfort to him. The court martial cited a letter in which she expressed much empathy for this lonely prisoner far from home. The letter did not allude to any familiarity or

---

[38] Feldurteil, Koblenz-Ehrenbreitstein, September 9, 1941, in PAAA, R 40884.
[39] Feldurteil, Linz, September 9, 1941, in PAAA, R 40884.

erotic dimension, however, and it used the formal address ("*Sie*" instead of "*Du*"). Both admitted only a hand kiss by the prisoner, which even the courts found trivial. Still, the court martial in Münster sentenced him to five months in prison. She received one month in prison from the district court in Hagen, but the judgment was cancelled by a higher instance because it was considered too mild. Her final punishment is unknown.[40]

Regardless of the war circumstances, the prisoner could easily appear as a savior to a woman in an unhappy or abusive marriage. This was the case of French POW Fernand Miquel, an office clerk from Belfort who was married and had one child. Miquel had served in the French medical service and now worked for the roofer Herrmann Dammert in Blücherthal near Trebnitz (Silesia). Frau Dammert complained to the prisoner that she was in an unhappy, forced marriage. The prisoner witnessed fights between the spouses, and the woman later argued that he had protected her from her husband's violence, although the husband denied that he had ever threatened his wife. Herr Dammert was aware that Miquel and his wife were close because they once both asked him to tolerate their relationship, and the husband agreed (he claimed in court that he was just joking). The prisoner was transferred to a farm not much later, but he kept visiting Frau Dammert in her home. The court martial in Breslau sentenced Miquel to three years in prison on October 7, 1941. The fact that the husband had tolerated the affair and not denounced him served as a mitigating factor. That Miquel had sometimes engaged in oral sex served as an aggravating factor, however, given that judges found oral sex "unnatural" and disgusting. The judges angrily reproached him with having played the gallant savior for a woman in an unhappy marriage. To the woman, the judges gave the paternalistic advice: "Many women face the same situation [an unhappy marriage] but resign themselves with their lot by dutifully caring for their household and their children."[41]

In a similar case, French POW François Bernard, a farmer, was assigned to the Schnitt family farm in Reichenberg (Sudetenland) that also employed an old German farmhand and a *Pflichtjahr* girl. Charlotte Schnitt accused her husband of infidelity, abuse, and even sodomy. She only refrained from suing for divorce because of their three children. The French prisoner provided much comfort to her. In the evenings, they sat together and taught each other French and German, while the husband

[40] Feldurteil, Münster, November 11, 1941, in PAAA, R 40898.
[41] "Viele Frauen tragen aber ein gleiches Los und finden sich damit ab, indem sie ihren Haushalt pflichtgemäß versehen und für die Kinder sorgen." Feldurteil, Breslau, October 7, 1941, in PAAA, R 40886.

was away. According to the farmhand and the *Pflichtjahr* girl, Frau Schnitt gave the POW extra food and asked the children to kiss him good night every day. The husband became suspicious. Together with two other witnesses, he decided to surprise his wife and the POW in the evening of April 19, 1942. He saw light in the house, but when he confronted the prisoner, Bernard only pointed at his fly and shook his head. The next day, Bernard was ordered back to his work detachment. Frau Schnitt cried when he left the farm, and both waved to each other in a very affectionate way. Upon interrogation, both admitted having had sex several times in the mudroom or the horse stable. Both retracted their confession later, arguing that the interrogating officers had blackmailed them into confessing. Testimony from the husband and the *Pflichtjahr* girl, however, suggested a close and tender relationship, and the court martial in Dresden therefore sentenced Bernard to three and a half years in prison on December 17, 1942.[42]

Pity for the situation of the prisoner and desire to cheer him up seems to have been a frequent motivation of German women, sometimes regardless of whether the prisoner asked for comfort and support or not. What exactly the doctor's wife, who was helping out as a medical assistant in her husband's practice, wanted from POW Roland Robert, who worked in a sugar factory in Markranstädt outside of Leipzig, is unclear. When the prisoner went to the doctor for a consultation, she smiled at him in the waiting room while registering him. He smiled back. A little later, she appeared at the fence of the local POW camp, looked for Robert, and threw a sack with apples to him with a little note, saying "*mes amitiés*" (in friendship). A few days later, she did the same thing with a sack of pears. This time, the note said "*mon cher*" (my dear) and asked the prisoner (in a mix of French and German) whether he liked fruit and whether he needed anything. The woman also asked him to write her after the war. The prisoner answered that he needed a razor. A few days later, the doctor's wife appeared again at the fence and threw him a razor with another little note, but this time somebody observed and denounced her. The court martial in Leipzig sentenced him to four months in prison, acknowledging that she had taken the initiative.[43]

In some cases, it was the prisoner who felt pity for a woman. In a Nürnberg brewery, for example, the thirty-year-old French POW Henri Albertin, a teacher from Algeria, noticed a woman who always seemed sad. The woman, Emma Eckerlein (twenty-eight), was divorced and had two children. The prisoner tried to cheer her up, and he occasionally

---

[42] Dossier François B., in AN, F9, 2361.
[43] Feldurteil, Leipzig, November 28, 1941, in PAAA, R 40900.

helped her during work. The contact came to the attention of the management, and Albertin was transferred to a more distant department of the brewery. Yet, he still passed by her workplace when he went to the bathroom. One day, he said to her: "Eckerlein *kaputt*. Too much work." Occasionally, they hugged and kissed each other. On May 27, 1941, a guard followed the prisoner and caught them. The woman offered the guard money, so that he would not denounce them, but the guard refused. According to the guard, the prisoner had had his hand under the clothes of the woman when he entered the room, but the court martial determined that the guard could have erred and sentenced the prisoner to only six months in prison on January 6, 1942. The special court had sentenced Frau Eckerlein to fifteen months in prison on August 4, 1941.[44]

Search for emotional comfort, mixed with erotic desire, characterized the relationship of French POW Maurice Leroux with Erna Rothe in Kriescht, a village between Küstrin and Landsberg an der Warthe in eastern Brandenburg. Leroux worked for Karl Steinborn, a local farmer who was also the NSDAP district leader. Rothe, born in 1901, was an elementary school teacher and herself a party member and leader of the local branch of the Nazi women's league. Rothe helped out on Steinborn's farm. She spoke French and often sought out French prisoners to practice her French. A guard had once admonished her because of this, but she always defended herself with her need to brush up on her French. Leroux told her that he missed his family (he was married and had three children) and that his enforced sexual abstinence was driving him crazy. What happened then was contested. Rothe initially admitted that they had made love several times on her couch. Later, she withdrew her confession and claimed to have been raped twice. She explained that she had not denounced the prisoner because he had asked her for forgiveness and she felt sorry for him. Leroux, however, told the court martial that there had been a long consensual relationship beginning in 1941 and continuing until discovery in the fall of 1943. Leroux and Rothe had a brief opportunity to meet after their arrest and apparently discussed their defense, exchanging little notes with instructions and tender messages. It seems that he advised her to claim rape because it would lead to a milder punishment for her. The court martial therefore dismissed the rape accusation and sentenced Leroux to three and a half years of prison for a long-lasting consensual relationship. The special

---

[44] Feldurteil, Nürnberg, January 6, 1942, in PAAA, R 40905; BStA Nürnberg, Akten der Anklagebehörde beim Sondergericht, 1196. The file for the woman is incomplete.

court in Frankfurt an der Oder also did not believe in rape and sentenced Rothe to twenty months of penal servitude on March 15, 1944.[45]

For Elisabeth Trottmann (forty-four), a married housewife in Frankfurt an der Oder, the encounter with a French POW occurred during a most stressful phase. Trottmann was married to a construction worker serving in the Wehrmacht and stationed in northern Finland. She was taking care of a six-year-old child her husband had brought into the marriage. Her husband visited briefly in December 1943 but left very soon to see his girlfriend in Königsberg. A few months later, he wrote Frau Trottmann that he wanted to divorce her and marry his girlfriend. She was extremely distressed, partly because she had become very attached to her stepchild and feared losing him. She even traveled to Königsberg to convince her husband's girlfriend to end the relationship, apparently to no avail. On the ground floor of her apartment building was a shop employing French POWs. They were always nice to her and her stepson. She began talking to one of them, Roger Leduc, and asked him to write down the words of the French love song *"Parlez-moi d'amour!"* (speak to me of love), a 1930 hit by Jean Lenoir. Leduc visited her several times in her apartment, and she served him dinner. Once, he stayed overnight. When he left the apartment in the morning, a neighbor saw him. She told her husband, a local NSDAP functionary, who promptly denounced Frau Trottmann. The special court in Frankfurt an der Oder considered her ruined marriage and deep sadness as extenuating circumstances and sentenced her only to ten months in prison on November 14, 1944.[46]

As in Trottmann's case, popular songs often served as sources of comfort in forbidden relationships. The sixteen-year-old daughter of a farmer near Mannheim knew that the French POW Raymond Bel-Hiba, who worked for her father, played the accordion. One day, she asked him to play the song "Lili Marleen" for her. Later she asked him to play the song *"Ich bin ja heute so verliebt"* (I am so in love today), a Lizzi Waldmüller hit from the film *Operette*. Every time he played a song for her, she gave him a kiss. The court martial sentenced him to seven months in prison.[47] The song "Lili Marleen" also played a role in the relationship of the farmer's wife Anna Müller in Stolberg (eastern Brandenburg) with Serb POW Alois Pesković. When she learned that her husband was reported as missing in action on the eastern front in January 1942, the Serb POW became her comforter, and she wrote him tender

[45] BLHA Potsdam, 12 C, Sondergericht Frankfurt an der Oder, 1221.
[46] BLHA Potsdam, 12 C, Sondergericht Frankfurt an der Oder, 1530–1533.
[47] Feldurteil, Mannheim, May 5, 1942, in AN, F9, 2419, folder 3004.

letters, using the text of "Lili Marleen" with some substitutions appropriate to their relationship.[48]

Some women and prisoners just fell so passionately in love that their attraction to each other transported them into a different reality. The Austrian worker Anna Leonhard, for example, was head over heels in love with French POW Henri Badinter. In August 1942, they took a walk in the company of another couple, and they hugged each other. Soon they met alone and had sex. She became pregnant but continued the secret meetings until the local police received an anonymous letter denouncing her. During her interrogation, Leonhard described the relationship as completely transforming. Badinter was handsome, funny, and sweet. She testified that he made her "entirely happy" and that she had never been involved with somebody so handsome and nice. The happiness of the moments with the prisoner made her forget the future and the consequences of the relationship. She and Badinter seem to have lived totally in the moment, in a state of amorous intoxication. The relationship provided emotional warmth and comfort by taking them out of their daily routines. It bordered on sincere love.[49]

Sincere Love

For many couples, the motivation was not primarily erotic desire nor merely the need for comfort and emotional warmth. These couples, officially enemies, looked for ways to settle into a new life routine either during the war or after its conclusion. Most of them discussed marriage, which sometimes meant divorcing their current spouses; some wanted to stay in Germany, others wanted to go to the home of the prisoner. Many of these couples embraced the alternative reality created by the war as a new long-term normalcy, although they knew their relationship was illegal under the present conditions. The judges had to punish these relations, but they often respected them and considered sincere love as a mitigating circumstance.

Georges Smets reports a love story of a Belgian POW who was working on a farm in Bismarck, a village near Heydekrug (Memel), alone with the farmer's wife and her two little children. The woman's husband was a soldier on the eastern front, and the prisoner himself was also married. Smets knew that the prisoner was seriously ill and went to see him, asking him to let himself be repatriated. The prisoner refused, however,

[48] BLHA Potsdam, 12 C, Sondergericht Frankfurt an der Oder, 926.
[49] Sentence of the special court Vienna, December 6, 1943, in WStLA, Sondergericht, 7207.

pointing out that he felt responsible for the woman and the two children, who were both holding on to his legs while he was talking with Smets. Smets learned later that the prisoner died only a few weeks after their conversation. The woman lovingly cared for his grave, bringing flowers and praying there every Saturday. The woman's husband never returned from Russia, but after the war, she and the prisoner's wife contacted each other. At the time of Smets's writing (1976), the two women regularly visited each other. Smets also established contact with the children, who were living in Kiel.[50]

The love story of Else Schneider and French POW Georges Kessler represents a typical case where the temporary reality created by wartime circumstances took over and invalidated their prewar lives – at least until the discovery of the forbidden relation on August 1, 1943. Else Schneider was a thirty-six-year-old cleaning lady in a wine tavern, and Georges Kessler was a thirty-three-year-old waiter from Paris. Both were married. Schneider's husband was a locksmith employed by the MAN machine works in Nürnberg. He had to work extremely long hours and was almost never home. He apparently was cold and distant toward his wife. Kessler, who was born in Alsace as a German citizen, knew German well and was often called as a translator. He had worked for a while on the Nazi Party meeting grounds in Nürnberg, but in August 1942 he was assigned to the wine tavern where Schneider worked. Kessler and Schneider fell in love with each other. They wrote each other passionate letters. She wrote to him: "I would rather die than live without you." When he expressed jealousy because he had seen her sit down on the bed of a guard, she wrote to "my dear Georg" (the German form of his first name): "But you do know precisely that I can love only you with my entire heart." Kessler eloquently expressed his longing for her. In one letter, he mentions a friend working in a hotel in Montpellier (southern France), and he suggested that they could both escape and join that friend. They kissed and hugged. In order to be able to see her more easily, Kessler became a transformed prisoner in June 1943. Apparently, she believed that having a relationship with him was legal now, and she invited him for coffee and cake. He wanted to become intimate with her, but she refused. On August 1, they met again in her apartment, and they both admitted that they would have had sex this time had they not been arrested. On September 10, 1943, the special court in Nürnberg sentenced her to one year in prison, acknowledging that she did not know that relations with transformed POWs were still forbidden and punishing her only for

[50] Smets to Mr. Georges Paulus, January 11, 1976, in Musée Royal de l'Armée et d'Histoire Militaire, Brussels, Fonds Hautecler, Farde 34.

the contact before Kessler's transformation. The court martial in Nürnberg sentenced Kessler to one and a half years in prison on November 10, 1943.[51]

In Darmstadt, twenty-one-year-old Liselotte Paetsch, a domestic servant employed by a high school teacher, noticed a good-looking French prisoner in a group of POWs who regularly marched to work in front of her window. After watching him for a long time, she once noticed in January 1943 that the POW was walking outside alone. She rushed out and started talking to him. She learned his name, François Dumoulin, that he was thirty-four, and that he worked for the coal merchant Philip Diehl at the *Ostbahnhof* (eastern rail station). When checking out Diehl's premises, Paetsch noticed that there were some rabbit cages. She then bought a rabbit and asked Diehl if she could keep it in one of his cages. Diehl approved, and Paetsch daily went to his firm to feed the rabbit, or rather, to see Dumoulin. They became intimate, finding various hiding places on the firm grounds. Diehl obviously noticed something, and he heard rumors about an affair. He therefore gently asked her not to come every day any more. Dumoulin took over the feeding of her rabbit on most days, but when she came to the coal depot, they still became intimate. Meanwhile, Paetsch's mother found out about the relationship. Initially, she was worried, but then she requested to meet the prisoner. To this end, she asked Diehl if he could send her Dumoulin to split some wood, which he did. The mother served him meals and warmly welcomed him.

In August 1943, Dumoulin was transformed and from then on wore civilian clothes. He had apparently started an affair with another woman but continued seeing Liselotte and told her and her mother that he wanted to marry her. He and Liselotte went to the cinema together, and when his room was destroyed in a bombing in September 1943, she arranged for him to move in with her grandmother, and she went shopping for him every day. They often gathered at her mother's apartment. For unknown reasons, they were caught in October 1943. Liselotte Paetsch stated in front of the court that she really loved Dumoulin and was serious about marrying him. Her mother also admitted that she liked him very much and that she had seen him as her future son-in-law. She did not want to stand in the way of her daughter's happiness, especially since her daughter had had disappointing experiences with German men. The special court in Darmstadt was amazingly lenient in this case, ignoring the contacts after August 1943 because mother and

[51] BStA Nürnberg, Akten der Anklagebehörde beim Sondergericht, 2298; Sergeant-chef Lavollé to Officier conseil du Wehrkreis XIII, December 15, 1943, in AN, F9, 2745.

daughter claimed that they did not know that contacts with transformed POWs were forbidden. Both were punished only for the contacts before the transformation – Liselotte with ten months in prison and her mother with three months in prison for having facilitated the relationship.[52] In the case of Liselotte Paetsch, sincere love is beyond doubt, although it is dubious whether Dumoulin was as serious as she was in light of his affair with another woman.

The love relation of French POW Clément Allier and the eighteen-year-old employee Ursula Rickau, in Landsberg an der Warthe in 1942, also inspired marriage plans. Both were working in the dispatch department of a net and cable factory. He packed the goods, while she prepared the address labels. One day, he noticed some piano music in her bag. He himself was a saxophone player. They started talking about music and soon became fond of each other. They wrote each other tender letters in which they discussed getting married and moving to France after the war, although she expressed fears that his family might not accept her because she was not French. She gave him the key to her apartment (she was living with her grandparents), and he visited her many times at night, escaping from his sleeping quarters through the toilet window and letting himself down to the street with the help of a rope. During the police interrogation, Rickau declared that she would do anything for Allier, even if it meant committing high treason. Partly because of this comment, the special court in Frankfurt an der Oder sentenced her to two and a half years of penal servitude, an extremely harsh sentence given her youth.[53]

One of the longest undiscovered love relationships involved Frieda Thomsen, a farmwoman in the village Norderstapel not far from Schleswig, and a Flemish prisoner. She was married to a farmer who was nineteen years her senior, and they had two children. The marriage was unhappy, and it was rumored in the village that Herr Thomsen sometimes beat his wife. She had once decided to get a divorce but changed her mind when she noticed that she was pregnant with her second child. One of the workers on her farm was POW Omer van den Broeck, an attractive car mechanic and sports teacher who was well liked in the village. Van den Broeck had quickly mastered *Plattdeutsch*, the local dialect, which has similarities with Dutch. Herr Thomsen greatly appreciated him. When he was drafted into the Wehrmacht in 1941, he asked his wife to treat van den Broeck well, so that he would not leave. In the

---

[52] Sentence of special court Darmstadt, March 7, 1944, in HStAD Fonds G 24, Nr. 955/2.
[53] BLHA Potsdam, 12 C, Sondergericht Frankfurt an der Oder, 1206.

fall of 1941, van den Broeck's relationship with Frau Thomsen became intimate. They began living like a married couple.

Sometime in 1942, the news arrived that Herr Thomsen had died of a stroke in Estonia. The relationship between van den Broeck and Frau Thomsen had meanwhile begun to spur rumors in the village. In the fall of 1942, van den Broeck was therefore transferred to a different farm-woman in the village Groß Rheide, twenty kilometers away. They kept in touch by writing letters to each other, either in Dutch or *Plattdeutsch*. Frau Thomsen was pregnant with van den Broeck's baby and gave birth on December 15, 1942, probably declaring the child to be the result of her husband's last home leave. She and van den Broeck maintained intensive contact, and he expressed much interest in seeing his child. Frau Thomsen and van den Broeck had every intention to marry after the war. He was married himself but said that his marriage was unhappy and that he would seek a divorce as soon as he could. He planned to stay in Germany with her after the war. His new employer, Frau Rohwedder, also a war widow, quickly learned of the relationship. Although she belonged to a family with good Nazi credentials, as the court files note, she felt compassion for Frau Thomsen and decided to support the relationship. She transmitted some of the couple's letters and made sure they could see each other, treating them to coffee and cake on her farm. Another woman, a neighbor of Frau Thomsen, also supported the rela-tionship and allowed van den Broeck to address his letters to her, so that suspicions would not fall on Frau Thomsen. The two guards who were responsible for the POWs in Groß Rheide were no less obliging. They did not report van den Broeck when they noticed that his bed was empty at night. For a long time, they even transported letters between the lovers and helped them to see each other.

The relationship was discovered on April 22, 1944, after two and a half years. Van den Broeck was returning from a trip (he was probably called as a translator) in the company of one of his guards. In Norderstapel they missed the last bus to Groß Rheide. Since the guard was severely handi-capped because of a war wound, he was unable to walk the remaining distance. Van den Broeck therefore proposed that they stay overnight at Frau Thomsen's place nearby, and the guard agreed. To celebrate the occasion, Frau Thomsen illegally slaughtered a pig on her farm (this was severely punished in wartime Germany). What exactly led to the discov-ery is not clear. According to one source, the illegal slaughter caught the attention of the police. According to another source, somebody recog-nized van den Broeck (who was well known in the village) and alerted the police. Frau Thomsen was severely punished; on August 2, 1944, the special court in Kiel sentenced her to two years of penal servitude for the relationship and one and a half years for the illegal slaughter, compressed into two and a half years of penal servitude. The judge recognized that her unhappy marriage had increased the temptation to start a relationship with the prisoner, but he used the fact that the transfer of the prisoner had not served her as a warning as an aggravating factor. Frau Rohwedder received a prison sentence of six months for her help in facilitating the relationship. The punishments meted out to the guards and the prisoner are unknown but must have been harsh, especially against the guards, who had actively supported the illegal relationship. The attorneys for the two women submitted several clemency pleas, pointing out van den Broeck's long-standing commitment and sincerity, his concern for his child, and the fact that he was pro-German and sincerely wanted to stay in Germany and marry Frau Thomsen. They also pointed to his Germanic descent, but to no avail.[54]

Some women in love with a prisoner did everything they could to protect him. An example is the twenty-eight-year-old Marie Wolf, who worked as an auxiliary laborer in the Pauker rail car factory in Vienna-Floridsdorf. In November 1941, Wolf noticed a French prisoner at work who occasionally smiled at her. She smiled back. One day, the prisoner wrote her a little love note in German: "I like you because you are so funny. Please, can I write again?" She destroyed his note and wrote him back that writing was too dangerous. Still, the exchange of notes continued, and in April 1942, they managed to spend some time at night outside the factory. They kissed and declared that they loved each other. They took a walk. A few days later, they met again in front of the factory. They lay down on a lawn. When she realized that he wanted sex, she undressed. According to her testimony, he took care not to get her pregnant (she disclosed no details). After this meeting, she wrote him a very tender love letter and deposited it in the men's room, together with a metal heart. She wrote: "Here, I offer you my heart." She expressed longing for his kisses and great fear that he would be arrested. Another worker, who used the toilet before the prisoner arrived, discovered the letter and the metal heart and notified the management. The police started an investigation. All female workers named Marie had to submit a sample of their handwriting, and this allowed the police to identify Marie Wolf. She confessed everything during interrogation and declared that she still loved the prisoner and that they wanted to live together after the war. Asked whether she regretted anything, she said that she only regretted the punishment both would get, but not the encounters. Marie

---

[54] LASH Schleswig, Abt. 358, 7013.

Wolf claimed to only know the first name of the prisoner, Jean (a very common French first name). The police led all French prisoners named Jean in front of her, but she denied recognizing him, very likely in an effort to protect him. She then had to look at every single French POW working in the factory but still did not identify him. To the police, she explained that it had always been dark during their intimate reunions (that was true, but she had also seen Jean in the factory during daylight). The special court in Vienna sentenced her to one and a half years of penal servitude on July 29, 1942, counting the fact that one of her brothers had been killed in France in 1940 as an aggravating factor because the court claimed that this should have made her resent French soldiers. Marie Wolf was kept in the local prison for a few months because the police were still hoping for her help in identifying Jean. But the police apparently never found him. In December 1942, she was sent to a penitentiary.[55]

Despite the increasingly bitter hostility of Nazi propaganda toward Britain at a time of intensifying bombings, some British POWs and German women also experienced sincere love and planned to marry after the war. In Danzig-Langfuhr, for example, British POW John Scholes fell in love with the secretary Ursula Fritz, who worked in the same company, sometime in 1942. He gave her chocolate and soap from his aid parcels, and they developed a long intimate relation. Fritz became pregnant and gave birth to a child in June 1943, and this probably triggered the discovery of the relationship. Scholes and Fritz wanted to marry after the war. The court martial of Danzig, which had been singled out by British officials as particularly harsh, sentenced Scholes to two years and nine months in prison, a relatively mild punishment. His desire to marry her counted as a mitigating factor. The judgment against her is unknown. How such an involved relationship could continue for a year without being discovered is unclear. Scholes was reputed to be a very good and trustworthy worker, which may have granted him some protection.[56]

Also in 1942, NCO Edward Hunter befriended Gertrud Schulze, a mother of two children, while working for the army provisioning service in Oels (Upper Silesia). Schulze told him that she was married to an officer but that they had separated already years before and planned to seek a divorce. A friendship developed between the two. In May 1944 Hunter was transferred to a different workplace, and the contact ended. But on October 10, 1944, Hunter suddenly knocked at her door (she had once told him where she lived) and asked her to hide him

[55] WStLA, Sondergericht, 6608.
[56] Feldurteil, Danzig, November 23, 1943, in BAR Bern, Bestand Vertretung Berlin, 79b.

because he had escaped from his new work detachment. She agreed and gave him a jacket belonging to her husband as camouflage. He slept in bed with her, and they had sex several times. After eight days, he was discovered and arrested. He declared that he intended to marry Schulze and take her and her two children to England after the war. The court martial in Breslau sentenced him to two years of penal servitude on January 11, 1945, a very light sentence even though the judges blamed him for having ruined her marriage (an argument his defense attorney tried to challenge in light of the separation and the divorce plans of the spouses). The special court sentenced her to six years of penal servitude, a very harsh sentence even considering that she had hidden Hunter after an escape. In Hunter's case, did the love for Schulze and a longing for her motivate his escape, or did he just see her home as a good hiding place that would facilitate an escape? Everything points to sincere love as the motivation because he seems to have had no further plans to escape from her home, and the judges would have punished him much more harshly had they suspected that he was exploiting her love to facilitate his escape.[57]

Charlie Marshall, a British POW working in the northern Sudetenland, fell in love with the married woman Gertrud Äppler in the fall of 1942. They discussed getting married and moving to England after the war. She was married to a railroad employee who was often absent, and she told Marshall that her marriage was unhappy. Marshall spent many nights in her apartment, and they lived together as a couple. When he was arrested in August 1943, almost a year after the beginning of the relationship, he immediately confessed everything. The court martial in Teplitz-Schönau sentenced him to three years in prison, considering his confession and his sincere love for her as extenuating circumstances, even though the long duration of the relationship and the fact that she was married counted as aggravating factors.[58]

Car mechanic Ernest Asher was convinced that he had found the love of his life in Germany. Asher was born in Birmingham in 1899 and had emigrated to Canada (New Brunswick). He was a widower and had one child. He had been captured in May 1940 and was working in a small forestry work detachment, quartered in an isolated farmhouse near Elbing (West Prussia). A married German woman, Frau Krause from Elbing, regularly took walks through the forest with her six-year-old son.

[57] Feldurteil, Breslau, January 11, 1945, and attorney Hochheiser to Swiss Legation, undated, both in BAR Bern, Bestand Vertretung Berlin, 81b.
[58] Feldurteil, Teplitz-Schönau, October 19, 1943, and attorney Lomatsch to Swiss Legation, October 21, 1943, both in BAR Bern, Bestand Vertretung Berlin, 81c.

One day in June 1942, she sent the boy to ask the prisoners for water. Asher gave it to him, and he also handed him some chocolate. A few days later, Frau Krause took an outing with her niece and sat down on a bench not far from the farmhouse in which the prisoners slept. Asher recognized her. When the women passed in front of the farmhouse, he started talking to them. He and Frau Krause from now on met regularly. He gave her chocolate, soap, honey, and a sweater, and she brought him baked goods and paper for letters. An intense love relationship developed. He wrote her extremely tender letters in which he mentioned his intention to take her to Canada after the war and to marry her. He pointed out that he had a lucrative business and would take good care of her. She declared that she would seek a divorce and marry Asher. On four or five occasions, they had sex in the brush, according to her confession. The relationship went on for many months until it was discovered for unknown reasons. Asher immediately admitted the contacts with Frau Krause during interrogation, but he denied having had sex with her. The court martial of Danzig did not hold that against him, however, because it believed that he was trying to protect her from harsh punishment. In front of the court, Asher repeated his sincere desire to marry her after the war. The justification of the judgment and the report of Asher's attorney to the Swiss legation reveal that the judges were genuinely touched by the love he professed for a German woman and that they found it hard to punish him with the required severity. They sentenced him to three years in prison, a lenient sentence for a very involved relationship that had not been facilitated by working together and that, as the court martial suggested, had probably ruined Frau Krause's marriage.[59]

If the courts martial saw signs of sincere love, they sentenced the POW with great lenience if no sexual intercourse had occurred. This applied, for example, to Victor Heart, a bank clerk from London, who worked in a company in Weisswasser (northeast of Dresden). Every day, he had to pick up a radio from the communication room of the company. He noticed the stenotypist Käthe Wünsch, and they soon felt a strong mutual attraction. They exchanged little gifts and letters. She spoke some English. She repaired Heart's socks and pajama pants. One day he came into her apartment in the company of an electrician to repair her iron, but no intimacies occurred. They did however meet secretly on the firm grounds in a shed where she stored her bicycle. They admitted hugs and kisses in the shed, but both denied having had sexual intercourse,

---

[59] Feldurteil, Danzig, May 11, 1943, and attorney Dr. Marx to Swiss Legation, May 11, 1943, both in BAR Bern, Bestand Vertretung Berlin, 86b.

and the judges believed them. When the affair was discovered, Wünsch's husband, a district forester, sued for divorce. Heart, who was married and had two small children, wanted to get a divorce himself and marry Käthe Wünsch after the war. The court martial in Neisse sentenced him to six months in prison on December 21, 1943, a mild punishment that considered his sincere love and rewarded his restraint.[60]

A similar case was the relationship of Australian POW Sidney Robert Pellman and the accountant Edith Gäbel in Odrau (Sudetenland). Both worked in a weaving mill. Although she worked in the office, she occasionally helped him load the finished products onto a horse wagon, and they began conversations and exchanged letters. Pellman wrote her that he would love to marry her and take her to Australia after the war. She expressed interest in going with him but warned him that a relationship was illegal during the war. They both kept their distance, and the court martial of Breslau therefore only sentenced him to four months in prison on August 30, 1944, considering his intention to marry her as an extenuating circumstance.[61]

For practical reasons, the thought of escaping together was rare for German–British couples. But a few of them did try to escape. British POW Peter Foot and the German housemaid Ursula Gengel, for example, were working on an estate in the village Berghausen near Stuhm (south of Danzig). They had an intimate relation for several months. When she discovered that she was pregnant from him, they decided to escape together and to get married. They made it as far as Gelsenkirchen in western Germany (more than 1,000 kilometers away and less than seventy kilometers from the Dutch border), where they were caught. The court martial of Danzig sentenced Foot to two and a half years in military prison in April 1944, a mild sentence. The judges recognized his sincere love for the woman. That she was not married also counted as a mitigating factor.[62]

For many French and Belgian prisoners desiring to marry their German partner, the thought of an escape suggested itself more easily. It opened the prospect of getting married in France or Belgium and freely living a relationship that was illegal in wartime Germany. Many of these couples were caught at or near the border, however. Even if the POW had civilian clothes and some money, he likely did not have valid papers. There were frequent controls in the trains, and crossing the green border to Switzerland or to occupied France or Belgium was difficult because

[60] Feldurteil, Neisse, December 21, 1943, in BAR Bern, Bestand Vertretung Berlin, 80a.
[61] Feldurteil, Breslau, August 30, 1944, and attorney Ernst Kranz to Swiss Legation, undated, both in BAR Bern, Bestand Vertretung Berlin, 79a.
[62] Feldurteil, Danzig, March 14, 1944, and attorney Klawitter to Swiss Legation, March 14, 1944, both in BAR Bern, Bestand Vertretung Berlin, 86b.

there were many patrols. Although some POWs undoubtedly promised marriage to a woman in order to get her to help them prepare an escape, most of these relationships seem to have been sincere.

French POW Jean Nivelle, for example, was assigned to a farmer in Oberndorf, a village in the Spessart Mountains east of Frankfurt am Main. The married daughter of the farmer, Marie Rombach, helped out on the farm and was working daily with Nivelle. Her husband was serving in the Wehrmacht. Nivelle felt attracted to Marie Rombach, and in October 1940 he told her that he loved her. She initially just laughed, but after a while, she hugged and kissed him. In December, her husband suddenly came home on leave, interrupting her relationship with Nivelle. When the husband left, in January 1941, Nivelle and Rombach resumed their tender relations, after Nivelle expressed some jealousy against her husband. In February, he tried to seduce her in the basement while they were sorting potatoes together. She initially resisted but then gave in. They repeatedly had sex in the basement, in the barn, and in the forest during the day (he had to return to the POW quarters at night). In May, she discovered that she was pregnant from him. When it became impossible to hide the pregnancy, they decided to escape to France and marry there. Because they believed that traveling together was too risky, they took separate trains. They agreed to reunite in Metz, a city in Lorraine *de facto* annexed by Germany, and to go to France from there. On August 27, 1941, Marie Rombach took a train to Metz, and the following night, Nivelle broke out of the POW sleeping quarters and also took the train to Metz. Marie had given him some civilian clothes belonging to her husband as well as some money. Nivelle did not make it to Metz, however. He was caught in Karlsruhe ten days after escaping, while Rombach was still waiting in Metz, where she was arrested. Both received extremely harsh punishments: the court martial in Kassel sentenced Nivelle to five years in prison. Love affairs with soldiers' wives did not yet lead to penitentiary sentences, but the fact that he had seduced the wife of a soldier was considered an aggravating factor, as was the pregnancy of Marie Rombach. The special court in Kassel sentenced Rombach to eight years of penal servitude, one of the harshest sentences ever against a German woman for a forbidden relationship. The fact that she had helped prepare Nivelle's escape by giving him money and her husband's clothes counted as aggravating factors. Rombach gave birth to a girl on November 1, 1941, during a release from pre-trial custody. Her punishment was so unusually harsh that that she was released on parole in 1944, after having served three years of her sentence.[63]

---

[63] Feldurteil, Kassel, November 27, 1941, in PAAA, R 40900.

In Greifswald, POW Jacques Kellerman, a trade representative from Paris, fell in love with Lotte Grabowski, who was married to a Luftwaffe officer and had a young child. Kellermann, who was born in Basel (Switzerland) and spoke German very well, served as a translator and therefore had more liberties than the usual French POW at this time (1941). Grabowski told Kellerman that she would seek a divorce and that she wanted to go to France with him and get married. She suggested that he escape and hide at her house and that, after some time, they would both go to France and marry. According to Kellerman, he always resisted the temptation to kiss her and to go farther than that, but he did agree to the plan for an escape and marriage. In July 1941, however, Grabowski's husband unexpectedly returned on leave and discovered the relationship. The court martial in Greifswald sentenced Kellerman to only two months in prison, but Frau Grabowski received one and a half years of penitentiary, a harsh sentence. The fact that she had actively encouraged and prepared an escape of a POW and that she had been unfaithful to her officer husband served as aggravating factors.[64]

One of the most involved and intimate relationships between a POW and a German woman, with a love-inspired escape, involved Edmond Bouvier (twenty-seven) and Gisela Behrle (twenty-three) in Stuttgart.[65] They met in 1941 while working in a factory, she as a typist, and he as a mechanic. They began talking and discovered a strong affinity for each other. They decided to get married. In November 1941, Gisela Behrle resigned from her position for unknown reasons, but the couple managed to stay in touch. In February 1942 she proposed that he escape and try to pass as a civilian worker, which would then allow them to get married legally. Behrle smuggled civilian clothes to him to facilitate the escape. One day in March 1942, he took off his uniform, put on the civilian clothes, and climbed over the fence of the factory. He joined Gisela in her parents' apartment, and she hid him in her room. His efforts to get papers as a civilian worker failed, however, and he remained hidden for a long time. The mother at some point learned about the relationship and protected it. Whenever Gisela heard somebody come toward her room, she locked Bouvier in a cabinet. He spent the days in her room and slept in her bed with her at night. On March 9, 1943, an anonymous denunciation letter arrived at the local police station stating that Gisela Behrle

[64] Feldurteil, Stettin, October 17, 1941, in PAAA, R 40894.
[65] Delattre to Gericht der Division 155, August 30, 1943; "Rapport sur la Défense des Prisonniers devant le tribunal militaire allemand," November 26, 1943; Delattre to Chef de la Délégation, September 6, 1943 and January 27, 1944; all in AN, F9, 2743, dossier "Stalag V-A." Feldurteil, Ludwigsburg, May 18, 1943, in AN, F9, 2487 (dossier 8280). The case is summarized in Delattre, Ma Guerre sans fusil, 136–40.

was hiding a French prisoner in her room. This led to their arrest after almost exactly one year of hiding.

French POW attorney Stéphane Delattre felt a special concern for this couple. He eloquently defended Bouvier during his trial, but the court martial of Ludwigsburg sentenced him to three years and three months in prison on May 18, 1943. The judges recognized Bouvier's noble motives but counted the long duration and great intensity of the forbidden relationship as aggravating factors. Delattre made heartfelt efforts on his behalf. In a five-page clemency plea spiced with allusions to characters and quotations from Goethe's works, he pointed out that Bouvier could have fled from Germany but decided to stay, wanting to continue working as a civilian laborer, and that the ultimate motivation for his "disobedience" was his overwhelming love for Gisela and his desire to marry her. Delattre stressed that Gisela was infertile as a result of a previous surgery and that therefore the relationship did not risk to produce potentially undesirable offspring and could not detract from the alleged duty of a German woman to produce children for the Reich. Delattre highlighted Bouvier's pure intentions and the risks he took in hiding: as Bouvier had written him, he had often been very hungry but had told Gisela that he needed no more food so as not to expose her to a greater risk of discovery. Bouvier had also remained in the room during bombing raids when everybody else had taken refuge in the basement (the files suggest that Gisela's family lived across the river from the Daimler-Benz factory, which was the target of many air raids[66]). Bouvier even expressed the desire to receive a death sentence if Gisela was sentenced to death because he would then feel as if he was her murderer. Delattre admitted that the couple had broken the law, but he appealed to a higher law that was evident in their heart. He argued that the "healthy feeling of the Volk" would certainly understand this deep love and forgive the "perpetrators," allowing them to do what they so ardently desired – to marry.

Delattre's rhetoric, which used sophisticated references to Goethe's works to underline the purity and intensity of their mutual love, impressed the highest judicial officer (*Gerichtsherr*) in the district, who supported the clemency plea. But the High Command rejected it. Delattre was convinced that the harsh circumstances in the German military prison Graudenz, where Bouvier was sent, would amount to a death sentence for such a sensitive human being and therefore fought unusually

---

[66] Elmar Blessing, *Die Kriegsgefangenen in Stuttgart: Das städtische Kriegsgefangenenlager in der Ulmer Straße und die "Katastrophe von Gaisburg,"* 2nd ed. (Stuttgart: Verlag im Ziegelhaus Ulrich Gohl, 2001).

hard on his behalf. He even involved Scapini in the case, but Scapini also could not help. Repeated clemency pleas by Delattre remained ineffective. Luckily, Delattre's fears were not confirmed. Bouvier survived his stay in Graudenz in good health, as a French medical examination after his repatriation on May 11, 1945, confirmed.[67]

Gender Dynamics

Whether the forbidden relationship involved primarily erotic desire or a deep commitment, one characteristic of many cases is the active and often very assertive role of the woman.[68] Many women, as the court documents reveal, defended their right to sexual satisfaction in ways that challenge contemporary notions of the woman as the more passive and "receiving" partner. Some women also defended their freedom to choose their male partner and to define the extent of their relationship, without state interference. This calls forth questions on the gender dynamics in the forbidden relations.

The relationship between a foreign male prisoner and a free local woman is not quite the same as the male–female relationship in the home society of both, and it is not comparable to the gender dynamics between a free soldier and a civilian woman, for example in the context of the American army presence in France in 1944–5.[69] As Birthe Kundrus argues, "For most nations during the Second World War, the victorious power's sexual 'occupation' of the 'body' of another nation symbolized both the military defeat of the enemy nation and the humiliation of its male population."[70] Yet, the situation of a POW is peculiar. He is a disarmed and, in a sense, a defeated soldier. In his host society, he is more or less stigmatized as an enemy and foreigner. By definition, being a POW means limited mobility, although we have seen that these limits became wider over the course of the war in Nazi Germany, especially for French and Belgian POWs. Moreover, the POW is still a mobilized soldier and therefore owes obedience to his superiors, be they officers from his own army or personnel from the detaining army. This duty to obey also applies to the prisoner's relationship with anybody who legally takes the position of the guard, for example a work supervisor, potentially a farmer. Should the farmer be absent, for example after being drafted into the army, the prisoner is strictly speaking obliged to obey the farmer's wife. The woman,

---

[67] Personnel file, SHD Caen, 22 P 244, 492; 22 P 244, 521; 22 P 709, 758; 22 P 259, 109.
[68] As noted in Arnaud, "Die deutsch-französischen Liebesbeziehungen," 189–90, and Usborne, "Female Sexual Desire and Male Honor," 486.
[69] Roberts, *What Soldiers Do*, 85, 110.   [70] Kundrus, "Forbidden Company," 204.

by contrast, is at home. She faces no legal restrictions on her mobility and is bound only to the law of her country, although that could of course be constraining, as it was in Nazi Germany. While the prisoner is marked as a POW, usually by wearing his army uniform with the insignia "KG" (for *Kriegsgefangener*, prisoner of war), the woman carries no such marking. In a factory, she speaks the language of the management. Do the relationships between POWs and German women therefore reveal a role reversal? Nazi authorities, including SS chief Heinrich Himmler, worried greatly about the apparent decline of morals in German wartime society, especially among women. The high number of these illicit relationships helped to conjure up anxiety about a crisis of gender norms, maybe a sexual revolution. Did the forbidden relations justify this fear?[71]

The judicial files suggest a more nuanced answer, especially in cases where one can access both the prisoner's and the woman's court proceedings. I would argue that every couple negotiated gender roles in its own ways, depending on the context, and that a comprehensive characterization is therefore difficult. It is important to note that the western POW and the German woman both had something to offer, including material goods and services (which often started the relationship). Moreover, both ran great risks and suffered potentially harsh consequences. Either the man or the woman might start the relationship. As many examples show, it was not unusual for the woman to be older than the prisoner. Generally, the love relations between POWs and German women tended to show a more egalitarian gender dynamic than was normal in German peacetime society or in the society of the prisoners. This undoubtedly represented a change, but characterizing it as a reversal of gender roles would seem to go too far.

It is tempting to see the POW in a weaker position, but it is important to keep in mind that the (western) prisoner was not without rights.[72] Unlike a forced laborer or POW from Eastern Europe, he could lodge a complaint against his supervisor and request a transfer to a different workplace. Article 42 of the Geneva Convention granted every prisoner the right to vent grievances through the man of confidence responsible for his work detachment, and this protected the prisoner from potential abuses. On farms, the POW's threat to request a transfer was serious given the labor shortage in agriculture. There were a few cases in which the accused woman claimed that the prisoner used the threat of requesting a transfer to a different work location as blackmail to obtain sexual favors, although the POW usually denied this. Some women argued that

[71] Schneider, *Verbotener Umgang*, 219.
[72] Spoerer, "Die soziale Differenzierung," 502–9.

they had tolerated the sexual advances of the prisoner because they had been afraid of losing a good worker.[73] These defenses may be suspicious given that an accused woman had an interest in defending herself by blaming the prisoner, but they do reveal the power a prisoner could have especially on a farm during a period of acute labor shortages.

An additional source of power for the POW were the goods from his aid parcels. In the context of increasing shortages in Nazi Germany, the items from the Red Cross parcels that western POWs received were a major asset, especially the high-quality goods not necessary for nutrition such as the chocolate, coffee, soap, and the decent cigarettes. There were few love relations between British POWs and German women, for example, that did not involve at some point the gift of chocolate or soap from the POW aid parcels. On the other hand, the woman also had resources that could be difficult for the prisoner to secure. She could offer the prisoner additional food and homebaked goods, which were much appreciated but pointed to traditional gender roles. The woman could offer the prisoner some services, too, but most of them were also grounded in traditional female gender roles, such as mending a prisoner's clothes or washing his laundry. This applies also to sex in a venal sense if the prisoner expected sexual favors as a payment for his goods. Traditional gender roles also applied to some of the services POWs performed for women, such as splitting wood or repairing doors and windows. In order to get such tasks done, women who were in charge of their households could request a prisoner since the proverbial *Mann im Hause* (man in the house) was absent.

One factor that prisoners and women had in common was that they both faced severe punishment. The prisoner, however, could expect that his punishment would not carry a social stigma after the war. Sentences for having committed "disobedience" might even be regarded as a form of heroism, and they would likely expire at the end of the war even if the prisoner had not served all of his time. The worst long-term legal consequence a married POW might have to expect would be a divorce suit from his wife. For the women, the social stigma of having gone to prison and, worse, the penitentiary, which also meant a loss of civil rights, was likely harder to bear. Losing her civil rights meant that a woman had almost no power if the husband sued for divorce, and it meant that she

---

[73] This transpired, for example, in the case of Roger Touche: Feldurteil, Baden-Baden, September 20, 1941, in PAAA, R 40883. See also BStA Nürnberg, Akten der Anklagebehörde beim Sondergericht, 1528. In this case, the farm woman claimed that the French POW had pressed her into sexual intercourse in the cow barn because he said he would work harder if they had sex. The special court in Nürnberg dismissed her excuse and sentenced her to two years of penal servitude in June 1942.

was excluded from a broad range of benefits and rights, such as a widow's pension if her husband died in the war.[74]

Granted, the court files do suggest that women did often play an active role in courtship and that many women were not ashamed to admit their attraction to a prisoner and to insist on their right to sexual satisfaction. But can we take the statements the women made to police interrogators at face value even though the women signed them at the end, confirming their accuracy? Considering that these statements came during a long and upsetting interrogation, with officers sometimes using threats and asking suggestive questions, we have to be careful with the precise wording of the confessions. In her article on women on trial in Munich, Cornelie Usborne admits that some investigators may have coaxed certain statements out of women and described them in their own words. Yet, she points out that one can usually find confirmation for the dynamics of the relationships in other, less controlled documents and in the particular features of the case.[75]

Lotte Birkl, for example, was a worker from Nürnberg who, according to the interrogation protocol signed by her, testified about her French partner: "Mourand is a handsome, dark blonde Frenchman, and I found him attractive. This is why I started smiling at him."[76] Margarethe Huber, on trial for a long relationship with a French POW also in Nürnberg, confessed: "he is a handsome man, and I liked to see him."[77] Another woman on trial in Nürnberg stated: "I engaged in sexual intercourse with the Frenchman Pollard because I am very hot-blooded and because I have not received sexual satisfaction for sixteen months."[78] Do these statements reflect the feelings of the accused women or the phantasies of the male police interrogator? Or perhaps both? One can certainly imagine that the interrogators put these statements into the mouths of the women. Yet, the dynamics of the relationships in all three cases show that the woman was quite active in initiating and pursuing the relationship.

In some cases, one can find independent confirmation of such statements, as Usborne points out. Elisabeth Amberger (thirty-seven), for

---

[74] Boll, "… das gesunde Volksempfinden," 672.

[75] Usborne, "Female Sexual Desire and Male Honor," 478.

[76] "Mourand ist ein schöner dunkelblonder Franzos und er gefiel mir, weshalb ich ihn zuerst angelacht habe." BStA Nürnberg, Akten der Anklagebehörde beim Sondergericht, 1744.

[77] BStA Nürnberg, Akten der Anklagebehörde beim Sondergericht, 1802.

[78] "Ich habe mich deshalb mit dem Franzosen Pollard auf einen Geschlechtsverkehr eingelassen, weil ich sehr vollblütig bin und bereits seit 16 Monaten keine geschlechtliche Befriedigung mehr fand." BStA Nürnberg, Akten der Anklagebehörde beim Sondergericht, 2046.

example, was a married worker in Darmstadt who had two relationships with French prisoners (one of them a transformed POW) in 1943–4. When asked to explain her behavior in court, she admitted that she had a happy marriage but a strong sex drive and that the first prisoner was "a beautiful man." Interestingly, her husband, a forty-nine-year-old hair stylist drafted into the Wehrmacht in 1943, indirectly confirmed her statements in a letter to the court, written without the intimidating context of a police interrogation and without knowing what she had said. He explained that he had been mentally ill and confined to bed for many years, and he felt grateful for his wife's committed care and support during that period. He was aware of her sexual frustration and admitted that he had sometimes been unable to satisfy her sexually because of problems with his nerves, and he forgave her infidelity.[79]

But the image of German women with unashamed sensuality chasing POWs, as portrayed by Francis Ambrière in *Les grandes Vacances*, cannot be generalized, even though many POWs used it in their defense. Gender roles could be mixed and contested in one and the same encounter. The French POW Henri Lombard, for example, claimed that the soldier's wife Marie Berger in a village near Darmstadt had started the forbidden contact: she had allegedly noticed that his cardigan had a hole and offered to fix it. Yet, Berger herself denied that she had offered her help and claimed instead that he had started the contact by asking her to fix his cardigan. Regardless, the way in which the relationship started was tied to traditional gender roles.[80]

When it came to sexual relations, it appears that the prisoner usually took the active role. Women on trial often stated that he had taken the first step and that they had to some degree resisted at first. Some women claimed to have been raped, at least the first time the sexual encounter occurred. It is difficult in each individual case to evaluate the claims and counterclaims based mostly on documents produced in the context of a trial, where the stakes were high. Clearly, it was in the interest of the accused woman to blame the prisoner, just as it was in the prisoner's interest to portray the woman as pursuer and temptress. It also has to be considered that the prevalent notions of the time expected the man to play the active role in initiating a sexual relationship and that the bar for a

[79] The special court in Darmstadt sentenced her to one and a half years of penal servitude for the first affair (it ignored the second affair because she claimed not to have known that contacts with a transformed POW were forbidden). Urteil, Sondergericht Darmstadt, May 23, 1944, in HStAD Fonds G 24, Nr. 955/2.
[80] HStAD, G 27 Darmstadt 1438.

woman to prove rape was high.[81] The special courts in most cases dismissed a woman's claim of having been raped by pointing out that she did not call for help or run away even though this would have been possible and by highlighting that she had repeated the sexual contact after the first occurrence rather than reporting the alleged rape or at least keeping more distance from the prisoner. In some cases, the fact that the woman had followed the prisoner to a hiding place or that sexual intercourse had occurred in a position that required significant cooperation from the woman, for example while standing, also indicated to the judges that the sexual advances of the prisoner were not unwelcome. But in certain environments, women could have a hard time resisting the advances of a prisoner. This applies in particular to farms, where a maid, for example, would often work alone with the prisoner. Some teasing, rough-housing, kissing, and touching could occur, and if a prisoner wanted to go farther, it could be difficult for a woman to say no given that she had already compromised (and inculpated) herself by cooperating in the more harmless forms of contact. There were a few clear-cut cases of sexual assault and rape, but the prisoners found guilty were sentenced under the German law code (*Reichstrafgesetzbuch*, §176) in addition to §92 of the military law code (disobedience). These cases were very rare, however. Historian Patrice Arnaud reaches the same conclusion based on a sample of cases involving French POWs and forced laborers, although he points out that the fantasy of rape often dominates French postwar accounts, providing the defeated and disarmed soldier with a "redemptive" victory over the enemy.[82]

An example for the ambiguity of some cases is the court martial against French POW Maurice Cordier, who was accused of having attempted to rape a sixteen-year-old girl who was performing her service year on the farm north of Munich where he worked milking the cows. The girl claimed that another woman, a forty-one-year-old divorced milkmaid, had dragged her onto the hay while she was feeding the chickens, so that the prisoner could touch her genitals and rape her. Cordier denied the accusation and only admitted having kissed the girl with her consent. During the prisoner's hearing, both women suddenly refused to testify, and the court martial therefore dropped the charge of attempted rape and sentenced him to nine months in prison on the basis of his own admission of a kiss.[83] Was the accusation a means by which the

[81] Regina Mühlhäuser, "Reframing Sexual Violence as a Weapon and Strategy of War: The Case of the German Wehrmacht during the War and Genocide in the Soviet Union, 1941–1944," *Journal of the History of Sexuality* 26, no. 3 (2017), 387.
[82] Arnaud, "Die deutsch-französischen Liebesbeziehungen," 187–8.
[83] Feldurteil, München, December 30, 1941, in PAAA, R 40905.

sixteen-year-old girl wanted to get rid of a POW who may have been harassing her? Or did she try to save herself after the older woman had perhaps seen her kissing the POW, trying to discredit the witness by accusing her of cooperation in a rape?

In one of the few cases where a court martial did sentence a POW according to §176, the German Foreign Office challenged the judgment because it found the evidence inconclusive. It concerned Julien Le Quellec, a twenty-nine-year-old butcher from Paris who was married and had one child. Le Quellec was assigned to a farm belonging to an older couple in Weissenbach (Northern Hessen). The daughter of the farmers, the married Helene Sterz, occasionally helped out on her parents' farm. Sterz had four children, and her husband worked in a quarry nearby. On July 12, 1941, her parents wanted to work on a remote field that belonged to their farm. Because they had to finish some chores near the house, they asked her and Le Quellec to walk ahead. Suddenly, Frau Sterz noticed a piece of wood in her sandal. She asked Le Quellec to continue walking while she took out the piece of wood. Le Quellec, who understood very little German, sat down in the grass next to her and rolled himself a cigarette. According to her testimony, he then suddenly grabbed her, pushed her back, and lay down on top of her, making movements reminiscent of sexual intercourse. In this moment, another farmer came by on his horse cart and noticed them. Le Quellec and Frau Sterz rose to their feet and continued walking to the field as if nothing had happened. When her parents joined them, she told her mother about the incident. The mother asked her not to tell the father because he had just suffered a mild stroke. Later, Frau Sterz told her niece about the incident, and her niece recommended that she mention it to her husband, so that he would report it. Frau Sterz refrained from telling her husband, however, because he was irascible and she feared that he might kill the prisoner. Her husband had suffered much as a POW in France during World War I, and he had bad memories of French soldiers from the 1940 campaign. What led to the arrest of the prisoner therefore was not a denunciation by Frau Sterz but the fact that the farmer who had witnessed the incident told his brother about it. The brother happened to be the local Nazi farm leader (*Bauernführer*), and he reported the prisoner.

During interrogation, Le Quellec denied all the allegations. He pointed out, in particular, that Frau Sterz had brought him food after his arrest and that she would hardly have done so if she really felt he had sexually assaulted her. But the testimonies of Frau Sterz and the witness convinced the court martial that he was guilty. An investigation of her health history revealed that she was suffering from attacks of nervousness and that she became paralyzed in moments of fear. That is how the court martial explained that she had not called for help and that she had not immediately asked the witness to intervene and take the prisoner to the police. The court martial in Kassel therefore saw the case as an attempted rape and sentenced Le Quellec to three years of penal servitude.[84] The German Foreign Office objected, however. Its legal expert Alfred Lautz argued that the assault had certainly not been planned and that it was not proven that the POW had really wanted to rape the woman, especially because the incident took place in an open location on a road, where the appearance of witnesses had to be expected. Lautz therefore suggested that the sentence be commuted into a prison sentence for violation of the order prohibiting closer contact with German women. After having seen thousands of judgments against POWs, he noted: "If one considers the flood of court martial cases based on sexual relations between prisoners of war and German women, it is apparent that violence matters only in a tiny fraction of cases."[85]

It is unclear what to make of this case. Frau Sterz revealed in court that they had been walking through a forest before they sat down in the grass, and that she had told Le Quellec that she would briefly go back to the forest to relieve herself and then catch up with him. In this sense, Lautz was right: if Le Quellec had really wanted to rape her, he would likely have done so while they were in the forest, or he would have followed her when she announced her intention to go back. Yet, the witness confirmed Frau Sterz's statement that the prisoner had placed himself on top of her and made movements reminiscent of sexual intercourse. Had Le Quellec misunderstood her? This was possible, perhaps likely, in light of his poor German. But why did he (or his attorney) not claim this in court? Le Quellec was killed during a bombing attack in his regular POW camp in September 1944, shortly after his dismissal from the penitentiary.[86]

In another case, the French POW Charles Pelletier, working on a farm near Würzburg (Bavaria), had allegedly been harassing the farmer's wife for a while. She had told her husband about it, but she claimed that the fear of losing a good worker had induced them to remain quiet. Yet, the prisoner's work performance deteriorated. According to the woman, he one day tried to rape her, but she defended herself effectively. The farmers denounced him after this incident. Pelletier received two years of penal servitude for attempted rape. He denied the allegations, but the

---

[84] Feldurteil, Kassel, September 19, 1941, in PAAA, R 40884.
[85] Lautz to OKW, October 17, 1941, in PAAA, R 40884.
[86] Personnel record, Julien Le G., SHD Caen.

court martial believed her testimony.[87] The farmers appear to have tolerated a certain degree of harassment as long as the POW worked well. But was the incident that led to the denunciation a case where the POW went farther than before, or had his declining work performance lowered the farmers' tolerance level, so that they did not care any more about losing him?

The one situation in which a reversal of gender roles could occur was when a woman hid an escaped prisoner, as demonstrated in the case of Edmond Bouvier and Gisela Behrle and Edward Hunter and Gertrud Schulze. Another typical case occurred in Jena in 1941. The French POW Marcel Aribaud was working in a small work detachment near the train station and befriended a woman who drove a truck and often passed by the train station. He gave her chocolate, and she gave him some extra bread in exchange. Her name was Anna Scholz. She was a widow with two children. They arranged for secret meetings in a tunnel under the railway, and they had sex. Later, Anna Scholz picked him up during some evenings and drove him in her truck to a cemetery, where they felt safer. They decided to get married after the war. On September 28, 1941, he escaped and went to her apartment. She agreed to hide him and provided for him. After three weeks, he was discovered. The court martial in Kassel sentenced him to three years of prison on January 22, 1942, and the special court in Weimar gave her three and a half years of penal servitude. Her punishment was higher because she had assisted him in his escape.[88]

On the surface, this relationship looks like a strong case in support of gender reversal. She drove him around in her truck and she was the prisoner's only contact to the outside world after his escape. He was entirely at her mercy, and she provided for him while he was watching her children. But when they had sex, did they also reverse traditional gender roles, which assigned the active part to the man and favored his satisfaction rather than hers? The trial documents are silent on this question because both immediately admitted consensual sex, and the judges therefore saw no need to probe into details. Like many of these couples, they planned to get married after the war. We cannot know for sure, but it seems unlikely that the role reversal would have continued under "normal" circumstances. It seems to have been a result of the specific situation where the woman had the power to hide the prisoner for a while.

---

[87] Feldurteil, Würzburg, October 22, 1941, in PAAA, R 40895.
[88] Feldurteil, Kassel, January 22, 1942, in PAAA, R 40909.

4   Discovery

The Process of Discovery

Many court records, especially those regarding the prisoners, do not disclose what led to the discovery of the forbidden relation. Even if there is information, it is not always clear how to classify it because several factors might be at play. For example, a guard might notice one night that a prisoner is missing and later find the prisoner coming out of the apartment of a certain woman and arrest him. But the fact that the guard knew where to look for the prisoner may be the result of earlier rumors, perhaps even a denunciation by a civilian that did not trigger an investigation. Denunciations, moreover, could occur for a variety of reasons that sometimes had little or nothing to do with the illegality of the relationship. For example, a neighbor might call the police because the single woman living in the apartment next door was noisy at night, and when the police arrived, they found two POWs and two women having a party. Similarly, a woman may be pregnant without being able to name the father of the child. The police may investigate and discover the forbidden relationship by following up local rumors about who could be the father. A guard finding an anonymous love letter during a routine search of the prisoner quarters could also trigger discovery. Given existing rumors, it often took little for the police to figure out the suspects.

Discovery often benefited from a cloud of rumors in villages and in factories. Sooner or later, these rumors would reach the police or a guard. A formal denunciation might not be necessary. Police officers, especially in small villages, were often aware of *Stammtisch* gossip. Historian Ela Hornung speaks in this context of "denunciatory chains."[1] Talkative neighbors might mention in a pub that a certain woman was

---

[1] Ela Hornung, "Denunziation als soziale Praxis. Eine Fallgeschichte aus der NS-Militärjustiz," in *Wehrmachtsjustiz. Kontext, Praxis, Nachwirkungen,* ed. Peter Pirker and Florian Wenninger (Wien: Braumüller, 2011), 203. See also Prieler-Woldan, *Das Selbstverständliche tun,* 83.

suspiciously close to the prisoner working on her farm. A male farm-worker, jealous that the milkmaid preferred the prisoner to him, may start a rumor, too.[2] Sometimes, fellow prisoners or foreign laborers contributed to this "denunciatory chain," perhaps to "get back" at the woman employing them or to humiliate a POW perceived as privileged.

Clearly, the Nazi regime put much effort into convincing Germans that affairs with men stigmatized as implacable enemies amounted to treason and called for denunciation and prosecution. Do the denunciations then vindicate the Nazi ideal of the "healthy feeling of the Volk?" Or do they suggest that denouncers acted more out of a sense of propriety or for entirely private reasons? We need to analyze the types of discovery. Who discovered and who denounced, and why? Discovery, in particular if it resulted from denunciations, provides a glimpse into the social fabric of wartime German factories and farm communities.

The Guards

Many forbidden relationships, perhaps most, were discovered by the guards. This was their duty. Guidelines distributed by the High Command repeatedly admonished guards not to tolerate any contact between prisoners and civilians that was not strictly necessary for work. In case of rumors, the guard had to investigate and to notify the commander of the work detachment or the camp under whose administration the POW worked. It was strictly forbidden to grant civilians access to the camps and sleeping quarters of POWs. Guards themselves had to keep their distance from POWs.[3] Discoveries by the guards therefore differed from willful denunciations by civilians. Yet, it is important to note that the behavior of the guards varied widely. While some did follow the rules closely, others warned the prisoner and often also the woman, sometimes repeatedly, instead of reporting them right away, as would have been their duty. Frequently, guards reported a forbidden relationship only after finding incontrovertible evidence or after feeling pressured to step in, for example if a forbidden relationship had become widely noted. Out of a spirit of camaraderie and humanity, some guards and even some camp commanders tolerated POW romances with German women.[4] Some guards were downright complicit by transporting letters or gifts

---

[2] For a typical case of denunciation by a jealous co-worker, see Feldurteil against Joseph L., Linz, November 28, 1941, in PAAA, R 40912.

[3] "Merkblatt für Führer von Arbeitskommandos," Nürnberg, August 1, 1941, in AN, F9, 3644.

[4] d'Hoop, "Les prisonniers français et la communauté rurale allemande," 46; Horn, "History from the Inside", 276.

between the lovers, ignoring the absence of a prisoner from his bed at night, and making possible illegal encounters. The German guard battalions were composed of men considered unfit for frontline service because of age or a physical handicap. Their training was brief and superficial, and their superiors often complained about their lack of discipline and lack of marksmanship (the guards had orders to shoot if a POW ran away). In my work on the guards in charge of French colonial prisoners in German-occupied France, I found that the guards were most tolerant in places where they were left to their own devices with the prisoners, without close supervision from officers. In the eyes of some prisoners, the guards were "good old papas." The same holds true for the guards in charge of prisoners in work detachments in Germany itself.[5]

American POW Jack Dower, who was man of confidence in a small work detachment in eastern Pomerania in 1944, described these guards in his memoirs. His work detachment (twenty prisoners) had three guards altogether (one each for several months), and all were laid-back and friendly. The nicest was the second guard:

This was a kindly white-haired man of about sixty-five who had been a librarian. There was absolutely no malice in him, and he was almost apologetic when he aroused us in the mornings. He was soon dubbed "Uncle Ben." The *Wehrmacht* was scraping the bottom of the manpower barrel for sure. ... He was a real gentleman, polite almost to the point of being courtly, and with just a trace of the schoolmaster about him. He was sincerely sorry for us, frequently inquired about our parents, and hoped that the war would soon be over so we could return to our kinfolk. This was the last thing we had expected, an idealistic pacifist in *Wehrmacht* gray.

Dower claims that the POWs had secretly taken out the firing pin of this gun when "Uncle Ben" arrived, but it is unlikely that he would ever have fired a shot while guarding the work detachment. "Uncle Ben" even once let Dower watch his rifle while he went to search some forgotten papers on a bicycle – a completely illegal act. One can easily imagine this kind of guard also feeling sympathy for a POW's amorous adventures, although Dower's work detachment, at least according to his account, never tested "Uncle Ben's" tolerance in this matter.[6] As Dower observed, it was standard practice of the Wehrmacht to change guards periodically, so that they would not get too close to the prisoners, but this did not help much.

---

[5] Scheck, *French Colonial Soldiers*, 91–102.
[6] Dower, *Deliverance at Diepholz*, 98, 123. For similar evidence of kind guards, especially after 1942, see d'Hoop, "Prisonniers de guerre français témoins de la défaite allemande," 80, 87.

Guards in many places marched the prisoners from their sleeping quarters to their work sites, be it a farm, a construction site, or a shop. Once the POW arrived, however, he was often only under the watch of his employer, while the guard moved on. In October 1941, the German High Command issued new guidelines that relaxed the rules for French prisoners. They could now be placed alone on individual farms or businesses if a German man was willing to act as an auxiliary or substitute guard, which meant that this man would be responsible for alerting the nearest command post if a prisoner had done something illegal or escaped. As a consequence of this arrangement, many French prisoners did not encounter a uniformed guard for days, weeks, or even months. Housing POWs on the farm or the business where they worked saved commuting time and guard personnel, but it multiplied opportunities for forbidden relations. In factories, POWs would normally sleep in a separate building with a guard, and they might occasionally see one in the factory, but they would be on their own for most of the day, and the foreman on the shop floor would be responsible for ensuring that they behaved according to their orders. The new guidelines even allowed French POWs to march to their place of work and back without guarding if they did not live on the factory grounds. By 1943, the German High Command officially extended these guidelines to Belgian and Serbian prisoners, although in practice this had already happened on a large scale much earlier, especially with respect to the Belgians, who were often mixed with French prisoners.[7] Guards remained in charge of the large camps, which were off limits to civilians, and they supervised the sleeping quarters of the work detachments, usually with an occupancy ranging from ten to 150 POWs. POWs traveling to a doctor or a different work detachment would likely be accompanied by a guard, although even that should no longer be taken for granted for French and Belgian prisoners after 1943. The lighter guarding became more common for British POWs only in 1943, although their contacts with civilians remained more restricted than the contacts of French and Belgian POWs. The lighter guarding meant that guards often had to be tipped off by rumors or by denunciations. Pervasive rumors or a recent rise in POW escapes could put pressure on the guards to act. Yet, the degree to which guards went out of their way to track down the prisoner and the woman varies considerably, as some examples will show.

---

[7] "Handbuch für Arbeitskommandoführer WK XIII," 1943, in AN, F9, 3644; OKW, "Auflockerung der Bewachung kriegsgefangener Franzosen," 3.10.1941, in NLA Oldenburg, Best. 135 B.

The French POW Charles Barbier worked on a farm in the mountains of southern Austria. The daughter of his farmer repeatedly teased him by undressing in front of him. In March 1941, they had sex for the first time, and they did it again multiple times. One day in May, the guard surprised them in the forest *in actu*.[8] As in many other cases, the guard must have heard rumors about the forbidden relationship. He needed to have a specific suspicion about the secret meetings in the forest to follow the prisoner, perhaps because the encounters had been observed before and become part of village gossip. Many guards were local men, and they were attuned to the local rumor mill. A similar case involved British POW James Ames, a career soldier, who had begun an intimate relation with Marta Sokolski in the village Klein-Sanskau in West Prussia during the summer of 1943. Sokolski was the wife of a soldier who had gone missing at Stalingrad. She had two children and belonged to the German people's list, category III. She had met Ames because she was washing the laundry for the prisoners. Ames frequently slipped out of his sleeping quarters and visited her for the night, returning before dawn. In the night of April 11–12, 1944, the guard noticed that three POWs were not in their beds. Two of them returned soon, but Ames remained missing. The guard, however, went straight to the place where Frau Sokolski lived and waited outside. When Ames appeared, he ordered him to stop. Ames ran away, and the guard opened fire, but missed him. Ames then stopped and raised his hands. The guard was acting according to his orders, but it is remarkable that the relationship went on for many months before he decided to check the beds of the prisoners at night and that he knew immediately where to look for Ames.[9]

Sometimes the prisoner triggered his own discovery because he was missing from work. In a factory in Düsseldorf, for example, French POW Jean Renaud noticed an unused shed in the courtyard. He transported carpets and fine wood shavings into the shed and transformed it into a cozy hiding place for his encounters with the married factory worker Helene Schiller, who brought beer and food to the rendezvous. Meanwhile, another Franco-German couple, Georges Bergeron and Emilie

[8] Feldurteil, Wolfsberg, August 26, 1941, in AN, F9, 2361. The prisoner got away with a very light punishment (one year in prison) at a time when the court martial sentences were still inconsistent, and the fact that the woman had teased and seduced him counted as an extenuating circumstance.
[9] Feldurteil, Danzig, September 28, 1944, and attorney Klawitter to Swiss Legation, October 16, 1944, both in BAR Bern, Bestand Vertretung Berlin, 78a. The special court in Graudenz sentenced the woman to two and a half years of penal servitude, while the court martial of Danzig sentenced Ames to three years of penal servitude on April 28, 1944.

Schröder, stood watch outside. Then the couples switched roles. The secret encounters took place repeatedly during work throughout September 1941, but one day a guard noted that Renaud was not at his workplace after break and started looking for him. Bergeron realized that the guard was trying to find Renaud and warned him. Renaud remained in hiding but was stopped when he was leaving the factory. Interrogations soon revealed that he and Frau Schiller had used the hideout almost daily to have sex. Bergeron and Schröder steadfastly denied having done more than hugging, but the judges did not believe them. The court martial in Krefeld sentenced Renaud to four years and Bergeron to three years in prison.[10]

A very large number of relationships were discovered because the guards found suspicious items during a search of the prisoner's quarters and possessions. Such searches were required periodically. They might reveal a love letter, a curl saved in an envelope, a photo, or another item that suggested a forbidden relationship, such as civilian clothes, which the POW sometimes obtained from a woman so that he could more freely visit her or disguise himself during an escape.

The bookbinder Lotte Birkl (twenty) and French POW Albert Mourand, both working at the cable and metal works Neumayer in Nürnberg, fell in love with each other. Fearing discovery, they mostly wrote each other letters. Once they met in secret under a stairwell in a seldom-used section of the factory and had sex. It was not the meeting that led to discovery, however. During a routine search, a guard found Birkl's letters in the prisoner's sleeping quarters. Birkl explained to the notorious Nazi judge Oswald Rothaug, the chairman of the special court in Nürnberg, that she loved the prisoner and wanted to marry him, but Rothaug had no pity and on October 12, 1942, sentenced her to two and a half years of penal servitude and three years' loss of her civil rights.[11]

When the husband of Elisabeth Allermeyer, a soldier, left his home in Itzehoe (Schleswig-Holstein) in early 1941, he suggested that she stay with his parents in Bavaria during his absence. In April 1941, she traveled to Bavaria with her child. After a while, she befriended Louis de Ridder, a French POW working on a local farm. They bonded because both felt homesick (her in-laws had pressured her to stay longer than she wanted).

[10] Feldurteil, Krefeld, January 15, 1942, in PAAA, R 40908.
[11] BStA Nürnberg, Akten der Anklagebehörde beim Sondergericht, 1744. On the career of judge Rothaug, see Ewald Behrschmidt, "Der Saal 600," in *Justizpalast Nürnberg: ein Ort der Weltgeschichte wird 100 Jahre. Festschrift zum 100. Jahrestag der feierlichen Eröffnung des Justizpalastes in Nürnberg durch König Ludwig III. am 11. September 1916*, ed. Ewald Behrschmidt (Neustadt an der Aisch: VDS, Verlagsdruckerei Schmidt, 2016), 118; Lutz, "Das Sondergericht Nürnberg 1933–1945," 258.

In August, Allermeyer and de Ridder became intimate. Yet, Allermeyer was so conflicted that she decided to go home with her child a few days later. Nothing happened for an entire year, but on August 14, 1942, a guard searching the possessions of the prisoner found a letter she had written to de Ridder, a curl in a little envelope, and a condom. Although de Ridder claimed that he had randomly found these objects, it did not take the police long to track down Allermeyer. The special court in Kiel sentenced her to one and a half years in prison, a relatively mild sentence because she had ended the relationship.[12]

Sometimes, the guard needed to make no special effort to discover a forbidden relation because the woman betrayed herself through careless behavior. In the village Panthen east of Hamburg, Luise Hartmann, the woman who later complained to the judge about the lack of German men in her age group, had started an affair with French POW Félix Le Bon. When Le Bon was transferred to a different work detachment, she tried to visit him. On May 21, 1944, she stood outside the POW quarters at five in the morning and called his name. A woman in the neighborhood heard her, knocked on the door of the guard, and woke him up. In his pajamas, the guard grabbed Hartmann and locked her up in a storage den. While he got dressed, however, Hartmann climbed up to the ceiling and opened the roof by removing the tiles. She went home unrecognized. Despite warnings from family members, Hartmann continued to look for Le Bon until one day she was arrested. During her trial, it transpired that she had been warned by guards multiple times to stay away from the prisoners. In one camp, she was well known to the guards because she came almost every day and waved to Le Bon. Amazingly, the relationship was able to continue for a long time. Le Bon found ways to slip out of his sleeping quarters, and the guards ignored clear evidence that she was interested in this prisoner. It took remarkable persistence on her part to move the guards to step in.[13]

An act of kind-hearted carelessness betrayed the secretary Margot Schneider, who worked for a transport company in Berlin-Wilmersdorf. When the office building suffered some bomb damage, French POWs repaired the building. Schneider, who knew French, started an affair with Marcel Letellier, but the POWs were sent to Stettin a few weeks later. She wrote to Letellier and one day took the train to Stettin to bring him a jacket and twelve cigarettes. She could not see him but naively gave the jacket and cigarettes to a guard, telling him that Letellier had forgotten his jacket. Her careless action triggered the discovery, since even the gift of cigarettes was forbidden (except as a reward for extra work). Her visit prompted a search of the prisoner's belongings, which revealed the letters she had written him.[14]

As some of these cases reveal, guards sometimes showed remarkable indulgence or solidarity with the couples involved in forbidden relations.[15] In the case of Frau Thomsen and Belgian POW van den Broeck, described in the preceding chapter, at least two guards transported letters between the lovers and even made it possible for them to meet. In the case involving French POW Jacques Kellerman, who had a relationship with the wife of a Luftwaffe officer in Greifswald, the guard was also a direct accomplice. Kellerman befriended the guard who always accompanied him on his translating missions. When Kellerman started seeing the woman, the guard delivered their letters. One day, he and Kellerman met the woman and a friend in the street, and they all went into a wine shop and drank wine together.[16] Belgian POW Albert Roland also had a sympathetic guard. When the court martial in Danzig sentenced him to one and a half years in prison for having repeatedly visited a brothel with Polish prostitutes, he asked his legal advisor to challenge the sentence because he pointed out that his guard had always accompanied him to the brothel and patiently waited outside.[17] In a small work detachment near Dresden, the French POW Jean Largillier had a relationship with the soldier's wife Melanie Janner in 1942. During his trial, Largillier explained that his guard had encouraged him to begin the relationship, telling him that he himself also had an affair and that he would close both eyes. The court martial in Dresden sentenced Largillier to only one year in prison, but he was dragged in front of a court martial again when the woman committed suicide in pre-trial custody and when the guard, on trial himself, suddenly denied having encouraged the prisoner. The court martial in Graudenz sentenced Largillier to three years in prison despite evidence that the guard had been supportive.[18]

Many guards integrated the prisoners into their own social circle, including civilians. A telling example comes from the village Dörrenbach on the picturesque *Weinstraße* (Rhenish Palatinate). A woman in charge of a local winery, Frau Liesel Fasch, had asked the nearby French POW detachment to send her two POWs to perform some urgent work in her vineyard on Sunday, July 27, 1941. Work was completed shortly after

[14] BLHA Potsdam, 12 C, Sondergericht Berlin, 6819.
[15] See the case study "The Wife of a Jew" in Chapter 7.
[16] Feldurteil, Stettin, October 17, 1941, in PAAA, R 40894.
[17] R. to Silva, November 15, 1944, in CEGESOMA, AA 263 Stalag XX-A, Papiers B. Sylva.
[18] Feldurteil, Graudenz, October 15, 1942, in AN, F9, 2381.

noon, and Frau Fasch prepared lunch for the prisoners and served them wine. When the guard arrived, at 1:30, the meal was not yet finished, but Frau Fasch offered him some wine and food, too. The guard gratefully accepted, and Frau Fasch brought out more wine after the meal. Since the wine had made the prisoners tired, the guard agreed to go to other vineyards and pick up more prisoners, so that the two prisoners could take a nap. As he was walking through the streets, however, he encountered three women dancing and playing an accordion. The guard, who knew how to play the accordion himself, asked the three women if they would like to visit Frau Fasch and dance there. They accepted, and Frau Fasch welcomed the group, pushing her living room furniture aside to make room for dancing. When the two prisoners woke up, they asked the guard to bring them back to their camp. The guard, however, began dancing with Frau Fasch and invited the prisoners to join him. Merry dancing and drinking continued, and it was late at night when the guard finally brought the prisoners to their sleeping quarters. It is unclear how the event came to the attention of the authorities, but the festivities had obviously happened without any secrecy and involved a number of people in the village. The guard was sentenced to four months in prison, and Frau Fasch received the same sentence. Two of the women who had joined the party also received punishments. The prisoners were acquitted because the guard confirmed that he had encouraged them to stay and dance.[19]

On a farm near Graudenz, the British POWs William MacCoy and Leonhard Gilgen became close to the Polish woman who worked as a cook on the landed estate (relations to non-German women were punishable in this district). They wrote each other love notes and kissed her occasionally in the winter of 1942–3. The guard on the estate suspected something and once lay in wait when MacCoy and the woman were exchanging letters and their addresses. The guard tore up the letters and addresses and told them to wait for the end of the war before writing to each other. But he did not denounce them, as would have been his duty. The affairs were discovered because the contacts continued despite the warning.[20] The guard of British POW Royce Ratner was obliging enough to transport bottles of wine and letters that two women in Beuthen (Upper Silesia) sent to Ratner. In March 1943, the guard even allowed Ratner to see the women. The visit apparently did not lead to intimate contact, but the court martial in Kattowitz sentenced Ratner to

[19] Feldurteil, Mannheim, December 2, 1941, in PAAA, R 40897.
[20] Auswärtiges Amt an Schweizerische Gesandtschaft, Verbalnote, Berlin, January 7, 1944, BAR Bern, Bestand Vertretung Berlin, 86b.

eight months in prison despite the complicit guard. The two women received the same punishment.[21]

British POW Edward Cochran also benefited from a generous guard. He had become fond of the fourteen-year-old daughter of his employer, a farmer in the Vogtland, in southern Saxony. He told her that he found her attractive (she looked much older than fourteen), and he gave her ten chocolate bars. When Cochran was transferred to a different work site in April 1944, he asked his guard whether he could send letters and chocolate to the girl and allow her to use the guard's name and address for the replies. The guard agreed, and for several months, Cochran kept a lively correspondence with the girl. He gave the guard chocolate and margarine as a thank-you gift. It is unclear who discovered the relationship, but Cochran was sentenced to fourteen months in prison for the relationship and for bribing the guard, who was himself punished and stripped of his rank.[22] In a cheese factory in Marienburg (West Prussia), British POWs William Hick and Thomas Fellman also benefited from a generous guard who allowed them to go out late at night. They regularly spent part of the night with women in town throughout the summer of 1944. The prosecutor requested three years in prison, but the court martial of Danzig sentenced them only to two years on December 28, 1944, because the guard had facilitated the relationships by tolerating the nightly outings.[23]

A love story with a tragic outcome for the guard occurred in a little village in the southern Sudetenland, not far from the former Austrian border. In the summer of 1941, Belgian POW Victor Delvaux fell in love with eighteen-year-old Ida Nellinger, the niece of the farmwoman for whom he worked. They repeatedly went into the forest, kissed, and made love on top of his coat. The guard responsible for the Belgians in the area, Josef Schadenböck, heard rumors about the affair from villagers and felt increasing pressure to investigate. Perhaps in an effort to protect the couple, he did not try hard and assured the police that the rumors were groundless. When the Gestapo in the next town received an anonymous denunciation letter and began seriously investigating the couple, Schadenböck committed suicide because he expected a severe punishment for his negligence.[24]

[21] Feldurteil, Kattowitz, May 18, 1943, and attorney Hans Kirsch to Swiss Legation, May 19, 1943, both in BAR Bern, Bestand Vertretung Berlin, 87b.
[22] Feldurteil, Leipzig, November 10, 1944, in BAR Bern, Bestand Vertretung Berlin, 81b.
[23] Feldurteil, Danzig, December 28, 1944, and attorney Hoffmann to Swiss Legation, December 28, 1944, both BAR Bern, Bestand Vertretung Berlin, 81b.
[24] "Anklageverfügung," September 25, 1941, in PAAA, R 40853, and Feldurteil, Linz, October 31, 1941, in CEGESOMA, AA 244.

Examples of tolerant guard behavior caused alarm in the highest circles of Nazi Germany. In a circular from November 1943, for example, Hitler's influential secretary Martin Bormann alerted local officials that guards too often misunderstood their role by thinking of themselves as protectors and caretakers of the POWs. Bormann alleged that this led to the POWs having a better life than the German worker, which he considered intolerable at a time when the German people were fighting for their very existence. The circular admonished local officials to watch more carefully that civilians and guards maintained a distant attitude toward POWs.[25]

Random Denunciations

Denunciations were widespread in Nazi Germany, and it is therefore not surprising that many forbidden relations were discovered because of a denunciation. Denunciations came from random witnesses, family members, neighbors, and co-workers. Often an anonymous letter or phone call triggered an investigation. The motivations varied widely. Random denouncers did not need to have a political motivation, and it could be a specific behavior, not the forbidden relationship, that they denounced. Many forbidden encounters took place in wild areas, particularly in forests, fields, or high grass. This meant that any passerby could become a witness. Sometimes it was obvious that the secret reunion involved a POW because he wore his uniform. At other times, especially in the case of transformed French prisoners, it was not obvious. But the fact that a man and a woman were seeking a hiding place and making efforts not to be seen always aroused suspicions. Intimacy in public was of course illegal and shunned, regardless of whether it involved a legal or illegal relationship (§183 and 183a of the German law code). Generally, random denouncers did not know the prisoner and the woman, although sometimes they recognized one or both, seeing for example that the man was the POW who worked on a certain farm. Often, the rumor cloud had already spread in a village community, and it was easy to assume a forbidden relationship if somebody spotted the woman and the prisoner outdoors. Sometimes children became witnesses of forbidden encounters. They might call a parent or, in the case of enterprising Hitler Youth boys, follow the couple, observe them, and alert the police. It is possible that the propaganda warning civilians about illegal schemes of the POWs toward the end of the war created a

[25] Rundschreiben 163/43, Reichsverfügungsblatt, published November 28, 1943, Ausgabe B, in CEGESOMA, AA 244.

heightened sense of awareness that made random witnesses more eager to report an observation involving POWs.

In May 1941, French POW Georges Grimaud was working on a farm in Vilsendorf near Bielefeld. Occasionally, Elfriede Färber, the twenty-four-year-old wife of a Wehrmacht soldier and mother of a small child, helped out on the farm. Grimaud and Färber felt a strong affection for each other but kept their distance, aware of the severe punishments. In early December, however, they met in the barn and had sex. The farmer came into the barn just as they were lying down, but he either did not notice them or decided to ignore them. But on January 21, 1942, a random villager saw them lying on the ground on top of Grimaud's coat. He went to the police and denounced them. The special court in Bielefeld sentenced Elfriede Färber to three years of penal servitude, and the court martial of Münster sentenced Grimaud to four years of prison on March 26, 1942.[26] Was outrage about a forbidden relation the cause for the denunciation? Or would the witness have denounced the couple in any case because they offended his sense of propriety by making love outdoors? The court records do not tell.

In July 1941, the accountant Hans Müller, who had his office on *Kantstraße* in Nürnberg, observed a POW and a woman who met across the road and then entered a house. After a while, they both left again. These meetings occurred almost daily, and Müller told his two colleagues about them. The woman usually wiped her mouth when she left the house, prompting one of Müller's colleagues to comment: "now she is wiping away the kisses, the swine." After two weeks, Müller informed a guard supervising some POWs working for a catering service adjacent to the house that served as the meeting point. The guard followed the couple to the attic and arrested them on July 26. The woman, Frieda Egelsdorfer (thirty-six), was a married employee in a nearby bookbinding firm, and the prisoner was Frenchman Marcel Farinaud (twenty-seven), a cooper from a village north of Paris. Farinaud was working for the catering service next to the house. Egelsdorfer stated that her marriage was happy but that she felt compassion for the quiet and gentle prisoner and therefore had given him some cigarettes. They could barely understand each other, but they had hugged and kissed. The judges could not prove that they had done more than that, but the special court nonetheless sentenced the woman to two years of penal servitude on August 20, 1941, a very harsh sentence. Farinaud was sentenced to only six months in prison. That he was an excellent worker spoke for him. His company

---

[26] Dossier 2663, in AN, F9, 2416.

desperately wanted to keep him.[27] What induced Müller to denounce the secret reunions remains unclear. Was his sense of propriety offended? Did he expect that somebody else in the office would sooner or later denounce the couple anyway?

A "bad" reputation of a woman made her more likely to be denounced and punished harshly. Denunciations from several random witnesses led to absurdly harsh punishments for the thirty-eight-year-old Mathilde Oppel and French POW Antonin Hébert in the village Tornesch north of Hamburg. Oppel lived in concubinage with a sixty-one-year-old gardener. Hébert (thirty-eight) was a truck driver from Lyon, married and with two children. All that the courts ever revealed was that they had occasionally met in the countryside, where she gave him cigarettes, and that she had once repaired his mittens. During their first meeting, they were seen by a locksmith who denounced them to the local church warden. The church warden warned Frau Oppel to stay away from the prisoner but did not report her to the police. The second time, a woman from the neighborhood saw them together and alerted the police. The court martial in Hamburg sentenced him to one year in prison on September 16, 1941. In a far-fetched argument, the judges pointed out that the prisoner had said that the conversation between him and Frau Oppel had occurred in French and German whereas she had said that they only spoke German. On the basis of this minor discrepancy, the judges argued that he was lying and that more must have happened than what they admitted. On October 1, the special court in Kiel, one of the harder ones in the Third Reich, went even farther by sentencing Frau Oppel to two years of penal servitude, a punishment that was normally reserved for relations involving proven sexual intercourse. The fact that she was divorced, lived with a man in concubinage, and had an illegitimate child from him likely made her so vulnerable to denunciation, and this must also have influenced the judge. That she had once been warned also counted as an aggravating factor.[28]

Random witnesses brought a tragic end to the short love affair between French POW Jules Brochart and the married farm daughter Leopoldine Graf from the village of Untersiebenbrunn east of Vienna. Brochart and Graf flirted while working in the fields, and on July 29, 1941, while walking to a cucumber field, they lay down in a cornfield and had sex. Some passersby witnessed their encounter and reproached the woman

[27] BStA Nürnberg, Akten der Anklagebehörde beim Sondergericht, 1215, and Feldurteil, Nürnberg, November 18, 1941, in PAAA, R 40900.
[28] Feldurteil, Kiel, September 16, 1941, in PAAA, R 40883; LASH Schleswig, Abt. 358, 4998.

for committing a shameful act. The witnesses continued on their way, but Brochart and Graf, now certain that they had been discovered, stayed put and had sex a second time. Some other witnesses saw them and expressed outrage. Frau Graf got dressed and left the scene. Three hours later she threw herself in front of a truck. Brochart initially denied the allegations, but he was shocked when he learned of her suicide and then admitted everything. The court martial in Linz sentenced him to eight months of prison, a very mild judgment.[29] The court files suggest that the impropriety of the act, conducted in public view, provoked the outrage of the witnesses, not specifically the forbidden relationship between a POW and a German woman.

A mean-spirited denunciation turned a summer outing into a nightmare for two women and two French POWs in Regensburg (Bavaria). In August 1942, they decided to go swimming together in the public beach along the river. While sitting in the grass, they flirted, and one of the women grabbed one of the prisoners by the hair and said to the others: "look at this red hair!" After a while, they swam to the other side of the river to have more privacy and pursued an animated and happy conversation there. But other bathers observed them from across the river and notified the police. One of the women tried to bribe the police officer by offering him 100 marks as well as free beer if he did not report them, but that only made her liable to prosecution for attempted bribery. She received fifteen months of penal servitude, an absurdly harsh punishment. The fact that she had once been warned – she had already come to the attention of the police because of excessive familiarity with a POW – counted as an aggravating factor. The other woman received five months in prison.[30] In this case, the denunciation reflected outrage at the fact that the women were spending their free time flirting with POWs because the court files mention no impropriety beyond the one woman grabbing one of the prisoners by his hair.

Australian POW Adam Gilson, who was working on a farm in southern Austria, met Jenny Happel, a soldier's wife with two children who had been evacuated from the heavily bombed west German industrial city Duisburg to the village Wenigzell in the Austrian Alps in 1943. Gilson and Happel had secret meetings in the forests. One day in December 1943, a local woman and her son noticed the couple when they tried to hide behind a tree. They followed and denounced them.[31]

---

[29] Feldurteil, Linz, September 30, 1941, in PAAA, R 40887.
[30] BStA Nürnberg, Akten der Anklagebehörde beim Sondergericht, 1803.
[31] Feldurteil Leoben, April 14, 1944, and attorney Viktor Glaser to Swiss Legation, April 14, 1944, both in BAR Bern, Bestand Vertretung Berlin 78a.

Whether the denouncing woman knew Happel or whether she just spotted two people doing something suspicious in the forest and wanted to find out what they were doing is unclear. It was common for farm communities to look askance at women evacuated from big cities far away, often from a region with a different dialect and religion. Especially in Austria, rumors circulated that evacuated German city women were leaving their children with Austrian nannies while pursuing amorous adventures.[32] The court martial could not prove more than hugs and kisses, but it sentenced Gilson to one year of penal servitude because he knew that Happel was married to a soldier.

Anonymous letters or phone calls sometimes triggered an investigation. We cannot know for sure whether they came from random denouncers, family members, or neighbors. Sometimes it is possible to guess who might have been the denouncer, and often the accused woman mentioned a suspicion during the investigation, but there is no certainty. One example is an anonymous letter that arrived at the police headquarters of Nürnberg on July 1, 1942, accusing Margarethe Schwilk, an employee at a local shoe factory, of having a relationship with a French POW. The letter contains a surprising amount of detail. It notes that Schwilk was pregnant and that her husband was being nursed in an army hospital in the Saar district. The letter also provided precise information on the location where the POW worked and the date when the relationship had started. The investigation revealed that Schwilk, whose job was to clean ducts at the shoe factory, had often been watched by a group of French POWs while she was working. One of the POWs, Ives Ropars from Brest, had expressed a special liking for her. He had followed her on several occasions, rung her door bell (she lived as a boarder in a dentist's apartment), and asked her to let him in. She initially rejected him but then gave in, and they had sex twice in the conjugal bedroom. Given that the denunciation is so specific, it must have come from somebody who was close to her, perhaps the dentist (or his wife) in whose apartment she was renting a room, a co-worker, or her husband. She had confessed the affair to him, and he had said that he no longer wanted to live with her but that he would not report her. She insisted that the child was from her husband (she had visited him in the hospital), but it could also have been from the prisoner.[33]

In numerous cases, discovery occurred because of the intervention of a person in an official function who did not usually have a duty to report.

---

[32] Torrie, *"For Their Own Good,"* 73–6. Form and Uthe, *NS-Justiz in Österreich*, introduction, xxxi.
[33] BStA Nürnberg, Akten der Anklagebehörde beim Sondergericht, 1724.

French POW Albert Josquin, for example, experienced a doubly unpleasant surprise when he visited a German doctor because of an ailment in late 1943. First, he learned that he had tested positive for a venereal disease and, second, he realized that the doctor had denounced him because Josquin had mentioned that he had recently had sex with a German woman named Anna. They had secretly met in the forest and had made love on his coat. Anna was a widow with two children whose husband had been killed in combat in 1941, when she was twenty. She had recently had sex with three different German soldiers and tested positive for the same venereal disease.[34]

An SS man played the decisive role in the discovery of the affair between Therese Tiller and Belgian POW Louis Bodard, a married painter, in Sulzbach-Rosenberg, a town with a large POW camp east of Nürnberg. Neighbors one day noticed that a Belgian POW was visiting Frau Tiller for coffee and cake. One of the neighbors sent her child over to Frau Tiller to ask for some kitchen supplies, but in reality as a spy. The curious neighbors did not denounce the couple, but they fired up the rumor mill, and the rumor reached the ears of Hans Hubmann, an SS member living in the vicinity. Although Hubmann had not seen anything, he felt a duty as an SS man to denounce illegal affairs and notified the police. Bodard declared that the invitation to coffee and cake was a "payment" for a portrait he had made for the woman, as he had done for other people in town, and denied any sexual contact, but the woman admitted that she was very much in love with him and that they had had sex six times, either at her workplace (she was a cleaning lady in a big orphanage) or at her home.[35] In this case, an SS man's sense of commitment to legality (on Nazi terms) triggered the denunciation, although the guard was already aware through the rumor mill that something was going on.

Rumors coming to the ears of a party official also were at the origin of the discovery of the affair between Anna Ettinger (thirty-six), a farmer's daughter in the village Siegritz, northeast of Nürnberg, and French POW Jean Ivars, a farmer ten years her junior. First, the mayor of this tiny

---

[34] BStA Nürnberg, Akten der Anklagebehörde beim Sondergericht, 2410. On December 28, 1943, the special court in Nürnberg sentenced her to two years of penal servitude, finding her behavior particularly revolting in light of the fact that she was a war widow and mother of two small children.

[35] BStA Nürnberg, Akten der Anklagebehörde beim Sondergericht, 2418. The special court in Nürnberg sentenced her to two years of penal servitude. The fact that she had become intimate with Bodard in the conjugal apartment while her husband was working for German rearmament counted as an aggravating factor. Her husband was working for the steelworks in town and was not home very much.

village heard something, and he then contacted the leader of the NSDAP section in the nearest town, who informed the police. When the police began investigating, they learned that the mother had surprised her daughter with the prisoner in the hay sometime in June 1941. Both parents had beaten up the daughter as a punishment. The parents could not confirm whether sexual intercourse had taken place, but Anna Ettinger herself admitted that she and Ivars had once met in the hay and had sex. The special court in Nürnberg sentenced her to two years of penal servitude. That she counted as mentally slightly impaired was an extenuating factor.[36]

A random soldier triggered the discovery of an illegal double affair of Anna Niessner, a forty-three-year-old cook working in the social welfare office of the German Labor Front in Frankfurt an der Oder. When the soldier observed her giving an ointment to a French prisoner in the street, he asked her to come to the police. On the way to the police post, she threw away two photos that she had been carrying on her. The soldier picked up the crumpled photos and delivered them to the police. The police interrogation revealed that Niessner had been involved with two French POWs, Pierre and Michel, over several months. She had met them during work – one prisoner delivered the vegetables for her kitchen, and the other one picked up the cooked meals and delivered them to factories. They visited her in her attic room or met her in the forest and had sex. She did not know their last names. Frau Niessner had been married to a German soldier, but he divorced her in the fall of 1943 because she had cheated on him with a German man. In April 1944, Michel, who had a rash around his mouth, had asked her for an ointment, and this triggered the discovery.[37]

A discovery by an official in plain clothes occurred on Good Friday 1944. When criminal assistant Eidmann was hiking outside Darmstadt with his son, he saw a man in a French POW uniform walking into the forest and a young woman following him. Eidmann found them lying on the floor behind some brush. The POW got up and ran away. When Eidmann confronted the woman, she talked to him in French and explained that her name was Louise Degrelle. He wrote down her name

---

[36] BStA Nürnberg, Akten der Anklagebehörde beim Sondergericht, 1223.
[37] BLHA Potsdam, 12C, Sondergericht Frankfurt an der Oder, volume 1017. Frau Niessner received a surprisingly mild sentence, one and a half years in prison, because the judge accorded her mitigating circumstances as she allegedly had a very strong sex drive. The judge also noted in her favor that she had taken up relationships with French POWs, who enjoyed more freedom and were more integrated into German society than other prisoners (judgment of May 19, 1944). The special court in Frankfurt an der Oder was among the most lenient courts in the matter of forbidden relations.

and birthdate and let her go, probably planning to initiate prosecution
later on (a foreign civilian worker had to expect punishment, while the
POW did not). Eidmann's son, however, told him later that he knew the
woman: she was the daughter of the new innkeepers in Darmstadt-
Eberstadt on *Adolf-Hitlerstraße!* A check in the police files quickly
revealed that the boy was right. The woman, who had learned French
in school, was really Walburga Lamm. When she pretended to be a
French worker, she had even given her correct birthdate. Walburga was
twenty years old and came from Cologne. In the heavy bombings, her
family had lost all their possessions and had relocated to Darmstadt in
October 1943, and they were operating an inn. Walburga worked there as
a waitress, and that is how she had met French POW René Tissot. They
became close and discussed getting married after the war. He gave her a
silver watch out of which she had two engagement rings made. Hers
carried the German name Richard Talk (the initials of the POW) – to
hide the illegal relationship. The special court in Darmstadt sentenced
her to one year in prison, a mild punishment in light of the fact that she
admitted having had sex with Tissot three or four times. Her youth
counted as a mitigating circumstance, however. That she had lied to
Eidmann did not weigh against her because he had been off duty and
worn civilian clothes when intercepting her.[38]

In several other cases, children helped an investigation and acted as
denouncers, especially Hitler Youth (HJ) boys. Although it is a myth that
Hitler Youths were trained as denouncers of their parents and neighbors,
their training did encourage vigilantism, enterprise, and persistence, and
some boys were eager to prove these qualities.[39] The thirty-three-year-
old French POW Robert Bertin belonged to a group of POWs occupied
with road building in Tharandt near Dresden in late 1940 and early
1941. The thirty-five-year-old married Magdalena Bergmann could see
the prisoners from her window. Bertin caught her attention. From time
to time, she walked by the work detachment and dropped a pack of
cigarettes near him, and he picked it up. With sign language, she

[38] HStAD, G 27 Darmstadt 1417.
[39] For children as denouncers, see, for example, Katrin Dördelmann, "Denunziationen im
Nationalsozialismus: Geschlechtsspezifische Aspekte," in *Denunziation: Historische,
juristische und psychologische Aspekte,* ed. Günter Jerouschek, Inge Marßolek, and
Hedwig Röckelein (Tübingen: Edition diskord, 1997), 160. On Hitler Youth boys as
vigilantes, see also Armin Nolzen, "Der Streifendienst der Hitler-Jugend (HJ) und die
'Überwachung der Jugend', 1934–1945: Forschungsprobleme und Fragestellung," in
"Durchschnittstäter": Handeln und Motivation, ed. Christoph Dieckmann et al. (Berlin:
Schwarze Risse, 2000). On the myth of Hitler Youth children trained as denouncers of
parents and neighbors, see Nicholas Stargardt, *Witnesses of War: Children's Lives Under
the Nazis* (New York: Alfred A. Knopf, 2006), 37.

indicated to him that they could meet unsupervised in a little forest nearby. They did meet several times, and she gave him cake and fruit as well as a photo of herself. On February 18, 1941, two HJ boys witnessed a meeting in the forest and denounced the couple. The boys claimed that Bertin and Bergmann had been lying on top of each other, but the judges determined that this was likely an optical illusion given the angle from which they had observed the couple. The court martial in Dresden sentenced Bertin to two months in prison on September 18, 1941. Tragically, Frau Bergmann committed suicide through hanging a few days after the discovery.[40]

Another example of active HJ boys is the case of Jensine Trulsen, a thirty-seven-year-old teacher's wife from a suburb of Kiel, and French POW Claudius Ludwig in Lüthjenburg, a small town near the Baltic coast in Schleswig-Holstein. Trulsen's husband, who was twenty-one years older, had been drafted to teach evacuated city children in Lüthjenburg in 1943. He and his wife had rented a tiny apartment, but he was rarely home. Ludwig was a French officer who had volunteered for work and who acted as man of confidence for the local work detachment. He wore a French uniform. He and Trulsen met in the street, greeted each other, and smiled. In December 1943, they started taking walks together several times per week, and in February 1944, they began to have sex in a forest. Their walks together fired up the local rumor mill, however. On April 19, 1944, somebody saw them out of town. On his way to the police, the witness encountered two HJ boys and asked them to follow the couple. The police surrounded the forest and, with the help of the HJ boys, found the couple. Trulsen was extremely upset and begged the policeman who arrested her to shoot her right away.[41] The HJ boys in this case did not make the denunciation, but they eagerly helped to track down the couple.

In Lebus, a small town north of Franfurt an der Oder, five children aged thirteen and fourteen (four girls and one boy) witnessed how two female farmworkers, married women aged thirty-four and forty-nine respectively, were very close to two French POWs also working on the farm estate. The children had been called out to help farmers with the potato harvest during their vacation. They once saw how one of the

[40] Feldurteil, Dresden, September 18, 1941, in PAAA, R 40883. Why there was a seven-month delay between the discovery and the court martial is unclear.
[41] LASH Schleswig, Abt. 358, 6996. The special court in Kiel sentenced her to one and a half years of penal servitude. It considered the forced move to a new town and her being neglected by her husband as mitigating factors. That Ludwig had volunteered to work and was very sympathetic to Germany also helped her, but the fact that she had started a relationship with a POW who did not work with her counted as an aggravating factor.

women hugged a prisoner and the other one laughingly put her head between the other prisoner's legs. Once, the prisoners grabbed the women between the legs. When the children confronted the two couples, one of the women threatened them: "Darned kids: I will hit you on the head with the hoe!" The other woman commented sarcastically: "Next time, do not forget to bring a lantern!" The children denounced the women. The investigation did not reveal more than what the children had seen, but the older woman was sentenced to one year in prison, the other one to eight months.[42]

In the summer of 1943, a girl walking through the forest near a village northeast of Regensburg (Bavaria) stumbled upon a POW who was lying on his coat together with a woman. The girl, who had heard that some Soviet prisoners had recently escaped, alerted the guards in a nearby POW camp. When the guards searched the forest, they discovered a French POW who had had sex with twenty-year-old Maria Pinkerl, the stepdaughter of a local farmer. The POW worked on the neighboring farm, and the couple had secretly met in the forest once before. The prisoner had started the relationship by befriending the woman's thirteen-year-old brother, giving him cigarettes for her and asking him to tell her that she was beautiful. The boy did not denounce them. The girl who did alert the guards was alarmed because of recent POW escapes.[43]

Letters were a common reason for discovery, but unless postal censors picked them out, the finder had to make a denunciation. French POW Victor Trochard, for example, wrote his parents about the love affair he was having with the two daughters of his employer, a baker in Vehlingen, near the Dutch border. He even included photos of the two women, aged twenty and twenty-eight. Mindful of postal censorship, Trochard looked for a safe way of getting the letter to his parents. Somebody told him that a young sailor stationed with the German navy in France was on leave in the town. With the consent of the POW, the middleman gave the sailor the letter, asking him to mail it in France, but the sailor opened it and denounced the prisoner.[44]

In the case of Martha Meier and Marius Delumeau, it was also a letter from the prisoner combined with a random denunciation that led to discovery. Frau Meier, who had four children and was divorced, had met Delumeau because he brought her the laundry of the prisoners in

---

[42] BLHA Potsdam, 12 C, Sondergericht Frankfurt an der Oder, 90–3.
[43] BStA Nürnberg, Akten der Anklagebehörde beim Sondergericht, 2366.
[44] Feldurteil, Münster, January 13, 1942, in PAAA, R 40909. The court martial in Münster sentenced Trochard to three years in prison, a relatively mild judgment given that he had had affairs with two women.

Hamberge, a village outside of Lübeck, to wash. Delumeau, a teacher who spoke German well, had visited her on several occasions overnight, but in November 1943, he was transferred to a work detachment in another village. He wrote her a letter, obtained a stamp, and asked some comrades to post it, but they asked a woman in town to bring the letter to the public mailbox. This woman opened it, read it, and notified the police. Martha Meier was pregnant from Delumeau at the time of her trial. She received two years of penal servitude on February 9, 1944.[45]

Neighbors As Denouncers

During the war, the Nazi regime encouraged vigilantism among neighbors in an effort to control the home front. Most Germans in urban areas lived in apartment buildings, meaning that they had numerous neighbors. Custodians were often party members and charged with watching over the renters (as *Blockwart*), for example to make sure everybody darkened their windows at night to better protect cities from bombing. These custodians might also report people who were in hiding. Neighbors often had already heard rumors or observed some suspicious activities before they notified the authorities, but they often denounced only when they felt that they had proof of illegal activity. In the countryside, neighbors might be more distant than in an apartment building. But in both places, tensions between neighbors made a denunciation more likely. In apartments, of course, it often could have been a complaint to the *Blockwart* or police because of excessive noise that triggered a discovery, especially if group dating occurred in a small apartment. The court files usually do not reveal the reason for the denunciation.

In a village outside of Nürnberg, French POW Fernand Rieu noticed a woman waving at him from her window. On July 23, 1941, in the evening, he entered her house. Neighbors saw him. One of them, Frau Seebald, notified the village mayor. The mayor came, and he knocked on the door, while Frau Seebald and her husband were watching. Nobody opened. After a while, the mayor went to the local POW camp and asked the guard if a prisoner was missing. The guard quickly noticed that it was Rieu, went to the house, called him, and arrested him. Why exactly the prisoner had entered the house and what happened inside remained unclear. The prisoner argued that the woman, Käthe Pross, wife of a Wehrmacht soldier and mother of two children, had called him inside, and then locked the door and tried to seduce him. He also said that she

[45] LASH Schleswig, Abt. 358, 2406–7.

had told him to stay inside so that they would not be discovered. The prisoner denied any sexual interest in the woman, who was ten years his senior ("much too old for me," according to him). The woman, however, presented him as an intruder who had wanted to attack her, and she accused him of having locked the door himself. She claimed that he was sexually aroused and kissed her against her will. The special court in Nürnberg sentenced her to one year of penal servitude, believing that she had lured the prisoner inside with the intention of becoming intimate with him because it was obvious that Rieu had not forced himself into the apartment. The court martial gave him only three months in prison, perhaps because of the age difference, even though it believed that his defense was dishonest. While the facts of the encounter remained the subject of dispute, the denunciation also was controversial. A lively discussion had occurred before Frau Seebald informed the mayor: her own daughters and some neighbors had argued that one should first speak to Frau Pross and figure out what exactly was happening before making a denunciation. Even the mayor, who knew Frau Pross and called her by her first name, seems to have looked for a way to resolve the issue without recourse to the judicial process, but he had no choice when nobody answered the door.[46]

A hostile neighbor denounced French POW Jean Marie Trévidic, a mason from western Brittany, and the farmer's daughter Elfriede Herder (twenty) in Kempfenbrunn (southeastern Hessen). The prisoner and the woman hugged each other several times outdoors. A neighbor with an old grudge against Herder's family took two photos and sent them to the mayor, leading to the arrest of the couple in July 1941.[47] The courts usually tried to make sure that a denunciation was not merely part of an old neighborhood feud, but in this case, the two photos served as convincing proof, and the judges therefore did not question the motives of the denouncer.

Neighbors also denounced French POW Jean Collard and Marianne Melzer, the daughter of his farmer, in 1941. A married couple snuck into the horse stable on August 31, 1941, and observed the couple while they were kissing each other. The witnesses even claimed that sexual intercourse had occurred, but the court martial dismissed this claim because it had been fairly dark in the horse stable. It sentenced Collard to one

[46] BStA Nürnberg, Akten der Anklagebehörde beim Sondergericht, 1278, and Feldurteil, Nürnberg, January 6, 1942, in PAAA, R 40905.
[47] Feldurteil, Kassel, November 27, 1941, in PAAA, R 40898. Trévidic was sentenced to four months in prison; Herder received eight months because the court believed that she had taken the initiative.

year in prison because he admitted that they had hugged and kissed. But the judges were rather critical of the couple who had denounced them, commenting that they had nothing better to do than to spy on their neighbors all day long.[48]

In Bremen, a denunciation from neighbors set the police on the trail of several forbidden relations, but the implicated women outsmarted the police. In February 1943, two women living together in a downtown apartment, Wilma Keller and Anne-Maria Held, invited two French officers who had volunteered to work at a nearby airplane factory for wine and cake. They kissed and hugged. Not much later, one of the French officers was arrested because the police had discovered that he had had an affair with another woman. In the spring, however, Held met another French officer, Paul Fabien, and invited him together with Pierre Proess, who had already visited in February. They had multiple gatherings in the apartment of the two women in June. Following an anonymous denunciation from a neighbor, two policemen decided to observe the apartment on June 26, 1943. They opened the apartment directly below, which was rented by the Nazi organization Strength through Joy but was currently unused. The police officers heard talking upstairs, but only from the women. One policeman then took a ladder and peeked through some of the windows, but he could not detect anything suspicious. Next, the two policemen knocked on the door to tell the women that there was a ladder leaning against the house and that somebody might try to break in. They were hoping to get an opportunity to peek into the apartment. Still, they could not spot any men. They even searched the apartment, pretending to look for the burglar, but to no avail. It later turned out that the women had heard something in the downstairs apartment, which was normally quiet. They had hidden the two POWs first in the attic and later in a little storage den, and they had placed empty wine bottles in front of the door to the den. When searching the apartment, the police officers did not look there. When the police knocked, Frau Held grabbed a photo of Fabien on her nightstand and hid it in her bra. Later in the night, the women took advantage of a bomb alarm and the spreading of artificial fog as camouflage for the nearby airplane plant to let the two prisoners slip out undetected. What did ultimately lead to the proof of the relationship is not clear, but it seems that the police found clues when they searched the hotel in which the French officers who had volunteered to work were housed.[49]

---

[48] Feldurteil, Hamburg, November 4, 1941, in PAAA, R 40893.
[49] Bremen, 4.89/5-312; Colonel de Pinsun, Officier de confiance, to Chef de la Dél., February 21, 1944, in AN, F9, 2746. For the officer arrested first, see AN, F9, 2400,

In Reichenwalde, a village southeast of Frankfurt an der Oder, a peculiar denunciation started a long investigation. On May 6, 1943, the widow Bertha Herrmann went to the police and told them that a former friend and neighbor, Berta Brenner, had admitted having a sexual relationship with a French prisoner and also with many of the guards from the nearby camp. As Frau Herrmann testified: "My parents and I, as German people's comrades, do not agree with the dealings of this woman, especially in light of the fact that my sister has to endure a harsh punishment in a similar matter (contact with Poles)." The background was that Frau Herrmann's sister had been sent to Ravensbrück concentration camp after a love affair with a Pole. That some women in the village were engaging in relations with French POWs with impunity irked Frau Herrmann. Frau Brenner had already received a police warning in late 1942 because she had been seen with French POW Aimé Bourbon (relationships with the guards were not punishable). After Frau Herrmann's denunciation, Frau Brenner had to face trial, but the special court in Frankfurt an der Oder acquitted her on July 5, 1943, because many witnesses seemed to bear personal grudges against her. Yet, there were strong indications of a forbidden relationship: a photo of Bourbon had been found in Brenner's possession. She had also given birth to twins who were clearly not from her husband (she ascribed paternity to one of the guards, but this was never confirmed). What saved her nonetheless was the fact that the judge refused to take seriously the testimony of a woman whose sister was in a concentration camp.[50]

Mean-spirited neighbors were the source of many denunciations, but some courts saw through the motives. The courts martial in southern Austria, for example, found themselves flooded with a series of what they considered frivolous denunciations against women and British prisoners in 1944. They often found out that hostile neighbors had used a denunciation to vent a grievance or avenge something. British POW Joseph Keyes, for example, was accused of having a forbidden relation with the woman with whom he worked on the farm of the village priest. The denouncers claimed that the woman was giving him extra rations and that she used to walk arm in arm with him. Yet, the judges at the court

---

case 48. The special court in Bremen sentenced Held to one and a half years and Keller to one year in prison on October 19, a relatively mild judgment. Held was punished more harshly because she had been involved with two French officers and because she seemed to have been the driving force. The local court martial sentenced Proess to two years and Fabien to one and a half years in prison. Both courts considered sexual intercourse likely, especially between Held and Fabien, but they could not prove it. That the officers had volunteered to work counted as a mitigating factor.

[50] BLHA Potsdam, 12 C, Sondergericht Frankfurt an der Oder, 125.

martial in Wolfsberg concluded that neighbors had taken offense merely because the woman had shown the prisoner his daily work routine. Also, the judges pointed out that giving a POW extra rations was not forbidden if the act constituted a reward for good work. Keyes was acquitted.[51]

In the case of British POW James Hobart, the judges went to extraordinary lengths to disprove the claims of three neighbors, one man and two women. They determined that the male denouncer had once been a suitor of the accused farm girl and was still angry because she had rejected him. The two female neighbors carried a grudge against the accused woman because she had once testified against them in a case of cow theft, and they were also jealous because she had received the most diligent POW in the village. All that the investigation revealed was that the prisoner and the woman had often been riding together on an oxcart and that they had occasionally rested in the grass next to each other, but neither act was punishable because they were working together. The denouncers pointed out that the prisoner and the woman had used the informal address "*Du*," but the judges remarked that this was the custom in many Austrian villages and that British POWs gladly accepted it because their language lacks a distinction between formal and informal pronoun. They acquitted Hobart.[52] These Austrian military tribunals in 1944 were remarkably proactive in refuting accusations against British prisoners. It might go too far, but one can ask whether some Austrian military judges began to revolt subtly against the Nazi law they had to enforce.

Discovery through the Employer or Fellow Workers

Many discoveries occurred in the workplace and resulted from denunciations by employers or other workers. We need to keep in mind that the civilian employers of POWs committed themselves not only to watching and disciplining the POWs but also to ensuring that they were not violating orders and laws. On farms with an absent farmer, the wife had to act in his stead. Similarly, the foreman in a factory was charged with watching over the POWs and the women, and many foremen caught couples when they tried to meet in secret. The denunciations of a forbidden relationship through employers or their deputies are therefore distinct from random denunciations by a civilian, a neighbor, or a co-worker who faced no legal obligation to report. But employers or their deputies, like the guards, also had some latitude. For example, they

---

[51] Feldurteil, Wolfsberg, May 19, 1944, in BAR Bern, Bestand Vertretung Berlin, 79a.
[52] Feldurteil, Graz, June 8, 1944, in BAR Bern, Bestand Vertretung Berlin, 78b.

could warn a couple or assign them to different shifts rather than denouncing them. Co-workers who denounced a couple acted more like random denouncers or neighbors, but sometimes co-workers were party members or occupied special positions of trust that gave them a perceived or real duty to enforce the law on the shop floor. It is not always clear whether the co-worker who discovered and denounced a secret encounter or who brought a love letter to the attention of the management was a person charged with such duties or a random denouncer.

The discovery of the relationship between farmworker Irmgard Mallmann and French POW René Marceau was one of the cases where the Nazi idea of the "healthy feeling of the Volk" seemed to work as planned. The setting was a large farm estate on the southern edge of Nürnberg in the summer of 1941. Farmworkers observed Mallmann and Marceau hugging each other in public and denounced them. During interrogation, she admitted that she liked the prisoner very much. He spoke German quite well and was charming and kind. They had met in the barn, kissed, hugged, and touched each other. They both denied having had sexual intercourse, and the judges believed them. The special court in Nürnberg still sentenced her to one and a half years of penal servitude on September 8, 1941, a harsh judgment. The outrage her relationship had caused on the estate counted as an aggravating factor, and the judges believed that she had seduced the prisoner because she was three years older. Marceau, a sailor born in 1922, received a very light punishment (six months in prison). His judges also cast the woman in the role of seductress, while acknowledging that Marceau was in an age "in which erotic desire can influence a person quite powerfully."[53]

In the Hessian town Battenberg, French POW Pierre Juilliard was working in a factory in 1941. Juilliard (twenty-six) was a lawyer and notary public from Paris. When walking to and from work, he noticed the sixteen-year-old Ingrid Jakobsen feeding her rabbits in the garden of the factory owner. Jakobsen was the director's daughter, and she had learned French. She and Juilliard began talking in French across the fence. When her father asked for a French POW who would perform garden work for him, Juilliard applied and was accepted. He from now on worked in Ingrid's household and participated in the daily coffee and cake breaks. The family warmly accepted this educated and well-mannered man. He and Ingrid liked each other very much, and they talked of getting married after the war. The parents voiced no objections. More intimate encounters do not seem to have occurred because the girl

---

[53] BStA Nürnberg, Akten der Anklagebehörde beim Sondergericht, 1222; Feldurteil, November 18, 1941, in PAAA, R 40894.

was always under the watch of her parents. But some workers in the factory were bothered by the relationship. Why should the prohibition apply to common people but not to a factory director's family? It was workers from the father's factory who denounced the couple, leading to Juilliard's arrest. Ingrid was left at home while the investigation took its course, and she attempted to commit suicide by shooting herself (she was not killed right away, but the medical prognosis at the time of the court martial said that she was unlikely to survive). The court martial in Kassel sentenced Juilliard to one year in prison on September 18, 1941, because it considered him responsible for having ruined a family and driven the girl to suicide. The judgment also blamed him for having divided the German home front because it noted that the employees of the factory were angry with the director and his daughter. As in many other cases in Nazi Germany, denunciation here was a weapon of the weak, allowing workers to "get back" at their factory director.[54]

In the Triumph bicycle and motorcycle factory in Nürnberg, the management used a spy among the French POWs, a man named Polosse, to investigate numerous thefts and suspected forbidden relations between female workers and POWs in 1943. One of the people Polosse tracked down was Gilbert Chanteloup. Polosse found a passionate love letter this prisoner had addressed to a woman. Polosse mentioned to the management that Chanteloup had shown him her photo. The suspect was Juliane Kanther, a thirty-seven-year-old divorced woman who had already been punished with one year in prison for kissing a French POW in 1941. Chanteloup, who was illiterate, claimed that another prisoner had written the letter for him and that it was for his wife, who was unfaithful to him. Indeed, the letter, which was written in French, included some jealous remarks about the adored woman having had wine with other men and about a photo showing her with a tall bicycle racer. The police did not believe this story, but Chanteloup managed to let the photo disappear and Polosse, who had only briefly seen it, did not think it resembled Juliane Kanther. The case seemed closed. A zealous guard, however, conducted another search of Chanteloup's possessions and found the photo sewn into the inner lining of Chanteloup's suitcase. It did indeed show Frau Kanther, and now the POW admitted that the letter was for her and that they had exchanged

---

[54] Feldurteil, Kassel, September 18, 1941, in PAAA, R 40884. Dördelmann, "Denunziationen im Nationalsozialismus," 159–60; Gisela Diewald-Kerkmann, "Politische Denunziation im NS-Regime: Die kleine Macht der 'Volksgenossen'," in *Denunziation. Historische, juristische und psychologische Aspekte*, ed. Günter Jerouschek, Inge Marßolek, and Hedwig Röckelein (Tübingen: Edition discord, 1997), 147.

kisses. He explained that he was deeply in love with this very beautiful woman and that he had been jealous when she had drunk wine with four other POWs. Frau Kanther argued that she had written to the prisoner to dissuade him from a relationship, but the special court in Nürnberg dismissed this justification as a "silly excuse." Chanteloup was a car mechanic, seven years younger than Kanther. He was married and had two children. When asked why he had hidden the photo, he explained that he desperately wanted to protect Frau Kanther but that he was too much in love with her to destroy the photo. The special court sentenced her to 16 months of penal servitude on May 3, 1943, a very harsh punishment for a few kisses and occasional gifts of food and wine. The fact that she had a previous conviction in this matter was an aggravating factor.[55]

Factories offered many hiding places, but they were risky meeting grounds because of the number of potential witnesses. Toilets or changing rooms were frequent meeting places. In the firm Elektroacustic in Neumünster (Schleswig-Holstein), the employee Käte Frick, the daughter of a police chief, had an affair with a French transformed POW. They had noticed that the wall separating the ladies' room and the men's room did not extend all the way to the ceiling. At agreed times, both went to the toilet, and the prisoner climbed over the separating wall into the ladies' room, where they had sex many times. Fellow prisoners stood watch outside the toilets. One day, however, the warning system failed, and a co-worker followed the prisoner and found him climbing over the wall. It is unclear whether this worker was a foreman or a random witness.[56]

The Cypriot POW Ramadaan Naftali and the married German woman Irma Lott met during work in a factory in the Sudetenland. They from time to time snuck into the basement of the factory, where they had sex. On September 25, 1944, however, a supervisor followed them and caught them in the act. As in other cases, the prisoner had requested a transfer to another workplace before the affair became intimate because he feared that he would not be able to resist the temptation forever, but the local POW commander had rejected the request. Prisoners like Naftali faced a dilemma: they could not reveal the real reason for their transfer request because the relationship might already have involved contact that was punishable, for example hugs, kisses, or letters. But in

---

[55] BStA Nürnberg, Akten der Anklagebehörde beim Sondergericht, 2078.
[56] LASH, Schleswig, Abt. 358, 6959. Frick was sentenced to two years of penitentiary on April 26, 1944.

the absence of specific reasons, such as abuses by employers or unsafe work conditions, the army authorities tended to reject transfer requests because they seemed gratuitous.[57]

In many other cases, co-workers did act as vigilantes, sometimes out of jealousy and sometimes because of a spontaneous observation. In a factory in Nürnberg, German women and French POWs were working in the same halls. On May 26, 1941, the worker Georg List noticed a woman and a prisoner kissing in front of the bathrooms. He notified a foreman, and with the help of a guard and another worker they established the name of the woman and the prisoner: Magdalena Fechl and Jean Pitioret. The pair worked right next to each other and had begun friendly conversations. Pitioret's German was very bad, but they did find out that they were both married. She often gave him sandwiches. She admitted liking the prisoner, although she said that her marriage was happy. Her husband was fighting on the eastern front, and she had not seen him for half a year. She and Pitioret kissed a couple of times. The guards in the factory had allowed the women to leave sandwiches for the prisoners at the end of a shift, so that the guards could later distribute them to the prisoners.[58]

The discovery of the carbon copy of a letter led to denunciation in the case of Fleuris Derocher and Irmgard Schenker in a battery factory in Hagen in the fall of 1941. Schenker had not noticed that the paper on which she was writing the letter lay above a carbon copy sheet, but nosy secretaries discovered the imprint of the letter and made a denunciation. The text clearly talked about captivity, mentioned the hometown of the prisoner, and used his first name (albeit misspelled). It was easy to deduce the prisoner and the woman after this discovery.[59]

In the Borgward motorworks factory in Bremen, Anna Bammerlin was cleaning up after a work shift on November 6, 1942. In the locker room, she encountered French POW Léon Rothewitz from Paris. Rothewitz had been flirting with her for a while. He had been born in Germany and spoke German. He had once given her a honey cake, and she had given

---

[57] Mitteilung, Dresden, October 14, 1944, in BAR Bern, Bestand Vertretung Berlin, 83a. There is no documentation here indicating whether Naftali and Lott were ever sentenced. Their trials would have occurred very late in the war.

[58] BStA Nürnberg, Akten der Anklagebehörde beim Sondergericht, 1194. The special court in Nürnberg sentenced Fechl to ten months in prison. The fact that she was married to a frontline soldier was an aggravating factor, but the judge acknowledged that the behavior of the guards had encouraged forbidden relations.

[59] Feldurteil, Münster, November 11, 1941, in PAAA, R 40898. She misspelled his first name "Floris" instead of "Fleuris." Derocher was sentenced to five months in prison and Schenker to one month in prison, but her sentence was cancelled by a higher court because it was considered to be too mild.

him three pears in return. Women working with her had told her that the prisoner was often staring at her. She had ignored his advances and replied to her co-workers that she knew that contact with POWs was forbidden. Yet, this one evening she felt differently. The prisoner had locked the door from the inside, and he began touching her. She lay down on the table, and they began sexual intercourse. Two other workers had noticed something, however, and they began knocking on the door. Frau Bammerlin pushed the prisoner into a locker and opened the door of the room, pretending that nothing had happened. The two witnesses searched the room and found the prisoner in the locker. Rothewitz claimed to have locked himself in, but this was impossible because one could lock the doors only from the outside. The two workers denounced the couple.[60]

In a dairy company in Neustadt (Saxony), the French POW Severin Sellier met Käthe Leber, who had a five-year-old daughter and was living on the firm premises together with some other German women. Sellier loved children and repeatedly gave Frau Leber chocolate for her child, meeting her in her room. One day, Frau Leber heard somebody coming when Sellier visited her, and they both fled into the bathroom. The intruder was Lucie Katzer, the daughter of the business owner. Katzer knocked on the bathroom door, and the prisoner answered that he was taking a bath. Frau Leber became very worried, and he fondled her cheeks and gave her some kisses in an effort to soothe her. When Katzer had left, he made sure Frau Leber could escape through the window. Lucie Katzer had meanwhile called the business owner and told him that she had peeked through the keyhole and seen the prisoner standing naked and Frau Leber kissing his penis. The investigation led the court martial to a different conclusion, however. Lucie Katzer, as the judges pointed out, had a reputation for wanting to stir up trouble for her co-workers, and the judges therefore found it hard to believe her testimony. Still, they assumed that the prisoner had lured Frau Leber into the bathroom with the intention to become intimate with her. They sentenced him to six months in prison.[61]

---

[60] Staatsarchiv Bremen, Hauptverfahren vor dem Sondergericht 4,89/5 – 204. See also Wrobel, *Strafjustiz im totalen Krieg*, vol. 2, 262. The special court of Bremen sentenced her to 15 months in prison, a mild punishment. The judge considered her transgression a one-time offense and accepted the fact that the prisoner had approached her and locked the door as an extenuating circumstance, although he did point out that she could easily have called for help. The court did not use the fact that her husband was at the time serving in the Wehrmacht in North Africa as an aggravating factor.

[61] Feldurteil, Dresden, January 21, 1942, in PAAA, R 40909. Both Sellier and Frau Leber made a very good impression on the judges.

Jealousy of a co-worker caused the discovery of a secret meeting between French POW Roger Mouret and Lydia Lenz (twenty-two), a lab technician, in a chemical factory in Ludwigshafen. Mouret and Lenz met in the locker room, and Mouret locked the door from the inside. They mostly wanted to talk, and their relationship was companionate, not sexual. Lydia Lenz was married to a sailor from the battleship *Graf Spee*, who was a British POW, and Mouret believed that she was kind to him because her husband was in a similar situation. Yet, another worker who himself had some interest in Lenz secretly followed them to the locker room and alerted the authorities when he noticed that the door was locked. The court martial in Mannheim sentenced Mouret to six months in prison, a rather high price for a simple conversation motivated by mutual desire for empathy. Lydia Lenz was dismissed from the factory but apparently not prosecuted. The judgment against the prisoner claimed that his behavior had triggered unrest among the workers and therefore endangered the cohesion of the German home front.[62] Clearly, the jealous denouncer had spied on the couple.

Jealousy likely also played a role in the denunciation of Katharina Gut and Georges Lacoute, a music student, who worked at the same machine in the cement factory Luitpoldhütte in Amberg (Bavaria). Both were twenty years old, and the daily contact while working on the same machine nurtured mutual feelings. They kissed and hugged. Their affection came to the attention of other workers, and one of them took offense. This worker warned Gut about the illegality of the relationship. On May 27, 1941, however, Gut and Lacoute decided to have sex in an unguarded place near the silos. When they heard some noise nearby, they decided to withdraw to the men's room, but the worker who had previously warned Gut followed them, climbed up the outer wall, and peeked through the top window. He spotted them in tender embrace and denounced them. Gut admitted that they would have had sex had they not been interrupted. The fact that she already had a three-year-old child born out of wedlock made her look like a woman without morals to the judges. It ensured that she received a harsher punishment than the prisoner (two years of penal servitude, whereas he received one year and nine months in prison).[63]

---

[62] Feldurteil, Mannheim, November 11, 1941, in PAAA, R 40992.

[63] BStA Nürnberg, Akten der Anklagebehörde beim Sondergericht, 1165; Feldurteil, Nürnberg, November 25, 1941, in PAAA, R 40896.

Denunciations by fellow employees often revealed interesting workplace dynamics. In the honey cake factory König in Brandenburg in the fall of 1941, for example, a denunciation took an unexpected turn. The workforce consisted of fifty women and twelve French POWs. Flirting during work was common, and the women repeatedly gave cigarettes and sandwiches to the prisoners. On October 2, 1941, the worker Margarete Engelmann went to a woman supervisor and denounced Helene (Leni) Schütz, a fellow worker, reporting that she had heard that Frau Schütz took gifts from the prisoners and from time to time went outside with one of them. Frau Engelmann also claimed that Frau Schütz had shown herself to the prisoners in her underwear. The police interrogated many of the women and the foremen, and found out that Frau Schütz was particularly close to French prisoner Camille Rougier. This contact had come to the attention of the supervisors, who moved Rougier to a different shift, but rationalization measures led to the elimination of shifts in this factory, so that Frau Schütz and Rougier were again working together. Frau Schütz, who was thirty-nine and married, initially denied the allegations, but after some probing admitted that she and Rougier had met several times in the air raid shelter and had sex. The story that Frau Schütz had shown herself to the French prisoners in her underwear turned out to be an unfounded rumor, however. The special court in Berlin sentenced Leni Schütz to two years of penal servitude plus three years' loss of civil rights. The judge stressed that a harsh punishment was necessary as a deterrent because other women in the factory had also become friendly with French prisoners. He considered her crime particularly severe because an NSDAP speaker had recently come to the factory and reinforced the "enemy remains enemy" propaganda against POWs.

Frau Engelmann, the woman who denounced Leni, was a party member. She claimed that Leni's behavior had triggered outrage among the truly "German" women in the factory. From the interrogations of the other workers, however, the police learned that it was Frau Engelmann who was ostracized after it became known that she had denounced Leni. Another revealing aspect is the behavior of the management. Instead of denouncing the couple when evidence of an illegal relationship appeared, the foremen assigned them to different shifts as long as this was possible. Given that friendly relations between the women and the French prisoners were widespread in the factory, the management may have feared multiple arrests and potentially the loss of much of their workforce. This likely explains why they called in the party functionary who warned the women. They tried to resolve the problem with soft methods, too soft for the taste of the court, which criticized the management for failing "to intervene with the necessary decisiveness."[64]

In another case, employee ostracism against a denouncer had an unexpected outcome. Maria Arnold and French POW Maurice Rey, who were working next to each other in a Berlin brewery in 1941, seemed fond of each other. One day they had a serious argument because Rey was jealous after another worker had given her a cigarette. Rey slapped her in the face, and she went to the management and denounced him for hitting her, whereupon many other workers severely reproached her, telling her that Rey might be shot. She felt terrible and secretly met with Rey, who apologized for having hit her and told her that he feared for his life. He asked if she would help him escape to Switzerland, and she agreed. Rey came to her apartment, where they had sex. They were arrested on the way home from the cinema three days later. Luckily for Rey, it turned out that Maria Arnold did not have German citizenship. She was originally from Latvia but had come to Germany as an orphan refugee in 1924 and had been taken in by a German couple. She had applied for German citizenship several times but had never received it because she could not prove her "Aryan" ancestry. This meant that Rey was acquitted. Arnold received a relatively mild punishment for a relationship that had involved multiple sexual encounters and help for an escape (six months in prison).[65]

The finding of a letter by a colleague or employer often triggered the discovery. In a small factory in Windsheim (today: Bad Windsheim), west of Nürnberg, the manager one day in July 1943 noticed that French POW Albert Liau had received a letter from a woman in Nürnberg. While the foreman went to report the observation, however, somebody mistakenly took the letter and delivered it to the prisoner. The foreman could not remember the name of the POW, but the police officer suggested that he wait for the next letter and seize it. Another letter promptly arrived a few days later, and its contents suggested that a tender meeting had taken place and that the woman would come to Windsheim by train the following Sunday. The Gestapo waited for her and arrested her, finding letters from a prisoner in her purse. Meanwhile, the investigation in the factory revealed that the prisoner implicated in the forbidden love relation was not Liau but Raymond Guittard; Guittard had asked the woman to write to Liau to camouflage the relationship. Upon interrogation, the woman refused to reveal her name, but the Gestapo found out

[64] BLHA Potsdam, 12C, Sondergericht Berlin II, 6845.
[65] Feldurteil, Berlin, January 23, 1942, in PAAA, R 40909, and BLHA Potsdam, 12 C, Sondergericht Berlin, 6200.

that it was Luise Grob, a worker from Nürnberg, the wife of a soldier who had gone missing in Stalingrad. The investigation revealed that she and Guittard had had an erotic relationship while working in the same factory in Nürnberg in late 1942 and early 1943. The prisoner had repeatedly managed to break out of his camp at night. The special court sentenced her to two years of penal servitude. That she was having sex with a prisoner while her husband was caught in the siege of Stalingrad counted as an exacerbating factor.[66]

Weighing the loss of one, or potentially two, valuable workers was a significant consideration for farmers and small entrepreneurs, given that it became increasingly difficult to find replacements. Denunciations by farmers or their wives seem to have occurred more frequently in 1941 than later, when the labor shortage was more acute. The case of the farmworker Anna Knorr, a mother of three children aged from three to twelve in Furth im Wald (Bavaria), illustrates the competing pressures on farmers. Knorr lived and worked on the farm of Alois Kiefl and his wife. According to the testimony of a neighbor, Knorr would often look out of the window when the prisoners returned from work and marched through town. This neighbor once warned her. The Kiefls also noticed that Anna Knorr often teased French POW Marie Arthur Moreau, who was assigned to their farm from late 1940 until July 1941, and warned her repeatedly. Knorr ignored the warnings and had sex with Moreau on five or six occasions beginning in February 1941. In July 1941, the farming couple confronted her. Knorr admitted having had an affair with Moreau but asked the farmers not to denounce her. She claimed that her husband would kill her and that, if she survived, she would drown herself rather than stand trial. She also appealed to the farmers' compassion by asking them to think of what would happen to her three children. Yet, Alois Kiefl explained to her that he would be prosecuted and punished himself if he did not report her. The special court sentenced her to three years of penal servitude on August 28, 1941; Moreau received three and a half years in prison. Both claimed that the other had been the seducer. The repeated earlier warnings show that the farming couple hesitated to denounce her, preferring instead to warn her. But the finding of new evidence and the fact that the forbidden relation had become part of the village rumor mill meant that they risked punishment themselves if they did not denounce her.[67]

[66] BStA Nürnberg, Akten der Anklagebehörde beim Sondergericht, 2307.
[67] BStA Nürnberg, Akten der Anklagebehörde beim Sondergericht, 1206; Feldurteil, Nürnberg, November 20, 1941, in PAAA, R 40887.

Farmers who "caught" a couple in front of witnesses almost always denounced them, probably expecting to be prosecuted if it became known to the police that they had not reported a forbidden relationship. In the village Schadwalde (southeast of Danzig), for example, British POW Joseph MacAllister was working on a farm compound together with three women, two of them German citizens and one a Russian forced laborer. The three women slept in the same room. One night in September 1943, MacAllister, who liked Irene Pankowski, one of the German women, climbed into the women's bedroom. He undressed and snuck into bed with her. The farmer, however, noticed something and opened the door to the bedroom, finding the naked couple in bed. He denounced them. The court martial in Danzig, meeting on March 20, 1944, believed that sexual intercourse had occurred, although the prisoner and the woman both denied it. The court martial sentenced MacAllister to nine months in prison, a mild sentence, because the judges believed him that he had mistaken the woman as Polish. In this area all relationships with women were forbidden, but relations with non-German women were punished more lightly.[68]

Foreign laborers could also act as denouncers or provide testimony after a denunciation had occurred. Especially on farms, POWs often worked together with civilian laborers, mostly eastern Europeans. Not all eastern laborers were forced; there were some volunteer workers from Nazi allies like Slovakia, Hungary, Croatia, and other countries. Some of the eastern workers might be jealous of the western POW because he had more rights and might be treated better by the German employers and employees. Judges tended to give little credit to testimonies from eastern laborers, however, so that a verdict usually required more evidence.[69]

A denunciation by Slovak worker Martin Pipiska on an Austrian farm, for example, failed to bring French POW Gilbert Moret into prison in late 1941: Pipiska reported Moret for an affair with the German farmworker Anna Obritzberger. Pipiska, as a citizen of a Nazi-allied state, parroted Nazi propaganda by saying that he found it hard to stomach that "a German woman is messing around sexually with a member of an enemy nation." He also told the police that one of the three Polish laborers on the farm had observed the couple having sex in the barn. The police investigation, however, found the evidence dubious. Upon re-interrogation, Pipiska said only that he had one night seen that the light

[68] Feldurteil, Danzig, March 23, 1944, in BAR Bern, Bestand Vertretung Berlin, 86b.
[69] Hinrich Rüping, "Denunziation und Strafjustiz im Führerstaat," in *Denunziation: Historische, juristische und psychologische Aspekte*, ed. Günter Jerouschek, Inge Marßolek, and Hedwig Röckelein (Tübingen: Edition discord, 1997), 129.

in the woman's bedroom was still on and that the prisoner had not gone
to bed. Pipiska had heard a conversation but could not be more specific
than that. The Polish farmworker Anna Smucha testified that she had
seen Moret and Obritzberger working together in the barn and that it
appeared that they were having sex while standing. More contextual
evidence suggested, however, that she may not have had a good view
and could have misinterpreted the motions of common work given that it
was relatively dark. The farmer and some other employees said that they
had never noticed anything suspicious. Moreover, it appeared as if
Pipiska himself had some interest in Frau Obritzberger and might have
been jealous of Moret. In typical fashion, the court martial in Linz
dismissed the testimonies of non-Germans: "The damning testimonies
come only from non-German persons, whose personalities do not seem
to indicate that they are credible and reliable." Moret was acquitted.[70]

In Neumünster (Holstein), Ida Müllner had to manage the farm with
the help of a French prisoner, a Polish maid, and two male German
laborers after her husband had been drafted. On October 31, 1941, the
Polish maid Katharina Skowronska went to the Gestapo and denounced
her and French POW Antoine Dujardin. Skowronska testified that
Dujardin often spent the night in Müllner's bedroom and locked the
door behind him. She had once confronted Dujardin, but he had
grabbed her by the neck and yelled at her, "You are crazy, you Polish
pig!" The Gestapo, however, dismissed her testimony because she was a
Pole and illiterate and because Frau Müllner and her husband were both
dedicated NSDAP members. Yet, the rumor spread, and a few days
later, a family friend found Müllner and Dujardin in tender embrace.
Whether it was he who denounced them or whether the Gestapo, motivated by the persistent rumors, decided to interrogate the other workers
on the farm is unclear. Ida Müllner at first denied everything but then
broke down crying and claimed that Dujardin had taken advantage of
tensions between her and her husband and that she had felt that she owed
him something because he had once saved the life of her two-year-old
daughter.[71] The motive for the denunciation by Skowronska was likely
the offensive reaction of the prisoner to her reproach, although the fact
that she did confront him may also have resulted from resentment at his
privileged position on the farm.

[70] "Die belastenden Aussagen stammen lediglich von nicht deutschen Personen, die nach
ihrer Persönlichkeit nicht geeignet sind, als glaubwürdig und verlässlich zu erscheinen."
Feldurteil, Linz, November 28, 1941, in PAAA, R 40904.
[71] LASH Schleswig, Abt. 358, 2406–7.

Family Members As Denouncers

Family members often acted as denouncers. In the case of in-laws and husbands, the motives appear to have been predominantly private. Many parents resented their daughter-in-law for having an affair with somebody else while their son, her husband, was fighting on the eastern front. Sometimes the marriage had been concluded in a hurry at the beginning of the war, and the parents may never have liked their daughter-in-law. That the daughter-in-law was involved with a POW might have been an additional insult, but it is fair to think that the in-laws would have resented the relationship regardless of the status of the man. In the case of husbands as denouncers, jealousy and anger serve as a sufficient explanation. The husband coming home on leave and finding his wife involved with another man would have been angry against the other man regardless of whether he was a prisoner or a German neighbor. Against the latter, he could only sue for insult, which resulted in a small punishment at worst, but against the POW, the regulations in force ensured a much harsher punishment.[72]

Clearly, married women whose husbands were away faced close scrutiny from family members, neighbors, and co-workers. Margarethe Huber, the wife of a soldier and NSDAP member, worked in the kitchen of a shoe factory in Nürnberg. The factory also employed many French POWs and foreign workers, mostly Belgian women. Huber was once warned by the Gestapo to keep her distance from the prisoners after somebody had reported her to the management. The warning did not help, however. In July 1942 the kitchen overseer witnessed how she kissed French prisoner Roger Boulet. She reported Huber to the management. Interestingly, the factory merely dismissed Frau Huber and did not alert the police. She soon found new employment at the local post office, but she stayed in touch with Boulet. A Belgian civilian worker, Jeanne Aerts, who herself had a busy love life involving a German soldier and a French POW, helped her maintain the contact. Aerts and Huber met "their" prisoners several times in the forest, drank wine, and had sex. What ultimately led to the prosecution of Huber's relationship was a denunciation by her father-in-law. He went to the Gestapo and reported that his daughter-in-law was often absent at night and that she seemed to be having an excessive social life while her husband was fighting on the eastern front. Judge Rudolf Oeschey sentenced Huber to two years of penal servitude on March 26, 1943. He argued: "That she went to a

---

[72] Kundrus, *Kriegerfrauen*, 384–6.

POW camp at night, together with a foreigner, to have sex with a prisoner of war shows an unusual squalidness."[73]

In a village near Nürnberg, French POW Edouard Jouvet worked on a farm. The farmer had been drafted into the Wehrmacht, and the farm-woman, Maria Rüst, was in charge. She had a small child. Her father-in-law occasionally helped out. Jouvet and Frau Rüst quickly realized that they liked each other very much. He gave her chocolate from his aid parcels and was helpful and kind. One day in early April 1942, he asked her if he could come to her bedroom. She said yes. They had sex nine times until the father-in-law discovered and denounced them. Jouvet portrayed her as the seductress, but the court martial in Weiden sentenced him to three and a half years in prison on June 23, 1942.[74]

In 1943, Else Hart met a German soldier through a marriage bureau. They got married in a hurry before he had to leave for another tour of duty. She moved in with his parents, but in August 1943, she began an affair with French POW Desmaraist Gemelle. They had sex three times, and she became pregnant. She confessed the affair to her husband, who forgave her and generously promised to accept the child as his own. On May 15, 1944, she gave birth to a girl, but on July 31 her husband was killed in action in Normandy. The death of her son prompted the mother-in-law to denounce Else Hart. The special court of Frankfurt am Main sentenced her to only one year in prison, a stunningly mild punishment. The fact that she had not had a chance to get to know her husband, whom she had married without a period of courtship, counted in her favor, as did her claim that her husband had never had sex with her, neither when they got married nor during his two home leaves thereafter. The fact that her in-laws had from the start rejected her also served as a mitigating circumstance.[75]

Like many people contracting war marriages, Ella Schult and NCO Horst Schult never got a taste of married life. They celebrated their wedding in 1939, when she was nineteen, and he left immediately for the front, leaving her behind with a baby. In April 1941 they divorced after both had started affairs with other partners. Ella, who lived in a rural suburb of Berlin, helped out during the harvest in a nearby village. French POW Adrien L'Heureux, who worked on another farm, flirted with her and told her: "Come on, beautiful blonde, just say yes." They

---

[73] "Es zeugt von einer starken Verkommenheit, dass sie sich mit einer Ausländerin zusammen nachts an ein Kriegsgefangenenlager begab, um dann nach Verabredung sich mit ihm geschlechtlich einzulassen." BStA Nürnberg, Akten der Anklagebehörde beim Sondergericht, 1802.
[74] Dossier Edouard J., in AN, F9, 2360.   [75] HHStA Wiesbaden, Abt. 461, Nr. 9851.

had sex in the fields. She soon noticed that she was pregnant, although she was not sure who the father was because she had also had affairs with German men. Ella was still living with her former in-laws. It was her ex-mother-in-law, annoyed by her affairs, who denounced her. Ella initially claimed to have been raped by L'Heureux, but later she admitted consensual sex. The special court in Berlin sentenced her to one and a half years of penal servitude on January 20, 1942.[76]

It even happened that the parents or step-parents of a German woman denounced the relationship. In many cases, it appears that they wanted to punish the prisoner while knowing that their daughter would not receive a harsh punishment because of her age or mental state. They were likely hoping that even a mild punishment would serve as a warning to their daughters. In Schleswig-Holstein, a nosy mother looking through the luggage of her seventeen-year-old daughter triggered the discovery of a group of relations between women and French POWs on an estate in Todendorf. The daughter, Margarethe Bielemann, was performing her mandatory service year on the estate, and her mother found a love letter to her from a French POW. She denounced her daughter, and the police found out that several *Pflichtjahr* girls on the estate as well as a married woman evacuated from Hamburg had had affairs with French POWs. The married woman and the POWs were severely punished, while the *Pflichtjahr* girls, including Bielemann, got away with relatively light sentences because of their youth.[77]

In another case, the mother of thirty-two-year-old Anna van der Lubbe caught her with French POW Antoine Vernier, a twenty-seven-year-old welder working on their farm in a small village near the Dutch border in September 1940. They had kissed, hugged, and touched each other's genitals in the cow barn. On January 20, 1941, the mother denounced the affair, probably knowing that her daughter would receive a mild punishment because she had been diagnosed as "feeble-minded" (the special court in Düsseldorf sentenced her to six months in prison). The court martial in Aachen gave Vernier two years in prison.[78] In the case of Emilie Hartmann (thirty-five), a soldier's wife, it was her mother's impatience with her lifestyle that led to the denunciation in 1944. Frau Hartmann was living with her own two children in the apartment of her mother in southwestern Germany. She left the apartment three to four times a week and stayed away for the night. She had several intimate encounters with a transformed French POW, a sales clerk five years

[76] BLHA Potsdam, 12 C, Sondergericht Berlin II, 6203.
[77] LASH Schleswig, Abt. 358, 2400–2405.
[78] Feldurteil, Aachen, August 1, 1941, in PAAA, R 40875.

younger than her. The mother disapproved of her lifestyle and denounced her.[79]

Many husbands denounced their unfaithful wives, sometimes in a fit of anger and jealousy shortly after discovery, other times after some hesitation. French POWs Pierre Ivère and Gustave Moriand were working in a factory in Bayreuth (Bavaria). They had to wash in the courtyard, which was connected to the apartment of the worker Amsler. In September 1940, Herr Amsler invited the two prisoners to his home, and his wife served them coffee and cake. Another woman, the unmarried Katharina Mellmann, was also present, perhaps because she was a boarder in the apartment of the Amslers. The prisoners and the three Germans frequently talked with each other. One day, as Ivère was taking a shower, Frau Amsler waived to him and invited him to the apartment. They had sex inside. They met four or five times, in the attic, the shower room, or the marital bed. Meanwhile, Moriand met with Mellmann in the courtyard, and they exchanged kisses and hugs. In December 1940 Herr Amsler surprised both couples and denounced them. The court martial in Weiden sentenced Ivère to two and a half years and Moriand to ten months in prison.[80]

Frieda Selke, a thirty-five-year-old woman living in Potsdam, noticed in the summer of 1941 that French POWs were working in the coal storage of a firm next door. She could see them from her kitchen window. After observing them for a while, she waved to one of them, the high school teacher Paul Leduc. He waved back. Selke trained her dog to go into the courtyard and deliver little notes to Leduc and to bring her his answers (the archival file contains a letter with the dog's teeth marks). The dog also carried a photo of her to him. Through their canine messenger, they agreed to meet in a rowboat on one of the many local waterways. She rented a boat, and when she made the dog bark, Leduc knew that it was safe to swim to the boat. They kissed while lying down in the boat but apparently did not go farther because of the danger of discovery. Selke, who was married, told her much younger sister-in-law Margarethe Bossler about the affair. Bossler was fascinated by it and soon also participated in the reunions, swimming and kissing with another French prisoner from the courtyard. Once, Frau Selke showed herself naked at the kitchen window, while Leduc was masturbating outside. Frau Bossler asked her to at least put on her bathing suit. The double affair was discovered by Frau Bossler's husband (Frieda Selke's

[79] "Session du tribunal des prisonniers du Wehrkreis V: Fiches de prisonniers," audience du 23.1.1945, in AN, F9, 2799.
[80] Feldurteil, Weiden, November 18, 1941, in PAAA, R 40897.

brother). He did already suspect that his sister was involved with a POW, and he had warned his wife to avoid contact with her. He became alarmed when his wife renewed her friendship with his sister and when she began to be frequently absent. His wife explained to him that she was visiting her sick father in Berlin, but when he found out that this was a lie, he confronted her on August 19, 1941, and she confessed everything. The husband hesitated at first, but six days later he denounced his wife and his sister. The special court sentenced Frau Selke to one and a half years of penal servitude and Frau Bossler to one year in prison.[81]

French POW Sauveur Esquibel, a farmer and mason from the Pyrenees region in southwestern France, worked for farmers in Külmla in Thuringia. Although the husband was present on the farm, Esquibel and the farm wife, Frau Graber, had a secret affair. They had sex on the hay in the barn several times in late 1941. It seems that the woman was hoping to end the relationship, but, on January 16, 1942, she had a fight with her husband and decided afterwards to meet the prisoner again. She told him that she would wait for him in the washroom. When Esquibel appeared, he suggested that they would be safer in the basement. He asked her to get a blanket, however. When she came down to the basement with the blanket, she did not notice that her husband had followed her. When the husband confronted the couple, just as they were undressing, the woman ran up into the courtyard and threw herself into the well. The prisoner climbed after her and saved her from drowning. The court martial in Kassel on April 10, 1942, sentenced him to three and a half years in prison even though his rescue of the woman counted as a mitigating factor.[82]

Unanticipated leaves of soldier husbands led to many discoveries and denunciations, often under painful circumstances. In Reichenbach near Görlitz (southeast of Berlin), for example, French POW Maurice Blois was working in a factory in early 1942, when he took note of a woman who was living in an apartment across from the factory. Through a coachman, he found out her name (Hildegard Ortner), but before he decided what to do next, the woman approached him on the street and invited him to visit her. They agreed to secretly meet at night. Early in the morning of February 8, 1942, he climbed over the fence surrounding the factory and visited her. They had sex, and after fifteen minutes, he returned to the factory. Just a few moments later, the woman's husband returned from the front, and the woman was so confused and embarrassed that she confessed everything to him. The husband denounced

---

[81] BLHA Potsdam, 12 C, Sondergericht Berlin II, 6407.   [82] AN, F9, 2383.

them. Blois at first claimed that she must have met with somebody else, but during a face-to-face encounter at the police station, she identified him by pointing to a small scar at the left of his mouth. The special court sentenced her to one year of penal servitude, and the court martial in Breslau gave him three years in prison on September 8, 1942. The woman's husband was killed in action in Russia a few months after the discovery.[83]

In the early morning of August 14, 1944, the soldier Hermann Kruse arrived in Wuppertal-Barmen. He had been wounded at the front and spent some time in a military hospital. After his release, he wanted to see his wife and children. When he entered his apartment, he found his wife naked and awake, lying in bed with one of the children, while the marital bed was empty but still warm. When Kruse opened the dresser to put away his jacket, he discovered a man inside. Kruse tried to grab the man, but he escaped. His wife confessed that it was Gabriel Soulard, a French transformed POW, who had taken up an erotic relationship with her. They had lived like a couple for many months.[84]

Another painful discovery, albeit with a delay, happened to another wounded German soldier returning to his home in eastern Pomerania in late 1943. His wife, Frau Michael, immediately told him that there were rumors in the village that she was having an affair with a prisoner but that they were groundless. The husband believed her, but after a week, he noticed that he had gonorrhea. Although he had once had an outbreak of this disease, he had been cured, and he claimed not to have had sex since his last home leave. Herr Michael therefore confronted his wife, who now confessed having had an affair with a French POW. Right after the confession, the wife tried to commit suicide by taking an overdose of sleeping pills. The husband intervened and dragged her to the local POW quarters to identify the guilty prisoner. Still drowsy, she pointed at POW Ernest Hortin. During the police investigation, it transpired that her friend, Frau Pankow, also had an affair with a POW. After Frau Michael had tested negative for gonorrhea, however, both women recanted. Yet, a neighbor reported to the police that she had overheard the two women talking to each other about sex with the prisoners. On the basis of this testimony, the special court sentenced Frau Michael to one and a half years and Frau Pankow to two years of penal servitude (apparently she had met "her" prisoner more frequently). Yet, on February 17, 1944, the

---

[83] Dossier 2837, in AN, F9, 2417.
[84] Feldurteil, Münster, December 5, 1944. SHD Caen, 25 P 11598. Soulard received four and a half years of penitentiary, an unusually harsh punishment. That he had gone to the cinema together with Frau Kruse counted as an aggravating factor.

court martial in Stettin acquitted Hortin, the POW Frau Michael had pointed out, because it could not prove that he had been her partner (Frau Michael had been under the influence of the sleeping pills when she "identified" him and then claimed that nothing had happened between her and a POW). The other suspect, Lucien Darnaud, received two and a half years of penal servitude for his relationship with Frau Pankow.[85]

British POW Harold Wells already had a disciplinary and criminal record as a POW when he stood trial before the court martial of Danzig on June 20, 1944. He had escaped in the summer of 1943 and received three weeks' arrest as a punishment (a normal disciplinary sanction). However, it came out at that time that he had also had a love affair with an underage girl, and for this affair the court martial had sentenced him to three years of penal servitude (soon converted to a prison term) on October 26, 1943. Yet, Wells escaped from the prison on Christmas 1943 and walked back to his old work detachment in a village south of Danzig. He hid among his former comrades who were working in a brickyard. On January 10, 1944, he visited the daughter of the local innkeeper, Edeltraut Brecht, with whom he had also had a love affair in the summer of 1943. Brecht lived in the inn of her father and was married to a Luftwaffe officer. She agreed to hide Wells in a storage den, where he spent two months. Yet, in March, Brecht's husband returned on home leave unannounced. He discovered and denounced the prisoner. Wells received four years of penal servitude in addition to his previous sentence. Frau Brecht was also sentenced to four years of penal servitude.[86]

It could sometimes be difficult for courts to decide what precisely had happened when angry husbands denounced their wives. In the case of Anna Rössler, the wife of a blacksmith in Berlin-Marienfelde, an abusive husband was a likely cause for the forbidden relationship and also the denouncer. Rössler, who was forty, had been married for half her life. Her husband drank, squandered money, and beat her, as neighbors confirmed. She had run away many times, and once, in 1938, she had filed for divorce, but she had withdrawn her petition because of threats from her husband. In 1939, the husband was drafted into the Wehrmacht, but he served in a garrison unit not far from home. In April 1941, she received French POW Anselme Larivière as a helper. Larivière was himself a blacksmith and a very good worker. He spoke a little German. Husband and wife were happy to have him. Yet, on December 10, 1941, another fight broke out between the husband and wife. A little later, Frau

---

[85] AN, F9, 2525.   [86] BAR Bern, Bestand Vertretung Berlin, 83b.

Rössler went into the rabbit hutch for a secret meeting with Larivière. While she was waiting for him, she took off her underpants. Her husband discovered and denounced her. She first admitted that she had been sexually aroused and wanted to have sex with the prisoner, but then she retracted the confession and claimed that she had only placed her underpants on the floor so that her husband would notice them and, believing in adultery, would finally agree to a divorce. While the court martial considered the evidence insecure and acquitted Larivière on February 13, 1942, the special court in Berlin argued that she had acted in an undignified manner regardless of what had motivated her to take off her underwear and sentenced her to nine months in prison on June 12, 1942.[87]

Another tricky case came before the court martial of Breslau on October 20, 1944. It involved British POW Thomas Walker, who was man of confidence of a work detachment in Breslau. He worked in a charity distribution center installed in a brewery and slept on the premises. The married woman Stefanie Wolters cleaned the rooms and washed the laundry of the POWs. In December 1943, her husband returned from the front and discovered another man's clothing in their apartment. He asked to whom the clothes belonged, and she mentioned Walker, whereupon the husband went to the brewery and beat Walker up. Although Frau Wolters had a good alibi, since she was washing the laundry of the prisoners, she confessed to her husband that she had had sex with Walker in his bed twice during an early morning. The special court in Mährisch-Schönberg sentenced her to two and a half years of penal servitude in April 1944 even though she retracted her confession several times and Walker denied any intimate relation. When Frau Wolters appeared as a witness during his court martial, she again confessed two intimate encounters and then withdrew her confession. She claimed that she had only confessed having had sex with Walker because she assumed that her husband would be punished for beating up Walker if the authorities found out that he had no reason to be jealous. Frau Wolters had previously been examined for insanity and been certified as sane, and therefore the court martial assumed that her initial confession was truthful and sentenced Walker to three years in prison. He did not receive penal servitude because the judges were not convinced that he had known that Frau Wolters was married to a soldier.[88]

---

[87] BLHA Potsdam, 12 C, Landgericht Berlin. Urteile 1943. Berlin II, 7/35.
[88] BAR Bern, Bestand Vertretung Berlin, 81c.

Denunciation through the Prisoner or the Woman and Discovery Chains

Several women denounced a prisoner, accusing him of having harassed or raped them, but the denunciation often backfired because the bar for proving rape was quite high, so that the judges often concluded that the relationship had been consensual and that the woman was only trying to get an alibi by accusing the prisoner of rape. This is what happened to the farmworker Marie Kelch who complained to a guard on June 11, 1941, that Gilbert Haus, the French POW working with her on a farm in a hamlet southwest of Nürnberg, was constantly harassing her. The farmer, perhaps hoping to keep the POW as a worker, told the guard that he had not noticed anything. Kelch was twenty-four and had a four-year-old child born out of wedlock. Haus was a blacksmith from the European minority in Algeria and one year older. The police investigation suggested that the woman and the prisoner had started a consensual intimate relationship in the fall of 1940. The prisoner was marched to the farm by a guard every morning and picked up at night, but he and Kelch had worked together unsupervised during the day. They admitted having had sexual encounters in the barn and the hayloft. In February 1941, they had a big fight and ignored each other for a while, but they became intimate again until they had another fight in June, which prompted her denunciation. She admitted that she was in love with him and that she was very passionate. The special court in Nürnberg, deliberating on September 5, 1941, showed strong bias against Kelch because she had an illegitimate child and seemed "anchorless" in sexual matters. She received two years of penal servitude. The only mitigating factor was the fact that she had twice ended the relationship after a fight. The court martial in Nürnberg sentenced Haus, who made a far-reaching confession but claimed to have ignored the prohibition, to three and a half years in prison.[89]

The denunciation of a POW also backfired on Anna Müller, a forty-seven-year-old farmwoman in a village near Schwandorf (Bavaria). Her husband was sixty and sickly. They had three children aged from ten to sixteen and there were two older children from the husband's first marriage. The French POW assigned to their farm was Léon Paradis, a thirty-seven-year-old mason from a village east of Paris. He was an appreciated worker and always ate at the family table. In October 1941,

---

[89] BStA Nürnberg, Akten der Anklagebehörde beim Sondergericht, 1214; Feldurteil, Nürnberg, November 20, 1941, in PAAA, R 40898. The judges provided the card with the prohibition that he had signed.

a guard stopped at the farm, doing his routine check on the prisoners. He asked Anna Müller whether she was satisfied with Paradis. Frau Müller answered that he was a good worker but that he had raped her three times. The guard immediately arrested Paradis. Yet, the investigation soon cast a shadow over Frau Müller. The POW claimed that she had seduced him three times and that she had denounced him as an act of revenge after he had decided to end the relationship because it was forbidden. He claimed that Frau Müller had not left him alone. He also believed she was angry because he had once complained about the food on the farm. When asked why she had not reported Paradis after the alleged rapes, Frau Müller answered that she had not had the time to do so. She claimed to have told her husband that Léon was not leaving her alone (something the husband vaguely confirmed), but that was all. Herr and Frau Müller were clearly afraid of losing a good worker. The district court in Schwandorf concluded that she had engaged in a consensual relationship with Paradis and sentenced her to twenty months of penal servitude. The court martial in Nürnberg sentenced Paradis to two years in prison. Revealing a typical bias toward relationships between an older woman and a younger man, the judges claimed that he had been seduced by "an ageing woman." They also rewarded him for having tried to end the sexual relationship.[90]

Although sexual violence was rare, it did happen that a prisoner did not take seriously the woman's defense and rejection. In a furniture factory in Bergisch-Gladbach (east of Cologne), the worker Rosalie Rötler from time to time gave candy to French POW Henri Decolas. The prisoner misread her kindness. On June 10, 1941, he hugged and kissed her when they were alone in a room. When he touched her breasts and waist, she bit his arm, and he let go of her. She denounced the prisoner, and the court martial in Bonn sentenced him to two years in prison. The judges considered her gifts of candy, which were forbidden, as a mitigating factor for the prisoner, arguing that she had not kept the required distance from him and therefore tempted him.[91]

The trial of French POW Robert Lemaire turned into an insult competition between him and the woman who had denounced him, the farmworker Maria Sandkühler (twenty-one). They had both been working on a farm in Westphalia throughout 1941. One day, Lemaire hugged Maria Sandkühler when she jumped off a horsewagon and asked her to kiss him. She slapped him in the face. She waited for a couple of

---

[90] BStA Nürnberg, Akten der Anklagebehörde beim Sondergericht, 1308; Feldurteil, Nürnberg, December 18, 1941, in PAAA, R 40905.
[91] Feldurteil, Bonn, November 7, 1941, in PAAA, R 40894.

weeks until the harvest work was over, and then she denounced Lemaire, accusing him of lewd talk and of inappropriate advances. Lemaire, in turn, made some of the same accusations against her and claimed that she had once urinated in the presence of the prisoners. He claimed that she had only denounced him because he had complained about the food on the farm, and she admitted that his complaint had prompted her to denounce him. The judges commented on the primitive circumstances on this farm, which did not have toilets and where a person who had to urinate regularly attracted lewd comments from the others. Still, they sentenced Lemaire to six months in prison because they believed her incriminating testimony despite the fact that she admitted having denounced him in anger over his complaint about the food.[92]

Some prisoners turned themselves in and thereby also denounced the woman. The POW Pierre Delannoy, a twenty-two-year-old student at an arts academy, worked as a milk distributor for a farmer northwest of Berlin and met twenty-six-year-old farm laborer Anna Akovieff, who had German citizenship but came from Persia. According to Delannoy, she seduced him twice in the summer and fall of 1941. He decided to turn himself in when he learned about the prohibition. The court martial in Berlin believed that he likely had not received the order of January 10, 1940, because he had been sent to a work detachment very early. Even though a guard testified that he had written the order on a sheet of paper and shown it to Delannoy before the relationship started, the judges pointed out that the prisoner might not have understood it (although he knew German). The judges even suspected that the guard predated this incident in an effort to cover up his own negligence. Delannoy was acquitted. It is not clear why in this case the judges went out of their way to defend the prisoner. Certainly, the fact that he had turned himself in provoked respect. The fact that the woman was of non-German origin and that she was older than the prisoner likely also worked in his favor.[93] Another case of a prisoner turning himself in and thereby exposing the woman to prosecution was George Linton, who had an affair with a married woman in Pless (Upper Silesia) but broke up with her when she made contemptuous remarks about her husband. In this case, too, the judges rewarded the honest action of the POW with a mild sentence and gave him only one year in prison even though they had had sex four times.[94]

[92] Feldurteil, Münster, December 18, 1941, in PAAA, R 40905.
[93] Feldurteil, Berlin, October 31, 1941, in PAAA, R 40895.
[94] Feldurteil, Kattowitz, April 12, 1944, in BAR Bern, Bestand Vertretung Berlin, 79a.

A very common cause of discovery was the chain reaction that occurred after one arrest and interrogation. This was more widespread among the women because they were usually exposed to more intimidating interrogations. The Gestapo always asked a woman whether she could name any others who had affairs with prisoners, and quite a few women, and sometimes also prisoners, revealed the names of other couples after their own discovery. Some defendants may have hoped to mitigate their own punishment; others may have believed that indicating somebody else's forbidden relationship before admitting one's own might lead the Gestapo onto a different track. In the case of groups dating each other, discovery was therefore often contagious. Even if the woman or the prisoner did not directly name another couple, a search of their possessions might reveal letters or clues pointing toward another forbidden relationship, and the interrogation of witnesses could easily identify other suspects. Discovery chains should be distinguished from random denunciations, given that the revelations usually occurred under the pressure of an interrogation by the police or a military justice official.

Many factories or workshops became notorious for harboring multiple forbidden relations. One of them was the tile factory Höcherberg in Bexbach (Saar). French prisoners met secretly with German women on a large scale, and discovery of one relationship led to at least a dozen arrests and trials in the fall of 1941. The court martial in Mannheim concluded that "an atmosphere of general licentiousness" reigned at the factory. The permissive environment, pointing to a lack of enforcement of the prohibition, served as a mitigating factor.[95] The worsted yarn factory "Amerika" in Penig near Chemnitz (Saxony) was another place with many intimate relations between French POWs and women employed in the factory. Couples met in the forest or in the homes of the women. One denunciation in late 1941 had a domino effect because the police interrogations kept revealing ever new relationships. In this case, the relations were more far-reaching and intimate because, unlike in Bexbach, the couples could easily meet outside the factory grounds.[96]

Also in late 1941, a series of arrests occurred on the Augsburg site of the MAN (Maschinenfabrik Augsburg-Nürnberg) motor works. From the trials of French POWs employed there, it emerged that the prisoners worked largely unsupervised with German women and that their sleeping quarters were unguarded. Many prisoners planned secret meetings with German women during work and then met them at night in the

---

[95] See, for example, Feldurteil, Mannheim, November 25, 1941, in PAAA, R 40896.
[96] See, for example, several cases tried by the court martial in Chemnitz on January 6 and 13, 1942, all in PAAA, R 40908 and 40909.

surrounding fields, in abandoned barns or haylofts, or on the sports facilities of the company. The earliest case seems to have involved Alphonse Robert, a young lathe operator from Luxemburg who served in the French army and fell in love with the German worker Elisabeth Gschmieder. They had sex in the fields at least seven times, and they spoke of getting married and moving to Luxemburg after the war. The court martial in Augsburg sentenced Robert to three and a half years in prison, a harsh punishment even though it considered the lax guarding on this factory site as a mitigating circumstance.[97] After this case, the police kept discovering many more forbidden relations that had sprung up during the warmer months of 1941, and trials continued into early 1942. The prisoners had convinced some of the women to meet them at night by pointing out that they were unguarded.[98]

In the mine and smelting works of Jenbach (western Austria), the police discovered a similar chain of forbidden relations in the winter of 1941–2, prompting the general prosecutor of the district court in Innsbruck to observe: "One can almost speak of a 'love nest' featuring the French and Belgian prisoners of war employed there and the female workers drafted for labor. It seems as if certain parts of the female population do no longer take seriously in this respect the instructions and warnings of the authorities." As elsewhere, the prosecutor concluded that poor guarding and the strong integration of the POWs into the working community favored illegal relationships.[99] Another case involved group relationships between British POWs and Austrian women in a dynamite factory in southern Austria during the spring of 1943. Several of the women accused of forbidden relations announced that the entire factory would need to be arrested if they were prosecuted.[100]

Discovery chains also occurred in many farming communities. In the small village Gülchsheim, south of Würzburg (Bavaria), the mayor denounced the twenty-one-year-old farmworker Luise Diehl in October 1942. She was pregnant, but she did not name a father. To her employer, she said that she had had a quick affair with a Luftwaffe soldier while visiting the cinema in Ochsenfurt, the closest town. The rumor mill claimed that Belgian POW Joseph Goffin was the father. During the police interrogation, she admitted it. She had been working with Goffin

---

[97] Feldurteil, Augsburg, November 13, 1941, in PAAA, R 40896.
[98] Feldurteil, Augsburg, November 13, 1941, in PAAA, R 40896, and Feldurteil, Augsburg, November 20, 1941, in PAAA, R 40898; Feldurteil, Augsburg, November 28, 1941, in PAAA, R 40912.
[99] Form and Uthe, *NS-Justiz in Österreich*, 79.
[100] See the case study "A Failed Group Escape" in Chapter 7.

daily for several years and claimed that he had become more and more pushy in early 1942 until she had finally given in to him. Diehl told the interrogator that there were quite a few other forbidden relations in the village, without mentioning names, but the police immediately discovered another affair between a pregnant farmworker and a Belgian POW, and others later on. The special court in Nürnberg was unusually lenient in Diehl's case and sentenced her to only one year in prison on March 24, 1943, considering the shared daily work with the prisoner and the fact that he had played the active role as mitigating factors. That her employer described her as an excellent worker with the strength of two others also influenced the judge. The court martial in Würzburg sentenced Goffin to three years in prison. Their child was born on October 27, 1942.[101]

In Möllendorf, west of Vienna, an anonymous denunciation alerted the police to the relationship of Anna Leonhard with French POW Henri Badinter. Upon interrogation, Leonhard mentioned five other women who were involved with POWs, although she did not know in each case how far they had gone. Interrogations of the other women, and re-interrogations based on new testimony obtained from them, quickly revealed a rich tapestry of love affairs. As usual, the investigators used small discrepancies in the testimonies to push for more extensive confessions, and they confronted one woman with the claims of another one, and sometimes with the testimony of the prisoner. As long as the women and the prisoner could not meet and discuss their defense strategy (although sometimes they did manage to do so), they almost inevitably revealed more during subsequent interrogations.[102]

Similar chain reactions occurred all over the Reich in factories and on farms. A shortage of guards and the long workdays fostered an environment that was conducive to flirting and amorous approaches. Knowledge that others were violating the prohibition lowered inhibitions because couples perceived security in numbers, but discovery of one relationship triggered a chain reaction. Perhaps in some cases the police were reluctant to dig into the full extent of forbidden relations because it would have paralyzed an entire farming village, workshop, or factory. In these cases, it is possible that the authorities limited themselves to a few exemplary cases as a deterrent, as Ulrich Herbert and others have suggested.[103] One must wonder, of course, how many factories and farming

---

[101] BStA Nürnberg, Akten der Anklagebehörde beim Sondergericht, 1973.
[102] WStLA, Sondergericht, 7207.
[103] Herbert, *Hitler's Foreign Workers*, 125; Theis, *Wehrmachtjustiz an der "Heimatfront,"* 387; Ambrière, *Les grandes Vacances*, 197.

villages existed that had networks of relationships that were never discovered.

Discovery Not Leading to Immediate Denunciation

Denunciation often was only the means of last resort. Guards, employers, and fellow workers who discovered a forbidden relation could warn the woman or the prisoner without a denunciation. If the couple persisted, it was possible for an employer to request a transfer of the prisoner or dismiss the woman, still without denunciation. Guards and military authorities in charge of assigning the POWs to work sites were sometimes complicit in these cases, knowing that there probably was an illegal relationship (or a threat that one may develop) but deciding not to investigate. Given that discovery could lead to an arrest of multiple workers, it was usually best to arrange a quiet transfer of the prisoner. As demonstrated, this occurred quite frequently. The cases that did come to court were often those where the prisoner and the woman maintained contact after his transfer by writing to each other or by visiting each other.

The farmworker Barbara Deggendorfer and French POW Robert Bal worked on a farm in Hannersgrün, a tiny village east of Nürnberg. One evening, the son of the farmer observed Deggendorfer going into the prisoner's bedroom. He followed her and saw how Bal pulled her into bed with him. The son reported the incident to his father. The court files of the prisoner and the woman differ slightly on what happened next, but they do not dispute that Bal was transferred to a different farm a few days later, and they show that neither the farmer nor the guard, who knew something about the incident, brought the matter to the attention of the police or the higher military authorities. After the transfer, however, Bal kept visiting Deggendorfer until the guard noticed one night that he was missing at his new workplace and found him with Deggendorfer on the original farm, leading to the arrest of the couple. Although the prisoner, who was married himself, denied intimate relations, the woman admitted having had sex once in the barn, and the farmer's son now also told the police what he had seen. Bal was a respected and cherished worker in the farm community, and this may have afforded him some protection after the initial discovery by the farmer's son.[104]

---

[104] BStA Nürnberg, Akten der Anklagebehörde beim Sondergericht, 1690, and Dossier Robert B., in AN, F9, 2365. The special court in Nürnberg-Fürth sentenced her to two years of penal servitude on October 20, 1942, and the court martial in Weiden sentenced Bal to three years in prison on November 20, 1942.

In a small village south of Vienna, Hedwig Linsbichler was working on the farm of the village mayor in 1941. From April to July, she had a sexual relationship with the French POW Etienne Meier who also worked in the village. The police interrogation revealed that several people, including her employer, had noticed her closeness to the prisoner. The farmer and some others had repeatedly warned her about the consequences: they told her that her head might be shorn and that she might be dragged through the village and shamed. When the warnings failed to break up the relationship, Meier was assigned to a different workplace. The relationship would not have been prosecuted had Meier not escaped from his new workplace to go back to his old farm. He was stopped in a train station, and during a search, the police found a photo of Hedwig Linsbichler. The farmer (who was also mayor), the guards, or any of the other witnesses in the village could easily have denounced the couple, but nobody did. During the police interrogation, the farmer had to defend himself because of this.[105]

In a garden center in Heidelberg, French POW Louis Soubise, a thirty-seven-year-old cook for the French merchant marine, worked in the company of sixteen-year-old Margarethe Gert, starting in 1940. Her father, who owned the garden center, had been a POW in France during World War I and wanted to show to Soubise that Germany was treating POWs better than France had. He therefore invited him to the family table and treated him with great consideration. While working in the greenhouse, Soubise and Margarethe Gert became increasingly intimate. She was influenced by a friend who told her that sex was beautiful and that she herself was proud to already have a child at age sixteen. In early 1941, Soubise was transferred to a different workplace. He and Margarethe wrote each other and continued their intimate relation when Soubise returned to the garden center in April. In August 1941, the father discovered the letters. He first refused to believe that more than flirtation was involved, but he decided to ask for a second transfer of the prisoner. Upon leaving, in September, Soubise confessed the affair to the father. Soubise assured the father that he did not want to inherit the garden center (he knew Margarethe had a brother who was considered the heir), but he declared that he wanted to marry her and stay in Germany. The father promised not to denounce the relationship but asked that his

[105] WStLA, Sondergericht, 6325; Feldurteil, Linz, February 24, 1942, in PAAA, R 40912. Linsbichler did not have to suffer the threatened shaming rituals because the court sentence would have mentioned them. That Meier had lived in Vienna before the war and spoke the local dialect facilitated his integration into the village, although villagers knew that he was a POW.

daughter take another year before she decided about marrying Soubise. While talking to the daughter, however, the father was more reproachful, and the daughter became so distressed that she turned herself in. In this case, the father likely hesitated to imperil his daughter through a denunciation, but he must have known that she would not be punished harshly in light of her youth. The fact that the relationship went on for a year suggests that the parents must have noticed it. They did accept the prisoner as a fine suitor for their daughter, although they did want her (understandably) to take more time before she decided. The father opted for a soft approach (request for transfer of the POW) rather than a denunciation when he found evidence of the forbidden relation.[106]

A remarkable, but not unusual, case of neighborly forbearance occurred in Berlin. When the housewife Berta Lagowski moved into a new apartment complex in Berlin-Ludwigsfelde in April 1941 with her husband and their two young children, the French POW Adolf Milewski came to finish the painting of the apartment. Frau Lagowski started a passionate affair with Milewski, who was a Polish citizen, while her husband was at work. Milewski kept visiting her even after his paint job was finished. She was very much in love with him and did not hide it. To one neighbor, she boasted that the prisoner "is a handsome blond boy" with a beautiful "Pillack" (a word for penis in her native East Prussian dialect). She even showed her the condoms she had bought at the neighborhood pharmacy. The neighbor just shrugged her shoulders and said: "oh well, there is no harm done if a little Frenchman results from this relationship." The husband of that neighbor apparently told Lagowski's husband that his wife was cheating on him with a prisoner, but Herr Lagowski dismissed the comment, saying, "Ah, my wife is crazy!" Other neighbors observed that Frau Lagowski always wore a scarf, presumably to hide love bites, and one neighbor testified that Milewski's guard had once come out of her apartment and made a comment suggesting that he himself had had sex with Frau Lagowski (she denied this, while admitting the relationship with Milewski). It is not clear what triggered the discovery, but it is remarkable that the relationship went on from April to August 1941 and that none of the many neighbors who knew about it made a denunciation over several months. Given that the apartment complex was brand new, the renters probably

---

[106] Feldurteil, Mannheim, December 19, 1941, in PAAA, R 40902. The court martial in Mannheim sentenced Soubise to three years in prison. The fact that Margarethe had apparently already had a sexual experience before meeting him counted as a mitigating factor, although the judges noted that he, as a much older man, should have acted with more restraint.

did not know each other before moving in, and there had been no time for neighborhood solidarity to develop.[107]

In Nürnberg, the boarder Frieda Graf noticed that her landlady, Maria Meyer, was often absent in the morning. She knew that her marriage with an office clerk, who was fighting on the eastern front, was in crisis, and she suspected an affair. One morning, in December 1942, she secretly followed the landlady and noticed that she was meeting with a Belgian prisoner. She confronted Frau Meyer, who admitted having an affair with the prisoner. Frau Meyer asked her not to say anything because the prisoner might kill himself if they were discovered. She said that she wanted to marry him after the war. Graf warned Frau Meyer and told her to burn the letters from the prisoner, which she did. But Graf did not denounce her even though all witnesses characterized her relationship with Frau Meyer as strained. The affair was likely discovered through new letters that the couple exchanged.[108]

On a farm estate in a tiny hamlet 100 kilometers south of Vienna, four women had affairs with three of the five French POWs assigned to the estate, starting in April 1941. The estate owner was a Polish woman, and the estate had an Austrian administrator, Herr Wandl. The five French POWs on the estate slept in a separate room. In late May 1942, the farmhand Johann Richter, who had to lock the POW sleeping room in the evening, had a suspicion that some prisoners were sneaking out at night. He told Wandl that he would check with his flashlight whether all prisoners were in their bed. Wandl, however, told Richter to mind his own business and dismissed him the next day. Richter went straight to the police station in the next town and denounced Wandl and the women on the estate. It became clear that Wandl had known about several forbidden affairs on the estate for a long time. He had likely not intervened because discovery threatened him with the loss of much of his labor force. One of the accused women had herself warned Richter not to say anything because otherwise the estate would lose its French prisoners. The other employees on the estate also kept their mouths shut, but it needed only one uncooperative employee to trigger the discovery, in revenge for his dismissal.[109]

The relationship between French saxophone player Clément Allier and Ursula Rickau in a factory in Landsberg an der Warthe came out

---

[107] BLHA Potsdam, 12 C, Sondergericht Berlin, 172, containing both judgments. The court martial sentenced Milewski to three and a half years in prison even though it considered Frau Lagowski, who was six years older, as the driving force. She received three years of penal servitude.
[108] BStA Nürnberg, Akten der Anklagebehörde beim Sondergericht, 2313.
[109] WStLA, Sondergericht, 6348 and 6532.

because a guard found her letters during a routine search of Allier's possessions. The investigation revealed, however, that a circle of employees and also her family had protected the relationship for a long time. A young worker who played the accordion and made music with Allier transported letters between the two on days when they could not see each other. Other employees and even members of the management knew of the relationship, but they liked the couple and refrained from denouncing them. Some of them told the police that they had warned Rickau, but the police believed that these statements were self-serving and that warnings, if they had happened at all, had not been serious. Her mother, and perhaps also her father and her grandparents, with whom she lived, had known about the relationship, but nobody had tried to stop it.[110]

Veronika Bachmann, an auxiliary worker in the champagne factory Kupferberg in Mainz in 1943, seems to have found an understanding foreman. This establishment employed thirty to forty German women and fifty French POWs. It had many caves for the cool storage of champagne dug in the hills at the southern edge of the old town. Bachmann, born in 1901, was married and had a seven-year-old daughter. The French POW Marcel Keusch, a thirty-two-year-old teacher, caught her attention during work. He once asked her for cigarette paper and matches, and she brought him all he wanted and also sandwiches. In the dark caves, they began kissing and hugging. They found a hiding place and had sex. Her foreman, however, noticed something and one day lay in ambush and surprised then. Bachmann began crying and asked the foreman not to say anything. He warned her but refrained from reporting her because, as he later explained to the police, he did not want to make her entire family unhappy. The intimate relationship continued, however. It is unclear whether the foreman reported them after catching them again or whether some other witness said something. But clearly this foreman gave in to her pleas at first and let a warning be enough even though he should have reported them right away.[111]

In Klein-Wesenberg, a small village southwest of Lübeck, the widow Antonie Preuß rented out the unused workshop of her husband to French POWs in 1941. In early 1942, she started intimate relations with the vintner Gustave Perrier, one of the POWs rooming in the workshop. The relationship attracted attention in the village, and Perrier was sent to

---

[110] BLHA Potsdam, 12 C, Sondergericht Frankfurt an der Oder, 1206.
[111] Sondergericht Darmstadt, November 19, 1943, in HStAD, Fonds G 24, Nr. 955/2. Her defense attorney argued that the women and the prisoners had often consumed alcohol together and that she may have been inebriated when seeing Keusch, but the special court dismissed this argument by suggesting that she perhaps drank in order to loosen her restraint.

different sleeping quarters, but Preuß kept visiting him, and they often had sex outdoors and at least once in her apartment. The contact went on for several years. Meanwhile, however, Frau Preuß's eighteen-year-old boarder, Helga Verheyen, also started a relationship with a French POW, possibly with the encouragement of Frau Preuß. Verheyen became pregnant in late 1943. Under increasing pressure to reveal the name of the father, she went to the police in February 1944 and confessed her forbidden relationship. During interrogation, she also revealed her landlady's involvement with Perrier. Verheyen mentioned yet another woman who was said to be close to French POWs, but the police could not find any evidence in this case. Obviously, Frau Preuß was able to maintain a forbidden relationship for two years even though it came to public attention relatively soon, prompting the transfer of the prisoner. It is not clear what exactly protected her. Perhaps it was compassion for her in the community. Frau Preuß's husband had been killed by an insane person in 1939, and she had two children. The special court sentenced her to two and a half years of penal servitude. Perrier was sentenced to three and a half years in prison.[112]

As was the case with some guards, a German employer could be openly complicit in a forbidden relationship. The rural worker Charlotte Bierhoff, married to a soldier, worked on a farm in Lebus (north of Frankfurt an der Oder) together with French POW Marcel Bruneteau. The farmer was very fond of Bruneteau. He often pointed out Frau Bierhoff to him, making crude allusions to her being a good sexual partner. A neighbor woman observed Bruneteau and Bierhoff together and probably denounced them. The fact that the farmer admitted having encouraged the sexual relationship counted as a mitigating factor in the court martial against the prisoner, who was sentenced to only two years in prison. But the High Command cancelled the judgment, stating that the farmer's encouragement could not be used as a mitigating factor. The court martial in Frankfurt an der Oder convened again and this time sentenced Bruneteau to three years in prison. The special court gave Frau Bierhoff one and a half years of penal servitude.[113]

---

[112] LASH Schleswig, Abt. 358, 6072. Perrier denied everything, probably because he was married and feared being sued for divorce if his wife found out. Frau Preuß's file includes the court martial judgment against Perrier.

[113] Feldurteil, Frankfurt an der Oder, November 21, 1941 (second sentence), in PAAA, R 40900, and BLHA Potsdam, 12 C, Sondergericht Frankfurt an der Oder, 102.

Other Discoveries

One of the most painful and difficult ways of discovery for a woman was pregnancy. Although condoms and other mechanical birth control devices were available in Nazi Germany, few couples in forbidden relations seem to have used them.[114] The most frequent birth control method was early withdrawal, which was of course unreliable. To be on the safer side, prisoners and women could engage in forms of sex that did not involve penetration. But many couples were not careful at all, and often the stressful circumstances of the sexual encounter, owing to fear of discovery, did not favor prudent steps to avoid pregnancy. As a result, a very large number of German (and some non-German) women became pregnant from intercourse with a prisoner, and the pregnancy often triggered discovery. Abortion, which had been widely practiced in the Weimar years, had become illegal for women of "desirable" stock, and the Weimar-era network of professional abortion help had largely disappeared.[115] Some prisoners tried to help the woman abort the fetus, but that exposed both to severe additional punishment.

Pregnancy without clear paternity always inspired rumors about the father of the child and often triggered a police investigation. Some married women claimed that the child was from their soldier husband, but if the police were suspicious (as they often were) they could search the dates of the husband's home leaves and determine whether the timing made sense. A very common explanation for women was to blame the pregnancy on a chance encounter with a German soldier on his way to the front who had only mentioned his first name. This seemed to be a plausible explanation given that many soldiers were on the move, and many engaged in short erotic adventures.[116] Yet, the Gestapo had heard too many "unknown soldier" stories to believe them. A closer investigation often revealed that the woman had invented the story. The rumor mill, or the interrogation of family members and other potential witnesses, usually provided clues leading to the discovery of a forbidden relationship. Some pregnant women had sexual relations with Germans as well as with a POW, and it was not clear who was the father. But even in these cases, the authorities' search for the father usually led them onto the trail of the prisoner, especially if there were already rumors.

---

[114] On the availability of condoms, see Herzog, *Sex after Fascism*, 24.
[115] Cornelie Usborne, *Cultures of Abortion in Weimar Germany* (New York: Berghahn Books, 2007), 220–2.
[116] Kundrus, *Kriegerfrauen*, 365.

A few women admitted that nobody except for the prisoner could be the father, and some of them filed a paternity claim against him to obtain child support. Some prisoners admitted their paternity, and they became liable to paying child support, but many rejected any responsibility, either by denying the relationship or by pointing out that the woman had also had relations with other men. A genetic identification of the father was not possible. Blood tests were available but could only exclude certain men from paternity. Whether it was legally possible to sentence a POW to pay child support was a question of international law and triggered some Franco-German correspondence, but a few courts did sentence prisoners to pay child support. In one case, French POW Etienne Clos, already sentenced for a forbidden relationship, had to be called back from military prison to stand trial in a paternity suit launched by the youth welfare office of Karlsbad (Sudetenland). The woman with whom he had been involved had given birth to a child in March 1942, while serving a six-year penitentiary sentence, and the local authorities wanted Clos to pay for the upkeep of the baby in the orphanage. Clos denied his paternity because the woman had also had sex with two German men. A blood test excluded the paternity of one of them, but the other one was at the front and could not be reached for testing. According to the legal advisor of the nearby Stalag, the paternity claim had no chance of winning under French law, but German law was different. The files do not reveal the outcome of this dispute. The Scapini Mission insisted, however, that French law applied to all paternity matters of Frenchmen in a foreign country and planned to take up this matter during negotiations for a peace treaty after the war, hoping to get reimbursed for the attorney fees and hoping also to reverse the German paternity judgments.[117] Yet, Hans K. Frey, the legal expert of the Swiss Legation who was dealing with paternity suits against British POWs, considered it legal for the courts of the detaining country to sue a POW for child support under its own laws.[118]

British POW John Bentley was accused of having had an affair with the Polish rural laborer Klothilde Szalkowski in the region of Marienburg (West Prussia). She became pregnant and gave birth to a child in March 1943. She listed Bentley as the father, but he denied everything during two interrogations in February and August 1943. During a third interrogation in December 1943, he admitted having had sex with Szalkowski

---

[117] Lenoble, report on trials in January 1944; Lenoble, report on trials in June 1944; and Lenoble to chef de la Délégation, February 2, 1944, all in AN, F9, 2745, dossier Stalag XIII-B.
[118] Frey, *Die disziplinarische und gerichtliche Bestrafung*, 54.

but claimed that it had taken place in February 1942 – before the order of the district commander forbidding relations with all women had been announced (March 25, 1942) and too early to have caused the pregnancy. He was acquitted, but Szalkowski launched a paternity suit against him, stating that sexual intercourse had occurred much later than he claimed. The first paternity trial in February 1944 ended inconclusively, but during a second trial on August 29, 1944, he admitted that she was right and agreed to pay child support. The court in Marienburg sentenced him to a one-time payment of 4,500 marks. His admission should also have triggered a court martial against him regarding the forbidden relation because it revealed that sexual intercourse must have happened *after* he had learned about the order of March 25, 1942 (during his first trial he had admitted that he had received the order on the following day). But the records do not disclose whether he ever came to trial for the forbidden relationship, nor do they reveal how he paid for child support.[119]

But the immediate concern of many women pregnant from a POW was not child support but rather to hide the forbidden relationship. Therese Pscharrer, in the village Parkstetten near Regensburg (Bavaria), was particularly inventive in this regard. Pscharrer was pregnant from the French prisoner who worked on the farm of her father. In August 1941, the pregnancy began to show, and the local rumor mill began to turn. Soon, an anonymous denunciation letter arrived at the police station stating that she was pregnant from a Frenchman. The denouncer claimed to have heard from other French POWs that the prisoner working with her was the father. Meanwhile, Pscharrer came up with a scheme that backfired and led to a second denunciation. She wrote to a former village sweetheart, who was now serving on the eastern front, and asked him to identify himself as the father of the child out of gratitude for all the favors she had granted him during their youth (this was a rather bold step because this affair must have occurred many years earlier; she was thirty-five). The ex-boyfriend was not amused. He sent Pscharrer's letter to his mother, complaining about the proposal. The mother, who had never liked Pscharrer, forwarded the letter to the police. It proved that the French POW was the father of her child. The special court in Nürnberg sentenced Pscharrer to one year of penal servitude, a relatively mild punishment. It worked in her favor that the French POW, Prosper Wegner, was from Lorraine and spoke very good German. He had even

---

[119] See the detailed summary of the case in Fulton (man of confidence) to Swiss Legation, November 8, 1944, in BAR Bern, Bestand Vertretung Berlin, 78a.

applied for German citizenship and declared that he wanted to remain in Germany permanently.[120]

In the case of Tilly Mosbauer, an employee in Schwabach (Bavaria), pregnancy also led to discovery. Mosbauer already had a two-year-old toddler. Her husband was serving in the Wehrmacht. She befriended French POW Roger Gras, with whom she took walks after work. They had sex in the forest three times. When she told him that she was pregnant, Gras shrugged his shoulders and said that he could not do anything about it, but that her husband was scheduled to be back on home leave soon and that she could declare the child as her husband's. Yet, the husband only arrived two and a half months later. After Mosbauer had given birth on July 6, 1943, she did declare that the baby was from her husband, but the doctor noticed that the baby was rather well developed for a premature infant. She received one and a half years of penal servitude. During her trial, the judges wondered aloud why she had not been sterilized because her mother and sister suffered from mental illness.[121]

In December 1942, Ottilie Merk, a thirty-six-year-old farmworker from Ingelheim on the Rhine, west of Mainz, noticed that she was pregnant. Questions soon arose about the identity of the father because it was known that her husband had been sentenced to two years of penal servitude in 1941 for an incestuous relationship with their daughter, leading to pregnancy and childbirth. He was still behind bars. To the authorities, Merk declared that she was pregnant from a German soldier, and she even supplied his name and residence: Johann Weiner from Mühldorf near Munich. The police, however, found out that nobody with that name was registered in Mühldorf and began investigating. Then, an eastern laborer who also worked on the farm came forward and mentioned having observed an intimate reunion of Merk and the French POW Jules Dumouriez, who worked on the same farm. The eastern worker did not denounce the couple after this observation, but she provided the decisive clue during a police interrogation triggered by the pregnancy. Merk had felt very lonely after the arrest of her husband, and in August 1942 she had started an intimate relationship with Dumouriez.[122]

Hertha Jäckel, a young innkeeper's daughter from a village south of Kiel, almost succeeded in deceiving the authorities. After she gave birth to a daughter on April 27, 1942, the police investigated because it

[120] BStA Nürnberg, Akten der Anklagebehörde beim Sondergericht, 1366.
[121] BStA Nürnberg, Akten der Anklagebehörde beim Sondergericht, 2327.
[122] Sondergericht Darmstadt, February 9, 1944, in HStAD Fonds G 24, Nr. 955/2.

suspected a POW as the father. Her parents' inn had closed and become the sleeping quarters for French and Belgian POWs. But the police did not find any clues, and Jäckel swore under oath that the child was from a German officer who had not given his full name. But then she started a relationship with French POW René Colas in December 1942. She became pregnant again and gave birth on September 8, 1943. Colas had been transferred elsewhere, but they had stayed in touch through letters. They wanted to marry after the war. The discovery of the letters made it impossible for her to deny the forbidden relationship. Moreover, a neighbor under interrogation revealed that she had once seen Colas climbing into her bedroom with a ladder (but she had not denounced them). The relationship with Colas prompted the police to re-examine Jäckel's earlier pregnancy, and they found out that the first child was really from Belgian POW Johann de Groote, one of the POWs sleeping in her parents' inn. They had started an intimate relation in July 1941. According to Jäckel, de Groote was very pushy, but the special court did not see any evidence for rape, partly because she admitted that the sexual contact had occurred six or seven times without her saying any-thing to her parents. On November 26, 1943, the special court in Kiel sentenced her to two years and one month of penal servitude, which included a five-month sentence because of perjury.[123]

Given that abortion was strictly punished in Nazi Germany, a stillbirth often triggered an investigation because of a suspicion of abortion. Elisabeth Renner from Raidelbach south of Darmstadt, for example, had a stillbirth on January 1, 1944, and the midwife declared that the fetus was approximately three months old. This triggered a police investigation. Although the police concluded that there was probably no abortion attempt, they began searching for the father of the baby. Renner's husband was out of the question because he had been on his last home leave in November 1942 and had been killed on the eastern front in August 1943. The tracks led to French POW Maurice Laborde who worked on a farm near the restaurant owned by Renner's parents. He had often given chocolate to her children, and she had given him beer and cigarettes. They had begun exchanging letters with the help of a young apprentice. The relationship had become intimate soon after her husband's last home leave. The special court in Darmstadt sentenced her to two years of penal servitude on April 20, 1944. That she had been unfaithful to her husband, an old NSDAP member, while he was still alive counted as an

[123] LASH Schleswig, Abt. 358, 6629.

aggravating factor. Laborde admitted having had sex with her approximately twenty times.[124]

Another common way of discovering a forbidden relation was postal censorship. This was different from the finding of letters that the lovers sent to each other without use of the postal service, for example by dropping them in an agreed-upon space or by having a third person deliver the letter. In these cases, discovery required that the finder follow up with a denunciation, and they are therefore random denunciations. Postal censors, like guards, had a duty to report illegal acts. They opened letters in circulation in Germany, while military camp censors read incoming mail to the POWs before it was distributed to the work detachments. A central military censorship office in Cologne monitored the POWs' correspondence with home, and some discoveries resulted from the censors in this office, for example if POWs alluded to a German girlfriend in letters to their parents.

Couples were most vulnerable if for some reason they became separated and had no other way to communicate than through regular mail. It often happened that a POW was transferred to a different work detachment, sometimes in reaction to rumors and suspicions. When writing to each other, the couple had to be very careful. For example, it was a good idea for the woman not to address the letter directly to the prisoner but to a third person (another prisoner or a complicit civilian). POWs were allowed to write a certain number of letters every month, but these letters were meant to facilitate their communication with home, and almost all of their mail was opened by censors. If the prisoner wanted to write to somebody in Germany, he needed to find paper and a stamp and post the letter himself or with the help of an accomplice. It was best either not to write a return address on the envelope or to use a false return address, perhaps that of a complicit civilian. It was also advisable to avoid using real names or to Germanize the name of the prisoner. Postal censorship might let the letter pass, assuming that it concerned a German relationship or one between a foreign civilian worker and a German woman. But many couples were not careful, and their relationships were discovered through censorship. This form of discovery is impossible to quantify because the police was secretive about postal surveillance.

A typical case was the love affair of French POW François Jacquet with the farmworker Anna Korbmeyer in the region of Linz (Austria). They had had sex in Jacquet's bedroom several times during the

---

[124] Sondergericht Darmstadt, April 22, 1944, HStAD Fonds G 24, Nr. 955/2.

summer of 1941. Then Korbmeyer saw a poster explaining the prohibition and decided to end the relationship. Not much later, Jacquet was
transferred to a different work detachment. He gave Korbmeyer's
employer his new address. After a while, Korbmeyer missed Jacquet
and wrote him that she would like to resume their relationship. The
postal censorship seized the letter. Given that Jacquet denied having
had any intimate relationship with Korbmeyer, the letter served as
conclusive evidence against him.[125]

French POW Jean Chaumont-Latour (thirty-one), a sculptor and
woodworker, was performing construction work for the Reich *Autobahn*
east of Dresden in 1941. The cook for his work detachment, Monika
Bader (thirty-two), fell in love with him. They kissed and hugged in
hiding. They spoke of getting married. When the prisoner had to go to
the military hospital because of a stomach ailment, Monika Bader cried.
He came back for a short time but was then sent to another work
detachment. They wrote each other passionate love letters, which led to
discovery through postal censorship. The letters played a favorable role
in the court martial of the prisoner, however, because they documented
the sincere love of the couple. Chaumont-Latour clearly considered
Bader his fiancée, and he wrote her about his efforts to learn German
so that he could better communicate with her. The letters also revealed
that sexual intercourse had never happened between them. In light of
these mitigating factors, the court martial in Dresden gave Chaumont-
Latour only five months in prison even though the special court in
Dresden had sentenced her to one and a half years in prison.[126]

In the case of Jean Richard (thirty-two), who was assigned to the
construction site for the Hermann-Goering apartments in Murdorf west
of Graz (Austria), it was a package sent to him that led to discovery. The
forty-four-year-old soldier's wife Marie Raab was also working on this
site, and she was quite smitten with Richard, following him every day and
handing him letters. One day, she had the imprudent idea of sending him
a package through regular mail, using full names of sender and receiver.
Although the package contained nothing incriminating, it is likely that
the post office alerted the guard, who seized the package when it arrived
and decided to watch the prisoner and the woman more carefully. One
day he followed them to a basement in a new building and caught them
during a secret meeting. The prisoner put up a mean-spirited defense in
front of the court martial, claiming that he found the woman physically

---

[125] Feldurteil, Linz, September 16, 1941, in PAAA, R 40886.
[126] Feldurteil, Dresden, October 22, 1941, in PAAA, R 40890.

revolting and that the two sexual encounters she had admitted were wishful thinking. But the other workers on the construction site testified upon interrogation that the prisoner and the woman had had an intimate relationship for some time. The special court in Leoben sentenced her to three years of penal servitude, while the court martial gave him three years of prison. The relationship had obviously been noted by co-workers, but it was the careless sending of a package to the prisoner that put the guard on the trail of the forbidden relation.[127]

Assessment

The question of discovery is intimately tied to the community reactions to the illegal relationships.[128] Had everything happened according to the ideals of the Nazi regime, guards would immediately have reported a forbidden relation, and German civilians would not have hesitated to denounce an offending woman and prisoner. The reality was much more complex. Although many relations did come to the attention of the authorities through guards or denunciations, there often was hesitation. A guard might warn the prisoner and the woman. A civilian witness might not say something for a while. Of course, the authorities in Nazi Germany were wary of frivolous denunciations and therefore often waited until evidence appeared to be sound before intervening.[129] But there are clear cases where the community covered up the forbidden relation and, if it did come out, ostracized the denouncer. If outrage was the motivation for a denunciation, moreover, it was often directed against particular offensive acts regardless of the fact that the couple consisted of a foreign prisoner and a German woman. This finding supports the results of new research about denunciations, namely that a large number of "crimes" were likely never denounced and that the population's eagerness to collaborate with the Gestapo has been exaggerated.[130]

Many discoveries were motivated by institutional processes. The guards had a duty to watch the prisoners, check their belongings

[127] Feldurteil, Wolfsberg, November 6, 1941, in PAAA, R 40893.
[128] On the importance of group norms for denouncing illegal behavior or keeping it secret, see Katrin Dördelmann, *Die Macht der Worte: Denunziationen im nationalsozialistischen Köln*, Schriften des NS-Dokumentationszentrums der Stadt Köln (Köln: Emons Verlag, 1997), 39–41.
[129] Rüping, "Denunziation und Strafjustiz im Führerstaat," 128–9, 135.
[130] Schneider, *Verbotener Umgang*, 184–5. See also Patricia Szobar, "Telling Sexual Stories in the Nazi Courts of Law: Race Defilement in Germany, 1933 to 1945," in *Sexuality and German Fascism*, edited by Dagmar Herzog (New York and Oxford: Berghahn Books, 2005), 141.

periodically, and report all illegal activity. The postal censors looking for forbidden relations were doing their job, although one may wonder what kind of person signed up for this work. In other cases, private motives or notions of public propriety that were not generically Nazi prompted a denunciation. The husband who dragged his wife to the police after he had just learned that she had cheated on him reacted out of distress, jealousy, and anger. Whether he approved of the prohibition and the ideology motivating it seems to be secondary at best. The neighbor calling the police because of noise in the apartment of the woman living upstairs may or may not approve of the prohibition and the ideology motivating it. The hiker witnessing an amorous encounter in the fields or the forest may be outraged because people are kissing and hugging in public or because he or she knows that the woman is committing adultery. The village rumor mill at the *Stammtisch* of the local inn was always grinding; that it often facilitated the discovery of a forbidden relation does not necessarily mean that the conveyors of the rumors were committed to Nazism and supportive of the prohibition.

Conversely, the protection of an illegal couple by a guard or a civilian did not always indicate an anti-Nazi attitude or at least a disagreement with the prohibition. Farmers risked losing two workers, the prisoner and a female farm hand, in case a relationship was discovered. They had to balance the risks of tolerating the affair against the potential loss of the couple as workers at a time when replacements were hard to find. The stakes were of course particularly high if the farmworker was the farmer's own daughter. Guards and employers may have become fond of a prisoner and disliked denouncing him, preferring to warn him or to actively foster and protect the forbidden relationship. Given that the guard often was a local man, he might also have felt reluctant to bring unhappiness to a family he knew.

Can one detect patterns over time? Belgian man of confidence Georges Smets wrote that in East Prussia, 95 percent of the population was pro-Nazi at the beginning of his captivity (May 1940) and that many Germans were arrogant toward the Belgian prisoners, saying they had no culture. Yet, Smets noticed a change beginning in 1941 with the invasion of the Soviet Union and mounting German losses. The change accelerated in later years, according to Smets, with most Germans becoming greatly worried about the war and a potential defeat. By 1944, Smets argued that the POWs had become so indispensable in many businesses that they enjoyed great respect. He mentions a woman running a restaurant and hotel in Königsberg who locked the doors when a group of POW representatives met in her establishment. While she was serving the POWs a multi-course meal, German soldiers and officers angrily knocked on the doors – to no avail.[131] It is difficult to quantify public reactions given the incomplete and inconsistent information and the frequent mix of factors that led to discovery. But it is clear that the most mean-spirited denunciations and the few cases of public outrage that corresponded to the Nazi notions of "healthy feeling of the Volk" and "enemy remains enemy" occurred mostly in 1941 and were rare later on. But even in 1941, a raw mix of motivations and factors led to discovery or to (often temporary) protection of a forbidden relationship.

---

[131] Georges Smets, reply to "Question 13: Quels-étaient vos rapports avec la population allemande?," in CEGESOMA, AA 244, Archives de la Commission d'Histoire de la Captivité de Guerre 1940–1945: verslagen, corr., vragenlijsten, 06/1940–15/04/1970.

5   The Trials

Two Legal Systems

The accused woman and prisoner stood trial in two different but connected legal systems. Because their violation fell under the *Wehrkraft* decree, the women normally came before a so-called special court (*Sondergericht*), which the Nazi regime had built up to deal with political opposition during its consolidation of power in 1933–4. From the beginning, the special courts had a reputation for extraordinary harshness and loyalty to Nazi ideology. During the war, Roland Freisler, a leading Nazi jurist and president of the highest special court, the *Volksgerichtshof*, claimed that the special courts were meant to be the "courts martial of the inner front," acting with a speed and power comparable to a *Panzer* division. While the military tribunals would ensure strict discipline within the army, the special courts would do the same on the home front, all in an effort to prevent the corroding influences that had allegedly led to the "stab in the back" in 1918.[1] As civilian defendants accused of a crime resembling treason, the women were often in the power of the Gestapo while waiting for their trial. They were therefore exposed to the most arbitrary branch of the Nazi system of law enforcement and justice, at least for some time.

The prisoner went through the channels of military justice. While much scholarship has debated the Nazification of military justice and highlighted its increasingly ruthless use of the death penalty to ensure strict obedience in the armed forces, the prisoners of war were judged with a different rationale that stressed, like the special courts, the maintenance of discipline and morale on the home front. The military judges staffing the courts martial inside wartime Germany were members of the reserve army and normally dealt with disciplinary problems of soldiers

---

[1] Ingo Müller, *Furchtbare Juristen: Die unbewältigte Vergangenheit unserer Justiz* (Munich: Kindler, 1987), 158–64. See also Lutz, "Das Sondergericht Nürnberg 1933–1945," 255; Angermund, *Deutsche Richterschaft 1919–1945*, 201.

while on home leave, not with ensuring discipline at or near the front. In contrast to German defendants, the POWs also had internationally guaranteed rights through the Geneva Convention. These rights sometimes clashed with German military judicial practice because Nazi Germany had neglected to bring its judiciary regulations in line with the Geneva Convention, but there was usually international oversight during the pretrial custody and during the trial itself. Prisoners awaiting trial were not in the clutches of the Gestapo but confined in the POW camps, with the exception of a few transformed POWs, but their arrest by the Gestapo triggered protests by the Scapini Mission, which pointed out that accused POWs had to stay under the military justice authorities, not the Gestapo, and that Germany could not hold transformed prisoners to the laws in effect for POWs while taking away their rights as POWs in the enforcement of justice.[2]

Generally, the special courts tried the woman first, and courts martial often waited and then used the woman's dossier to convict the prisoner. The timing may have had to do with the delays required for the courts martial against POWs, such as the notification of the protecting power three weeks before the hearing. But having the woman tried first was convenient for the courts martial especially in the frequent cases where a prisoner denied the allegations. Clearly, it was more difficult to bully a POW than a woman to reach a confession. The POW usually had a translator and sometimes a legal advisor with him (both potentially fellow prisoners). Most accused women also had to appear as a witness during the hearing of the prisoner, and the POW was often interrogated by the police investigating the woman; he sometimes had to attend her trial as a witness. A confession by the woman almost automatically counted as proof against a prisoner who denied the relationship because courts martial argued that the woman would not make frivolous allegations that exposed her to severe punishment and ostracism. The only exception were cases in which the woman was considered not completely sane or where the judges believed that she was making up things in an act of revenge or boasting. Under these conditions, the judges usually acquitted the prisoner. But in many cases, the POWs were judged on the basis of a woman's confession, leading exasperated French legal advisors to exclaim that it was not worth holding a court martial if the woman's confession was to be taken as the last word.[3]

[2] See, for example, Roger Liagre, Stalag IX-C, to Chef de la Délégation, February 18, 1944, in AN, F9, 2731.
[3] See the case of Raymond G., who apparently became the victim of a German jealousy drama because a Frau B., who "admitted" having had a relation with him, wanted to get

The tendency of courts martial to wait until the woman had been sentenced meant that POWs often spent a long time in pre-trial custody, sometimes up to half a year. Late in the war, the High Command asked for POWs to be tried first, hoping that rapid and harsh judgments would act as a deterrent to other POWs, but the increasing transportation problems in a country under bombing made it hard to comply. In the last months of the war, almost every second court martial had to be postponed at least once because either the prisoner, the woman who was called as witness, or the defense attorney could not attend the hearing because of traffic disruptions. Some courts martial proceeded without the defense attorney present, but this violated the Geneva Convention and was likely to trigger a protest from the protecting power. The special courts also failed to live up to the expectation of quick judgments. The investigations took time, which may be a sign that these courts often hesitated to abandon the standards of judicial normalcy in the interest of speed.[4]

Courts martial and special courts shared conservative and paternalistic ideas about sexual behavior. They tended to rate the sexual need of men more highly than the sexual need of women, although it is striking that judges of special courts did sometimes consider sexual need in the case of women, especially married women separated from their husbands, as a mitigating factor, which seems to be a reflection of reform tendencies from the 1920s that promoted sexual satisfaction for both marriage partners.[5] But all judges shared conceptions about "proper" sexual intercourse and despised couples who did not conform to them. Manual stimulation and, especially, oral sex – which many judges called "lesbian sex" and some women called "satisfaction in French" (*Befriedigung auf*

---

the husband of her friend jealous because he was cheating on his wife. When Frau B. appeared as a witness in front of the court martial, she withdrew her confession, which had already cost her two years of penal servitude, but the court martial still sentenced the prisoner to three and a half years of penitentiary: "Audience," October 14, 1943, in AN, F9, 2742, Dossier Stalag I-A.

[4] Can Bozyakali, *Das Sondergericht am Hanseatischen Oberlandesgericht: Eine Untersuchung der NS-Sondergerichte unter besonderer Berücksichtigung der Anwendung der Verordnung gegen Volksschädlinge* (Frankfurt am Main: Peter Lang, 2004), 309–11. One woman in my sample had an affair with a French POW in January 1942 that was discovered as part of a cluster of affairs in July 1942, but her trial took place in Kattowitz only on August 2, 1944, because she (and her husband) claimed that medical problems would make it impossible for her to stand trial. There was growing evidence that she similated seizures before police interrogations and court dates. She apparently avoided going to a penitentiary to serve her sentence of one and a half years by continuing the same tactics: case of Helene P., in Archiwum Państwowe w Katowicach, Sondergericht, 1330.

[5] Herzog, *Sexuality in Europe*, 49–50.

französisch) – could provoke bitter reprimands in the courtroom and function as a circumstance of aggravation.[6] The judge of Belgian POW Gaston Thyssen, for example, noted in the judgment that Thyssen had repeatedly practiced oral sex until the woman had had an orgasm, and he publicly called the practice a *"Schweinerei"* (an act of swinishness).[7] Many judges punished manual stimulation and oral sex the same way as "natural" intercourse, and this was consistent with Nazi legal practice.[8] Although most judges were inclined to consider the fact that these alternative forms of sex could not result in pregnancy as a mitigating factor, their censure of "unnatural" sexual behavior usually cancelled out all the benefits to the defendant.

The Trials of the Women

Following discovery, an accused woman would normally be interrogated. Who carried out the first interrogation of an accused woman depended largely on location: in remote villages, it was the local policeman; inside or near cities, it was a Gestapo officer. The local policeman, who often knew the accused woman and her family, was not likely to threaten her.[9] But women from small villages were often transferred to a prison in the next city and re-interrogated by the Gestapo. Gestapo officers occasionally used bullying, threats, and false promises to induce a confession. Some Gestapo officers asked the woman to confess so that she could go home rather than spend the night behind bars. Some interrogators tricked women into confessing by falsely claiming that the prisoner had already admitted everything and that the woman's denial therefore would only lead to harsher punishment. Sometimes, the interrogating officer threatened the woman that she would be publicly shamed and that her head would be shaved if she did not confess.[10] A significant number of women made a far-reaching confession during interrogation but withdrew it at the court hearing, accusing the interrogating officer of having

---

[6] The men dominating sexologist discourse in the interwar period tended to believe that a man giving oral sex to a woman was perverse and would sooner or later become homosexual: Angus McLaren, *Twentieth-Century Sexuality: A History* (Oxford: Blackwell, 1999), 100.
[7] Judgment against Gaston Th., Stuttgart, September 18, 1941, in PAAA, R 40853.
[8] The legal expert Karl Peters argued that "unnatural," "degenerate," and "irregular" intercourse had to be treated as harshly as "normal, natural" intercourse. Peters, "Das gesunde Volksempfinden," 347.
[9] Usborne, "Female Sexual Desire and Male Honor," 463.
[10] BStA Nürnberg, Akten der Anklagebehörde beim Sondergericht, 2046.

pressured them.[11] Privately, some judges expressed unease about the Gestapo interrogation methods, which tended to create unexpected obstacles and complications during the trial or court martial if a woman suddenly retracted her confession.[12] Sometimes the judge or the prosecutor asked the interrogating officer to testify in court that the woman had really made the statements as noted in the protocol and that she had freely signed her confession, but this made no difference because the officers almost always denied having used pressure.[13]

While the Gestapo sometimes used physical threats and torture in interrogations of women accused of involvement with Poles or Soviet citizens, this seems to have been much less common in the case of forbidden relations with western POWs.[14] If it did happen, it seems to have concerned mostly women who were already stigmatized as "asocial" by the Gestapo. In my sample, there is one case where an accused woman declared that a Gestapo officer had slapped her in the face when she refused to admit sexual intercourse with a prisoner, and she stated that she had only confessed because she feared getting a seizure (she was prone to get nervous seizures). The officer did admit that he proceeded "energetically" during the interrogation. Interestingly, the special court of Kiel condoned his behavior by saying that general experience dictated that the woman must have had sex with the prisoner even though both denied it. The woman had been sterilized on the grounds of "inherited feeble-mindedness" and therefore already counted as an outcast. But this case is not typical because she belonged to a group of three milkmaids in Schleswig-Holstein who were accused of having had sex not only with French POWs but also with two eastern laborers.[15]

Many women who at first denied the allegations but admitted the relationship in a second or third interrogation did so when they were confronted with inculpating evidence, for example a love letter or photo found during a search of the POW's possessions or the testimony of an eyewitness, not in reaction to Gestapo pressure. In some cases, women withdrew their initial confession after hearing that the prisoner had

---

[11] See also Ludewig and Kuessner, *"Es sei also jeder gewarnt,"* 152; Boll, *"… das gesunde Volksempfinden,"* 665–6.
[12] Wrobel, *Strafjustiz im totalen Krieg,* vol. 3, 327–8.
[13] See, for example, the case of Hedwig B., WStLA, Sondergericht, 5284.
[14] Gisela Schwarze insinuates that the Gestapo used violence also in interrogations of women accused of forbidden relations with western POWs: Schwarze, *Es war wie eine Hexenjagd,* 72–4; 166–7, 170. Usborne is more critical: "Female Sexual Desire and Male Honor," 463. For a case in which the sentenced woman did claim that she had made a false confession after being beaten, see Prieler-Woldan, *Das Selbstverständliche tun,* 100.
[15] Judgment against Annelise B., February 18, 1942, in LASH Schleswig, Abt. 358, 2760 and also vol. 2839.

denied a sexual encounter, but it is hard to determine whether they did so because a Gestapo officer had bullied them to confess or because they saw an opportunity to get a lighter sentence through a denial from both partners. The postwar applications for cancellation of a sentence or for indemnification by women sentenced for a forbidden relation with a western POW generally do not refer to threats during interrogation, and very rarely do they claim that the sentence was based on a false confession. If Gestapo officers had more routinely used violence or physical threats, these women (or their attorneys) would likely have mentioned it. All things considered, it therefore seems fair to say that the Gestapo pressured women in cases involving western POWs to make a quick and comprehensive confession – the special courts were expected to mete out hard and *rapid* sentences – but that most of the confessions were truthful even if they did not serve the best interests of the defendants.[16]

Depending on how the police and the court evaluated the risk of escape or obfuscation of evidence, they might take the accused woman into custody while awaiting trial, but some women remained free until the conclusion of the trial, especially if they were pregnant. The police meanwhile heard witnesses, including the prisoner, gathered more evidence, and conducted background checks on the accused woman, inquiring about her membership in Nazi organizations or anti-Nazi groups (before 1933) and requesting reference letters from a foreman, peasant leader, or town mayor. Some of the evidence required translation and transcription (for example hand-written letters by the prisoner). If enough incriminating evidence had been gathered, the court formulated an arrest warrant against the woman. This could take a few weeks. During this phase, the woman often had to appear for a second and sometimes a third interrogation, during which she would be confronted with new evidence and asked to explain herself.

In this phase, the judge might also order humiliating tests, whose results would be reported during the hearing. Some women had to undress in front of a university professor specializing in heredity and "racial hygiene" so that he could examine their bodies for physical signs of "degeneration." In a similar setting, these women also had to take intelligence tests with questions such as "what is the capital of France?" in order to determine whether they were "feeble-minded" (*geistesschwach*). Article 51 of the German law code (formulation of January 1, 1934) stipulated that persons who were unable to grasp the illegality of

---

[16] Bozyakali, *Das Sondergericht am Hanseatischen Oberlandesgericht*, 261–3, 305–11.

their acts could not be punished, and persons whose ability to understand it was impaired needed to be judged more leniently. A diagnosis of feeble-mindedness would therefore count as a mitigating factor in court, but it often led to compulsory sterilization.[17] Some women also had to take a pregnancy or virginity test, especially young women who denied ever having had sex.

The investigation probed into every detail of the relationship, especially its sexual dimension. How often, when, and where had sexual intercourse occurred? In which position – standing, sitting, lying? Many officials would ask further: Had the prisoner practiced early withdrawal? Had the woman had an orgasm? Had she enjoyed the experience? Some witnesses, such as Belgian man of confidence Georges Smets, accused these judges and prosecutors of voyeurism, and many historians concur. Clearly, some questions the judges asked were gratuitous and deliberately humiliating, but some of the detail was important to determine the dynamics of the relationship, which influenced the sentence. Who had been the driving force? Who had arranged the first meeting? Who had undressed first? Given that some women claimed that the prisoner had forced himself on them, judges had to establish specifics about the sexual encounter to determine whether it counted as rape in German law (requiring that the woman had to have tried to defend herself and to get help if possible). For example, a woman who claimed the prisoner had used force but who described that sexual intercourse had occurred while they were both standing and within earshot of potential witnesses would not be believed. Circumstances mattered, too: if intercourse had occurred in the marital bed and in the presence of the woman's sleeping children, judges would mete out a more severe punishment than if it had happened in the forest, a hayloft, or barn. For the accused woman, as for the prisoner, the number of intimate encounters was relevant, given that judges considered recurrent sexual intercourse as a repeated violation or act of disobedience and judged it more harshly than a one-time transgression, which they might classify as an aberration, especially if the woman had been under the shock of a recent event, for example the death of a close relative or the destruction of her apartment. The detail

---

[17] An example is the milkmaid Helene A. who had sex with one French POW, one Polish POW, six Polish civilian workers, three Ukrainian and three Belorussian workers. She was sterilized during her trial. Despite the diagnosis of feeble-mindedness, she still received four years of penal servitude on February 18, 1942, because of her numerous forbidden contacts and because the special court of Kiel found a harsh sentence necessary for deterrence: LASH Schleswig, Abt. 358, 2760, and 2761 (with the diagnosis recommending sterilization).

from the hearing of the woman often served as evidence in the prisoner's court martial as well.

The accused women had the right to a defense attorney, but the attorney was usually not in a position to stop the humiliating questions and tests. Many women had difficulties finding and paying a defense attorney, moreover. A study of the special court in Frankfurt am Main shows that while all defendants had an attorney in 1939, this was true only for half of them in 1943.[18] Although before the war it was standard practice to use a defense counsel assigned by the court in case the defendant could not pay, this was no longer done consistently during the war.[19] Many women in my sample seem to have had no attorney during the trial, although their families often used an attorney to submit a clemency plea later on.

Standing trial in the special court was a horrifying and humiliating experience for most accused women. They were exposed to an all-male court and a mostly male audience (the trials were public[20]) who mustered them with a demeaning gaze as the prosecutor read the charges and as he or the judge probed into intimate details. Most accused women had to undergo this ordeal twice – at their own trial and at the trial of the POW, when they appeared as a witness. Not surprisingly, a number of women committed, or attempted to commit, suicide after discovery.

An example of a woman's public humiliation by a judge is the trial of Erna Rothe at the special court of Frankfurt an der Oder on March 15, 1944. As mentioned before, Rothe, a forty-three-year-old teacher and district leader of the Nazi women's league, had first admitted consensual sex with a French POW but then claimed to have been raped twice, probably at the suggestion of the prisoner who hoped to get her a lighter sentence. The judge noted that the prisoner was attractive whereas she was over forty, had a limp, wore glasses, and had never been married (all ways to say that in the eyes of the court she was not attractive). The condescending conclusion was: "One can therefore believe her that never in her life has a man ever approached her." The judge argued that she had fallen in love with the prisoner in a "kind of late spring that had awoken her womanly feelings."[21] Similarly, the special court of Frankfurt am Main commented on the "unattractive and physically retarded" looks of a cleaning lady from Wiesbaden on trial for a relationship with a

---

[18] Weckbecker, *Zwischen Freispruch und Todesstrafe*, 98.
[19] Bozyakali, *Das Sondergericht am Hanseatischen Oberlandesgericht*, 271.
[20] Christiane Oehler, *Die Rechtsprechung des Sondergerichts Mannheim 1933–1945* (Berlin: Duncker & Humblot, 1997), 62–3.
[21] BLHA Potsdam, 12 C, Sondergericht Frankfurt an der Oder, 1221.

Frenchman in 1941, stating that "it is therefore not surprising that she quickly succumbed to the seduction when she was suddenly – and against all expectations – seen as desirable by a French prisoner of war."[22] The fact that such insulting passages made it into the written sentence suggests that the actual trial was even more hurtful and demeaning.

The special court of Darmstadt provided a particularly heinous example in the case of Maria Harder, a farmer's wife accused of a relationship with a French POW in a village south of Mainz lasting from 1941 to 1944. Harder stated in her defense that the prisoner had at first pressed her to have sex with him by threatening to leave the farm and to incite the other POWs not to work for her. The judge then launched a tirade, calling her explanations "impertinent excuses" and claiming that she could easily have found another prisoner in the village (in 1941 when labor shortages were not yet drastic) and that she had approved of the contact because she had never reported any harassment and continued the relationship for years. When asked about her husband, who was serving in the Wehrmacht, she stated that he was lazy, drank too much, and occasionally hit her. The judge then asked whether she had had sex with him when he was on his last home leave. She answered affirmatively, leading the judge to conclude that her claims about her abusive husband must have been false and that therefore her defense about the prisoner having used pressure was also unconvincing.[23]

Stéphane Delattre, a committed and inventive French POW lawyer, unintentionally illustrated how humiliating and shaming the court hearings could be for the accused woman, both during her own trial and during the court martial of the prisoner. Recapitulating the case of a POW who had frequently engaged in sexual intercourse with a sterilized woman, Delattre characterized the woman as "repelling, misshaped, and unbearable to the eyes. The entire audience feels nauseated, especially at the thought of … The facial expressions of all members of the audience suggest, as I note, that we are in a dissection hall." He insinuated that the prisoner had already been punished enough by consorting with a "scarecrow" and that there was in this case no "dignity of the German woman" that the prisoner could have attacked.[24] In other cases, Delattre speaks of German women as "merchandise" and highlights the "immoral" lifestyle of some accused women, thus reinforcing the double standard that

---

[22] Sentence of February 6, 1942, in HHStA Wiesbaden, Sondergericht, Abteilung 461, vol. 8354.

[23] Sondergericht Darmstadt, February 15, 1944, in HStAD Fonds G 24, Nr. 955/2.

[24] Delattre, *Ma Guerre sans fusil*, 110–11.

condemned the promiscuity of women while accepting the "sexual conquests" of men. It is clear from Delattre's remarks that he used his misogynistic impressions of a woman's appearance and lifestyle during the defense of POWs in the courtroom.[25]

Several factors influenced the verdict. Nazi jurisprudence placed increasing emphasis on the personality and persuasions of the offender in judging a crime, based on a theory of criminal types (*Tätertypen*), and Justice Minister Thierack repeatedly emphasized this approach in his missive on forbidden contact with POWs.[26] People characterized as particular "criminal types," such as "asocials," "habitual criminals," or the nearly untranslatable *Volksschädling* ("pest to the people"?) would receive harsher punishments for the same deed as others.[27] To determine whether a woman belonged to a criminal type, her political past, her reputation, and her present attitude required examination. For this reason, the police collected detailed information about an accused woman's membership in Nazi organizations, about the quality and intensity of her engagement in these organizations, and about past membership in anti-Nazi organizations. Women who had belonged to left-wing organizations before 1933 received harsher sentences, and their judges sometimes disregarded the standards of proof.

In Kiel, for example, Käthe Frick was sentenced to one and a half years of penal servitude simply for meeting with a French POW in a drying room of the factory in which they worked. A foreman had observed that they were both missing from their workplace for a few minutes and had followed them, seeing them coming out of the drying room. The prisoner claimed that the woman had ambushed and kissed him, but she denied that. No sexual intercourse had been proven or observed, but Käthe Frick had belonged to a communist organization before 1933, and this obviously influenced the police and the court in judging her as "an entirely debauched character." In an evaluation of Frick, the NSDAP district leader of Neumünster (Schleswig-Holstein) pointed out that she came from a troubled family and was a "character of inferior value" ("*minderwertiger Charakter*") who deserved a "long-lasting removal from the *Volksgemeinschaft*." The judge assumed on the basis of her reputation that sexual intercourse must have happened and punished her with penitentiary, normally reserved for relations involving proven sex.[28]

---

[25] Ibid., 95, 113, 14, 17, 23.   [26] Boberach, *Richterbriefe*, 88, 90, 92.
[27] Theis, *Wehrmachtjustiz an der* "Heimatfront," 230–4; Bozyakali, *Das Sondergericht am Hanseatischen Oberlandesgericht*, 288; Löffelsender, *Strafjustiz an der Heimatfront*, 302–3.
[28] Kreisleiter NSDAP Neumünster to state prosecutor, December 12, 1940, and other documents in LASH Schleswig, Abt. 358, 2078.

Similarly, the special court in Nürnberg considered Else Schneider's membership in a socialist swimming club before 1933 as an aggravating factor when she was on trial for a relationship with a French POW from Alsace in September 1943.[29] In the case of Anna Bittner, a thirty-nine-year-old worker from Groß-Gerau (Hessen), who had to stand trial at the special court in Darmstadt in April 1943, it was undisputed that she had helped other women to hide two escaped French POWs and sent love letters to one or two POWs who could not be identified. There were rumors that she had had sex with a prisoner, but she denied this, and nobody could prove the contrary, especially since it remained impossible to identify the prisoner in question. On these flimsy grounds, the special court sentenced her to three and a half years of penal servitude, punishing her for sexual intercourse with at least one POW. The reason for this absurd sentence was that Bittner and her husband had been communists until 1933. In the eyes of the court, her previous political orientation "had created in her an inner opposition to decrees of the German state," and this was enough to "prove" her guilty.[30]

Ursula Rickau, the employee in Landsberg an der Warthe who had an intense love affair with French POW Clément Allier in the spring of 1942, did not have a damaging political past, but her letters to Allier, which had triggered the discovery, contained critical political comments. Rickau deplored the lack of freedom in Nazi Germany and complained to Allier that countless women had already suffered severe punishment because of a forbidden relation "with you guys." She also mentioned that she had heard many people doubt a German victory, and she made critical remarks about a Hitler speech. When her police interrogator asked her whether she loved the Führer, she said no. When the officer asked whether she would do anything for Allier even if it meant committing high treason, she said yes. These statements counted as severe aggravating factors, and the special court in Frankurt an der Oder sentenced her to two and a half years of penal servitude, a very harsh punishment for a woman who had just turned nineteen at the time of the trial (women under twenty normally were only sentenced to prison, not penitentiary). She avoided an even harsher punishment because of the fact that she had lost her German fiancé early in the war and because the judge believed that she had not been properly supervised by her grandmother and her parents, who lived in Berlin.[31]

[29] BStA Nürnberg, Akten der Anklagebehörde beim Sondergericht, 2298.
[30] See the case study "A Frenchman for Everybody?" in Chapter 7.
[31] BLHA Potsdam, 12 C, Sondergericht Frankfurt an der Oder, 1206.

While most women on trial were not particularly active in Nazi organizations, some did get lighter sentences if a local leader of the Nazi women's league testified on their behalf. But women who occupied a leading position in a Nazi organization risked being judged more harshly than others because the judges expected them to act as a role model.[32] The social standing of the accused woman also played a role. Women from wealthier families often received milder sentences and early releases.[33] Justice Minister Thierack also highlighted the importance of marital status. A woman married to a German soldier, he argued, did not only commit adultery and an undignified act against the *Volksgemeinschaft*; she moreover committed "treason against a soldier who was fighting also for this woman." But Thierack by the same token cautioned against judging unmarried women more leniently than married women. With married women, especially with soldiers' wives, the judges had to consider the relationship of the marriage partners. As Hitler had demanded, if the husband was willing to forgive his wife and to continue the marriage, the judge could be lenient.[34]

Some judges considered sexual neediness (*Sexualnot*) as a mitigating factor in trials of women, as was standard practice in courts martial against POWs and also against German soldiers accused of rape in enemy territory. Women who claimed that they had been receptive to the advances of the prisoner because they no longer obtained sexual satisfaction from their husbands sometimes received a more lenient sentence.[35] This was true also for soldier's wives who had not seen their husband for a long time. Thierack was critical of this practice, however: "The judge has to be very careful when weighing the motive of sexual neediness because it must be expected of the German woman that she control herself, especially in the case of sexual intercourse with prisoners of war."[36] A number of accused soldiers' wives took a defiant stance during their trial by blaming their "crime" on the long-enforced

[32] Case of Elisabeth G., sentence special court Vienna, September 30, 1941, in WStLA, Sondergericht, 5991.
[33] See, for example, the case study "Two Wehrmacht Auxiliaries" in Chapter 7. On the bias of special court judges against defendants with a left-wing past and low social standing, see also Angermund, *Deutsche Richterschaft 1919–1945*, 143–5.
[34] Boberach, *Richterbriefe*, 94.
[35] Beck, *Wehrmacht und sexuelle Gewalt*, 331. For an example, see the case against Elisabeth A., Sondergericht Darmstadt, May 23, 1944, in HStAD Fonds G 24, Nr. 955/2. But the special court in Frankfurt am Main, in a sentence of May 15, 1942, refused to accept the sexual frustration of a soldier's wife as a mitigating factor: case against Berta M., HHStA Wiesbaden, Sondergericht, Abteilung 461, vol. 8387.
[36] Boberach, *Richterbriefe*, 94.

separation from their husbands, but this usually angered the judges because it implied a critique of the war.[37]

Special courts and courts martial almost always considered the woman the driving force if she was older than the prisoner. In their misogynistic mindset, they believed that an older woman was desperate to find a lover and therefore would go out of her way to seduce a man. Conversely, an older prisoner involved with a young woman usually received the blame as the initiator of the illegal relationship, except if the woman had acted in a blatantly seductive way, looked much older than she was, or already had much sexual experience. Article 176 of the German law code prohibited sexual acts with children, defined as people under fourteen. For male homosexual acts, the adult defendant was punished much more severely if his partner was younger than twenty-one (§175a). Girls aged fourteen to eighteen would be punished more leniently, but the judges always punished a young woman with previous sexual experience more harshly than a woman for whom the relationship with the prisoner was the first sexual experience (the prisoner was punished more harshly in the latter case). Special courts also considered some other mitigating or aggravating circumstances. Mindful of the Nazi idea of criminal types, for example, a woman considered promiscuous and anchorless always received a harsher punishment. A previous conviction, regardless of the cause, also counted as an aggravating factor.

To what extent did the background of the prisoner with whom a woman had been involved influence the special courts? As demonstrated, Thierack and other justice officials pondered the question whether a woman involved with a French or Belgian POW should be punished more leniently because of the growing popular esteem for Frenchmen and Belgians. In his discussions with Bormann in November 1942, Hitler did suggest that women involved with POWs whose armies were still fighting Germany (mostly British and American) should be judged more harshly than women involved with POWs from "nations that are currently undergoing a political reorientation process" – defined as Nazi-occupied countries except for eastern Europe. Hitler also suggested that the attitude of the POW toward Germany was important. A woman involved with a POW who was known to be particularly anti-German deserved a harsher punishment.[38]

---

[37] See, for example, the case of Käthe P., BStA Nürnberg, Akten der Anklagebehörde beim Sondergericht, vol. 1278. See also the example of the same argument in a father's clemency plea for his daughter: case against Marie B., Sondergericht Darmstadt, January 12, 1945, in HStAD, G 27 Darmstadt 1438.

[38] Missive of Thierack to court presidents, November 1942, and Bormann to Lammers, December 3, 1942, in Bundesarchiv Berlin-Lichterfelde, R-43 II/1544a. I thank Rüdiger Overmans for this reference.

Occasionally, a judge pointed out a relationship with a British POW as an aggravating factor, especially in the context of Nazi hate propaganda in the wake of major bombing attacks, and some judges sentenced a woman more leniently because she had become involved with a French rather than a British POW.[39] But these judgments seem to have been aberrations. The sentences overall show little difference if one considers the date and place of the trial. Some judges tended to see a relationship with a prisoner who spoke good German as less offensive because, they argued, it was easier for the woman to forget that he was a stranger and enemy. Others, however, punished the woman more harshly because they pointed out that a German-speaking POW could be particularly dangerous because he was potentially a better spy.[40]

Given the ethnic, national, and racial diversity of western POWs, did women face harsher punishment if they had a forbidden relation with a POW with a particularly stigmatized background, for example a Jew or a Pole? Surprisingly the race and ethnicity of the prisoner – as long as he was a western POW – played a small role in the trials against German women. The judge sometimes counted the ethnic background of the POW or his hostility to Germany as an aggravating factor for the woman, but the punishments were hardly different. In the small village Auffen near Graz, for example, a farmmaid married to a soldier was accused in October 1944 of having had sexual relations with two French POWs with Polish citizenship over several years. The special court of Graz did not see enough proof for the earlier affair but considered the second relation proven. The fact that this relationship involved a Pole counted as an aggravating factor. Yet, the sentence was fifteen months in penitentiary, a typical punishment.[41] Although sex with a Jew or Pole normally stood under a much harsher penal regimen in Nazi Germany and counted as "racial defilement" (*Rassenschande*),[42] the special courts generally sentenced these women the same way as women engaged with other western POWs. The fact that the records from the woman's trial often served as evidence in the court martial of the prisoner meant that the sentences against German women were also to some extent exposed to the

[39] See the case against Anna N, May 19, 1944, BLHA Potsdam, Sondergericht Franfurt/ Oder, Rep. 12C, vol. 1017.
[40] WStLA, Sondergericht, 6325.
[41] Sentence of January 17, 1945, Sondergericht Graz, in StLA Graz, KLs 209/44. It was clear that the woman had known that the prisoner was a Pole (he even needed a Polish translator in court). For a case involving a Jew, see the case study "British Jew and Polish German" in Chapter 7.
[42] Alexandra Przyrembel, *'Rassenschande': Reinheitsmythos und Vernichtungslegitimation im Nationalsozialismus* (Göttingen: Vandenhoeck & Ruprecht, 2003).

international limelight, and this may explain why the special courts here let the principles of international law, in the shape of the Geneva Convention, override Nazi law.

Sometimes special courts revealed their racial bias in case the woman had become involved with a prisoner who had Flemish or German ancestry by pronouncing a mild sentence. In the case of Hermine Halbarter, a farm girl who had a relationship with British POW Johann Weller, the special court in Graz (Austria) sentenced her to only ten months in prison on February 16, 1943, an unusually lenient sentence given that she had admitted sexual intercourse, which normally led to at least one year of penitentiary. Weller had been born in London, but his parents were German citizens, and his father had been interned in Britain as an enemy alien during the First World War. His parents now lived in Germany and had been allowed to visit him in captivity once. Three of his brothers served in the Wehrmacht (two of them had been killed). Although Weller considered himself to be a British citizen, the judge of Hermine Halbarter clearly saw his German ancestry as a mitigating factor, as did the court martial in Wolfsberg, which sentenced Weller to only one year in prison. As his defense attorney argued, this relationship could not have led to a mixture of foreign blood with German blood.[43] Women involved with Belgian or French POWs who had Flemish background or with South African POWs with German ancestry also fared better. But judges tended to ignore German ancestry in cases where the POW or his parents had emigrated from Germany for political reasons. If other factors in the relationship or the woman's background appeared to be offensive, the "Germanic" ancestry of the POW also tended to evaporate as a mitigating factor.

While the punishment of the prisoners became harsher during the course of the war, German women received more lenient sentences over time. Manfred Weckbecker's examination of the trials in front of the special court in Frankfurt am Main shows that the sentences declined from an average of 28.8 months of penal servitude for a relationship involving three to five sexual contacts in 1941 to 19.3 months in 1943 and 15.1 months in 1945. A comparison of two relatively similar cases reveals that two women sentenced in early 1942 received six years in penitentiary while two other women sentenced in 1944 received two and two and a half years, respectively (although I would argue after seeing these and many other cases that the six-year sentence was exceptionally harsh for its time. It also involved preparations for an escape).

---

[43] Karl Petrischek, Wolfsberg, to Swiss Legation, May 3, 1943, in BAR Bern, Bestand Vertretung Berlin, 87a.

Weckbecker finds that married women were punished more harshly (although my sample suggests that clemency pleas on their behalf, especially if supported by a forgiving husband, were more likely to succeed) and that repeated intercourse counted as an aggravating factor. An active pursuit and seduction by the POW counted as an extenuating factor, as did sexual need. The facilitation of the relationship through a common workplace, especially the often very intimate work situation in a close-knit farming community, could act as a mitigating factor. Young women and mentally handicapped women received lighter sentences, as did non-German women involved with prisoners.[44]

While Weckbecker's general conclusions agree with my own findings, the mitigating trend evident in Frankfurt am Main did not materialize to the same degree everywhere, and there were always significant differences among the special courts. The special court of Nürnberg-Fürth remained harsher than others and only slightly softened its judgments, which is not surprising given that it included some of the most fanatical Nazi judges including Oswald Rothaug and Rudolf Oeschey, who both received life sentences during the Nürnberg jurists' trial in 1947 (albeit not for their handling of trials on forbidden relations).[45] Michael Löffelsender has found no softening trend in the special court of Cologne, although it has to be pointed out that for organizational reasons cases involving a forbidden relationship did not generally come to this court before 1942. The survey therefore excludes the year (1941) during which punishments were the hardest.[46] Although an examination of the judgments of the special court in Kiel suggests that the punishments did become softer, this court remained very strict in some cases and only slightly reduced the average sentences for forbidden relations.[47] Yet, in Frankfurt an der Oder, defense attorneys perceived a clear trend toward more lenient sentences, especially against women involved with French and Belgian POWs. In Vienna, judicial officials observed that the sentences were becoming more lenient in 1942. The special court of Bremen was generally lenient, but a trend cannot be established because it tried only a few women accused of forbidden relations while most local cases went to the harder special courts in Oldenburg or Hamburg. A relative of a woman sentenced by the Nürnberg special court argued in August 1944 that the special court in Munich was clearly softer than the one in

---

[44] Weckbecker, *Zwischen Freispruch und Todesstrafe*, 204–5.
[45] Behrschmidt, "Der Saal 600," 117–18; Lutz, "Das Sondergericht Nürnberg 1933–1945," 250.
[46] Löffelsender, *Strafjustiz an der Heimatfront*, 301.
[47] Colmorgen and Godau-Schüttke, "Verbotener Umgang mit Kriegsgefangenen," 148.

Nürnberg.[48] In southern Austria, the special court of Leoben, under a judge who took seriously the argument of Nazi legal theorists that the perceived interests of the *Volksgemeinschaft* trumped strict standards of proof, passed much harsher sentences than the one in Klagenfurt, with the special court of Graz following a middle line.[49] Given that the judgments were published in the press, it was possible for a keen observer to compare the legal practices of different courts and also to detect trends. The brother of a woman convicted by the special court in Nürnberg to five years of penal servitude on July 22, 1941, for example, submitted a clemency plea for her in June 1944 pointing out that punishments for forbidden relations had become more lenient.[50]

A special case was the prosecution of women involved with transformed French or Belgian prisoners (*transformés*) in 1943–5. Here, German courts were highly inconsistent. A complicating factor was that many relationships had started before the transformation of the POW, and it is not always clear how much weight the court gave to intimate relations before and after the transformation. The special court of Kiel-Neumünster took a hard line by insisting that contacts with transformed POWs also fell under §4 of the Decree for the Protection of the Will to Resist of 1939. It therefore sentenced a woman to two years in penitentiary for having had sex with a transformed French POW in the toilet of the electronics factory where both worked. The first event had occurred before the transformation of the POW and the second thereafter, but the woman was not punished for a one-time transgression but rather for a continuous and repeated offense, disregarding the prisoner's changed status.[51] The special court of Nürnberg-Fürth, too, often punished women involved with transformed POWs as if they had been involved with regular POWs, although it was occasionally more lenient if the woman claimed not to have known that contacts with transformed POWs were forbidden or that her French partner was a transformed POW.[52]

---

[48] Therese W. to Josef Goebbels, August 22, 1944, in BStA Nürnberg, Akten der Anklagebehörde beim Sondergericht, 2031. Defense attorneys in Nürnberg said the same thing in other matters, too, and used the comparison to the special court of Munich in favor of their clients: Lutz, "Das Sondergericht Nürnberg 1933–1945," 256.

[49] Unfortunately this judge followed orders of the Reich Ministry of Justice to destroy legal documents before the Allies arrived: Polaschek, *Im Namen der Republik Oesterreich!*, 105, 125–8.

[50] BStA Nürnberg, Akten der Anklagebehörde beim Sondergericht, 1180.

[51] Case of Käte F., LASH Schleswig, Abt. 358, 6959, sentenced on April 26, 1944.

[52] See the case of Tilly (Ottilie) M., vol. 2327; Sophie H., vol. 2350; Gunda H., vol. 2383; Käthe F., vol. 2314; Else S., vol. 2258, all in BStA Nürnberg, Akten der Anklagebehörde beim Sondergericht. For an example of greater leniency, see the case of Georges Q. and Else Sch. (vol. 2298).

On the other hand, the special court in Vienna tended to judge all contacts with transformed POWs leniently. In October 1944, it even dismissed a case against twelve women working in an armaments factory in Lower Austria who had entered into intimate relations with French transformed POWs. That the women were almost all very young and that for a long time nobody had taken offense, not even a foreman and a police officer who were aware of the relations, motivated this decision. Moreover, it played a role that the factory management had indirectly encouraged the relations by housing the women in the same barracks as the prisoners, which violated regulations for the housing of POWs.[53]

Other special courts were lenient in cases with transformed prisoners, too. The special court in Hannover and Hildesheim, for example, prosecuted Mimi Berkner for relations with the transformed French POW Roland Gallois. Both worked for a beer company. He drove a delivery truck, and she accompanied him and did the paperwork. Their relationship had become intimate already before his transformation in August 1943, but they lived it openly thereafter, attending the cinema and taking long walks together. She introduced the prisoner to her family, and they lived like a couple. She claimed that she had not known that relationships with transformed POWs were forbidden (although he admitted having been aware of it). The special court only sentenced her to the minimum sentence, one year in penitentiary, for the intimate contact before Gallois' transformation while acquitting her for the long and intensive contact after his transformation. The prosecutor immediately appealed against the judgment, which he found much too lenient, but the late date (March 5, 1945) made it unlikely that it was ever reversed.[54] In some areas, the women involved with transformed POWs were not prosecuted at all; in others, they received acquittals or light sentences if they claimed not to know that the prohibition applied to transformed POWs or if they argued that they had considered the prisoner to be a civilian worker. This was usually hard to refute because the transformed POW lived and dressed like a civilian. It appears that the standards for proving this ignorance to the justice authorities were not very high.[55]

Persons sentenced by a special court had no right of appeal.[56] The woman, family members, or the attorney could only submit clemency pleas or request temporary dismissals, but the decision depended on the director of the penitentiary or prison and the state prosecutor.

[53] Sammelmitteilung, October 7, 1944, in WStLA, Sondergericht, 3191.
[54] NSTA Hannover 172, Hildesheim Acc. 22/57, Nr. 18 (case of Minna [Mimi] B.).
[55] Boll, "… das gesunde Volksempfinden," 676 (note 33).
[56] Schwarze, Es war wie eine Hexenjagd, 157.

The convicted woman was responsible for the court costs, but in most cases, she was too poor to pay. All penitentiary sentences also carried a loss of civil rights that matched or exceeded the term in the penitentiary. The court normally counted the pre-trial custody of the woman toward the length of the sentence, but only if she had confessed.

The Courts Martial

A prisoner suspected of a forbidden relation was usually transferred to the next larger camp and placed under stricter guard while the investigation proceeded. Some POWs had to join penal battalions and work under close watch with POWs serving disciplinary punishments or lighter sentences. Others were locked up in arrest cells inside the main camps, while still others were simply transferred from the farm where they had worked to a large camp without any special arrangements. The Geneva Convention mandated that pre-trial confinement be deducted from the sentence if permitted for members of the detaining state's forces (§47), but German legal practice was inconsistent. The German law governing military trials stipulated that courts martial had to deduce pre-trial custody "in whole or in part" from the sentence but did not specify any guidelines (§64, *Kriegsstrafverfahrensordnung*). A special instruction regarding trials against POWs did, however, demand that pre-trial custody be fully deducted from the sentence.[57] Most courts martial complied with this rule, but some refused recognition of pre-trial custody to POWs who were found guilty but who denied the allegations; the courts martial argued that this practice was analogous to procedures against German servicemen and therefore in agreement with the Geneva Convention. Differences of opinion also arose over what exactly counted as pre-trial custody because some military judges argued that the confinement the POW had experienced before the hearing did not differ significantly from the normal conditions of captivity and therefore did not qualify as pre-trial custody. By 1944, the Wehrmacht prisons reserved for soldiers in pre-trial custody were hopelessly overcrowded because of the flood of forbidden relations cases, and the prisoners awaiting trial therefore had to remain in the main camps under circumstances that did not differ dramatically from the conditions of "normal" prisoners in these camps.[58] Delegates of the protecting powers and

[57] *Reichsgesetzblatt* (RGbl.) 147, August 26, 1939, p. 1467 and p. 1478.
[58] For an instructive example, see attorney Gustav Sellner (Vienna) to Swiss Consulate General in Vienna, July 12, 1944, in BAR Bern, Bestand Vertretung Berlin, 79b.

defense attorneys spilt much ink over this issue, which was never completely resolved.

Once a POW was awaiting trial, the German Foreign Ministry had to notify the protecting power about the charges and the court date. The notification had to be received at least three weeks before the hearing. The prisoner also had to be notified of the precise charges, and he had the right to choose a defense attorney. The delegates of the protecting powers created a list of German attorneys and sometimes drafted lawyers from among the prisoners, as was the case with Delattre. These attorneys specialized in the defense of POWs. A prisoner could use the service of the lawyers on the approved list without charge, but he had to pay the attorney if he wanted to make his own choice (which almost never happened). Some defense attorneys received much praise from the officials of the protecting power and from the prisoners themselves, while a few of them seemed uninterested or not up to their task. Still, Sir Harold Satow, the director of the British POW department, concluded in a review of POW matters after the war: "Taken as a whole, the German lawyers did well for their clients and performed their duties conscientiously."[59] Some of the best attorneys, for example Dr. Hanns Marx, who defended many French POWs and also some women in Nürnberg, knew the language of the prisoner and needed no translator.[60]

A variety of practical problems hampered the work of the defense attorneys. In response to criticism of his work, attorney Dr. Heinz Melchert from Münster explained to the Scapini Mission in 1943 that transportation difficulties had made it increasingly difficult for him to visit the accused prisoner and confidentially discuss strategies for his defense. Bombings had destroyed rail connections, and trains were running late, if at all. Many POW camps were not close to train stations, and often the accused POW was on a work detachment outside the camp when the attorney arrived. If Melchert did track down the accused prisoner, he also had to find a capable translator because he did not speak French. Sometimes Melchert could not get home in the evening after a visit to a POW camp because his return train would not arrive. Melchert also complained that the schedule during the day of the

[59] Sir Harold Satow and M. J. Sée, *The Work of the Prisoners of War Department during the Second World War* ([London]: Foreign Office, 1950), 45.

[60] The estimation of the French men of confidence and legal advisors for Marx is evident in the Dossier "Stalag XIII-D" in AN, F9, 2745. Other attorneys receiving special praise were Dr. Birkl in Amberg (Bavaria) and Dr. van Hoboken in Berlin. See Man of confidence to Chef de la Délégation, March 8, 1944, in AN, F9, 2745, dossier "Stalag XIII-C," and Jean Lassalle to Scapini, January 19, 1944, in AN, F9, 2742, dossier "Stalag III-D."

hearings often changed at the last minute; the case of a certain prisoner he had to defend might be moved up if an earlier case was postponed because a witness had failed to appear. Melchert therefore often had to defend a prisoner without having had any opportunity to talk to him.[61]

A shortage of competent translators exacerbated the problems.[62] British POW William Ogden Donovan, for example, had signed a confession during interrogation saying that he had sex with a Polish woman. But during his trial he claimed that the translator had completely misunderstood him. Donovan had good luck because the translator present during the hearing stated that the first translator was not up to the task and that this had already led to problems in other trials. In the end, Donovan received a very mild punishment (two weeks of arrest) for having given candy to the woman.[63] In the case against British POW William Howard in front of the court martial in Leoben (Austria), the prosecutor relied, among other statements, on an incriminating testimony a Ukrainian forced laborer had made to the police. Given that the statement contained contradictions, however, the court martial wanted to hear the Ukrainian as a witness, but no competent translator could be found. This worked in favor of the POW, who received only six months in prison because he was sentenced only for the (minor) charges that could be proven without the witness. A less conscientious judge might have taken the most damning statements from the testimony and used them as proof.[64]

In light of the communication problems between accused POWs and attorneys, the Scapini Mission proposed in 1943 to select in each major camp a prisoner with legal knowledge who would act as an advisor to the accused prisoners. The German High Command approved this measure on August 25, 1943, and French and Belgian legal advisors began working with the large number of accused POWs. Although shortages made it difficult to equip the legal advisors with German law books, they did receive instructions on how to prepare POWs for the hearing. "Manly" and soldierly appearance was important. As Georges Smets learned, the judges tended to be harsher on POWs who wore sideburns or goatees. He once asked a German attorney why this was the case, and the attorney suspected that the judge might mistake these prisoners for Jews or for friends of Jews (although in my sample there are numerous

---

[61] Attorney Dr. Heinz Melchert to SDPG, July 17, 1943, in AN, F9, 2731.

[62] The Scapini Mission often complained about bad translators. See, for example, "Renseignements concernant la visite à faire au Kriegsgerichtsrat Dr. Peterson, Tribunal Militaire de Graudenz," May 14, 1943, in AN, F9, 2721.

[63] Feldurteil, Danzig, September 28, 1943, in BAR Bern, Bestand Vertretung Berlin, 84a.

[64] Feldurteil, Leoben, September 18, 1943, in BAR Bern, Bestand Vertretung Berlin, 84a.

cases in which judges did not sentence Jewish POWs more harshly). Henceforth, Smets made sure that all of the defendants in his district went to the hearing clean shaven.[65] The legal advisors also evaluated whether – or rather at which point – a POW should confess in order to receive a more lenient sentence. Many legal advisors contacted the attorney before the hearing and coordinated defense strategy, an important factor given that the attorney was often unable to speak to the POW. By 1944, however, the High Command restricted the mobility of the French legal advisors in reaction to some escapes and resistance activities. In conversation with Reinecke in 1943, Scapini had given his word that the legal advisors would not abuse their travel privileges, but apparently some did, although the High Command remained vague about the charges.[66] The legal advisors probably helped in many cases, although it has to be kept in mind that the possibility to influence sentences was limited given that the military judges were under strict instructions from Keitel. The prisoners also did not always heed the advice of the attorney and legal advisor to confess in spite of clear evidence against them, leading to harsher sentences. Some prisoners hoped to protect the woman by denying the allegations; others wanted to reduce their own sentence. Some defense attorneys complained about this habit. As attorney Dr. Knipp from Stettin pointed out, a prisoner's stubborn denial often undermined the attorney's efforts to portray the woman as the active part and thus to reach a milder sentence for the POW.[67]

The Belgians adopted similar defense arrangements and often coordinated their procedures with the French. The French legal advisors also helped Belgian POWs, and Belgian officials or men of confidence helped the French. Unlike the French POWs, however, the Belgians had to pay the attorney first because Belgium did not have a recognized protecting power after the American entry into the war. Comrades raised the money through a collection among other prisoners, and the DSLP later

[65] Musée Royal de l'Armée et d'Histoire Militaire, Brussels, Fonds Hautecler, Farde 33: Le questionnaire aux hommes de confiance. Réponse de Georges Smets (Stalag I-A), Question 14 (no pagination).
[66] "Entretien du 13 février 1943," and "Compte-rendu de l'entretien avec le Général Reinecke le 19 mai 1944," both in AN, F9, 2176. Reinecke mentioned a Lieutenant Fortin as an example of abuse, but he did not disclose what this prisoner had done.
[67] Dr. Knipp to SDPG, April 29, 1942, in AN, F9, 2731; Dr. Nehlert, Neisse, to Schweizerische Gesandtschaft, May 5, 1944, BAR Bern, Bestand Vertretung Berlin, 80a; Dr. Rudolf Glaser, Leoben, to Schweizerische Gesandtschaft, September 20, 1943, BAR Bern, Bestand Vertretung Berlin, 83b. See also Stéphane Delattre, "Rapport sur la Défense des Prisonniers devant le tribunal militaire allemand," September 29, 1943, in AN, F9, 2743, dossier Stalag V-A; "Observations fournies par les docteurs Pechmann & Heuser, le 16 janvier 1942," in AN, F9, 2731.

reimbursed them. Attorneys for the French and British prisoners sent a bill and a report of the court martial to the Scapini Mission or the Swiss legation, which paid them after the hearings. Defending a POW was lucrative. Melchert, for example, mentioned that his good pay for defending a POW (eighty to a hundred marks per case, twice as much as for a "normal" job) had triggered jealousy among colleagues.[68]

In approximately half the cases where the demand of the prosecutor is known, the court martial pronounced a more lenient sentence, usually thanks to the attorney's interventions.[69] The attorney could undermine the credibility of the witnesses or insist on the prisoner's good conduct in captivity or his good work performance. He could portray the woman as the seductress and denigrate her character, as demonstrated. In cases involving relationships with soldiers' wives, he could spread doubt that the prisoner had known this fact. Similarly, he could demonstrate that the prisoner had reason to believe that the woman was not German, leading to a milder sentence in those districts where all relationships with women were forbidden and to acquittal in the others. In the earlier trials, he could support the POW's claims that he had not known (or understood) the prohibition.

Given the strict guidelines from the highest military authorities, however, the attorney could often do nothing more than prevent the court martial from exceeding the minimum punishment. This fact at first created the impression among the agencies of the protecting powers that the attorneys were not worth their pay. The attorneys justified themselves by pointing out that the higher authorities had squashed all judgments they considered too mild. The Scapini Mission acknowledged in an internal memo in July 1942 that, despite impressive efforts by some attorneys, the latitude of the defense was small.[70] By 1943, one had to expect at least one year in prison for hugs and kisses, three years of prison for a relation involving one-time sexual intercourse, and more (usually penitentiary) in case the POW had known that the woman was married to a soldier. The Belgian POW agency, after reviewing the cases it had overseen, also concluded that the minimum punishments were largely set in stone and constructed a table of what a POW had to expect, albeit with large margins of error:

- attempt to approach a woman: 3–18 months in prison
- kisses: 3–12 months; attempted kiss: 4 months

[68] Dr. Melchert to SDPG, July 17, 1943, in AN, F9, 2731.
[69] This is consistent with the practice of the special courts: Bozyakali, *Das Sondergericht am Hanseatischen Oberlandesgericht*, 311.
[70] Untitled memo, July 17, 1942, in AN, F9, 2731.

- delivering letters for another POW or a woman: 6 months
- friendship (repeated meetings, exchange of gifts, letters): 1–2 years in prison
- tender touching (without indecent behavior): 1–1.5 years in prison
- sexual relations: attempted: 12–18 months in prison, and in case of a very young woman 2–3 years in prison; in case of rape or contact with a girl under 15: up to 8 years of penal servitude; in case of a married, divorced, or widowed woman: 3 years in prison (but slightly less if the woman was very active); with a woman married to a soldier: at least 3 years in penitentiary.[71]

Some attorneys openly criticized the High Command's influence on military tribunals. Attorney Franz Peterson from Salzburg was the most outspoken among them. He found the punishments excessive and even argued that treating the forbidden relations under the provisions of §92 (disobedience) of the military law code was a glaring misuse of this article. Like other attorneys, Peterson bemoaned that there was no possibility for the POW or his attorney to refer a case to a higher judicial authority (not that this would have mattered given the mindset of the higher authorities).[72] According to the legal expert of the Swiss Legation in Berlin, Hans K. Frey, even the German judges often complained to him that the High Command left them little freedom.[73]

The court martial was composed of three members, usually one qualified military judge and two assistants, including a man of the same rank as the accused (§9 of the procedural regulation for German military tribunals); in the case of most POWs that was a rank-and-file soldier. The judgment was decided in secret deliberation by majority vote among the three members (§62), although the presiding judge played the dominant role because he was usually the only member of the court with legal training.[74] Being a judge at a court martial for POWs was not a prestigious role. Judges who were considered not harsh enough in trials against German frontline soldiers were occasionally relegated to courts martial in the rear area, which dealt with POWs, and they experienced this transfer

---

[71] "Notes pour servir à la rédaction d'un rapport sur le service juridique et sur l'observance des articles 60 à 65 de la Convention de Genève," in CEGESOMA, AA 257.

[72] Dr. Peterson to SDPG, July 7, 1942; Dr. Melchert to SDPG, July 17, 1943; Dr. Knipp to SDPG, April 29, 1942, all in AN, F9, 2731. Dr. Wabnitz to Swiss Legation, April 22, 1944, and Dr. Nehlert to Swiss Legation, May 5, 1944, both in BAR Bern, Bestand Vertretung Berlin, 80a.

[73] Frey, *Die disziplinarische und gerichtliche Bestrafung*, 63.

[74] *Kriegsstrafverfahrensordnung* (KStVO), August 17, 1938, published in *Reichsgesetzblatt* 1939, no. 147, August 26, 1939, pp. 1457–76. Snyder, *Sex Crimes under the Wehrmacht*, 39–40.

as a symbolic demotion.[75] The prosecutor (called "representative of the accusation") also had legal training. In some courts martial, the prosecutor and the presiding judge traded seats from case to case.

Georges Smets attended many courts martial in Königsberg and left a lively description of the procedures. He and the German attorney met approximately one hour before the start of the hearings in a small restaurant near the court building to discuss the last details of the defense with the accused prisoners, who arrived in the company of their guards. Often, the women with whom the prisoners had been involved also gathered in this restaurant because they were called as witnesses. "These young ladies were not guarded and did not hide their affection for their sweethearts. Touching scenes occurred despite the intervention of the furious guards. The women often brought goodies to the site. Pieces of bread and sausages discreetly slipped into the vast pockets of the prisoners." At the start of the hearing, Smets and the attorney sat down in the front row, and when the court martial entered, an old sergeant acting as master of ceremonies ordered the audience to rise. The members of the court martial, before sitting down, raised their right arms for a shattering "Heil Hitler!" The judge, Smets claimed, "was invariably between seventy and eighty years old; he wore a general's uniform and looked as if he had escaped from the marionette theater of High Street [*Rue Haute*] in Brussels." The other members of the court were mostly disabled soldiers. Smets likely exaggerated with respect to the age of the judges; in a sample examined by historian Kerstin Theis, only ten percent of the judges in courts martial of the reserve army were over sixty in 1944, and the average seems to have been around forty-five years.[76]

During the hearing, Smets argued, "the judge must be a pervert because he wants to know every slight detail about the relationship between the prisoner and the woman." Nonetheless, Smets concluded that the court martial was usually conscientious and fair in its proceedings; the problem was the harshness of the punishments.[77] After the judge had pronounced the sentence, Smets often witnessed that he upbraided the woman because she had "soiled the beautiful German race" and cheated on her soldier husband. Some women retorted that they had not seen their husbands in years or that they knew their husband was flirting with French or Belgian women in the west. Smets concluded: "I could write a book about all I have heard and seen at this ghastly

[75] Snyder, *Sex Crimes under the Wehrmacht*, 42.
[76] Theis, *Wehrmachtjustiz an der "Heimatfront,"* 456–7.
[77] This is what he said to a DSLP official at the time: Smets to t'Serclaes, September 22, 1943, in CEGESOMA, AA 244.

tribunal. There would be much to laugh if the consequences had not been so tragic."[78]

Judges could consider a series of extenuating circumstances. For example, they respected true love and the prisoner's desire to marry the woman or the prisoner's chivalrous efforts to take blame away from the woman. They also appreciated evidence of the prisoner's good conduct and work performance provided by letters from employers and camp or work detachment commanders. Evidence of seduction by the woman or even the fact that the woman had offered no resistance to the advances of the prisoner could also count as extenuating circumstances. As pointed out, a woman who was significantly older than the prisoner was automatically seen as the seducer. A frank confession by the prisoner led to a lighter sentence. Judges generally recognized that prisoners, especially young ones, were under considerable sexual pressure because they had been forced to be abstinent for a long time, although this did not necessarily lead to lighter sentences.[79]

Often, the best conduct, the most chivalrous behavior, and the sincerest love only served to avert an increase of the minimal punishment, while many forces were pulling in the other direction. A prisoner involved with a very young woman would be blamed as seducer unless there was evidence that the woman had already had sexual contacts before. If the woman was married, the prisoner also had to expect a harder punishment, although the fact that many prisoners were married themselves made little difference to most judges. Some POWs were judged more harshly if the contacts had led to, or risked, pregnancy, as was often the case, but the courts martial were far from consistent in this matter. The Belgian POW officials believed that pregnancy of the woman was not an aggravating factor in the courts martial, but some cases in my sample suggest the contrary.[80] An example is the sentence for French POW Roger Lepelletier, who had a long-time sexual relationship with farm maid Ursula Mitterholzer in the village Indorf northeast of Munich. Mitterholzer became pregnant. On September 7, 1941, she secretly gave birth in the toilet of her parents' farm and immediately strangled the baby with her underskirt. The court martial judging Lepelletier considered his

[78] Musée Royal de l'Armée, Brussels, Fonds Hautecler, Farde 33: Le questionnaire aux hommes de confiance. Réponse de Georges Smets (Stalag I-A), Question 14 (no pagination). Smets claims that the court martial also sentenced the women, but the women had to stand trial in front of a civilian court.
[79] It was standard practice to consider "sexual neediness" in cases against German soldiers prosecuted for sexual violence: Beck, *Wehrmacht und sexuelle Gewalt*, 331.
[80] "Notes pour servir à la rédaction d'un rapport sur le service juridique et sur l'observance des articles 60 à 65 de la Convention de Genève," in CEGESOMA, AA 257.

carelessness that had led to the pregnancy as an aggravating factor but gave him credit for his sincere shock and regret when he heard about the killing of the baby. He received three years in prison, while she was sentenced to six years of penal servitude (including a sentence for infanticide).[81]

If a prisoner had consorted with a sterilized woman, the prisoner or his attorney would often argue that the sexual contact could not be perceived as an attack on the purity of the German blood (the woman or her attorney usually made the same argument), but the judges angrily dismissed this point even though it cut to the heart of the racial justification for the order of January 10, 1940.

Defense attorneys sometimes tried to use the "new" justification of the courts martial, namely that the prisoner had through his relationship attacked the honor of the German woman, by arguing that the woman in question did not have any honor to violate and that therefore the prisoner ought to be punished more lightly. Attorney Nehlert in Neisse (Upper Silesia) made the most elaborate, albeit misogynistic, argument in this matter. In a clemency plea for two British POWs sentenced in May 1944, he argued that German women and girls who became involved with POWs "show such serious neglect of their national duty that they automatically exclude themselves from the *Volksgemeinschaft*." In case of sexual intercourse, Nehlert claimed that the woman always acted as the seducer because the POW, as a captive, could not use his seductive skills:

If German women and girls get involved with POWs, there is therefore only one possible conclusion, namely that they are predestined to be prostitutes. Prostitutes, however, are not even international, they are a-national. If POWs touch prostitutes, the honor of the German woman is hardly affected because prostitutes are no German women. Prostitutes need no special protection [of their honor] because fornication is their profession.[82]

Other attorneys, including Delattre, made similar arguments in trials and in clemency pleas. Although this strategy rested on established notions of female sexual honor, or rather dishonor, the judges usually countered that what was at stake was not the honor of the woman with whom the prisoner had been involved but rather the honor of "the" German woman and the dignity of the German people as an abstraction.[83]

[81] Feldurteil, München, November 28, 1941, in PAAA, R 40897.
[82] Nehlert to Gericht der Division 432, Neisse, May 5, 1944, in BAR Bern, Bestand Vertretung Berlin, 80a.
[83] For a good discussion of female sexual honor in German judicial practice, although focused mostly on the treatment of German soldiers' transgressions against non-German women, see Beck, *Wehrmacht und sexuelle Gewalt*, 285–92.

Although it was usually unknown whether the prisoner had a criminal record before being captured, most courts martial took the prisoner at his word if he denied having had earlier convictions (it would have been difficult to verify this under wartime conditions). Disciplinary punishments while in captivity, for example for escaping, would be noted but did not count as aggravating factors because the Geneva Convention considered the desire to escape and join one's own forces a patriotic impulse. In the few cases where a prisoner had a previous conviction because of an illegal relationship, this fact of course counted as an aggravating factor, as it did in the case of women in front of the special courts.

Many POWs denied the forbidden relationship or at least tried to claim that it had not led to sexual intercourse. But, as demonstrated, this did not help if the woman had made a confession. There were only a few cases where the courts martial dismissed a confession of a woman because they believed that she was mentally unbalanced. One such case led to a spectacular discrepancy between the special court and the court martial: the special court in Nürnberg sentenced the farmer's daughter Maria Fitzler to two years of penal servitude in the summer of 1941 for her relationship with French POW Marcel Giraud, the POW assigned to her parents' farm. Fitzler admitted having had sex with Giraud twice in the fall of 1940. She had already been sent to a penitentiary when the court martial in Nürnberg requested her as a witness in the trial against Giraud on December 16, 1941. She repeated her confession but then claimed that they had only had sex once, not twice. Yet, she spoke very hesitantly and did not seem to know the difference between intercourse in the sense of contact ("*Verkehr*") and sexual intercourse ("*Geschlechtsverkehr*"). After hearing a police testimony that called the woman "dumb, naïve, and inconsiderate," the court martial concluded that she was mentally handicapped and that she had merely imagined sex with the good-looking prisoner. He was acquitted. When her attorney heard of this decision, he requested a re-trial of Fitzler and a psychiatric examination, but to no avail. She did only receive a medical examination by a family practitioner, who concluded that she was normal. Interestingly, when she successfully requested in 1949–50 that her sentence be deleted from the penal registry, she pointed out that she was now married to the man for whom she had been sentenced. The name does not match the prisoner's name, but she had already in 1941 talked in vague terms about having had a relationship with another man, and she had had a stillbirth at the time of her trial in late July 1941. It is likely that she was sentenced by mistake, perhaps because she had not wanted to reveal her sexual relationship with the German man who she later married.[84]

In general, courts martial decided without much consideration for the ethnic or racial identity of the prisoner, as required by the Geneva Convention. National stereotypes often appear in the judgments, for example allusions to "impulsive" Italian-born prisoners or allegedly theft-prone Jews, but negative stereotypes seem not to have led to harsher judgments. In one case, a Catholic French POW and a Hungarian Jew had to stand trial for having had a love affair, one after the other, with an unhappy innkeeper's wife. They both had had sex with her the same number of times. The judge clearly resented the Hungarian Jew, but the sentence for both defendants was the same: three and a half years in prison. The Foreign Office even protested against any mention of racial questions in the judgment to the High Command, and it notified the Scapini Mission of the verdict only after cutting out the objectionable statements about the Hungarian Jew.[85] Courts martial also made no significant difference among French, Belgian, and British POWs. The price for violations of the order of January 10, 1940, was remarkably consistent for all western POWs, once steering efforts from above had eliminated the big discrepancies that were still noticeable in the judgments against French and Belgian POWs in the middle of 1941 (there are no recorded trials of British POWs from 1941 on the basis of the prohibition). Defense attorneys who defended prisoners from several armies did not mention a difference.

As was the case for the women tried by the special courts, however, positive stereotypes did occasionally lead to milder sentences, as happened to some Flemish POWs from the Belgian or French army and some British POWs with German ancestry. In the court martial against Gérard Florimont Meunier, who had Flemish ancestry despite his French name, the sentence stated:

In considering the appropriate punishment, the court considered as mitigating factors the confession of the defendant, his integrity, and in particular the fact that the defendant is a Fleming and thus from a tribe of people that still carries within itself significant Germanic elements; it appears entirely possible that the

---

[84] BStA Nürnberg, Akten der Anklagebehörde beim Sondergericht, 1228; Feldurteil Nürnberg, December 16, 1941, in PAAA, R 40902.

[85] Feldurteil, Memmingen, January 9, 1942, in PAAA, R 40908. The Jewish POW stated that his mother was Jewish and that he was circumcised. He claimed that he did not know whether his father, who was in exile in Britain, was Jewish. It seemed very likely, but the court martial did not pursue the question. For the Foreign Office's reaction, see Lautz to High Command, February 7, 1942, and Auswärtiges Amt to Dienststelle Scapini, April 23, 1942, both in PAAA, R 40908.

defendant, conscious of his ancestry, did not fully understand the objectionable nature of his act.

Meunier received only four months in prison for hiding in the home of an Austrian woman, who herself received one year of penal servitude.[86] One controversial procedure for lighter offenses of POWs was the German *Strafverfügung* (punishment order), a decision by the camp commander to convict the POW to up to six months in prison without any hearing.[87] The western governments claimed that the punishment order violated the judicial regulations of the Geneva Convention by sentencing a prisoner to more than 30 days of prison without a hearing and a defender (§54). The German High Command countered that the POW or his attorney had the right to challenge the punishment order and get a regular court martial following all international rules, but the judges usually threatened to pronounce a harsher sentence in that case.[88] In 1943, German camp commanders began handing out punishment orders for up to six months in prison to the French and Belgian POWs. Initially, they limited punishment orders for British and American POWs to one month, but in 1944, they also imposed longer sentences on British and American prisoners. The Scapini Mission as well as the Swiss legation demanded that the German authorities use punishment orders only for sentences up to thirty days, which would have approximated it to a disciplinary punishment in conformity with the Geneva Convention. But the German Foreign Office argued that it could apply a method of punishment as it was used in the German army because the laws in force in the army of the detaining power also applied to POWs. The Scapini Mission replied by pointing to the fact that the Geneva Convention required signatory states to bring their military law codes into agreement with the Geneva Convention, but to no avail. Many French, British, Belgian, and some American POWs received punishment orders, almost always prison terms from one to six months.[89] For German military justice, which was being flooded with trials because of violations of the

[86] "Bei der Strafbemessung war mildernd das Geständnis des Angeklagten, der gute Eindruck, seine Unbescholtenheit, und insbesondere der Umstand, dass der Angeklagte Flame ist, ein Volksstamm, welcher noch ganz bedeutende germanische Elemente in sich trägt, und es erscheint durchaus möglich, dass der Angeklagte im Bewusstsein seiner Abstammung das Verwerfliche seiner Handlung nicht voll eingesehen hat." Feldurteil, Linz, July 31, 1941, in PAAA, R 40853.
[87] Initially, the *Strafverfügung* allowed only up to three months in prison, but the maximum sentence was lengthened to six months in 1942, and almost all POWs who received one fell under the revised provision: Snyder, *Sex Crimes under the Wehrmacht*, 45–6.
[88] Frey, *Die disziplinarische und gerichtliche Bestrafung*, 132–5.
[89] Chef de Delégation to Homme de confiance Henri Erbs, November 4 and December 8, 1943, in AN, F9, 2744, and Dossier "Affaires judiciaires, Dossier de principe et

order of January 10, 1940, the punishment order was an efficient way to
deal with small transgressions such as an occasional kiss, hug, or letter
between POWs and women without having to organize a court martial
and to follow the elaborate protocol required by the Geneva Convention.

Some POWs decided to challenge a punishment order, but they did
usually receive the same or a slightly harsher punishment. The Belgian
legal advisor Jean Thisquen therefore recommended in a POW newspaper not to challenge a punishment order unless the prisoner had very
strong reasons to do so.[90] Sometimes, the punishment order was an
advantage for a POW because it did not uncover aggravating circumstances that would have surfaced during a trial: British prisoner James
Garrett, for example, was accused of having given German employee
Ottilie Duda at the Blechhammer factory site a love letter and a package
with dried raisins. Garrett confessed but claimed that Duda had told him
that she was a Pole. The camp commander, inundated with cases,
accepted this claim and gave Garrett a punishment order of three months
in prison in July 1944. Although this was a comparatively light punishment, Garrett challenged it, but when he learned that Duda had testified
that she had never told him that she was Polish, he wisely withdrew his
objection before the court martial met. He would have received a harsher
punishment had he persisted.[91]

Once the court martial had pronounced a sentence, the judgment went
to the commander of the military district, who served as the next highest
judicial authority (*Gerichtsherr*). He could confirm the sentence (which
happened in the majority of cases) or reverse it, which was almost always
coupled with the request for a harsher sentence. After confirmation by
the district commander, the judgment was forwarded to the High Command and the Foreign Office. As we have seen, the High Command used
its right to reverse a sentence to steer the trials into a harsher direction.
The Foreign Office usually sent the sentence to the protecting power of
the POW. Like the woman sentenced by the special court, the prisoner
had no right of appeal,[92] but his attorney could ask the *Gerichtsherr* not to
confirm the sentence or to mitigate the punishment, but only if new

correspondance générale," in AN, F9, 2185; "Procès-verbal de la réunion du 2 juin
1944," in AN F 9, 2177. For a collection of punishment orders against French POWs,
see the dossier "Peines disciplinaires" in AN, F9, 2799. For the British POWs getting
punishment orders, see dossier "Strafverfügungen," BAR Bern, Bestand Vertretung
Berlin, 84a.

90 Jean Thisquen in *S'Unir*, Stalag X-A. #13, November–December 1944. In
CEGESOMA, AA 257 (Conseiller juridique Jean Thisquen).
91 Strafverfügung, Breslau, July 15, 1944, BAR Bern, Bestand Vertretung Berlin, 84a.
92 KStVO, 17 August 1938, §76.

evidence had come to light since the hearing. The standards for what constituted "new evidence" were restrictive, and rarely did a higher authority reverse a judgment considered too harsh or reduce a punishment. One of the few successful examples involved two French POWs who had left their camp and visited a woman who treated them to coffee and cake in her apartment. The court martial in Neustettin sentenced them both to six months in prison. When the French judicial officer of the camp learned that the woman had been sentenced to only four months in prison, he asked the defense attorney to request a reduction of the sentence. As he argued, the woman who had invited the POWs should not be punished more lightly than the POWs who had accepted the invitation. He also pointed to the fact that the POWs had performed work for the woman and that the invitation was meant to "pay" them back for their services (and this was not forbidden). In this case, the *Gerichtsherr* slightly reduced the punishment to five months in prison.[93]

After the prisoner had served part of his sentence, the prisoner himself, the protecting power, or the attorney could submit a clemency plea, but the German authorities rarely granted early releases from a military prison or penitentiary. The Scapini Mission made a concerted effort in 1943 to go through thousands of files of convicted prisoners (except Jews, because it was known that they might be deported after release) and select the harshest sentences with an eye to potential clemency pleas, but such requests almost always met with rejections even if the conduct of the prisoner was good.[94] Military justice officials knew that they were under intense scrutiny for being too soft, and the sentences against the POWs accused of forbidden relations tended to become more severe over the course of the war.[95] This made it counter-intuitive for military justice authorities to reduce earlier (lighter) sentences.

Justifications

Generally, the courts martial and special courts formulated a justification for the sentence. Most court martial judgments throughout the war

---

[93] "Audience du Tribunal de Neustettin du 28 février 1944," and Conseiller juridique to Chef de la Delégation, August 29, 1944, both in AN, F9, 2742.

[94] In the case of the Hungarian Jew and the non-Jew sentenced to three and a half years in prison, for example, the Scapini Mission only considered a clemency plea for the non-Jew. They knew at this time that it was safer for a Jew to remain in a German POW camp than to return home. See Dossier 2060 in AN, F9, 2410.

[95] Harold Satow claimed that the sentences against British POWs in general became milder, but this does not apply to the forbidden relations cases. Satow and See, *The Work of the Prisoners of War Department*, 46.

invoked the danger of espionage, sabotage, and escapes, and they high-lighted dangers for the security of the Reich. Cordial relations with "enemies" might paralyze the German will to resist, especially given that relations between prisoners and German women could become contagious. Many judgments throughout the war also argued that the prisoner had attacked the honor of the German woman and the dignity of the German people. Until early 1942, the courts martial were very elaborate in explaining the "signifi-cant disadvantage" caused by the act of disobedience, often stressing racial hygienic motives. Formulations such as the prisoner threatening "to add unwanted admixtures to the German blood" or the need "to keep the German blood pure and to prevent that children of a foreign race are born in German marriages, thus introducing a foreign element into the German family" appear frequently.[96] The court martial in Dresden, for example, justified a six-months prison term for Henri Michaud, who had only met a German woman in secret and written love letters to her, by stating: "Through his actions, he has violated an important interest, namely the protection of the purity of the German blood and of the German woman's honor."[97] The court martial in Salzburg elaborated on this theme in a judgment against a French prisoner who had fondled a young German worker in a sawmill:

[The act] represents a danger for the security of the Reich because there cannot be any doubt that a contact of prisoners of war with civilians, especially with German women, leads to a dulling of hostility toward the enemy and therefore to war weariness and to corrosion of the German people's defensive abilities. Moreover, one has to consider that sexual intercourse would produce a mixture of races, which would lead to the degeneration of the German people.[98]

On other days, the same court martial conjured up the danger of "con-tamination of the German blood." The court martial in Breslau, in a trial against a Belgian POW, also warned that the illicit sexual encounters threatened to undermine the German racial laws.[99]

---

[96] One example: Feldurteil, Memmingen, December 15, 1941, in PAAA, R 40912.

[97] "Durch sein Tun wurde ein wesentliches Rechtsgut verletzt, nämlich die Reinerhaltung des deutschen Blutes und die deutsche Frauenehre." Feldurteil, Dresden, September 26, 1941, in PAAA, R 40884.

[98] "Er bedeutet eine Gefahr für die Sicherheit des Reiches ..., denn es kann gar keinem Zweifel unterliegen, dass ein Verkehr von Kriegsgefangenen mit Zivilpersonen, insbesondere deutschen Frauen, eine Abstumpfung gegenüber dem Gegner und sonach eine Kriegsmüdigkeit und dadurch Zersetzung der Wehrkraft des deutschen Volkes verursacht. Darüber hinaus würde durch einen Geschlechtsverkehr eine Rassenmischung erfolgen, die die Entartung des deutschen Volkes zur Folge hätte." Feldurteil, Salzburg, October 30, 1941, in PAAA, R 40895.

[99] Feldurteil, Salzburg, December 4, 1941, in PAAA, R 40912, and Feldurteil, Breslau, October 17, 1941, in PAAA, R 40854.

The court martial in Regensburg (Bavaria) provided one of the most convoluted variations on this theme in a trial against two French POWs who had intense erotic relations with two nuns in a convent. After rehashing the regular formula about espionage, sabotage, and escapes, the judgment stated in a style that would be unacceptable even by the more indulgent rules of German syntax:

> In particular, it has to be considered from the point of view of the cleanliness and cohesion of the *völkisch* community that the fatherland experiences a significant disadvantage in the determined execution of the German people's struggle for survival if prisoners of war take up sexual relations with German women and girls. ... Moreover, it speaks against the defendants that they did not shy away from using sisters of a religious order for their sexual desires. An aggravating factor that has to be considered is, especially, the generally subversive effect that the behavior of the defendants had to have on the German population.

It is safe to assume that the prisoners' German was not fluent enough for them to understand this fearful justification, and one can only pity the interpreter who had to translate it into French.[100] Of course, the concern for the protection of the nuns was hypocritical given that the Nazi authorities had stepped up their campaign against German monasteries at the beginning of the war.[101]

After the protests from the German Foreign Office against the racial hygienic justifications, the court martial sentences became shorter and more formulaic and increasingly defined "significant disadvantage" primarily as acts intended to weaken the home front. By causing a woman to be severely punished, for example, judgments argued that the prisoner had brought the woman to a penitentiary and that her absence from her workplace or family had weakened the home front. Ultimately, this line of argument made the POW responsible for the prohibition. This happened in a context where the punishments for the women were still much harsher than those for the prisoners (1941). The court martial in

---

[100] "Insbes. ist aber von [sic] Standpunkt der Sauberkeit und Geschlossenheit der völkischen Gemeinschaft der Heimat ein sehr erheblicher Nachteil für die entschlossene Durchführung dieses Überlebenskampfes des deutschen Volkes dann gegeben, wenn Kriegsgefangene in sexueller [sic] Beziehung zu deutschen Frauen und Mädchen treten. ... Ausserdem sprach es zu ihren Ungunsten, dass sie sich nicht scheuten, Ordensschwestern zum Gegenstand ihrer Gelüste zu machen. Erschwerend musste vorallem auch die allgemein zersetzende Wirkung, die das Verhalten der Angeklagten auf die deutsche Bevölkerung haben musste, in Betracht gezogen werden." Feldurteil, Regensburg, September 25, 1941, in PAAA, R 40887. Nonetheless, the court martial sentenced the prisoners only to one and a half years in prison, at a time when the punishments were not yet standardized.

[101] E.D.R. Harrison, "The Nazi Dissolution of the Monasteries: A Case-Study," *English Historical Review* 109, no. 431 (1994).

Nürnberg, for example, wrote in a judgment against two French prisoners who had both had intensive affairs with female workers at the local AEG electric factory: "If such cases multiply, the distinction between friend and enemy will disappear. Moreover, the women have been removed from the *Volksgemeinschaft* through their penitentiary sentences." The POWs received a prison sentence of 20 months while the women received four years of penal servitude and loss of civil rights.[102] The same court martial harkened back to this theme a month later and added that the food the prisoners were getting from many women damaged the food supply of the German people (ignoring that many gifts of food also went from prisoners to women).[103]

With the German losses mounting on the eastern front, some courts martial argued that relations of POWs with wives of soldiers were a particularly heinous offense because they undermined the morale of husbands fighting at the front. The court martial of Münster formulated this concern: "It is obvious that a contact of prisoners of war with German women at a time when German husbands, sons, and brothers are engaged in combat has to be seen as disgraceful and that the home front needs to make sure that such incidents are impossible and remain impossible."[104]

Courts martial increasingly used the formula "insult to the honor of the German woman and to the dignity of the German people" as the standard justification, in addition to the old arguments about espionage, sabotage, escapes, and corrosion of the will to resist. Some judgments elaborated on the danger to the security of the Reich by invoking the potential of sexual bondage into which a POW could bring a German woman so as to exploit her unconditional devotion for espionage. This idea reflected the notion of women as easily manipulated and, of course, greatly underestimated the agency of German women. There was in my sample not a single case in which a prisoner manipulated a woman for espionage purposes, although there were a few cases where the POW exploited the contact with a woman to prepare an escape (although there

---

[102] "Bei einer Mehrung solcher Fälle verschwände die Unterscheidung zwischen Freund und Feind und es kommt noch hinzu, daß die Frauen durch die Verbüßung der Zuchthausstrafen aus der Volksgemeinschaft ausgeschieden sind." Feldurteil, Nürnberg, September 25, 1941, in PAAA, R 40885.

[103] Feldurteil, Nürnberg, October 16, 1941, in PAAA, R 40891.

[104] "Es liegt auf der Hand, dass ein Verkehr von Kriegsgefangenen mit deutschen Frauen zu einer Zeit, da deutsche Ehemänner, Söhne und Brüder im Felde stehen, als schmachvoll angesehen werden muß und daß die Heimat die Gewähr bieten muß, daß solche Vorfälle unmöglich sind und unmöglich bleiben." Feldurteil, Münster, October 14, 1941, in PAAA, R 40899.

were more cases in which the escape was motivated by a desire of both, the prisoner and the woman, to live together uninhibited).[105]

The special courts invoked similar motives, and they stigmatized the accused women as traitors to their nation and people, essentially because they had refused to hate the POW as an enemy. The special courts did not need to prove "significant disadvantage," but they often referred to the "healthy feeling of the Volk" that had allegedly been violated by the relationship. The racial hygiene argument appeared in sentences against women in 1941, but it was less common than in the courts martial at this time.[106] Increasingly, the justifications for the sentences against the women stressed the need to protect the German *Wehrkraft* (will to resist) and to preserve national solidarity rather than the racial pollution argument. A landmark case is the trial and re-trial of Hedwig Linsbichler, who was involved with a French prisoner who had lived in Vienna during his childhood. The prisoner, Etienne (he sometimes used the German form "Stephan") Meier, spoke fluent German with a Viennese accent. His last name was a common German family name. He told Linsbichler that his father was Austrian, and he acted very much like a local man. In her defense, Linsbichler argued that she did not think it was forbidden to get involved with a man who had German ancestry. During the hearing on December 23, 1941, the district court in Znaim sentenced her to only seven months in prison even though she admitted having had sex once, which would normally have led to penitentiary of at least one year (and that was what the prosecutor required). Linsbichler used the racial argument behind the prohibition, which made a sexual relation with Meier inoffensive – perhaps even desirable. The court had to punish her for having become involved with a POW, but it accepted her reasoning as a powerful mitigating circumstance.

Yet, the prosecutor brought the case to the German supreme court. In his evaluation, the supreme prosecutor (*Oberreichsanwalt*) asked the supreme court to scrap the sentence. He argued that it represented "a significant miscarriage of justice," because a German-speaking prisoner was particularly dangerous as a potential spy. He called the woman's decision to consort with the POW an "extremely undignified form of

---

[105] For a typical judgment invoking the danger of sexual bondage, see Feldurteil, Chemnitz, January 13, 1942, in PAAA, R 40909. For a case of a POW who at least in part cultivated a relationship with a woman for an escape, see Nehlert to Gerichtsherr der Division 432, November 18, 1943, BAR Bern, Bestand Vertretung Berlin 78a.

[106] See, for example, BStA Nürnberg, Akten der Anklagebehörde beim Sondergericht, 2327, in a statement of December 10, 1943: "This case shows, in particular, that in the interest of keeping the German blood clean, such relationships of German women with prisoners of war need to be prevented."

confidentiality." The *Oberreichsanwalt* found in her behavior "a particularly contemptuous mentality" and "extraordinary indignity" while she was "ignoring the duties that her belonging to the *Volk* dictated to her." The supreme court accepted this argument, stating that the prohibition for German women was based on the protection of the *Wehrkraft* and not on the desire to protect racial purity. The supreme court also stressed that Meier's German ancestry was not proven (his file contains contradictory information about his birthplace – some documents say Budapest and others Vienna) and that he signed with the French version of his first name. The district court in Znaim therefore re-tried Linsbichler on July 8, 1942, and this time sentenced her to one year of penal servitude.[107] In this case, the highest judicial authorities confirmed that the decree applying to the women was to be handled for the purpose of preventing espionage and maintaining national unity and coherence, not racial purity.

The notion that the German soldier heroically fighting for the people must be severely disturbed when hearing about the forbidden relations was another theme that appeared frequently, often with allusions to male relatives of the accused woman who served in the Wehrmacht. The special court in Nürnberg, under the direction of the notorious Nazi jurist Rudolf Oeschey, sentenced Margarethe Schwilk to two years of penal servitude on October 19, 1942, claiming that her relationship to a French POW was particularly shameful: "While her husband was risking his life and health on the ice fields of Russia, she received a French prisoner in the conjugal bedroom," a heinous "betrayal of honor and race."[108] War widows were held to the same strict standards. On February 10, 1944, for example, the special court in Darmstadt sentenced forty-year-old Katharina Speckner to sixteen months in prison simply because she had once tried sexual intercourse with a French POW who turned out to be impotent. The sentence stressed "her duty to preserve the dignity and honor of the German woman and mother" especially in light of the fact that she was a soldier's widow. The punishment was deemed necessary "to satisfy the need of the *Volksgemeinschaft* for atonement."[109] After a litany about hateful enemies who brought so much

---

[107] The second sentence only prolonged her time in prison because she had already been behind bars for eight months, and it made no sense to transfer her to a penitentiary for the short remainder of her sentence. She was kept in the local prison and released not much later, two months before the end of her sentence. WStLA, Sondergericht, 6325.

[108] BStA Nürnberg, Akten der Anklagebehörde beim Sondergericht, 1724. Regarding Oeschey's career at the special court, see Lutz, "Das Sondergericht Nürnberg 1933–1945," 254.

[109] Sondergericht Darmstadt, February 10, 1944, in HStAD, Fonds G 24, Nr. 955/2.

suffering to the German people, a sentence by the special court in Nürnberg stated:

This did not prevent her from entering into a relationship with an enemy of her people, somebody who went to war in order to annihilate the German people. Many Germans had to give their lives in an effort to foil these aims of enemies full of hatred. The behavior of the defendant therefore not only defiles the German reputation and the German honor, it also implies a desecration of the memory of the war dead, who paid with their lives for their struggle on behalf of the German people.[110]

Many special courts insisted that French and Belgian POWs also had to be treated as irreconcilable enemies because they had taken up arms against Germany, wanted its annihilation, and had caused tens of thousands of German deaths. The special court of Nürnberg, judging a woman involved with a Belgian POW, stated, "The prisoner of war remains an enemy of the German people. He strove for the annihilation of the Reich," and berated the woman for not being worth the thousands of sacrifices of German men that this prisoner and his comrades had allegedly made necessary.[111] The special court of Berlin sentenced two women involved with French POWs to fifteen months of penal servitude on June 12, 1942, "because they became involved with enemies of the German people, for whose defeat German men had to sacrifice their lives."[112] The special court in Vienna elaborated on the same theme:

The German people have not forgotten that France wanted to assault us without any understandable reason, just for the sake of the hateful encirclement and annihilation policy of the western democracies. All French prisoners of war have to bear all the consequences arising from the failure of these plans until the Führer orders a change of policy.[113]

---

[110] "Das hat sie nicht gehindert, sich mit einem Feind ihres Volkes einzulassen, der in den Krieg gezogen ist, um das deutsche Volk zu vernichten. Viele deutsche Menschen mussten ihr Leben einsetzen, um dieses Ziel des hasserfüllten Feindes zunichte zu machen. In dem Verhalten der Angeklagten liegt daher nicht nur eine Schändung des deutschen Ansehens und der deutschen Ehre, sondern auch eine Beschimpfung des Andenkens an die Gefallenen, die ihren Einsatz für das deutsche Volkstum mit ihrem Leben bezahlten." Judgment against Katharina G., BStA Nürnberg, Akten der Anklagebehörde beim Sondergericht, 1165.

[111] "Der Kriegsgefangene bleibt Feind des deutschen Volkes. Er hatte sich für die Vernichtung des Reiches eingesetzt." BStA Nürnberg, Akten der Anklagebehörde beim Sondergericht, 1311.

[112] BLHA Potsdam, 12 C, Landgericht Berlin. Urteile 1943. Berlin II, 7/35.

[113] "Das deutsche Volk hat noch nicht vergessen, dass Frankreich uns ohne jeden Grund, der noch verständlich wäre, nur der gehässigen Einkreisungs- und Vernichtungspolitik der westlichen Demokratien zu Liebe überfallen wollte. Sämtliche Folgen des Misslingens dieser Pläne haben sämtliche französischen Gefangenen bis zu dem Zeitpunkt zu tragen, in dem der Führer eine Änderung anordnen wird." Judgment,

Echoing the notion of some military judges about POWs making women sexually dependent and exploiting them for espionage, the special court in Berlin justified a sentence by arguing that a rapprochement between a prisoner and a woman was almost always sexual in nature and that, given the naïve character of women, it created a greater danger of espionage than a relationship with a German man.[114] In other sentences, the special courts highlighted the risk that the POW might go home after the war and tell about his adventures with a German woman, leading to a loss of prestige: "The dishonor of a German woman in this way severely damages the German prestige in the world for a long time. People's comrades [*Volksgenossen*] who feel healthy national pride can only react with disgust and outrage to such behavior."[115]

The relentless stigmatization of all POWs as enemies triggered resistance. Farmworker Marie Gericke, on trial in Berlin for a relationship with a French prisoner on January 29, 1943, announced defiantly that what she had done would be judged differently after the war. She pointed out – very reasonably given that she had just been divorced – that her actions had not hurt anybody. The judges angrily dismissed her defense and sentenced her to three years of penal servitude, a harsh sentence at that time.[116] In cases involving French POWs, women on trial often alluded to Franco-German collaboration, and in cases involving French or Belgian prisoners, they occasionally mentioned the fact that Frenchman and Belgians were fighting together with German forces on the eastern front. The farmer's daughter Anna Preisinger, for example, countered the hateful rhetoric against France in the courtroom of Nürnberg: "The Frenchmen told us that they, too, did not want a war and that Pétain is a comrade of Hitler."[117] She had to stand trial together with her mother because both had been extremely welcoming to French POWs. Gertrud Schulze, a farm maid from a village near Lübeck who had engaged in two affairs with French prisoners, claimed that the French were not real enemies like the Poles or Russians, with whom she would not have started a closer relationship.[118] Rosa Birkenmeier, a divorced

Sondergericht Wien beim Landesgericht Znaim, July 8, 1942, in WStLA, Sondergericht, 6325.
[114] BLHA Potsdam, 12C, Sondergericht Berlin, judgment of November 14, 1941, 6407.
[115] "Die Ehrvergessenheit einer deutschen Frau bewirkt auf diese Weise eine ausserordentliche Schädigung des deutschen Ansehens in der Welt auf lange Zeit hinaus. Den von gesundem Nationalstolz erfüllten Volksgenossen kann ein derartiges Verhalten nur mit Abscheu und Empörung erfüllen." Judgment against Käthe P., BStA Nürnberg, Akten der Anklagebehörde beim Sondergericht, 1278.
[116] BLHA Potsdam, 12 C, Landgericht Berlin. Urteile 1943. Berlin II, 7/35.
[117] BStA Nürnberg, Akten der Anklagebehörde beim Sondergericht, 1240.
[118] Gertrud S., LASH Schleswig, Abt. 358, 5382.

woman from Erlangen, defended herself in front of the Nürnberg special court by saying: "I want to stress that I acted toward this 'transformed' prisoner only as a human being and a woman. I never considered him to be an enemy. In my entire life, nobody has ever been as nice to me as this Frenchman, not even my own husband."[119] When Hermine Braun, a young Alsatian woman, had to stand trial in 1942 for having made love with a French POW in a cemetery in Freiburg, she stated: "I knew that intercourse with Frenchmen is forbidden, but I did not think it was such a bad thing because, after all, Germany and France are united now."[120]

Relatives or defense attorneys sometimes argued that the woman consorting with a French prisoner had not consciously committed a crime because she had not seen him as an enemy; as a defense attorney in Schleswig-Holstein pointed out in the fall of 1942: "popular understanding does not necessarily consider France as an enemy nation any more. After all, some Frenchmen are fighting together with Germans against the Soviets."[121] In her clemency pleas, the mother of Maria Wolf, an auxiliary laborer from Vienna, always stressed that her daughter had not recognized the French POW with whom she had become involved in the spring of 1942 as an enemy because "France is fighting with us against bolshevism."[122] Similarly, the attorney of Marie Wildermuth, sentenced by the special court of Hildesheim to one and a half years of penal servitude, argued in November 1942 that one has to consider that she became involved with a French POW: "It is known that the attitude of France toward Germany has become increasingly favorable. The French prisoner occupies a special position."[123] On trial, the farmworker Grete Ehlert also defended herself with the argument that "the French are no longer our real enemies." She pointed to the fact that the farmers employing her and several French POWs had allowed the POWs to take photos with them. Although this (illegal) behavior of the farmers counted as a mitigating factor, the special court in Kiel still sentenced her to two years of penal servitude.[124] When attorney Dr. Grzimek in Berlin wrote a clemency plea for Käthe Deuter, who had been sentenced to penitentiary in the context of a big group affair with French POWs in a factory in Oranienburg (north of Berlin), he stated: "The French workers, who are

---

[119] BStA Nürnberg, Akten der Anklagebehörde beim Sondergericht, 2774. For a similar example, see the case of Maria M., ibid., 2313.
[120] SHD Caen, 25 P 6495.
[121] Attorney Maßmann to special court Kiel, October 30, 1942, in LASH Schleswig, Abt. 358, 5420.
[122] WStLA, Sondergericht, 6608.
[123] NSTA Hannover 172, Hildesheim, Acc. 82/78 5, Nr. 3.
[124] Sentence of March 3, 1943, in LASH Schleswig, Abt. 358, 5667.

working in Germany in great numbers, are generally well-loved by the population and are without a doubt the most appreciated and popular group among the foreign laborers. The same holds true for the French prisoners of war, who receive much praise." Grzimek pointed out that the press was highlighting European cooperation and the role of France in it. "I therefore sincerely doubt that, given the popular opinion about French POWs, penitentiary sentences are appropriate any more for forbidden relations with them."[125] Even some judicial officials questioned the advisability of harsh punishments for relations with French POWs at a time when they were so integrated into German everyday life.[126]

Confronted with reproaches about having besmirched national honor, some accused women had the courage during trial to expose the double morality that tolerated the affairs of German soldiers stationed in France or Belgium while severely penalizing the relations of German women with French and Belgian POWs. Some married women cast doubts about the fidelity of their husband, especially if he was a soldier. In one case, the judge learned that the accused woman's husband, an officer stationed in France, had brought his illegitimate child with him on home leave.[127] A woman from Meldorf (Schleswig-Holstein) sentenced to two years and two months of penal servitude in July 1943 explained in court that her husband had written her that he had a girlfriend in France and that this information had greatly weakened her resistance to the French POW with whom she became close.[128] Gertrud Küster, a married employee at a milk processing plant in Neustadt (Holstein), also explained to the court that she had agreed to an intimate relationship with a French POW after hearing that her husband had caught a sexually transmitted disease during his service in the Wehrmacht. She was arrested in December 1944, too late to come to trial.[129]

Assessment

The trials against the women were more humiliating and shattering than the courts martial against the prisoners because they always meant public shaming. The woman was torn out of her normal environment in disgrace; her sentence was often published in the newspapers with her name

[125] BLHA Potsdam, 12C Sondergericht Berlin, 112/1.
[126] See, for example, Oberstaatsanwalt Krems to Generalstaatsanwalt Wien, October 27, 1941, WStLA, Sondergericht, 8259.
[127] Delattre, *Ma Guerre sans fusil*, 109, 27, 29.   [128] LASH Schleswig, Abt. 358, 5801.
[129] LASH Schleswig, Abt. 358, 6167.

and with moralizing comments, and she was forced to reveal sexual details in the course of the interrogation and the court hearing. The interrogating officers, often Gestapo men, could be intimidating, bullying, even abusive. If the woman was married, her husband would hear about her infidelity. By contrast, the prisoner would be drawn out of his "German" life, but his family would only hear that he was sentenced for disobedience, and it was not apparent that this meant a relationship with a German woman. If married, the prisoner might have to think about if and how to reveal the affair to his wife, but he had much time to contemplate this. Except in cases where the judges berated the prisoner for having used "lesbian" practices or in cases where the woman might testify that the prisoner had been impotent, the trials were less humiliating for the POW.

The special courts were from the beginning expected to mete out fast and harsh punishments that would serve as a deterrent. They severely limited the rights of the defense and rested on what the judges considered to be the "healthy feeling of the Volk," an arbitrary and vague orientation.[130] The increasing tendency of the special courts to try to classify the defendants as "criminal types" softened the standards of proof, leading to some judgments influenced more by the social standing of the defendant and local gossip than by critically examined evidence. Women on the margins of society and without a supportive and politically unobjectionable husband were particularly vulnerable. Yet, the degree to which special courts deviated from more rigorous judicial norms varied from place to place. Some judges did believe a woman who withdrew her confession in court, arguing that the Gestapo had bullied her, and most investigations were more time-consuming and rigorous than the authorities expected.[131]

The punishments for women and POWs changed over time. In 1941, women often received very harsh sentences (up to six years of penal servitude), while many prisoners got away with punishments of one or two years in prison – even though the High Command already considered three years the default sentence for a sexual relation. The special courts and the courts martial were aware of this discrepancy, and Keitel endorsed it in a memorandum to all court martial presidents in June 1941: "It is right to consider that a German woman who throws herself away for a prisoner of war must be punished more harshly than the prisoner of a foreign race and that she, as a rule, deserves a punishment

[130] Helmut Paulus, "Das Sondergericht Bayreuth 1942–1945 – Ein düsteres Kapitel Bayreuther Justizgeschichte," *Archiv für Geschichte von Oberfranken* 77 (1997): 486–7.
[131] Bozyakali, *Das Sondergericht am Hanseatischen Oberlandesgericht*, 309–11.

that robs her of her honor [a penitentiary sentence and loss of civil rights]."[132] Yet, many special courts became more lenient. This change contradicts the way the Nazi courts treated many other transgressions during the war, and it is not certain what explains it. One factor likely was Hitler's patronizing view of women as passive objects of male desire, which he communicated to Justice Minister Thierack in 1942.[133] Part of the explanation may also have been the severe disruptions and negative economic and social consequences provoked by the prolonged incarceration of thousands of women, treated in the next chapter. Did judges realize that the forbidden relations were not a security risk despite the justifications they wrote into countless sentences? Did they understand that the "healthy feeling of the Volk" often did not object to consensual relationships between western POWs and German women, as long as they did not violate common norms of decency? Did they appreciate that the war placed enormous stresses on women while depriving them of much of their usual male network, making them more receptive to amorous advances from POWs? Is the greater leniency of special courts in these cases one of Hitler's compromises, a decision to (temporarily) appease a *Volksgemeinschaft* not ready for the full force of doctrinaire Nazism? The documentary record does not provide a clear answer. Prosecutors and defense attorneys were aware of the softening trend, but they did not explain it.

For POWs, by contrast, the punishments became harsher in 1941–3 as a result of the steering practice of the higher authorities who rejected sentences they considered too mild and in late 1943 insisted on penitentiary in cases involving the wives of soldiers even if the marriage was already ruined. These directives came from the highest quarter, likely with Hitler's direct input. If at first the hardening sentences could have been meant to ensure better compliance with the order, this reasoning soon made no sense because the number of cases kept increasing rapidly despite harsher punishments. Deterrence clearly did not work. Unlike the women, the prisoners benefited from international oversight during their trials, but the habit of courts martial to accept the confession of the woman as incontrovertible proof indirectly held the POWs hostage to the interrogation methods of the Gestapo officers who "produced" the woman's confession.

---

[132] "Dabei wird mit Recht berücksichtigt, dass eine deutsche Frau, die sich an einen Kriegsgefangenen wegwirft, schwerer strafbar ist als der Gefangene fremden Volkstums und dass sie in der Regel eine Strafe verdient, die sie ehrlos macht. "Chef OKW (Keitel), "An alle Reichskriegsgerichtspräsidenten," Führerhauptquartier, June 5, 1941, in PAAA, R 40852.

[133] Angermund, *Deutsche Richterschaft 1919–1945*, 237–9.

The Path of the Convicted Women

The women and the prisoners experienced different challenges following their trials. When women went to prisons or women's penitentiaries, they were separated from their families and often had to deal with the difficult fallout from the trials. They left behind the networks in which they had lived before, often their entire lives, even though these networks had been altered by the war. In a sense, women made the transition that the prisoner had made when he was mobilized. A big difference was, however, that the prisoner had left in good standing and with honor, whereas most women left publicly humiliated. Moreover, the family the prisoner left behind received allocations from the state whereas the family of an imprisoned woman received nothing except bills for the court costs and, if she had given birth in a penal institution, the costs of delivery. Many women had children and older parents who depended on their care. For her family and her environment, the incarceration of a woman often created an emergency situation. If married, the woman had to cope with a marital crisis, knowing that she was powerless if the husband sued for divorce because she had been convicted for an act that involved infidelity, which meant that the court would almost always consider her the guilty party and give the husband custody of the children and property. The loss of civil rights that accompanied all penitentiary sentences made a woman even more powerless.

Penitentiary sentences usually meant that the woman had to travel a long distance from home. Some penitentiary institutions for women supervised labor detachments where women were forced to do hard and dangerous physical labor, for example clearing rubble after bombings or handling chemicals without adequate protection.[1] Visiting a woman in a penitentiary was much harder than visiting a woman in the prison, not least because of the distance. Women sentenced to

---

[1] Wachsmann, *Hitler's Prisons*, 237–8.

penitentiary in Vienna or Graz, for example, were usually sent to Aichach near Augsburg (Bavaria), more than 500 kilometers away. Women sentenced in Kiel or Lübeck often had to travel to the women's penitentiary in Anrath (near Krefeld), a distance of nearly 500 kilometers. Women sentenced in Nürnberg also went to Aichach (a little less than 150 kilometers from Nürnberg), but Aichach quickly became overcrowded, and many women were transferred either to Hagenau in Alsace, to the *Elbregulierung* penal camp system in Griebo near Wittenberg, or to penal institutions in southern Bavaria (Bernau am Chiemsee and Laufen). Women sentenced in Darmstadt and Wiesbaden went to the Ziegenhain penitentiary south of Kassel (110–150 kilometers), and most women sentenced in Berlin and Frankfurt an der Oder went to the Cottbus women's penitentiary, which was somewhat closer. Women sentenced to prison did not usually have to travel so far, although some of them were sent far away owing to overcrowding in the nearest prison. Family members who were not deterred by the physical distance to a penitentiary needed to wait for special permission, given that penitentiaries severely restricted visits. Most allowed no visit during the first six months, and then only one family visit of 15 minutes every four months. Correspondence was highly restricted, especially in the first six months. The penitentiary staff seized letters that mentioned conditions of captivity or alluded to the sentence, without telling the convict.[2]

Conditions in the penitentiaries and prisons ranged from difficult to miserable. Hitler said many times during the war that the penal system should not preserve "asocial" and criminal people while "the most noble German blood" was being spilled on the battlefield. He was convinced that this kind of "negative selection" had occurred in World War I and that it helped to explain the revolution and defeat of 1918.[3] Although this maxim, which led to active collaboration of the legal system in mass murder, applied mainly to men and people considered habitual criminals and who had very long penitentiary sentences (eight years or more), women punished for a forbidden relationship also suffered from the consequences. The rations in penal institutions were so low that most inmates suffered from malnutrition and all the ailments and diseases associated with it. Given that the number of convicted women grew far beyond peacetime levels, the women's penitentiaries were hopelessly

---

[2] For the rules in the penitentiary Amberg (Bavaria), see SHD Caen, 25 P 6785. For materials on the women's penitentiary in Cottbus, see BLHA Potsdam, Rep. 29 (ZH Cottbus). See also Gabriele Hackl and Brigitte Sack, *Das Frauenzuchthaus Waldheim (1933–1945)* (Dresden: Leipziger Universitätsverlag, 2016), 74.

[3] Wachsmann, *Hitler's Prisons*, 284–9.

overcrowded. On June 30, 1944, there were 19,466 women in larger regular penal institutions, exceeding their maximum capacity by 8,600. Many more women were therefore sent to satellite camps and outside commandos, where conditions were hardly better. Everywhere, beatings by guards or civilian foremen were common. Medical service was often rudimentary.[4]

Clemency Pleas for Incarcerated Women

Although there was no higher recourse against a special court sentence, family members or an attorney could submit clemency pleas, triggering an elaborate consultation procedure. In theory, the Reich Ministry of Justice had the final say, but the prosecutor's office often made the decision after asking the local police or Gestapo chief or other authorities such as the NSDAP district leader or the mayor whether the circumstances used as reasons for a clemency plea were valid. These local authorities interviewed family members and neighbors and inspected the farm or apartment of the woman. An inquiry also went to the director of the penitentiary or prison regarding the behavior of the convicted woman. The woman herself, her family, or her attorney could also ask the Reich Interior Ministry or the chancellery of the Führer to support a clemency plea.

The prosecutor's office had several possibilities. It could commute a penitentiary sentence into a prison sentence. It could decide on an early release by shortening the sentence, and it could grant a temporary release or decide for an early release on parole. A temporary release meant that the convict had to return behind bars after the leave and that the leave time was added on to the sentence, postponing the date of the definitive release. Temporary releases were often granted for pregnancy, important work at home, and home leaves of a soldier husband who had forgiven his wife. For the same reasons and under the same conditions, courts could agree to postpone the summons to serve the sentence. Release on parole meant that the convict was released early on condition that she would not

---

[4] Ibid., 241–5. In the Waldheim women's penitentiary, beatings of the inmates apparently did not happen, and women were assigned "female" work much longer than in other women's penitentiaries, but overcrowding, lack of food, and bad medical care also characterized this institution: Hackl and Sack, *Das Frauenzuchthaus Waldheim (1933–1945)*, 83–94, 151–60, 81. Rothmaler cites a contemporary statistic listing 48,000 women inmates in 1943/4: Christiane Rothmaler, "Volksschädlinge und Gemeinschaftsfremde: Frauenstrafvollzug im Nationalsozialismus," in *"Der Stand der Frauen, wahrlich, ist ein harter Stand": Frauenleben im Spiegel der Landesgeschichte*, ed. Elke Imberger (Schleswig: Landesarchiv Schleswig-Holstein, 1994), 167.

commit another offense. The sentence expired after four or five years if the woman's behavior was good. Releases on parole for women sentenced to penal servitude were usually granted only if less than a quarter of the sentence remained and if the authorities agreed that the punishment had served its purpose (*Strafzweck*). This meant that the penitentiary or prison director needed to be confident that the woman regretted her "crime" and was unlikely to commit something similar again.[5]

For the prosecutor's offices handling clemency pleas, similar factors mattered that had already influenced the judgments. Aside from the attitude of the husband and the utility of the woman as a worker, the prosecutor's offices took into consideration the following questions: Did the woman's family have a good reputation? What was her (and potentially her husband's) political past? Did she have a previous conviction or a record of behavior considered "a-social" or deviant? Did the woman's custodial sentence lead to severe hardship for children or parents? In addition, the woman's behavior after incarceration played a role. Did she have a proper understanding of her crime and show sincere regret? Was she a disciplined and hard-working inmate?

The clemency pleas often show that the arrest of a woman wreaked havoc on her family and community. In the case of Anna Müller, a forty-seven-year-old farmer's wife from Schwandorf (near Regensburg) sentenced to twenty months of penal servitude for a relationship with the French POW assigned to her farm, her children (aged ten, eleven, and sixteen) had already submitted a clemency plea at the time of the trial, in November 1941. In March 1942, her daughter Anna Junior, now twelve, wrote to Angela Raubal, Hitler's cousin, asking her to sway Hitler to grant an early release to her mother. Anna pointed out that her father was sixty-one and not in good health and that the arrest of her mother had brought "endless misfortune" to her family. Anna also mentioned that her stepbrother (her father's son from a previous relationship) had received a medal "in the struggle against bolshevism" but had gone missing in January. One of Müller's sons, "Hitlerjunge" Johann Müller, also submitted a clemency plea for his mother, pointing out that the potential loss of the son on the eastern front had severely shaken his father. Finally, the husband himself made several petitions for an early release of his wife, declaring that he had forgiven her. He mentioned that his son had meanwhile been confirmed dead, while his other son had been drafted into the Wehrmacht. Anna Müller was sent to Aichach and

[5] Löffelsender, *Strafjustiz an der Heimatfront*, 430–4, 38–41.

then to Anrath, but the woman directing the Anrath penitentiary opposed an early release because Müller did not really regret her "crime" (not surprisingly, given that she had always claimed that the POW had been pushy). The local official charged with checking into the merits of clemency pleas pointed out that neither Anna Müller nor her husband belonged to the NSDAP or to any organization associated with it. Nevertheless, he confirmed that the husband was handicapped as a consequence of several accidents, and he therefore advocated a temporary release. Anna Müller was allowed to go home for several months in June 1942 and again a year later, coinciding with the busiest farming months. She was finally released on parole on September 14, 1943, with four and a half months of her sentence remaining. Since she was already on a temporary leave, this meant that she was allowed to stay home.[6]

Fanny Hoffer and Martha Löffler, both married to soldiers, were sentenced to four years of penal servitude by the Nürnberg special court on April 12, 1943. Their sentences were so high because the judge had found it particularly disgusting that the two women had had sex with French prisoners in the back of a furniture truck, and also because both women were older than the prisoners. Hoffer (born in 1906) had six children aged from four to nineteen years, and she was pregnant at the time of the trial, probably from her husband. Löffler (born 1904) had two children (aged eight and fourteen). Both women had to go to Aichach, but neither stayed there very long. Löffler soon developed a serious mental illness and was transferred to a psychiatric institution. With regard to Hoffer, the Aichach administration immediately requested permission to send her home so that she could deliver her baby at home. The delivery room in the penitentiary was overcrowded, and it was very difficult to place the children of convicts with foster families. The prosecutor's office denied this request. Meanwhile diphtheria broke out in Aichach, and the director again asked for permission to send Hoffer home for the delivery, this time with success. She went home in July 1943 but had to report back on January 1, 1944, even though her attorney requested an extension of her leave because nobody was able to take care of the baby. In August 1944, a neighbor of Frau Hoffer, a Frau Wachheit, wrote one of the most remarkable clemency pleas to none less than propaganda minister Josef Goebbels: "Given that you are so well known to be for mother and child, I allow myself to bring this petition to you." She explained that Hoffer's husband was a brutal alcoholic who had often mistreated her: "I myself witnessed that this

---

[6] BStA Nürnberg, Akten der Anklagebehörde beim Sondergericht, 1306.

poor woman was sent to the delivery room with blackened eyes." Wachheit also complained that Hoffer had not had a chance to be with her new baby for long and that she had suffered enough, being sent to a work detachment in a Munich armaments factory where "she had been exposed to the bombing terror." Wachheit asked why the special court in Nürnberg was much harsher than the one in Munich. With some delay, her request came to the director of the Aichach penitentiary, who rejected it, claiming that Hoffer was "just as negative, obstinate, and impertinent as this petitioner."[7]

Marie Wolf, who had had a love affair with a French prisoner, was twenty-eight at the time of her arrest (May 1942) and not married. She was sentenced to one and a half years of penal servitude on July 29, 1942, but because the police were still hoping for her cooperation in identifying the prisoner, she remained in the local prison in Vienna until December 1942. She then came to Aichach. From the beginning, her mother begged for her release. The mother had given birth to eleven children (two had died in infancy). Three of her sons had been drafted into the Wehrmacht. One of them was killed during the campaign in France, and the two surviving sons were deployed on the eastern front. One of her daughters had a young illegitimate child for whom the mother cared. The mother, whose health was failing, worked on a farm and badly needed her daughter's help, especially during the harvest. The father, who had been wounded twice in World War I, was no longer alive. Many clemency pleas by the mother and the daughter herself remained unsuccessful, but in July 1943, the prosecutor's office and the director of the penitentiary agreed that she could be released a few months before the end of her sentence. The suffering of the mother was the decisive factor. Wolf became free on August 4, 1943, three months before the end of her sentence.[8]

In the case of four women from a farm in the village Scharndorf (between Vienna and Bratislava), Ottile (Tilli) Haberl had received a penitentiary sentence (three and a half years) on July 22, 1942, following over four months of pre-trial custody. She was sent to Aichach with a significant delay because she was needed as a witness in the trials of the other women (including her sister) and the courts martial of the prisoners. Tilli Haberl repeatedly requested temporary leaves and an early release. She had a one-year-old child, her husband was a soldier on the eastern front, and she took care of a so-called *Erbhof* (a small farm that had been in the possession of the family for several generations and that

---

[7] BStA Nürnberg, Akten der Anklagebehörde beim Sondergericht, 2031.
[8] WStLA, Sondergericht, 6608.

enjoyed special protection in Nazi Germany). Her mother was sixty-four and sick (she had given birth to 12 children). In January 1943, her husband sued for divorce. Following desperate petitions by the local farmers' leader (*Bauernführer*) and clemency pleas by her lawyer, she received a temporary leave in August 1943 and again in August 1944, each time for the harvest. In October 1944, Tilli Haberl made a desperate petition for a pardon, arguing: "Now I want to sacrifice all my strength in agriculture at home, so that I can contribute as a German woman to the sacrifices required by the war and by our victory." During her stay in the penitentiary, one of her sisters took care of her son. During each leave, Haberl had to work on her farm and report to the *Bauernführer* for work wherever she was needed. During her last leave, she became pregnant (but not from a prisoner). She and her sister urgently asked for permission for her to stay home longer to give birth, but the prosecutor's office in Vienna insisted that she return to Aichach. Yet, on February 22, 1945, the governor in Aichach requested permission to send her home. The penitentiary was completely overcrowded. There was no room in the infirmary, and it was impossible to care for the children born in the institution. The Aichach governor criticized the prosecutor's office, which had insisted that Haberl travel late in her pregnancy, even though the Reich Justice Ministry had apparently not objected to a longer leave. Haberl did return home in April 1945, a few weeks before her due date, but she was not paroled. Despite strong support from the local *Bauernführer* and even from the NSDAP Gau office Niederdonau for an early release, she (and her sister) received only temporary leaves for helping out in the harvest. Both were apparently very good workers.[9]

The conviction of war widow Katharina Spickermann from Pfungstadt (south of Darmstadt) also created enormous hardship for her children. Spickermann had been sentenced to sixteen months of prison by the special court in Darmstadt for trying to have sex outdoors with a French POW in October 1943. The prisoner was impotent, and she decided to end the relationship, but a married couple had observed their meeting and denounced her. The police arrested her on November 1, 1943. She had a seventeen-year-old daughter and a nine-year-old son. The daughter, Minna, had to serve her mandatory service year, and the son was given to the care of Spickermann's sister, a dubious, money-grubbing character. Minna sent her mother letters, and her mother wrote her, too, but the prison authorities did not deliver some letters because they contained criticism of the judicial authorities. Minna often visited her

---

[9] WStLA, Sondergericht, 6315.

mother in prison, bringing her letters, cigarettes, and toiletries, but her aunt denounced her for that in June 1944, albeit apparently without consequences. But then the aunt's apartment was bombed, and Minna herself had to take care of her brother. On September 27, 1944, she wrote a desperate clemency plea on behalf of her mother. She described the hardship that had befallen the family after the death of the father in March 1942 and explained that she was unable to watch her brother given her work commitment. Her brother was wandering around on his own all day and, during alarms, had to go to a bomb shelter alone. She admitted that she and her brother were suffering "terrible fear for our mother" during bombings and concluded: "I am only seventeen years old, and I have been confronted with very difficult challenges over the past years. Now, it is really too much and I can no longer go on." The prosecutor's office granted the mother only a two-week leave on October 15, 1944. In November 1947, the mother sued the couple that had denounced her, but it is very unlikely that they were ever punished. By this time, the mother had married again.[10]

Elisabeth Amberger, who had pursued two affairs with French POWs in Darmstadt, was sentenced to one and a half years of penal servitude on May 23, 1944, and sent to the women's penitentiary Ziegenhain. Her husband, who forgave her, was serving in a coastal navy unit, but their two children (twelve and fourteen years old) were left on their own in the apartment. In the night of September 11–12, 1944, a bombing attack destroyed the apartment, but the children survived. The husband obtained a brief home leave, but he could not find a new home for the children. With the help of an attorney, Amberger received a temporary leave on October 12, 1944, and saw her children, discovering that her twelve-year-old daughter was covered with lice. Her son also seemed neglected. Amberger asked for an early release to find a permanent place for her children, but the director of the Ziegenhain penitentiary denied her request.[11]

Many clemency pleas combined arguments based on family hardship and the woman's qualities as a laborer. In the fall of 1944, the court in Peine (between Hannover and Braunschweig) sentenced the farmer's wife Frieda Bücking (forty-three) to eight months in prison simply for having asked a French POW for a cigarette. A woman had seen her in a forest and assumed that the relationship had involved more, although this seems never to have been proven (the judgment is lost). Bücking was allowed to stay at home until December 1, 1944, and then had to report

[10] HStAD, G 27 Darmstadt, Nr. 1396, and G 30 Darmstadt, Nr. 1961.
[11] HStAD, G 27 Darmstadt 1411.

to the district prison in Hannover. Her two lawyers immediately submitted a clemency plea, arguing that she was an excellent voluntary worker, had just lost her mother in a bombing attack, and had nine siblings who were all living in bombed cities. Bücking was also caring for one of her sisters and her children. The husband of this sister had been killed in combat, and the sister's apartment had been destroyed by bombs. Bücking's husband had just been drafted into the Wehrmacht and had to join a unit with older reservists near Berlin. He also submitted a clemency plea on her behalf on February 3, 1945, arguing that a release of his wife was necessary because their daughter, who would soon return from her mandatory service year and start professional training, needed the attention of the mother. The pleas were all rejected, but the police chief of her home town, supported by the mayor, also asked for her release a month later, emphasizing that Bücking was an excellent worker and respected citizen. Owing to the chaos of the last weeks of the war, a favorable answer to this plea materialized only in September 1945 (after her sentence had expired anyway), but the prosecutor's office found out that Bücking had been liberated by Allied troops on April 20, 1945, in the prison of Lüneburg, where she had been transferred three weeks earlier.[12]

In the case of the farmer's daughter Gertrud Ripke from the village Hohenstein near Strausberg (east of Berlin), family emergencies also combined with the need for her as a laborer on the farm. Ripke had been sent to the women's penitentiary in Cottbus, but shortly after her departure, in March 1943, the police chief of her village wrote an urgent clemency plea for her. Her mother had died, and her father and sixteen-year-old sister were both sick (the sister died a few weeks later). Left on the farm were her fifteen-year-old brother and her four-year-old daughter born out of wedlock. Her three older brothers all served in the Wehrmacht. Interestingly, the police chief pointed out that the local population felt much compassion for the family. This dire situation convinced the director of the Cottbus penitentiary to support a temporary release, and she was sent home in May 1943 with an open-ended leave permission, probably with the provision that she would have to serve the rest of her sentence after the war.[13]

The behavior of women in the prisons and penitentiaries was a factor in considering temporary releases and paroles. Klara Liebl and Amalie Moll, both sentenced to two years of penal servitude for relationships with Belgian POWs, conducted themselves very well in the Aichach

---

[12] NSTA Hannover 172, Peine Acc. 42/58, Nr. 36.
[13] BLHA Potsdam, 12 C, Sondergericht Berlin, 6828.

penitentiary. The director of the institution advocated release on parole for both of them and even proposed to revoke their loss of civil rights, which would have lasted until the end of the sentence. Moll was released after having served three-quarters of her sentence, and her civil rights were restored upon release, but the prosecutor's office in Nürnberg rejected the same arrangement for Libl, who was older and seen as more responsible. Still, Libl was released three months before the end of her sentence.[14]

The farmworker Marie Wildermuth in Algermissen (near Hannover) was first sentenced to two years in prison by the district court of Hildesheim in July 1942 for a love affair with a French POW, but the prosecutor appealed against the sentence because they had had sex one to three times per week, which called for a penitentiary sentence. The court did indeed change the judgment to one and a half years of penal servitude and five years loss of civil rights. Her father, a seventy-year-old town clerk, sent several clemency pleas, as did her attorney, asking for the penitentiary sentence to be (re-)commuted to a prison sentence, which would have kept her nearby. They pointed out that the lack of supervision by the farmer who had employed Wildermuth had favored the forbidden relationship, that her brother was on the eastern front and suffering from the fact that his sister had to go to a penitentiary, and that her mother was sick. Wildermuth, as several local officials confirmed, was also a very good worker. All the pleas were rejected, and Wildermuth was transferred to Anrath. She had not told anybody that she was pregnant from the prisoner, and none of the judicial officials had bothered to ask. On November 8, 1942, she gave birth to a baby girl in the penitentiary. The woman who directed the institution sent the prosecutor's office a bill for the delivery (thirty marks) and the midwife (thirty-six marks). On August 9, 1943, her attorney asked the prosecutor for an early release on parole. The prosecutor consulted the woman directing the penitentiary in Anrath, and she agreed on August 18, 1943. Apparently Wildermuth's conduct in the penitentiary had been very good, and she had shown sincere regret. The consideration for her old father who badly needed her given the sickness of his wife was also a strong factor. Wildermuth was released on September 11, 1943, a little more than three months before the end of her sentence.[15]

Some women attracted the negative attention of the prison authorities and consequently had to serve out their sentences. Irmgard Mallmann,

[14] BStA Nürnberg, Akten der Anklagebehörde beim Sondergericht, 1311.
[15] NSTA Hannover 172, Hildesheim, Acc. 82/78 5, Nr. 3. The documents say nothing about what happened to the baby.

for example, sentenced to one and a half years of penal servitude in Nürnberg on September 8, 1941, was considered by the penitentiary directors to be "impertinent, unthankful, superficial and unreliable at work." She came first to Aichach and later to the *Elbregulierung* penal camp in Griebo. She did not even receive a temporary release.[16] In the case of Hedwig Bossel, who had been sentenced to fifteen months of penal servitude, all clemency pleas failed even though her mother repeatedly begged for a release. Bossel, who lived in a small village south of Vienna, had two very young children born out of wedlock, and the mother, who was sick, had to care for them. The mother also had to house a sister who had a child herself. The mother even wrote to Hitler personally, but to no avail. Bossel came to Aichach and then to Laufen and Bernau in Southern Bavaria, but the directors of all three institutions refused an early release, saying that Bossel was rebellious. She received several disciplinary punishments of several days arrest each, which were all added to her sentence. This meant that she was released seventeen days after the end of her original sentence.[17] In the eyes of the authorities, her behavior in the penal institution ruled out any concession.

In the case of Sophia Hardmeyer, the director of the Aichach penitentiary also rejected all clemency pleas from her mother and her attorney even though the situation of her family was difficult. Hardmeyer, who was sentenced to sixteen months of penal servitude on October 25, 1943, had a ten-year-old child born out of wedlock. Her sister first took care of the child, but then the sister had to go work, and the old mother had to take in Hardmeyer's child and also the sister's children. Despite an elaborate clemency plea by attorney Dr. Hanns Marx in Nürnberg, the director in Aichach remained implacable. The reason was that he considered Hardmeyer cheeky and impertinent. She had received multiple disciplinary punishments in the penitentiary. She was a diligent worker, but her behavior ruled out a pardon and early release.[18]

The political attitude and connections of the sentenced woman played a major role in what happened after the trial. Although the judges usually emphasized that women who were in the NSDAP and who occupied leadership positions in the *NS-Frauenschaft* were held to a higher standard than others, they were more likely to receive an early release. A blatant case is Ida Müllner, the farmer from Eilsdorf (Schleswig-Holstein) who had an affair with a French POW. Müllner was sentenced to one and a half years of penal servitude on February 14, 1942. She went

---

[16] BStA Nürnberg, Akten der Anklagebehörde beim Sondergericht, 1222.
[17] WStLA, Sondergericht, 5284.
[18] BStA Nürnberg, Akten der Anklagebehörde beim Sondergericht, 2350.

to the penitentiary, but because of an eye ailment she was transferred to a hospital after a few weeks. After leaving the hospital she went home, and her attorney succeeded in getting her a leave until October 31, 1942, because she managed a large farm with several workers and had two young children (aged two and four at the time of the trial). Although the prosecutor's office rejected several clemency pleas, it did commute her sentence into a prison sentence (which reinstated her civil rights) and agreed to another leave until the end of October 1943. In April 1943, Müllner gave birth to a third child, apparently from her husband. Her trail is lost after that, but it seems that she never had to go back behind bars. The fact that her husband had forgiven her and wanted to continue the marriage was important but not sufficient to explain this stunning leniency. The real reason likely was that both Ida Müllner and her husband were committed NSDAP members and had very good connections to the Nazi farmer's organization in the province. Her husband was an SA member and serving in the Wehrmacht. He sent clemency pleas from the various places where he was stationed. A Nazi woman, Müllner had to go to the penitentiary only for a few weeks and then was unofficially and discreetly pardoned.[19]

As a comparison, the twenty-one-year-old farmworker Irma Linke was sentenced to fifteen months of penitentiary by the same special court only four days later for a superficial sexual contact with a Belgian POW working on the farm with her. She had a three-year-old child born out of wedlock from a German man in the village (who had recognized his paternity). She was sent to the penitentiary in Lübeck-Lauerhof, perhaps with the same transport as Müllner, but she had to stay there for the full duration of her sentence. The prosecutor's office rejected all clemency pleas from her parents even though the director of the penitentiary was in favor of an early release. Linke obviously lacked the party connections that favored Müllner.[20] Ursula Rickau, the eighteen-year-old woman who had taken up an intense romantic affair with a French POW, was sentenced to two and a half years of penal servitude by the special court in Frankfurt an der Oder on September 7, 1942. Despite many clemency pleas by her attorney, her father, and other family members, and despite her good behavior in the women's penitentiaries in Berlin-Lichtenberg and Cottbus, she had to serve her very harsh sentence to the very end. The woman directing the Cottbus penitentiary supported a release on parole in late 1944, but the prosecutor rejected it on January 13, 1945, a few weeks before the end of her sentence. The reason for this rigidity was

[19] LASH Schleswig, Abt. 358, 2406–2407.   [20] LASH Schleswig, Abt. 358, 2740–2741.

that her letters to the prisoner had contained critical comments on the German war effort and the Nazi dictatorship, and that she had admitted under interrogation that she did not love the Führer. It is possible that the politically motivated intransigence of the authorities cost her her life because the women's penitentiary in Cottbus was hit during a bombing raid on February 15, 1945, and many inmates perished.[21]

The reputation of the woman in the eyes of the judicial authorities influenced not only her sentence but also the outcome of clemency pleas. Margarethe Zeidler, sentenced in Nürnberg in October 1941 to two years of penal servitude for some sexual contacts with a French POW during work, had had a colorful career. Born in 1912, she had joined a traveling circus as a belly dancer at the age of sixteen. A year later, she had a child born out of wedlock. Yet, she had become such a diligent and useful presser that her employer, the director of the machine factory Lauer in Nürnberg, urgently requested an early release. Her seventy-two-year-old mother also submitted several clemency pleas because she was sick and had to take care of Zeidler's daughter. Zeidler was sent to Aichach and later to Hagenau. The penitentiary authorities rejected all clemency pleas because they considered Zeidler to be a woman of loose morals. Her past as a belly dancer hurt her, after already having led to a very harsh sentence. In early 1943, the prison authorities did consider a release one or two months before the end of the sentence, but that was not generous in comparison to other cases.[22]

When Alwine Modrow, a farmworker in Wülfingen (south of Hannover), was accused of having exchanged kisses and hugs with the French POW Armand Müller, her husband beat her up. After this confrontation, Modrow admitted the sexual charges to the police. A Polish woman working on the same estate also accused her of having stolen a men's jacket and forty marks from her closet, allegedly for the French prisoners, but Modrow denied this charge. Given that she had spent two years in a home for struggling youths after an incestuous relationship with her stepfather at age fifteen (leading to pregnancy and a stillbirth), the court ordered the usual tests for "feeble-mindedness" (she had already been tested in 1936), but she passed all of them. Still, her past kept haunting her. On October 28, 1942, the district court in Hildesheim sentenced her

---

[21] BLHA Potsdam, 12 C, Sondergericht Frankfurt an der Oder, 1206/2 and 3. Some Cottbus inmates arrived in the women's prison Waldheim near Dresden in February 1945, but it is not clear whether these inmates were survivors of the bombing: Hackl and Sack, *Das Frauenzuchthaus Waldheim (1933–1945)*, 95.

[22] BStA Nürnberg, Akten der Anklagebehörde beim Sondergericht, 1262.

to one year and seven months of penitentiary for the forbidden relationship and for having given the prisoner and another French POW civilian clothes from her husband so that they could escape. The court also sentenced her for the theft of the jacket but could not prove the theft of the money. Modrow was sent to Anrath. Yet, soon after her trial, she claimed that she had only made the confession in anger after her husband had beaten her, hoping that he would divorce her. Her attorney, her mother, and her suddenly regretful husband submitted several clemency pleas on her behalf, pointing out that even the POW had meanwhile admitted that it was he who had stolen the clothes and the money from the Polish woman. But the director of the Anrath penitentiary claimed that Modrow did not show much regret and pointed out: "The fact that she already engaged in incest with her step-father at age fifteen has negatively influenced her character." She had to serve her sentence to the last day (June 4, 1944). When she asked for the sentence to be deleted from the criminal record in 1950, the prosecutor's office did strike the punishment for the forbidden relation but left the punishment for the theft on her record.[23]

The Reaction of the Husbands

The arrest and conviction of a married woman usually triggered a marital crisis. How would the husband react if he learned that his wife was on trial for having cheated on him with a foreign POW? How would he deal with the intimate detail of the adulterous relationship that often became public knowledge through newspaper articles and posters? How would he take the fact that his wife might be pregnant from the prisoner? The husband had the right to sue for divorce if his wife had become unfaithful to him (§1565 German Law Code), and she would be in a weak position. Serving a custodial sentence far away from home, she would not be allowed to attend the divorce trial. But, as demonstrated, the prosecutor's offices, in agreement with Hitler's preferences, often showed leniency if the husband had forgiven the wife and wanted to continue the marriage. The reaction of the husbands had a strong influence on the penal sentence of married women.[24]

Some husbands wasted no time to sue for divorce. The husband of Elisabeth Allermeyer, who had engaged in a very brief affair with a

---

[23] NSTA Hannover 172, Hildesheim Acc. 82/78 5, Nr. 8.

[24] Local studies reach the same conclusion: Boll, "... das gesunde Volksempfinden," 673; Mechler, *Kriegsalltag an der "Heimatfront,"* 243–5; Löffelsender, *Strafjustiz an der Heimatfront*, 304–5, 440.

French POW while visiting her in-laws in Bavaria, immediately sued for divorce when the affair was discovered in August 1942. He had seen her for the last time in early 1941, and the affair had occurred in August 1941. Plagued by a bad conscience, she had ended the affair promptly and returned home. The divorce went through even before her trial, and she lost custody of her son. She was sentenced to one and a half years in prison.[25] Anna Dach belonged to a group of women employed by a factory in Traiskirchen (south of Vienna) who all had affairs with French POWs working with them in 1943. Dach had ended her affair after two sexual encounters. Her husband, a soldier on the eastern front, initially decided to forgive her, but then he changed his mind and announced already before her trial that he would sue for divorce, maybe because the investigation brought to light rumors that his wife had also had affairs with Austrian men.[26]

In the case of the farmworker Magdalene Scharnagl (born 1901), the husband cared so little for her that he did not even bother to sue for divorce. She had been sentenced to two and a half years of penal servitude in October 1942 for intimate relations with a French POW on a farm in a Bavaria. Her husband was already living in concubinage with another woman who was also married, and Scharnagl had known this long before she started the affair with the prisoner. The husband occasionally talked of divorce, but there is no record of it in her file. In September 1944, her two daughters (both eighteen) submitted a clemency plea. Scharnagl had already spent the vast majority of her sentence behind bars, her health was failing, and her son had been wounded in combat. Yet, the director of the Aichach penitentiary turned a deaf ear to all requests.[27]

Hertha Schmittke's husband, a film painter from Babelsberg outside of Berlin serving in the Wehrmacht, heard of her indictment while he was on his way from Norway to the eastern front in early January 1942. He received permission to attend her trial in Berlin. During the trial, he heard details about his wife's relationship with a French prisoner, to whom she had written letters in which she warned him of her husband's home leaves while reassuring him that she would remain loyal to him (the prisoner) even while her husband was visiting. During the trial, it also transpired that Hertha Schmittke had relations with other men. Upon leaving the courtroom, her husband promptly filed for divorce.[28]

[25] LASH Schleswig, Abt. 358, 5493.   [26] WStLA, Sondergericht, 7207.
[27] BStA Nürnberg, Akten der Anklagebehörde beim Sondergericht, 1716.
[28] BLHA Potsdam, 12 C, Sondergericht Berlin II, 6207.

Annelise Scholl, a mother from Burgdorf near Hannover, suffered a particularly bitter fate. Her husband, a railway worker, had accused her of an intimate relationship with a Belgian POW because she occasionally came home with real coffee, a prized possession of POWs. She denied the allegations, but one night, her husband secretly followed her and found her sitting in the lap of the Belgian prisoner. A brawl ensued during which the Belgian apparently tried to blind the husband with his flashlight, so that he would not recognize him. The court in Celle sentenced Frau Scholl to eight months in prison on June 7, 1944, although no closer contact was ever proven. Her husband sued for divorce and won custody of the couple's four children (aged two to twelve). Frau Scholl's mother had to represent her in the divorce suit because she had already been sent to the penal camp Lichtenau.[29]

In some cases, a husband initially forgave his wife but reconsidered later. When Walther Irmer, a painter from a village east of Frankfurt an der Oder, was drafted into the Wehrmacht and sent to France in February 1941, he jokingly announced to Gustave Vilain, the French POW working on the farm of his in-laws, that he would have sex with Vilain's wife in France. Meanwhile, Irmer's wife remained on her parents' farm with her two children and spent many hours working alone with Vilain. The relationship became intimate, and Vilain requested a transfer several times, but his requests, as usual, were unsuccessful because he did not give a reason and continued to state (truthfully) that he was treated well at his present workplace. In January 1942, Frau Irmer realized that she was pregnant from Vilain. When her husband returned on leave not much later, she confessed everything to him. The husband generously forgave her, and according to the court documents, they resumed an intimate relation. Yet, a few days after her husband's renewed departure, she had sex with Vilain again, and this time they were caught. The husband sued for divorce, which was finalized in December 1942, while she was in the Cottbus penitentiary. Frau Irmer, who had given birth to a girl in June, was released on parole six weeks before the end of her sentence, and she vouched to fight to get back her three children, the two older ones living with her ex-husband's family and the baby being in a Berlin orphanage.[30]

Still, only a few husbands sued for divorce, and in these cases the marriage was often already in troubled waters. The wife's involvement

---

[29] NSTA Hannover 172, Peine Acc. 42/58, Nr. 29.
[30] BLHA Potsdam, Sondergericht Frankfurt an der Oder, 12C, 546 and 546/1-3. The court martial in Frankfurt an der Oder sentenced Vilain to two and a half years in prison on April 21, 1942: Dossier 2821, in AN, F9, 2417.

with the POW might have been the last straw and possibly one among several other affairs. As a survey of the examined files from the special courts in Nürnberg, Vienna, and Kiel/Neumünster shows, far more husbands chose forgiveness and continuation of the marriage rather than divorce.[31] In Nürnberg, of seventy-seven women where the marital status is clear, thirty-five were married and forty-two unmarried, divorced, or widowed. Of the thirty-five cases involving married women, only four demonstrably led to divorce as a consequence of the affair with the POW. In sixteen cases, the husband forgave the wife and wanted to continue the marriage. In fifteen cases, there is no information on the effects of the trial on the marriage. The cases in front of the special court in Vienna and in Kiel and Neumünster show a similar ratio. Of the women in my sample tried in Vienna whose marital status is clear, twenty-six were unmarried, divorced, or widowed and fourteen were married. Only in one case did the relationship with the POW demonstrably lead to divorce. In six cases, the husband forgave the wife. Seven cases are unclear because the documentation is incomplete or because the husband went missing in action or was killed before he had time to react. For the special court of Kiel and Neumünster, I have seventy-six files where the marital status is documented. Forty-two women were single, divorced, or widowed, and thirty-four married. In six cases, the husband sued for divorce. In nine cases, the husband forgave the wife. In nineteen cases, the husband's reaction is unknown. Adding all three special courts, we arrive at a ratio of almost three to one for forgiveness where the husband's decision is documented (slightly more than half of all cases in this sample). These numbers confirm Hester Vaizey's argument that marriages were rather resilient and that married partners somehow understood that the circumstances created by the war were in many ways exceptional and transitory.[32]

Practical considerations (care for the children and the household) often encouraged forgiveness, but many husbands also tried to understand what had motivated their wives to become involved with a prisoner of war. If the wife was pregnant from the prisoner, some husbands declared that they would forgive her but not accept the child, but a few husbands even accepted the child fathered by the prisoner as their own or

[31] See also Mechler, *Kriegsalltag an der "Heimatfront,"* 244.
[32] Hester Vaizey, "Husbands and Wives: An Evaluation of the Emotional Impact of World War Two in Germany," *European History Quarterly* 40, no. 3 (2010); Vaizey, "Empowerment or Endurance? War Wives' Experiences of Independence during and after the Second World War in Germany, 1939–1948," *German History* 29, no. 1 (2009); Vaizey, *Surviving Hitler's War: Family Life in Germany 1939–1948* (New York: Palgrave Macmillan, 2010).

decided to not ask questions if paternity was insecure.[33] It is possible that the conviction of his wife relieved a husband of a bad conscience because he might himself not have been faithful, especially if he was serving in the armed forces.

Some husbands missed their wives and wrote clemency pleas that revealed tenderness and concern. The husband of Frieda Egelsdorfer, who had been sentenced to two years of penal servitude on August 20, 1941, for making out with a POW in the attic of a house in Nürnberg, wrote her a warm letter while she was awaiting trial. He said that he missed her badly and did not want to go home any more after his long shifts at the factory because she was not there. He concluded that she had made a rash and headless decision, and he wrote that their neighbors thought the same thing (although, in fact, she had regularly met the POW over a longer period). After her trial, the husband submitted several clemency pleas for her. The director of the Aichach penitentiary rejected them; although he admitted that she was a good and disciplined worker who regretted her transgression, he found it important for reasons of deterrence that she stay behind bars. Like many Aichach prisoners, she was later transferred to Hagenau. In April and July 1943, the director of the Hagenau penitentiary supported a release two to three months before the end of the sentence, which was common in cases where the husband was forgiving. But the Gestapo Nürnberg objected to an early release because it discovered in its files that the husband had once been a communist party deputy in the local parliament and that he had a run-in with the police in May 1933 after allegedly distributing communist party pamphlets (although no charges were filed against him).[34]

Paula Grupp, a married farmwife with a seven-year-old son from a tiny village on the North Sea coast of Schleswig-Holstein, had an intimate relation with a Belgian POW assigned to her farm in the spring and summer 1942, interrupted by a home leave of her husband in April and May. She became pregnant, and the pregnancy likely led to the discovery of the affair (the court assumed that the Belgian POW was the father). Because of the pregnancy, Frau Grupp was allowed to stay home during the investigation. On April 2, 1943, she gave birth to twins, but one of them soon died. On April 12, a local official urged the authorities to

---

[33] For an example of a husband agreeing to accept the child of a POW, see the case against Else H., in HHStA Wiesbaden, Abt. 461, Nr. 9851. For another case, this time involving the child of a Polish POW, see case of Else R., BLHA Potsdam, 12 C, Sondergericht Berlin, 232. For a case where the husband forgave his wife but refused to accept the child of the prisoner, see BStA Nürnberg, Akten der Anklagebehörde beim Sondergericht, 2305.

[34] BStA Nürnberg, Akten der Anklagebehörde beim Sondergericht, 1215.

imprison her because she did not nurse the surviving baby and because she had threatened to shoot herself and her older son. She was taken into pre-trial custody and sentenced to one and a half years of penal servitude on June 4, 1943. Her husband forgave her immediately and asked for her release after the trial. She did obtain temporary releases and became pregnant again, likely from her husband during a home leave. She gave birth on September 10, 1944, and this time nursed the baby. Her sentence was commuted into a prison sentence reinstating her civil rights. She was allowed to stay home and was officially "released" on parole on January 23, 1945. A forgiving husband who served in the Wehrmacht and some supporting documents about the woman as a good worker and mother mollified the prosecutor's office. As in some other cases, the fact that Grupp's family owned an *Erbhof*, an inherited family farm enjoying special protection in Nazi Germany, also worked in her favor.[35]

Soon after Magdalena Fechl was sentenced to ten months in prison for having exchanged kisses with a French POW in a factory in Nürnberg in 1941, her husband, a soldier on the eastern front, forgave her and asked for an early release. He believed that she had committed a one-time offense. Both said that their marriage was happy. Her attorney claimed that her offense had only happened because she had a warm heart and felt compassion for the prisoner, and he requested a temporary leave because she was needed on her parents' farm for the harvest. The prison directors were initially opposed to a release. They had read the letters she sent to her husband and concluded that she did not really regret her "crime." All that seemed to worry her was whether her husband would leave her. But the justice authorities finally agreed to release her on parole three months before the end of her sentence.[36]

Bertha Knipp, working in a factory in Wittenberge, northwest of Berlin, had been sentenced to prison because she had exchanged tender letters and kisses with a French POW. Knipp had also given him many photos of her. The prisoner was married, but his wife had left him before the war. Knipp's husband was serving in the Wehrmacht. The prisoner had talked of marrying her after the war if she divorced her husband, but she balked at the thought of leaving him. The special court in Berlin sentenced her to two years in prison, a rather harsh punishment given that the relationship never seems to have involved more than letters and kisses. Knipp's husband visited her in prison in Leipzig and Breslau while he was on home leave. When he was wounded in May 1942, he asked for

[35] LASH Schleswig, Abt. 358, 5763.
[36] BStA Nürnberg, Akten der Anklagebehörde beim Sondergericht, 1194.

an early release of his wife. Her mother-in-law also submitted a clemency plea on her behalf to Hitler. The prison director in Breslau advocated an early release, probably around half a year before the end of her sentence, and she seems to have been released in early 1943. Clearly, her relationship with her husband and his family survived the affair with the prisoner. That she had told the prisoner that she did not want to leave her husband and that the erotic dimension of the affair seems to have remained limited likely helped.[37]

Emma Marquardt's husband also reconciled with her after she had become close to a French POW, even though she had spoken of marrying him and of having a child with him. Herr Marquardt owned a trading company in Luckenwalde outside Berlin that his wife had been managing alone while he had volunteered for the Wehrmacht. After her arrest, he resigned from the Wehrmacht (which he was allowed to do given that he was aged fifty-six) and tried to save the business, but to no avail. His wife, who had complained about her husband's disinterest in sexual matters, became very fond of him after arriving in the prison. The director of the prison in Berlin-Alt-Moabit supported a release on parole four months before the end of her fifteen-month prison sentence, a generous arrangement, but not unusual in cases where the husband had forgiven his wife.[38]

When Hildegard Welchow was arrested because of a love relation with a French officer who had volunteered to work as a streetcar operator in Cottbus in March 1943, her husband Walter, a railroad employee, sent countless clemency pleas to the judicial authorities and to Hitler. He assured the authorities of his sincere love for his wife and their two young children, and he used every possible argument to excuse her "mistake." He visited her in pre-trial custody and in the penitentiary as often as he could. When he learned that she was pregnant, he tacitly accepted the child as his own, although his paternity was not beyond doubt. The special court in Frankfurt an der Oder sentenced Hildegard Welchow to fourteen months of penitentiary on April 28, 1943, claiming that this was an unusually mild sentence because of her husband's dedication to her. The husband's persistence also impressed the prosecutor's office, which agreed to release her from Cottbus penitentiary three months before the end of her sentence. Perhaps the husband had a bad conscience himself: Hildegard Welchow told the French officer that her

---

[37] BLHA Potsdam, 12 C, Sondergericht Berlin, 991 and 991/1–2; Feldurteil, Berlin, October 17, 1941, in PAAA, R 40891.
[38] BLHA Potsdam, 12 C, Sondergericht Berlin, 182.

husband had admitted having cheated on her once and that she was still angry about it.[39]

For some husbands, forgiving their wife's infidelity was a long and agonizing process. The husband of Babette Späth, for example, attended her court hearing in Nürnberg on September 22, 1941. He heard how she confessed having had sex with a Belgian POW three times, including one time where she manually stimulated him. This had happened during work at the Siemens-Schuckert electronics factory and despite the fact that Späth claimed to have a good marriage. She and her husband had been married for thirteen years, and they had two children. She was sentenced to two and a half years of penal servitude and three years of loss of civil rights. Babette Späth was sent to Aichach and later to Hagenau, and her case was discussed in the newspapers under the title "A Dishonorable Woman." The anger of her husband was boundless. In his letters to her, he fulminated against the prisoner ("dirty swine") and against her hypocritical behavior, with her having pretended to be a good wife and mother while having a lover in the factory. He announced that he would sue for divorce, that it would be better if she were dead rather than alive, and that her behavior was worse than that of a prostitute. He told her that he would never visit her in the penitentiary and that she would lose all rights to the children.

Yet, after a little more than a year, he submitted a clemency plea on her behalf. He had withdrawn the divorce request. He desperately missed the two children – and his wife. The children had first come into an orphanage, but he had taken the older child (fourteen) in with him. This was extremely difficult, however, because he worked in the armaments industry and had long hours and changing shifts. The husband claimed that his wife's behavior was a psychological riddle because their marriage had indeed been very good. He begged the authorities to release her for Christmas 1942. Yet, the prosecutor's office rejected his petition after being assured by the local police station that the situation of the husband and children was not dire enough to warrant even a temporary release. In March 1943, the husband again submitted a clemency plea. He had been forced to take in the younger child (eight), too, because the foster mother had been called up for labor service. The family apartment had been partly destroyed by bombs. The director of the Hagenau penitentiary rejected the husband's requests as premature although he noted that a release perhaps two to three months before the end of the sentence might

[39] BLHA Potsdam, 12 C, Sondergericht Frankfurt an der Oder, 1621, and 1621/1–2. For the judgment against the officer (who received three years of prison), see AN, F9, 2400 (case 52).

be appropriate because Späth conducted herself well and showed sincere regret. The husband renewed his plea in June 1943. The documentation ends here, but she was likely released soon afterwards, since she had only three months left of her sentence.[40]

On September 27, 1943, Maria Meyer was sentenced to sixteen months of penal servitude for a relationship with a Belgian POW in Nürnberg. Although sexual intercourse had not been proven, she and the prisoner had confessed their love to each other, and they had talked about divorcing their partners and getting married after the war. Both were in unhappy marriages, and the local rumor mill considered Meyer's husband to be no model of marital fidelity himself. At the time of the trial, Meyer's husband was stationed on the eastern front. Two weeks after the trial, he paid the court costs and requested the trial documents. He claimed that he wanted to reconcile with his wife but that he first needed to know what exactly had happened. In November 1943, the physician in the Aichach penitentiary noticed that she was pregnant and due in March. Although his paternity was not beyond doubt, her husband was convinced that she carried his child, and he was touched by the prospect of becoming a father. He requested a temporary release for her in January 1944, so that he could see her during a home leave and so that she could give birth at home. He wrote that it pained him to think that his wife had to go into labor in the penitentiary and explained: "I am willing to forgive her the big mistake she made, so that the child has a father and mother." She came home in December 1943 and, on March 9, 1944, she gave birth to twin girls. She requested an extension of her leave because she wanted to nurse the babies. The matter went all the way to the Ministry of Justice, which on April 2, 1944, decided to grant her release on parole in exchange for a fine of 300 marks to be paid to the Red Cross.[41]

Willi Schneid, the husband of Dora Schneid, also wanted to know all the facts when he heard that she had been sentenced to fourteen months of penal servitude on January 6, 1944, while he was serving in the Wehrmacht. When he received a home leave in May, he wanted to see her and requested a temporary release, but he emphasized that he had not forgiven her for the intimate affair with a French POW for which she had been sentenced. But seeing her completely changed his mind, and he wrote to the prosecutor's office that he had decided to forgive her and asked for a pardon. Perhaps the fact that she had ended the relationship with the prisoner because she felt sorry for her husband motivated his

[40] BStA Nürnberg, Akten der Anklagebehörde beim Sondergericht, 1230.
[41] BStA Nürnberg, Akten der Anklagebehörde beim Sondergericht, 2313.

decision. The couple had a two-year-old child in the care of his parents, and the local *Bauernführer* badly wanted Schneid back because she was a good worker. At the end of August 1944, her sentence was commuted into a prison sentence, and her civil rights were restored. She was allowed to return home. The decision took into consideration the damaging effect of the wife's sentence on the fighting morale of the husband, who was meanwhile stationed in Greece.[42]

For some husbands, the infidelity of their wife prompted painful soul-searching. The car mechanic Georg Schneider, the husband of Else Schneider, a groundkeeper in a Nürnberg factory, was shocked when he heard that his wife was on trial for an intensive love affair with an Alsatian POW in the summer of 1943. In repeated clemency pleas on her behalf, he argued that he himself was to blame for her misstep. He had had no idea that his wife yearned for deep love, and he reproached himself for having dismissed her expressions of love for him. They had lived in different worlds, which explains why their marriage had remained childless. The husband could briefly see her when she received a short leave following the death of her father, and he was deeply pained to see her disappear behind prison doors again. Her attorney sent the authorities a copy of Georg Schneider's will, in which he named his wife as his sole heir and repeated his claim that her misstep was only his fault. The prosecutor's office at first remained unimpressed, but she was released approximately one month before the end of her sentence (she had been sentenced to only one year in prison).[43]

When Berlin secretary Margot Schneider received one and a half years of penal servitude for an affair with a French POW in 1943, her husband, a car mechanic who had been dismissed from the Wehrmacht because of a hand injury, critically examined his own behavior toward his wife. In a clemency plea, he explained to the prosecutor's office that he had neglected his wife and driven her into the arms of the prisoner. He wanted to continue the marriage and wrote that he urgently needed her help. They had two children (aged seven and nine), and his injury made it hard for him to take care of the children alone. The prosecutor rejected the clemency plea because Frau Schneider had only served half her sentence but indicated that she might obtain an early release later, which seems to have happened.[44]

Concern for the well-being of the children was an important factor in the decision of many husbands to forgive. The farmer's wife Käthe Pross

---

[42] BStA Nürnberg, Akten der Anklagebehörde beim Sondergericht, 2427.
[43] BStA Nürnberg, Akten der Anklagebehörde beim Sondergericht, 2298.
[44] BLHA Potsdam, 12 C, Sondergericht Berlin, 6819.

from a village near Nürnberg had been sentenced to one year of penal servitude in 1941. Her husband was a soldier on the eastern front. On a home leave in June 1942, he traveled all the way to Hagenau, and he was allowed to speak to her. He confronted her with heavy reproaches, but she insisted on her innocence, arguing that she had tried to send the French POW who had entered her house away (she had been sentenced on dubious evidence). In a clemency plea submitted on August 21, 1942, her husband explained: "Worries about the well-being of my two children who are left without their mother has undermined my fighting spirit." The prison director at first hesitated but then agreed to release her on parole a few weeks before the end of the sentence, arguing that she was "just congenitally dumb."[45]

Farmworker Anna Knorr, a mother of three young children, had told her employers that her husband would kill her if he heard of her relationship with French POW Arthur Moreau. Yet, the husband submitted a clemency plea for her only three days after the special court in Nürnberg had sentenced her to three years of penal servitude (on August 28, 1941). He pointed out that his wife sincerely regretted her actions and that he did not want their children to go into foster care. Because the youngest child (three) was physically handicapped and needed special care, Anna Knorr was allowed to stay home until January 1, 1942, but then she had to report to Aichach. Later, she was sent to Hagenau. Clemency pleas based on the situation of the children met with rejection because they were well cared for by the stepmother of Anna Knorr's husband. The director of the Hagenau penitentiary claimed that Knorr did initially not appreciate the extent of her transgression, but in the summer of 1944, he supported an early release on parole, finding that her sentence had likely served as a deterrent. He called her a diligent and good worker but "a congenitally rather primitive woman." Knorr seems to have been released in the fall of 1944, three months before the end of her sentence.[46]

Ilse Paetz had been sentenced to three and a half years of penal servitude by the special court in Kiel on July 22, 1942, for having helped two French POWs escape and for having had an affair with one of them. Paetz was married to a Luftwaffe officer who was serving on a base nearby, and they had one daughter. The husband forgave his wife and wrote clemency pleas on her behalf. Like other military husbands, he pointed out that he could only perform good military service if his wife

---

[45] BStA Nürnberg, Akten der Anklagebehörde beim Sondergericht, 1278. The children were in the care of another family.
[46] BStA Nürnberg, Akten der Anklagebehörde beim Sondergericht, 1206.

was free and at home. He also expressed concerns because he felt that his daughter, without the care of the mother, was becoming increasingly alienated from him. The prosecutor's office granted Paetz several temporary leaves (two weeks) to be with her husband. She was released on parole on March 23, 1945, several months before the end of her sentence.[47]

In the case of Margarethe Huber, who had been sentenced to two and a half years of penal servitude in Nürnberg on March 26, 1943, everything pointed to a divorce. As soon as she was arrested, her in-laws began emptying the marital apartment. The police noted that her mother-in-law was already wearing Margarethe Huber's fur coat. Yet, the husband, a soldier, wanted to see his wife when he came back on leave in July 1943. He contemplated a divorce, but when he saw her for the second time in May 1944, he decided to forgive her for the sake of their six-year-old child, and he requested an early release. The prosecutor's office agreed. The local police post, asked for its input, voiced a very low opinion of the in-laws while pointing out that Margarethe Huber had always been "orderly and clean." She was paroled in the second half of 1944 but had to perform volunteer work for the Red Cross. Once, she asked for her volunteer service to be postponed because she was already working sixty hours per week in a factory and had no time for her child. The request was granted.[48]

When the two soldiers' wives Margarethe Schäfer and Erna Nordmann, living in a village north of Berlin, were sentenced to two years in penitentiary in August 1942 after having been caught in a remote sand pit with two French POWs, divorces also appeared very likely. Frau Nordmann's brother-in-law wrote her an angry letter outlining the harsh consequences of her actions for her two children (aged nine and twelve years) and her husband. At the request of the husband, who was stationed on the eastern front, his parents picked up both children, who were terribly distraught. Schäfer's husband, also stationed on the eastern front, announced his intention to divorce his wife and requested a copy of the judgment in support of the request. But then Paul Nordmann visited his wife in pretrial custody in a Berlin prison. He was touched by how much she was suffering in prison, and he began to doubt that she was guilty. He wrote a clemency plea to Hitler, but to no avail. After the court hearing, he wrote another clemency plea to the Ministry of Justice, declaring that he wanted to continue the marriage regardless of what had happened in the sand pit: "Should my wife have forgotten herself, which I do not believe, the only

[47] LASH Schleswig, Abt. 358, 5525.
[48] BStA Nürnberg, Akten der Anklagebehörde beim Sondergericht, 1802.

reason is my long absence." Neumann was a career soldier and had seen his wife for the last time in November 1940, more than a year and a half before the incident in the sand pit. He also believed that Frau Schäfer had exercised a bad influence on his wife. Amazingly, the Justice Ministry released Erna Nordmann on parole at the end of February 1943, after she had served only seven months of a two-year sentence.

Wilhelm Schäfer, however, sued for divorce with the help of his attorney on February 2, 1943. His wife had meanwhile been released temporarily to give birth to a girl in March 1943, and her temporary release was renewed several times because she took care of the baby and her six-year-old son. On October 1, 1943, the divorce went through. Yet, on January 14, 1944, Margarethe Schäfer submitted a clemency plea, explaining that her ex-husband had been on home leave over Christmas and that they had decided to remarry each other. Wilhelm Schäfer confirmed this information. He even mentioned that he and his (ex-) wife had resumed a sexual relation during his leave. In April 1944, however, Schäfer suddenly denied that he intended to remarry his ex-wife. Yet, a month later he supported another clemency plea on her behalf, as did his mother, who pointed out that her son could not stand the thought of his two children being abandoned. The pleas pointed out that Frau Nordmann had already been paroled. The prosecutor's office finally agreed to parole Margarethe Schäfer at the end of July 1944. Whether the couple ever remarried is unclear. Margarethe Schäfer had spent even less of her two-year sentence behind bars than Frau Nordmann because she had obtained a long temporary release to give birth and to nurse her baby.[49]

Many husbands who forgave their wives placed the blame for the adulterous relationship on the POW or the negative influence of friends. This denied the wives agency, but it facilitated the decision to forgive. The husband of Anne Freytag, a married milkmaid from a village southwest of Lübeck sentenced to one and a half years of penal servitude for a relationship with a French POW, pondered her case while he was stationed on the eastern front. In May 1944, he decided that he wanted to put the entire matter behind him. He believed that his wife had been under the bad influence of her sister, who had also been involved with a POW. He asked for a commutation of the penal servitude to a prison sentence and for an early release. It seems that the prosecutor's office had granted both requests by April 1945.[50]

The husband of Rosina Wölkl, a factory laborer in a small town near Sankt Pölten (west of Vienna), fought particularly hard for the release of

---

[49] BLHA Potsdam, 12C Sondergericht Berlin II, 218 and 218/1–4.
[50] LASH Schleswig, Abt. 358, 6101.

his wife, and blaming the incident on a bad influence helped him to forgive. He was deeply shocked when he came home on leave from the eastern front in April 1943 and learned that she had just been arrested for having had sex twice with a French POW in the apartment of an older friend. The prisoner had even promised to marry her in case her husband did not return from the war, but Wölkl had ended the relationship rather soon. The husband immediately petitioned the special court to grant his wife a mild judgment. He pointed out that he had forgiven her, believing that the prisoner had seduced her. Nevertheless, the Sankt Pölten branch of the special court of Vienna sentenced her to one and a half years of penal servitude on May 26, 1943, and she was sent to Aichach two days later.

The husband had meanwhile returned to the eastern front, but he kept asking the prosecutor's office for an early release of his wife, declaring that the marriage had been happy and would be happy again, that he had forgiven her, and that the transgression his wife had committed was the result of the seduction by the prisoner and the bad influence of a friend. Despite a stream of bad news – Wölkl's sixty-year-old mother was dying of cancer and Wölkl's sister, who was taking care of her child and her mother, had lost her husband – the director of the Aichach penitentiary rejected all petitions even though he admitted that Wölkl was a disciplined and diligent inmate. Yet, the prosecutor's office granted her a two-month temporary release, and Wölkl was allowed to go home on September 1, 1943. She received several extensions because her husband had meanwhile been wounded on the eastern front. While recovering, he wrote yet another passionate clemency plea. He explained that, before her arrest, he had seen his wife for the last time in May 1941, more than a year and a half before her affair with the prisoner. He confirmed that the marriage was happy again and that all the trouble had been due to his long enforced absence. Having to return to the front knowing that his wife was in the penitentiary was a "terrible thought" for him. The director in Aichach again rejected the plea, but somehow the matter came to the attention of the Reich Ministry of the Interior. A ministry official overruled the Aichach director and granted Wölkl a release on probation for May 1944, urging the husband (somewhat disingenuously, given that he was expected to return to the eastern front) to watch more carefully over his wife in the future. Wölkl had effectively served only a little less than half of her sentence. The Interior Ministry stressed that the original sentence was appropriate but that the circumstances warranted an early release.[51]

---

[51] WStLA, Sondergericht, 7164.

Women as Essential Workers

In the context of an ever-increasing labor shortage in wartime Germany, the arrest and custodial sentence of a woman caused economic in addition to emotional hardship, especially in the countryside. Farmers' leaders (*Bauernführer*) were under pressure to fulfill production quotas, and they needed all hands on board. The departure of a woman often deprived them of a good worker and sometimes caused a family farm to fail. A replacement was difficult to find. Quite a few women sentenced to penitentiary or prison counted as such precious workers that they had to spend rather little time behind bars, getting temporary releases, extensions of temporary releases, and early releases on parole. This sometimes occurred even though the judicial authorities were not convinced that the woman sincerely regretted her "crime." In a few cases, however, these requests were not successful because the woman was performing important war-related work under the auspices of the penitentiary administration itself.

Marie Keim was known as such a good worker in the farmlands southwest of Nürnberg that no fewer than three local employers petitioned for an early release to get her to work for them. She had been sentenced to two years of penal servitude on September 5, 1941. The director of the Aichach penitentiary considered her to have "an arrogant, cheeky, and obstinate character" and rejected the first clemency pleas, but she was released on parole in April 1943, approximately three months before the end of her sentence.[52] In a similar case, Albine Löck was also released three months prior to the end of her sentence even though, according to the penitentiary director, she did not recognize the wrong she had done. But she was an unusually diligent worker in the penitentiary, and she had worked in an armaments factory outside Vienna.[53]

Therese Pscharrer was sentenced to one year of penal servitude on May 14, 1942, after having tried to get her former village sweetheart to declare himself as the father of her child, which was in truth fathered by French POW Prosper Wegner. Pscharrer had given birth in January 1942, but she was so badly needed on the family farm that she was allowed to stay at home during the trial and even for half a year afterwards. Her father was eighty-three and her mother sixty-eight. She had a handicapped sister (twenty-eight) and three brothers, who were all fighting on the eastern front. Only on December 10, 1942, did she have to report to Aichach. Yet, both the local and the regional *Bauernführer*

---

[52] BStA Nürnberg, Akten der Anklagebehörde beim Sondergericht, 1214.
[53] WStLA, Sondergericht, 7207.

requested a temporary release because of the spring work to be done on the farm, and she was allowed to return home on March 15, 1943, having spent just over three months in Aichach. The peasant leaders considered her so indispensable that she received multiple extensions, allowing her to remain home for several years. Only on January 30, 1945, did she finally return to the penitentiary. Her new end of sentence was set for October 16, 1945, but she was likely released in late April 1945 after the arrival of Allied troops. One may be tempted to ascribe the leniency of the judicial authorities in her case to the fact that she had been involved with a Lorrainer who had German ancestry and had applied for German citizenship (and this explains her comparatively light sentence), but the prosecutor's office quite consistently rejected pleas for a release on parole and only agreed to temporary leaves because she was so essential for the family farm.[54]

The arrest of four women involved with French prisoners in a hamlet 100 kilometers south of Vienna in May 1942 created an emergency. The women were such good agricultural workers that a series of clemency pleas or petitions for temporary releases arrived at the prosecutor's office. The estate had received a few new French prisoners, but they had no experience handling the cattle and were unreliable with milk deliveries, leading to much milk being spoiled. One of the women died in Aichach, but the three others did receive temporary releases during the busiest periods of the agricultural year, and one of them, partly owing to her higher age (she was forty-nine), was released on probation a few months early. Despite the temporary releases, the estate was near collapse in the fall of 1944 because the few foreign laborers assigned to the estate often had to dig entrenchments for the Wehrmacht at a time when the lack of fuel required ever more manual labor for many tasks. The local *Bauernführer* confirmed that one of the women was able to milk twice as many cows as was normally expected of somebody in her position, and the special court in Vienna advocated an early release, arguing that the sentences for the women (two and a half to four years of penal servitude) exceeded the usual punishments meted out later. The director of the Aichach penitentiary, however, refused an early release on parole. The case even went to the Ministry of Justice, but without resolution.[55]

Therese Schwamendinger, a farmworker from a village near Regensburg (Bavaria), had been sentenced to two years of penal servitude on August 19, 1943, for a love relation with Italian-born French POW Angelo di Poggia. Her father urgently requested her release, portraying

[54] BStA Nürnberg, Akten der Anklagebehörde beim Sondergericht, 1366.
[55] WStLA, Sondergericht, 6348, 6532, and 6587.

her as a daughter who always had to work hard (one of twelve children) and who understandably could not resist the temptation presented by the prisoner. His plea was rejected, but – as was often the case – a local *Bauernführer* again asked for her release because her labor was so badly needed. She did obtain a temporary release from Aichach for the summer of 1944 to help with the harvest. On December 20, 1944, the director of the Aichach penitentiary advocated an early release on parole because she had conducted herself well and because he saw her mistake as a consequence of the circumstances in which she lived, and she appears to have been released at the end of the year.[56]

Farmworker Margarethe Kohl, however, had the bad luck of getting into war-related work under the auspices of the penitentiary system. She had been sentenced to two years of penal servitude in Nürnberg on November 10, 1941. At the time of her trial, she was pregnant from the French prisoner with whom she had been involved. Because of her pregnancy, she was allowed to stay on the farm during the investigation, but soon after the trial she was sent to Aichach, where she had to give birth. From Aichach, she was transferred to the *Elbregulierung* penal camp. A farmwoman from her village asked for her release because she needed her as a laborer, but the authorities rejected the request because Kohl was working for the Junkers airplane factory and an ammunitions factory. She seems to have been released only on the very last day of her sentence in December 1943. Before giving birth to the prisoner's child, Kohl already had two children born out of wedlock (aged two and nine). What happened to her three children is unclear. The authorities did not care.[57]

The End of Incarceration for the Women

As Kohl's case shows, the inmates of penitentiaries and prisons were increasingly mobilized for war-related work, and this meant that the penal institutions had to send them into factories and other work sites where they might come into contact with civilians and where guarding would be harder to enforce than in the walled penal institutions.[58] Some women took an opportunity for an escape, especially during the disruptions caused by bombing raids. Most women were recaptured, and a few of them turned themselves in when they realized the difficulties of surviving in hiding. Recaptured inmates were punished with half rations, isolation, and beatings. As Allied troops closed in on the Reich in early 1945, the

---

[56] BStA Nürnberg, Akten der Anklagebehörde beim Sondergericht, 2243.
[57] BStA Nürnberg, Akten der Anklagebehörde beim Sondergericht, 1298.
[58] Wachsmann, 231–6.

penitentiaries and prisons tried to evacuate the inmates, but this often happened so late that the directors had to tell the inmates to go home and await further instructions. Many inmates used the general confusion to abscond. Their trail often gets lost in this period. Sometimes the judicial authorities searched for them after the end of the war.

Gertrude Pfaff, a nineteen-year-old woman living in Regensburg, was serving a penitentiary sentence of two years and three months for a relationship with French POW Charles Mourand and also for theft. After her trial in Nürnberg on December 15, 1941, she was sent to far-away Anrath for unclear reasons (perhaps because she was originally from Duisburg, not far from Anrath). On a work detachment at the Rheika silk factory in Krefeld, she managed to escape early in the morning of September 14, 1942. She was recaptured in Austria a few months later and put on trial again because she had committed another theft during her escape. On June 7, 1943, the special court in Graz sentenced her to ten years of penitentiary, in addition to the remaining sentence from her Nürnberg judgment, an absurdly harsh punishment. She came to Aichach and later to Hagenau.[59]

Anna Zehetmeier had been sentenced to two years of penal servitude in Nürnberg in December 1943. She was a war widow with two children. She spent some time in Aichach and was then sent to a work detachment at the Agfa camera factory in Munich. During a bombing attack on July 16, 1944, she escaped and decided to walk home. But realizing the hopelessness of her situation, she turned herself in to the police a week later.[60] Franziska Hamm, sentenced to two and a half years of penal servitude on March 30, 1944, also took advantage of a bombing raid on Munich in July 1944 to escape. She wanted to return to her farm in northern Bavaria. Her and her husband's petitions for a temporary release had all been rejected. Her husband was in poor health, and her young child had to be admitted to a hospital. She was desperate to return home, but she was recaptured a day after her escape in Ingolstadt.[61] Antonie Preuß, a widow with two children who had been sentenced to two and a half years of penal servitude on July 14, 1944, was luckier. A month after her trial, she was sent from the Lübeck penitentiary to Anrath and from there to a work detachment in Düsseldorf. On November 2, 1944, during a bombing attack, she disappeared. When the judicial authorities searched for her after the war, it became clear that she had made it home and lived there without being bothered again.[62]

[59] BStA Nürnberg, Akten der Anklagebehörde beim Sondergericht, 1286.
[60] BStA Nürnberg, Akten der Anklagebehörde beim Sondergericht, 2410.
[61] BStA Nürnberg, Akten der Anklagebehörde beim Sondergericht, 2046.
[62] LASH Schleswig, Abt. 358, 6072.

The farmworker Margarethe Ollenberg, who had been sentenced to three years of penal servitude in Kiel on October 1, 1942, came to the penitentiary in Lübeck-Lauerhof. She was deployed in a work detachment outside the institution and escaped during a night shift in June 1944. Three months later, she was captured again and had to resume her penitentiary sentence, with time added for the escape. On May 1, 1945, however, an official from the prosecutor's office called the penitentiary and asked for her release. British troops were in place outside Lübeck, and the local Wehrmacht commander was negotiating the surrender of the city.[63]

Late in the war, transportation difficulties often made it impossible for women to return to a penitentiary after a temporary leave. When two women from the hamlet south of Vienna tried to take the train to Aichach to report back at the penitentiary after a temporary release in early February 1945, the train officials in Vienna refused to let them on board because the trains were reserved for people with higher priority. The two women returned home.[64] Herta Jensen, who had been sentenced to three and a half years of penal servitude in April 1943 for an affair with a French POW and for having hidden him in her home for seven weeks, was in Anrath when Allied troops began shelling the area in early March 1945. The director of the institution then ordered all women inmates to go home, and Jensen joined her parents near Lübeck. Like other Anrath prisoners sent home in early March, she received a summons to report to the penitentiary in Lübeck in April, but it is safe to assume that she remained with her parents.[65]

The special court in Oldenburg sentenced Erna Berg, a war widow with four young children from Brake (north of Bremen), to one and a half years of penal servitude for a relationship with a Belgian POW on February 15, 1945. On March 7, she arrived with a transport of convicts at the women's penitentiary Rheda near Gütersloh (Westphalia). Yet, Allied troops were already nearby, and the convicts were transferred to one of the sections of the Oberems prison camp inside Gütersloh not much later. She did not stay there very long because Allied troops liberated the city in early April.[66] In July 1945, the welfare office in Oldenburg began searching for her because of custody questions regarding her children. After three months, the welfare office learned from the police in her hometown that Erna Berg had returned home.[67]

[63] LASH Schleswig, Abt. 358, 5444.
[64] WStLA, Sondergericht, 6348, 6532, and 6587.
[65] LASH Schleswig, Abt. 358, 5704.
[66] Karina Isernhinke, *Das Strafgefangenenlager Oberems: Das nationalsozialistische Lagersystem im Gebiet des heutigen Kreises Gütersloh*, (Bielefeld: Verlag für Regionalgeschichte, 2015), 77–88, 96.
[67] NLA Oldenburg, Best. 140–5, Nr. 496.

On February 15, 1945, the women's penitentiary in Cottbus, which detained most of the women sentenced to penal servitude in Berlin and Frankfurt an der Oder, was hit by bombs. The woman director of the institution survived, but she mentioned that a number of inmates had been killed while others had used the confusion to escape. Who was killed and who had escaped was still unclear at the end of March 1945 because it had not been possible to clear the ruins. The director believed that many corpses were buried under the ruins.[68]

Some women suffered severe mental or physical crises behind bars, and some did not survive their time in the penitentiary. Frau Löffler, the friend of Frau Hoffer, sentenced like her to four years of penal servitude by the Nürnberg special court on April 12, 1943, went to Aichach with her, but Frau Löffler's mental health rapidly deteriorated. She claimed to have syphilis and that nobody could touch her, and she believed that she would be beheaded. In November 1943, she was transferred to a psychiatric clinic in Munich. Her examiner noted that she refused to eat because she claimed all food was poisoned and that she had extremely sharp mood swings. She was put under strong medication and transferred to the psychiatric clinic of Erlangen. Her trail is lost thereafter. It occasionally happened that mentally ill patients were quietly murdered.[69]

Hedwig Ungerböck (twenty-one) was the cook of the estate in the hamlet south of Vienna where four women were sentenced for affairs with French POWs. Before her trial on July 24, 1942, Ungerböck had to endure various intelligence and physical tests to determine whether she was "feeble-minded" (she passed all tests), but nobody had the idea to request a pregnancy test even though she had said already in May that she had not had her period after her last meeting with the POW. The four women were held in a Vienna prison until the POWs had had their court martial and were then sent to Aichach at the end of October. On December 12, 1942, somebody in Aichach noticed that Ungerböck was in an advanced stage of pregnancy and notified the prosecutor's office in Vienna. Nothing happened, and her file ends with a death notice, informing the prosecutor's office that Ungerböck had died in Aichach late at night on January 6, 1943. No reason was given. Had she had a miscarriage? Was it a suicide?[70] Another death in Aichach also went unexplained. Frieda Mutzbauer had been sentenced to four years of penal servitude by the special court in Nürnberg on October 10, 1941. She died in the penitentiary on March 28,

[68] BLHA Potsdam, 12 C, Sondergericht Frankfurt an der Oder, 849/3.
[69] BStA Nürnberg, Akten der Anklagebehörde beim Sondergericht, 2031. Wachsmann, *Hitler's Prisons*, 313–14.
[70] WStLA, Sondergericht, 6348.

1942. She received some posthumous rehabilitation because her husband Peter asked in 1950 for her name to be struck from the registry of crimes, with success.[71]

In some cases, it proved difficult after the war to trace the fate of incarcerated women before and after liberation. Katharina Heilmann, for example, was a married housewife from a village near Worms who had been sentenced to three years of penal servitude in March 1941. She was released on parole in June 1943, seven months before the end of her sentence, but her tracks seemed lost after that because all of her trial and post-trial documents had been destroyed during a bombing attack. In 1949, the prosecutor's office, still searching for her, found out that she had burned to death in her room during a bombing attack shortly after her release.[72]

Luise Hartmann, who had been sentenced by the special court in Lübeck to two and a half years of penal servitude for a relationship with French POW Felix Le Bon on October 16, 1944, was interned in various penitentiaries in northern Germany and released by the British authorities on May 13, 1945. She returned to the village where she had worked before, but a year later, she submitted a request for indemnification to the prosecutor's office in Kiel. She described that she had been put into iron chains after her arrest and that she had witnessed the execution of a Polish prisoner. She was slapped in the face many times and suffered great hunger. She had to sleep on cold cement floors and claimed that she was still suffering from the effects of her incarceration. She even claimed to have spent some time in a concentration camp, which could have been the case after evacuation (several women held in the Lübeck-Lauerhof penitentiary claimed to have been in a concentration camp at the end of the war). Her request for indemnification was rejected, but she was asked to testify as a witness in a trial involving crimes against humanity in Lübeck in July 1950.[73]

A Soldier's Concentration Camp? The Specter of Graudenz

"GRAUDENZ. One hears in this simple word a growl that makes one tremble."[74] This is how French POW lawyer Stéphane Delattre characterizes the reputation of the German military prison of Graudenz, to which most POWs convicted to prison terms were sent. He cites a camp

---

[71] BStA Nürnberg, Akten der Anklagebehörde beim Sondergericht, 1258. Her trial records are lost.
[72] HStAD, Darmstadt, G 27, 889.
[73] LASH Schleswig, Abt. 358, 6111. See also the case of Käthe S., 6172.
[74] Delattre, *Ma Guerre sans fusil*, 14.

inspector's memoirs that compare Graudenz to Rawa-Ruska, the grue-
some penal camp for POWs who had escaped multiple times, and he
evokes the analogy to the hell of a concentration camp: Graudenz, a cold,
dark, damp fortress on the Vistula, whipped by glacial winds, far away
from the friendly skies of France, a concentration camp without crema-
toria. After the war, former French, Belgian, and British POWs
requested that Graudenz be assimilated to other dreadful Nazi camps
and that the survivors of Graudenz receive indemnification payments
similar to people deported to concentration camps. Historian Peter Lutz
Kalmbach points out that the conditions in Wehrmacht prisons generally
resembled concentration camp conditions and that some judicial experts
and (German) prisoners called them "*Soldaten-KZ*" (concentration camp
for soldiers).[75] This image requires some modification when considering
POWs, rather than German convicts, however. What is the reality behind
the fearsome image of Graudenz?

Harsh military discipline had been a hallmark of the Prussian and
German state before 1919, and the army had been allowed to treat its
members without much consideration for their health. Brutal corporal
punishments were standard fare in military prisons. The Weimar Consti-
tution of 1919 had abrogated these practices, but the Nazi regime had
quickly reinstated a powerful military justice system. Time in military
prison was meant to be a deterrent to ensure maximum discipline among
the German troops in combat. Transfer into the German military prison
system certainly exposed a POW to much harsher treatment than he
experienced in a normal camp or work detachment. It often meant severe
hardship, abuse, and hunger. The German authorities justified this treatment by pointing out that German soldiers punished with military prison
had to suffer the same penal regime, or even worse.

Once the judicial district commander (*Gerichtsherr*) confirmed their
judgments, POWs convicted to a prison sentence longer than three
months were sent to German military prisons if their custody before
confirmation had not taken up so much of their sentence that a transfer
to a prison made no sense (provided that the court martial had counted
the pre-trial custody). There were several German military prisons that
normally held German military convicts, for example in Torgau-Fort
Zinna (Saxony), Germersheim (Palatinate), Hamburg, Berlin, Anklam

---

[75] Kalmbach, *Wehrmachtjustiz*, 157–8. See also Delattre, *Ma Guerre sans fusil*, 14–15;
Scapini, *Mission sans gloire*, 214–18. For the French camp inspector who compared
Graudenz to a concentration camp, see: Georges Baud, Louis Devaux, and Jean
Poigny, eds., *Mémoire complémentaire sur quelques aspects du Service Diplomatique des
Prisonniers de Guerre: SDPG-DFB-Mission Scapini, 1940–1945* ([Paris]: G. Baud,
1984), 123 and 148.

(Pomerania), and Graudenz (West Prussia; today Grudziądz, Poland). At first, POWs were sent to a military prison close to the area where they had been working, although they were usually kept separated from German military convicts. But in early 1942, the Wehrmacht earmarked Graudenz as the principal place of confinement for convicted POWs, and the German inmates there were transported to other prisons. For unclear reasons, some POWs also continued to be sent to other detention centers, especially to Torgau-Fort Zinna, which served as the nerve center of the German military penal regime.[76] As was typical in Nazi Germany, the POWs jailed in a certain institution were often sent to work detachments outside the prison walls. Graudenz established several detachments nearby and also a more distant cluster of work camps in the Heydebreck industrial complex in eastern Upper Silesia, not far from Auschwitz. Here, convicted POWs helped build synthetic fuel plants and canals or worked in chemical factories. Late in the war, Graudenz also established a work detachment at the Leuna synthetic fuel plant in Merseburg near Leipzig.[77]

Before 1943, only POWs convicted for carrying out or attempting the most heinous acts had to go to a penitentiary, and the number of these convicts was very small. But the shift to an automatic penitentiary sentence for a relationship with a soldier's wife in 1943–4 meant that thousands of POWs began to appear in German penitentiaries, where they were under the oversight of the German Ministry of Justice and no longer inside the military penal system. Prisoners in penitentiaries lost touch with the protecting power, which had channels of communication only with the Wehrmacht and the German Foreign Office. These POWs were integrated into the same system as the women sentenced to penal servitude, although they usually remained separated. Conditions in penitentiaries were harsh during the war, although one has to wonder whether being sent to a penitentiary, which was supposed to be a more severe punishment than prison, was really worse for a POW than being transferred to a German military prison.

In prison or penitentiary, the POWs lost the relative freedom of movement that many of them had enjoyed before, especially if they had worked on a farm. Even in the work detachments outside the military prisons, the regimen was very strict. Prisoners would be housed in barracks under rigid discipline. It was hard to escape, and contacts with

---

[76] Kalmbach, *Wehrmachtjustiz*, 57; Eberlein, Haase, and Oleschinski, *Torgau im Hinterland*, 61–90.

[77] Peter Hayes, *Industry and Ideology: IG Farben in the Nazi Era*, 2nd ed. (New York: Cambridge University Press, 2001), 334.

civilians were largely limited to encounters with concentration camp inmates and other convicts. The German military prison regime contained many harsh and cruel aspects that contradicted the right of the POW to be treated in a humane fashion. Although the sections of the Geneva Convention dealing with penal sanctions did not explicitly state that convicted POWs preserved all their rights, this was certainly expected, given that articles 2 and 3 emphasized that POWs had to be treated humanely and with respect under all conditions and that they preserved their civil rights. Article 46 of the Geneva Convention stressed in reference to the prison regime: "All forms of corporal punishment, confinement in premises not lighted by daylight and, in general, all forms of cruelty whatsoever are prohibited," while article 67 guaranteed that the convicted POW did not lose the right to communicate his grievances to the protecting power (covered by article 42). At first, however, the Wehrmacht refused to allow international inspections of the prisons and penitentiaries or communications of their inmates with the protecting power. Convicted POWs also lost other rights protected by the Geneva Convention, such as the right to letters, aid parcels, work security, leisure time, reading materials, decent accommodations, religious services, and basic health care. The German authorities initially defended these restrictions by arguing that POWs had to follow the rules in place for German convicts.

Informal reports, including testimonies from POWs who had served out their sentence, soon revealed that conditions in Graudenz and its dependent work detachments were extremely harsh. Some prisoners had to go into solitary confinement under conditions forbidden by the Geneva Convention. There were beatings, abuses, and random murders. Rooms in Graudenz were damp and sometimes unlighted. Prisoners were forbidden to read in certain work detachments. Medical services were inadequate, and in many places the work was detrimental to the health of the prisoners. In one work detachment in Graudenz, for example, POWs were suffering from acidic burns and debilitating head and stomach aches because they had to extract recyclable chemicals from used batteries without protection. In other work detachments, POWs had to stand knee-deep in the Vistula River to build dikes or to break up ice in the winter, without boots. Most alarmingly, the food rations were much too low. Some inmates had lost twenty kilos (forty-four pounds).[78] POWs described the commander of the Graudenz prison, Colonel

---

[78] See, for example, Lt-Col. Lescrauwaet to Commission belge des crimes de guerre, January 14, 1946, citing letters by a Belgian POW from March and April 1943, in CEGESOMA, AA 120/C/64.

Dallmer-Zerbe, as a small, mean man with a glass eye who bore a
particular grudge against French POWs because his wife had allegedly
once had an affair with a Frenchman. Several prisoners remembered
Dallmer-Zerbe greeting new French and Belgian arrivals by saying:
"You are dead meat" or "You are lost meat for your families."[79] Some
of his staff members were no better: Belgian ex-POW Robert Vanparys
remembered a Major Rose as "the prototype of the sadistic Prussian
barracks rat" and a Captain Heuer as a sadist with the face of a hyena
who used to boast that he had lined up Belgian generals against a wall
when he was stationed in Liège. His transfer to Graudenz was rumored
to be a punishment for misconduct.[80]

The vast majority of the POWs exposed to this harsh penal regime –
over 90 percent of the Frenchmen and Belgians – had been sentenced for
forbidden relations with German women. Although the percentage of
love-related trials against French and Belgian POWs was lower (75–80
percent), the fact that forbidden relations led to long sentences meant
that the soldiers convicted for this reason were overrepresented in the
military prisons. POWs with lighter sentences would not be sent to
Graudenz but served out their sentences in the main camps. As Dr.
Brucker, the medical expert of the Berlin delegation of the SDPG, wrote
in May 1943:

Ninety-five percent of the prisoners of war in Graudenz were sentenced for
forbidden relations with German women on grounds that, normally, would
lead to neither a judicial nor a disciplinary punishment. They rightly feel that
there is a disproportion between the violation they committed and the
punishment inflicted on them. ... Only a tiny minority has committed acts that
normally would come before a tribunal.[81]

---

[79] Fernand Caire, "Sous le joug. Mémoires 1939–1945," manuscript in CEGESOMA, AB
1249, 29, 31. A German translator who befriended many French and Belgian POWs,
however, passed a milder judgment on Dallmer-Zerbe, while concurring with their
condemnation of some of the other officers: Victor Hanewald to Belgian Government,
Heidelberg, November 20, 1945, and "Bericht über meine Tätigkeit und Erfahrungen
als Dolmetscher im Wehrmachtsgefängnis Graudenz," both in CEGESOMA, AA 120/
C/64.

[80] Robert Vanparys to Ministère des Affaires étrangères, September 30, 1945, and
Vanparys to Belgian Minister in Moscow, July 21, 1945, and Victor Hanewald,
"Bericht über meine Tätigkeit und Erfahrungen als Dolmetscher im
Wehrmachtsgefängnis Graudenz," all in CEGESOMA, AA 120/C/64, Commission
belge des crimes de guerre: Camp de Graudenz.

[81] "95% des prisonniers de guerre de Graudenz ont été condamnés à la suite de rapports
interdits avec des femmes allemandes pour des motifs qui, normalement, ne
provoqueraient ni peine judiciaire ni sanction disciplinaire; ils considèrent à juste titre
qu'il y a une disproportion entre la faute commise et la punition infligée. Les mesures
envisagées ci-dessus amélioraient considérablement l'état moral et matériel des
prisonniers de guerre détenus à Graudenz dont une infime minorité seulement a

The Belgian authorities determined that a similar proportion (94 percent) of their prisoners in Graudenz and its work detachments had been sentenced for forbidden relations, and the Swiss pointed out that the majority of the British POWs were there for the same reason.[82]

The French POWs were the first to arrive in the penal institutions in large numbers, and the Scapini Mission soon became worried about their fate, especially in Graudenz. Not even the ICRC had been allowed to inspect the Graudenz prison and its work detachments.[83] The problem came at a difficult time for the Scapini Mission because Hitler, in a hysterical fit of rage, had ordered that all French camp inspections be suspended after the escape of General Henri Giraud from an officer camp on April 17, 1942.[84] When the German High Command began to quietly subvert Hitler's order and to readmit French camp inspectors in the fall of 1942, a visit to Graudenz was at the top of Scapini's list. Reacting to the High Command's refusal to allow inspections of military prisons because there were no inspections for German military convicts, he insisted that the protecting power, according to the Geneva Convention, had the right to visit and inspect *all* places in which POWs might be detained (article 86), including military prisons and penitentiaries. The High Command backed down, and on November 12–15, 1942, the Scapini Mission could for the first time inspect Graudenz and some of its work detachments. Scapini himself led this inspection, demonstrating the importance he attached to the fate of the inmates.

The inspection revealed deficiencies in all work detachments (although all arriving POWs spent some time in the fortress of Graudenz, at the time of the inspection, all French POWs were in work detachments). Food was insufficient, especially in light of the hard work, clothing and shoes were worn out, and living areas were severely crowded and not adequately heated. In one large work detachment on the Vistula in Graudenz itself (with 576 French POWs), the German officer had reduced food rations as a collective punishment for minor infractions of some POWs, a clear violation of the Geneva Convention, which outlawed collective punishments. The POWs in several places spoke of physical abuses, albeit mostly in the past tense. Some brutal guards had apparently been replaced with friendlier guards. There were some

commis des fautes relevant normalement des tribunaux." Inspection report on the fortress of Graudenz and work detachments, May 19, 1943, by Dr. Brucker and Scapini, in AN, F9, 2721.
[82] Rapport du Lt. med. Van Doornick, April 14–15, 1943, in Musée Royal de l'Armée et d'Histoire Militaire, Evere, dossier captivité, #12, 19–21.
[83] ICRC report on Graudenz, August 6, 1942, in AN, F9, 2918.
[84] Scheck, "The Prisoner of War Question and the Beginnings of Collaboration," 382–3.

severely sick prisoners who should have been repatriated. In the final meeting with Major Otto, the deputy commander, Scapini and his team suggested several improvements. Above all, the POWs should receive aid parcels to mitigate malnutrition. Major Otto rejected this demand, however, arguing that he had to follow the same rules as those in place for German convicts. On some other questions, for example the repatriation of severely ill POWs and religious services, he was more accommodating, pending approval from the High Command.[85]

In his memoirs, Scapini left a depressing description of the visit. His North African valet Ahmed Bella, who guided him by the arm because of Scapini's blindness, told him of a desert-like atmosphere in some commandos and about the dreadful impression the fortress of Graudenz made with its high walls, dark rooms, and barred windows:

It was a sinister fortress-prison. ... I visited it together with the man of confidence, staff sergeant Vilat [Maurice Vila], who was anguished and extremely worried about the fate of his comrades.

I found men who were in a terribly deficient physical state, with obvious signs of lack of vitamins: bloated appearance, total fatigue, resigned weariness. Dr. Brucker [the medical expert of the Scapini Mission] confirmed this impression.

The treatment was harsh and the work exhausting.

We felt a rising anger that we had to control. Nonetheless, it broke out piecemeal during our conversations at the command office.

The German colonel always answered the same way: he had no power to change the rules, but if he did receive orders from the High Command, he would do it.

I broke off the conversation and told him that I would speak directly to General Reinecke and the German Foreign Office.[86]

Scapini kept his word and immediately contacted Reinecke, explaining to him: "Almost all the prisoners of Graudenz are not really criminals. If it is indeed just that they have to suffer the proscribed punishment for the crime they have committed, is it in the interest of Germany, from a human perspective, to inflict on them an irreversible physical and psychological decay?" Repeatedly, Scapini requested permission to send aid parcels to the Graudenz prisoners, and he urged the sending of a priest, special Christmas gifts, and improvements in the physical structure of many work detachments.[87]

[85] Inspections of the work detachments Graudenz, Königsdorf, Georgenhof, Steindorf, Thorn (Einheit 14A), and Zoernowitz, November 12–15, 1942, in AN, F9, 2721.
[86] Scapini, *Mission sans gloire*, 215–16. Scapini predates Dr. Brucker's visit to November 1942. According to the inspection records, however, Dr. Brucker visited Graudenz only in May 1943, but he confirmed many of Scapini's initial impressions.
[87] "Entretien du 15 décembre 1942," in AN, F9, 2176.

As so often, the High Command's reaction was slow. The German authorities always pointed out that the POWs had to abide by the same rules as German convicts and that it was impossible to treat the POWs convicted for love relations any differently than the remaining 5 percent. But Reinecke seemed sympathetic, and the High Command indicated that it might allow the delivery of aid parcels under certain conditions and the dispatch of French physicians and priests. It also allowed more inspections. On April 14–15, 1943, a Belgian delegation under Dr. van Doornick visited Graudenz and some of the work detachments with approximately 500 Belgian POWs. Van Doornick reported similar problems as Scapini had noted before, above all inadequate nutrition, poor accommodation, and occasional abuses. Some POWs in the camp hospital were seriously ill, one of them being as thin as a skeleton, yet the camp physician, a Dr. Polstorff, refused to acknowledge the serious illness of some POWs. According to van Doornick, Polstorff was "either a big ignoramus or a huge hypocrite." Van Doornick also reported severe tensions between the Belgian and British POWs. The Belgians considered the British uncouth and were jealous because the British did receive aid parcels and were generally better treated. Also, the Belgians looked down on the British because, according to van Doornick, many British had been sentenced because of homosexual relations, often with their guard.[88] This seems to be a misperception, however. Most British inmates, according to the records of the Swiss Legation in Berlin, were there for the same reasons as the Belgians and Frenchmen: a forbidden relation with a woman.

Like the Scapini Mission, the Belgian delegation immediately requested a meeting with the German authorities, asking for an amnesty for the POWs sentenced because of a forbidden relation and urging improvements for the POWs held in the Graudenz complex. (A German Foreign Office official had counseled the Belgians to always make two requests to the High Command because one was certain to be denied while the other might be approved.)[89] On April 30, van Doornick met with the Scapini Mission in Berlin and coordinated the dispatch of aid parcels to the Graudenz inmates, which the High Command had approved on condition that the bulk of the supplies would be delivered to the kitchen rather than to individual prisoners. Deliveries did start in

[88] Rapport du Lt. med. Van Doornick, April 14–15, 1943, in Musée Royal de l'Armée et d'Histoire Militaire, Evere, dossier captivité, #12, 19–21.
[89] "La commission t'Serclaes," in Musée Royal de l'Armée et d'Histoire Militaire, Evere, Fonds Gillet, Boîte 1, #4: Affaires juridiques, 312.

May or June 1943.[90] At the same time, the ICRC received permission to conduct its first inspection of the prison and some work detachments, and it reached the same conclusions as the French and Belgian officials.[91] The Scapini Mission made another large inspection in May 1943, this time led by Dr. Brucker, its medical expert. The grievances remained the same. Dr. Brucker urgently requested improved nutrition, more aid parcels, and better work conditions and hygiene. Some guards still were pushy and violent. After the inspection, Dr. Brucker again petitioned the High Command and the German Foreign Office for a comprehensive amnesty for the POWs incarcerated in the Graudenz complex because of a love affair, but to no avail.[92]

Scapini brought up Graudenz again when he met Reinecke in June 1943. Having heard complaints about the situation in the Heydebreck detachments, he suggested that aid parcels should be sent there, too, and he tried to get approval for sending vitamin pills and other supplementary goods to the prisoners. Reinecke accepted many of the suggestions, and conditions improved slowly. A French inspection of the four Heydebreck detachments, which held approximately 3,000 convicted POWs (2,600 Frenchmen and 400 Belgians), occurred in October 1943 and revealed that three of the detachments (Ehrenforst, Hugoslust, and Heydebreck) were in good shape. Only in Blechhammer were there reports of abuses and insufficient food.[93] An ICRC inspection in January 1944 pointed out that some of the work detachments near Graudenz were now also in good condition. Only the work detachment in Thorn-Süd still had insufficient rations and harsh guards. The Königsdorf work detachment even received high praise, expect for air raid protection, which was largely non-existent despite the fact that the detachment was working on an airfield, which had been bombed in October 1943 (the POWs were just asked to disperse into the fields during air raids). According to the inspectors, however, the POWs had displayed exemplary behavior and put out many fires in their own quarters and beyond. The bombing had created a bond of solidarity between the guard staff and the POWs.

[90] Rapport du Lt. med. Van Doornick, April 14–15, 1943, in Musée Royal de l'Armée et d'Histoire Militaire, Evere, dossier captivité, #12, 32, and Lilienthal (German Foreign Office) to Scapini Mission, March 31, 1943, in AN, F9, 2721 (indicating that the High Command would soon allow the delivery of aid parcels under certain conditions). Start of deliveries: SDPG, Délégation de Berlin, to SDPG Paris, May 31, 1943, and Codechèvre to Maurice Vila, June 12, 1943, both in AN, F9, 2336.
[91] Inspection of Graudenz and work detachments, April 17, 1943, by Dr. Bubb and E. Mayer (ICRC), in AN, F9, 2721.
[92] Inspection report of Graudenz and work detachments, May 19, 1943, and various notes of Brucker to the Foreign Office, June 22, 1943, all in AN, F9, 2721.
[93] "Visite des camps disciplinaires de Heydebreck," October 5, 1943, in AN, F9, 2715.

The commander of the detachment was committed to doing his best for the prisoners. Overall, the ICRC drew an encouraging conclusion:

One can no longer consider the passage of a prisoner through Graudenz to be a dangerous period for his health. ... The German authorities have visibly alleviated the penal regime in Graudenz, taking into consideration that they are not dealing with criminals but rather with prisoners of war who, for the most part, have committed a violation of the rules, mostly by consorting with German women or girls.

The delivery of aid parcels from the French and Belgian POW agencies as well as the ICRC had led to a massive improvement of the health of the prisoners. Those prisoners who had lost weight had regained it. Discipline continued to be very strict, but the behavior of the guards now was by and large correct and not randomly abusive.[94]

The Scapini Mission, which inspected the Graudenz complex again in February 1944, concurred. Although the German authorities remained unwilling to distribute the full content of packages to individual prisoners because it contradicted the rules for German convicts, they allowed them to take a part of the content while putting the rest at the disposal of the camp kitchens. The nutrition had become adequate, and the French POWs had even been able to give some food to the Italian military internees in the prison, who were undernourished. The High Command, prompted by the Scapini Mission, had ordered to give those POWs who were performing particularly hard labor the rations that were standard for German workers. Abuses had become rare. The camp inspectors pointed out one abusive officer who had beaten up a prisoner, but Dallmer-Zerbe had apparently threatened this officer with consequences if he did not stop his behavior. Two new problems worried the Scapini Mission, however: first, there were indications that among the prisoners themselves a mafia-like gang had formed, which intimidated and starved new arrivals. The French man of confidence, Maurice Vila, seemed to be powerless to intervene, although the inspectors believed that he did not form part of the secret organization. Second, there were signs of corruption in the camp, an impression confirmed by the Belgians. Some of the German kitchen employees and some of the guards, as well as some prisoners, seem to have helped themselves to a share of the aid parcels, with the help of the French kitchen personnel. As the French inspectors noted: "Clearly, the regime in any prison is not particularly cut out to develop biblical virtues ..."

---

[94] ICRC inspection report of Graudenz and work detachments, January 26, 1944, in AN, F9, 2721.

Still, there seemed to be unanimity that the conditions had strongly improved since the arrival of the first inspection team a little more than a year earlier. The corporal punishments and the bullying guards had largely disappeared. The callous camp physician had been replaced by a more understanding colleague, and there were now two French physicians (although one of them was apparently as cold-hearted as the first German doctor).[95] An informal report mentioned that some guards continued to be abusive, hitting prisoners on the head with heavy key chains, and it confirmed the rumors about corruption in the kitchen. The report also spoke of strong tensions between some French officers and NCOs who had volunteered to work and been sentenced on the basis of a forbidden relation and those who had not worked but been sentenced because of some rebellious act. The latter considered the former to be traitors. Still, even the critical informal witness concluded: "Nonetheless, the Graudenz inmates are unanimous in recognizing that over the last year, the penal regime has completely changed thanks to the efforts of the ambassador [Scapini] and his mission. The worries of the prisoners are greatly reduced and their mood is much better as a consequence."[96]

In the spring and summer of 1944, the Scapini Mission protested against the re-trials of many French POWs who had been sentenced to prison for a relationship with a soldier's wife. These second trials occurred in Graudenz without the required notification of the protecting power, and they automatically resulted in a penitentiary sentence. The local defense attorney, a Dr. Mielke, was not up to his task, and sometimes the courts martial went ahead without any defense attorney. The Scapini Mission successfully insisted that the system of French legal advisors already in place in the Stalags be extended to Graudenz, however, and the legal advisor of Stalag XX-B in nearby Marienburg helped out during some re-trials. After the confirmation of the second court martial sentence, the convicted prisoners were transferred to a penitentiary.[97] Similar re-trials occurred against Belgian POWs involved with soldiers' wives. If there were ever any re-trials of British POWs in Graudenz for this reason is unclear, but it is unlikely because most of the British soldiers convicted of a forbidden relation were sentenced at a time when penal servitude was already the standard punishment for a relationship with a soldier's wife (1943–5). Although the Scapini Mission

---

[95] Inspection of Graudenz and work detachments, February 26, 1944, by Col. Laureux and Dr. Copreaux, and Renseignements sur Graudenz, March 20, 1944, both in AN, F9, 2721.
[96] "Renseignements sur le Camp de Graudenz," February 12, 1944, in AN, F9, 2721.
[97] For material on this problem, see "dossier Graudenz," in AN, F9, 2746.

was right in its insistence on the judicial procedures required by the Geneva Convention, it is noteworthy that the re-trials could lead to shorter sentences. A French prisoner, for example, who was sentenced to three and a half years of prison for a relationship with a soldier's wife in January 1944 was re-tried after arriving in one of the Heydebreck camps and sentenced to two years in penitentiary (which was the equivalent of only three years in prison). Moreover, the time already spent in prison was counted toward the sentence.[98]

For the Belgian POWs in the Graudenz complex, their man of confidence, Léon Nailis, launched a series of appeals for help. In February 1943, Nailis wrote to the men of confidence in all major camps with Belgian POWs and asked them for deliveries of food and clothing to Graudenz, based on the reasoning that the camps still received aid parcels for "their" prisoners who were now in the Graudenz complex. Nailis also made appeals for help to newspapers in Belgium and to the ICRC, all with success. But his activities involved him in a turf battle with the man of confidence of the nearest POW camp, Stalag XX-B in Marienburg, Robert Duchesne. Duchesne believed that Graudenz, since it was in "his" military district, should be supplied through the Marienburg camp. Nailis complained, however, that the parcels channeled through Marienburg did not all reach the prisoners in Graudenz (perhaps as a consequence of the corruption networks there). In October 1943, Nailis emphatically addressed his comrades and told them that they only had Duchesne to blame for the next famine in the Graudenz complex. He then sent a letter to Duchesne, signed by eighty-four POWs, asking him to leave Nailis in charge of organizing aid and protesting against the treatment of Graudenz as simply a sub-camp of Duchesne's Stalag. Duchesne defended himself by saying that Nailis had done great things for the inmates but that he, as a punished prisoner, could not do as much as a man of confidence from a regular camp could do. The Belgian POW authorities mediated and reconciled the two men in early 1944.[99]

Information on the British POWs in Graudenz is sparse for the first period (1942–3). From the documents relating to French and Belgian inmates, it becomes clear that the British (and a few Americans) were at first lodged separately from the other prisoners. Until 1943 there were only very few of them. When the convictions of British POWs increased,

---

[98] Case of Robert B., Feldurteil, Königsberg, January 31, 1944, and Feldurteil, Neisse, August 23, 1944, both in SHD Caen, 25 P 5424.

[99] Léon Nailis to other prisoners, October 6, 1943; Nailis and 84 prisoners to Duchesne, November 8, 1943; Duchesne to DSLP, September 26, 1943; t'Serclaes to Duchesne, February 8, 1944, all in Musée Royal de l'Armée et d'Histoire Militaire, Evere, Dossier Captivité, Boîte 1, farde 1 #8 et 9 et 10 Documents de l'homme de confiance Graudenz.

the conditions in Graudenz were already improving. Van Doornick's inspection from April 1943 suggests that the British had received aid parcels earlier than the French and Belgians and that this had triggered resentments among the other inmates. The ICRC inspection of Graudenz and its work detachments in January 1944 confirmed that the jealousy still existed because the British and Americans were always better supplied than the French and Belgians.[100] Swiss delegates charged with watching over the British and American POWs visited Graudenz on March 18, 1944. The fortress itself held 283 British and two American POWs at this time, and there were several work detachments reserved for British POWs. The delegates complained about lacking hygiene, dark and crowded rooms, and insufficient toilets in the night quarters (the prisoners had to get out twice during the night to urinate all together). The German food rations were insufficient, but the aid parcels ensured adequate nutrition for POWs in Graudenz itself but apparently not always for those in work detachments. The prisoners complained about two guards who shouted very much and provoked them, but Dallmer-Zerbe rejected all criticism, arguing that the guards had orders to treat all prisoners correctly. He refused to increase the rations for the POWs in the work detachments because he claimed that they were already above the level typical for German reserve troops. The inspector criticized the treatment of one British air force officer whose mail the commander had withheld because the officer had allegedly made critical remarks in his letters. The inspector demanded that the mail be delivered to the prisoner, and the commander complied.[101]

An ICRC inspector visiting the British and American POWs in Graudenz on October 17, 1944, recognized improvements but also pointed out severe abuses against some inmates. A British officer (the same one whose mail had been withheld in March 1944) had been shot and killed in his cell after an attempted escape on July 4, 1944. Dallmer-Zerbe claimed that the officer had reached for a weapon, but this seemed to be a flimsy excuse. According to an unconfirmed postwar report by Belgian POW Robert Vanparys, a German NCO named Oestrich shot the British officer into the belly without provocation and left him bleeding to death for three hours. According to Vanparys, Dallmer-Zerbe was mad at Oestrich because he believed that it was his fault that the officer had escaped. Dallmer-Zerbe then allegedly asked Oestrich to make things

---

[100] ICRC inspection report of Graudenz and work detachments, January 26, 1944, in AN, F9, 2721.
[101] Inspection Graudenz, by Walter Braun, March 18, 1944, in BAR Bern, Bestand Vertretung Berlin, 80a.

"right" again after the recapture of the officer.[102] Vanparys probably heard this version of the story from British POWs with whom he was evacuated from Graudenz in 1945, but this British officer had already been identified in the first inspection report as very nervous and perhaps mentally ill after a trauma suffered during the crash of his plane. In April 1944, the Swiss inspector had suggested to Dallmer-Zerbe that he needed psychiatric care, but Dallmer-Zerbe and the camp physician had countered that the officer was just a neurasthenic and needed no treatment. In another case, a guard had fired a shot at a prisoner who wanted to complain in the commander's office, shattering his knee. Dallmer-Zerbe explained that the POW was running toward the roof where he could have taken a hook and injured the guard. The inspector strongly protested against these abuses. The conclusion of the inspection of October 1944 for British and American POWs called the material conditions "quite good" but contrasted the callous regime in the fortress itself with the much better situation in the work detachments: "The Prison commandant as well as the German physician do not show any interest in the prisoners. The prisoners who have been sent on working detachments are far better off and receive more humanly treatment."[103]

On January 21, 1945, Dallmer-Zerbe received orders to evacuate the prison complex and lead the POWs to the west and south. A column of 1,200 Graudenz prisoners from several nations left in late January under the leadership of Dallmer-Zerbe. Exhausted prisoners stayed behind in barns and villages, and some deliberately went into hiding to wait for the arrival of the Red Army. After a trek of more than 1,100 kilometers (with many detours), all the way to southern Bavaria, only four hundred prisoners were left. On April 23, Dallmer-Zerbe abandoned them in a village not far from Memmingen and continued walking toward the Alps. Seventy of these POWs were briefly interned in the nearby POW camp of Memmingen, and most others seem to have walked on toward Switzerland. Food was extremely scarce. Louis Fontaine, a French officer who participated in the march, told Hans K. Frey, the Swiss delegate who tried to track down the Graudenz POWs in May 1945, that the prisoners once had no food for nine days. They did have some rest days in the POW camp of Hammerstein (Pomerania) early on and in Ansbach in Bavaria later, and they seem to have been transported by rail for a section

[102] Robert Vanparys to Ministre des affaires étrangères, September 30, 1945, in CEGESOMA, AA 120/C/64.
[103] Inspection report on Graudenz, by Albert Kadler, October 17, 1944, in BAR Bern, Bestand Vertretung Berlin, 72a (for the British government) and 80a (for the American government).

of the trip.[104] According to the Graudenz translator Victor Hanewald, groups of SS officers searching for German stragglers and lost POWs likely killed some prisoners. Hanewald, who participated in the trek, argues that conditions became better toward the end because the POWs were able to get some food from farmers.[105]

Belgian POW Robert Vanparys was in a different column of 2,500 Frenchman, one hundred Belgians, and seventy-eight British POWs commanded by the notorious Captain Heuer, who threatened to shoot POWs who could not keep up. They had to march through deep snow in extreme cold, and one prisoner had to walk on with frozen feet. Vanparys claims that seventeen prisoners were shot during the march, although he does not disclose whether Heuer or the SS groups mentioned by Hanewald were responsible. He confirms that many prisoners took advantage of a shortage of guards to hide and leave the column quietly. The prisoners did get rail transport for a part of the trip to POW camp Hammerstein, but they had to spend twenty-seven hours in open cattle cars. Vanparys later heard that another column of Belgian and British prisoners under the leadership of a Colonel Daehnik was led astray by Polish villagers who gave them wrong directions. In this group, a German NCO named Fuchs beat the slow prisoners with his rifle butt. The New Zealander Webb apparently walked up to Daehnik and told him that the prisoners would kill Fuchs if he did not stop, prompting him to rein in the brutal guard.[106]

The evacuation of the Graudenz prisoners happened under similar circumstances as the evacuation of other POWs from the eastern regions of the Reich. Georges Smets also experienced it. He recorded meeting a group of Belgian POWs coming from Graudenz. They complained that their own man of confidence (Smets mentions no name) had abandoned them, taking with him a large amount of badly needed supplies. Smets noted that prisoners of different nations mixed with each other and that the convicts blended in with the regular POWs. There were starving Soviet POWs, and the guards shot many of them when they were trying to get some milk from civilians. The Americans were well supplied and aroused the anger and contempt of other prisoners because they spread their dried milk powder on the roads and had difficulties keeping up even though they had the best shoes. They stopped from time to time to heat

[104] Report of Lt.-Col. Louis Fontaine, in BAR Bern, Bestand Vertretung Berlin, 72a.
[105] Victor Hanewald, "Bericht über meine Tätigkeit und Erfahrungen als Dolmetscher im Wehrmachtsgefängnis Graudenz," in CEGESOMA, AA 120/C/64.
[106] Robert Vanparys to Belgian minister in Moscow, July 21, 1945, and Vanparys to Ministre des affaires étrangères, September 30, 1945, both in CEGESOMA, AA 120/C/64.

Nescafé in the farmhouses, to the great joy of the farmwomen with whom they shared a cup. The German guards, who appeared constantly hungry and nervous, were standing by.[107]

The western POWs liberated by the Soviet army often experienced additional hardship and danger. Although I have not found an account of a Graudenz prisoner who fell into Soviet hands, testimonies clearly suggest that some did. Accounts of POWs from the eastern regions of the Reich indicate that especially French and Belgian POWs were often treated harshly because they were considered to be collaborators or because the Soviets thought that they were Germans hiding in foreign uniforms. Some French and Belgian POWs were shot.[108] The Belgian POW Louis Flament remembered a very unfriendly reception when he was liberated by the Soviets who suspected the Belgians were Germans. Flament and his comrades had to put on uniforms of killed German soldiers. He remembers that his uniform pants had a huge dried blood spot on the inside. As they were marched to the rear, they were grouped together with German POWs. They walked by civilians flattened by tanks. Repatriation took many months.[109]

The archival record, combining official inspection reports and informal sources, strongly suggests that the conditions in the Graudenz complex were very hard in 1942 and early 1943 for the French and Belgian POWs and possibly also for the first British prisoners arriving there. Yet, it also shows that the situation improved in the spring of 1943, as the German High Command authorized aid parcels and allowed regular inspections of the fortress and the various work detachments and branch camps. Discipline remained strict, and not all problems were resolved. Some abusive officers stayed at their post until the end, and escaping POWs or POWs recaptured after an escape were occasionally mistreated and killed. Living conditions of the POWs deteriorated again late in 1944, as supplies in Germany became tighter due to bombings, shortages, and disrupted transportation. Aid parcels failed to arrive in Graudenz in late 1944. But this problem affected all POWs, not only those sentenced to military prison. Undoubtedly, the French and Belgian

---

[107] Smets to Mr. Georges Paulus, January 11, 1976, in Musée Royal de l'Armée et d'Histoire Militaire, Brussels, Fonds Hautecler, Farde 34. For more detail on evacuation marches from the region of Graudenz, see Nichol and Rennell, *The Last Escape*, 174–80. The observation of Americans wasting their own plentiful supplies is not uncommon in the memoirs of other POWs. See, for example, Ambrière, *Les grandes Vacances*, 371.

[108] Durand, *Prisonniers de Guerre*, 276–7.

[109] Louis Flament, "Du conscrit à la captivité russe: rapport, juillet 1934–décembre 1945," in CEGESOMA, AB 1582.

inmates suffered much hardship in the first year after Graudenz became the default military prison complex for POWs, and some other inmates (for example Italians) suffered also in the later period. But the POWs had certain rights, and once their protecting agencies insisted on them, they received services and parcels. Their experience was from then on very different from the experience of German military convicts. Comparing Graudenz and its work detachments to a concentration camp is therefore misleading.

Little information is available about POWs in other military prisons and in the penitentiaries. Some British POWs came to Torgau-Fort Zinna and were treated well. The ICRC inspected the prison in October 1944 and found that the man of confidence of a nearby Stalag was visiting them frequently and supplying them with food.[110] Working for the interests of British and American POWs, Swiss legal expert Hans K. Frey worried about the lack of information about POWs in a penitentiary and the curtailment of correspondence and aid parcels, even though relatively few British and American POWs did receive penitentiary sentences (thirty-two British POWs in my sample, and only one American).[111] Yet, a moderately positive picture comes from a Swiss inspection report of the Wartenburg penitentiary in East Prussia, where some British POWs were held. They were well nourished and had actually gained weight since their arrival, but there were problems with shouting, door-slamming guards, and the inmates complained about hard work and mail restrictions.[112]

A French witness, Charles Kalfayan, experienced several penitentiaries: Bromberg, Wartenburg, where he spent most of his sentence, Brandenburg-Görden, and Hamburg-Fuhlsbüttel. From Wartenburg, he was sent to work on fortifications for the Wehrmacht in Riga. Kalfayan described long work hours; the food was scarce given the hard work, but not grossly insufficient. The discipline was not strict, and he mentioned no abuses. Medical care was inadequate largely because of the lack of medication. The prisoners received pay of fifteen to forty Pfennig (cents) a day, which was higher than the pay for the POWs working in military prisons (ten Pfennig a day). The ICRC visited the penitentiaries a few times and made some suggestions for improvement, but they were ignored.[113] Altogether, the conditions in penitentiaries that Kalfayan

[110] Inspection Torgau-Fort Zinna, October 6, 1944, Gabriel Naville, in BAR Bern, Bestand Vertretung Berlin, 80a.
[111] Frey, *Die disziplinarische und gerichtliche Bestrafung*, 136–40.
[112] Inspection Wartenburg penitentiary, June 22, 1944, Gabriel Naville, in BAR Bern, Bestand Vertretung Berlin, 80a.
[113] "Renseignements Concernant le Regime des Zuchthaus," in AN, F9, 3576.

described appear comparable to the conditions in Graudenz after the improvements.

Worried about the lack of communication with POWs in penitentiaries, the Scapini Mission made access to them a high priority in 1944. They knew that French POWs were in Brandenburg-Görden, Luckau, and Amberg, but they lacked precise information, as Scapini complained to the High Command on March 20, 1944. In accordance with the Geneva Convention, he asked for a list of POWs in penitentiaries, permission to send aid parcels to them, inspections, and more generous rules for correspondence.[114] At a meeting with High Command representatives in Paris on June 2, 1944, Scapini reiterated his demands. The German officials at first made the usual point that POWs were treated the same way as German military convicts but then agreed to implement some changes. Henceforth, the directors of penitentiaries should inform the Scapini Mission of French POWs in their institutions. The POWs should also receive mail, and the High Command agreed to consider a concentration of all French penitentiary inmates in one institution, so as to facilitate correspondence and inspections.[115] At the end of 1944, the German High Command did begin to concentrate the French POWs sentenced to penal servitude in Brandenburg-Görden. But the chaotic state of transportation and communication in the last months of the Third Reich slowed the transfers. Before all French POWs with penitentiary sentences had arrived, Brandenburg-Görden had to begin evacuations because of the Soviet advance. At the end of March 1945, the director told the French POW agencies that only seventy-seven French POWs with penitentiary sentences remained in Brandenburg. Large groups had been sent southwest to Untermaßfeld and Arnstadt in Thuringia.[116]

Even though penitentiary was supposed to be a harsher form of punishment than prison, it appears that for POWs the penitentiary experience was perhaps better, and certainly no worse, than Graudenz. Many aspects of the German penal regime that the POWs experienced, be it in penitentiaries or in Wehrmacht prisons, reflected the general "fare" of the Nazi prison system even if it contradicted the official rulebooks: physical abuses, detention in dark cells, exposure to cold, hard labor, and low food rations.[117] These practices contradicted the Geneva Convention, but it has to be said that the German authorities did make

---

[114] "Notes remises le 20 mars 1944," in AN, F9, 2176.
[115] "Proces-verbal de la réunion du 2 juin 1944," in AN, F9, 2177.
[116] "Prisonniers punis de Zuchthaus," March 29, 1945, in AN, F9, 2731.
[117] Wachsmann, *Hitler's Prisons*, 87–8, 90–1.

significant improvements. As in many other areas, the Scapini Mission was the trailblazer in negotiations leading to German concessions. The other prisoners benefited from them, although it seems that the British and American POWs in the Graudenz complex were treated better from the start.

The Fallout for the Prisoner of War Families

Unlike the trials against the women, the courts martial against the prisoners had no publicity. The POWs were not shamed by posters and newspaper articles that mentioned their names and provided details about their actions. The POW authorities usually told their families only that the POW had been convicted for disobedience, that he would be sent to a military prison where his correspondence would be restricted and where he would not be able to receive individual packages. Many married prisoners did not tell their wives the real reason for the conviction, and some lied. The Scapini Mission tried to make sure the information did not leak out.

Whether the families suspected something is hard to say. The French POW agencies did receive quite a few letters from POW wives who were alarmed about the transfer of their husbands but did not seem to suspect the real reason for the conviction. One wife of an NCO expressed a touching concern for the well-being of her husband and worried greatly about him being in a military prison without her packages. She had not received a letter from him in six months. She obviously was not aware of the reason for the conviction.[118] Another wife told the Scapini Mission that she struggled to understand why her husband had been sentenced for "disobedience," stating that he had never been a rebellious person. When the Scapini Mission replied that the conviction had happened in accordance with the rules, she asked the town mayor to inquire about the matter. The Scapini Mission told the mayor the truth but asked him to keep it secret.[119]

Some prisoners lied to their wives. Joseph Chapellier, for example, wrote his wife that he had been transferred to a disciplinary company in Graudenz for having conducted anti-German propaganda. His wife was quite upset and asked the Scapini Mission to intervene. She suspected

[118] Madame C. to Ambassador Scapini, October 15, 1942, and Scapini to Madame C., November 16, 1942, both in AN, F9, 2407, dossier 1781.
[119] Mme G. to Scapini, March 1, 1943, Desbons to Mme G., March 23, 1943, Maire de Pavillons-sous-Bois to Scapini, March 25, 1943, Desbons to Maire, April 15, 1943, all in AN, F9, 2185.

that her husband had been sentenced on trumped-up charges because he had never been a politically interested person. She also believed that disciplinary companies were forbidden. The Scapini Mission knew the truth. Its officials tried to find a way to reassure the wife that all was in order without divulging the real reason for the conviction.[120]

Sometimes, however, POW families asked the German Red Cross about the transfer and new address of a prisoner, and answers from the German Red Cross usually contained information on the reason for the conviction. The wife of Lucien Balladur, for example, learned the truth through this channel. She gracefully asked the Scapini Mission about her husband's well-being, apparently having forgiven him.[121] Some wives were clearly aware of the truth, perhaps through a confession from the husband. In these cases, the Scapini Mission usually reassured the wife that the conviction of her husband would expire at the end of the war.

Admitting the real cause for thousands of sentences would not only have angered thousands of POWs, it would also have undermined an important legitimating factor for the Vichy regime. The social policy of Vichy France stigmatized and sought to punish the unfaithful prisoner wife, while Vichy propaganda mythologized the prisoner as the sacrificial lamb of a hedonistic prewar France who would redeem his country through his suffering. This notion of course assumed that the POW would be abstinent. That so many French POWs engaged in amorous relations in Nazi Germany challenged the foundations of this myth.[122] The degree to which the convictions of POWs for forbidden relations became known to the families of Belgian and British POWs is unclear. Silence and cover-up are most likely, given that the topic has received so little attention even in the scholarly literature after the war.

[120] Mme Ch. to Scapini, July 10, 1943, and Mr. Bouffanais to Philippe Comte, both in AN, F9, 2185.
[121] Délégué en France de la Croix Rouge allemande to Mme B., November 23, 1943, in AN, F9, 2185.
[122] Fishman, *We Will Wait*, 131–4.

7 Case Studies

The Wife of a Jew

In the summer of 1941, Josefine Rosenfeld went to the village Kalten-brunn in northern Austria (northwest of Vienna) together with her friend Hildegard Jirik for *Sommerfrische* (summer holidays in the countryside). Rosenfeld, née Schlager, was born in Vienna in 1914 and had met Albert Rosenfeld in 1931. Four years later they got married. Her husband owned a taxi company in Vienna. In March 1938, following the annex-ation of Austria, her husband lost his business, which was "Aryanized" (stolen) as Jewish property. In June 1938, he was arrested and sent to Dachau concentration camp for undisclosed reasons. In October 1939 he had to emigrate to an unknown place. Josefine Rosenfeld had last heard from her husband in the spring of 1941, but she did not know where he was. After the arrest of her husband, Josefine Rosenfeld lived with her father, a bakery assistant in Vienna, who provided for her. She did not have a job.[1]

In Kaltenbrunn, the two women stayed on a private farm but had lunch in a restaurant. Rosenfeld signed the official papers (one needed to sign a confirmation of residence for the local authorities) with her maiden name (Schlager) because she was afraid of being taken for a Jew if she used her married name. During lunch, she and her friend met rifleman Weber, who was in charge of the local POW work detachment, and some other guards. They ate together daily and engaged in pleasant conversation. They flirted. One day, during a stroll in the countryside, Rosenfeld noticed a POW on an ox cart. The POW gave her a "sharp look," as she said. She looked at him, too. She felt a strong spontaneous attraction to the prisoner.

During one of the lunches with the guards, the topic of conversation turned to the prisoners. Weber noticed that Frau Rosenfeld was inter-ested in them and proposed that she accompany him in the evening when

---

[1] Her file is in WStLA, Sondergericht, vol. 8259; the POW's file is in PAAA, R 40912.

he picked up the prisoners from the surrounding farms. She agreed, and, to her delight, she met the prisoner from the ox cart again. They began to talk, and Weber left them alone while he went to gather some more prisoners from other farms. The prisoner told her in broken German that he was twenty-eight and a peasant from a village forty kilometers outside of Paris. His name was Maurice Lafarge. When Frau Rosenfeld accompanied Weber on his tour on the next day, she tried to talk to Lafarge again, but Weber, who had noticed the earlier conversation, told her: "Girlie [*Mäderl*], it is not allowed to speak with the prisoners!" But another prisoner secretly gave her a note from Lafarge: "Madame – please. Want to speak to me. The Sunday I free 9 o'clock morning. I should Wait for you street of Schafberg [a neighboring village]. Please would you answer. Best wishes. Thanks and beautiful see you again." Frau Rosenfeld answered Lafarge, telling him that a meeting would be too dangerous. But then she felt bad and wrote him another note saying that she would meet him. She managed to slip both notes to him in secret.

On Sunday, July 27, 1941, Frau Rosenfeld met Lafarge on the road to Schafberg. They walked together and began kissing. After a while, they both sat down in the grass and kissed more intensely. Lafarge asked if she was ready for sexual intercourse. She answered yes. They lay down. He practiced early withdrawal. She became very afraid of discovery, and the prisoner started to cry. Two weeks later, they met again, and they had two more reunions on the following Sundays. They had sex every time. On August 24, they exchanged photos because Frau Rosenfeld had to return to Vienna the next day. On the back of the photo that she took of Lafarge, she wrote: "My great yearning. Big love, big suffering. My poor Maurice. Your Finni [Josefine] loves you so much, loves you infinitely."

To the farmwoman with whom Frau Rosenfeld stayed, she said that she would return alone in a few weeks to help out during the poppy harvest. Indeed, on September 5, Frau Rosenfeld returned to Kalten-brunn, this time without her friend. She had another secret reunion with Lafarge on Sunday, September 7. She could not meet him again on the following Sundays because she was busy with the poppy harvest, but she managed to speak to him on Friday, September 26, in front of the POW camp, and arrange for a meeting the following day.

During her second visit, Frau Rosenfeld continued to be close to the guards. Rifleman Weber, with whom she had flirted (and perhaps been more intimate), had been sent to a different location, but he still wrote her letters. A current guard, Kellner, was also in love with her. They kissed, but when Kellner wanted to have sex with her in a barn, she refused. Kellner expressed jealousy against Weber. He was married but wanted to get a divorce and marry Frau Rosenfeld.

When Frau Rosenfeld met Lafarge on September 27, a guard surprised and arrested them. The files do not note whether it was Kellner or, if it was a different guard, whether Kellner had sent him. But the previous five meetings with Lafarge and her frequent contacts with prisoners had not gone unnoticed. Somebody had denounced her to the police, saying that she had been repeatedly observed in the presence of POWs. It is therefore possible that the police alerted the guards. The guard who surprised her allowed her to go to her room and pack her things while waiting for the police. When the police officers arrived, they announced that they would search her room, whereupon she grabbed a photo, tore it up, and tried to hide it in her nightstand. The police seized the photo. It was the picture she had taken of Lafarge and on the back of which she had written the love declaration for him. It rests in the Vienna state and city archives in the crumpled state in which the police seized it.

The investigation, conducted by the Gestapo in Zwettl, the next town, was simple because Frau Rosenfeld admitted everything without hesitation, as did Lafarge. But the chief prosecutor at the district court in Krems an der Donau, where she was scheduled to stand trial, was not sure how to handle forbidden relations with French POWs in light of new army regulations that allowed them greater freedoms. He therefore wrote to the Vienna prosecutor's office on October 27, 1941, asking whether relations with French POWs still had to be punished severely given that some Frenchmen were now fighting on the German side against the Soviet Union and given that the guarding of French POWs had stopped in many places, making closer contacts between them and the German population unavoidable. The prosecutor even proposed to acquit her! The prosecutor's office in Vienna, however, answered that there were no new regulations regarding relations with French POWs and that he should proceed as usual.

On November 20, 1941, Frau Rosenfeld had to stand trial before the district court in Krems an der Donau, which in this case served as a special court. After summarizing the facts, the prosecutor demanded one and a half years of penal servitude. The judge asked her whether she was divorced from her husband, and she answered that she had not wanted a divorce earlier on and that now she was forbidden to divorce him. The judge considered her regretful confession as an extenuating circumstance. In his view, she had sincerely fallen in love and lost control of herself. The fact that the guards had facilitated her contact to the POW also helped her; for example, the judge did not punish her for taking the picture of Lafarge (even though it was forbidden to take photos of prisoners) because a guard had apparently told her that it was permitted. Frau Rosenfeld was sentenced to fifteen months of penal servitude, a mild punishment for this time period. On January 16, 1942, she was transferred to the women's penitentiary Aichach in Bavaria. She did not have to pay the court costs because she had no financial resources. Her trial documents were sent to the court martial of the 187th Infantry Division in Linz for Lafarge's trial. Lafarge had meanwhile been taken to the disciplinary barrack of the POW camp in Krems-Gneixendorf.

The court martial met on February 27, 1942, and sentenced Lafarge to two years in prison. This was also a relatively mild punishment. Apparently Frau Rosenfeld had made a witness statement for the court martial and testified that she had been the driving force (it is unclear whether she wrote this statement or testified in person. Given that Lafarge admitted everything, her presence may not have been deemed necessary). Lafarge said that he liked her very much and had stood under great sexual pressure. The court martial counted these factors as extenuating circumstances, together with his frank confession. His time in the disciplinary barracks of the POW camp counted as pre-trial custody toward the sentence. On April 28, 1942, Lafarge was sent to Graudenz, which had just become the default site for convicted POWs. He experienced the prison during its harshest phase until he was transferred in a transport of 972 sentenced POWs to one of the Heydebreck camps in Upper Silesia a year later. He survived the war in good health, although a medical examination in May 1945 stated that he had bad teeth, perhaps as a result of malnutrition during his captivity in Graudenz.[2]

Frau Rosenfeld submitted a clemency plea on April 19, 1942, pointing out that her incarceration had caused enormous grief to her father (her mother had died during the flu pandemic in 1918). She repeated her sincere regret. The director of the Aichach penitentiary pointed out that she was diligent, modest, obedient, and a good worker, but he rejected her clemency plea because he argued that she had persistently sought the contact to the POW. In July 1942, she submitted another clemency plea, offering to work in agriculture as a volunteer, pointing to her experience with the poppy harvest in Kaltenbrunn. She also described her isolation and loneliness after the enforced separation from her husband. After a long period of abstinence, she explained that she had fallen prey to her passions. The director rejected the plea again. She was set free only on December 27, 1942, having served her sentence to the very last day. During her pre-trial custody, in October 1941, she learned that her

---

[2] Personnel file, SHD Caen, including lists 22 P 671 and 22 P 520 and 703.

husband had been deported to the Soviet Union. According to the Yad Vashem database of Holocaust victims, he was murdered immediately after his deportation. On August 12, 1949, she requested that her sentence be deleted from the penal registry, with success. She was married again at this time.

The connection to the guards had encouraged Frau Rosenfeld and probably given her a false sense of security. But, as the denunciation revealed, it was dangerous for a stranger in the village to be seen with POWs. Still, the behavior of the guards was remarkably lax. Weber, the first detachment commander, might have looked for a way to impress Frau Rosenfeld and therefore invited her to accompany him on his evening tour gathering the POWs. He even left her alone with Lafarge the first evening while he was getting some prisoners from other farms. Kellner, especially in light of his jealousy, also must have noted that she was suspiciously close to the prisoner. It is hard not to feel compassion for her, with her husband forcefully taken from her side in 1938, after his business had been stolen. Lafarge, who was married himself but without children, comes across as a sensitive man, very homesick and frustrated by the seemingly indefinite captivity. Lafarge's relationship with Rosenfeld mixes the need for emotional comfort and erotic attraction (she obviously was attractive to the guards, too), and perhaps more. The secrecy of the meetings and the constant fear of discovery made it difficult for the couple to explore further options.

The Mother of a Prisoner of War

During the night of September 8–9, 1942, Belgian POWs Joseph Hubert and Raoul Bodart escaped from their POW camp in Mechtal (Upper Silesia) through a crack in the fence. The commander of the work detachment, however, noticed that they were missing and intercepted them when they returned to the camp in the early morning. Hubert immediately confessed that he and Bodart had visited two women. He stated that it was his second visit and that the woman (Maria) had seduced him after following him for several days. Bodart had accompanied him only during the second visit and had apparently not had sex with the other woman (Ruth). The prisoners were carrying photos of the two women. The commander seized them, and they are preserved in the Polish state archives in Katowice. Hubert was born in 1913, Bodart in 1912. Both were married and had three children. They were miners from the Belgian coal belt and now worked in a local coalmine.

On the basis of Hubert's confession and the photos, the police quickly identified the women: Maria Czuba (née Trost) and Ruth Czuba. They lived together in an apartment in Mechtal, a small town in a region where many people had mixed Polish and German ancestry. Mechtal had ended up just on the German side of the prewar German–Polish border determined by a popular vote in 1921, and both Maria and Ruth had German citizenship. Maria Czuba was a widow, mother of five children aged from one to twenty-one. She was born in 1902. She had four children from her husband Wilhelm and one child born out of wedlock in 1941. She had abandoned that child to an orphanage in nearby Gleiwitz. Her husband, who died in Danzig in January 1940, had apparently been a violent and abusive alcoholic and addicted gambler. The cause of his death remained vague; according to one source, it was due to heavy drinking, according to another one, it was suicide. He was at that time separated from his wife. Ruth (born 1919) was Maria's sister-in-law. She had worked as a conductor for the German state railroad (*Reichsbahn*) in Kattowitz but had recently been dismissed because she had neglected her duties. Maria's oldest son, Helmuth, had volunteered for the German navy at age seventeen and served on a submarine. In May 1941, his boat was lost at sea and Maria was told that her son had been killed. A couple of months later, however, she heard that he had survived and was a POW in Canada. Through the mediation of the Red Cross, she occasionally sent him parcels with homemade gingerbread and other goods.[3]

According to Hubert, Maria Czuba one day waited for him when he was leaving the coalmine and grabbed him by the arm, calling him by his first name. She did not tell him how she knew his name, but she invited him to visit her. The next day, he followed her to her apartment after work. She asked him to come in and showed him photos of her oldest son, the POW, and gave him the photo of herself. She also asked him whether he was treated well in captivity. Hubert answered yes. She told him that she had a soft spot for the Belgians in her heart. Hubert claimed that he got bored after a while and left for the camp, where he arrived after midnight. Over the next days, Maria Czuba always waved to him when he was passing under her window to and from work. On September 8, she talked to him again as he was leaving work in the afternoon, asking him to visit her at 11 PM and encouraging him to bring his comrade Bodart, who was walking with him. She said that she would have another woman for Bodart. Hubert and Bodart agreed to visit her if they could leave the camp, which they managed to do.

[3] For file of the two women, see Archiwum Państwowe w Katowicach (Poland), Sondergericht, 494. The prisoners' file is in CEGESOMA, AA 244, Archives de la Commission d'Histoire de la Captivité de Guerre de 1940–1945.

According to the prisoners, Maria Czuba welcomed them in her apartment that night and served them beer. Bodart stayed in the kitchen with Ruth Czuba, but apparently they mostly talked and looked out the window – although later she claimed that they had kissed and that he had touched her genitals against her wish. Bodart's interrogation proved to be very difficult because the translator was inept and because Bodart, unlike Hubert, spoke practically no German. Bodart admitted that Ruth Czuba gave him her photo. While he talked with Ruth, Maria began kissing and caressing Hubert. They withdrew into her bedroom. She undressed and invited him into her bed. They had sex. He practiced early withdrawal. Around 2:45, the prisoners left the apartment.

In her own interrogation by the police in Mechtal, Maria Czuba presented a different story. She claimed that she had met Hubert for the first time several months earlier in a forest, where he was listening to music from a radio with some comrades. She noticed a woman in a group of civilians passing by the POWs spitting and exclaiming *"Pfui, Schweine!"* to the POWs. She then started talking to Hubert, who asked her whether she also thought that POWs were pigs, but Czuba told him that she respected every honest soldier regardless of nationality. She complimented him on his good German. Initially, Maria Czuba denied any intimate relationship with Hubert. She only admitted having given him her photo, allegedly during a chance encounter on a walk. She also claimed not to know that contact with Belgian POWs was forbidden. But gradually, she admitted that he had visited her in her apartment, although she denied having invited and kissed him. Then she also admitted having had sex during the second meeting, although she did not agree with the details Hubert had described, namely that she had invited the POWs, pulled Hubert into her bed and undressed in front of him. She claimed that he had promised to marry her after the war and that she loved him. The police in Mechtal stated that her reputation in the village was bad because men sometimes visited her at night.

During the interrogation of Ruth Czuba, it came out that she had been present for two meetings with the two POWs, not only one. The police in Beuthen, where Maria Czuba had meanwhile been transferred, therefore interrogated Maria again. They believed that their colleagues in Mechtal had done a poor job during the first interrogation. This time, confronted with Ruth's statements, Maria admitted that Hubert had visited her a total of three times, and that they had had sex on two occasions. She claimed that he told her he was Flemish and owned a mine, that he was divorced and had only one child, and that he was serious about marrying her after the war. He would even stay in Germany to that end.

Maria was becoming increasingly anxious during this interrogation, pleading with the officer not to punish her because she had three young children under her care, had had a terrible marriage, and had been abandoned pregnant by a ruthless man after the death of her husband. She repeated that she had had absolutely no idea that relationships with Belgians were forbidden. She pointed out that the Belgians marched to the mine without any guard and that they saluted townspeople with "Heil Hitler." She had not perceived them to be enemies. Hubert, she said, had been immensely kind to her. She also repeated her concerns about her son, who was himself a POW. She hoped that nobody yelled "pigs" at him and his comrades, and she wished that he had somebody caring for him.

On September 17, Maria sent a petition to the prosecutor's office, asking to be released until the trial. She was terribly worried about her children (her thirteen-year-old daughter had a heart disease), and she herself was still suffering from the effects of an abdominal surgery from 1941 and also had a sick heart. She repeated that she deeply regretted her act but that she was driven by concerns for her son in Canadian captivity. "I can only assure you that I will never do something that is not becoming to the dignity of a German woman. ... Have pity on an unhappy, desperate mother!" On September 21, Ruth Czuba also asked for a release until the trial because her brother was on home leave from the eastern front. She emphasized that she was not aware of having committed a crime. The repeated requests of both women received no answer from the authorities. They had to remain in prison.

On September 26, Maria sent the prosecutor's office some letters from her husband to demonstrate that he was a drunkard who regularly lost his job and who made debts everywhere, leading to the blackening of her own reputation. She again begged for a release, telling the prosecutor that she had never done anything criminal and that she would never have believed that she could end up behind bars for consorting with a Belgian man. She implored the court to let her go and send packages to her son in captivity. She explained that it was only her good heart that had made her willing to do Hubert a favor and have sex with him. He had allegedly begged her for it. Maria repeated her requests many times, beseeching the authorities to let her go to her children. She even argued that the *Führer*, with his interest in the future of Germany, would let her go and care for her children because they were the future of Germany. Yet, the prosecutor remained implacable, and everything indicates that she had to remain in the prison of Beuthen.

From the prison, Maria wrote her children, initially replying to letters from them. She worried about every detail, from getting winter shoes for the younger children to finding money to buy potatoes for them. She asked about everything that had happened in school and about the children's health. She was just horrified about being in prison, dying of longing for her children, and completely stunned that a little favor to a Belgian, who was not guarded and spoke German (according to her he spoke it perfectly; according to the police, he spoke broken German) was landing her in front of the special court and likely in a penitentiary. As she wrote in one letter: "Am I a murderer? For a little dumb, meaningless love I am being tormented so much!" Once, she even compared her fate to the fate of a Jew: "It is as if I was a Jewess and not a German mother who has given her son to the fatherland." Maria implored her children to write back and worried greatly because of long silences from them.

Maria did not know that the prison authorities seized her letters to her children because she regularly criticized their decision to keep her locked up and commented on the reasons why she had become involved with the Belgian prisoner. It was forbidden to people on pre-trial custody to write anything to the outside that pertained to the case under investigation, and the censor underlined all of her criticism of the authorities and her case-related statements with a green pen. Maria also wrote to her sister, explaining that she was not expressing her full desperation to the children because they would not be able to handle it. She begged her sister to bake gingerbread for her captive son and to send it to him. Maria also repeated her defense argument, namely that only the longing for her son in captivity had made her so receptive to the Belgian prisoner and that she had not had the slightest idea that this contact was forbidden. But to her sister, she also complained that she, as a mother of five, was being slowly killed inside the prison walls, a passage the prison censor again underlined in green and that also led to the seizure of the letter. When Maria received the act of accusation, she emphasized again that she had not tried to meet a prisoner but had felt sorry for him when she witnessed the woman spitting at the prisoners and calling them pigs. She said that her longing for her son had guided her behavior. She repeated that she had no idea that she was doing something forbidden, and she denied having invited Hubert to bring a comrade to her apartment.

On November 27, 1942, both Maria and Ruth were transferred to the prison in Kattowitz in anticipation of the trial. On December 1, meanwhile, the court martial against Hubert and Bodart took place before the military tribunal in Kattowitz. It is possible that the two women were present, although the court martial may not have seen a need for them as witnesses given that the prisoners had immediately confessed. The military judges, after studying the police files of the women, concluded that Maria Czuba had been the driving force in the entire affair, and the prisoners therefore received comparatively light sentences: two years in prison for Hubert, one year for Bodart.

It is possible that the POWs were present during the trial of the two women in front of the special court in Kattowitz on December 10, 1942, although the protocol does not mention any question for them. The judge did not believe Maria's explanation of the beginning of the relationship because Hubert had never confirmed the story of the woman spitting at the Belgians and calling them pigs. In court, Maria reiterated her earlier arguments and added that Hubert had told her that he knew somebody in Canada who could help her son. In contrast to her interrogation, Ruth Czuba stated that she and Bodart had done nothing more than talking. She claimed that he wanted to kiss her and touch her breasts and buttocks but that she did not allow it. The judge did not believe her and insisted on the more far-reaching confession she had made during the first interrogation. Moreover, Ruth's claim that she did not know that Bodart was a POW did not convince the court because both Hubert and Bodart had worn a uniform. The court also rejected the claim of both women that they did not know that contacts with POWs were forbidden. The newspapers and the radio had reported many times on forbidden relationships. In any case, since the prohibition for the German women was a law, ignorance of the law did not lead to acquittal. The judge sentenced Maria to three years of penal servitude and three years' loss of civil rights, a harsh sentence for this time. That she was eleven years older than Hubert made her appear as the seducer. Ruth was sentenced to one year in prison. The pre-trial custody counted toward the sentences because the women had confessed.

The day after the trial, Maria asked for a short leave to go home to look after her children. As a widow, she received her husband's pension and needed to make sure that the payments for the following year would arrive. Ruth also asked for a temporary release to take care of some administrative tasks for her mother, who was in psychiatric care. The court records do not note whether these requests were granted.

In the second half of January 1943, Ruth was transferred to the prison in Leobschütz (Sudetenland) and Maria to the women's penitentiary in Jauer near Liegnitz in western Silesia. Ruth was released on parole at the end of June 1943, approximately three months before the end of her sentence, following a clemency plea in which she stressed that she had two brothers serving in the Wehrmacht and that her mother was being treated for mental illness. Maria submitted a clemency plea in October 1943, but the director of the Jauer penitentiary recommended rejection because she had not even served half of her sentence yet. In October and November 1944, things began to look more hopeful for her. Her sisters submitted a clemency plea for her, and Maria herself also asked for an early release again. The director of the penitentiary in Jauer this time supported a release on parole, and on January 13, 1945, the police in Kattowitz advocated an early release for Maria as well. She had behaved well in the penitentiary and had shown intense regret for her actions from the beginning. Her concern for her children had not diminished. We learn from some of the court documents that her three minor (legitimate) children were in the care of Ruth's mother (Maria's mother-in-law) after she had been released from psychiatric care. The mother-in-law had moved into Maria's apartment, but she was apparently as addicted to alcohol and gambling as her son had been. Whether and where Maria reunited with her children is unclear. What is known is that the Soviet army, when it entered Mechtal on January 25, 1945, began massacring the civilian population, killing approximately two hundred people over three days, mostly men and teenage boys. The list of people killed does not include anybody from Maria's immediate family, however.[4]

One striking aspect of the case is the discrepancy between Hubert's and Maria Czuba's description of the relationship. Hubert's testimony portrayed her as an annoying woman who pursued and seduced him. Maria, however, described him as a wonderful person who promised her marriage and a good life after the war and who was much better to her than her deceased husband, although the bar was admittedly very low. Both claims might have been meant to help their own defense. Hubert made no effort to protect her in his interrogations and during his court martial, in contrast to many other prisoners, and he seemed oblivious to the disastrous consequences of the arrest of a mother with three minor children and without a husband. The interrogation files of Maria suggest that she became increasingly irritated when confronted with his statements. Unlike the prisoners, she had no defense attorney, and the judge, relying on local police reports about her "bad" (promiscuous) reputation, was biased against her.

It is entirely plausible that she and Ruth did not consider the Belgians as enemies. Maria once specifically alluded to the fact that Belgians were fighting as volunteers against the Soviet Union, and her sympathies for the Belgians sound heartfelt. The pervasive Nazi propaganda about the foreign POWs as implacable enemies obviously did not impress Maria and Ruth Czuba. Convinced that these prisoners were friends, not enemies, they may very well not have realized that they were doing something strictly illegal. For Maria, concern for her son, who had at

---

[4] Joachim Stopik, *Beuthen-Miechowitz/Mechtal* (Dülmen: Laumann-Verlag, 2008), 385–97, 519–22.

first been listed as dead, strengthened her empathy for the POWs. With the number of German prisoners increasing rapidly in the second half of the war, parents and relatives of captured German soldiers probably looked at the foreign POWs in their communities with growing empathy.

A Frenchman for Everybody?

On April 20, 1943, Hitler's fifty-fourth birthday, the special court in Darmstadt held a big trial against four married women. They were accused of having had forbidden relations with three French POWs and of having hidden one of the prisoners to facilitate his escape to France. The "crime site" was a house in the *Bahnhofstrasse* in Groß-Gerau, a little town between Darmstadt and Mainz, just southwest of today's Frankfurt International Airport. Three of the four women lived there, one in the front section of the house, two in the back. The fourth woman was a friend living nearby. They all worked either in the *Süddeutsche Zuckerfabrik* (south German sugar factory) or in the *Helvetia* canned goods factory in town. There was a camp with French POWs on the grounds of the sugar factory, and many prisoners worked there.[5]

On the street level of the house on *Bahnhofstrasse* was a Wehrmacht office, probably serving the administration of the local POW camp. On the second floor were some rooms occupied by soldiers, possibly guards of the POWs. A recently divorced couple was renting a three-bedroom apartment on the third floor (or second floor according to German counting), just above the rooms rented by the soldiers, in the front section of the house. The man, Alphons Krebl, was serving in the Wehrmacht and had locked all his possessions in one room, and his ex-wife had put her things into the other. They had sublet the third room and the kitchen to Anna Margarete Mühlberger with her four-year-old daughter. Mühlberger, born in 1917, had married a packer in 1938, who was now serving in the Wehrmacht. She had worked as a cleaning lady at a local school and, for a short time, in the canteen of the locomotive depot at the Darmstadt main train station. Now she was an employee of the sugar factory in Groß-Gerau. Her marriage was troubled. Her husband had tried to divorce her in 1941 because he had a relationship with another woman, but the court had rejected his divorce request because it found his reasons frivolous. While working at the sugar factory, Mühlberger noted French POW Roger Carnot. Carnot was born in 1908 and worked as a vegetable trader in Maisons-Laffitte, a suburb northwest of

[5] The file for all four women is in HStAD, Sondergericht Darmstadt, G 27, 1180 (181 pages).

Paris. He was married but had no children. Mühlberger and Carnot arranged secret meetings on the factory grounds in the fall of 1942. They exchanged love letters. She told him that she was divorced. They had sex in an empty hall of the factory one night. He told her that he found her very pretty and asked if he could visit her, but she said that she was afraid that they might be discovered by the soldiers living below her. But Mühlberger told her friend Anna Bittner about Carnot. Bittner was born in 1904. Like Mühlberger, she had worked as a cleaning lady at a local school before getting a job at the sugar factory. Bittner had married a truck driver in 1930, but they had separated, and she used her maiden name (Laut). Her husband had been serving in the Wehrmacht since 1939. They had not had contact since then, and she did not know where he was. Bittner had a seventeen-year-old son from a premarital affair, who was performing his mandatory labor service (*Reichsarbeitsdienst*). According to the police, the father of her son was a soldier from the French occupation army in the Rhineland. Bittner and her husband had been communists until 1933. They had sometimes worn party uniforms.

Bittner, who had already known Mühlberger when she was a child, encouraged her to invite Carnot to her home, and she gave her a coat belonging to her husband, so that Carnot would not be recognized on his way to Mühlberger's house. On December 7, 1942, Carnot climbed over the fence of the POW camp and met Mühlberger, who was waiting for him outside with the coat. They walked to Mühlberger's apartment, and she took him in. She gave him a big hug when he entered her apartment and said: "Finally you are here with me." During the day, she went to work and shopping. During the night, she slept with Carnot in the marital bed. Her child slept on the couch. Carnot spent his days reading and smoking.

In the back section of the house on *Bahnhofstrasse* lived two married women, Gertrud Stiehl and Marie Bäcker. Stiehl, born in 1918, was married to a sergeant stationed in France. They had a five-year-old child. She worked in the canned goods factory. Frau Bäcker was married to a toolmaker who was also serving in the Wehrmacht. They had two children (aged nine months and two and a half years). To reach their apartment, Frau Stiehl and Frau Bäcker had to go up the main staircase and turn in front of Frau Mühlberger's door. Both soon noticed something. Stiehl and Mühlberger were friends. Mühlberger had shown Frau Stiehl some of the letters from Carnot, and she introduced her to him soon after he arrived in her place. Frau Bäcker became curious and asked Frau Stiehl what was going on. Frau Stiehl finally told her that Frau Mühlberger was hiding an "amazingly beautiful" French POW. The three women began to socialize in Frau Mühlberger's apartment and to take walks with Carnot, who wore the coat from Bittner's husband and clothes from Frau Bäcker's husband as camouflage.

After a few days, Frau Stiehl – according to Mühlberger and Carnot – hinted to Carnot that she would love to have a Frenchman for herself. Carnot said that he could arrange for a comrade to visit, and he wrote a letter to his comrade Marcel Trochu, a car mechanic from a village in the Marne valley (east of Paris). Either Mühlberger or Bittner delivered the letter during work in the sugar factory, and Trochu indeed visited not much later, sneaking out of the camp the same way Carnot had done before. He slept in Frau Stiehl's apartment and went back to the camp early in the morning. Frau Stiehl, according to the testimony of the others, sent him another letter and asked whether he would like to join them and hide in the house. He agreed to come a few days later, and he moved in with Frau Stiehl (his personnel record states that he escaped on December 21, 1942, three days before his thirty-second birthday).[6]

The women and the two POWs had to be careful for a while because Krebl, Mühlberger's landlord, returned on home leave on December 17, 1942, staying until January 2, 1943. Krebl did not notice anything; he stayed somewhere else and only occasionally visited the house on *Bahnhofstrasse* to get something from his room. Whenever he came, the two POWs hid in the apartments of Frau Stiehl and Frau Bäcker. One day, Krebl prepared an inventory of his possessions stored in his room in the presence of two witnesses. After Krebl returned to the eastern front, Mühlberger broke open the door to his room and prepared a little hiding place for the prisoners in case of surprise visits.

On December 30, 1942, Frau Mühlberger visited her aunt in northern Hessen overnight. She asked Frau Bäcker to hide Carnot during her absence, and Frau Bäcker agreed. She served him meals and allowed him to sleep in the marital bed, while she slept with her older child in another bed in the same room. When Mühlberger came back on the second night, she slipped into Frau Bäcker's marital bed with Carnot. A few days later, Mühlberger, Bäcker, and Carnot decided to go to Frankfurt for an outing. Mühlberger and Carnot took the train together and met Bäcker in a café. They then watched an operetta in the Schumann Theater, a famous music hall with attached restaurants. In order to better camouflage Carnot, Mühlberger took a shirt belonging to Krebl and gave it to Carnot. Frau Stiehl warned Mühlberger not to take the shirt because she was afraid that Krebl would notice something when he returned, but Mühlberger claimed that he had so many shirts that he

---

[6] Personnel records, SHD Caen, including lists in 22 P 559, 412, 22 P 583, 454, and 22 P 567, 915.

would not remember this one. The outing went well. Mühlberger and Carnot discussed getting married after the war. Carnot repeatedly offered to leave and escape to France because he was worried about Mühlberger having to go to prison if they were discovered, but he later explained to the police that he loved her too much to leave her behind. As he always stressed, he did not really want to escape. All he wanted was to hide until after the war and then stay in Germany and marry Frau Mühlberger, the beautiful woman he loved.

All the testimonies portray a passionate and tender relationship. Carnot told the police that they once had sex sixteen times in one afternoon. The police also asked him about "French" (or as the police also called it "perverse") sexual practices (oral sex), and he admitted that he "taught" Frau Mühlberger, who initially was not interested, the "French" way of making love. The three women living on *Bahnhofstrasse*, sometimes with Frau Bittner, spent several entertaining evenings with the two POWs. Carnot showed them folk dances from his home region, and they drank, smoked, ate, and listened to music in Mühlberger's apartment.

Meanwhile, Frau Stiehl had heard that her husband might soon return on home leave. She prepared for that eventuality by asking Frau Bäcker if she would take in Trochu during her husband's leave, which she agreed to do. The eventuality happened sooner than expected. At 5 AM on January 7, 1943, Herr Stiehl rang the doorbell, having arrived from France with a troop transport. While Frau Stiehl answered the door, Trochu, in the style of a *commedia dell'arte* character, climbed in his pajamas through the bedroom window onto a balcony and from there into Frau Bäcker's apartment. While Herr Stiehl went to bed to recover from the trip, his wife brought Trochu a pillow and blanket and provided him with breakfast and lunch at Frau Bäcker's place. With Frau Stiehl's husband at home, Trochu did not feel safe any more. Unlike Carnot, he had seriously considered escaping from Germany. He moved into Mühlberger's apartment for one night and then left for France. At Frau Stiehl's request, Frau Mühlberger provided him with bread and sausage for the trip. Frau Bäcker offered him some old civilian trousers from her husband, but Trochu refused to take them because they were too damaged. He likely helped himself to some of Krebl's clothes. Trochu made it home to his village. According to his French army personnel file, he was never recaptured.[7]

Frau Bittner had meanwhile also befriended a French POW named "Albert" in the sugar factory. She wrote him tender love letters, but

---

[7] Ibid.

because she could not write well, she dictated the letters to Frau Stiehl or Frau Mühlberger. The rumor mill had it that Bittner had met this POW secretly and had sex with him in her apartment or in the house on *Bahnhofstrasse*, but Bittner steadfastly denied this in court, and "Albert" could never be identified. According to the testimony of the other women, Frau Bittner also wrote tender letters to other prisoners, but the police did not find any of them. She sometimes slept in Frau Stiehl's apartment, but neither the other women nor Carnot claimed that she had intimate relations with Carnot or Trochu.

The discovery occurred through a mist of rumors and more or less indirect denunciations. In the front of the house, next to the Wehrmacht office, was a small store run by Karl Schaffner. Schaffner clearly knew something about the affairs in the house. One day, Georg Baillé, a neighbor of Anna Bittner, told him that he had seen Frau Stiehl visit Bittner in the presence of a French POW who he knew from the sugar factory but who was wearing civilian clothes – which was suspicious. Schaffner claimed that he urged Baillé to report the matter to the nearby Wehrmacht office, but neither Schaffner nor Baillé did anything for a while. A few weeks later, Baillé talked to the director of the sugar factory, who called in the foreman of the department in which Carnot and Trochu had worked. It turned out that the foreman knew that Trochu had been seen in Bittner's apartment after his escape but that the foreman had not done anything about this. It is possible that the director of the sugar factory, after his talk with Baillé, alerted the guards, perhaps hoping that the prisoners might be recaptured. But it is also possible that Schaffner prompted the discovery because he one day asked an officer shopping in his store whether Baillé had talked to him, and when the officer said no and inquired about the matter, Schaffner repeated what Baillé had told him. But it is obvious that none of the witnesses was in a hurry to denounce the women.[8] Baillé might have hesitated because he had an arrangement with Frau Bittner according to which his daughter could sleep in her apartment.

Baillé and Schaffner were not the only witnesses. It became clear during the investigation that Frau Mühlberger's sister and her parents knew that she was hiding a prisoner. The sister had seen Carnot during a visit, and the parents took care of Mühlberger's daughter while she was at work, and the daughter said something about a certain Roger and "Uncle Marcel" being in her mother's apartment. Her parents once confronted

[8] This hesitation to denounce, conflicting with the feeling that it was dangerous *not* to do so, was a typical phenomenon in Nazi society: Dördelmann, "Denunziationen im Nationalsozialismus," 162.

and warned Frau Mühlberger, but she told them that the Frenchmen visiting her were civilian laborers she had met while working in the canteen of the locomotive depot in Darmstadt the previous summer. There is no question that the local POW guards and employers were on high alert because of a recent spike in POW escapes (Carnot and Trochu were not the only ones). Given that Frau Bittner was writing letters to POWs, it appears that the rumor mill in the factory soon pointed to a connection between her and the disappearance of prisoners. On January 20, 1943, the police appeared at the house on *Bahnhofstrasse* and arrested the four women and Carnot.

Carnot immediately admitted everything. He testified that he found Frau Mühlberger very beautiful and was determined to marry her after the war. He did not want to escape; he just wanted to be with the woman he loved. Frau Mühlberger and Frau Bäcker also confessed, although in the case of the latter, the charges involved mostly helping to hide escaped French POWs because the court did not believe that she had had sexual contact with a prisoner. Frau Mühlberger only denied having stolen the shirt; she claimed that she had just borrowed it and wanted to return it before Krebl came back. But the fact that Carnot had been wearing it frequently and that it was found in her apartment convinced the court that she had stolen it, and this was a serious charge because she had essentially exploited the war situation (in this case the absence of a soldier drafted into the Wehrmacht) to commit a theft, which meant that she would be judged under a harsher wartime law.[9] Frau Bittner admitted having written love letters to several French POWs and having helped to hide Carnot and Trochu, but she denied ever having had sex with a POW. The court did not believe her. Frau Bittner had apparently told a witness that she had also had sex with a prisoner, but she later claimed that this was untrue. She had spent two nights in Stiehl's apartment, and the court was convinced that she had met with a prisoner during those nights, even though this third prisoner could not be identified and the other women remained tight-lipped about this matter. Frau Stiehl admitted that she had kissed Trochu but denied all intimate contact with him or other prisoners, but the fact that Carnot and Mühlberger testified that she had more or less asked for a French POW reduced her credibility in the eyes of the judge. Carnot said during interrogation that Trochu had told him that he had had sex with Frau Stiehl, up to four times per night. Trochu's dramatic escape over the balcony after Herr Stiehl's early return also spoke against her.

---

[9] Löffelsender, *Strafjustiz an der Heimatfront*, 110.

Shortly after the arrest, Krebl received a telegram, asking him to come home immediately because of the break-in into his room. He came back from the eastern front fairly quickly and found that more things were missing than the one shirt that Carnot had worn (the inventory he had made in December served as proof). The court assumed that Trochu, who had access to Krebl's room while he was hiding in Frau Mühlberger's apartment, had taken some of his things with him. In February 1943, while the women were in pre-trial custody, Frau Bäcker received the news that her husband had been killed on the eastern front. Meanwhile, the father of Frau Mühlberger visited her in prison and wrote a long letter to the court, explaining that her husband had cheated on her many times and told her that she had become old and unattractive after giving birth to their daughter. He mentioned that his daughter had become extremely addicted to smoking as a consequence. That her mother had a heart sickness and that her brother had been killed on the eastern front had helped to destabilize her.

The trial on the Führer's birthday was laden with moralistic statements. The court found it most outrageous that the four women had engaged with "enemy" prisoners and supported their escape while the German army was fighting its biggest battle, the battle of Stalingrad. As the judgment stated: "At a time when the thoughts of the entire German people are more than ever before with this war and with the soldiers, who are locked in the hardest defensive struggle, the defendants engaged in a shameless way with French prisoners of war." The judge claimed that the women had thrown away their feminine honor and light-headedly violated their duty to be loyal to their soldier husbands – conveniently ignoring that two of the husbands were demonstrably unfaithful themselves. "They [the women] therefore disgracefully betrayed and disappointed their husbands and brothers who are standing at the front and who are also fighting for them; they have also severely violated their own national dignity and engaged in a very dangerous activity for the *Volksgemeinschaft*, namely helping prisoners to escape."

In the case of Frau Mühlberger, the duration and intensity of her relationship with Carnot counted as aggravating factors, as did the fact that she had played a key role in the escape of both prisoners. The court did consider as mitigating factors, however, that her marriage was unhappy and that Carnot had promised to marry her after the war. Considering the details of their erotic relationship, the court believed that she had become sexually dependent on Carnot. The special court sentenced her to five years of penal servitude for the relationship and the help in the escapes, and additionally to fifteen months of penal servitude for the theft of the shirt, both very hard punishments. The theft fell under a draconian decree against "people's pests" (*Volksschädlinge*).[10] As was common in German law, the two sentences were amalgamated into a shorter one: five and a half years of penal servitude. Frau Stiehl's relationship with Trochu was shorter than Mühlberger's liaison with Carnot, but the court found her request for a French prisoner particularly distasteful, at a time when she already knew that her husband would be home on leave soon. She had obviously supported the escape of both prisoners. She was therefore punished the same way as Mühlberger (for the relationship), five years of penal servitude. Frau Bäcker received two years of penal servitude, a very harsh punishment given that she had not had an affair herself. Her consistent support for the affairs of the other women and her help in hiding the two escaped French prisoners, however, convinced the court to treat her transgression as a "serious case" meriting penitentiary. Frau Bittner received three and a half years of penal servitude, an outrageously harsh punishment given that the court could not prove anything beyond her letters to POWs and her encouragement to Mühlberger. Her communist past obviously influenced the court, which stated that her previous political orientation "had created in her an inner opposition to decrees of the German state." That she was significantly older than the other women also counted as an aggravating factor. According to the judge, she should have warned them immediately. As was typical, the pre-trial custody (three months) counted only for Frau Mühlberger and Frau Bäcker given that the two others denied the allegations. It seems that only Frau Stiehl had a defense attorney.

When Frau Mühlberger's husband heard of the affair, he wasted no time and filed for divorce again. This time, the court saw no reason to deny the request. Frau Stiehl's husband, now stationed on the eastern front, was much less certain about what to do. In May 1943, he asked to see the court documents. He knew that his wife had been on trial, but he did not know the precise charges and findings of the court. He hinted that he might file for divorce, but he does not seem to have done so. At least, the Stiehls were still listed as married in late 1944. Frau Bäcker was released on parole on May 1, 1944, a generous decision given that she had only served fifteen months of her two-year sentence. Frau Mühlberger (now divorced and using her maiden name Ruhland) was sent to the women's penitentiary in Hagenau (Alsace). On October 23, 1944, the director of the sugar factory in Groß-Gerau requested a temporary release for her until mid-January 1945. He urgently needed her work. But the director of the penitentiary rejected the request. A little later,

[10] Angermund, *Deutsche Richterschaft 1919–1945*, 210–13.

Frau Stiehl's mother also requested a temporary release for her daughter, who also was serving her sentence in Hagenau. The house on *Bahnhofstrasse* had been destroyed in a bombing. The mother had been injured during a separate bombing of her home town (Kaiserslautern). She requested the leave so that her daughter might visit her and see what was left of her and her husband's possessions in Groß-Gerau. The penitentiary director did grant Frau Stiehl a short leave in November 1944, but before she could leave, a general evacuation order arrived, as the front was nearing. In great haste, the director had to evacuate the penitentiary with the 275 remaining women in the night of November 22–23. During the march through the night, in total darkness because of the danger of strafing Allied planes, several women escaped, among them Frau Stiehl.

Bittner and Mühlberger, probably marching in the same group, did arrive at a penal camp in Ebersbach an der Filz (near Göppingen in Württemberg), where they had to work in an armaments factory. Mühlberger's father submitted a request for a temporary release of one year on January 25, 1945, because her mother's health was deteriorating, but it was rejected. Anna Bittner's son Heinz, who was now serving in the Wehrmacht, also submitted a clemency plea on her behalf, explaining that his fighting morale was suffering because he had nobody at home sending him packages to the eastern front. Heinz had already been wounded once but was back again at the front. The director of the Ebersbach penal camp praised Bittner lavishly as a good worker and disciplined prisoner but considered a release premature. On April 22, 1945, the American army reached Ebersbach and freed Bittner and Mühlberger.

All four women had returned to Groß-Gerau by November 1945. Their trial documents were used in early 1948 in the denazification proceedings against the judge of the special court, Dr. Paul Stimmel, who had sentenced them. A few years later, Frau Mühlberger requested a cancellation of her sentence from the penal registry. In January 1952, the court in Darmstadt cancelled the sentence for the forbidden relation and converted the sentence because of theft to three months in prison, considering it served through her pre-trial custody. The statement of the court condemned her behavior, however, finding the theft of a shirt for the POW with whom she had "a crudely adulterous relationship" rather heinous. Frau Mühlberger was listed as having two children in 1945, but there is no record of a birth in the penitentiary. Was she pregnant from Carnot?

Among other things, the case illuminates the strain on marriages during the war. Bittner and Mühlberger were separated from their husbands and more or less waiting for a divorce. Frau Stiehl cheated on her husband, who was stationed in France and perhaps also unfaithful. Frau Bäcker, as becomes clear in the court documents, had affairs with German men, which were not punishable. The landlords of Frau Mühlberger had just divorced. Given the prolonged absence of their husbands, the four women formed a community of friends, centered on the house in which three of them lived but also including Frau Bittner through her friendship particularly with Frau Mühlberger. This community was a support network. Once Frau Mühlberger and Carnot had "proven" that it was possible for a prisoner to escape and for a woman to hide him, the example appealed to the others. The widespread notion that French men were particularly attractive and excellent lovers, although not mentioned in detail in the court files, must also have played a role.

A Failed Group Escape

Around midnight in the night of June 19 to 20, 1943, two watchmen employed by the Dynamite Factory in Sankt Lambrecht in the Austrian Alps made their usual round.[11] When they passed the barrack where the women workers slept, they noticed light in one room. They thought that the women who inhabited the room were at home on vacation and therefore decided to take a look. They could not see much through the shutters. When they knocked, the two women who were supposed to be on vacation answered. The watchmen also saw a third woman and two men lying on the floor – one of them trying to hide between the beds. The two men were British POWs. Because there were three women but only two men in the room, the watchmen suspected that a third man might be hiding nearby. After some searching, they found another British POW crouching in a locker in the same building. The three POWs belonged to a work detachment employed by the factory.[12] They slept in a separate, fenced-in barrack on the factory grounds.

---

[11] Sources: Verbalnote, Foreign Office to Swiss Legation, April 22, 1944, in BAR Bern, 84a (summarizing the trial against B.; apparently his judgment was lost); Dr. Glaser to Swiss Legation, September 20, 1943, BAR 84a; Feldurteil against Charles C. and Harold H., Leoben, September 18, 1943, BAR 84a; StLA Graz, BH (Bezirkshauptmann) Murau 14, 1943, Karton 479.

[12] Given that Article 31 of the Geneva Convention outlawed the deployment of POWs "in direct connection with the operations of the war," including "the manufacture or transport of arms or munitions," one may wonder why POWs were working in a dynamite factory. Dynamite, however, could be used for civilian purposes, too, for example the building of tunnels. POWs had the right to protest against infractions of Article 31, but there is no archival record of such a protest, which suggests that the deployment was not objectionable.

The watchmen asked the women to wait while they brought the POWs back to their barrack and locked them up. The women agreed, but two of them (Gisela Pölzweiler and Erna Kirchner) said that they wanted to go outside because they needed some fresh air. While the watchmen walked the POWs back to their barrack, the two women waiting outside ran away. The third woman, Ludmilla Filipitsch, tried to catch up with them, but the watchmen captured her. While the watchmen were preoccupied with the women, the three POWs also escaped. As it turned out later, the POWs had long ago sawn off some screws belonging to the grill outside a window of their barrack, so that the grill could be removed and replaced without showing any sign of damage. There was a small hole beneath the fence surrounding the barrack, hidden by high grass, through which the prisoners could slip out. The three POWs had used this escape path earlier that night to meet the three women, and the beds of the women showed traces of grass from the uniforms of the POWs. Later in the night, a fourth woman employed by the factory, Regina Osterwalder, joined the two fugitive women. She had heard that Filipitsch had been arrested and feared that she would reveal Osterwalder's own relationship with a POW to the police. Osterwalder knew the meeting point where the other women would be waiting.

The police identified the three POWs as William Bolton, Harold Hingham, and Charles Clover. All three had been captured on Crete on June 1, 1941. A search warrant went out for the six fugitives. The police investigation revealed that the women and the POWs had been in contact for some time. Afraid of discovery, they had discussed escaping together, and they had tentatively agreed on two meeting points: a field with a church called Schönanger on a steep mountain right behind the dynamite factory (today a ski resort), and a ruined castle called Steinschloß approximately twelve kilometers away. The women did go directly to the Schönanger but could not find the POWs. Since this site was not far from the factory, they were afraid to wait and trekked through the night to Steinschloß. The POWs meanwhile made it across the mountain range to the Gurk valley south of Sankt Lambrecht, camping out in the forests. They were recaptured in the small town Friesach on June 21, twenty-eight kilometers away if one uses the hiking paths in the valleys, much less if one uses the mountain paths. The women meanwhile hid in haylofts on the hillslopes near Steinschloß. Information on their arrest is contradictory. According to one police report, the three women decided to go to Pölzweiler's parental home in Oberwölz, approximately a three-hour walk from Steinschloß. When they arrived there, Pölzweiler's father, a policeman, took them to the police post and had them arrested. According to another source, the police found the women near Steinschloß after having learned of the meeting point through letters discovered in the women's room and interrogations of Ludmilla Filipitsch, the one woman already in police custody. The women were all arrested by June 25.

The police investigation took several weeks. The POWs denied having had any forbidden relations, which was typical for British prisoners because they violated not only the German prohibition but also their own army regulations if they consorted with an enemy civilian. But the women confessed to the local police that they had amorous relations with the POWs, although only Pölzweiler admitted having had sexual intercourse with Clover (a confession she withdrew later on). Testimonies from factory employees and the watchmen confirmed that many people had noticed a suspicious closeness between women and POWs working in the factory. The POWs had been able to leave their sleeping quarters for some time, and there were undoubtedly other nightly encounters. One watchman had seen a POW together with Kirchner and Pölzweiler at night two or three weeks before the escapes but could not catch or recognize him. Several watchmen, employees, and a female social worker employed by the factory had repeatedly caught women and POWs talking with each other and hanging out in places where they had no reason to be. A popular meeting place was the washing room of the boiler house. The women and POWs had received several warnings not to socialize with each other, and the social worker and watchmen had told the women repeatedly to wash in their own shower rooms, not in the boiler house, where the prisoners took their showers. Once, a witness noticed that the backs of the women looked dirty, indicating that they had been lying on the floor of the boiler house. The work detachment had two guards, but they seemed very passive. One of them was under investigation because of illegal deals with a female French worker.

The testimonies of the women and the letters found in their rooms provided further information, as did interrogations of the women's relatives, the watchmen, and other women working at the factory. Gabriele Wirt, a co-worker, admitted having had tender encounters with Clover in the boiler house and having received letters from him (which she destroyed). Wirt had then gone on vacation in Graz for three weeks, but when she returned, a colleague told her that Clover ("Charli") was now involved with Pölzweiler. She got mad and confronted him several times, as she explained to the police: "Once I said to Charles that he should not think that I am stupid just because I am a German girl." Charles Clover did not stay with Pölzweiler very long, however. He soon left her for Regina Osterwalder (although he told the police that he did not know her). Osterwalder herself stated that she had dated Clover but broken up with him after eight days and then started going out with a POW named Norman (who remained unidentified). Harold Hingham had relationships with Filipitsch and another woman worker, Christina ("Tini") Leibl, triggering intense jealousy between the two women. William Bolton was deeply in love with Erna Kirchner.

Bolton's letters to Kirchner, in broken German with many Anglicisms, expressed his sincere love and warned her to be careful: "Please taking care and not play with others because I know talking always remain loyal with you, you my entire life and happiness and I with you am very happy."[13] He called her "My eternal angel" (*"Meine Ewig Engle"* [sic]). The letters revealed that he had given her chocolate and cigarettes from his aid parcels. Both were aware that their relationship had been noticed. She wrote him shortly before the escape that she was planning to commit suicide because she was certain that they would be caught: "I am dying with the great love for you in my heart, and I will not die lightly. I love you so much, it is hard to leave you. I cannot help it."[14] In a letter to her mother on the day before the escape, Erna Kirchner also mentioned a planned suicide together with Gisela ("Gisa") Pölzweiler. If caught, she expected to be brought to Leoben, the district capital, and to be beaten and killed slowly by the Gestapo or in a penitentiary. But she also told her mother about the escape plan and gave her the address of Pölzweiler's mother in Oberwölz, asking her not to say anything to the police. Pölzweiler also wrote her sister about the escape plan, but she mentioned no intended suicide. Harold Hingham's letters to Ludmilla Filipitsch stated that he was totally in love with her and felt sick when he could not see her for a while. He said he would never forget her. Hingham signed with "King Harold." Interestingly, Hingham wrote her one letter in Slovenian, her mother tongue. Whether he used a local translator or knew Slovenian is unclear. Filipitsch likely belonged to the Slovenian minority in southern Austria.

The women involved with the three POWs all came to trial before the special court in Leoben, which was one of the harshest in Nazi Austria.[15] Their trial records are not preserved (the special court of Leoben carried out the order from the Justice Ministry to destroy all files at the end of the war), but from the trials of the prisoners we learn that Erna Kirchner was sentenced to two years in penitentiary on September 15, 1943. The court

[13] "Bitte auf Passen und nicht spiel mit andere, denn ich weis sprechen immer bei dir treu bleiben, Du bist mein ganze Leben und Glück und mit dich ich bin sehr glücklich."
[14] "Ich sterbe mit der großen Liebe zu dir im Herzen und sterbe nicht leicht. Ich habe dich ja so lieb, es fällt mir schwer von dir zu gehen. Ich muß ich kann nichts anders [sic]."
[15] Polaschek, *Im Namen der Republik Oesterreich!*, 127.

martial considered it proven that Bolton had written her ten letters and that they had had sex on several occasions (he denied everything, even the letters). Erna Kirchner, who was twenty-one and had an illegitimate child, admitted having had sex with Bolton at night in early June. He may have been the POW who had once been seen by a watchman. Filipitsch received a punishment of eight months in prison. She never admitted having had sex. Wirt was sentenced to four months in prison, Pölzweiler to eight months, and Osterwalder to ten months. When Pölzweiler withdrew her earlier confession that she had had sex with Clover, the judge believed her. He also believed that Wirt and Osterwalder had not had sexual intercourse, although in the case of Osterwalder the contacts must have been quite intimate. Martina Leibl had admitted sexual intercourse, but her sentence is unknown. She came before a youth court because she was not yet eighteen, and she likely received a mild sentence. It is noteworhty that the judge of the special court was uncharacteristically lenient in the trial of the women. Given that the POWs had been able to break out of their sleeping quarters at night as they pleased, the special court would normally have assumed that sexual intercourse had taken place in more cases than the women admitted. Given the traces of grass in the women's beds, judges would typically have treated the reunion during the night of the discovery as an interrupted attempt at sexual intercourse and punished it as if intercourse had actually happened.

The prisoners had to stand trial together in front of the court martial in Leoben on September 18, 1943. Bolton was born in 1909, a hairdresser from Walsall (near Birmingham), married with three children. The letters he had written to Erna Kirchner, the testimony of the watchmen and other witnesses, and her confession that they had had sex served as proof despite his denials. He was sentenced to three and a half years in prison. Hingham, an unmarried mechanic born in 1920 in Yeovil (Somerset), received three years in prison for having had sex with Martina Leibl, who had confessed. He did confess having had a romance and correspondence with Filipitsch but was not punished for it because he claimed that he mistook her for a Yugoslav citizen. The judges found this credible because her German was accented and because she admitted having told him that she was Yugoslav although she did have German citizenship. Unlike the other two prisoners, who had both arrived in Sankt Lambrecht only in May 1943, Hingham had been there much longer. The court martial believed that he was involved with Leibl from January 1943 on. Ironically, his partial confession regarding his relationship to Filipitsch (for which he was acquitted) counted as a mitigating factor. Clover, an unmarried glass worker from Cardiff (Wales) born in

1916, was punished seperately for his romances with Pölzweiler (ten months), Wirt (six months), and Osternig (two years), amalgamated into three years in prison. The court martial believed that he had not engaged in sexual intercourse with any of them but that he came very close, at least with Osterwalder. That all three prisoners (with the partial exception of Hingham) denied their relationships irked their defense attorney Dr. Viktor Glaser, who complained to the Swiss legation that he could have defended them more effectively if they had made confessions.

The circle of people involved in forbidden relations at the factory was much wider than the five women and three POWs who had to stand trial. From the letters and eyewitness testimonies, it emerged that several other British POWs had also used the unsecured window to escape at night and met with other women employed in the factory over the preceding six months. There was a strong perception at the factory that the forbidden relations were a mass phenomenon in Sankt Lambrecht. When Gabriele Wirt asked one of the watchmen on June 21 whether the fugitive women had been caught, she told him that their capture would cause a major commotion in the factory because their interrogations would compromise many other employees and even members of the management. When one female employee confronted Stenka Petschuch, also a member of the Slovenian minority in Austria, about her relationship to another British POW around the time of the trials, Petschuch angrily retorted that if she was arrested because of this, then the entire facory would have to be jailed. The two guards deployed on the factory grounds were on friendly terms with the prisoners. One of them (the one under investigation for illegal deals with a female French worker) had to stand trial himself because he traded nude photos of Petschuch and another woman to the British POWs for chocolate (the women had agreed to the nude photos but not to them being sold). But there is no archival trace of other trials for forbidden relations at this location, even though the investigation of the five women and three POWs revealed other names. This points to a deliberate decision to prosecute only some relations to make an example, as Ulrich Herbert and others have suspected in other cases. Had the police tracked down every single forbidden relation on the factory grounds, it would likely have had to arrest so many people that the factory would have been forced to shut down. The men and women involved in the failed escape had come to public notice because of the search warrants, and the courts had little choice but to prosecute them. But they did not go much farther, and the verdicts of the special court in Leoben were uncharacteristically mild, perhaps also indicating a desire to quickly make an example and put the matter to rest.

Two Wehrmacht Auxiliaries

On September 6, 1943, a Wehrmacht auxiliary (*Nachrichtenhelferin*) in training discovered a photo album at an electric bus stop near the Verdun barracks in Gießen (Hessen), which housed a school for female auxiliaries of the Wehrmacht. The young woman began browsing through the album, which showed two other Wehrmacht auxiliaries in uniform during outings in tender poses with two French POWs. She knew that contacts with POWs were strictly forbidden and brought the album to the police. It did not take long for the police to identify the two women and the two prisoners on the photos. The women were twenty-three-year-old Gertrude Petschau from Vienna and nineteen-year-old Maria von Griebnitz from Berlin. Both women were in training as female auxiliaries. The parents of von Griebnitz had emigrated to the United States in 1928, settling in New York. They were presently interned in the United States as enemy aliens, but Maria had returned to Germany in 1939 to live with her grandmother and to start training as a designer. After performing her *Pflichtjahr* (mandatory labor year), she started studying at an art school in Berlin. Together with her grandmother, she then moved from Berlin to Vienna to study at the women's art academy in Vienna. This is where she met Gertrude Petschau, a highly talented art student whose father was a justice official in Vienna. In the fall of 1942, both women decided to sign up as female auxiliaries and came to the school in Gießen. They were sent to the drawing department because of their artistic talents.[16]

The Verdun barracks also employed some French POWs. In January 1943, the prisoners Paul Durocher and Richard de Marco delivered beds into the room of the two women. Gertrude gave Durocher some cigarettes, and they started talking. In broken German, he one day invited Gertrude to meet him in the coal cellar. Gertrude accepted, but she brought her friend Maria with her. They talked and smoked, and they decided to take a walk together. They met several times in the coal cellar and in the forest as a trio, but Durocher was obviously only interested in Gertrude. To make Maria feel less alone, they decided to invite de Marco to join them. The two couples met frequently, exchanging gifts, photos, and kisses. In May 1943 they began to have sex in the coal cellar and in the forest. In July, the two prisoners were sent to a different work detachment, but the couples kept up correspondence and occasionally visited each other, going to their old hiding spots in the forest. The

---

[16] The file for the two women is in HStAD, G 27 Darmstadt 1215. The judgment (November 8, 1943) is in HStAD Fonds G 24, Nr. 955/2 Mitteilungen in Strafsachen.

relationship was only discovered when Gertrude Petschau accidentally left the photo album at the bus stop. On the day following the discovery, they were dismissed from the Wehrmacht auxiliaries' school and arrested. Petschau was soon transferred from the prison in Gießen to the prison in Mainz because the Gießen institution was completely overcrowded and normally did not take women. It appears that von Griebnitz was interned in a youth prison.

During a search of their room the police seized their diaries, which provided additional evidence about the amorous relations. In the case of Gertrude Petschau, the diary revealed that she had already had a friendship with a French POW in Vienna, Emile Leblond. She had met him in the fields while painting, and she had visited him in his camp several times, speaking with him across the fence. The relationship had apparently not become intimate, however. Petschau's diary also contained some of the letters she had written to Durocher, and these letters as well as the diary itself alarmed the police because Petschau always spoke of "Austria" (*Oesterreich*) rather than the official Nazi term "*Ostmark.*" Was she perhaps an Austrian separatist and critic of the *Anschluss* (the annexation of Austria in March 1938)? During interrogation, Petschau claimed that she had used the term Austria in her communications with the prisoner because she was not sure he would understand *Ostmark.* She pointed out that her father and she herself had secretly supported the NSDAP already in 1933 and welcomed the *Anschluss.* She stated that Austria was better off now than before the *Anschluss.*

Both women came from wealthy families, and both had defense attorneys. Petschau's father Carl immediately wrote to the justice authorities (through her lawyer). He was deeply worried about his daughter and pointed out that she had a history of absent-mindedness. He requested that she receive a psychiatric examination. The prosecutor's office complied, and she was tested and interviewed by a psychiatrist, who concluded that she could not be classified as mentally ill. He found her depressive and tense, but very focused and artistically highly talented.

The trial of the two women took place in Darmstadt on November 8, 1943, two months after their arrest. The judge berated them for having consorted with "enemies" while wearing a Wehrmacht uniform. Petschau's case was considered to be more serious. The judge saw her as the driving force in both relationships because she was the older of the two women. The judge also considered her German patriotism dubious, claiming (without providing an example) that she had displayed a negative attitude toward "Germandom" in her contacts with the two Frenchmen. The police evaluation spoke of Maria von Griebnitz as a still very immature and dependent youth who had followed the leadership of her more experienced friend. Petschau received a sentence of nine months in prison for her first relationship in Vienna (converted to six months in penitentiary) and fifteen months in penitentiary for her relationship with Durocher. The two sentences were amalgamated to eighteen months of penitentiary. The court sentenced Griebnitz to only fourteen months in prison because the judge considered her to be deprived of parental guidance since she had not been with her parents since 1939. Both sentences were unusually lenient, considering that the relationships had lasted over many months and involved much sexual intimacy.

After the trial, Petschau was sent to the penal camp Oberems in Gütersloh (Westphalia). She received a temporary release in late 1944 under condition that she refrain from contacting Maria von Grieb-nitz again. During her leave, her father submitted a clemency plea for her, and she was released on parole. She did not have to return to the penitentiary to serve the remaining four months of her sentence. Maria von Griebnitz served much of her sentence in the youth prison Frankfurt-Preungesheim. She was released on parole in July 1944, also four months before the end of her sentence, and returned to her grandmother in Vienna. On August 8, 1944, she informed the prosecutor's office in Vienna that she was working as a volunteer. Although both women did conduct themselves well in jail, it is hard not to see a class bias at work in the generous enforcement of already very lenient sentences.

British Jew and Polish German

On September 19, 1943, twenty German staff sergeants searched the British POWs in the work detachment E 593 in Beuthen-Schomberg, a branch camp of Stalag VIII-B with headquarters first in Lamsdorf and later in Teschen (Upper Silesia). This work detachment, located not far from Kattowitz in the area of Poland annexed to the Reich in 1939, was holding Jews from the British army, many of them captured in Greece in April 1941. Given that there had been some escapes recently, the camp commander thought it was time for a thorough search of the POW quarters. In the back pocket of the work pants belonging to POW Shlomo Edelmann, the staff sergeants found six letters written in Polish. They seized the letters and had them translated into German. They were passionate love letters written by a woman named "Lucia" to a man she called "Siomus" or "Siomusia." She explained that she knew that he was married and hinted that she was married herself, but she spoke of true love for him and expressed her desire to kiss him and to rest in his arms. She claimed that his voice completely hypnotized her, and she thanked him for gifts of chocolate and cheese from his Red Cross parcels. In one letter, she told him that her brother had been severely wounded in combat and wrote a potentially subversive sentence: "Our grief is boundless. A child, who loved his fatherland so much, had to sacrifice his life for these tyrants." In another passage she used the potentially seditious phrase "we slaves." Her letters revealed that she had also received letters from the man, presumably also in Polish. She asked him in one letter whether he was a Pole himself and apologized for the grammatical mistakes in her letters. She also admonished him to burn her letters and to be careful with his choice of messenger for the letters and gifts. She indicated that there was a guard and a "little one," and another woman, who had either transferred the letters and goods or tolerated the transfer, but who could not be fully trusted. She also spoke of a meeting with the prisoner and gave him her address, a street in Godullahütte, a nearby village.[17]

Interrogated by the criminal police in Beuthen on October 18, Edelmann claimed to have found the letters approximately one and a half months before the discovery near a train overpass on his way back to the camp. Edelmann, who knew German, pointed out that he was a translator and that he had therefore been marching on the side of the POW column and had seen the letters before the other prisoners had spotted them. He claimed to have picked them up to use them as toilet paper and then to have forgotten them in his back pocket. When the police officer asked how he could have forgotten letters in his back pocket for six to seven weeks, he answered that he had received new pants and not worn the old ones for a while. Edelmann was born in Warsaw, but he claimed that he had never learned Polish because he had gone to Jewish schools where he spoke Yiddish and then emigrated to Palestine at a young age.

Two days later, the Gestapo in Kattowitz arrested Luzie Rybnik, an employee at a garden center in Godullahütte who lived at the address given in one of the letters. Rybnik initially refused to reveal any information except that she was married to miner Leo Rybnik. The police found out that she and her husband were prewar Polish citizens who had been admitted to the German people's list, category III, which meant that they had German citizenship. The woman's maiden name was German (Krüger), and she claimed to have been raised bilingually. After a night in prison, she confessed that she had written the letters to the prisoner "Schloma" who she had met in September, allegedly just to tease him. She also confessed having received five letters from the

---

[17] The woman's file is in the Archiwum Państwowe w Katowicach (Poland), Sondergericht, 680. The court martial record for the prisoner and the correspondence of his attorney with the Swiss legation in Berlin is in BAR Bern, Vertretung Berlin, 80a.

prisoner with declarations of love as well as chocolate and cheese. She had immediately destroyed his letters. Asked about the reference to tyrants and slaves, she explained that she had referred to the fact that the prohibition of contacts between German women and POWs made her and the prisoner slaves. She claimed that she did not know Edelmann was a Jew, a statement the Gestapo officer interrogating her underlined in red and adorned with a big question mark.

When the police interrogated Edelman again and showed him her confession, he admitted that she had written the letters to him and that "Siomus" and "Siomusia" were terms of endearment she had used for him. He denied having had sex with her but admitted having kissed her once. He claimed that he wrote the letters mostly in search of intellectual engagement and explained that he had initially denied any connection to the author of the letters in order to protect her. Contrary to her testimony, he stated to have told her that he was a Jew. Born in Warsaw as the son of a milkman in 1912, Edelmann had emigrated to Palestine in 1931 and taken a job as construction worker in the docks of Haifa, where he had married and started a family. He had two children. After the outbreak of the war, he volunteered for the British army and was sent to Greece, where he was captured by the German army at the end of April 1941. Like many British POWs captured in Greece, he was sent to Austria and later to Stalag VIII-B in Silesia. He was not only a translator but also a foreman on a construction site in Godullahütte, where British POWs were digging foundations for new houses. That is how he had met Frau Rybnik, who worked at a garden center nearby, together with other Polish-speaking women. The women occasionally waved to the prisoners on the construction site and tried to talk to them. Given that Edelmann knew Polish, he answered. He found one woman particularly likeable. After one week, he wrote her a letter in Polish and dropped it at the edge of a brook while making sure she could see him. She replied, and they exchanged a dozen letters. He also admitted having given her five bars of chocolate and some cheese from his aid parcels. Although it appears likely from her letters that there were some persons who transmitted some of the letters and goods, both Edelmann and Frau Rybnik were careful not to implicate anybody else, and the police never found out who had helped them.

After his confession, Edelmann was sent back to the main camp of the Stalag in Teschen to await his trial. Meanwhile, the Gestapo in Kattowitz concluded its investigation, complaining to the prosecutor's office that Frau Rybnik was stubborn and potentially anti-German. She was interrogated once more, but she only specified that she had accepted the chocolate and cheese from the prisoner because she had wanted to send these goods to her brother who had been transported to a military hospital in Przemysl and who had meanwhile died of his wounds. She did have an attorney, Dr. G. Schaefer, who requested that she be set free until the trial because her husband, a worker in the Hohenzollern mine in Beuthen who also had to take care of his sick mother-in-law, was suffering severely from his wife's absence. Given that the Gestapo considered her crime to be a "severe case," however, she had to stay in the Kattowitz prison. Her trial was scheduled for February 2, 1944.

The court martial for Edelmann took place a week earlier, on January 25, 1944. The day before, he visited his defense attorney, Dr. Hans Kirsch in Kattowitz, to discuss defense strategy – very likely in the company of a guard and perhaps a translator, although Edelmann probably did not need one. According to Dr. Kirsch, the most promising strategy was to spread doubt that Edelmann had known that Frau Rybnik was a German citizen and that he had therefore assumed that the relationship was not forbidden. Although the commanders of some army districts straddling the prewar German–Polish border had decreed that *all* POW relations with women were punishable, no corresponding order existed for army district VIII to which Edelmann's Stalag belonged. If Kirsch could show that Edelmann had taken Frau Rybnik to be Polish, the judges would have to acquit him, as had happened in quite a few cases of British POWs in Upper Silesia and the German–Czech borderlands where women with German citizenship sometimes claimed not to be German. Even if Kirsch could not prove that Edelmann had considered Rybnik to be Polish, the ambiguity might be a mitigating factor.

During the court martial of the 432nd Infantry Division in Kattowitz, the prosecutor argued that Edelmann knew, or could have known, that Frau Rybnik was German because she had spoken of her brother's service in the Wehrmacht on the eastern front. Regarding the extent of the forbidden contact, the prosecutor acknowledged that "sexual intercourse cannot be proven" but demanded one and a half years in prison for the kisses, the letters, and the gifts of chocolate and cheese, all forbidden to POWs in relation to German women. Attorney Kirsch insisted first on Edelmann's good behavior in captivity and pointed out that he had been a capable and trusted construction worker, as evidenced by his appointment as foreman in the prisoner company working in Godullahütte. A letter from an officer highly praised Edelmann. Regarding the question of Frau Rybnik's nationality, Kirsch pointed out that Edelmann must at least have doubted that she was German because she wrote him in Polish and sometimes even signed with "your little Pole." The court, however, sided with the prosecutor in the question about his knowledge of her nationality, but it reduced the sentence to one year in prison on account of Edelmann's good behavior and excellent work performance.

The day after the court martial, Kirsch wrote to the *Gerichtsherr* (highest judicial officer of the division) requesting a non-confirmation of the sentence because he had meanwhile received another glowing letter about Edelmann's conduct from the commander of a camp where he had stayed earlier. The *Gerichtsherr*, however, turned down this request, arguing that the letter presented no facts that had not already been considered in the judgment. The British government, via the Swiss legation in Berlin, asked for a re-trial because they had not received the mandatory advance notice of Edelmann's trial. The Swiss legation learned, however, that the notice of Edelmann's trial – together with many others – had likely been burned during the bombing of the German High Command headquarters in Berlin in November 1943. Kirsch still urged the Swiss legation to insist on a re-trial because he believed that Edelmann would receive a lower sentence if he, Kirsch, could read the late letter in court. But the British authorities did not persist, probably because the court martial, aside from the missing notification, had proceeded in accordance with international legal standards including the presence of a defense attorney accredited by the Swiss legation.

Meanwhile, things did not look good for Frau Rybnik. The prosecutor, in his bill of indictment written two weeks before the trial, repeated the Gestapo's claim that this was a serious case. He argued that in her letters she had declared her love "in a shameless way." The prosecutor found it particularly disturbing that she knew that he was a Jew. Another plea by her attorney for a temporary release was rejected again, and the director of the judicial press service in Kattowitz wrote to the president of the special court that he was eagerly waiting for the sentence to publish a report about the case. At the hearing on February 2, 1944, the prosecutor demanded one and a half years in penitentiary and two years of loss of civil rights. This was a severe punishment that would have been typical for cases where sexual intercourse was proven.

When asked by the judge why she had started the contact with the POW, Frau Rybnik said that her only motivation had been to obtain chocolate for her wounded brother. The court did not quite believe her, but there was a witness who confirmed that she had visited her brother in the hospital in Przemysl and brought him some chocolate. The judge conceded that desire for chocolate may have been one motivating factor, but he did not believe it was the decisive one. The love letters had been too tender and intimate. The special court agreed with the court martial regarding the extent of their relationship, believing her that she had not tried to have sex with the prisoner. It also saw him as the initiator of the relationship. But did she know that he was a Jew? The judge thought it likely because of the prisoner's last name. Moreover, Edelmann had testified during his interrogation that he had told her that he was a Jew, and he was present at Frau Rybnik's trial as a witness. When the judge asked him to confirm his statement from the interrogation, however, Edelmann suddenly denied ever having revealed his Jewish identity to her and claimed that he had only told her that he was from Warsaw. The judge therefore considered it likely but unproven that she had known that he was a Jew. The judge conceded that "Edelmann has no typical Jewish looks" and concluded with respect to his interrogation statement: "Such shaky testimony from a Jewish witness is not fit to convict a German citizen." The judge also did not think that Frau Rybnik could have known that the work detachment in Beuthen-Schomberg was all-Jewish. Still, he considered her behavior undignified and deserving of severe punishment. He gave her a sentence of fifteen months in prison, a little more than half of what the prosecutor had demanded (one and a half years in penitentiary were equivalent to two years and three months in prison). As in many other cases, the support of Frau Rybnik's husband was an important factor in support of leniency. The sentence stated: "Her husband, after all, has forgiven her aberration because she has always been an orderly wife." Her pre-trial custody counted toward the sentence because she had confessed.

After the trial, Frau Rybnik had to stay in the prison of Kattowitz until she was transferred to the prison in Leobschütz (Sudetenland) on March 14, 1944. Her husband submitted a clemency plea even before she arrived there. He argued that the prisoner had seduced his wife and lured her with chocolate. He offered to pay a cash fine for her and explained that he urgently needed her at home. His plea was rejected, as was a later one by Luzie Rybnik herself, even though the director of the Leobschütz prison admitted that she was a good worker. On September 5, 1944, her attorney submitted another clemency plea, pointing out that the husband was a hard-working, upright citizen who now had to perform additional labor on entrenchments for the Wehrmacht and who could not maintain his home alone. Ten days later, the director of the prison answered and advocated an early release, pointing out that Frau Rybnik sincerely regretted her "crime" and that the punishment had suitably impressed her. The record stops at this point, but it seems that she was released not much later, approximately three months before the official end of her sentence (January 2, 1945).

According to his POW personnel card, Edelmann was brought to Graudenz on March 23, 1944.[18] He must have been released in October or November 1944, one year after his transfer to pre-trial custody in Teschen. After his release, Edelmann was likely sent to nearby Stalag XX-B (Marienburg), where many Graudenz prisoners who had served out their sentence were held. He did survive the war because he filled out a questionnaire regarding his captivity for the British army on May 13, 1945, after his liberation. Interestingly, he did not mention his court martial sentence in the questionnaire, perhaps because the British army itself prohibited POW contacts with enemy civilians.[19]

The case reveals the problems and inconsistencies of Nazi racial categories. It is striking that a Jew from Warsaw received a regular German court martial in Kattowitz, only some thirty miles from Auschwitz, at a time when almost all Jews from Warsaw – likely including many members of Edelmann's extended family – had already been murdered. Edelmann was even allowed to meet his attorney in town on the day before the trial, and his attorney defended him vigorously. This was noteworthy. German attorneys were forbidden to defend a Jew in court, and it had taken some diplomatic wrestling between Vichy and Berlin in early 1941 to establish that this law would be suspended in the case of trials against Jewish POWs.[20] Some defense attorneys nonetheless decided to hide behind the prohibition and refused to defend "non-Aryans." But the Geneva Convention did not allow discrimination on the basis of race or nationality (Article 4). Jewish POWs in British, French, or Belgian uniform, regardless of their citizenship, had to be treated as members of the army whose uniform they wore, and the German authorities had confirmed this rule. They generally respected it with respect to Jewish prisoners from the western armies out of consideration for the fate of German POWs in western Allied hands.[21]

While there was no doubt that Edelmann was a Jew, Frau Rybnik's status was initially unclear. The police at first needed to confirm whether she was a German citizen. A note from the mayor's office in Godullahütte proved that she and her husband had been accepted to the German Ethnic List, category III, on June 23, 1942, and received German citizenship. Persons assigned to category III had been allowed

---

[18] National Archives, Kew, WO 416/141/257.
[19] National Archives, Kew, WO 344/120/2 (G).
[20] Scheck, "Collaboration of the Heart," 378.
[21] Rüdiger Overmans, "German Treatment of Jewish Prisoners of War in the Second World War." Translated by Helen McPhail, in *Wartime Captivity in the Twentieth Century: Archives, Stories, Memories*, edited by Anne-Marie Pathé and Fabien Théofilakis (New York: Berghahn Books, 2016), 50–1.

to become German citizens only in January 1942, albeit with the proviso that citizenship could be revoked.[22] Frau Rybnik was initially threatened with harsh punishment for having declared her love for a Jew, but then the judge vindicated her as a German against the "shaky testimony of a Jew" – even though her letters suggested an insecure identification with Germany or at least with Nazi Germany – and gave her the benefit of the doubt regarding her knowledge of Edelmann's background, although a strong suspicion remained. Edelmann very likely tried to protect her when he retracted his initial statement and denied in court that he had ever told her that he was a Jew. The forgiving attitude of Frau Rybnik's husband helped her, and it is likely that his heavy work in the coalmine and digging entrenchments for the Wehrmacht helped her to get an early release.

The files of course leave many empty spaces. What explains Frau Rybnik's romance? She and Leo had been married since 1933. Was it that he was extremely busy and did not have time for her? Did she feel that her life was dreary and empty? Was she concerned about the war situation? Were the combat injury and then the death of her brother a shock that made her crave emotional comfort that she did not get from her husband? Her letters suggest all of these possibilities, but we do not know for sure. It is obvious, however, that she sincerely regretted her flirtation with the POW and that her husband, rather than judging her, forgave her and wanted to continue the marriage. An interesting detail is that she was listed as having one child when she was released from prison, although there is no information on that anywhere else. She was listed as childless during her interrogations, and her husband never spoke of a child in his clemency pleas (he would certainly have mentioned it if he had been forced to care for a child). Had she given birth in prison? Or was the notice simply a mistake?

What did Edelmann know about the fate of the European Jews, especially those in Poland, including his extended family? Occasional contacts between Jewish forced laborers and POWs happened. Although there is no evidence for this in Edelmann's file, Jewish POWs did sometimes exchange information with Jewish forced laborers from various ghettos and camps. The fact that Edelmann spoke Polish and Yiddish would have facilitated his communications with Jewish forced laborers. He was in an all-Jewish work detachment, and it is likely that

[22] "Deutsche Volksliste" on the site "Online-Lexikon zur Kultur und Geschichte der Deutschen im östlichen Europa" at the University of Oldenburg, ome-lexikon.uni-oldenburg.de/begriffe/deutsche-volksliste/ (last visited: May 30, 2019).

somebody had information on the fate of the Jews in Nazi-occupied Europe.[23]

Edelmann's case is consistent with other trials against Jews from the British, French, Belgian, Yugoslav, and American armies in German captivity. While some judges felt obliged to make disparaging remarks about the Jew on trial, the sentences were generally in line with those pronounced against non-Jews. In the trial of Frau Rybnik, as in other trials against women involved with Jewish (and Polish) soldiers from the western armies, the judges ultimately treated the act of the woman as if she had been involved with a non-Jew despite the Nürnberg Laws, which called for much harsher punishments. The Geneva Convention in these cases colored Nazi legislation.

---

[23] Yoav Gelber, "Palestinian POWs in German Captivity," *Yad Vashem Studies* 14 (1981): 118–19; Russell Wallis, *British POWs and the Holocaust: Witnessing the Nazi Atrocities*, International Library of Twentieth Century History Series (London: I.B. Tauris, 2016), 58–63. Whether Edelmann knew of the mass gassings at Auschwitz is questionable, however. Even British POWs working nearby and smelling burned flesh did apparently not know the truth until the end of the war: Rolf, *Prisoners of the Reich*, 73.

On September 20, 1945, the Allied Control Commission for Germany abrogated all Nazi legislation based on racial, religious, and political discrimination, and this included the prohibition of contacts with POWs. A few weeks later, a general amnesty followed for all sentences pronounced according to these laws. Corresponding laws were passed in the separate occupation zones, in Austria, and later in the two independent German states. All sentences based on §4 of the decree of November 25, 1939, were voided, although women had to apply individually for a cancellation of their sentence from the penal registry. Many women submitted such applications in the late 1940s or early 1950s, and they were always approved, although the courts sometimes made derogatory and moralistic statements to the applicants, as for example in the response to Frau Mühlberger in Groß-Gerau in 1952.[1] If a woman had only been sentenced for a forbidden relationship, she therefore became free of previous convictions and no longer had a criminal record. Had a woman also been sentenced for other infractions related to the forbidden relationship, such as an abortion, a theft, or helping a prisoner escape, she could not get that sentence struck, and a few women had to struggle with the legal authorities and prove to them that their incarceration before May 1945 should cover the punishment for the offense that did not fall under the cancellation laws. The cancellation of the sentence did not remove the social stigma especially for women who returned from penitentiary and had to live with continued public censure because a stay in the pentientiary counted as shameful.

Indemnification payments for the victims of Nazism formed part of the earliest postwar discussions, but differences of opinion on how exactly to define a victim of Nazism and fears about too extensive payments soon hampered progress on this question, leaving it to the four Allied powers

---

[1] Landgericht Darmstadt 1 to Anna Margarethe R., January 24, 1952, in HStAD, Sondergericht Darmstadt, G 27, 1180. See case study "A Frenchman for Everybody" in Chapter 7.

and later the Federal Republic of Germany (FRG), the German Democratic Republic (GDR), and Austria to work out their own regulations.[2] With respect to indemnification, the women and prisoners punished for a forbidden relation were in a weak position because, unlike political dissidents, they had not fought for a democratic, or socialist Germany, and they had not consciously resisted the evil of the Nazi regime. They usually had not even criticized the Nazi regime, unlike many other people convicted by the special courts or courts martial.[3] Unlike many victims of Nazism, they had not been persecuted on the basis of their race, ethnicity, or religion. They had made what appeared to them like a private choice (although that is not how the Nazi regime saw it) and been punished harshly for it. Yet, the women were not in a common sense criminals. The law had simply turned things that normally belong to the private sphere into a subject of prosecution and public shaming. The women therefore stood in sharp competition to other groups who were more clearly victims of National Socialism and, increasingly, also with groups who were considered victims of war and expulsion (Germans who had lost everything during bombings and refugees or deported people from the German eastern regions or foreign countries).[4]

Several convicted women tried to get indemnification payments following the three major indemnification laws that the Federal Republic passed in 1953, 1956, and 1965.[5] But if one did not belong to a racial or religious group targeted for persecution under the Nazis, political conviction was the paramount criterion for indemnification.[6] In practice, only people who had been punished for an action resulting from "an ethically firm world view" opposed to Nazism could be considered for indemnification (aside from those persecuted on the basis of their identity). Even those Germans sentenced for "racial defilement" did not qualify because the authorities alleged that they had acted simply to satisfy their sexual desire. Although a few officials advocated restitution for people who had been sent to concentration camps because of sexual relations with a Polish or Soviet POW as "erotically persecuted people,"

---

[2] Constantin Goschler, *Wiedergutmachung: Westdeutschland und die Verfolgten des Nationalsozialismus (1945–1954)* (München: Oldenbourg, 1992), 71–3.

[3] See Raffael Scheck, "Western Prisoners of War Tried for Insults of the Führer and Criticism of Nazi Germany," *Journal of Contemporary History*, published online, April 27, 2020: doi.org/10.1177/0022009420907670.

[4] Goschler, *Wiedergutmachung*, 89.

[5] Cornelius Pawlita, *"Wiedergutmachung" als Rechtsfrage? Die politische und juristische Auseinandersetzung um Entschädigung für die Opfer nationalsozialistischer Verfolgung (1945 bis 1990)* (Frankfurt am Main: Peter Lang, 1993), 289–322.

[6] Goschler, *Wiedergutmachung*, 156.

the majority opinion rejected the merits of these cases and insisted on a well-defined political worldview as motivation.[7]

A typical case was forty-one-year-old Sabine Becker, a servant from a hamlet near Bad Hersfeld (northern Hessen). She was arrested on September 7, 1941, after having a love relationship with Polish POW Josef Jurkiewicz. She considered Jurkiewicz her fiancé, and she was pregnant from him at the time of her arrest. Jurkiewicz was hanged soon after discovery, and Becker was sent first to the forced labor camp Breitenau in Guxhagen (south of Kassel) and, in March 1942, to the concentration camp Ravensbrück, all without a trial.[8] She reported after the war that she was forced to deliver the baby with a very painful caesarian section, and that the baby was taken away from her and died not much later (she did not know whether it had died because of the premature and brutal delivery or if it was killed by the SS guards). Becker had to stay in the concentration camp until the end of the war. She made a compelling case for having suffered damage to her health. Yet, the authorities did not approve her repeated requests for indemnification, starting in 1953, because she was not a victim of political persecution and had not been targeted because of her worldview. She persisted into the late 1960s, but her indemnification file suggests that she never received payments.[9] One would have to assume that the bar was even higher for women sent to a penitentiary or prison for a relationship with a western POW.

Resistance to indemnification of people sentenced under §4 of the decree of November 25, 1939, also characterized the attitude of the Austrian authorities, who in principle argued that Austria, as the first foreign victim of National Socialism, had no obligation to pay any reparations or indemnifications to victims. The Republic of Austria was willing to pay some support for victims of Nazism, but under conditions difficult to fulfill. For example, a woman who had spent two years in Ravensbrück concentration camp for helping Polish POWs did not receive recognition as a victim of National Socialism or as a political opponent, even though she had to wear the red angle in Ravensbrück, which identified her as a political prisoner. But the Austrian authorities did not think that she had acted out of fundamental opposition to Nazism and a commitment to an independent, democratic Austria. Austria also did not accept §4 of the decree of November 25, 1939, as an example of

---

[7] Ibid., 157–8.
[8] Martin Weinmann, ed., *Das nationalsozialistische Lagersystem (CCP)* (Frankfurt am Main: Zweitausendeins, 1990), 158.
[9] HHStA Wiesbaden, Abt. 518, Nr. 4061.

specifically Nazi legislation because other countries also penalized contacts to POWs (albeit, one would have to add, in fundamentally different ways). Not even a Social Democratic woman who had been sentenced for helping a POW escape won indemnification because the political motivation for her act did not seem clear enough to the court. This woman pointed out that she did not act out of erotic or amorous motivations.[10] Although a new law in 1988 facilitated indemnification payments for women who had been sent to a concentration camp for a forbidden relation, the women sentenced for amorous relations with western POWs had not much hope to be recognized as victims in Austria.[11]

Even women who had been forcibly sterilized found it hard to receive compensation. Although forced sterilizations stopped in 1945, the judgments of the Nazi courts that had decided for sterilization were not voided until 1998.[12] Indemnification payments were for a long time only possible if the victim could prove that the expert committees ordering the sterilization had acted unlawfully – by the standards of the 1933 law, which gave doctors the latitude to make extremely subjective decisions.[13] It took until 1980 for the victims of forced sterilization to get some compensation, initially with tight restrictions. The argument against compensating sterilization victims was that forced sterilizations were not a genuinely Nazi policy given that other countries, even democracies, had also used legal "eugenic" sterilizations.[14] Of course, like other victim groups in the 1950s and 1960s, the sterilized women (and men) faced bureaucrats, doctors, and, if they took legal steps, judges who had been active under the Nazi regime and were not sympathetic to their demands.[15] Even Jewish survivors sometimes had a hard time convincing

[10] Brigitte Bailer, *Wiedergutmachung kein Thema: Österreich und die Opfer des Nationalsozialismus* (Vienna: Löcker, 1993), 165–6.
[11] Prieler-Woldan, *Das Selbstverständliche tun*, 200.
[12] Stefanie Westermann, *Verschwiegenes Leid: Der Umgang mit den NS-Zwangssterilisationen in der Bundesrepublik Deutschland*, Menschen und Kulturen (Köln, Weimar, Wien: Böhlau, 2010), 61–2.
[13] Timm, *The Politics of Fertility in Twentieth-Century Berlin*, 133–4.
[14] On this aspect, see in particular Rolf Surmann, "Was ist typisches NS-Unrecht? Die verweigerte Entschädigung für Zwangssterilisierte und 'Euthanasie'-Geschädigte," in *Lebensunwert zerstörte Leben: Zwangssterilisation und "Euthanasie,"* ed. Margret Hamm (Frankfurt am Main: VAS, 2005), 201–2.
[15] Margret Hamm, ed., *Ausgegrenzt! Warum? Zwangssterilisierte und Geschädigte der NS-"Euthanasie" in der Bundesrepublik Deutschland* (Berlin: Metropol, 2017); Goschler, *Wiedergutmachung*, 196; Hermann-Josef Brodesser et al., *Wiedergutmachung und Kriegsfolgenliquidation: Geschichte – Regelungen – Zahlungen* (Munich: Beck, 2000), 211–12; Westermann, *Verschwiegenes Leid*, 81–8.

the authorities that their time in hiding or in a concentration camp had caused significant damage to their physical and mental health.[16]

In the German Democratic Republic, the emphasis was on indemnification of political opponents of Nazism, primarily communist resisters, and the GDR saw itself as a state of victims of Nazism, thus rejecting any obligation to indemnify other victims or (as a communist state) to restitute capitalist property.[17] The end of the cold war opened the path for German agreements with eastern European states and a special foundation for the former forced laborers, many of whom had been deported from eastern Europe. The latter agreement resulted from a combination of domestic efforts to widen the circle of people considered to have suffered under National Socialism and pressure from American class action lawsuits. For a long time, the government of the Federal Republic had argued that foreign forced laborers should be indemnified through the reparations paid to their home countries. In 1998–2000, however, the German government established a foundation to indemnify former forced laborers with contributions from the German state and from private firms that had benefited from forced labor. But this arrangement was widely seen as the last major step of the restitution and indemnification process.[18]

Whatever women sentenced for forbidden relationships with POWs did to receive indemnification, it usually happened through private initiatives, and no pressure group ever formed. The result was that the issue was quickly forgotten.[19] It took until the publication of Rolf Hochhuth's historical novel *Eine Liebe in Deutschland* (*A Love in Germany*) in 1978, made into a film by Andrzej Wajda in 1983, that the topic was revived. Hochhuth traced the real love story of a Polish POW and a woman in southwest Germany, ending in the public hanging of the prisoner and the transfer to a concentration camp of the woman.[20] In the context of the new interest in everyday life under Nazism (*Alltagsgeschichte*) in the 1980s and 1990s, the topic became more widely known and received coverage in local histories centering on the role of the special courts during the war.[21]

---

[16] Christian Pross, *Paying for the Past: The Struggle over Reparations for Surviving Victims of the Nazi Terror*, trans. Belinda Cooper (Baltimore and London: Johns Hopkins University Press, 1998), 106–64.
[17] Constantin Goschler, *Schuld und Schulden: Die Politik der Wiedergutmachung für NS-Verfolgte seit 1945* (Göttingen: Wallstein, 2005), 361–411.
[18] Ibid., 450–71.   [19] Maiwald and Mischler, *Sexualität unter dem Hakenkreuz*, 218.
[20] Rolf Hochhuth, *Eine Liebe in Deutschland* (Reinbek bei Hamburg: Rowohlt, 1978).
[21] For a summary, see the section on literature in the Introduction.

Most returning prisoners had no interest in highlighting the convictions on the basis of the prohibition, and they were largely forgotten. Convictions on the basis of the order of January 10, 1940, expired upon liberation, and they were not part of the soldier's penal registry. If anything, having been convicted of disobedience by a Nazi court could count as a badge of honor if one disregarded the precise nature of the disobedient act. The French and Belgian Graudenz prisoners wanted to be recognized on par with other prisoners who had been sent to particularly brutal camps, for example for NCOs refusing to work or for prisoners who had repeatedly escaped. The German army had set up special disciplinary camps in Rawa-Ruska (Stalag 325) near Lvov and in Kobierzyn (Stalag 365) near Krakow. The Rawa-Ruska camp, for repeat escapers, was called *"le camp de la mort lente"* (the camp of slow death), and conditions there were not much better than in a concentration camp. Kobierzyn, for NCOs refusing to work, was better, although the food supply was insufficient in the beginning (Francis Ambrière was a man of confidence in Kobierzyn and left a detailed description of this camp).[22] Survivors of these disciplinary camps formed their own associations after the war and lobbied for indemnification in analogy to the resistance fighters deported to a concentration camp. This was an arduous but ultimately successful struggle. The NCOs who had refused to work could argue that they had actively resisted, although the case was less clear for those POWs who had repeatedly escaped, perhaps simply to get home. In France, returning POWs had initially been recognized as victims of war in 1945, but the indemnification arrangements negotiated internally and in conjunction with the Federal Republic of Germany limited claims to former resisters and people deported for political reasons. POWs were also excluded from the Franco-German indemnification treaty of 1960.[23]

Prisoners who had experienced Graudenz and its sub-camps argued that they had performed an act of resistance (because they had disobeyed German orders), and they lobbied for compensation. In their political struggle, the Graudenz prisoners even employed the epithet of Rawa-Ruska ("camp of slow death") and applied it to Graudenz, although this comparison, as demonstrated, is misleading if one considers the significant improvements occurring in 1943. Like the German women requesting indemnification, the former Graudenz prisoners had suffered harsh

[22] Ambrière, *Les grandes Vacances*, 299–334.
[23] Claudia Moisel, "Pragmatischer Formelkompromiß: Das deutsch-französische Globalabkommen von 1960," in *Grenzen der Wiedergutmachung: Die Entschädigung für NS-Verfolgte in West- und Osteuropa 1945–2000*, ed. Hans Günther Hockerts, Claudia Moisel, and Tobias Winstel (Göttingen: Wallstein, 2006), 261.

punishment for an act motivated mostly by a normally private interest, not a political agenda. In order to overcome this quandary, former Graudenz prisoners always tried to downplay the fact that "disobedience" in the vast majority of cases had consisted of getting involved with a German woman. But Scapini published his memoirs in 1960, in which he described conditions in Graudenz, efforts to improve them, and the fact that 95 percent of the French prisoners there had been sentenced for love relations.[24]

In 1979, the former French Graudenz prisoners founded their own interest organization to better fight for recognition as victims and as resisters.[25] In order to achieve their aims, they had to give a very low profile to the reason for most convictions. Conveniently, their first chairman, Fernand Caire, was one of the few Graudenz prisoners sentenced for something other than a forbidden relation: the court martial in Dresden had sentenced him (falsely, he claimed) to six months in prison for forging a document after a spurious denunciation by a fellow prisoner. Caire arrived in Graudenz in October 1944, and he was transferred to the detachment in Thorn after one day. He therefore spent only three months in the Graudenz complex before the evacuation and had to rely on other sources for the period preceding his arrival.[26]

In 1981, the French government rejected recognition of the Graudenz prisoners as resisters, pointing to the real reason for most convictions and arguing that a relationship with a German woman served merely the *preparation* of a resistance act, especially an escape, but did not in itself constitute an act of resistance.[27] Although even this rhetorical concession was wide of the mark by ascribing a patriotic functionality to the forbidden relations, the government response prompted the association of former Graudenz prisoners to publish a book that used the epithet of Rawa-Ruska in its title: *Graudenz-Pologne: La forteresse de la mort lente* (1983). The editor argues that Graudenz was a prison for resisters, and he uses the term "the forgotten resisters of Graudenz" indiscriminately for all Graudenz inmates. The book consistently downplays the importance of convictions for amorous relations and, if it does acknowledge them, highlights the most harmless forms (prisoners giving chocolate or speaking to a German girl) or functionalizes them by suggesting that all relations to German women served subversive purposes, for example the

---

[24] Scapini, *Mission sans gloire*, 214–18.
[25] Their website is still active: www.uipf-graudenz.org/ (last visited on February 12, 2019).
[26] CEGESOMA, AB 1249: Sous le Joug, 1939–1945: mémoires, 1939–1945 / Fernand Caire. – Beziers. – 59 p.
[27] Jean-Charles Lheureux, *Graudenz-Pologne: La forteresse de la mort lente* (Nîmes: Le Camariguo, 1983), 150.

preparation of an escape, securing additional food (for one's comrades, of course!), or getting access to a radio to hear foreign news. While a few French POWs did indeed exploit a relationship to a German woman in hopes of escape, the vast majority had either no demonstrable intention to escape or, if they did want to escape, were motivated by private factors, usually the desire to live the relationship with the woman freely in France. Moreover, only very few prisoners came to Graudenz after having given chocolate to a German woman and hardly anybody merely for having talked to a German girl! The book belittles and desexualizes the forbidden encounters in order to argue that even the prisoners sentenced for forbidden relations were resisters. It portrays Graudenz as a detention site for upright opponents of racism, injustice, and political violence, a place "for the stubborn heads who had difficulties keeping their tightened fists in their pockets when a guard harassed them too much. And for those who were incautious enough to express aloud what others merely thought quietly."[28] This depiction, of course, had nothing to do with the actual reasons leading the vast majority to Graudenz.

The book contains a brief reflection by the former French man of confidence, Maurice Vila, that echoes the many problems registered by the Scapini Mission (insufficient supplies, dangerous work, abusive guards). But Vila, in fairness, concedes that the situation improved and that abusive guards were sent to the eastern front if the POWs complained about them enough (this would not have happened in Rawa-Ruska). He also acknowledged that the guards used later in the war were mostly World War I veterans and generally friendly. In order to still portray the Graudenz prisoners as resisters, however, Vila claims that the Graudenz prisoners did not matter to the Scapini Mission because they were overwhelmingly opposed to collaboration. There is absolutely no confirmation for that in the documents, and Vila should have known that. During the war, he was involved in the efforts of the Scapini Mission to improve conditions, and he was perfectly aware that whatever frustration remained for the Graudenz prisoners was due to German lack of cooperation and not to any indifference on the part of the Scapini Mission.[29] Moreover, opposition to collaboration, while it may have become a widespread feeling of the Graudenz prisoners late in 1944 (as for most French POWs in general), practically never played a role in the love-related trials. To the contrary, quite a few POWs involved with German women stressed their willingness to stay in Germany, not only in front of the courts, but also in private documents.

---

[28] Ibid., 84, 133.   [29] Ibid., 51–63.

The Belgian commission for war crimes gathered testimonies from former prisoners and other witnesses immediately after the war, planning to bring Dallmer-Zerbe and the most abusive officers and guards to trial. One of the most detailed testimonies was the report of the translator Victor Hanewald, a city clerk from Heidelberg. Hanewald, who came to Graudenz in December 1942 as a translator for French-speaking prisoners, mentioned several abuses of prisoners by German officers and guards. His testimony was influenced by his interest in defending his own role (he wrote during the first wave of denazification in 1945), but it does largely confirm the evil acts of some officers witnessed by prisoners. Hanewald only defended Dallmer-Zerbe as a Prussian officer of the old school and at heart well intended, while several former prisoners accused him of at least shared responsibility for eight murders of POWs (two Belgians, three Frenchmen, two Italians, and one British POW). Hanewald listed more than a dozen French, Belgian, and British prisoners as references for himself and included some endorsements from them. One of the endorsements came in the form of a poem dedicated to him by the Belgian hair stylist of Tilsit, Jean ("Jonny") Descoteaux, whose legendary good looks had inspired a group affair of four Belgian POWs with two German women in the spring of 1942.[30] The records do not disclose whether any of the abusive officers serving in Graudenz was ever charged with war crimes.

The Belgian government also gathered descriptions about the behavior of German civilians and foremen in some areas, asking the former men of confidence to create lists of people who had been supportive or hostile to POWs. Some examples from the region of Stalag XIII-B (Weiden in northeastern Bavaria) have survived. The man of confidence divided civilians into three groups: "A" for people who had helped POWs and treated them fairly, "B" for Nazi party members and officials who were not known to have interacted positively or negatively with POWs, and "C" for specific persons who had been mean or abusive to POWs. The lists give the addresses of the Germans and the names of former POWs who witnessed the good and bad behavior. Some women appear in group "A" for having been particularly helpful to a POW or for having hidden him during an escape attempt, but there is no mention of amorous relations even though they were very widespread in this region. These lists, created in July 1945, may have been intended for use during

---

[30] CEGESOMA, AA 120/C/64, Commission belge des crimes de guerre. Camp de Graudenz. The story is told in Chapter 3 in the sub-chapter "Erotic Encounters."

denazification proceedings and perhaps war crimes trials, but it is unclear if they ever served that purpose.[31]

The Belgian federation of former POWs first tried to achieve recognition of Rawa-Ruska as a concentration camp, but a parliamentary vote in 1954 rejected this equation despite support from King Leopold III. But in the 1970s, the camps of Rawa-Ruska, Kobierzyn, and now also Graudenz and its sub-camps were indeed recognized as sites of persecution.[32] But when former man of confidence Georges Smets in a television interview in 1975 revealed that 6 percent of the prisoners in his camp (Stalag I-A in East Prussia) had to stand trial because of forbidden relations and that he spent 75 percent of his time caring for their defense, he triggered much criticism in the press and through private channels. To a critic and friend, he wrote a long letter, explaining that it was all true and that he could prove the full extent if he had not been forced to abandon his files on the flight from East Prussia in early 1945. Smets explained that some convicted POWs were so desperate to avoid Graudenz that they volunteered to join one of the Belgian Waffen-SS divisions, and that he had been called as a defense witness in some postwar trials against these men to explain the horrors of Graudenz and the reason for the conviction.[33] Although German officials at the time denied that the Waffen-SS recruited among western POWs, there was, according to Smets, a German officer in Stalag I-A who quietly arranged the transfer of volunteers to the Walloon or Flemish Waffen-SS division, among them quite a few people on trial for a forbidden relation.[34]

The British authorities did conduct some trials against commanders who had mistreated POWs, possibly including some convicts from the Graudenz complex, during the evacuation marches in early 1945. In front of a British court, Captain Willi Mackensen was charged with having caused the death of at least thirty POWs during a march from

[31] CEGESOMA, AA 120/C/84.
[32] Musée Royal de l'Armée et d'Histoire Militaire, Evere, Fonds Gillet, Boîte 1, #4 affaires juridiques.
[33] Smets to Mr. Georges Paulus, January 11, 1976, in Musée Royal de l'Armée et d'Histoire Militaire, Brussels, Fonds Hautecler, Farde 34. For confirmation that some Belgians signed up for the Waffen-SS to escape punishment for a forbidden relation, see Schwarze, *Es war wie eine Hexenjagd*, 171.
[34] About the notion of a "pan-Germanic" SS army including Belgians, see Bernd Wegner, *Hitlers politische Soldaten. Die Waffen-SS 1933–1945: Studien zu Leitbild, Struktur und Funktion einer nationalsozialistischen Elite*, 5th edn (Paderborn: Schöningh, 1997), 310–11. Recruitment among Soviet prisoners was more common, however: Peter Black and Martin Gutmann, "Racial Theory and Realities of Conquest in the Occupied East: The Nazi Leadership and non-German Nationals in the SS and Police," in *The Waffen-SS: A European History*, ed. Jochen Böhler and Robert Gerwarth (Oxford and New York: Oxford University Press, 2017), 25–6.

Stalag XX-A in Thorn. Although Mackensen could have effectively defended himself by arguing that most of the deaths resulted from terrible conditions on the march, he did plead guilty and was sentenced to death; he was executed in March 1946. Wilhelm Menzel, an NCO in charge of evacuating mostly British POWs from Blechhammer, also was on trial for gratuitous abuses of POWs and the miserable conditions during a thirteen-week march that in many ways resembled the trek of Dallmer-Zerbe's column from Graudenz to southern Bavaria. Menzel admitted having hit POWs with his rifle butt, but he claimed that he had acted under ever stricter orders to prevent escapes and become very frustrated by the many prisoners who absconded during the march. He was first sentenced to ten years in prison, but his defense attorney objected by arguing that Menzel was not responsible for the terrible supply situation on the march and by pointing out Menzel's low rank. The higher judicial officer reduced his sentence to five years in prison.[35]

The British government negotiated an indemnification treaty with the FRG in 1964, but this treaty focused on refugees who had come to Britain and on concentration camp inmates or inmates of camps characterized by similar circumstances. POW camps were excluded, and many former POWs who had suffered grievous human rights abuses were not considered. A prominent POW demand for indemnification came from the survivors of the "Great escape" from Stalag Luft in Sagan, where the SS had murdered fifty recaptured prisoners, and this interest group, powerfully supported in the press, did achieve later inclusion in the indemnification definitions. The POWs interned in Graudenz and Torgau also received some recognition when the British government accepted these prisons as equivalent to concentration camps (erroneously in my opinion), but many former inmates of the military prisons still saw their applications for indemnification rejected. The handling of POW applications remained inconsistent.[36]

Veteran POWs sometimes undertook trips to their former detention sites, alone or in groups. Edouard Frankignoul left a detailed description of one such trip organized by an *amicale* (club) of former Belgian POWs in July 1972. He and his comrades went to Weiden in Bavaria, site of the

[35] Margaretha Franziska Vordermayer, *Justice for the Enemy? Die Verteidigung deutscher Kriegsverbrecher durch britische Offiziere in Militätgerichtsprozessen nach dem Zweiten Weltkrieg (1945–1949)* (Baden-Baden: Nomos, 2019), 149–54.
[36] Susanna Schrafstetter, "'What About Paying BRITISH Victims of Nazi Hell Camps?' Die Entschädigungsfrage in den deutsch-britischen Beziehungen," in *Grenzen der Wiedergutmachung: Die Entschädigung für NS-Verfolgte in West- und Osteuropa 1945–2000*, ed. Hans Günther Hockerts, Claudia Moisel, and Tobias Winstel (Göttingen: Wallstein, 2006), 612, 614, 618, 621–9.

former Stalag XIII-B, and they visited various villages in which they had spent important years of their youth. Frankignoul reflected benevolently on the German population, claiming that many foremen in the factories and most farmers had been friendly to the Belgians. In villages and senior citizen homes, the group visited many farm wives who had been their bosses during the war. Alluding to the much-loved goods POWs used to give to their employers from their aid parcels, he mentioned that they brought the farm wives coffee and chocolate from Belgium. While sitting down for a "*großes Bier*" with a few comrades in a village restaurant where they used to work, he described an emotional encounter:

Suddenly an old lady appears, confused, and four among us get up, squeeze and hug her. She cannot believe her eyes but remembers the first names of her former Belgian guests one after the other. Younger folk join in, as well as children, who had heard much about the prisoners of war. One of the older ones goes out into the fields and gathers sturdy workmen in their work clothes, all children thirty years ago, now adult men. Our comrades disappear into the building that used to be their sleeping quarters. The barred windows are still there.

The village people cordially celebrate the visitors and beg the travel guides to let them stay as long as possible. At the end, a pensive old man with a pipe says, with tears flowing down his face: "I ask you for forgiveness for all that we made you suffer. We did not know. We were tricked."[37]

Another Belgian veteran, Jules Delforge, chairman of the *amicale* of former POWs in district VIII (Silesia), attended the inauguration of a memorial for a POW camp in July 1976. On his return trip, he and his comrades stopped in northern Bavaria, where they met a woman, Anna Krämer, who told them that she had a church marriage with a POW from Brussels during the war despite the prohibition. The prisoner, Jean Vervois, had worked in a local sawmill. He had a secret relationship with Anna Krämer, and she became pregnant. Somehow she managed to convince the local priest to marry them in church, pretending that the name of her fiancé was Hans Busch. In early 1945, she gave birth to a boy. She showed Delforge a photo of the child that, according to Delforge, "left no doubt about Belgian paternity." As Anna Krämer had recently learned, Jean Vervois, alias Hans Busch, had returned to Brussels and died in 1967 without ever having married again. She had married another man after the war, but only in a civil ceremony, since her church marriage to the prisoner was still valid. She told Delforge that

---

[37] Eduard Frankignoul, "Retrouvailles," in CEGESOMA, AA 244 (Archives de la Commission d'Histoire de la Captivité de Guerre 1940–1945: verslagen, corr., vragenlijsten, 06/1940–15/04/1970).

now that she knew of the death of her first husband, she could also marry her current husband religiously. Delforge tracked down the village priest, who confirmed all the information.[38]

German women who had been denounced, or their families, could sue the denouncer on the basis of laws regarding crimes against humanity after the war. If a denunciation had occurred in full awareness of the potentially lethal consequences for the victim, it could retrospectively be punished even if the denouncer had acted in order to ensure respect for existing law. But the denunciation needed to be motivated by an inhumane mindset, and that was often difficult, even impossible, to prove in cases of forbidden relations.[39] Austria theoretically allowed high sentences for denunciations having led to the death of the denounced person (even life in prison), but the sentencing of the courts in practice was inconsistent, and many convicted denouncers obtained early releases.[40] A few cases of denunciations for "racial shame" and relationships with POWs did come before the courts (even though very few denounced persons died as a result of incarceration), but they almost always led to acquittal. Courts would only consider those cases in which the denunciation had, for example, led to the hanging of the Polish POW and the deportation of the woman into a concentration camp, and even there, judges followed a lenient line by arguing that the non-fraternization orders were not unique to Nazi Germany. Notions concerning "racial shame" sometimes continued to influence judges and juries. Sometimes courts concluded that the defendant did not know that the denunciation would endanger the life of the denunciation victim – although this was a spurious argument, for example, for a denouncer of a Polish or Soviet POW involved with a German woman, given that the hangings were public.[41]

The very marginal consideration of the people sentenced for forbidden relations in the indemnification proceedings and in courts has contributed to forgetting. Even a small, symbolic monetary compensation means recognizing the suffering of a person sentenced under National

---

[38] Jules Delforge to Georges Hautecler, August 4, 1976, in CEGESOMA, AA 244 (Archives de la Commission d'Histoire de la Captivité de Guerre 1940–1945: verslagen, corr., vragenlijsten, 06/1940–15/04/1970).

[39] Rüping, "Denunziation und Strafjustiz im Führerstaat," 136–7.

[40] Polaschek, *Im Namen der Republik Oesterreich!*, 181–201, 232.

[41] Heimo Halbrainer, "'Der Angeber musste vorhersehen, dass die Denunziation eine Gefahr für das Leben des Betroffenen nach sich ziehen werde': Volksgerichtsverfahren wegen Denunziation mit Todesfolge in Österreich," in *Holocaust und Kriegsverbrechen vor Gericht. Der Fall Österreich*, ed. Thomas Albrich, Winfried R. Garscha, and Martin F. Polaschek (Innsbruck: StudienVerlag, 2006), 255–6.

Socialism and anchors this suffering in public memory.[42] But the POWs
and the German women sentenced by the Nazi courts to harsh prisons
and penitentiaries did not generally benefit from this. The few successes
of the former Graudenz inmates, moreover, came at the cost of severe
distortion.

The forbidden relations and the harsh treatment of convicted POWs in
German prisons did have an impact on international law, however. When
the ICRC convened a conference on the drafting of a new POW convention in Geneva in 1949, both Hans K. Frey, the Swiss diplomat who had
overseen the trials against British and American POWs, and French
POW lawyer Stéphane Delattre submitted memoranda to the drafting
committee that reflected their experiences with German military justice.
As a result, Article 82 of the 1949 convention on POWs references the
convictions for forbidden relations with German women. "If any law,
regulation or order of the Detaining Power shall declare acts committed
by a prisoner of war to be punishable, whereas the same acts would not
be punishable if committed by a member of the forces of the Detaining
Power, such acts shall entail disciplinary punishments only."[43] As ICRC
director Jean Pictet, who oversaw the drafting of the 1949 POW Convention, states with respect to Article 82: "This provision ... is based on
the experience of the Second World War, when certain Powers adopted
repressive measures in regard to prisoners of war, sometimes entailing
very severe penalties, particularly in the case of relations between prisoners of war and the female population."[44] The article therefore adopts as
binding the practice of the British and American army with respect to
their POWs and echoes the line of argument the Scapini Mission and the
Belgian DSLP had presented to the High Command during the war.

The initial refusal of the German authorities to allow the protecting
powers and the ICRC inspections of the military prisons and penitentiaries, as well as the harsh conditions there, also inspired clearer guidelines after the war. Although the right of the protecting power to visit *all*
sites of detention with POWs had already been stated in the 1929 Geneva
Convention, the 1949 convention specifically included sites of imprison-
ment and clarified that the ICRC also needs to be given access to these

[42] For a collection of essays dealing with the connection between monetary restitution and
memory, see Dan Diner and Gotthart Wunberg, eds., *Restitution and Memory: Material
Restoration in Europe* (New York and Oxford: Berghahn Books, 2007).

[43] Vance, *Encyclopedia of Prisoners of War and Internment*, 555.

[44] Jean Pictet, *The Geneva Conventions of 12 August 1949: Commentary. III Geneva
Convention Relative to the Treatment of Prisoners of War* (Geneva: International
Committee of the Red Cross, 1960), 409.

sites (Article 126).[45] Moreover, the 1949 convention introduced a passage on the conditions in penal institutions that reflected the POW experiences in the Graudenz complex in Article 108: "These conditions shall in all cases conform to the requirements of health and humanity."[46] The same article also confirms the convicted POW's rights to receive correspondence, aid parcels, medical care, and spiritual assistance. The 1949 convention therefore vindicated all the demands made during the war by the Scapini Mission, the DSLP, and the Swiss legation in Berlin.

---

[45] Pictet, *The Geneva Conventions of 12 August 1949*, 602–13 (especially 609).
[46] Vance, *Encyclopedia of Prisoners of War and Internment*, 562; Pictet, *The Geneva Conventions of 12 August 1949*, 500–5.

Conclusion: Resistance, Dissent, Opposition?

How should we classify the forbidden relations? The people who chose to be involved with somebody "forbidden" did, in almost all cases, knowingly disobey a German military order (the POWs) or Nazi decree (the women). But was this a private act driven by self-interest that only became criminal because of the Nazi regime's intrusion into the private sphere? Were the people sentenced for forbidden relations victims of Nazi persecution, as some of the women claimed in the context of restitution claims? Or was it, as the Graudenz veterans insisted, somehow a political act, a case of conscious resistance, even if it did not necessarily serve a subversive act?

Scholars of the Third Reich and the Holocaust have considerably broadened the definition of resistance over the past three decades. No longer can armed and violent acts, such as the plot to blow up Hitler, the partisan resistance in Nazi-occupied countries, or the uprisings in ghettos and concentration camps, be considered the only forms of resistance.[1] Resistance could be non-violent, for example through distribution of anti-Nazi leaflets, as practiced by the White Rose student group. It could consist of breaking the rules in a ghetto or concentration camp, and it could involve intelligence-gathering for resistance groups. The broadening of the range of acts qualified as resistance considered people previously ignored, for example women in the resistance movements. One can even argue that the preservation of previous habits and traditions could be subversive, for example by maintaining Christian rituals and organizations or, in the case of Jews in a ghetto, the deliberate fostering of Jewish religious practice and identity. Historian Martin Broszat introduced the German term *"Resistenz"* for adherence to traditional ways of life against the ideological and organizational mandates

---

[1] For a helpful overview, see Ian Kershaw, *The Nazi Dictatorship: Problems and Perspectives of Interpretation*, 5th ed. (London: Bloomsbury, 2015), 213–51. On the subject of Jewish resistance, arguing for a broader definition, see Yehuda Bauer, *The Jewish Emergence from Powerlessness* (Toronto: University of Toronto Press, 1979), 27–40.

and expectations of the Nazi state. *Resistenz* implies the notion of "being resistant to" – something typically more passive and inert, although it could become an active and even subversive posture in a push-back reaction to the regime's efforts to infringe on cherished traditions or private life. Other examples of acts placed under a broad umbrella of resistance and dissent include various types of non-conformity in groups that chose to foster cultural practices condemned by the regime. Detlev Peukert, for example, has researched the fate of the "swing youth," groups of mostly middle-class and urban youngsters listening and dancing to American or British swing music. Contrary to *Resistenz*, such acts of non-conformity did not emerge from a preservation of traditional beliefs and ways of life but involved a conscious choice for something relatively new and forbidden. Moreover, similar to the forbidden relations, the adulation for swing and the use of English words and Anglo-American music during the war defied the vilification of the enemy in Nazi propaganda. SS chief Heinrich Himmler considered this behavior highly subversive, even treasonous, and he insisted on harsh punishments.[2]

Were the forbidden relations a case of *Resistenz*? One can certainly argue that the women and prisoners adhered to older traditions insofar as they insisted on their individual freedom to choose their love partners. Like people who committed "racial shame," they refused to accept Nazi prohibitions on dating and sexual partners. This notion works less well for the POWs than for the women, however. As mobilized soldiers in captivity, the POWs were still subject to army discipline – including the laws and orders of the German army. As pointed out in the beginning, POWs do not usually have unrestricted access to civilians. This is not a peculiarity of the Nazi regime, although the racial hygienic reasoning behind the prohibition and the severe penalization of the relationships are probably unique to Nazi legal practice. If the POWs insisted on their right of free choice when it came to a sexual partner, they were therefore in a sense revolting against their status as POWs, perhaps more than against a Nazi order. But the *Resistenz* paradigm fits less well in light of the fact that the forbidden relations emerged in an entirely new situation created by the war. Both the absence of many younger German men and also the presence of many poorly guarded foreign prisoners among the German population were highly unusual conditions. Arguing for the preservation and active defense of older traditions fails in light of these circumstances because the partners in the forbidden relations would not

[2] Detlev Peukert, *Inside Nazi Germany: Conformity, Opposition, and Racism in Everyday Life*, trans. Richard Deveson (New Haven: Yale University Press, 1987), 166–9.

have had the opportunity to meet and to get involved with each other in peacetime.

The term non-conformity fits the forbidden relations better. Both partners consciously and deliberately broke Nazi law. The women and the many civilians and guards who did not denounce a forbidden relationship refused to accept the Nazi propaganda line that the POWs were implacable enemies who ought to be hated or at least treated with a hostile distance. The POWs disobeyed a German order (they were not punished if they or their attorneys could prove that they did not know the order), and the British POWs violated also their own army regulations, which forbade "fraternization" with enemy civilians. Non-conformity would suggest a behavior contradicting prevailing norms, and here one has to consider whether the attitude of German communities undermines the non-conformity argument. As demonstrated, German communities to a large extent accepted the POWs, especially the French and Belgians. If the communities did object to the forbidden relations, they often did so not because they involved a POW but rather for reasons informed by broader notions of propriety, such as the condemnation of adultery and of public displays of affection and sexuality. Given the widespread danger of discovery, however, the women and prisoners did engage in an act of non-conformity even if the majority of the community, be it the farming village or the factory workforce, did not object to the relationship – or at least did not object to it because it involved an "enemy."

This leads to the question of motivation and intent. The dismissal of the forbidden relations as a purely private and self-interested choice, as prevalent during the restitution and indemnification debates in the Federal Republic of Germany, is not satisfactory because the Nazi regime so insistently politicized the private sphere. Almost all the couples treated in this book did make a conscious choice to defy a Nazi prohibition, knowing that this would lead to harsh punishment if they were discovered. Yet, their intent was not to damage or bring down the Nazi regime. Hardly any of the couples thought in these terms, and that is why the argument of the Graudenz veterans – namely that they engaged in an act of resistance designed to undermine the German war effort – made no sense even though it reflected the (flawed) reasoning in the court sentences against the POWs and the women. There is practically no evidence that POWs violating the order of January 10, 1940, hoped to damage the German war effort. Even the very small number of prisoners who planned to take advantage of a forbidden relation to prepare an escape were hardly thinking in these terms. For French and Belgian POWs, escape would not have been an effective way to sabotage the

German war effort because – directly or indirectly – they would have to work for it at home, too, unless they escaped in order to join a resistance group in the wilderness, which probably only very few prisoners in Germany were planning to do. German women, too, certainly did not calculate that their liaison with a prisoner would undermine the German war effort. Traces of dissent do appear in some cases where women, for example, criticize the war and the Nazi regime in their letters to a prisoner, but they are exceptional.

In a sense, however, the forbidden relations were acts of protest. For the French POWs, in particular, the protest targeted their continuing captivity at a time when their government collaborated with Nazi Germany. Being largely assimilated to a civilian worker, yet still being restricted by POW status, made little sense under these conditions, especially given the growing presence in Germany of French and Belgian civilian workers without dating prohibitions. For the British POWs, Clare Makepeace has uncovered a prevalent rebellious mindset, but her sample draws largely from officers and educated prisoners.[3] Granted, one can easily imagine that some British (and other) POWs who undertook parties with German women took delight in fooling their guards and in defying German regulations, but there is no evidence that this was the prevalent motivation for POWs to enter into a forbidden relationship. For the German women, the illicit relations often implied a protest against the situation created by the Nazi regime and its seemingly endless war – the absence of husbands and potential German boyfriends coupled with the tempting presence of many young but "forbidden" foreign men. For both, the POWs and the German women, love between enemies expressed a common bond of humanity transcending national boundaries, and this was a truly subversive action in the context of hatred and vilification in Nazi Germany.

As historian Nathan Stolzfus argues in *Hitler's Compromises*, Hitler sometimes backed down or chose to compromise if a policy he advocated encountered much opposition and protest within the German population, as did for example the removal of crucifixes from schools in Catholic regions, the euthanasia program, or the planned deportation and murder of Jewish men married to non-Jewish women in Berlin in early 1943. Hitler may have condemned and despised the motives for the opposition, but he could settle for a temporary halt of controversial policies while hoping that victory in the war and continued indoctrination would sooner or later wear down opposition. Such tolerance for

[3] Makepeace, *Captives of War*, 56–63.

opposition and protest also applied to certain wartime exigencies, for example the evacuation of women and children from urban areas targeted by bombings. Many people ignored the evacuation orders and returned home, and the authorities reacted with leniency in these cases, which also involved an intervention of the Nazi regime in the private sphere and the family.[4]

In the case of the forbidden relations, however, there is little indication that the regime backed down out of such considerations. It is true that the sentences for the women became more lenient throughout the war. But there is no evidence that the regime decided for compromise in this matter even though Hitler personally tended to deny women's agency and was not sure that the women, unlike the POWs, had to be severely punished. The normative judges' letters (*Richterbriefe*) by Justice Minister Thierack emphasized a hard line even in cases involving relationships with French POWs, consciously contradicting a more accepting popular feeling. The judges and prosecutors' offices, however, were aware of the disruptions caused by the arrest and incarceration of thousands of women. The myriad clemency pleas alerted them to the severe economic, social, and emotional fallout of incarceration for the women's communities and families, affecting in many cases a soldier husband. The punishments were obviously much more disruptive to the German war effort than the amorous relations themselves. There is no paper trail on this, but it is possible that these considerations motivated more lenient sentences against the accused women in the later years of the war. Clearly, the "healthy feeling of the *Volk*," which served as the underpinning of the prohibition for the German women, rarely worked as planned by the regime.

The regime did not need to compromise toward the foreign POWs, and it showed no inclination to do so despite discreetly shared misgivings against the harsh punishments among some military judges, the German Foreign Office, and even some members of the High Command such as General Reinecke. To the contrary, the punishments against the POWs quickly became harsher in the course of 1941, and the order to punish sexual relations with a soldier's wife with penitentiary instead of prison intended to harden penal practice even more, although I have found that

---

[4] Nathan Stoltzfus, *Hitler's Compromises: Coercion and Consensus in Nazi Germany* (New Haven: Yale University Press, 2016); Torrie, *"For Their Own Good,"* 99–112; Robert Gellately, "Police Justice, Popular Justice, and Social Outsiders in Nazi Germany: The Example of Polish Foreign Workers," in *Social Outsiders in Nazi Germany*, ed. Robert Gellately and Nathan Stoltzfus (Princeton: Princeton University Press, 2001); Nathan Stoltzfus, *Resistance of the Heart: Intermarriage and the Rosenstrasse Protest in Nazi Germany* (New York: Norton, 1996).

the conditions in the penitentiaries were hardly worse than in the Graudenz military prison complex. The Nazi authorities only compromised insofar as they agreed to improve conditions in the Graudenz complex and to allow communication with POWs incarcerated in penitentiaries. In both cases, the changes brought German penal practice, when applied to POWs, closer to the requirements of the Geneva Convention, while opening a gap between the extremely brutal treatment of convicted German soldiers and the more considerate treatment of POWs.

Increasingly, the prohibition served the purpose of steeling the German people's community in solidarity and bitter hostility against all outsiders. The racial hygienic motivation, which influenced the order to POWs in January 1940 and appeared in almost every court martial sentence in 1941, faded. In light of the ethnic and racial diversity of the POWs, including many people considered racially desirable and precious by Nazi standards, and in light of the absence of similar prohibitions for western civilian laborers (and, one might add, for German soldiers in many occupied countries), the Nazi regime would have had to apply a racial screen to the prohibition by punishing only racially "undesirable" prisoners and the women involved with them. Such a racial screen would have made it easier to apply the Nürnberg laws and other legislation against unwanted sexual relations, for example the decrees concerning Poles and workers from the Soviet Union, but this would have contradicted the Geneva Convention, which prohibits harsher treatment on the basis of race, ethnicity, and religion. It remains noteworthy, however, that the Nazi regime, out of international considerations, chose to ignore its own racial legislation in the trials of women involved with Jews or ethnic Poles from the French, Belgian, or British armies. Although some prosecutors saw involvement with a Jew or Pole as an aggravating factor and involvement with a "racially related" person such as a Fleming or a South African with German or Dutch ancestry as a mitigating factor, the courts by and large sentenced women with little consideration for the ethnic or racial background of the prisoner, although they did occasionally pronounce lenient sentences in the cases involving relationships with "racially related" prisoners. International law here clearly influenced German legal practice, which would normally have punished the women much more harshly for having consorted with a Jew or a Pole.

The shift of emphasis from the racial hygienic arguments to the unity of the *Volksgemeinschaft* at war represents an intriguing parallel to the treatment of the "Jewish Question" in Nazi propaganda. As other scholars have pointed out, the Nazi regime increasingly instrumentalized the vague but widespread public awareness of German atrocities against Jews to forge an iron community united not least in fear of collective punishment for its active or passive participation in the persecution and murder of Jews. As the Nazi leaders hoped, this community of fate would hold the home front together, for better or worse, and avoid another 1918. The link between ideological insistence on the purity of the race and unity of the *Volksgemeinschaft* of course existed from the start, given Hitler's obsession with the Jews as a subversive group fomenting rebellion behind the front lines, which he believed to have led to the "stab in the back" of 1918. But after most Jews had been "removed" from the *Volksgemeinschaft* and the occupied territories, the focus shifted to a dichotomy between the "Jewish enemy" outside and the purged and fanaticized *Volksgemeinschaft* within.[5]

While the Nazi regime encouraged Germans to burn all bridges behind them and to cast aside all moral concerns, the POWs and foreign laborers were representatives of the wider world and of Germany's enemies in the midst of the German population. German women getting involved with them, and German civilians tolerating the forbidden relations, were helping to preserve a link with wider humanity and defying the Nazi regime's disastrous course toward a situation where collective suicide or total annihilation were the only alternatives as a total Nazi victory became completely illusory.[6] Certainly, this was a less pressing concern in early relationships, but by 1944 it likely played an important role in the motivation of the women and in the reactions of their communities. Herein lies the most subversive aspect of the forbidden relationships from the sides of both partners: through their amorous encounters, western prisoners and German women affirmed a common bond of humanity that transcended national and often also racial boundaries and undermined the increasingly shrill and depraved hate rhetoric of the Nazi regime. In this sense, the love relations were acts of resistance, broadly defined.

---

[5] Stargardt, *German War*, 375–9; Peter Fritzsche, *Life and Death in the Third Reich* (Cambridge, MA, and London: Belknap, 2008), 265–6; Frank Bajohr and Dieter Pohl, *Der Holocaust als offenes Geheimnis: die Deutschen, die NS-Führung und die Alliierten* (Munich: Beck, 2006). The Nazi propaganda strategy to use guilt feelings about the treatment of the Jews to forge a community of fate was clearly perceived already in an intelligence report coming to the State Department through the American legation in Bern in June 1944: "The Nazis are systematically attempting to convince the German people that they are accomplices in Nazi crimes and therefore are inextricably linked with the fate of the Party." The report, which drew from some German sources, mentioned large-scale massacres of Jews, although it did not acknowledge the existence of death camps and thus reflected well the widespread state of awareness among the German population. American Legation Bern to State Department, June 16, 1944, in NACP, RG 59, 711.62114A, Box 2218.

[6] For the notion of a choreographed heroic defeat amounting to collective suicide, see Bernd Wegner, "Hitler, der Zweite Weltkrieg und die Choreographie des Untergangs," *Geschichte und Gesellschaft* 26 (2000): 493–518.

Bibliography

Published Primary Sources

Althusser, Louis. *Journal de Captivité: Stalag XA/1940–1945: Carnets, correspondances, textes.* n. p.: Stock/IMEC, 1992.

Ambrière, Francis. *Les grandes Vacances 1939–1945.* Paris: Les Éditions de la Nouvelle France, 1946.

Bartsch, Robert. "Das 'gesunde Volksempfinden' im Strafrecht." Dr. phil. dissertation, law faculty, Universität Hamburg, 1940.

Baud, Georges, Louis Devaux, and Jean Poigny, eds. *Mémoire complémentaire sur quelques aspects du Service Diplomatique des Prisonniers de Guerre: SDPG-DFB-Mission Scapini, 1940–1945.* [Paris]: G. Baud, 1984.

Boberach, Heinz, ed. *Meldungen aus dem Reich: Auswahl aus den geheimen Lageberichten des Sicherheitsdienstes der SS 1939–1944.* Neuwied and Berlin: Luchterhand, 1965.

Meldungen aus dem Reich 1938–1945: Die geheimen Lageberichte des Sicherheitsdienstes der SS. Herrsching: Pawlak, 1984.

Richterbriefe. Dokumente zur Beeinträchtigung der deutschen Rechtsprechung 1942–1944. Boppard: Boldt, 1975.

Delattre, Stéphane. *Ma Guerre sans fusil. Décembre 1942–avril 1945: Une chronique judiciaire de la captivité.* La Rochelle: Rumeur des Âges, 1991.

Domarus, Max, ed. *Hitler: Speeches and Proclamations, 1932–1945,* Vol. 3. Wauconda: Bolchazy-Carducci, 1990–2.

Dörken, Georg, and Werner Scherer. *Das Militärstrafgesetzbuch und die Kriegssonderstrafrechtsverordnung.* 4th ed. Berlin: Verlag Franz Vahlen, 1943.

Dower, Jack. *Deliverance at Diepholz: A World War II's Prisoner of War Story.* Stackpole Military History Series. Mechanicsburg, PA: Stackpole Books, 2016.

Folcher, Gustave. *Les carnets de guerre de Gustave Folcher paysan languedocien (1939–1945).* Paris: François Maspero, 1981.

Form, Wolfgang, and Oliver Uthe, eds. *NS-Justiz in Österreich. Lage- und Reiseberichte 1938–1945.* Schriftenreihe des Dokumentationsarchivs des österreichischen Widerstandes zu Widerstand, NS-Verfolgung und Nachkriegsaspekten, Vol. 3. Vienna: LIT Verlag, 2004.

Kadecka, Ferdinand. "Gesundes Volksempfinden und gesetzlicher Grundgedanke." *Zeitschrift für die gesamte Strafrechtswissenschaft* 62 (1942/1944): 1–27.

Kallfelz, Walter. "Strafbarer Umgang mit Kriegsgefangenen." *Deutsches Recht* 10, no. 43 (1940): 1811–13.

Kübler, Robert, ed. *Chef KGW: Das Kriegsgefangenenwesen unter Gottlob Berger. Nachlass.* Lindhorst: Askania, 1984.

Moll, Martin. *"Führer-Erlasse" 1939–1945: Edition sämtlicher überlieferter, nicht im Reichsgesetzblatt abgedruckter, von Hitler während des Zweiten Weltkrieges schriftlich erteilter Direktiven aus den Bereichen Staat, Partei, Wirtschaft, Besatzungspolitik und Militärverwaltung.* Stuttgart: Franz Steiner Verlag, 1997.

Müller-Hill, Werner Otto. *"Man hat es kommen sehen und ist doch erschüttert": Das Kriegstagebuch eines deutschen Heeresrichters.* Munich, 2011.

Münch, Ingo von. *Gesetze des NS-Staates: Dokumente eines Unrechtssystems.* 3rd ed. Paderborn: Ferdinand Schöningh, 1994.

Perrin, Marius. *Avec Sartre au Stalag 12D.* Paris: Delarge, 1980.

Peters, Karl. "Das gesunde Volksempfinden: Ein Beitrag zur Rechtsquellenlehre des 19. und 20. Jahrhunderts." *Deutsches Strafrecht: Strafrecht, Strafrechtspolitik, Strafprozeß* 5 (Neue Folge), no. 10/11 (1938): 337–50.

Satow, Harold (Sir), and M. J. Sée. *The Work of the Prisoners of War Department during the Second World War.* [London]: Foreign Office, 1950.

Scapini, Georges. *Mission sans gloire.* Paris: Editions Morgan, 1960.

Waltzog, Alfons. *Recht der Landkriegsführung: Die wichtigsten Abkommen des Landkriegsrechts.* Berlin: Verlag Franz Vahlen, 1942.

Secondary Sources

Anders, Freia. *Strafjustiz im Sudetengau 1938–1945.* Veröffentlichungen des Collegium Carolinum. Munich: Oldenbourg, 2008.

Angermund, Ralph. *Deutsche Richterschaft 1919–1945: Krisenerfahrung, Illusion, Politische Rechtsprechung.* Frankfurt am Main: Fischer Taschenbuch Verlag, 1990.

Arnaud, Patrice. "Die deutsch-französischen Liebesbeziehungen der französischen Zwangsarbeiter und beurlaubten Kriegsgefangenen im 'Dritten Reich': vom Mythos des verführerischen Franzosen zur Umkehrung der Geschlechterrolle." In *Nationalsozialismus und Geschlecht: Zur Politisierung und Ästhetisierung von Körper, "Rasse" und Sexualität im "Dritten Reich" und nach 1945*, edited by Elke Frietsch and Christina Herkommer. GenderCodes, 180–96. Bielefeld: transcript Verlag, 2009.

Les STO. Histoire des Français requis en Allemagne nazie 1942–1945. Paris: CNRS Editions, 2010.

Bästlein, Klaus. "Zur 'Rechts'-Praxis des Schleswig-Holsteinischen Sondergerichts 1937–1945." In *Strafverfolgung und Strafverzicht. Festschrift zum 125-jährigen Bestehen der Staatsanwaltschaft Schleswig-Holstein*, edited by Heribert Ostendorf, 93–167. Köln: Heymann, 1992.

Bailer, Brigitte. *Wiedergutmachung kein Thema. Österreich und die Opfer des Nationalsozialismus.* Vienna: Löcker, 1993.

Bajohr, Frank, and Dieter Pohl. *Der Holocaust als offenes Geheimnis: die Deutschen, die NS-Führung und die Alliierten.* Munich: Beck, 2006.

Bauer, Yehuda. *The Jewish Emergence from Powerlessness.* Toronto: University of Toronto Press, 1979.

Beck, Birgit. *Wehrmacht und sexuelle Gewalt: Sexualverbrechen vor deutschen Militärgerichten 1939–1945.* Paderborn: Schöningh, 2004.

Beer, Helmut. *Widerstand gegen den Nationalsozialismus in Nürnberg 1933–1945.* Schriftenreihe des Stadtarchivs Nürnberg. Nürnberg: Stadtarchiv Nürnberg, 1976.

Behrschmidt, Ewald. "Der Saal 600." In *Justizpalast Nürnberg: ein Ort der Weltgeschichte wird 100 Jahre. Festschrift zum 100. Jahrestag der feierlichen Eröffnung des Justizpalastes in Nürnberg durch König Ludwig III. am 11. September 1916,* edited by Christoph Strötz and Ewald Behrschmidt, 111–26. Neustadt an der Aisch: VDS, Verlagsdruckerei Schmidt, 2016.

Bennewitz, Nadja, and Gaby Franger. *Am Anfang war Sigena: Ein Nürnberger Frauengeschichtsbuch.* Nürnberg: Anthologie ars vivendi, 1999.

Bethmann, Dirk, and Michael Kvasnicka. "World War II, Missing Men and Out of Wedlock Childbearing." *The Economic Journal* 123, no. March (2013): 162–94.

Bjork, James. *Neither German nor Pole: Catholicism and National Indifference in a Central European Borderland.* Ann Arbor: University of Michigan Press, 2008.

Black, Peter, and Martin Gutmann. "Racial Theory and Realities of Conquest in the Occupied East: The Nazi Leadership and non-German Nationals in the SS and Police." In *The Waffen-SS: A European History,* edited by Jochen Böhler and Robert Gerwarth, 16–41. Oxford and New York: Oxford University Press, 2017.

Blanke, Thomas. *Die juristische Aufarbeitung des Unrechts-Staats.* Baden-Baden: Nomos, 1998.

Blessing, Elmar. *Die Kriegsgefangenen in Stuttgart: Das städtische Kriegsgefangenenlager in der Ulmer Straße und die "Katastrophe von Gaisburg."* 2nd ed. Stuttgart: Verlag im Ziegelhaus Ulrich Gohl, 2001.

Bock, Gisela. *Zwangssterilisation im Nationalsozialismus: Studien zur Rassenpolitik und Frauenpolitik.* Opladen: Westdeutscher Verlag, 1986.

Bock, Gisela, and Pat Thane, eds. *Maternity and Gender Policies: Women and the Rise of the European Welfare States, 1880–1950s.* London and New York: Routledge, 1991.

Böhler, Jochen, and Robert Gerwarth, eds. *The Waffen-SS: A European History.* Oxford and New York: Oxford University Press, 2017.

Boll, Bernd. "'… das gesunde Volksempfinden auf das Gröbste verletzt'. Die Offenburger Strafjustiz und der 'verbotene Umgang mit Kriegsgefangenen' während des Zweiten Weltkrieges." *Die Ortenau: Zeitschrift des Historischen Vereins für Mittelbaden* 71 (1991): 645–78.

Bozyakali, Can. *Das Sondergericht am Hanseatischen Oberlandesgericht: Eine Untersuchung der NS-Sondergerichte unter besonderer Berücksichtigung der Anwendung der Verordnung gegen Volksschädlinge.* Frankfurt am Main: Peter Lang, 2004.

Brodesser, Hermann-Josef, Bernd Josef Fehn, Tilo Franosch, and Wilfried Wirth. *Wiedergutmachung und Kriegsfolgenliquidation: Geschichte – Regelungen – Zahlungen.* Munich: Beck, 2000.

Buckinx, X. "Belgen in duitse Krijgsgevangenschap 1940–1945." *Spiegel Historiael,* no. 11 (1984): 503–11.

Capdevila, Luc. "The Quest for Masculinity in a Defeated France, 1940–1945." *Contemporary European History* 10, no. 3 (2001): 423–45.

Carlson, Lewis H. *We Were Each Other's Prisoners: An Oral History of World War II American and German Prisoners of War.* New York: Basic Books, 1997.

Carrard, Philippe. *The French Who Fought for Hitler: Memories from the Outcasts.* New York: Cambridge University Press, 2010.

Colmorgen, Eckard, and Klaus-Detlev Godau-Schüttke. "'Verbotener Umgang mit Kriegsgefangenen'. Frauen vor dem Schleswig-Holsteinischen Sondergericht (1940–1945)." *Demokratische Geschichte: Jahrbuch zur Arbeiterbewegung und Demokratie in Schleswig-Holstein* 9 (1995): 125–49.

d'Hoop, Jean-Marie. "Les prisonniers français et la communauté rurale allemande (1940–1945)." *Guerres mondiales et conflits contemporains*, no. 147 (1987): 31–47.

"Prisonniers de guerre français témoins de la défaite allemande (1945)." *Guerres mondiales et conflits contemporains* 38, no. 150 (1988): 77–98.

Diewald-Kerkmann, Gisela. "Politische Denunziation im NS-Regime: Die kleine Macht der 'Volksgenossen'." In *Denunziation: Historische, juristische und psychologische Aspekte*, edited by Günter Jerouschek, Inge Marßolek, and Hedwig Röckelein. Forum Psychohistorie, 146–56. Tübingen: Edition discord, 1997.

Diner, Dan, and Gotthart Wunberg, eds. *Restitution and Memory: Material Restoration in Europe.* New York and Oxford: Berghahn Books, 2007.

Dokumentationszentrum NS-Zwangsarbeit der Stiftung Topographie des Terrors, ed. *Zwischen allen Stühlen. Die Geschichte der italienischen Militärinternierten 1943–1945/Tra più fuochi: La storia degli internati militari italiani 1943–1945.* Berlin: Spree Druck, 2016.

Dombrowski, Nicole Ann, ed. *Women and War in the Twentieth Century: Enlisted with or without Consent.* Vol. 13, Women's History and Culture. New York and London: Garland Publishing, 1999.

Dördelmann, Katrin. "Denunziationen im Nationalsozialismus: Geschlechtsspezifische Aspekte." In *Denunziation: Historische, juristische und psychologische Aspekte*, edited by Günter Jerouschek, Inge Marßolek, and Hedwig Röckelein. Forum Psychohistorie, 157–67. Tübingen: Edition diskord, 1997.

Die Macht der Worte. Denunziationen im nationalsozialistischen Köln. Schriften des NS-Dokumentationszentrums der Stadt Köln. Köln: Emons Verlag, 1997.

Doyle, Robert C. *Voices from Captivity: Interpreting the American POW Narrative.* Modern War Studies. Lawrence: University Press of Kansas, 1994.

Drolshagen, Ebba D. *Nicht ungeschoren davongekommen: Das Schicksal der Frauen in den besetzten Ländern, die Wehrmachtssoldaten liebten.* Hamburg: Hoffmann und Campe, 1998.

Wehrmachtskinder: auf der Suche nach dem nie gekannten Vater. Munich: Droemer, 2005.

Durand, Yves. *La Captivité: histoire des prisonniers de guerre français, 1939–1945.* Paris: Fédération nationale des combattants et prisonniers de guerre et combattants d'Algérie, de Tunisie et du Maroc, 1982.

Les Prisonniers de guerre dans les Stalags, les Oflags et les Kommandos, 1939–1945. Paris: Hachette, 1987.

Ebbinghaus, Angelika, ed. *Opfer und Täterinnen: Frauenbiographien des Nationalsozialismus. Die Frau in der Gesellschaft.* Frankfurt am Main: Fischer, 1996.

Eberlein, Michael, Norbert Haase, and Wolfgang Oleschinski. *Torgau im Hinterland des Zweiten Weltkriegs: Militärjustiz, Wehrmachtgefängnisse, Reichskriegsgericht.* Leipzig: Kiepenheuer, 1999.

Eismann, Gaël, and Corinna von List. "Les Fonds des tribunaux allemands (1940–1945) conservés au BAVCC à Caen." *Francia* 39 (2012): 347–78.

Feltman, Brian K. *The Stigma of Surrender: German Prisoners, British Captors, and Manhood in the Great War and Beyond.* Chapel Hill: University of North Carolina Press, 2015.

"'We Don't Want Any German Off-Spring After These Prisoners Left Here': German Military Prisoners and British Women in the First World War." *Gender & History* 30, no. 1 (2018): 110–30.

Fishman, Sarah. "Grand Delusions: The Unintended Consequences of Vichy France's Prisoner of War Propaganda." *Journal of Contemporary History* 26, no. 2 (1991): 229–54.

We Will Wait: Wives of French Prisoners of War, 1940–1945. New Haven and London: Yale University Press, 1991.

Fout, John. "Homosexuelle in der NS-Zeit: Neue Forschungsansätze über Alltagsleben und Verfolgung." In *Nationalsozialistischer Terror gegen Homosexuelle. Verdrängt und ungesühnt,* edited by Burkhard Jellonnek and Rüdiger Lautmann, 163–72. Paderborn: Schöningh, 2002.

Foy, David A. *For You the War Is Over: American Prisoners of War in Nazi Germany.* New York: Stein and Day, 1984.

Fraenkel, Ernst. *The Dual State: A Contribution to the Theory of Dictatorship.* Oxford and New York: Oxford University Press, 1941.

Frey, Hans K. *Die disziplinarische und gerichtliche Bestrafung von Kriegsgefangenen: Die Anwendung des Kriegsgefangenenabkommens von 1929 auf die angelsächsischen und deutschen Kriegsgefangenen während des Zweiten Weltkrieges.* Vienna: Springer, 1948.

Fritzsche, Peter. *Life and Death in the Third Reich.* Cambridge, MA, and London: Belknap, 2008.

Gascar, Pierre. *Histoire de la captivité des Français en Allemagne (1939–1945).* Paris: Gallimard, 1967.

Gebhardt, Miriam. *Crimes Unspoken: The Rape of German Women at the End of the Second World War.* Translated by Nick Somers. Cambridge: Polity Press, 2016.

Gedenkstätte Roter Ochse, ed. *"... das gesunde Volksempfinden gröblichst verletzt": "verbotener Umgang mit Kriegsgefangenen" im Sondergerichtsbezirk Halle.* Halle: Heinrich-Böll-Stiftung Sachsen-Anhalt, Stiftung Gedenkstätten Sachsen-Anhalt, 2009.

Gelber, Yoav. "Palestinian POWs in German Captivity." *Yad Vashem Studies* 14 (1981): 89–137.

Gellately, Robert. "Police Justice, Popular Justice, and Social Outsiders in Nazi Germany: The Example of Polish Foreign Workers." In *Social Outsiders in Nazi Germany,* edited by Robert Gellately and Nathan Stoltzfus, 256–72. Princeton: Princeton University Press, 2001.

Gilbert, Adrien. *POW: Allied Prisoners in Europe, 1939–1945*. London: John Murray, 2006.

Gillet, E. "Histoire des sous-officiers et soldats belges prisonniers de guerre, 1940–1945." *Belgisch tijdschrift voor militaire geschiedenis/Revue belge d'histoire militaire*, XXVII (1987–8): 227–54, 299–320; 355–79; XXVIII (1989–90): 45–78, 123–66, 217–54, 299–335, 351–82.

Gillies, Midge. *The Barbed-Wire University: The Real Lives of Allied Prisoners of War in the Second World War*. London: Aurum Press, 2011.

Goschler, Constantin. *Schuld und Schulden: Die Politik der Wiedergutmachung für NS-Verfolgte seit 1945*. Beiträge zur Geschichte des 20. Jahrhunderts. Göttingen: Wallstein, 2005.

Wiedergutmachung. Westdeutschland und die Verfolgten des Nationalsozialismus (1945–1954). Quellen und Darstellungen zur Zeitgeschichte. München: Oldenbourg, 1992.

Grau, Günther. "Die Verfolgung der Homosexualität im Nationalsozialismus." In *Homosexuelle im Nationalsozialismus: Neue Perspektiven zu Lebenssituationen von lesbischen, schwulen, bi-, trans- und intersexuellen Menschen 1933 bis 1945*, edited by Michael Schwartz, 43–52. Oldenburg: De Gruyter, 2014.

Greiner, Bettina, and Alan Kramer, eds. *Die Welt der Lager. Zur "Erfolgsgeschichte" einer Institution*. Hamburg: Hamburger Edition, 2013.

Haase, Norbert. "Aus der Praxis des Reichskriegsgerichts: Neue Dokumente zur Militärgerichtsbarkeit im Zweiten Weltkrieg." *Vierteljahrshefte für Zeitgeschichte*, no. 3 (1991): 379–411.

Hackl, Gabriele, and Brigitte Sack. *Das Frauenzuchthaus Waldheim (1933–1945)*. Zeitfenster: Beiträge der Stiftung Sächsische Gedenkstätten zur Zeitgeschichte. Dresden: Leipziger Universitätsverlag, 2016.

Halbrainer, Heimo. "'Der Angeber musste vorhersehen, dass die Denunziation eine Gefahr für das Leben des Betroffenen nach sich ziehen werde'. Volksgerichtsverfahren wegen Denunziation mit Todesfolge in Österreich." In *Holocaust und Kriegsverbrechen vor Gericht: Der Fall Österreich*, edited by Thomas Albrich, Winfried R. Garscha and Martin F. Polaschek, 229–61. Innsbruck: StudienVerlag, 2006.

Hamburg, Justizbehörde, ed. *"Von Gewohnheitsverbrechern, Volksschädlingen und Asozialen ...": Hamburger Justizurteile im Nationalsozialismus*. Hamburg: Ergebnisse Verlag, 1995.

Hamm, Margret, ed. *Ausgegrenzt! Warum? Zwangssterilisierte und Geschädigte der NS-"Euthanasie" in der Bundesrepublik Deutschland*. Berlin: Metropol, 2017.

Hansen, Lulu Anne. "'Youth Off the Rails': Teenage Girls and German Soldiers – A Case Study in Occupied Denmark, 1940–1945." In *Brutality and Desire: War and Sexuality in Europe's Twentieth Century*, edited by Dagmar Herzog, 135–67. New York: Palgrave Macmillan, 2009.

Harrison, E.D.R. "The Nazi Dissolution of the Monasteries: A Case-Study." *English Historical Review* 109, no. 431 (1994): 323–55.

Harvey, Elizabeth. *Women and the Nazi East: Agents and Witnesses of Germanization*. New Haven: Yale University Press, 2003.

Hautecler, Georges. *Évasions réussies*. Liège: Éditions Solédi, 1966.

"La Vie religieuse des prisonniers de guerre Belges (1940–1945). Faits et documents." *Cahiers d'Histoire de la Seconde Guerre mondiale* 3 (1974): 49–64.

Hayes, Peter. *Industry and Ideology: IG Farben in the Nazi Era.* 2nd ed. New York: Cambridge University Press, 2001.

Heineman, Elizabeth D. *What Difference Does a Husband Make? Women and Marital Status in Nazi and Postwar Germany.* Berkeley and Los Angeles: University of California Press, 1999.

Held, Renate. *Kriegsgefangenschaft in Großbritannien: Deutsche Soldaten des Zweiten Weltkriegs in britischem Gewahrsam.* Veröffentlichungen des Deutschen Historischen Instituts London. München: Oldenbourg, 2008.

Herbert, Ulrich. *Hitler's Foreign Workers: Enforced Foreign Labor in Germany under the Third Reich.* Translated by William Templer. Cambridge and New York: Cambridge University Press, 1997.

Herzog, Dagmar. "Hubris and Hypocrisy, Incitement and Disawowal: Sexuality and German Fascism." In *Sexuality and German Fascism*, edited by Dagmar Herzog, 3–21. New York and Oxford: Berghahn Books, 2002.

"Introduction: War and Sexuality in Europe's Twentieth Century." In *Brutality and Desire: War and Sexuality in Europe's Twentieth Century*, edited by Dagmar Herzog, 1–15. New York: Palgrave Macmillan, 2009.

Sex after Fascism: Memory and Morality in Twentieth-Century Germany. Princeton and Oxford: Princeton University Press, 2005.

Sexuality in Europe: A Twentieth-Century History. Cambridge and New York: Cambridge University Press, 2011.

Sexuality and German Fascism. New York and Oxford: Berghahn Books, 2002.

Hett, Benjamin Carter. "Introduction." In *The True German: The Diary of a World War II Military Judge*, by Werner Otto Müller-Hill, xv–xxxii. New York: Palgrave Macmillan, 2013.

Heusler, Andreas. "'Strafbestand' Liebe: Verbotene Kontake zwischen Münchnerinnen und ausländischen Kriegsgefangenen." In *Zwischen den Fronten: Münchner Frauen in Krieg und Frieden 1900–1950*, edited by Sybille Krafft, 324–41. Munich: Buchendorfer Verlag, 1995.

Higonnet, Margaret Randolph, Jane Jenson, Sonya Michel, and Margaret Collins Weitz, eds. *Behind the Lines: Gender and the Two World Wars.* New Haven and London: Yale University Press, 1987.

Hinz, Uta. *Gefangen im Großen Krieg: Kriegsgefangenschaft in Deutschland 1914–1921.* Essen: Klartext Verlag, 2006.

Hochhuth, Rolf. *Eine Liebe in Deutschland.* Reinbek bei Hamburg: Rowohlt, 1978.

Höhn, Maria. *GIs and Fräuleins: The German–American Encounter in 1950s West Germany.* Chapel Hill: University of North Carolina Press, 2002.

Horn, Karen. "'History from the Inside': South African Prisoner-of-War Experience in Work Camp 1169, Dresden, 1943–1945." *War & Society* 33, no. 4 (2014): 269–82.

Hornung, Ela. "Denunziation als soziale Praxis: Eine Fallgeschichte aus der NS-Militärjustiz." In *Wehrmachtsjustiz:. Kontext, Praxis, Nachwirkungen*, edited by Peter Pirker and Florian Wenninger, 100–17. Wien: Braumüller, 2011.

Hornung, Ela, Ernst Langthaler, and Sabine Schweitzer. "Zwangsarbeit in der Landwirtschaft." In *Das Deutsche Reich und der Zweite Weltkrieg: Die deutsche*

Kriegsgesellschaft 1939 bis 1945, edited by Jörg Echternkamp, 577–666. Munich: Deutsche Verlags-Anstalt, 2005.

Irmen, Helmut. *Das Sondergericht Aachen 1941–1945*. Berlin: De Gruyter, 2018.

Isernhinke, Karina. *Das Strafgefangenenlager Oberems: Das nationalsozialistische Lagersystem im Gebiet des heutigen Kreises Gütersloh.* Veröffentlichungen aus dem Kreisarchiv Gütersloh. Bielefeld: Verlag für Regionalgeschichte, 2015.

Jellonnek, Burkhard, and Rüdiger Lautmann, eds. *Nationalsozialistischer Terror gegen Homosexuelle: Verdrängt und ungesühnt.* Paderborn: Schöningh, 2002.

Joshi, Vandana. *Gender and Power in the Third Reich: Female Denouncers and the Gestapo (1933–45).* Houndmills and New York: Palgrave Macmillan, 2003.

"Soldier's Morale and War Wife's Morality: Gendered Images of Righteousness and Citizenship in Nazi Germany." *Feministische Studien* 33, no. 2 (2015): 229–45.

Kalmbach, Peter Lutz. "Das System der NS-Sondergerichtsbarkeiten." *Kritische Justiz* 50, no. 2 (2017): 226–35.

"Eine 'Hauptwaffe gegen Defaitismus' – der Tatbestand der 'Wehrkraftzersetzung' als Instrument der NS-Justiz." *Neue Zeitschrift für Wehrrecht* 54, no. 1 (2012): 25–32.

"The German Courts-Martial and Their Cooperation with the Police Organizations during the World War II." *Journal on European History of Law* 8, no. 1 (2017): 2–5.

"'Schutz der geistigen Wehrkraft': NS-Strafrechtsreformen für den 'totalen Krieg'." *Juristenzeitung* 17 (2015): 814–19.

Wehrmachtjustiz. Berlin: Metropol-Verlag, 2012.

Keldungs, Karl-Heinz. *Das Duisburger Sondergericht 1942–1945.* Forum juristische Zeitgeschichte. Baden-Baden: Nomos, 1998.

Kershaw, Ian. *The Nazi Dictatorship: Problems and Perspectives of Interpretation.* 5th ed. London: Bloomsbury, 2015.

Kleinz, Angelika. *Individuum und Gemeinschaft in der juristischen Germanistik: die Geschworenengerichte und das "Gesunde Volksempfinden."* Heidelberg: Winter, 2001.

Koch, Hannsjoachim Wolfgang. *In the Name of the Volk: The Political Justice in Hitler's Germany.* New York: Barnes & Noble, 1989.

Kochavi, Arieh J. *Confronting Captivity: Britain and the United States and Their POWs in Nazi Germany.* Chapel Hill and London: University of North Carolina Press, 2005.

Koehl, Robert Lewis. "The 'Deutsche Volksliste' German Nationality List in Poland, 1939–1945." *Journal of Central European Affairs* 15, no. 4 (1956): 354–66.

Kotek, Joël, and Pierre Rigoulot. *Le Siècle des camps. Détention, concentration, extermination … Cent ans de mal radical.* [Paris]: Lattès, 2000.

Kroener, Bernhard. *Generaloberst Friedrich Fromm. Der starke Mann im Heimatkriegsgebiet: Eine Biographie.* Paderborn: Schöningh, 2005.

Kuller, Christiane. "Dimensionen nationalsozialistischer Verfolgung." In *Nach der Verfolgung: Wiedergutmachung nationalsozialistischen Unrechts?*, edited by Hans Günther Hockerts and Christiane Kuller. Dachauer Symposien zur Zeitgeschichte, 35–59. Göttingen: Wallstein Verlag, 2003.

Kundrus, Birthe. "Forbidden Company: Romantic Relationships between Germans and Foreigners, 1939 to 1945." *Journal of the History of Sexuality* 11, no. 1/2 (2002): 201–22.

Kriegerfrauen. Familienpolitik und Geschlechterverhältnisse im Ersten und Zweiten Weltkrieg. Hamburger Beiträge zur Sozial- und Zeitgeschichte. Hamburg: Christians, 1995.

Le Naour, Jean-Yves. *La honte noire: L'Allemagne et les troupes coloniales françaises 1914–1945.* Paris: Hachette Littérature, 2003.

Lebzelter, Gisela. "Die 'Schwarze Schmach': Vorurteile – Propaganda – Mythos." *Geschichte und Gesellschaft* 11, no. 1 (1985): 37–58.

Lehmann, Gertraud. "Von der 'Ehre der deutschen Frau': Nürnbergerinnen vor dem Sondergericht 1933–1945." In *Am Anfang war Sigena: Ein Nürnberger Frauengeschichtsbuch,* edited by Nadja Bennewitz and Gaby Franger, 199–210. Nürnberg: Anthologie ars vivendi, 1999.

Lheureux, Jean-Charles. *Graudenz-Pologne: La forteresse de la mort lente.* Nîmes: Le Camariguo, 1983.

Löffelsender, Michael. *Strafjustiz an der Heimatfront: Die strafrechtliche Verfolgung von Frauen und Jugendlichen im Oberlandesgerichtsbezirk Köln 1939–1945.* Beiträge zur Rechtsgeschichte des 20. Jahrhunderts. Tübingen: Mohr Siebeck, 2012.

Lorenz, Gottfried. *Todesurteile und Hinrichtungen wegen homosexueller Handlungen während der NS-Zeit: Mann-männliche Internetprostitution und andere Texte zur Geschichte und zur Situation der Homosexuellen in Deutschland.* Berlin and Münster: Lit Verlag, 2018.

Lower, Wendy. *Hitler's Furies: German Women in the Nazi Killing Fields.* Boston, MA: Houghton Mifflin Harcourt 2013.

Ludewig, Hans-Ulrich, and Dieter Kuessner. *"Es sei also jeder gewarnt." Das Sondergericht Braunschweig 1933–1945.* Quellen und Forschungen zur Braunschweigischen Landesgeschichte. Braunschweig: Selbstverlag des Braunschweigischen Geschichtsvereins, 2000.

Lutz, Nina. "Das Sondergericht Nürnberg 1933–1945: Eingespielte Justizmaschinerie der gelenkten Rechtspflege." In *Justizpalast Nürnberg. Ein Ort der Weltgeschichte wird 100 Jahre: Festschrift zum 100. Jahrestag der feierlichen Eröffnung des Justizpalastes in Nürnberg durch König Ludwig III. am 11. September 1916,* edited by Störtz, 250–63. Neustadt an der Aisch: VDS Verlagsdruckerei Schmidt, 2016.

MacKenzie, Simon Paul. "British Prisoners of War in Nazi Germany." *Archives* 28, no. 109 (2003): 183–7.

The Colditz Myth: British and Commonwealth Prisoners of War in Nazi Germany. Oxford and New York: Oxford University Press, 2004.

"The Treatment of Prisoners of War in World War II." *The Journal of Modern History* 66, no. 3 (1994): 487–520.

McLaren, Angus. *Twentieth-Century Sexuality: A History.* Oxford: Blackwell, 1999.

Maiwald, Stefan, and Gerd Mischler. *Sexualität unter dem Hakenkreuz: Manipulation und Vernichtung der Intimsphäre im NS-Staat.* Hamburg and Vienna: Europa Verlag, 1999.

Majer, Dietmut. *"Non-Germans" under the Third Reich: The Nazi Judicial and Administrative System in Germany and Occupied Eastern Europe, with Special Regard to Occupied Poland, 1939–1945.* Translated by Peter Thomas Hill, Edward Vance Humphrey, and Brian Levin. Baltimore and London: The Johns Hopkins University Press, 2003.

Makepeace, Clare. *Captives of War: British Prisoners of War in Europe in the Second World War.* Cambridge: Cambridge University Press, 2017.

Mattiello, Gianfranco. *Prisoners of War in Germany 1939–1945: Camps, Nationalities, Monthly Population.* Lodi: n. p., 2003.

Mattiello, Gianfranco, and Wolfgang Vogt. *Deutsche Kriegsgefangenen- und Interneteneinrichtungen 1939–1945: Handbuch und Katalog: Lagergeschichte und Lagerzensurstempel.* 2 vols. Koblenz: Selbstverlag, 1987.

Mechler, Wolf-Dieter. *Kriegsalltag an der "Heimatfront": Das Sondergericht Hannover im Einsatz gegen "Rundfunkverbrecher," "Schwarzschlachter," "Volksschädlinge" und andere "Straftäter" 1939 bis 1945.* Hannoversche Studien. Schriftenreihe des Stadtarchivs Hannover. Hannover: Hahn'sche Buchhandlung, 1997.

Messerschmidt, Manfred. *Die Wehrmachtjustiz 1933–1945.* Paderborn: Schöningh, 2005.

Moderow, Hans-Martin. "Französische Kriegsgefangene und Fremdarbeiter in Leipzig während des Zweiten Weltkriegs." In *Franzosen in Leipzig: damals und heute,* edited by Grazyna-Maria Peter. Schriftenreihe Europäer in Leipzig damals und heute, 5, 51–6. Leipzig: Europa-Haus, 2000.

Moisel, Claudia. "Pragmatischer Formelkompromiß: Das deutsch-französische Globalabkommen von 1960." In *Grenzen der Wiedergutmachung: Die Entschädigung für NS-Verfolgte in West- und Osteuropa 1945–2000,* edited by Hans Günther Hockerts, Claudia Moisel and Tobias Winstel, 242–84. Göttingen: Wallstein, 2006.

Monteath, Peter. *P.O.W.: Australian Prisoners of War in Hitler's Reich.* Sydney: Macmillan, 2011.

Moore, Bob. "Enforced Diaspora: The Fate of Italian Prisoners of War during the Second World War." *War in History* 22, no. 2 (2015): 174–90.

"Illicit Encounters: Female Civilian Fraternization with Axis Prisoners of War in Second World War Britain." *Journal of Contemporary History* 48, no. 4 (2013): 742–60.

"The Treatment of Prisoners of War in the Western European Theatre of War, 1939–1945." In *Prisoners in War,* edited by Sibylle Scheipers, 111–25. Oxford and New York: Oxford University Press, 2010.

Muggenthaler, Thomas, and Jörg Skriebeleit. *Verbrechen Liebe. Von polnischen Männern und deutschen Frauen: Hinrichtungen und Verfolgung in Niederbayern und der Oberpfalz während der NS-Zeit.* Viechtach: Ed. Lichtung, 2010.

Mühlhäuser, Regina. "Between 'Racial Awareness' and Fantasies of Potency: Nazi Sexual Politics in the Occupied Territories of the Soviet Union, 1942–1945." In *Brutality and Desire: War and Sexuality in Europe's Twentieth Century,* edited by Dagmar Herzog, 197–220. New York: Palgrave Macmillan, 2009.

Eroberungen. Sexuelle Gewalttaten und intime Beziehungen deutscher Soldaten in der Sowjetunion, 1941–1945. Hamburg: Hamburger Edition, 2010.

"Reframing Sexual Violence as a Weapon and Strategy of War: The Case of the German Wehrmacht during the War and Genocide in the Soviet Union, 1941–1944." *Journal of the History of Sexuality* 26, no. 3 (2017): 366–401.

Müller, Andreas. "Das Sondergericht Graz von 1939 bis 1945." Magisterarbeit, Universität Graz, 2005.

Müller, Ingo. *Furchtbare Juristen: Die unbewältigte Vergangenheit unserer Justiz.* Munich: Kindler, 1987.

Münch, Ingo von. *"Frau komm!" Die Massenvergewaltigungen deutscher Frauen und Mädchen 1944/45.* Graz: Ares, 2009.

Nagel, Jens, and Jörg Osterloh. "Wachmannschaften in Lagern für sowjetische Kriegsgefangene (1941–1945): Eine Annäherung." In *"Durchschnittstäter": Handeln und Motivation,* edited by Christoph Dieckmann et al. Beiträge zur Geschichte des Nationalsozialismus 16, 73–93. Berlin: Schwarze Risse, 2000.

Naimark, Norman. *The Russians in Germany: A History of the Soviet Zone of Occupation.* Cambridge, MA: Harvard University Press, 1995.

Nathans, Eli. *The Politics of Citizenship in Germany: Ethnicity, Utility and Nationalism.* Oxford: Berg, 2004.

Nichol, John, and Tony Rennell. *The Last Escape: The Untold Story of Allied Prisoners of War in Europe 1944–1945.* New York: Viking, 2002.

Nolzen, Armin. "Der Streifendienst der Hitler-Jugend (HJ) und die 'Überwachung der Jugend', 1934–1945: Forschungsprobleme und Fragestellung." In *"Durchschnittstäter": Handeln und Motivation,* edited by Christoph Dieckmann et al. Beiträge zur Geschichte des Nationalsozialismus 16, 13–51. Berlin: Schwarze Risse, 2000.

Oehler, Christiane. *Die Rechtsprechung des Sondergerichts Mannheim 1933–1945.* Berlin: Duncker & Humblot, 1997.

Overmans, Rüdiger. "German Treatment of Jewish Prisoners of War in the Second World War." Translated by Helen McPhail. In *Wartime Captivity in the Twentieth Century: Archives, Stories, Memories,* edited by Anne-Marie Pathé and Fabien Théofilakis. Studies in Contemporary European History, 45–53. New York: Berghahn Books, 2016.

"Die Kriegsgefangenenpolitik des Deutschen Reiches 1939 bis 1945." In *Das Deutsche Reich und der Zweite Weltkrieg,* edited by Jörg Echternkamp, 729–875. Munich: Deutsche Verlags-Anstalt, 2005.

Paulus, Helmut. "Das Sondergericht Bayreuth 1942–1945 – Ein düsteres Kapitel Bayreuther Justizgeschichte." *Archiv für Geschichte von Oberfranken* 77 (1997): 483–527.

Pawlita, Cornelius. "Der Beitrag der Rechtssprechung zur Entschädigung von NS-Unrecht und der Begriff the politischen Verfolgung." In *Nach der Verfolgung: Wiedergutmachung nationalsozialistischen Unrechts in Deutschland?,* edited by Hans Günther Hockerts and Christiane Kuller. Dachauer Symposien zur Zeitgeschichte, 79–114. Göttingen: Wallstein Verlag, 2003.

"Wiedergutmachung" als Rechtsfrage? Die politische und juristische Auseinandersetzung um Entschädigung für die Opfer nationalsozialistischer Verfolgung (1945 bis

1990). Europäische Hochschulschriften. Frankfurt am Main: Peter Lang, 1993.

Petschnigg, Edith. "'The Spirit of Comradeship': Britische Kriegsgefangene in der Steiermark 1941 bis 1945." In *Kriegsgefangene des Zweiten Weltkrieges: Gefangennahme, Lagerleben, Rückkehr*, edited by Günter Bischof, Stefan Karner, Barbara Stelzl-Marx and Edith Petschnigg, 421–37. Munich: Oldenbourg, 2005.

Von der Front aufs Feld: Britische Kriegsgefangene in der Steiermark 1941–1945. Veröffentlichungen des Ludwig Boltzmann-Instituts für Kriegsfolgen-Forschung. Graz: Verein zur Förderung der Forschung von Folgen nach Konflikten und Kriegen, 2003.

Peukert, Detlev. *Inside Nazi Germany: Conformity, Opposition, and Racism in Everyday Life.* Translated by Richard Deveson. New Haven: Yale University Press, 1987.

Picaper, Jean-Paul. *Le Crime d'aimer: Les enfants du STO.* Paris: Éditions des syrtes, 2005.

Pictet, Jean. *The Geneva Conventions of 12 August 1949: Commentary. III Geneva Convention Relative to the Treatment of Prisoners of War.* Geneva: International Committee of the Red Cross, 1960.

Pine, Lisa. *Hitler's "National Community": Society and Culture in Nazi Germany.* 2nd ed. London: Bloomsbury, 2017.

Pirker, Peter, and Florian Wenninger, eds. *Wehrmachtsjustiz: Kontext, Praxis, Nachwirkungen.* Wien: Braumüller, 2011.

Polaschek, Martin F. *Im Namen der Republik Oesterreich! Die Volksgerichte in der Steiermark 1945 bis 1955.* Veröffentlichungen des Steiermärkischen Landesarchives. Graz: LAD Zentralkanzlei, 1998.

Ponzani, Michela. *Figli del nemico: le relazioni d'amore in tempo di guerra, 1943–1948.* Rome: Laterzo, 2015.

Prieler-Woldan, Maria. *Das Selbstverständliche tun: Die Salzburger Bäuerin Maria Etzer und ihr verbotener Einsatz für Fremde im Nationalsozialismus.* Innsbruck, Vienna, Bozen: StudienVerlag, 2018.

Pross, Christian. *Paying for the Past: The Struggle over Reparations for Surviving Victims of the Nazi Terror.* Translated by Belinda Cooper. Baltimore and London: Johns Hopkins University Press, 1998.

Przyrembel, Alexandra. *'Rassenschande': Reinheitsmythos und Vernichtungslegitimation im Nationalsozialismus.* Veröffentlichungen des Max-Planck-Instituts für Geschichte. Göttingen: Vandenhoeck & Ruprecht, 2003.

Rachamimov, Alon. "The Disruptive Comforts of Drag: (Trans)Gender Performances among Prisoners of War in Russia, 1914–1920." *American Historical Review* 111, no. 2 (2006): 362–82.

Reiss, Matthias. "Bronzed Bodies behind Barbed Wire: Masculinity and the Treatment of German Prisoners of War in the United States during World War II." *Journal of Military History* 69, no. 2 (2005): 475–504.

Controlling Sex in Captivity: POWs and Sexual Desire in the United States during the Second World War. London: Bloomsbury, 2018.

Reiter, Raimond. *Frauen im Dritten Reich in Niedersachsen: Eine Dokumentation.* Frauen in Geschichte und Gesellschaft. Pfaffenweiler: Centaurus, 1998.

Reither, Dominik, Karl Rausch, Christine Fößmeier, and Elke Abstiens. *Auf den Spuren verlorener Identitäten: Sowjetische Kriegsgefangene im Stalag VII A Moosburg*. Norderstedt: Books on Demand, 2018.

Roberts, Mary Louise. *What Soldiers Do: Sex and the American GI in World War II France*. Chicago: The University of Chicago Press, 2013.

Röger, Maren. *Kriegsbeziehungen: Intimität, Gewalt und Prostitution im besetzten Polen 1939 bis 1945*. Frankfurt am Main: Fischer, 2015.

Rolf, David. *Prisoners of the Reich: Germany's Captives 1939–1945*. London: Cooper, 1988.

Rothmaler, Christiane. "Volksschädlinge und Gemeinschaftsfremde: Frauenstrafvollzug im Nationalsozialismus." In *"Der Stand der Frauen, wahrlich, ist ein harter Stand": Frauenleben im Spiegel der Landesgeschichte*, edited by Elke Imberger. Veröffentlichungen des Schleswig-Holsteinischen Landesarchivs, 143–85. Schleswig: Landesarchiv Schleswig-Holstein, 1994.

Rüping, Hinrich. *Bibliographie zum Strafrecht im Nationalsozialismus. Literatur zum Straf-. Strafverfahrens- und Strafvollzugsrecht mit ihren Grundlagen und einem Anhang: Verzeichnis der veröffentlichten Entscheidungen der Sondergerichte*. Texte und Materialien veröffentlicht vom Institut für Zeitgeschichte. Munich: Oldenbourg, 1985.

"Denunziation und Strafjustiz im Führerstaat." In *Denunziation: Historische, juristische und psychologische Aspekte*, edited by Günter Jerouschek, Inge Marßolek and Hedwig Röckelein. Forum Psychohistorie, 127–45. Tübingen: Edition discord, 1997.

Saldern, Adelheid von. *Victims or Perpetrators? Controversies about the Role of Women in the Nazi State*. London and New York: Routledge, 1994.

Sandweg, Jürgen. "Schwabacher vor dem Sondergericht: Der Alltag der Denunziation und die 'Justiz des gesunden Volksempfindens'." In *Vergessen und verdrängt? Schwabach 1918–1945*, edited by Sabine Weigand-Karg, Sandra Hoffmann and Jürgen Sandweg, 226–37. Schwabach: Stadtmuseum Schwabach, 1997.

Scheck, Raffael. "Collaboration of the Heart: The Forbidden Love Affairs of French Prisoners of War and German Women in Nazi Germany." *The Journal of Modern History* 90, no. 2 (2018): 351–82.

French Colonial Soldiers in German Captivity during World War II. Cambridge and New York: Cambridge University Press, 2014.

"Léopold Sédar Senghor prisonnier de guerre allemand: Une nouvelle approche fondée sur un texte inédit." *French Politics, Culture & Society* 31, no. 2 (2014): 76–98.

"The Prisoner of War Question and the Beginnings of Collaboration: The Franco-German Agreement of 16 November 1940." *Journal of Contemporary History* 45, no. 2 (2010): 364–88.

"The Treatment of Western Prisoners of War in Nazi Germany: Rethinking Reciprocity and Asymmetry," *War in History* (forthcoming).

"La victoire allemande de 1940 comme justification de l'idéologie raciale nazie." In *La Guerre de 40. Se battre – subir – se souvenir*, edited by Stefan Martens and Steffen Prauser, 143–53. Villeneuve d'Asq: Presses universitaires du Septentrion, 2014.

"The Danger of 'Moral Sabotage:' Western Prisoners of War on Trial for Homosexual Relations in Nazi Germany," *Journal of the History of Sexuality* (forthcoming).

"Western Prisoners of War Tried for Insults of the Führer and Criticism of Nazi Germany," *Journal of Contemporary History*, published online April 27, 2020, doi.org/10.1177/0022009420907670.

Schimmler, Bernd. *Recht ohne Gerechtigkeit: Zur Tätigkeit der Berliner Sondergerichte im Nationalsozialismus.* Berlin: Wissenschaftlicher Autoren-Verlag, 1984.

Schneider, Silke. *Verbotener Umgang. Ausländer und Deutsche im Nationalsozialismus: Diskurse um Sexualität, Moral, Wissen und Strafe.* Baden-Baden: Nomos, 2010.

Schöggl-Ernst, Elisabeth. "Das Ende der persönlichen Freiheit: Zwangsarbeit und Kriegsgefangenschaft." In *Geschichte der Steiermark: Bundesland und Reichsgau. Demokratie, "Ständestaat" und NS-Herrschaft in der Steiermark 1918–1945*, edited by Alfred Ableitinger, 479–92. Wien, Köln, Weimar: Böhlau, 2015.

Schöttler, Peter. "Der französische Historiker Fernand Braudel als Kriegsgefangener in Lübeck." *Zeitschrift für Lübeckische Geschichte* 95 (2015): 275–87.

Schrafstetter, Susanna. "'What About Paying BRITISH Victims of Nazi Hell Camps?' Die Entschädigungsfrage in den deutsch-britischen Beziehungen." In *Grenzen der Wiedergutmachung: Die Entschädigung für NS-Verfolgte in West- und Osteuropa 1945–2000*, edited by Hans Günther Hockerts, Claudia Moisel and Tobias Winstel, 568–629. Göttingen: Wallstein, 2006.

Schreiber, Gerhard. *Die italienischen Militärinternierten im deutschen Machtbereich 1943–1945.* Munich: Oldenbourg, 1990.

Schwarze, Gisela. *Es war wie eine Hexenjagd: Die vergessene Verfolgung ganz normaler Frauen im Zweiten Weltkrieg.* Münster: Ardey, 2009.

Seidler, Franz W. *Die Militärgerichtsbarkeit der deutschen Wehrmacht 1939–1945: Rechtsprechung und Strafvollzug.* Munich and Berlin: Herbig, 1991.

Shneyer, Aron. *Pariahs among Pariahs: Soviet-Jewish POWs in German Captivity, 1941–1945.* Translated by Yisrael Cohen. Jerusalem: Yad Vashem, 2016.

Siemssen, Iris. "Das Sondergericht und die Nähe: Die Rechtsprechung bei 'verbotenem Umgang mit Kriegsgefangenen' am Beispiel von Fällen aus dem Kreis Plön." In *"Standgericht der inneren Front": Das Sondergericht Altona/Kiel 1932–1945*, edited by Robert Bohn and Uwe Danker, 233–62. Hamburg: Ergebnisse-Verlag, 1998.

Snyder, David Raub. *Sex Crimes under the Wehrmacht.* Studies in War, Society, and the Military. Lincoln and London: University of Nebraska Press, 2007.

Solzhenitsyn, Alexander. *August 1914.* Translated by Michael Glenny. New York: Farrar, Straus and Giroux, 1972.

Spoerer, Mark. "Die soziale Differenzierung der ausländischen Zivilarbeiter, Kriegsgefangenen und Häftlinge im Deutschen Reich." In *Das Deutsche Reich und der Zweite Weltkrieg*, edited by Jörg Echternkamp, vol. 9/II, 485–576. Munich: Deutsche Verlags-Anstalt, 2005.

Stargardt, Nicholas. *The German War: A Nation Under Arms, 1939–1945: Citizens and Soldiers.* New York: Basic Books, 2015.

Witnesses of War: Children's Lives Under the Nazis. New York: Alfred A. Knopf, 2006.

Steinacher, Gerald. "' ... verlangt das gesunde Volksempfinden die schwerste Strafe ...': Das Sondergericht für die Operationszone Alpenvorland 1943–1945. Ein Vorbericht." In *Tirol zwischen Diktatur und Demokratie (1930–1950). Beiträge für Rolf Steininger zum 60. Geburtstag,* edited by Klaus Eisterer, 247–66. Innsbruck: StudienVerlag, 2002.

Stephenson, Jill. *Hitler's Home Front: Württemberg under the Nazis.* London and New York: Hambledon Continuum, 2006.

Women in Nazi Germany. Harlow: Pearson, 2001.

Stibbe, Matthew. *Women in the Third Reich.* London: Arnold, 2003.

Stoltzfus, Nathan. *Hitler's Compromises: Coercion and Consensus in Nazi Germany.* New Haven: Yale University Press, 2016.

Resistance of the Heart: Intermarriage and the Rosenstrasse Protest in Nazi Germany. New York: Norton, 1996.

Stopik, Joachim. *Beuthen-Miechowitz/Mechtal.* Dülmen: Laumann-Verlag, 2008.

Stopsack, Hans-Hermann. *Stalag VI A Hemer. Kriegsgefangenenlager 1939–1945: eine Dokumentation.* Hemer: Volkshochschule Menden-Hemer-Balve, 1995.

Surmann, Rolf. "Was ist typisches NS-Unrecht? Die verweigerte Entschädigung für Zwangssterilisierte und 'Euthanasie'-Geschädigte." In *Lebensunwert zerstörte Leben: Zwangssterilisation und "Euthanasie,"* edited by Margret Hamm, 198–211. Frankfurt am Main: VAS, 2005.

Swillen, Gerlinda. *De Wieg van WO II: Oorlogskinderen op de as Brussel–Berlijn.* Brussels: ASP, 2016.

Szecsi, Maria, and Karl Stadler. *Die NS-Justiz in Österreich und ihre Opfer.* Das einsame Gewissen. Beiträge zur Geschichte Österreichs 1938–1945. Vienna and Munich: Herold, 1962.

Szobar, Patricia. "Telling Sexual Stories in the Nazi Courts of Law: Race Defilement in Germany, 1933 to 1945." In *Sexuality and German Fascism,* edited by Dagmar Herzog, 131–63. New York and Oxford: Berghahn Books, 2005.

Tanguy, Alain. *Livre d'or du prisonnier de guerre belge 1940–1945.* Merendree: Editions du Livre d'Or, 1986.

Theis, Kerstin. *Wehrmachtjustiz an der "Heimatfront": Die Militärgerichte des Ersatzheeres im Zweiten Weltkrieg.* Studien zur Zeitgeschichte. Berlin and Boston: De Gruyter/Oldenbourg, 2016.

Théofilakis, Fabien. "Le Prisonnier de guerre dans l'historiographie française et allemande: Étudier la Seconde Guerre mondiale à front renversé." *Guerres mondiales et conflits contemporains,* no. 274 (2019): 17–26.

"La Sexualité du prisonnier de guerre: Allemands et Français en captivité (1914–1918, 1940–1948)." *Vingtième Siècle, revue d'histoire* 99 (2008): 203–19.

Thonke, Christian. *Hitlers langer Schatten: Der mühevolle Weg zur Entschädigung der NS-Opfer.* Wien, Köln, Weimar: Böhlau, 2004.

Timm, Annette F. *The Politics of Fertility in Twentieth-Century Berlin.* Cambridge and New York: Cambridge University Press, 2010.

Todd, Lisa M. *Sexual Treason in Germany during the First World War.* Gender and Sexualities in History. Cham: Palgrave Macmillan, 2017.

"'The Soldier's Wife Who Ran Away with the Russian': Sexual Infidelities in World War I Germany." *Central European History* 44 (2011): 257–78.

Torrie, Julia S. *"For Their Own Good": Civilian Evacuations in Germany and France, 1939–1945*. New York and Oxford: Berghahn Books, 2010.

German Soldiers and the Occupation of France, 1940–1944. Cambridge and New York: Cambridge University Press, 2018.

Usborne, Cornelie. *Cultures of Abortion in Weimar Germany*. New York: Berghahn Books, 2007.

"Female Sexual Desire and Male Honor: German Women's Illicit Love Affairs with Prisoners of War during the Second World War." *Journal of the History of Sexuality* 26, no. 3 (2017): 454–88.

Vaizey, Hester. "Empowerment of Endurance? War Wives' Experiences of Independence during and after the Second World War in Germany, 1939–1948." *German History* 29, no. 1 (2009): 57–78.

"Husbands and Wives: An Evaluation of the Emotional Impact of World War Two in Germany." *European History Quarterly* 40, no. 3 (2010): 389–411.

Surviving Hitler's War: Family Life in Germany 1939–1948. New York: Palgrave Macmillan, 2010.

Vance, Jonathan, ed. *Encyclopedia of Prisoners of War and Internment*. Santa Barbara: ABC-CLIO, 2000.

ed. *Objects of Concern: Canadian Prisoners of War Through the Twentieth Century*. [no place]: UBC Press, 1994.

Vascik, George S., and Mark R. Sadler, eds. *The Stab-in-the-Back Myth and the Fall of the Weimar Republic: A History in Documents and Visual Sources*. London: Bloomsbury, 2016.

Virgili, Fabrice. *La France "virile": Des femmes tondues à la Libération*. Paris: Éditions Payot & Rivage, 2004.

Naître ennemi: Les enfants des couples franco-allemands nés pendant la Seconde Guerre mondiale. Paris: Editions Payot, 2009.

Shorn Women: Gender and Punishment in Liberation France. Translated by John Flower. Oxford and New York: Berg, 2002.

Vordermayer, Margaretha Franziska. *Justice for the Enemy? Die Verteidigung deutscher Kriegsverbrecher durch britische Offiziere in Militärgerichtsprozessen nach dem Zweiten Weltkrieg (1945–1949)*. Historische Grundlagen der Moderne. Baden-Baden: Nomos, 2019.

Vourkoutiotis, Vasilis. *Prisoners of War and the German High Command: The British and American Experience*. New York: Palgrave, 2003.

"What the Angels Saw: Red Cross and Protective Power Visits to Anglo-American POWs, 1939–1945." *Journal of Contemporary History* 40, no. 4 (2005): 689–706.

Wachsmann, Nikolaus. *Hitler's Prisons: Legal Terror in Nazi Germany*. New Haven and London: Yale University Press, 2004.

Wallis, Russell. *British POWs and the Holocaust: Witnessing the Nazi Atrocities*. International Library of Twentieth Century History Series. London: I.B. Tauris, 2016.

Warring, Anette. "Intimate and Sexual Relations." In *Surviving Hitler and Mussolini: Daily Life in Occupied Europe*, edited by Robert Gildea, Olivier Wieviorka and Anette Warring, 88–128. Oxford and New York: Berg, 2006.

Weckbecker, Gerd. *Zwischen Freispruch und Todesstrafe: Die Rechtsprechung der nationalsozialistischen Sondergerichte Frankfurt/Main und Bromberg.* Baden-Baden: Nomos, 1998.

Wegner, Bernd. "Hitler, der Zweite Weltkrieg und die Choreographie des Untergangs." *Geschichte und Gesellschaft* 26, no. 3 (2000): 493–518.

Hitlers politische Soldaten. Die Waffen-SS 1933–1945: Studien zu Leitbild, Struktur und Funktion einer nationalsozialistischen Elite. 5th ed. Paderborn: Schöningh, 1997.

Weigand-Karg, Sabine. "'Ausländer-Einsatz': Fremdarbeiter in Schwabach." In *Vergessen und verdrängt? Schwabach 1918–1945*, edited by Sabine Weigand-Karg, Sandra Hoffmann and Jürgen Sandweg, 238–44. Schwabach: Stadtmuseum Schwabach, 1997.

Weikart, Richard. "Hitler's Struggle for Existence against Slavs: Racial Theory and Vacillations in Nazi Policy toward Czechs and Poles." In *Eradicating Differences: The Treatment of Minorities in Nazi-Dominated Europe*, edited by Anton Weiss-Wendt, 61–83. Newcastle upon Tyne: Cambridge Scholars Publishing, 2010.

Weinmann, Martin, ed. *Das nationalsozialistische Lagersystem (CCP).* Frankfurt am Main: Zweitausendeins, 1990.

Werther, Thomas. "Kriegsgefangene vor dem Marburger Militärgericht." In *Militärjustiz im Nationalsozialismus: Das Marburger Militärgericht*, edited by Michael Eberlein, 245–92. Marburg: Geschichtswerkstatt Marburg, 1994.

Westermann, Stefanie. *Verschwiegenes Leid: Der Umgang mit den NS-Zwangssterilisationen in der Bundesrepublik Deutschland.* Menschen und Kulturen. Köln, Weimar, Wien: Böhlau, 2010.

Wolf, Gerhard. "*Volk* Trumps Race: The *Deutsche Volksliste* in Annexed Poland." In *Beyond the Racial State: Rethinking Nazi Germany*, edited by Devon O. Pendas, Mark Roseman, and Richard F. Wetzell, 431–54. Cambridge and New York: Cambridge University Press, 2017.

Wrobel, Hans, Henning Maul-Backer, and Ilka Renken, eds. *Strafjustiz im totalen Krieg. Aus den Akten des Sondergerichts Bremen 1940 bis 1945.* 3 vols. Vol. 2. Bremen: Bremen Verlags- und Buchhandelsgesellschaft, 1994.

Wüllenweber, Hans. *Sondergerichte im Dritten Reich: Vergessene Verbrechen der Justiz.* Frankfurt (M): Luchterhand, 1990.

Wylie, Neville. *Barbed Wire Diplomacy: Britain, Germany, and the Politics of Prisoners of War, 1939–1945.* Oxford and New York: Oxford University Press, 2010.

"The 1929 Prisoner of War Convention and the Building of the Inter-war Prisoner of War Regime." In *Prisoners in War*, edited by Sibylle Scheipers, 91–108. Oxford and New York: Oxford University Press, 2010.

Zühl, Antje. "Zum Verhältnis der deutschen Landbevölkerung gegenüber Zwangsarbeitern und Kriegsgefangenen." In *Faschismus und Rassismus: Kontroversen um Ideologie und Opfer*, edited by Werner Röhr, Dietrich Eichholtz, Gerhart Hass, and Wolfgang Wippermann, 342–53. Berlin: Akademie-Verlag, 1992.

Index

Abetz, Otto, 27, 69
abortion, 60, 196, 200, 339
Aichach (penitentiary), 250, 252, 254, 257, 259, 261, 263, 266, 269, 272, 275–6, 278–81, 305
  death of inmates, 277, 281
  diphtheria outbreak, 253
  overcrowding, 250, 255
  pregnant inmates, 253, 255, 270, 278, 281
Allied Control Commission for Germany, 339
Alsace-Lorraine, 76, 79, 119, 128, 198
Althusser, Louis, 18
Amberg (penitentiary), 299
Ambrière, Francis, 2–4, 11, 19, 135, 344
  on revolt of women, 5
  on undiscovered relations, 31
American POWs, 11, 23, 40–2, 296, 298, 338
  in Graudenz, 293–5, 300
  punishment orders for, 235
  relations with women, 23, 41–2
Anrath (penitentiary), 250, 252, 258, 262, 279
  evacuation of, 280
anti-Semitism, 52
Arab POWs, 38, 40
Auschwitz, 284, 336
Australian POWs, 12, 21, 38, 127, 153

Bartsch, Robert, 81
Bau- und Arbeitsbataillon (BAB), 95
Bella, Ahmed, 288
Berger, Gottlob, 92
birth control, 196, 212, 303, 308
Blechhammer, xiv, 110, 236, 290, 349
Bormann, Martin, 84, 150, 218
Brandenburg-Görden (penitentiary), 298–9
  concentration of French POWs in, 299
Braudel, Fernand, 18

Breitenau (labor camp), 341
brothels: *see* prostitution
Brucker, Dr., 286, 288, 290

Caire, Fernand, 345
Canadian POWs, 12, 38, 125
Colditz, 12, 17
concentration camps, 5, 15, 17, 48, 61, 282, 285, 344, 349, 354
  as punishment for women involved with eastern POWs or laborers, 44, 163, 340, 342–3, 351
  Graudenz compared to, 282–3, 298, 349
Cottbus (penitentiary), 250, 257, 264, 268
  bombing of, 261, 281
criminal types, 81, 84, 215, 218, 247
Cypriot POWs, 38, 104, 167
Czechs, 13, 25, 77

Dachau (concentration camp), 302
Dachdecker-Bataillon, 95
Daehnik, Colonel, 296
Daimler-Benz, 130
Dallmer-Zerbe, Colonel, 286, 291, 294–5, 347
  and evacuation of Graudenz, 295–6, 349
de t'Serclaes et Wammerson, count, 34
Delattre, Stéphane, 225
  comments on accused women, 214–15, 232
  defending transformed POWs, 74
  defense of a sincere lover, 130–1
  on Graudenz, 282
  role in drafting 1949 Geneva convention, 352
Delforge, Jules, 350
Deutsche Volksliste (German People's List), 43, 77, 79, 105, 144, 331
  categories, 77
Didelet, Henri, 75
Dower, Jack, 41, 96, 142–3